Drug Use in America

Drug Use in America

Social, Cultural, and Political Perspectives

Peter J. Venturelli, Editor

Department of Sociology
Valparaiso University
Valparaiso, Indiana

JONES AND BARTLETT PUBLISHERS

Boston London

Editorial, Sales, and Customer Service Offices

Jones and Bartlett Publishers
One Exeter Plaza
Boston, MA 02116
1-800-832-0034
1-617-859-3900

Jones and Bartlett Publishers International
P.O. Box 1498
London W6 7RS
England

Library of Congress Cataloging-in-Publication Data

Drug use in America : social, cultural, and political perspectives /
Peter Venturelli, editor.
p. cm.
Includes bibliographic references and index.
ISBN 0-86720-752-3
1. Drug abuse—United States. 2. Alcoholism—United States.
I. Venurelli, Peter J., 1949–
HV5825.D7773 1994
362.29'-973—dc20 93-39419
CIP

Production Editor: Anne Noonan
Production Service and Composition: Book 1
Designer: Sixten C. Abbot
Cover Designer: Marshall Henrichs

Printed in the United States of America
97 96 95 94 93 10 9 8 7 6 5 4 3 2 1

Contents

Foreword

Drug and alcohol use and abuse are deeply interwoven into the social and economic fabric of American society. Furthermore, drug and alcohol use is more often a symptom and consequence of social inequalities and problems than a direct cause of or important contributor to the many social problems to which drugs and alcohol are often linked.

The 29 articles that make up this book provide varied approaches to support this theme. The editor, Dr. Peter Venturelli, has managed a major accomplishment by soliciting the contributions of the many eminent authors in the drugs-alcohol field, reviewing and editing their essays, developing an integrative structure, and providing introductory remarks that place each essay within a larger analytic context.

The articles in this anthology strike a cogent balance between those primarily focused on alcohol and upon illicit drug use. The special emphasis on ethnic issues is often overlooked in other anthologies. The methodological approaches range from quantitative studies examining the patterns of adult and adolescent drinking behavior in America and tests of theories of drug use, to ethnographic studies of heroin gangs and mobilizing communities against drugs, to social and historical analyses of the origins of alcohol movements and anti-drug campaigns, as well as provide systematic analyses of American drug policies and the AIDS crisis.

All of the articles provide a cogent and critical approach in their examination of important issues in the drugs-alcohol field. As is often the case, reasonable solutions to the intractable problems documented by these essays are seldom provided by the authors—a difficulty afflicting the entire field. What is clear from the essays, however, is that alcohol and drug abuse are "a symptom, a manifestation of deeper, more serious problems, and . . . certain types of human predicaments." It logically follows that restructuring society in order to avoid or reduce the inequalities would have the result of softening the worst consequences of illicit drug use.

Of course, many of these articles were written before Bill Clinton assumed the U.S. presidency in 1993, so the fundamental restructuring being attempted by his administration is not addressed. Nevertheless, the Clinton Administration is attempting to dramatically restructure the delivery and financing of health care so that everyone has health insurance. This proposal, if passed and implemented in roughly the form proposed in the fall of 1993, would greatly alter the health-care status of millions of alcoholics and illicit drug users—who currently are heavily overrepresented among the one-third of Americans without health insurance. The Clinton plan would make standard health care and preventive services available to the lowest-income Americans, and would provide medical pharmaceuticals that they cannot afford now. For the first time, the national standard package of health insurance could mandate the funding of 30 days of alcohol or drug detoxification for an individual. Although many in the alcohol and drug treatment field would argue that such new "health care" money will be wasted on a relatively ineffective intervention, and would suggest instead their favorite form of treatment, this new financing would generate resources not currently available to the majority of alcohol and drug abusers.

The essays on the decriminalization and legalization of drugs come closest to addressing such broad-based solutions. The authors of essays on drug policy are in general agreement that the punitive policies of the Reagan and Bush years have incarcerated hundreds of thousands, probably increased the social costs, and had a negative impact upon millions of low-income Americans. Yet most authors stop short of outright legalization. The most attractive model appears to be the Dutch model of "normalization," which consistently attempts to "de-moralize" and "de-politicize" illicit drug use and remove the stigma experienced by abusers. In the Netherlands, the harm-reduction model allows prohibitionist laws to stay on the books, but persons who use—and even abuse—drugs are permitted to discretely obtain and use them without major fear of arrest or prison. Moreover, the Dutch national health-care system attempts to maintain contact with and care for even the most serious heroin abusers—to prevent them from harming others. Addicts are provided with free methadone with almost no regulation, given clean needles to prevent the spread of HIV, and offered entry into treatment when and if they want it.

The diverse essays in this anthology provide important readings in this increasingly diverse field. They will be appreciated by scholars in the field, and will also provide an interesting reader for students taking courses in alcohol or drug abuse, deviant behavior, ethnicity, and many other areas.

Finally, the articles reflect the increasing breadth and sophistication of the analysis now being developed in the alcohol and drug use fields. Many authors are members of the Drinking and Drugs section of the Society for the Study of Social Problems (and, since 1991, the Alcohol and Drugs section of the American Sociological Association). The conferences of these groups provide a major opportunity for faculty members who are the "drug expert" or "alcohologist" at their college or university to present papers, receive intellectual feedback, meet informally and share common interests, and participate in each other's intellectual work. At the 1990 meetings in Washington, D.C., Dr. Venturelli first invited many of the authors to revise and submit their conference papers, many of which became the articles that appear in this book. Members of these organizations thank the editor for his commitment to this project, and for advancing the field.

Bruce D. Johnson, Ph.D.
Director
Institute for Special Populations Research
National Development and Research Institutes, Inc.
New York, New York

Preface

In an effort to answer the question, what are the social, cultural, and political ramifications of drug use, this anthology examines the use and abuse of drugs from a wide range of perspectives. The articles comprising this volume explore some crucial issues covering the use of specific drugs, patterns of individual drug use, the effects of drugs on certain groups, the differential impacts drugs have on people of color and those who identify with different ethnicities, the dynamics of drug abuse prevention including various models and strategies, controversial issues surrounding decriminalization, the effects of drugs on health care professionals, athletes, and expectant mothers, and a case study example of the politics behind a needle exchange program in New York City.

Specifically, each of the six parts comprising this volume addresses:

Part I: Alcohol and Alcoholism—the extent of alcohol use in the United States; causes of alcohol addiction; and identification of the types of drinkers.

Part II: Youth and Drugs—adolescent use and abuse of alcohol; theoretical explanations for use; comparisons of adolescent users of different types of drugs; and the relationship between adolescent drug use and leisure activity.

Part III: Race, Ethnicity and Drug Use—alcohol consumption among American Indians and Caucasian youth; use of heroin in two Chicano groups; the relationship of black male drug use to parents, peers and racial prejudice; and the way definitions of substance problems among African Americans are linked to the larger social structures of culture and power.

Part IV: Drug Abuse Prevention—historical twentieth century analysis of alcohol and drug control movements; analysis of the largest coordinated voluntary mass media campaign against drug use in advertising history; collegiate drinking patterns and legislation to address the problem; efforts to deter drunk driving; measures for preventing alcohol-impaired driving among youth; various approaches used for preventing alcohol and drug abuse among America's children and youth; use of addiction models for developing intervention strategies; and the application of strategic planning for drug abuse prevention.

Part V: Drug Decriminalization—historical review of drug control legislation; assessment of the merits and problems of our current drug control policy; and the social origins of the Marihuana Tax Act and other anti-marijuana propaganda.

Part VI: Special Populations, Dilemmas and Debates—Drug abuse by health care professionals; participation in sports and drug use; use of drugs by pregnant women; fetal rights versus the constitutional rights of child-bearing women; evaluation of punishing maternal substance abusers; and an example of a needle exchange program.

While ranging widely, the contributions are thematically linked to problems of substance use and abuse. The variety of substance abuse perspectives and topics contained in this volume matches the reality that substance abuse touches many aspects of daily life and often is inextricably linked to other serious psychological and social problems. In short, the plurality of perspectives contained in this volume corresponds to the nature of drug use in our society.

The newcomer studying substance abuse often believes that it is singularly linked to the individual's problem. This assumption will be challenged by the research offered in this anthology. The articles should leave the reader with an awareness that substance abuse is not an isolated problem but is woven into the structure and texture of a range of social problems. *Drug use is a symptom, a manifestation of deeper, more serious problems, and substance abuse is symptomatic of certain types of structured human predicaments.* For example, we cannot isolate the use of drugs from such related problems as: addiction, dysfunctional families, violence, poverty, discrimination and prejudice, troubled adolescence, low self-esteem, immaturity, stress, intense competition, and ignorance.

How is substance abuse symptomatic of other social problems? First, we must remember that people use and abuse drugs for many reasons. The reasons can range from using drugs to find relief from illness (as with morphine used to sedate terminally ill cancer patients), to self-gratifying physical and psychological pleasure-seeking activity (such as recreational cocaine use to relieve boredom and experience the pleasures of an "orgasmic" high). Second, drugs are attractive, pleasurable and satisfying to the human psyche. The psychoactive properties in drugs allow users to escape, postpone and disguise serious "root" problems. Third, the most troubled people are substance abusers. It is not uncommon to find that drug use occurs with: poverty (Anderson, 1990; Wilson, 1988; Williams, 1989); homelessness (Lubran, 1987), and crime (Wilson, 1990). Drug addiction is also found in dysfunctional families (Beschner & Friedman, 1986); it occurs with violent behavior (Williams, 1989); and latchkey children are likely to experience early experimentation with drug use (Richardson, 1989). Fourth, drug use can result from unrealistic competition, such as the use of anabolic steroids to improve sport performance and recreation (Kaplan, 1984); and finally, the elderly report an unusual amount of drug misuse and abuse (Peterson & Whittington, 1977).

This first-edition collection contains a total of thirty articles, twenty-eight of which have been carefully written for this anthology, and the remaining two published elsewhere. The authors have worked closely with the editor, often patiently revising their work in an effort to achieve a broad diversity of concerns.

This anthology has been written for two types of audiences. First, at the college or university level it can be used to accompany and complement an introductory drug text. Further, this text is challenging enough to be used as a main text in college-level substance abuse courses. Second, researchers in the field of substance abuse should also find that the articles in this anthology are informative and substantive enough for use as resource material.

This editor feels privileged to have worked with such respected authorities in the field of substance abuse, and anticipates inviting many of them back for future editions of the anthology.

For initial encouragement when this anthology was just an idea, I am grateful to James Keating, vice-president at Jones and Bartlett Publishers. Joseph Burns, also a vice-president at Jones and Bartlett Publishers, expressed early enthusiasm for the anthology and remained steadfast in his support of this project. His continual support and faith in my ideas allowed this anthology to materialize. My appreciation goes out to our production editor, Anne Noonan, at Jones and Bartlett Publishers for the outstanding job of coordinating and supervising this publication and in seeing it through to completion. I also acknowledge those who have supported the preparation of this book. For their helpful suggestions and comments, I would like to thank the following: Stewart Cooper, Stella Hughes, Joan Moore, David Pittman, Ernest Quimby, David Rudy, Ted Westermann, and my former student assistant, Ericka Shrontz. Extensive patience and help were graciously given by Ellen Meyer, and other last-minute bibliographic cross-checking by Patricia Hogan-Vidal at Valparaiso University's Moellering Library. Special thanks to my current student assistant, Leah Piepkorn, who now realizes the extensive amount of detail that goes into an anthology. My appreciation also includes other last-minute proofreading by another student assistant, Wendy Turner. All the teamwork provided by the people above further improved the quality of this anthology.

For their initial support and encouragement, I would also like to express my appreciation to Richard Baeplar, Valparaiso University's former Vice-President for Academic Affairs, and Philip Gilbertson, Dean in the College of Arts and Sciences. Their trust and initial monetary support for travel expenses to the 1990 annual meetings of the Society for Social Problems and the American Sociological Association, in Washington, D.C., to recruit contributors for this volume, are greatly appreciated. Last, but never least, is the encouragement, support and critical advice offered by my wife Shalini, to whom this book is dedicated.

References

Anderson, E. (1990). *Streetwise.* Chicago, IL: University of Chicago Press .

Beschner, G., & Friedman, A. (1986). *Teen drug use.* Lexington, MA: D. C. Heath.

Kaplan, J. (1984, May 28). Taking steps to solve the drug dilemma. *Sports Illustrated,* pp. 36–45.

Lubran, B. G. (1987). Alcohol-related problems among the homeless. *Alcohol and Health Research,* 11, 1–6, 73.

Peterson, D. M., & Whittington, F. J. (1977). Drug use among the elderly: A review. *Journal of Psychedelic Drugs,* 9, 25–37.

Richardson, J. L., Dwyer, K., McGuigan, K., Hansen, W. B., Dent, C., Anderson, C., Johnson, C. A., Sussman, S.Y., Brannon, B., & Flay, B. (1989). Substance use among eighth-grade students who take care of themselves after school. *Pediatrics,* 84, 556–566.

Williams, T. (1989). *The cocaine kids.* Reading, MA: Addison-Wesley.

Wilson, W. J. (1988). *The truly disadvantaged.* Chicago, IL: University of Chicago Press.

Wilson, J. Q. (1990). Drugs and crime. In M. Tonry, & J. Q. Wilson *(Eds.), Drugs and crime* (pp 521–545). Chicago, IL: The University of Chicago Press.

Wolfgang, M. E., & Ferracuti, F. (1967). *The structure of violence: Toward an integrated theory in criminology.* London: Tavistock.

Contributors

Patricia A. Adler, Ph.D.
Associate Professor of Sociology
University of Colorado
Boulder, Colorado

Robert Agnew, Ph.D.
Associate Professor of Sociology
Emory University
Atlanta, Georgia

Marsha E. Bates, Ph.D.
Assistant Research Professor in Psychology
Center of Alcohol Studies
Rutgers University
Piscataway, New Jersey

John R. Baumann, Ph.D.
Assistant Project Director for Grant and Proposal Development
National Development and Research Institutes, Inc.
New York, New York

Randall W. Conforti, B.A.
Director of Human Resources
Ranch Rehabilitation Service
Menomonee Falls, Wisconsin

Stewart E. Cooper, Ph.D.
Director, Student Counseling and Development Center
Associate Professor of Psychology
Valparaiso University
Valparaiso, Indiana

Richard A. Dodder, Ph.D.
Professor of Sociology and Statistics
Oklahoma State University
Stillwater, Oklahoma

Michael C. Elsner, Ph.D.
Department of Sociology and Anthropology
Howard University
Washington, D. C.

Ruth C. Engs, R.N., Ed.D.
Professor of Applied Health Science
Indiana University
Bloomington, Indiana

Ronald W. Fagan, Ph.D.
Professor of Sociology and Chairperson of the Social Science Division
Pepperdine University
Malibu, California

Ronald F. Ferguson, Ph.D.
Associate Professor of Public Policy
John F. Kennedy School of Government
Harvard University
Cambridge, Massachusetts

Thomas C. Froehle, Ph.D.
Professor, Department of Counseling and Educational Psychology
Indiana University
Bloomington, Indiana

Cherni Gillman, Ph.D.
Former contributing editor to the *International Journal on Drug Policy*
Former teacher and researcher at New York State Psychiatric Institute, Columbia University School of Public Health, and Drug Research, Inc.

David J. Hanson, Ph.D.
Director of Assessment and Professor of Sociology
State University of New York at Potsdam
Potsdam, New York

Anthony C. R. Hernández, Ph.D.
Research Psychologist, Chicano Studies Research Center
University of California, Los Angeles
Los Angeles, California

Michael L. Hirsch, Ph.D.
Assistant Professor of Sociology
Central Methodist College
Fayette, Missouri

Allan V. Horwitz, Ph.D.
Professor of Sociology
Department of Sociology and Institute for Health, Health Care Policy, and Aging Research
Rutgers University
New Brunswick, New Jersey

Stella P. Hughes, Ph.D.
Professor of Sociology
South Dakota School of Mines and Technology
Rapid City, South Dakota

Mary S. Jackson, Ph.D.
Assistant Professor of Criminal Justice
Department of Social Work
Cleveland State University
Cleveland, Ohio

Valerie Johnson, Ph.D.
Assistant Professor, Center of Alcohol Studies
Rutgers University
Piscataway, New Jersey

Keith M. Kilty, Ph.D.
Professor of Social Work
Ohio State University
Columbus, Ohio

Hugh Klein, Ph.D.
Senior Statistical Researcher
Nova Research Institute
Bethesda, Maryland

DeWayne J. Kurpius, Ed.D.
Professor, Department of Counseling and Educational Psychology
Indiana University
Bloomington, Indiana

Erich Labouvie, Ph.D.
Associate Professor of Psychology
Center of Alcohol Studies
Rutgers University
Piscataway, New Jersey

John C. McWilliams, Ph.D.
Associate Professor of American History
Penn State University-DuBois Campus
DuBois, Pennsylvania

Rustem S. Medora, Ph.D.
Professor of Pharmaceutical Sciences
University of Montana School of Pharmacy and Allied Health Sciences
Missoula, Montana

Martin A. Monto, Ph.D.
Assistant Professor of Sociology
University of Portland
Portland, Oregon

Joan Moore, Ph.D.
Professor of Sociology
University of Wisconsin-Milwaukee
Milwaukee, Wisconsin

Michael D. Newcomb, Ph.D.
Professor of Counseling Psychology
University of California, Los Angeles
Los Angeles, California

Maureen A. Norton Hawk, M.S.W., M.S.
Doctoral candidate, Department of Sociology
Northeastern University
Boston, Massachusetts

Michael R. Nusbaumer, Ph.D.
Associate Professor of Sociology
Co-coordinator of the Peace Studies Program
Indiana University-Purdue University at Fort Wayne
Fort Wayne, Indiana

Alexander Pearsall, B.A.
Graduate Student
San Francisco, California

David M. Petersen, Ph.D.
Professor of Sociology
Georgia State University
Atlanta, Georgia

David J. Pittman, Ph.D.
Professor Emeritus in Psychology
Washington University
St. Louis, Missouri

Ernest Quimby, Ph.D.
Associate Graduate Professor of Sociology and Criminal Justice
Department of Sociology and Anthropology
Howard University
Washington, D. C.

Jerome Rabow, Ph.D.
Professor of Sociology
University of California, Los Angeles
Los Angeles, California

James F. Rooney, Ph.D.
Professor of Sociology
Penn State University at Harrisburg
Harrisburg, Pennsylvania

Thaddeus Rozecki, M.S.
Doctoral candidate, Department of Counseling and Educational Psychology
Indiana University
Bloomington, Indiana

David R. Rudy, Ph.D.
Professor and Chair of the Department of Sociology, Social Work, and Corrections
Morehead State University
Morehead, Kentucky

William J. Staudenmeier, Jr., Ph.D.
Associate Professor of Sociology
Chair of the Social Science and Business Division
Eureka College
Eureka, Illinois

Peter J. Venturelli, Ph.D.
Chair and Associate Professor of Sociology
Valparaiso, University
Valparaiso, Indiana

Emilio Viano, Ph.D.
Professor, Department of Justice, Law, and Society
American University
Washington, D. C.

Alexander C. Wagenaar, Ph.D.
Associate Professor of Epidemiology
Director of the Alcohol/Tobacco/Drug Epidemiology Department
University of Minnesota School of Public Health
Minneapolis, Minnesota

Alisse Waterston, Ph.D.
President, Surveys Unlimited
Department of Cultural Anthropology
Fordham University
Bronx, New York

Helene Raskin White, Ph.D.
Associate Professor of Sociology
Center of Alcohol Studies and Sociology Department
Rutgers University
Piscataway, New Jersey

I

Part I—Alcohol/Alcoholism

In 1988 there were 106 million Americans who consumed alcohol on a regular basis (Witters, Venturelli, & Hanson, 1992). Teenagers are also heavily involved with this drug. "Adolescents who use alcohol and other drugs are much more likely than their nonusing peers to experience other serious problems" (Clayton, 1981; U.S. Dept. of Health & Human Services: Public Health Services, 1992). From 1979 to 1990, 88 percent of young adults (18–25) and 87 percent of older adults (26+) used alcohol (NIDA, 1990). With such statistics, we can see that alcohol continues to be the most widely used and abused drug in our nation today (Moskowitz, 1989). Other estimates are that approximately 18 million adults, 18 years and older, currently experience alcohol-related problems (Wodarski, 1990).

> Alcohol abuse and alcoholism cost the United States $116.8 billion in 1983. Costs due to premature death were $18 billion; reduced productivity cost $75.6 million; and treatment cost $13.5 billion. Alcohol is a factor in nearly 50 percent of all accidental deaths, suicides, and homicides, including 42 percent of all deaths from motor vehicle accidents. (Wodarski, 1990, p. 667)

Dryfoos (1991) reports that in a survey from *Weekly Reader,* 26 percent of fourth graders and 42 percent of sixth graders had already tried wine coolers. Such findings show that even to the present day, alcohol use continues to start very early. Further, if we consider fetal alcohol syndrome, alcohol use can begin involuntarily even before a child is conceived!

The fact that alcohol continues to be the most widely used and abused psychoactive drug is no great revelation. Because use is widespread, Part I devotes four articles to alcohol and alcoholism. These four articles pose the following questions: Who is likely to use alcohol? How do different people vary regarding their consumption of beer, wine and distilled spirits? What major explanations are given for alcohol abuse, and how do different explanations affect our perceptions of alcohol abusers? Finally, how can we distinguish between users and abusers?

The first article in Part I, "The Distribution of Alcohol Consumption in American Society," by Klein and Pittman, is based on a national probability sample of 2,041 Americans aged 21 and over (1,069 of whom were deemed "drinkers" on the basis of having drunk at least one alcoholic beverage in the past seven days before the interview). Klein and Pittman investigate the distribution of alcohol consumption in American society, both for total amount of alcohol consumed and for beer, wine, distilled spirits, and wine coolers, each considered separately. Differences based on sex, race, education, income, and marital status are examined, but are not found to be significant. The distribution of alcohol consumption by the location of the drinking (at home versus away from home; in different away-from-home locations; and in commercial versus noncommercial settings) is also studied, and many significant differences emerge. For example, distilled spirits are the only beverage type that is more likely to be consumed away from the home than at home. Results also indicate that beer, while being much more likely to be consumed in noncommercial than in commercial settings, is more *heavily* imbibed by drinkers in commercial settings. The policy implications of these research findings are also briefly discussed.

The second article, "Governmental Control of Deviant Drinking: The Manipulation of Morals and Medicine," by Nusbaumer, provides an analysis of the historical evolution of the two models that explain deviant drinking, by exploring the social history of governmental efforts to control deviant drinking (drinking to excess). Unlike Klein and Pittman, who give the reader some interesting data on the extent of alcohol consumption in our society, Nusbaumer provides some perspectives on how deviant drinking has been perceived.

The author outlines the two major models used to explain deviant drinking in American society: the moral model and the medical model. The moral model maintains that people drink alcohol to excess because they choose to do so, while the medical model postulates that they do so because of some uncontrollable biological condition. In examining the content of each of these models and the nature of their social support, Nusbaumer's article tries to explain why and how government used each of these models at different points in time. In general, this study shows how the government's use of these models may have affected its eventual success in controlling deviant drinking

The third article, "Perspectives on Alcoholism: Lessons from Alcoholics and Alcohologists," by Rudy, critiques how professionals who study alcohol use (known as alcohologists) view alcoholism from their discipline's orientation. Although this article expands on Nusbaumer's discussion of the moral and medical models of alcohol use and abuse, it differs in that special emphasis is placed on differentiating knowledge of alcohol use from beliefs about it. Further, this timely study also critiques some of the more recent research dealing with the inheritability of alcoholism.

Rudy highlights the limitations of the disease model of alcoholism and suggests alternative ways of conceptualizing alcoholism. Finally, the author points out that what has come to be regarded as alcoholism in contemporary America is a mythical form of social knowledge.

The fourth article, "Identifying Types of Normal and Problem Drinking," by Kilty, stresses that drinking is a form of social activity that can only be understood by examining normative (status quo) expectations that prescribe its use and the situational contexts where drinking occurs.

Kilty argues that since drinking involves many different activities and events, a system of classification is necessary to understand why people drink. Further, such a classification system should distinguish "normal" from "problem" types of drinking activities. The author suggests that drinking is not always problematic and that empirical and observational research should be conducted to understand the relationships among different drinking behaviors. Kilty also reviews several studies that attempted to develop different classification systems. Finally, Kilty outlines and discusses four types of drinking; they are: convivial drinking, drinking alcohol as a thirst-quencher, drinking alcohol as part of one's lifestyle, and drinking alcohol to change one's mood.

References

Clayton, R. R. (1981). The delinquency and drug use relationship among adolescents: A critical review [Monograph]. NIDA Research 31. In D. J. Letieri & J. Ludford (Eds.), *Drug abuse and the American adolescent.* Washington, DC: U. S. Dept of Health and Human Services.

Dryfoos, J. D. (1991). *Adolescents at risk.* New York: Oxford University Press.

Moskowitz, J. M. (1989). The primary prevention of alcohol problems: A critical review of the research literature. *Journal of Studies on Alcohol, 50*(1), 54–88.

National Institute on Drug Abuse (NIDA). (1990). Overview of the 1990 National Household Survey on Drug Abuse, *NIDA Capsules.*

U. S. Dept. of Health and Human Services: Public Health Services. (1992). *Healthy people 2000. National health promotion and disease prevention objectives.* Boston, MA: Jones & Bartlett Publishers, Inc.

Witters, W., Venturelli, P., & Hanson, G. (1992). *Drugs and society* (3rd ed.). Boston, MA: Jones & Bartlett Publishers, Inc.

Wodarski, J. S. (1990). Adolescent substance abuse: Practice implications. *Adolescence XXV, 99,* 667–688.

The Distribution of Alcohol Consumption in American Society

Hugh Klein David J. Pittman

Hugh Klein is currently a Senior Statistical Researcher with the Nova Research Institute (NRI), Ltd. in Bethesda, Maryland. Dr. Klein received his A.B. degree in sociology in 1983 from Washington University in St. Louis, and his Ph.D. in sociology in 1990 from Washington University in St. Louis. His major research interests are in the fields of substance abuse studies (particularly alcohol studies), sexual behavior and human sexuality, social aspects of AIDS, and the mass media. In recent years, Dr. Klein has been coprincipal investigator (with David J. Pittman) on the "Drinking Occasions Study," principal investigator of studies on college student drinking practices, and author of "Content and Changes in Gay Men's Personal Ads, 1975 to the Present." Most recently, he was awarded a grant from the National Institute on Alcohol Abuse and Alcoholism, to examine the portrayal of alcohol use and alcohol abuse in children's animated cartoons from 1930 to 1989.

Address correspondence to the author at: Nova Research Institute (NRI), Ltd., 4600 East-West Highway, Suite 700, Bethesda, MD 20814.

David J. Pittman is professor emeritus in psychology at Washington University, St. Louis, Missouri. He received his B.A. and M.A. degrees from the University of North Carolina—Chapel Hill. His Ph.D. degree was conferred by the University of Chicago. Dr. Pittman has been concerned with alcohol use, alcohol problems, and alcohol policy for many years. He is the author with C.W. Gordon of *Revolving Door: A Study of the Chronic Police Case Inebriate* and is the author of more than 200 published scientific articles, reports, and essays in the areas of alcoholism, drug addiction, criminology, and mass media. Dr. Pittman served as chairman of the 28th International Congress on Alcohol and Alcoholism in 1968; he is a former president of the North American Association of Alcoholism Programs; and he received the Silver Key Award from the National Council on Alcoholism (NCA) in 1978 for his "excellent and devoted service to NCA over the years." He is currently researching the economic effects of alcohol use and misuse and is working on a monograph focused on alcohol control measures.

Claims are frequently made regarding the distribution of alcohol use in the United States. For example, Kinney and Leaton (1987) assert that 7 percent of the drinking population consumes half of the alcohol ingested. In addition, they state that 70 percent of the drinkers consume only 20 percent of the alcohol, but no citation for these figures is provided. Royce (1981) also gives consumption distribution estimates for the U.S. drinking population, stating that 7 percent of all drinkers consume 40 percent of the alcohol, and that 10 percent drink 60 percent of our annual supply of alcoholic beverages. Yet Royce does not document his source of information either. Similarly, Haglund and Schuckit (1982) also provide unsubstantiated consumption figures, indicating that 2 percent of the population drinks about 25 percent of the alcohol consumed. These reported distribution patterns appear to have been derived impressionistically, not empirically.

In contrast, a few other researchers have documented their distribution-related findings. For example, Malin, Coakley, Kaelber, Munch, and Holland

(1982) report that the 11 percent of the drinking population that drinks most heavily consume half of all alcohol consumed, with the remaining 89 percent of the drinkers imbibing the other half.

Thus, while there are several estimates for the distribution of alcoholic beverage use in our society, there have been few empirical studies—especially recent ones—to substantiate these claims. This is an important omission, since taxation and other alcohol-related regulatory policies are premised on certain assumptions concerning the consumption of alcoholic beverages.

This is especially relevant when the issue becomes one of whether alcohol use takes place in commercial or noncommercial settings. Nowadays some individuals and groups are advocating that taxes be increased for alcoholic beverages, both in on-premise and off-premise settings. The justification for such tax hikes usually stems from the belief that significant amounts of alcohol are consumed in public, commercial settings; thus, a specific tax on each alcoholic beverage served would not only generate additional revenue for the state, but would also cause many drinkers to drink less alcohol (resulting in lower rates of alcohol-related problems such as driving while intoxicated).

The present study has three main purposes. First, it examines the distribution of alcohol consumption in a national probability sample of American adults aged 21 and over, to determine the concentration of alcohol use in the United States. Second, the distributions of alcohol consumption are compared for the demographic variables of sex, age, education, income, and marital status, to determine if these control variables affect the concentration of alcohol use. These variables were chosen because they have been shown to be influential in determining various aspects of alcohol consumption in previous research (Klein & Pittman, 1990b; Hilton & Clark, 1987; Haglund & Schuckit, 1982). Third, based on data on where respondents last drank alcoholic beverages, information is reported on the location-related distribution of consumption. This could provide an empirical foundation on which to base social policy decisions regarding the taxation of alcoholic beverages in various settings.

Method

The data were collected in November 1986 by a national research firm, for a study of drinking occasions. A national probability sample was obtained via telephone interviewing between the hours of 3:00 and 9:00 P.M. on weekdays, and between 10:00 a.m. and 4:00 P.M. on weekends. Random digit dialing was used to obtain access to potential respondents, to ensure the inclusion in the sample of people whose telephone numbers were unlisted. Approximately equal numbers of respondents were interviewed on each of the seven days of the week.

To be included in the sample, respondents had to be at least 21 years of age, and had to have consumed either beer, distilled spirits, wine, or wine coolers within the past week. People who had not consumed any alcoholic beverages within the past seven days were deemed nondrinkers, interviewers recorded the sex and age of nondrinkers, and then terminated the interview. The drinkers (i.e., those people who had consumed at least some alcohol during the past week), on the other hand, were asked a series of questions about their alcohol use. Drinking context information was gathered about the *last* time that respondents had had a particular beverage within the past week, but each person was asked about *each* type of alcoholic beverage that he or she had consumed within the past seven days. A seven-day reference period was chosen because it has been reported (Kendall, 1987) that it is difficult to remember accurately more than seven days in the past, but people's drinking habits vary so much from one day to another that any shorter time period than a week is likely to be misleading.

The survey instrument included separate sections for each of the four types of alcohol, but questions were otherwise identical within each of these sections. Questions dealt with how much of a particular type of alcohol people had consumed, who else was present during the drinking episode, what was going on at the time of the drinking, and when the drinking episode took place. Demographic data (sex, age, race, educational status, employment status, income, marital status, and state of residence) were obtained from each subject. Generally, these interviews took approximately 15 minutes to complete.

In all, of 4,104 telephone contacts, 1,603 people (or 39.1 percent) refused to be interviewed. Of the remaining 2,501 respondents, 1,432 (or 57.3 percent) were deemed nondrinkers on the basis of the criterion given above. Thus, 1,069 interviews were completed with eligible respondents, showing that fewer than half of the American adults sampled (or 42.7 percent) had actually drunk an alcoholic beverage in the past week.

Of all of the people contacted—including drinkers and nondrinkers alike—45.7 percent were male and 54.3 percent were female. Detailed data were collected only for the drinkers in this group, however; therefore the sample on which this research is based is actually 55.4 percent male and 44.6 percent female. This is consistent with national estimates of the sex ratio of drinkers in the population at large (Haglund & Schuckit, 1982; Cahalan, 1982). The contact sample ranged in age from 21 to 94, with a median age of 44.4 years; respondents in the drinking sample ranged in age from 21 to 90, with a median of 34.8 years. Thus, in general, the drinkers are much younger than the nondrinkers, as the proportion of people who drink declines with increasing age. This, too, is consistent with previous research on the relationship of age to drinking (Hilton & Clark, 1987; Cahalan, 1982). Other indicators (e.g., race, educational attainment, income level, and marital status) also suggest that this research is based on a relatively representative sample of American adult regular drinkers aged 21 or over (Hilton & Clark, 1987; Haglund & Schuckit, 1982; Cahalan, 1982). Further details about the sample can be found in Klein and Pittman (1990a).

Throughout this report, amounts of alcoholic beverages consumed during the past week are reported. These figures are based on the ethanol equivalencies for the various types of alcoholic beverages under study, rather than on the number of drinks consumed, *per se.* These ethanol equivalencies were calculated by multiplying the number of drinks of a given beverage type that each respondent reported having on his or her *last* drinking occasion by the estimated number of ounces contained in the drink (respondents' estimation) by the ethanol equivalency factor. The average ounces-of-alcohol-by-volume estimates (Williams, Doernberg, Stinson, & Noble, 1986) were used for these calculations. Thus, the ethanol equivalency factor for beer was .045, while those for distilled spirits, wine, and wine coolers were 0.411, 0.129, and 0.05, respectively. In this manner, a person who reported having 2 four-ounce glasses of wine the last time he drank would be said to have consumed 1.032 ounces of ethanol from that wine (2 glasses × 4 ounces per glass × 0.129 ounces of ethanol per ounce of wine consumed).

The data were analyzed utilizing two primary methods. One of these is the Statistical Analysis System (SAS), used here for all regression analyses. The other analytical technique employed in this study is the means-difference test, or the proportions-difference test, which was used to compare subjects' response breakdowns or amounts of consumption. The formulae for these latter computations are documented in Bohrnstedt and Knoke (1982). Results are reported as significant whenever they reached or exceeded an alpha level of .05.

Results

Distribution of Consumption among Drinkers

Table 1 presents the distribution of alcohol consumption for total ethanol ingestion, and separate comparisons for drinkers of the various beverage types. For all four beverages, alcohol consumption is quite unevenly distributed in the drinking population. By and large, wine, distilled spirits, and wine coolers show similar patterns of consumption distribution. For those types of alcohol, the heaviest-drinking 10 percent of the drinkers surveyed drank approximately three and a half times their proportionate share of the alcohol consumed. The top 20 percent of the drinkers of these beverages ingested around two and a half times their projected amount, while the heaviest-drinking one-third of the study participants drank just over twice their expected portions of alcohol.

While ostensibly similar results were obtained for beer consumption, the distribution of consumption for this particular beverage type is even more concentrated among the heaviest drinkers. Rather than drinking three and a half times their expected share of the alcohol, the top 10 percent of the beer drinkers surveyed consumed four and a half times their proportionate

Table 1
Distribution of Alcohol Consumption among Drinkers, by Beverage Type and Total Ethanol Intake

Distribution Ranking	Beer (N=675)	Wine (N=431)	Distilled Spirits (N=445)	Wine Coolers (N=148)	Total Amount (N=1-69)
Top 1%	9.5%	10.1%	6.7%	9.6%	8.4%
Top 5%	28.9	24.2	22.6	24.2	26.1
Top 10%	43.0*	35.7	35.8	35.3	39.0
Top 20%	59.7*	51.0	52.3	51.1	55.5
Top 33%	74.5*	65.8	69.3	65.2	71.0
Bottom 20%	2.9	6.4	5.0	8.1	4.4
Bottom 33%	6.6	10.7	9.5	13.5	8.5
Bottom 50%	13.8	20.9	17.9	20.8	16.6

* = significant (p<.05) versus all other beverage types

amount—a significantly greater concentration than those noted for wine (p<.009), distilled spirits (p<.009), and wine coolers (p<.05). Likewise, among the upper one-fifth of the beer drinkers, consumption is nearly triple the amount expected by their numbers—a proportionate share that is significantly more concentrated than the distributions noted for wine (p<.004), distilled spirits (p<.009), and wine coolers (p<.04). The same also occurs among the top third of all beer drinkers, compared to drinkers of wine, distilled spirits, and wine coolers (p<.003, p<.04, p<.03, respectively).

The converse is generally true as well. Among the bottom 20 percent of the drinkers surveyed, beer consumption is significantly less concentrated than consumption of wine (p<.006), distilled spirits (p<.05), or wine coolers (p<.03). The same statement can be made for the lightest-drinking one-third of all drinkers (p<.02, p<.05, p<.02, respectively) and the lower one-half of all drinkers (p<.003, p<.04, p<.03, respectively).

Even among the 5 percent heaviest drinkers of beer, consumption is significantly more concentrated than is true for wine (p<.05) or distilled spirits (p<.01). And finally, for the upper l percent of all alcohol consumers, consumption of distilled spirits is *least* concentrated, especially compared to the very heaviest drinkers of beer (p<.05) and wine (p<.04).

Distribution of Consumption, by Demographic Variables

Analyses for sex, age, income, education, and marital status were also performed separately. No pairwise significant differences were found. In a few instances (e.g., for wine cooler consumption among the lightest drinking l/5, 1/3, and l/2 of the youngest and oldest respondents), large absolute differences (i.e., concentration differentials greater than 20 percent) were noted between comparison groups. However, because of the small number of cases being compared, standard error terms were large, rendering the differences obtained statistically nonsignificant. Since no significant differences were noted, all of these data have been excluded from presentation.[1]

Distribution of Consumption by Drinking Location: Likelihood of Drinking

Given that alcohol consumption is by no means evenly distributed among drinkers, it was decided to investigate the distribution of alcohol consumption further, by beverage type, and by location of drinking. Tables 2 and 3 present the results of these analyses. Regarding the location of the drinking episodes, Table 2 indicates that people are significantly more likely to drink beer, wine, and wine coolers at home than away from home (p<.0001 for beer; P<.0001 for wine; P<.000l for wine coolers), while drinkers of distilled spirits are more likely to drink away from home than at home (p<.000l).

When the away-from-home drinking locations are analyzed, we find one consistency among all four beverage types: respondents are significantly less likely to drink at work than at any of the other away-from-home drinking locations. But other significant differences were also noted. For example, beer drinkers are more likely to drink at a bar than at a restaurant (p<.04), while the opposite is true for drinkers of distilled spirits (p<.03) and wine (p<.0001). Respondents are about equally likely to drink wine coolers in bars and restaurants, however (n.s.). Consumers of distilled spirits and wine are significantly more likely to drink these beverages in a restaurant than at a friend's home (p<.000l, p<.0001, respectively), while the reverse is true for wine cooler drinkers (P<.000l). Beer drinkers, on the other hand, are no more likely to drink at a friend's home than at a restaurant (n.s.). But when the likelihood of drinking at a friend's home and at a bar are compared, we find that wine and wine coolers are more likely to be consumed in the former setting (p<.000l, p<.0001, respectively), distilled spirits in the latter setting (p<.0001), and beer almost equally likely at either location (n.s.).

Since controversy has arisen in recent years over the consumption of alcoholic beverages in commercial versus noncommercial settings (especially in reference to drunk driving), analyses were performed to study the use of alcohol in these different types of settings. For the purposes of these analyses, drinking at home, at a friend's home, and at work were all considered noncommercial settings, while restaurants and bars were deemed commercial locations.

All four beverage types are much more likely (significantly so, in fact) to be consumed in noncommercial than in commercial settings. But it is also important to note that, of the four beverages under study, the type most likely to be consumed in a commercial location is distilled spirits—by a significantly greater proportion of the drinkers than is true for beer (p<.0001), wine (p<.0001), and wine coolers (p<.0001).

Table 2
Alcohol Consumption by Location of Drinking, by Beverage Type
(in percentage of drinkers)

	Beer (N=675)	Distilled Spirits (N=445)	Wine (N=431)	Wine Coolers (N=148)
Location of Drinking				
At home	57.6	42.2	61.3	60.1
Away from home	42.4	57.8	38.7	39.9
Away-from-home drinking locations				
At a friends' home	27.3	16.7	33.5	50.0
At a restaurant	22.4	41.6	52.1	20.7
At a bar	29.0	32.3	3.0	13.8
At work	3.5	0.4	1.2	3.4
Commercial setting?				
Yes	23.8	45.1	22.2	13.8
No	76.2	54.9	77.8	86.2

Analyses also revealed that wine coolers are significantly less likely than the other beverage types to be drunk in a commercial setting (p<.003 for beer: p<.0001 for distilled spirits: p<.01 for wine). Respondents were about equally unlikely to drink beer and wine in commercial settings, however (n.s.).

Distribution of Consumption by Drinking Location: Amount Consumed

When it comes to the amount consumed in each location, quite a different picture emerges. For example, while beer is three times as likely to be drunk in a noncommercial as in a commercial setting, beer drinking in commercial locations is significantly *heavier* than that noted for noncommercial locations. (Mean consumption in commercial settings = 4.58 oz., versus 3.01 oz. for noncommercial settings, p<.007.) The opposite is true for distilled spirits, however. (Mean consumption in commercial settings = 3.27 oz., versus 3.94 oz. in noncommercial settings, p<.04.) Wine and wine cooler consumption are approximately the same in commercial and noncommercial drinking locations (Mean consumption of wine = 1.57 vs. 1.85 oz., n.s.; mean consumption of wine coolers = 1.98 vs. 1.35 oz., n.s.)

Table 3 provides the results for the beverage-by-beverage analyses of the distribution of consumption in commercial and noncommercial settings. This table shows that the beverage types have quite different patterns of consumption distribution. For example, the use of beer or wine coolers is most heavily concentrated when they are consumed in commercial settings: the opposite is true for the use of distilled spirits and wine, however.[2]

Discussion

In the United States, alcohol consumption is unevenly distributed throughout the drinking population. The heaviest-drinking 10 percent of the population ingest nearly four times their proportionate share of alcohol. Likewise, 20 percent of all drinkers consume slightly more than half (55.5 percent) of the alcohol drunk each week, and the heaviest-drinking one-third of the drinkers ingest more than twice their suspected amount (71 percent). Conversely, on this other end of the drinking spectrum, 33 percent of all drinkers drink less than 10 percent of the alcohol. Even the lightest-drinking half of the drinking population consumes only about one-sixth of the total amount of alcohol drunk each week.

Table 3
Distribution of Consumption in Commercial and Noncommercial Settings, by Beverage Type

Distribution of Consumption	Beer (N=675)	Distilled Spirits (N=445)	Wine (N=431)	Wine Coolers (N=148)
Commercial Settings	(N=162)	(N=200)	(N=95)	(N-21)
Top 5%	32.3	19.9	16.7	30.8
Top 10%	49.8	34.7	27.4	40.0
Top 20%	66.4	52.0	43.5	56.9
Top 33%	79.4	66.4	60.1	70.8
Noncommercial Settings	(N=513)	(N=245)	(N=336)	(N=127)
Top 5%	25.7	23.3	26.3	23.8
Top 10%	39.3	37.4	37.2	34.7
Top 20%	57.6	54.3	52.5	50.9
Top 33%	73.0	70.9	66.7	64.3

These findings are both in agreement with *and* in contrast to previous reports in the literature. They mirror earlier work by demonstrating that alcohol consumption is unequally distributed throughout the drinking population. However, these findings differ from previous claims in that they show that alcohol consumption is not *as* skewed as has been presented. For example, in contrast to Royce's unsubstantiated claims (1981) that 10 percent of the drinkers consume 60 percent of our nation's alcohol, or the empirically-supported findings of Malin, Coakley, Kaelber, Munch, and Holland (1982) that this latter figure is about 50 percent, our results indicate that the 10 percent heaviest drinkers drink 39 percent of this country's alcohol. Clearly, this confirms that alcohol intake is concentrated in the heaviest-drinking segment of the population, but not to the extent previously stated.[3]

The findings for the different alcoholic beverage types show that distilled spirits, wine, and wine coolers all share similar distribution-of-consumption profiles, with the heaviest-drinking one-fifth of these populations consuming a little more than half of the alcohol, and the top one-third of these drinkers drinking around two-thirds of the distilled spirits, wine, and wine coolers consumed in any given week. Beer consumption, these results suggest, is even more concentrated among the heaviest drinkers—significantly more so, in fact, than is true for wine, distilled spirits, and wine coolers. This finding is consistent with previous work on beer drinkers, suggesting that these individuals drink more heavily and drink to the point of intoxication more frequently than do their wine- and distilled spirits-drinking counterparts (Klein & Pittman, 1990c; Berger & Snortum, 1985; Banks & Smith, 1980).

Also of importance is the finding that the distributions of alcohol consumption did not differ significantly by sex, age, education, income, or marital status. This is all the more impressive when one considers that no paired comparison yielded a significant difference, despite the large number of significance tests performed. The distribution-of-alcohol-consumption analyses based on the location of the drinking indicate that people are more likely to drink beer, wine, and wine coolers at home than away from home, while the opposite is true for distilled spirits. Interestingly, however, while drinkers of distilled spirits are more likely to drink away from the home than at home, they drink more heavily when at home (data not presented). In contrast, wine drinkers are not only more likely to drink at home, but they ingest more wine in that location than when they drink away from home. For beer and wine cooler drinkers, the amount consumed did not vary significantly by the location of their drinking (data not presented). Significant differences were also found for the likelihood of drinking in various away-from-home locations. Essentially, wine coolers are most likely to be consumed at a friend's home, wine and distilled spirits in a restaurant (or to a lesser extent, at a friend's home or in a bar, respectively), and beer either in a bar or at a friend's home. Therefore, the place in which individuals find themselves strongly influences whether or not they drink alcohol, which beverage(s) they will drink, and how much they will consume.

When the data are analyzed in terms of the commercial or noncommercial nature of the drinking setting, the results become even more distinct. Beer, wine, and wine coolers were all *much* more likely (all by more than a factor of three) to be consumed in noncommercial settings than in commercial settings, but only beer consumption was heavier in commercial than in noncommercial settings. Distilled spirits, too, were significantly more likely to be consumed noncommercially than commercially, although the difference here was much smaller than those noted for the other beverage types. Consumption of distilled spirits was actually heavier in the noncommercial drinking locations, however. Results also indicated a tendency (nonsignificant) for beer and wine cooler consumption to be more highly concentrated among the heaviest drinkers in commercial settings than among those drinking in noncommercial settings, while the opposite trends (nonsignificant) were observed for distilled spirits and wine consumption.

These findings have several implications for alcohol policy. First, they suggest that legislation aimed at further regulating the commercial sale of alcoholic beverages may not have a significant impact on alcohol-related harm, given the strong tendency for drinkers to consume their alcoholic beverages in noncommercial settings. Most drinking occurs in the home and in noncommercial settings; other recent research (Shanken, 1989) also bears this out. Therefore, attempts to reduce the number of on-premise sales outlets, their hours of sale, or their days of sale will affect consumption only to a limited extent.

Moreover, such laws would affect drinkers of the various beverage types differently. Regulatory policies aimed at commercial establishments would affect consumption of distilled spirits most (since this beverage type is most likely to be consumed in commercial settings), despite the tendency for drinkers of distilled spirits to do their heaviest drinking in noncommercial settings. Since beer drinkers drink only in commercial settings about one-quarter of the time, such laws would be less likely to have an impact on them, despite their tendency to drink most heavily when in a commercial settling. These laws would affect wine and wine coolers about equally, but these beverages are almost always consumed moderately (in this sample, at least), and are less frequently drunk in commercial settings in any case. This, too, has been reported elsewhere in the literature (Shanken, 1989).

In conclusion, the distribution of alcohol consumption in our society is very uneven, and exhibits much variation based on the beverage type under consideration and the location and nature of the drinking setting. Understanding who the heavy drinkers are and where they do their heaviest drinking is crucial if successful measures are ever to be implemented to decrease alcohol-related problems in our society. Regulatory policies for alcoholic beverages must be take into account the factors affecting the distribution of consumption of alcoholic beverages and the various settings of use. Such policy issues as the taxation of alcoholic beverages raise questions about whether two-thirds of the drinkers, who consume about 30 percent of the alcohol, should be required to pay for the problems affecting—and caused by—the heaviest drinkers. Our results suggest that taxing alcohol by the drink in commercial settings will not significantly affect alcohol consumption in these locations. Such legislative measures may have *some* impact on alcohol use in commercial settings, but this study indicates that this impact is likely to be minimal.

Notes

1. Readers who would like further information about the specific findings (not presented here) obtained for the distributions of consumption for beer, wine, distilled spirits, and wine coolers, based on sex, age, education, income, and marital status, should contact the first author.
2. None of these attained statistical significance. This is probably the result of the small cell sizes obtained when comparing only small proportions of the drinkers of each beverage type in commercial and noncommercial settings. Undoubtedly, had these cells been larger (say, with an N of 50 or 100), and had the same results been obtained, the findings (especially those for beer, wine, and wine coolers) would have reached significance.
3. Of course, we are aware that the amount of alcohol *reported* consumed by the drinking population does not equal the amount reported by the alcoholic beverage industry as being *produced.* Although some ethanol is undoubtedly "lost" to wastage and nonconsumption, these amounts are not significant. Recent research (Williams, Aitken, & Malin, 1985) has also indicated that self-reported ingestion of alcoholic beverages is relatively reliable, and that underreporting of alcohol consumption is not substantial.

References

Banks, E., & Smith, M. (1980). Attitudes and background factors related to alcohol use among college students. *Psychological Reports, 46,* 571–577.

Berger, D., & Snortum, J. (1985). Alcoholic beverage preferences of drinking-driving violators. *Journal of Studies on Alcohol, 46,* 232–239.

Bohrnstedt, G., & Knoke, D. (1982). *Statistics for social data analyses.* Itaska, IL: F. E. Peacock Publishers, Inc.

Cahalan, D. (1982). Epidemiology: Alcohol use in American society. In E. L. Gomberg, H. R. White, & J. A. Carpenter (Eds.), *Alcohol, science, and society revisited* (pp. 96–118). Ann Arbor, MI: University of Michigan Press.

Haglund, R. M. J., & Schuckit, M. A. (1982). The epidemiology of alcoholism. In N. J. Estes, & M. E. Meinemann (Eds.), *Alcoholism: development, consequences, and interventions* (2nd ed. pp. 32–48). St. Louis, MO: C.V. Mosby.

Hilton, M., & Clark, W. (1987). Changes in American drinking patterns and problems, 1967–1984. *Journal of Studies on Alcohol, 48*, 515–522.

Kendall, R. E. (1987). Drinking sensibly. *British Journal of Addiction, 82*, 1279–1288.

Kinney, J., & Leaton, G. (Eds.). (1987). *Loosening the grip: A handbook of alcohol information* (3rd ed.). St. Louis, MO: C.V. Mosby.

Klein, H., & Pittman, D. J. (1990a). Social occasions and the perceived situational appropriateness of consuming different alcoholic beverages. *Journal of Studies on Alcohol, 51*, 59–67.

Klein, H., & Pittman, D. J. (1990b). Perceived consequences associated with the use of beer, wine, distilled spirits, and wine coolers. *International Journal of the Addictions, 25*, 471–492.

Klein, H., & Pittman, D. J. (1990c). Drinker prototypes in American society. *Journal of Substance Abuse, 2*, 299–316.

Malin, H., Coakley, J., Kaelber, C., Munch, N., & Holland, W. (1982). An epidemiologic perspective on alcohol use and abuse in the United States. In National Institute on Alcohol Abuse and Alcoholism. Alcohol consumption and related problems [Monograph] *Alcohol and Health, 1*, 99–153. Washington, DC: U. S. Government Printing Office.

Royce, J. E. (1981). *Alcohol problems and alcoholism: A comprehensive survey.* New York: Free Press.

Shanken, M. R. (Ed.), (1989, August 1). SIP Releases new demographic data on alcoholic beverage consumption. *Impact, 19*, 1–5.

Williams, G. D., Aitken, S. S., & Malin, H. (1985). Reliability of self-reported alcohol consumption in a general population survey. *Journal of Studies on Alcohol, 46*, 223–227.

Williams, G., Doernberg, D., Stinson, F., & Noble, J. (1986). State, regional, and national trends in apparent per capita consumption. *Alcohol Health & Research World, 10*, 60–63.

Discussion Questions

1. In the research by Klein and Pittman, how does at-home consumption of alcohol differ from away-from-home consumption?
2. In most sociological studies, demographic variables such as gender, age, education, income, and/or marital status are found to have a strong influence on researchers' findings. Why do you suppose that this was not typically the case in Klein and Pittman's work?
3. Klein and Pittman report that the top 5 percent of all drinkers consume more than five times their proportional share of the alcohol ingested, and that the top 10 percent drink nearly four times their proportional share of the alcohol. At the opposite extreme, fully half of all drinkers consume about one-sixth of the alcohol. How do you interpret/explain these findings?
4. In your examination of the second block of data in Table 2, you will notice that there are large differences across beverage types in terms of which types of alcohol are ingested in different away-from-home locations. What do you think accounts for these particular differences?

Government Control of Deviant Drinking

The Manipulation of Morals and Medicine

Michael R. Nusbaumer

Michael R. Nusbaumer is currently an Associate Professor of Sociology and Co-coordinator of the Peace Studies Program at Indiana University-Purdue University at Fort Wayne. He received his B.S. in Education from Indiana University at Ft. Wayne, his M.A. in sociology from Ball State University, and his Ph.D. from Western Michigan University. His primary area of research interest deals with the definition and control of deviant drinking. His recent publications in this area have appeared in: the *Research Annual of Social Policy*, the *International Journal of the Addictions*, and *Sociological Focus*. His current research focus in this area deals with the politics of the study of drug use.

Beverage alcohol has been the most widely used psychoactive substance in humankind's history. Its use predates recorded history, and it has been ingested for its psychoactive properties in every culture that has fruit or grain and the knowledge of fermentation available to it. The consumption of alcoholic beverages is usually considered socially acceptable and even encouraged, if it reduces anxiety and alienation, or aids social adjustment and group cohesion. At the same time, almost every culture also has some conception of deviant drinking, or drinking behaviors that are viewed as disruptive to social interaction or societal functioning.

Since any disruptive behavior is potentially threatening to the stability of the social group, every society attempts to exert some type of control or pressure upon its deviant drinkers, to reduce or even eliminate these disruptive drinking patterns. Just as with the conception of deviant drinking, the form and content of these controls depend upon the particular society's beliefs about the cause and nature of deviant drinking and the culture's commonly held views about the deviant drinker. Furthermore, the form and content of societal controls are often restricted by the resources available to a particular society. For example, nomadic societies rarely have jails or prisons available to them for the confinement of deviants.

Within many societies, various individuals and social groups disagree over what constitutes appropriate and inappropriate drinking behaviors. However, in order for any society to control disruptive drinking behaviors successfully, at least some level of agreement or consensus must be reached regarding what are appropriate and inappropriate drinking patterns, and what are the most appropriate means of controlling these patterns. Typically, the social groups holding competing views on these issues attempt to operate as "moral entrepreneurs" (Becker, 1963). Moral entrepreneurs represent individuals and groups who not only have strongly held views on particular subjects, such as drinking, but who also strive to convince others to accept their views. Thus, moral entrepreneurs with conflicting views often enter into competition with each other, in an effort to establish greater support for their viewpoints.

In bureaucratically organized industrial societies, the ultimate goal for these moral entrepreneurs is to gain government acceptance of their particular views. Such government acceptance may take a variety of forms, including the passage of certain laws and the adoption of certain viewpoints by government agencies such as the National Institute on Alcohol Abuse and Alcoholism (NIAAA). Not only does this official acceptance serve as the ultimate societal sanctioning of these views, but it also brings to bear a wide array of government resources to aid in controlling the deviant behavior and enforcing the rules (beliefs).

In this light, the current inquiry will examine the social and political history of the United States with regard to the two major theoretical views relating to deviant drinking, government adoption of these two views, and how the nature of government utilization of these views has altered control activities. Within the context of limited government resources and powers, attention will focus particularly upon how government involvement in the control of disruptive drinking behaviors changes theoretical control approaches, which ultimately affects their success.

Two Models of Deviant Drinking

Throughout the history of the United States there have been two predominant explanations for deviant drinking: the moral model and the medical model. Although there have been numerous variations of these two views, there remain certain common core beliefs about the cause of such drinking behaviors, the level of responsibility of the deviant drinker for his or her drinking behavior, and the necessary and appropriate ways of controlling these behaviors.

The moral model of deviant drinking assumes that individuals have control over their own drinking practices and behaviors, and that they choose how much to drink. In a sense, drinkers are making such drinking choices as weighing the costs of drinking against the rewards. The drinker who persists in drinking in a manner considered disruptive and deviant by society is viewed as choosing to do so despite societal disapproval. Deviant drinkers always have the power to reform and bring their behavior in line with society's approved drinking patterns. These deviant drinkers simply do not want to change their behavior, because they feel that the rewards outweigh the costs.

Efforts to control deviant drinking under the moral model attempt to diminish or eliminate such behaviors by attaching additional costs to these behaviors. Theoretically, if enough costs or punishments are attached to these behaviors, the costs of continuing them will outweigh the rewards, and individuals will decide to stop their deviant drinking. The punishments may take the form of fines, loss of certain privileges, such as the revocation of driver's licenses, mandatory alcohol or driving education, or incarceration.

In contrast to the moral model, the medical model views deviant drinkers as having at least some level of diminished control over their drinking patterns. In other words, because of some biological condition within the individual, or some chemical property of the drug itself, the drinkers' ability to make rational choices regarding their drinking practices is impaired. Continued disruptive drinking practices therefore are not simply the consequence of the drinker's decision, but also the consequence of these biological or chemical factors. Thus, societal efforts to control these behaviors through the application of additional punishments is considered unethical, as it is inappropriate to punish individuals for behavior they do not have under complete control. Under the medical model, the deviant drinker is considered sick and eligible for placement in the sick role (Parsons, 1951). Such people deserve kindness, sympathy, and care, not punishment. While the sick role allows deviant drinkers to escape certain societal punishments, and relieves them of at least some of the responsibility for their drinking behaviors, it also requires them to fulfill two obligations. They are expected to want to get better and to seek out and cooperate with those who are best qualified to help them get better. Treatment approaches for this illness have never recognized the existence of a cure, but the symptoms can always be controlled if one completely abstains from alcohol consumption. Symptoms of the disease never appear unless alcohol is consumed.

Early American Drinking History

The heaviest alcohol consumption in this country's history occurred during the colonial period (Peele, 1989; Rorabaugh, 1979). Three major conditions supported this level of consumption. First, alcohol was viewed primarily not as a consciousness-altering substance, but as a healthy, even medicinal substance that improved both physical health and social well-being. Second, at the time, the distillation of grain into alcohol was one of the most efficient means of protecting and preserving the caloric value of grain from spoilage, and alcohol was easier to transport than the grain itself. Finally, in this new, vast, rugged, wilderness alcohol was viewed as an often necessary fortifier against the harsh, dangerous environment. Intoxication, although publicly condemned, was seen as acceptable behavior within the tavern setting, as long as one did not become disruptive. Even then, frequent disruptive public intoxication was viewed as a personal indiscretion or moral weakness, not as a problem with the drug itself.

Beginning just before the turn of the century, however, these views of drinking began to undergo change, as American society itself changed. Eastern cities were experiencing dramatic population growth, primarily because of industrialization and the increasing waves of European immigration. These rapid changes often hampered or destroyed traditional control mechanisms that had previously held certain forms of disruptive drinking in check. Additionally, intoxication within these urban industrial settings came to be recognized as disruptive to an industrious life that required disciplined labor (Levine, 1983; Rumbarger, 1989).

Support for the definition of heavy alcohol consumption as deviant also came from the struggle for cultural dominance between the traditional cultural base, made up of predominantly rural and small town, middle- and upper-class Protestants who had been in the states for a few generations, and the more recent immigrants, who were typically urban, Catholic, industrial workers (Gusfield, 1963). Differing views of appropriate drinking became a significant point of contention. The Protestants viewed intoxication as self-indulgence and a loss of self-control, while the European Catholics viewed it as a cultural right and a basis of socializing, especially among young men.

These conflicts and changes gave birth to the temperance movement. Although there were various groups involved with this movement, there appeared to be a general consensus within the movement on the nature and cause of frequent intoxication. Temperance advocates were the first moral entrepreneurs to utilize a medical model of deviant drinking. Generally, they felt that if one began drinking in an intemperate manner, the chemical nature of the drug alcohol took control of one, producing an uncontrollable desire to consume ever increasing amounts. The only possible consequence of such drinking was an ever downward spiral of physical and moral decay whose sole course led to the inevitable death of a drunkard. Given that the root cause of such drinking patterns lay within the drug itself, anyone could become enslaved by it.

The temperance movement was officially concerned with the immoral, disruptive, and deviant nature of intoxication; any form of alcohol consumption was a point of contention within this movement. While some believed that it was still possible to consume alcoholic beverages in a temperate manner, many believed that the powers of the drug were so insidious that even the most well-intentioned, moral drinkers could not be sure they would not succumb. As a result, a growing proportion of the temperance movement supported total abstention from the consumption of all alcoholic beverages. The decision to abstain from the consumption of alcohol was, however, clearly considered a moral one. The major thrust of early temperance activities was to get people to voluntarily take a pledge not to consume alcoholic beverages. By 1835, more than 1,000,000 people had voluntarily promised not to drink distilled spirits (hard liquor), and 500,000 had pledged not to drink any form of alcohol at all (Peele, 1989). Through most of the 1800s the temperance movement experienced ups and downs, and even though there were literally millions of Americans who signed pledges, drunkenness remained a major growing concern in American society. Beginning around 1890, the temperance movement underwent significant change. The attempt to produce changes in drinking behavior by pressuring drinkers to voluntarily take the pledge lacked success in controlling much deviant drinking. Thus, the temperance movement moved from an "assimilative" attitude towards drinkers to a "coercive" one (Gusfield, 1963).

Assimilative reformers perceive the targets of their reform as victims deserving kindness and sympathy, who can be converted to the "appropriate" moral position when given enough education and understanding; coercive reformers do not. Coercive reformers view violators of their moral standards as enemies who have repudiated (the reformers') morality and are beyond redemption. Simply relying on the morality of drinkers to make them abstain was not sufficient to thwart the overwhelming powers of alcohol and maintain the temperance supports' cultural norms.

From the moral model's perspective, the inability of drinkers to become and remain abstinent, as the morally appropriate way to protect themselves from the drug's powers, meant that additional costs needed to be applied to the decision to drink. This coercive orientation led to an all-out push to enact laws prohibiting the sale and use of alcoholic beverages.

Prohibition

Although many states had passed similar legislation earlier in the twentieth century, the national prohibition of alcohol did not occur until 1919, with the passage of the Eighteenth Amendment to the Constitution and its enabling legislation, known as the Volstead Act. This law made it illegal to produce, sell, or transport "intoxicating liquors." The law did not make it illegal to drink or possess alcoholic beverages, and it allowed for a grace period in which those with the financial means could stockpile as much liquor as they could afford. Furthermore, there was a variety of loopholes with regards to production and distribution. The fermentation of fruit juice at home was not outlawed, nor was the sale of distilling equipment. Physicians were not restricted from prescribing alcoholic beverages for "medicinal" purposes. Alcohol could also be legally manufactured for industrial uses.

In 1920, the first year of prohibition, the federal government provided only a little more than $2 million for its enforcement. Some 1,500 enforcement agents were hired at an average salary of $1,500. Not only were these agents underpaid (garbage collectors' wages compared favorably) and generally untrained, they were also political appointees hired through a spoils system. Out of a total of 17,972 appointments to the federal government's Prohibition Bureau in its first eleven years, 11,982 left on their own, and 1,604 were fired (Sinclair, 1962). Given these inadequate enforcement resources and the opportunity for graft and corruption among the politically appointed agents, federal enforcement activities had limited success. Because the Eighteenth Amendment gave states concurrent enforcement responsibilities, however, enforcement of the law was largely the responsibility of the individual states. Thus, depending upon the social and political makeup of different states, enforcement varied greatly in different parts of the country. In 1933, the Twenty-First Amendment to the Constitution passed in Congress, repealing national prohibition. Two major explanations have been given for this repeal. A major concern of many was the increasing lawlessness that resulted, not only from the anger, frustration, and despair stemming from the great economic depression of the 1930s, but from the fact that prohibition itself made lawbreakers out of a large percentage of otherwise law-abiding citizens (Cahalan, 1987; Levine, 1985). Indeed, by 1930, 4,000 out of 12,000 inmates in the federal prisons were there for trafficking in alcohol (Bakalar & Grinspoon, 1984). The second prominent explanation for prohibition's repeal relates to the general economic pressures brought on by the depression. If prohibition were repealed a resurgent alcohol industry could provide jobs, profits, and tax revenues, while the government costs of prohibition enforcement would be eliminated (Bakalar & Grinspoon, 1984; Cahalan, 1987).

Prohibition also represents a major turning point of society's orientation toward deviant drinking, appropriate control strategies, and the role of the federal government in that control. The repeal of prohibition at least officially signaled the failure and ultimate demise of the moral model of deviant drinking. Although drinkers were not directly punishable under prohibition law, the decision to drink was more costly under prohibition. Not only was alcohol more difficult to obtain and more expensive, but the safety of the alcoholic could not be guaranteed, and many went blind or died from drinking poisonous alcohol. Proponents of the moral model of deviant drinking, having been given their "ultimate" chance to prove their views correct through the enactments of prohibition, were discredited by its failure. The repeal of the Eighteenth Amendment signaled the demise of cultural dominance by the traditional rural-oriented middle-class Protestants. Many now viewed temperance advocates as moral or religious zealots lacking understanding of both the cause and solution of deviant drinking, and of the limitations of legitimate government intervention in a democratic society.

Prohibition was, however, the first major attempt by the federal government to control deviant drinking. This experience indicated that the mere passage of coercive legislation does not necessarily alter behavioral patterns (at least in regards to drinking), and that to attempt such coercion may prove embarrassing and discrediting to the government. It also made evident the fact that without widespread societal consensus, or an almost limitless supply of enforcement resources, such criminalistic and highly politicized approaches to controlling behavior are likely doomed to failure.

Enter the New Medical Model

In 1935, only a couple of years after the repeal of prohibition, two men, one a stockbroker, the other a physician, formed a self-help group for deviant drinkers attempting to control their drinking practices. They called the group Alcoholics Anonymous (AA). Although similar groups had existed as much as 100 years before, the birth of AA occurred under different social conditions.

To begin with, its two founders were strongly influenced by another physician named Silkworth. Silkworth suggested that deviant drinking (now defined as "alcoholism" by this group) was the result of a physiological reaction to alcohol, much like any allergic reaction (Jellinek, 1960). Just as certain people are allergic to pollen or cat fur, some people, because of their biological makeup, have a particular biological reaction to alcohol. Thus, alcoholics (deviant drinkers) have a "disease" for which they are not responsible, and over which they have little control. Unlike the previous medical model of deviant drinking, this new model posited that not everyone was susceptible to deviant drinking, only that small segment of the population who had the biologically-based allergic reaction. Like other allergies, alcoholism was incurable, so the best one could hope for was relief from the symptoms of the disease. Given that the symptoms of alcoholism only appeared when one consumed alcoholic beverages, the only way to control the symptoms was to abstain from alcohol consumption. AA believed that the task of remaining sober (abstaining) was very difficult for these diseased individuals, and could best be achieved through the fellowship and group support provided by the organization. It was also AA's belief that only those who had experienced the struggles for sobriety themselves could understand and help others attempting to do the same thing. AA had little place for professionals who had not gone through this ordeal, and they firmly believed that the only knowledge necessary to help others control their drinking was one's own personal experience.

AA was a voluntary, non-profit operation that had no paid staff members and no dues or membership fees. The voluntary nature of the organization was central, as they believed that individuals could not be helped until they recognized on their own the severity of their deviant drinking and their inability to control it. In this regard, AA felt that alcoholics had to "hit bottom" in terms of costs related to their drinking, before they could recognize the need and value of the AA fellowship.

AA's overall approach to the control of deviant drinking is best characterized in their now somewhat famous Twelve Steps for continued sobriety. While these twelve steps contain a variety of implications, there are three that are particularly relevant for current discussion. First, there is clearly a religious orientation, reminiscent of the earlier temperance movement. This religious orientation reflects traditional Protestant beliefs in one's powerlessness before God and the need to repent and reform one's ways (especially as they relate to alcohol-based disruptive behaviors). Many analysts have charged AA with being a religion unto itself (Peele, 1989). The second point relates to the twelfth step, which maintains that once one has achieved reform, it becomes one's duty to proselytize actively for AA. This twelfth step therefore produces increasing numbers of moral entrepreneurs advocating the AA approach. Finally, implicit within this disease model framework, moral aspects again come into play, as it is ultimately up to the individual to make and stay with *his/her* decision to abstain from alcohol.

AA's size, support, and influence grew rapidly in the following years. As time passed, more and more "twelfth steppers" were becoming active in gaining new recruits, as well as serving as living proof of the success of AA. In fact AA has long claimed to have the highest success rate of any treatment or intervention program dealing with alcoholics, although this claim remains largely unsubstantiated in the research literature. By 1980, it was estimated that AA had some 26,000 groups and between 800,000 to 1,200,000 members in the United States alone (Maxwell, 1982; Mecca, 1980).

Through the next three decades, a variety of factors provided support and legitimacy to AA's basic views.

One form of support came from the spouses and children of AA members, who joined either Alanon or Ala-teens in an effort to understand the situation, help keep the deviant drinker sober, and become public advocates for AA. Another source of support came from the newly developing professional treatment programs. Many successful AA members began careers as professional alcoholism counselors in these facilities, and these facilities typically mirrored AA's philosophy (Babow, 1975; Wiseman, 1970). The disease model of deviant drinking was also quite appealing to the producers and marketers of alcoholic beverages. Indeed from this point of view the cause of deviant drinking resided not with the drug itself, but with the flawed biochemistry of faulty individuals. Thus, alcoholic beverages could be consumed in a non-disruptive or non-deviant manner by most citizens.

Support for AA's views on deviant drinking also received significant scientific legitimacy from the various activities of the Yale Center for Alcoholic Studies (MacAndrew, 1969; Schneider, 1978). Developing out of a group composed primarily of physicians and natural science researchers at Yale University in the mid-1930s, the Yale Center became the major scientific research center on alcohol consumption in the United States. Through the publication of the *Quarterly Journal of Studies on Alcohol* and the writings of its first director, E.M. Jellinek, the Yale Center provided key scientific support for a disease model of alcoholism similar to that proposed by AA. The center's activities were essential to the eventual recognition of deviant drinking as a disease by the American Medical Association in 1956 and the American Hospital Association in 1957.

Furthermore, as part of the center's activities, a summer school was begun in 1943. These annual educational programs were designed to aid local leaders around the country in redirecting policy dealing with alcohol consumption. A major element of the school's efforts was to gain acceptance of the notion that alcoholism is a disease. One particular result of this summer school was the development of what was to become known as the National Council on Alcoholism (NCA). The NCA quickly became the leading voluntary organization in the United States whose primary mission was to "educate" the lay public about the disease of alcoholism.

After the Great Depression, numerous changes were occurring in American society that again altered our attitudes towards deviant drinking. The post-war baby boom, the increasing concentration of the population in urban centers, and the altruistic orientation of many New Deal programs all made people more aware of the need to control behaviors that may harm others. We also became increasingly concerned with issues of health as the basis of a happy and fulfilling life. The workplace was also undergoing changes for most workers. As the power of labor unions grew, corporate owners could no longer wield a free hand in dealing with absenteeism, and the easy replacement of workers became increasingly difficult. With the passage of workers' compensation laws, on the job accidents became more costly for employers. As more workers were covered by health insurance programs that were at least partially underwritten by employers, costs associated with health problems resulting from heavy alcohol consumption became additional burdens. Consequently, not just frequent intoxication, but intoxication of any kind became disruptive, and even long-term patterns of heavy drinking, regardless of intoxication, proved costly and were subsequently viewed as deviant.

The system of treatment at the time seemed unable to deal successfully with the growing problem. AA remained the predominant type of treatment available, but its reliance on voluntary recognition of the problem left many deviant drinkers uninvolved. The growth in the number of treatment professionals remained limited because many deviant drinkers simply could not afford such treatment services. The proponents of the disease model also experienced great difficulty overcoming the derelict or "skid row" image of deviant drinkers that was born during the temperance/ prohibition years (Roman & Blum, 1987). This meant that deviant drinkers who did not fit that stereotype typically did not think of themselves as having any drinking problems. Furthermore, many professionals working in related fields, as well as the general public, were reluctant to accept the disease definition of deviant drinkers (Chalfant & Kurtz, 1971; Haberman & Sheinberg, 1969). Eventually, a coalition of groups that supported the disease conception of deviant drinking, including AA, NCA, various professional treatment providers, and the alcoholic beverage industry, pushed for involvement by the federal government. The result was the establishment of the National Institute on Alcohol Abuse and Alcoholism (NIAAA).

NIAAA

In 1969, the U.S. Senate established the Special Subcommittee on Alcoholism and Narcotics, headed by Harold Hughes, a longtime member of AA and a recovering alcoholic. As a result of the subcommittee's activities, Congress passed the Comprehensive Alcohol Abuse and Alcoholism Act of 1970. Although the act established a variety of new policy precedents, most notable was the creation of the National Institute of Alcohol Abuse and Alcoholism (NIAAA). Under this act, NIAAA could give grants for the treatment and prevention of alcohol abuse and alcoholism.

With the establishment of NIAAA, the federal government formally accepted and supported the disease model of deviant drinking (Roman & Blum, 1987; Wiener, 1981). NIAAA therefore initially served as an advocate for the medical model of deviant drinking and through these efforts placed alcoholism in the mainstream of medicine. Funding for NIAAA's activities grew very rapidly in its first few years of existence. NIAAA's budget allocation in 1971 was $17 million, but by 1974 the allocation had grown to over $200 million. Much of this money was granted to groups supporting the disease model (Cahalan, 1987; Lewis, 1982). This practice quickly led to the emergence of an even larger constituency of disease model supporters, existing in a symbiotic relationship with NIAAA. By 1974, even Harold Hughes was expressing distress over the size and influence of these vested interest groups when he stated, "We have, in effect, a new civilian army that has now become institutionalized. The alcohol and drug industrial complex is not as powerful as its military-industrial counterpart, but nonetheless there are some striking similarities" (cited in Wiener, 1981, p. 3).

By the late 1970s, the ability of the federal government to continue to increase financial support for the medical model of control was limited, especially at a time of growing federal expenditures and declining revenues. An obvious solution to this funding problem rested with the ability of NIAAA to encourage acceptance of the disease model of deviant drinking by the health care system. To the extent that much of the workforce was currently covered by some form of medical insurance, the funding problem would be largely solved if deviant drinking could qualify for coverage under these policies. To accomplish this, NIAAA had to press state legislatures to mandate health insurance coverage for the treatment of alcoholism. It was also crucial to convince employers and employees alike that such coverage was valuable, and that the workplace was an appropriate arena to identify deviant drinkers and coerce them into treatment.

Beginning in 1982, NIAAA was no longer responsible for funding treatment and prevention services, and it now functions primarily as a research-support organization. Nonetheless, it has clearly institutionalized the medical model of deviant drinking. For example, by 1987, thirty-seven states required that alcoholism treatment coverage be at least an option available on all group health insurance plans (Cahalan, 1987). The growth and acceptance of the disease model of deviant drinking and the acceptance of the workplace setting for intervention can be seen in the growth of work-based programs dealing with deviant drinking. Evidence indicates that in 1972 only 25 percent of the fortune 500 companies had such programs; however, by 1979, 57 percent had programs (Roman, 1980).

Despite the federal government's role in establishing a major system of social control, certain changes in the nature of control (treatment) have occurred. Even though NIAAA spent millions of dollars on research projects to identify the most effective types of treatment for different individuals, the treatment approaches utilized remain extremely monolithic. Almost every treatment program is fundamentally based upon AA's original approach, including its twelve steps (Babow, 1975; Peele, 1989). Yet there have clearly developed two separate tracks or paths in the delivery of treatment services.

For those whose treatment is covered by health insurance (or those who are wealthy enough to afford it themselves), treatment is usually inpatient, associated with a hospital and located in a specialized facility staffed by professionals. Increasingly these treatment facilities are also run on a for-profit basis rather than a not-for-profit one. The other track is usually for those unable to afford such care, and is therefore more likely to be outpatient in form and in a social setting. Most commonly this treatment track is served by AA.

There are many implications of this two-track structure. To begin with, there is little evidence to suggest that inpatient treatment is more successful than outpatient, despite its comparatively higher cost (Miller & Hester, 1986; Zimmerman, 1986). For-profit treatment operations also raise questions as to whether their primary purpose is treatment or turning a profit.

Treatment for deviant drinking has also changed in its orientation towards deviant drinkers and their processing. Whereas AA holds that one must voluntarily seek help and recognize the need for it, much treatment is now more formally coerced. In the last two decades, clientele of treatment facilities have come increasingly from work-based programs, which threaten them with loss of job in order to coerce them into treatment, or from the criminal justice system as part of sentencing (Weisner and Room, 1984). Also, if clients exhibit the symptoms of the disease (become intoxicated) during treatment, they are expelled from the program. AA has always recognized and accepted the possibility of losing control over the disease and "falling off the wagon" at any time. Intoxication does not force someone out of treatment; it only reinforces the continued need for AA (Marlatt et al., 1985). Finally, AA believes that one must recognize on one's own that one has a drinking problem and that one has "hit bottom" with it; most treatment professionals, however, believe that they have the right to determine the nature of one's drinking, and that to deny the accuracy of their judgments only serves as further evidence of one's deviancy. Frequently underlying this evaluation of drinking behaviors by professionals is the assumption that if one were not drinking inappropriately one would not be seeing them in the first place. This orientation serves to produce more deviant drinkers and therefore more job security for treatment professionals.

Conclusion

Despite differing beliefs about the causes of deviant drinking and appropriate mechanisms of control, the nature of government involvement may have as much to do with the success or failure of these control efforts as do the beliefs themselves. Clearly, the predominant moral model that led to the passage of prohibition was part of a larger struggle between social groups for power and cultural dominance in society. This conflict had already shifted prohibition proponents into a coercive mode of operation, and it required them to push the government to operate in the same coercive fashion. The enactment of prohibition laws represented the ultimate form of coercion available to the government by making criminals out of many who were law-abiding citizens just the day before.

In contrast, under the medical model of deviant drinking, "alcoholics" were not seen as enemies or even competitors for power; rather they were seen as individuals who frequently shared our moral views but violated them only because of a disease beyond their personal control. In this context the push for government involvement was not from a coercive orientation, but an assimilative one. The reason the government established NIAAA was to assimilate the medical model of deviant drinking into mainstream society. Its funding went for educational efforts and the provision of more and better treatment, not for the passage of coercive laws. Indeed, if the government could convince the public that deviant drinking was a disease, then the almost universal value of health over illness would serve to support government intervention and control, in the name of health. Still it should be pointed out that government policies never quite follow the theoretical model being used. The ways in which the prohibition laws were written deviated dramatically from the types of prohibition legislation proponents had hoped for. The numerous loopholes failed to make consumption illegal and restrict some sources of supply. The lack of commitment of financial resources sufficient to enforce the laws, along with the lack of professionalism among the enforcement officers, often led to weak enforcement of the laws. Thus, the ability of many to continue to produce, sell, and consume alcoholic beverages meant that even prohibition was not an accurate test of the moral model of deviant drinking. The nature of government involvement was by itself partially responsible for prohibition's failure. Yet one must ask whether such problems of law creation and enforcement are not inherent when societal consensus is lacking. Government involvement in the control of deviant drinking under the medical model also strayed from the original beliefs. Through the creation of NIAAA, the government made possible the creation of the treatment industry whose concerns for successful control are often secondary to concerns for profits. Such a shift towards professional treatment has also led to increasing amounts of coercion in the control process.

Finally, the availability of government resources, particularly related to the funding of control efforts, is a key to successful government involvement. The government's inability to fund major, long-term control efforts clearly hampered the prohibitionist approach. The same impediment would have afflicted the government's efforts under the medical model if not for government's ability to utilize an alternative funding source.

To date, it must be recognized that government involvement in the control of deviant drinking appears to have experienced greater success operating from a medical model than from a moral one. Further, although government involvement alters the nature and form of control activity, such changes have been less damaging to control efforts under the medical model than under the moral model. The implications of this analysis seem relevant and applicable to government control efforts in the larger area of deviant drug use.

References

Babow, I. (1975). The treatment monopoly in alcoholism and drug dependence. *Journal of Drug Issues, 5,* 120–128.

Bakalar, J. B., & Grinspoon, L. (1984). *Drug control in a free society.* New York: Cambridge University.

Becker, H. S. (1963). *The outsiders.* New York: The Free Press.

Cahalan, D. (1987). *Understanding America's drinking problem: How to combat the hazards of alcohol.* San Francisco, CA: Jossey-Bass.

Chalfant, H. P., & Kurtz, R. A. (1971). Alcoholics and the sick role: Assessments by social workers. *Journal of Health and Social Behavior, 12,* 66–72.

Gusfield, J. R. (1963). *Symbolic crusade: Status politics and the American temperance movement.* Urbana, IL: University of Illinois.

Haberman, P. W., & Sheinberg, J. (1969). Public attitudes toward alcoholism as an illness. *Journal of Public Health, 59,* 247–256.

Jellinek, E. M. (1960). *The disease concept of alcoholism.* Highland Park, NJ: Hillhouse.

Levine, H. (1983). The committee of fifty and the origins of alcohol control. *Journal of Drug Issues, 13,* 95–115.

Levine, H. (1985). The birth of American alcohol control: Prohibition, the power elite and the problem of lawlessness. *Contemporary Drug Problems, 12,* 63–115.

Lewis, J. (1982). The federal role in alcoholism research, treatment and prevention. In L. Gomberg, H. R. White, & J. Carpenter (Eds.), *Alcohol, science and society revisited* (pp. 385–401). Ann Arbor, MI: University of Michigan.

MacAndrew, C. (1969). On the notion that certain persons who are given to frequent drunkenness suffer from a disease called alcoholism. In S. C. Plog, & R. B. Edgerton (Eds.), *Changing perspectives in mental illness* (pp. 483–500). New York: Holt, Rinehart and Winston.

Marlatt, G. A., Miller, W., Druchert, F., Gotestam, G., Heather, N., Peele, S., Sanchez-Craig, M., Sobell, L. C., & Sobell, M. B. (1985). Abstinence and controlled drinking: Alternative goals for alcoholism and problem drinkers? *Bulletin of the Society of Psychologists in Addictive Behaviors, 4,* 123–50.

Maxwell, M. (1982). Alcoholics Anonymous. In E. Gomberg, & H. White (Eds.). *Alcohol, science and society revisited* (pp. 295–305). Ann Arbor, MI: University of Michigan.

Mecca, A. M. (1980). *Alcoholism in America: A modern perspective.* Belvedere, CA: California Health Research Foundation.

Miller, W. R., & Hester, R. K. (1986). Inpatient alcoholism treatment: Who benefits? *American Psychologist, 41,* 794–805.

Parsons, T. (1951). *The social system.* New York: The Free Press.

Peele, S. (1989). *Diseasing of America: Addiction treatment out of control.* Lexington, MA: Lexington Books.

Roman, P. M. (1980). Medicalization and social control in the workplace: Prospects for the 1980s. *The Journal of Applied Behavioral Analysis, 16,* 407–22.

Roman, P. M., & Blum, T. C. (1987). Notes on the new epidemiology. *Journal of Drug Issues, 17,* 321–32.

Rorabaugh, W. J. (1979). *The alcoholic republic.* New York: Oxford University.

Rumbarger, J. J. (1989). *Profits, power and prohibition.* Albany, NY: State University of New York.

Schneider, J. W. (1978). Deviant drinking as disease: Alcoholism as a social accomplishment. *Social Problems, 25,* 361–372.

Sinclair, A. (1962). *Prohibition: The era of excess.* Boston, MA: Little, Brown.

Weisner, C., & Room, R. (1984). Financing and ideology in alcohol treatment. *Social Problems, 32,* 167–184.

Wiener, C. (1981). *The politics of alcoholism.* New Brunswick, NJ: Transaction Books.

Wiseman, J. P. (1970). *Stations of the lost: Treatment of skid row alcoholics.* San Diego, CA: University of California.

Zimmerman, R. (1986). Social model: As effective, cheaper than hospital. *U. S. Journal of Alcohol and Drug Dependence, 10,* 12.

Discussion Questions

1. Nusbaumer defines and discusses the concept of "moral entrepreneurs" as originally presented by Howard Becker (1963). In your own words, who are moral entrepreneurs and what do individuals who hold this view advocate?
2. List and describe the two models of deviant drinking outlined by Nusbaumer.
3. Discuss our early American drinking history, giving main periods and historically significant events.
4. What was the prohibition period? How did it evolve?
5. What is the medical model of deviant drinking?
6. What is the NIAAA? How did it originate, and why?

3

Perspectives on Alcoholism

Lessons from Alcoholics and Alcohologists

David R. Rudy

David R. Rudy, professor and chair of the Department of Sociology, Social Work and Corrections at Morehead State University, earned his Ph.D. in sociology at Syracuse University. He is the author of *Becoming Alcoholic: Alcoholics Anonymous and the Reality of Alcoholism* (1986, Southern Illinois University Press), and the co-author with Edward Reeves of *Uncommon Sense: An Introduction to Macro and Microsociology* (forthcoming). Professor Rudy's work has appeared in *Qualitative Sociology, Sociological Inquiry, Sociological Focus, Sociological Analysis,* and the *Journal of Studies on Alcohol.* His current research interests include radical identity transformation, the Adult Children of Alcoholics movement, and symbol work.

Introduction

Knowledge, whether it is folk knowledge held by people on the street or scientific knowledge held by researchers, is a social product. Knowledge about alcohol and alcoholism is produced by persons and groups, and is influenced by their social location. For example, people who treat alcoholism, people who sell alcohol, drinkers, and recovered alcoholics have views on alcohol that are shaped by their experience and location. Alcohol researchers (alcohologists) also produce knowledge about alcohol that is influenced by their disciplines, values, and personal experiences. Sociologists emphasize the role of group affiliations, socialization, and drinking subcultures in the development of alcohol problems. Biologists search for genetic, metabolic, or physiological factors that relate to alcoholism, and psychiatrists emphasize personality issues and conflicts in understanding alcoholism. Because so many persons with different political interests are involved in the alcoholism enterprise, the definition, study, and treatment of alcoholism are marked with debate and confusion. There is much confusion and conflict between alcohol knowledge generated by systematic research and alcoholism knowledge generated by social experience, clinical observations and social location. Conflict is particularly intense in the alcoholism treatment business because the economic stakes are large. Recent estimates of the alcohol and drug treatment business indicate an industry of nearly $4 billion in 1989, with prediction of over $6 billion by the mid-1990s (Rothman, 1990). Other economic sectors have a stake in the ways in which drinking, alcohol, and alcoholism are defined. Producers and distributors of alcohol, the restaurant and entertainment business, governments that tax and license alcohol and alcohol-related activities, and publishers who produce the books, films, and training materials for alcohol education and treatment are all dependent upon alcohol in specific ways.

With so much at stake and with so many factions involved, knowledge about alcohol is political and ideological as well as scientific. Some researchers (Schneider, 1978; Rudy, 1986; Fingarette, 1988a, 1988b; Peele, 1989, 1990) have argued that alcoholism and specifically the disease conception of alcoholism are social and political constructs rather than scientific ones. I believe it is useful to update and refine this argument within the context of popular understandings about alcoholism. In this essay I describe a number of areas and issues within the alcoholism enterprise, from the perspective of what we know versus the perspective of what we believe. This essay also suggests other ways of viewing alcoholism, and argues that what has come to be regarded as "alcoholism" in contemporary America is a particular type of social knowledge—a myth.

Alcohol: The Hard Facts?

Alcohol is a psychoactive drug because it affects the mind; it also alters the physiological process, or the way in which your body operates. However, alcohol is also a social object or drug. By this I mean that people have beliefs about what alcohol does or can do. These beliefs are more important than the actual properties of the drug in shaping behavior. Research and everyday experience demonstrate that various motor behaviors are affected when people drink alcohol. For example, reaction time slows when people drink, and drivers will take longer to stop and will hit more objects—including persons—when they are under the influence. Research also shows that if you drink enough alcohol over a relatively short time, it can kill you. Death will result because the depressant action will affect the central nervous system in such a way that your breathing will stop.

However, as powerful as alcohol is, there is clear evidence that much alcohol-related behavior is normative behavior. By this I mean that people learn, through normal processes of socialization, their society's expectations of the behavior of people under the influence of alcohol. These expectations are more important in shaping the way that people act when they are drinking than are the actual pharmacological properties of alcohol. In a classic work, MacAndrew and Edgerton (1969) argue that even drunken behavior is normative behavior. We assume that generally people act worse when they are drunk, but MacAndrew and Edgerton provide us with numerous examples that demonstrate that drunken behavior is clearly not uniform across cultures, and that some peoples act no worse when drunk than when sober. In fact, some peoples demonstrate fewer verbal arguments and greater sociability when drunk than when sober. People act "drunk" differently, and these differences are largely due to social or cultural factors. Despite what these research data tell us, there is a strong belief that alcohol makes us act in certain ways. Goode (1989) refers to this tendency to attribute specific complex behaviors to the ingestion of a certain type of drug, or to a given amount of some type of drug, as a "chemicalistic fallacy."

This line of reasoning (social versus pharmacological effects of alcohol) can be extended to include alcoholism as well. True, people may act drunk differently, but some people, "alcoholics," drink to excess and lose control over alcohol; these people become hopelessly enslaved to a physiological disease process called alcoholism. The belief is that this process is physiological (organic); once alcoholics begin to drink, their bodies respond in such a way that they will drink to intoxication whether they want to or not. The term that refers to this assumed process is "loss of control." The best example of the numerous research studies that challenge this view is a study by Marlatt and Rosenhow (1981). In a double blind study, neither the researcher nor the research subject knows whether a placebo or a drug is being used. In the Marlatt research, alcoholics participated in a taste-testing experiment that, unknown to them, monitored the frequency and quantity of their drinking. In the study, some respondents were given plain tonic water and were told that it was vodka and tonic, while others were given vodka and tonic and told that it was plain tonic. Two other groups actually received what they thought they were receiving. Marlatt and his colleagues hypothesized that if loss of control were physiological, then the actual beverage administered would be a better predictor of the amount consumed than what respondents were told they were drinking (response set). What the researchers found, however, is that response set was a better predictor. This means that, even among alcoholics, what people believe they are drinking is a better predictor of increased consumption (loss of control) than the alcohol itself. Heather and Robinson (1981), in a detailed and exhaustive review of research, argue that the concept of loss of control has little scientific merit, and that alcoholics consistently demonstrate that their drinking behavior is essentially operant behavior. Put more simply, there is considerable evidence that ". . . alcoholic drinking is modifiable in the same essential way as normal drinking . . . " (p. 127).

Studies of treatment outcomes also raise serious questions about the universality of loss of control. There are nearly 100 research studies that document a return to social drinking by some alcoholics. While these studies are ignored by many and attacked by some, they challenge the belief that "once an alcoholic always an alcoholic." The lack of acceptance or integration of these findings into the popular understanding of alcoholism has more to do with personal and ideological stances than with scientific analysis. Levine (1984) cogently argues that the belief that abstinence is necessary for treatment has much more to do with temperance ideology than with factual data. However, we so strongly *believe* in the necessity of lifelong abstinence that we routinely ignore and fail to consider systematic data that challenge our view.

Contemporary disease models of alcoholism, and the emphasis in Alcoholics Anonymous upon an allergy conception of alcoholism, are seriously questioned by these lab studies. However, to say that there is nothing intrinsic to alcohol that makes people lose control, or to say that "loss of control" is not physiological, is not to diminish the seriousness of the problems that some people have with alcohol. In terms of personal, social and economic costs, alcohol is an incredibly destructive drug—much more so than marijuana, heroin, or cocaine.

Another cornerstone of contemporary disease models of alcoholism is "blackouts." Blackouts are memory lapses believed to occur in alcoholics after moderate drinking. In my research among AA groups (Rudy, 1986), I found that some AA members were socialized to believe that they had experienced blackouts, when in fact there appeared to be no evidence that this was the case. Sometimes members confused blacking out with passing out. Some members were told that "alcohol fogs your brain, and if you cannot remember that you had blackouts, you probably did but just forgot them." As is the case with loss of control, there are research studies that call into question the value of blackouts as an early stage predictor of alcoholism. For example, Pokorny and Kanas (1980) demonstrate that seven out of 10 drinkers who experience blackouts will not become alcoholics. Clearly, blackouts are a poor predictor of alcoholism.

Failure to substantiate the physiological basis of loss of control and the uniqueness of blackouts for alcoholics is significant because it shows that alcoholics are not distinct from non-alcoholics. You may recall the recent research (Blum et al., 1990) that drew considerable attention because it argued that alcoholics are genetically different from non-alcoholics. When closely examined, this argument is also suspect—or at least a *long way* from being conclusive. While the popular media and those invested in alcoholism treatment hailed the significance of this research study, others were more cautious and critical. Robert Bazell (1990), in the *New Republic* commented:

> Because so many people want to believe that a tiny bit of DNA inherited from one or both parents can open the door to the devastation of alcohol, *The Journal of the American Medical Association (JAMA),* the two researchers, and their universities were able to portray the study as far more important than it is. As Dr. Paul Billings of the Harvard Medical School, who directs the Clinic for Inherited Disease at New England Deaconess Hospital, pointed out: "If this type of genetic research was carried out for a disease or a behavior less attractive than alcoholism, it would never get published . . . . It tells you nothing of significance . . . . The study is from the genetic dark ages." (p. 13)

Genetic/heredity theories of alcoholism were popular in America during the mid-1800s but lost favor shortly after the beginning of the twentieth century. Like contemporary genetic research, the older "degeneration theories of alcoholism" were assumed to be true, and persons searched every avenue to prove their worth (Levine, 1984; Fillmore, 1988). Just as the early "degeneration" theories developed within the context of the temperance movement, the renewed interest in genetic explanations also occurs in a new temperance era marked by a consistent decline in alcohol consumption and drug use.

Why Do We Regard Alcoholism as a Disease?

You might be thinking, "If alcoholism isn't a disease, why do so many people say it is?" It is not that we have scientifically discovered that the condition of alcoholism logically fits with our understanding of "disease." Rather, out of humane and practical concerns, we decided that alcoholics would be better treated under a medical/disease model than under alternative models. An examination of past views of alcoholism in the United States reveals definitions of alcoholism as sin, crime, moral weakness, and disease (Gusfield, 1963). Rather than view alcoholics as weak, evil, or criminal, we adopted a disease definition and treated them under a medical model. While the original intent of this approach was humane, I believe that it has a number of serious consequences.

An overemphasis on the disease model detracts from the fact that drinkers, their significant others, and society as a whole share in the responsibility for the development of drinking problems. Some drinkers use the lack of responsibility implied by the disease model to justify their drinking, or to verify its hopelessness (Fingarette, 1988a). During months of observation in AA, I observed members who used the disease view of alcoholism to "get on with their drinking," while others used the definition to lessen the stigma of alcoholism and to initiate recovery (sobriety). The disease model also does a disservice in that it divides drinkers into alcoholics and normal drinkers. Most drinkers are somewhere between these ends of the continuum but are more likely to regard themselves as normal drinkers than as alcoholics. Consequently, most people with drinking problems never seek help. A more profitable approach is that of Cahalan (1970), who defines problem drinkers by using quantity and frequency of alcohol consumption along with a measurement of the problems (social, marital, occupational, etc.) caused by drinking.

Perhaps the most serious consequence of the disease model is that by focusing upon AA, it excludes other approaches. A recent experience provides a good illustration. A few months ago a colleague came to see me, to talk about some research I was doing. After several minutes of conversation, she began to talk about her husband's drinking. She knew he was drinking over a quart of vodka a day, because she had located his stash and was measuring his daily consumption. Things were beginning to deteriorate at home. He was spending most evenings and weekends in a dulled state, and was beginning to withdraw from family life. They had discussed his heavy drinking, and he had admitted that he had a problem, but no action was taken.

In a later conversation it became obvious that her husband was drinking even more and that there were additional family consequences of the drinking. She was desperate. We talked about possible help for her (Alanon, counseling, etc.) and for him (AA, counseling, etc.), even though it seemed unlikely that he would follow through. When she mentioned that her husband was being treated for ulcers by Dr. X, I thought I had an answer. I knew that Dr. X had overcome a serious drinking problem through involvement with AA. I suggested that she contact Dr. X and raise the issue of heavy drinking and what effects it might have on her husband's stomach problem. I felt that the physician could confront her husband with the drinking problem, or hospitalize him and force him into withdrawal, thus forcing a therapeutic crisis. However, the physician was so strongly tied to the AA program that he believed that it wouldn't do any good to intervene. He told my colleague, "Your husband must figure this out for himself. It is not my role to say anything." In his view, the AA model is the "only game in town." In my view, this demonstrates a direct conflict between the physician's role of practitioner and his role of AA member. AA is not the only thing that works. Behavioral modification, aversion therapy, community reinforcement, relapse prevention, and other techniques all work for some alcoholics. In fact there is no evidence that any single treatment intervention is more successful than another in treating alcoholism. A review of inpatient alcoholism treatment studies (Miller & Hester, 1986) shows "... no overall advantage for residential over nonresidential settings, for longer over shorter inpatient programs, or for more intensive over less intensive interventions in treating alcohol abuse" (p. 794). Different things work for different people, and by overemphasizing AA we seriously harm those who don't respond well to the AA program.

Alcoholism as a Career

Alcoholism can be characterized as a career. Just as people have occupational careers, they can also have alcohol or drug careers. Careers involve several aspects, including identity, world view, and behavior systems. Because I am a sociologist, my behavioral system includes teaching and doing research. My world view emphasizes social structure, system, interaction, roles, and related ideas. So too for alcoholics. They drink alcohol and they organize, define, and experience their lives from the perspective of a drug, ethyl alcohol. Fingarette (1988a) views alcoholism as a central activity, in that all other aspects of the drinker's life are planned with reference to it. Maxwell (1984) writes about the increasing strength of the relationship between drinkers and their drugs. Some persons are able to drink large quantities of alcohol for long periods and retain normal social, familial and economic lives. Others withdraw from life and become more and more attached to alcohol. There is no single answer and no single pattern that explains alcoholism. There are as many ways of becoming an alcoholic as there are of becoming a sociologist or anything else, and there are also many ways out of alcoholism.

There are other analogies between occupational careers and alcoholic careers. Both are influenced by "career contingencies," factors that make career outcomes more or less likely. For example, the occupational characteristics of your parents are factors that relate to your occupational outcome. If your parents are physicians, you are more likely to become a physician than are children of non-physicians. This relationship is the result of social, not genetic, factors. Similarly, children of alcoholics are more likely to become alcoholics than are children of non-alcoholics. While some argue that this is because of a genetic predisposition, that is only partially true at best. Role modeling, drinking socialization, and self-fulfilling prophecies are factors that could be behind this relationship (Rudy, 1991) .

While we know that certain categories of persons may be more vulnerable than others, we also know that most vulnerable people never become alcoholics. For example, in the heavily cited Goodwin (1979) research, 18 percent of the biological sons of alcoholics developed alcoholism, and only five percent of the sons of non-alcoholics developed alcoholism. While this means that sons of alcoholics are nearly four times more likely to develop alcoholism, it also means that 82 percent of them do not develop alcoholism. Even if the recent genetic marker research (Blum et al., 1990) were totally accurate and predictive, it would reveal that more than 80 percent of persons possessing the gene variant predicting alcoholism would not be alcoholic (Peele, 1990) .

The Stereotype and Myths of "Alcoholism"

Knowledge is a social product, and knowledge on alcoholism is no exception to this principle. Knowledge based on observation and facts constitutes "truth," while knowledge based on values, beliefs, errors, and biased perceptions falls into the realm of myth, stereotype, or lie. What we "know" about alcoholism draws disproportionately from personal experience, the stories of alcoholics, clinical studies, and other popular accounts. Consequently, we produce more stereotypes and myths than facts. It is a fact that some people begin drinking, develop drinking problems, and continue to the point of destruction. However, more people develop drinking problems and resolve these problems, whether by treatment or by themselves. It is certainly a fact that alcoholism and heavy drinking produce numerous and costly consequences for America and Americans. However, it is also a fact that we overemphasize the role of alcohol in many maladies. For example, according to the state police in most states, alcohol-related traffic accidents not only include accidents where the driver is legally intoxicated, but also accidents where the driver, any passenger in any of the cars involved, or an involved pedestrian has been doing any drinking. Likewise, innocent victims are murdered by drunken drivers, but 52 percent of the people killed are the drunken drivers themselves, and another 20 percent are passengers who have chosen to ride with these drivers. When you add the statistic that another 11 percent are drunken pedestrians who walk into traffic, that leaves about 17 percent as innocent victims (Chafetz, 1990). Any victims, particularly innocent ones, are too many, but these data are a far cry from the picture of the "slaughter of innocent victims" portrayed by the media and advocacy groups. Overstatements and stereotypes are commonplace in daily discourse regarding alcohol problems. In our zealousness to overcome alcoholism and alcohol-related problems, we are willing to hope, stretch the truth, and define alcoholism in any way that we think will reduce its consequences. It is a myth that alcoholism is a disease. Alcoholism produces disease (cirrhosis, ulcers, etc.), but it is not a disease. Rather, alcoholism is a behavior. We may never find the cause(s) of alcoholism. Searching for causes of specific types of cancer is immensely simple compared to searching for causes for complex behaviors. Seeking the causes of alcoholism is logically similar to, and just as difficult as, seeking the causes of crime, violence, and suicide, or altruistic behavior, reading, and eating. Just as simple explanations for these phenomena have never been discovered, so too for the search for explanations of alcoholism.

Our views on alcoholism treatment are also mythical and stereotypical. Most people who resolve serious drinking and drug problems do it without formalized treatment. While AA is effective for some alcoholics, there are no systematic data that demonstrate that it is more effective than a range of other treatments. Different approaches work for different people. By maintaining a belief in the superiority of AA, we may be doing severe harm to alcoholics who could be better served in some other setting. There are as many ways out of an alcoholic career as there are into one, and most people leave alcoholic careers without formalized treatment.

Our argument is more than semantic and intellectual. It is unlikely that the application of flawed models will reduce problems associated with heavy drinking and alcoholism. Policies, public health strategies, and interventions must be based on sound models that are constructed from data, not from beliefs and ideologies, *if* we hope to make significant progress in the reduction of alcohol-related problems.

References

Bazell, R. (1990, May 7). The drink link. *The New Republic*, pp. 13–14.

Blum, K., Noble, E., Sheridan, P., Montgomery, A., Ritchie, T., Jagadeeswarn, P., Nogami, H., Briggs, A., & Cohn, J. (1990). Allelic association of human dopamine D2 receptor gene in alcoholism. *Journal of the American Medical Association, 263*, 255–60.

Cahalan, D. (1970). *Problem drinkers: A national survey.* San Francisco: Jossey Bass.

Chafetz, M. (1990, October 15). Unhealthy research on health. *The Cincinnati Enquirer*, p. A8.

Fillmore, K. M. (1988). The 1980's dominant theory of alcohol problems—genetic predisposition to alcoholism: Where is it leading us? In B. Segal (Ed.), *Alcoholism etiology and treatment: Issues for theory and practice* (pp. 69–87). New York: Haworth Press.

Fingarette, H. (1988a). *Heavy drinking: The myth of alcoholism as a disease.* Berkeley: University of California Press.

Fingarette, H. (1988b). Alcoholism: The mythical disease. *The Public Interest, 91*, 3–22.

Goode, E. (1989). *Drugs in American society.* New York: Alfred A. Knopf

Goodwin, D. W. (1979). Alcoholism and heredity: A review and hypothesis. *Archives of General Psychiatry, 36*, 57–61.

Gusfield, J. (1963). *Symbolic crusade: Status passage and the American Temperance Movement.* Urbana, IL: The University of Illinois Press.

Heather, N., & Robertson, I. (1981). *Controlled drinking.* London: Methuen & Co.

Levine, H. (1984). The alcohol problem in America: From temperance to alcoholism. *British Journal of Addiction, 79*, 109–119.

MacAndrew, C., & Edgerton, R. B. (1969). *Drunken comportment: A social explanation.* Chicago, IL: Aldine Publishing.

Marlatt, G., & Rohsenow, D. (1981, December). The think-drink effect. *Psychology Today*, pp. 60–69, 93.

Maxwell, M. A. (1984). *The Alcoholics Anonymous experience: A close-up for professionals.* New York: McGraw-Hill.

Miller, W., & Hester, R. (1986). Inpatient alcoholism treatment: Who benefits? *American Psychologist, 41*, 794–805.

Peele, S. (1989). *Diseasing of America: Addiction treatment out of control.* Lexington, MA: D. C. Heath & Company.

Peele, S. (1990) Second thoughts about a gene for alcoholism. *The Atlantic, 266*(2), 52–58.

Pokorny, A., & Kanas, T. (1980). Stages in development of alcoholism. In W. Fann, I. Karacan, A. Pokorny, & R. Williams (Eds.), *Phenomenology and treatment of alcoholism* (pp. 45–68). New York: Spectrum Publications.

Rothman, S. (1990). Treatment field to grow in 90's. *The U. S. Journal of Drug & Alcohol Dependence, 14*(2), 1, 7.

Rudy, D. (1986). *Becoming alcoholic: Alcoholics Anonymous and the reality of alcoholism.* Carbondale: Southern Illinois University Press.

Rudy, D. (1991). The adult children of alcoholics movement: A social constructionist perspective. In

D. Pittman, & H. White (Eds.), *Society, culture, and patterns re-examined* (pp. 716–732). New Brunswick, NJ: Rutgers Center on Alcohol Studies.

Schneider, J. (1978). Deviant drinking as disease: Alcoholism as a social accomplishment. *Social Problems, 25,* 361–72.

Discussion Questions

1. What are some of the different ways in which alcoholism has historically and contemporarily been defined? What are the consequences of different alcoholism definitions for treatment?
2. What are the strengths and weaknesses of the disease definition of alcoholism?
3. What are some advantages and disadvantages of alcoholism as a career?
4. Drawing from Rudy's article and your own views, logically support or refute the argument that alcoholism is a disease.

4

Identifying Types of Normal and Problem Drinking

Keith M. Kilty

Keith M. Kilty is Professor of Social Work at the Ohio State University in Columbus, Ohio. For nearly twenty years, he has been involved in research on alcohol and drug use and abuse. One of his interests has been to develop a taxonomy of drinking behavior, and he has published several studies on this topic, including "Styles of Drinking and Types of Drinkers," *Journal of Studies on Alcohol*, 1983; "Drinking Styles and Drinking Problems," (with P. Leung and K. M. Cheung), *International Journal of the Addictions*, 1987; and "Drinking Styles of Adolescents and Young Adults," *Journal of Studies on Alcohol*, 1990.

Alcohol is by far the most commonly used drug in this country, with over six of every 10 adults acknowledging that they drink at least "on occasion" (Royce, 1989). Yet the social science literature on drinking tells us very little about the role that alcohol plays in everyday life or the relation of normal drinking to problem drinking. In fact, the predominant emphasis in studies about alcohol use has not been on what most people do, or on how drinking affects their lives. Instead, researchers have been most concerned with a relatively small group of drinkers: those who have problems related to their use of alcohol (Kilty, 1982). As a result, social scientists have focused their attention almost entirely on drinking as a "problem behavior."

When viewed in historical context, a focus on pathology rather than on "normal" drinking is not surprising. As Pittman and Snyder (1962) noted, many of the early researchers in the field of alcohol studies were abstainers and did not drink on a "normal" or social basis. Furthermore, during the nineteenth century, when research—especially medical research—began in earnest on the problems of drinking and alcoholism in the United States (Strug et al., 1986), the consumption of alcohol was substantially higher than it is now, and serious problems caused by saloons and public drunkenness were widespread. It is no wonder, then, that the goal of the temperance movement gradually changed from moderation in drinking to total abstinence, ultimately leading to the prohibition era in this country from 1920 to 1933.

The consumption of alcoholic beverages still creates problems. Alcoholism and alcohol abuse impact on many lives in a variety of ways. Yet, by ignoring the reality of drinking, and by failing to differentiate between use and abuse, we have made it more difficult to understand the nature of the problems associated with alcohol. Most people live out their lives without serious problems due to the use of alcoholic beverages, and drinking is simply a minor part of their everyday social lives. The question becomes whether it is possible to understand what is pathological, when we do not understand what is normal.

We need to appreciate that drinking is an integrated and normative element of daily life in many different societies, including the United States (Heath, 1986a, 1986b). By "integrated and normative," we mean that drinking behavior occurs in patterns that are recognizable and predictable. Drinking is a *social* phenomenon that can be understood only by examining normative expectations about its use and the situational contexts in which that use takes place (MacAndrew & Edgerton, 1969).

Unfortunately, the social and medical sciences have generally failed to look at drinking as anything other than a problem. In fact, drinking behavior is usually treated as a single entity, and distinctions are not made about different kinds of drinking. On one side of the coin, there is a type of drinking that we label "normal," and then, on the other side, there is another type of drinking that we might categorize as "problem" or "alcoholic" drinking.

This approach is narrow. Not only does it ignore the context surrounding the consumption of alcohol, but it also assumes that social factors do not affect when people drink or how they act after they have been drinking (Kilty, 1980). Studies about alcohol and behavior have generally assumed that alcohol is a drug with certain properties (e.g., consumption leads to loss of inhibitions), and that these properties are the primary factors that influence what people do when they have been drinking. Only recently have efforts been made to separate the influence of pharmacological factors from what are called "expectancies" or "social learning factors" (Christiansen et al., 1982; Miller et al., 1990; Zinberg, 1984). As a result, the measurement of alcohol use and misuse has generally focused on the frequency and quantity of drinking (Cahalan et al., 1969; Armor et al., 1978), on counts of so-called indicators of problem drinking (Robinson, 1976; Vaillant, 1983), or on some combination of both methods (Skinner, 1987). What has been lacking is a focus on the broad range of contexts or situations within which drinking occurs and the reasons (personal and social) influencing the use of alcoholic beverages.

Classification and Theory-Building

Drinking involves many different activities and events. We drink to celebrate a marriage or to remember someone who has died. We drink to "loosen up" at a party. We drink for symbolic purposes in religious ceremonies or to acknowledge a special relationship with certain individuals or groups. We drink to "drown our sorrows." We drink to prove that we can "hold our booze." In sum, we drink in many different ways and contexts and for many different reasons. Therefore, we need to look at drinking as a complex social phenomenon that consists of a wide variety of activities or behaviors.

As a first step in understanding alcohol use, recognizing this wide range of behavior is well and good. However, if our goal is to explain a phenomenon according to scientific principles, we need to bring some order and coherence to our observations. One option is to try to organize the various elements of the phenomenon into a set of categories, based upon the similarities and differences that we can observe among them. In the case of drinking, we might try to identify those behaviors that are similar enough to each other to be classified into a particular category. That process of classification would provide the basis for creating a typology of alcohol use.

One of the fundamental goals of the scientific process is the classification of events or objects (Sanders & Pinkney, 1983). If phenomena are to be described, observations must be organized. Even if our ultimate goal is to develop theoretical understanding, classification is at least a necessary beginning point. The field of alcohol studies is a good example of the need for classification. As we have seen, our conceptual understanding of the nature of alcohol use and abuse is quite limited, which means that we have concepts that are vague, confusing, and overlapping—in essence, inadequate for developing sound explanations.

There are different ways in which typologies can be developed. One that could have particular value in the case of drinking behavior is the "taxonomy." According to Chafetz (1978), "A taxonomy is a classification scheme which is developed systematically by specifying a series of attributes and creating categories that exhaust the logical combinations of those attributes" (p. 67). Taxonomies are not simply meant to summarize the elements of a particular phenomenon. Rather, the goal is to develop categories that can be used as concepts, allowing interconnections to be identified among or derived from the categories, and connections to be made to other variables. Furthermore, the taxonomy needs to reflect actual physical or social conditions; it should not be based solely on abstractly defined categories. As Denzin (1989) points out, taxonomies stress two important issues: *interdependence among the categories* and *grounding in empirical reality.*

Using a taxonomic approach to studying drinking behavior could lead to new insights into the role of drinking in everyday life and the relationship between "normal" and "problem" drinking. One of the major problems in the alcohol literature has been its reliance on old and unsubstantiated ideas (Peele, 1989); much of what passes for "scientific wisdom" on alcohol use and misuse has more the flavor of ideology than specific principles (Rudy, 1986). Scientific theory is supposed to be based on empirical observation and a willingness to test one's ideas, not on one's commitment to a set of beliefs or point of view (i.e., faith).

Models of Drinking Behavior

Cultural Attitudes toward Drinking

Since the pioneering work of Bales (1946), a number of theoretical models have been offered that distinguish between different types of drinking (Fallding & Miles, 1974; Pittman, 1967). While Bales was mainly concerned with explaining "compulsive" drinking, his model could be applied to normal drinking as well. He identified four cultural attitudes toward drinking, each of which promoted a certain type of drinking. The first was an attitude favoring complete abstinence, usually associated with religious beliefs prohibiting all drinking. The second was described as a ritual attitude toward drinking, where alcohol is used as a part of certain religious ceremonies. In both of these cases, alcohol is not valued for its own sake. Even where religious beliefs allow drinking, appropriate situations are rigidly defined, and there is little consumption of alcohol in secular settings.

The third type of attitude was described as one of conviviality. While drinking retains a ritualistic nature, it is no longer an expression of religious values, but rather of social ones. Alcohol use in this case is typically an expression of social unit or group solidarity. That is, this type of drinking—which might also be labeled social—"loosens up emotions which make for social ease and good will" (Bales, 1946, p. 487).

Bales (1946) described the last type of attitude as utilitarian. While this type of drinking includes the use of alcohol as a medicine, its primary function is to provide "personal satisfaction." It often involves solitary drinking, but it can occur in group settings. What distinguishes the utilitarian use of alcohol from the convivial is the focus on drinking for its "psychological" effects: "The distinction is that the purpose is personal and self-interested rather than social and expressive" (p. 487).

According to Bales, rates of pathological drinking should be relatively low in cultures characterized by the first two types of attitudes. In the case of cultures where the convivial attitude was predominant, members of those societies were "protected" from pathological drinking patterns to the extent that drinking remained a ritualistic behavior. However, as drinking became more associated with drinking for effect (or to "feel good"), the convivial attitude would move toward the utilitarian. That is, Bales depicted the convivial attitude "as a mixed type, tending toward the ritual in its symbolism of solidarity, and toward the utilitarian in the 'good feeling' expected" (p. 494). Thus, the convivial attitude could be easily converted into the utilitarian. In general, as drinking patterns became less a display of social solidarity and more an expression of personal satisfaction, rates of alcoholism were expected to increase.

Personal vs. Social Effects

Fallding and Miles (1974) elaborated these ideas by presenting another typology consisting of four "basic" types of drinking behavior: ornamental, facilitation, assuagement, and retaliation. By definition, only ornamental drinking could be considered a positive or socially functional form of drinking. With its stress on the ritualistic and expressive aspects of drinking, ornamental drinking appears to be essentially the same notion as Bales's concept of convivial drinking, restricted to its function as a symbol of group solidarity. The other three types of drinking are subcategories of what Bales described as utilitarian drinking.

Mulford and Miller (1959) developed a model that essentially identified "socially positive drinking" and "drinking for personal satisfaction" (p. 386) as the key attributes in distinguishing between different types of drinking.

> There are suggestions in the literature that heavy consumption and alcoholism are associated with drinking to induce direct personal effects; that moderate and light consumption is associated with drinking for interpersonal or social effects; and that non-drinkers tend to define alcohol in terms of negative personal and social consequences.

Problems with Existing Typologies

Most of these models have suffered from various problems. Bales's theory was more a typology of cultural attitudes than a typology of individual drinking. It was a broad, general model, consisting of concepts that have been difficult to measure (Knupfer & Room, 1967). Furthermore, it assumes that there will be little or no variation within a particular culture.

Typologies that focus on explaining individual drinking behavior have generally emphasized pathological drinking (Fallding & Miles, 1974; Mulford & Miller, 1959) rather than drinking behavior in general. Classifications of problem drinking behavior certainly have significance for practitioners who work with alcoholics and problem drinkers, but the models proposed by Fallding and Miles or Mulford and Miller have apparently proven disappointing. Their failure may be due to an emphasis on defining drinking from a deviance perspective, with one type of drinking typified as drinking for "social" or "group-supportive" reasons, while a second is characterized as drinking for "personal satisfaction." This still produces nothing more than a bipolar conception of drinking. However, a value perspective has now been added: "normal" drinking is seen as "social-facilitative" or "good," while "problem" drinking is seen as representing "personal satisfaction" and therefore "bad" (Kilty, 1982).

An alternative approach would be to develop a typology of drinking behavior in general, with the emphasis on behavior. For this purpose, a wide variety of activities—both "normal" and "pathological"—would have to be included. The intent of the typology would be to identify those behaviors that form meaningful clusters or categories. Such a general taxonomy of drinking behavior could well be useful in defining alcoholism and alcohol abuse, discovering what varieties there may be of both, and explaining both how they differ from normal kinds of drinking and what they have in common with normal drinking.

Developing a Taxonomy of Drinking Behavior

In order to develop a typology of drinking behavior, both "normal" and "problem" drinking behaviors need to be examined, and the typology should be based on an empirical identification of the interrelationships among the various behaviors. Most previous research has failed to include a wide range of such behaviors, and, as noted earlier, the focus of study was generally on either "normal" drinking (e.g., the research about "drinking practices" by Cahalan et al., 1969), or on "problem" drinking (Armor et al., 1978). If we are to understand the complex phenomenon of drinking behavior, we need to change the way we look at it. Drinking behavior is not simply one behavior; it consists of many different acts. Therefore, we need to develop a multiple-act criterion for measuring it, rather than a single-act one (Fishbein & Ajzen, 1974; Kilty, 1978).

During the past several years, I have carried out three studies whose intent was to develop a typology of drinking behavior. For two of the projects, I collected the data, while I used an existing data base for the third project. Perhaps the most striking aspect of this research has been the consistency in the findings—even when I made use of data collected by other social scientists, eliminating any bias on my part in the data collection process. At least within the context of North American culture, there appear to be several types of drinking that can be identified from sample to sample and across different kinds of data sets.

Drinking Styles

The first study used an inventory of drinking behavior that included 37 questions regarding drinking in various situations (Kilty, 1983). By design, most of the situations could be characterized as "normal." The purpose of this research was to identify interrelationships among different drinking behaviors that represented a wide variety of relatively normal situations, although some of the behaviors were open to interpretation as indicators of problem drinking. The variables included social and family relations, participation in recreational activities, eating and food preparation, and moods, as well as the use of different kinds of alcoholic beverages (i.e., wine, beer, and distilled spirits).

In order to find relationships among the variables, the data were analyzed using a statistical technique called factor analysis. This statistical method is useful in finding clusters among large sets of variables. In this case, four distinct factors (or types of drinking) were identified. The first type suggested "convivial drinking," including such activities as drinking for special occasions or celebrating, drinking at parties, and drinking during social events away from home. In general, this drinking style was consistent with the convivial cultural attitude described by Bales (1946) and others.

The second type revolved around the use of "alcohol as a thirst quencher." These behaviors included drinking alcoholic beverages when thirsty, drinking after doing chores at home, and drinking beer with meals. The consumption of beer was strongly associated with this style of drinking, especially with drinking while watching sports or other programs on TV—stereotypical male behaviors.

The third type reflected a more "sophisticated" use of alcoholic beverages and was labeled "alcohol and lifestyle." These activities focused on using wine at meals, as well as using alcoholic beverages in cooking. The use of both wine and distilled spirits was highly related to this drinking style.

The last type suggested the consumption of alcohol as a way of "changing one's mood." These behaviors included drinking after getting bad news, drinking when upset about something, and drinking to help one in dealing with large groups. Some individuals might interpret this type of drinking as pathological, at least to some degree, but it could suggest just the opposite. One of the dominant conceptions of drinking in North American society is that it is calming and relaxing, i.e., that it acts as a sedative (Brecher, 1972). Furthermore, other variables that might suggest problem drinking, such as drinking at work, were not related to this style of drinking (Kilty, 1983).

Adolescent Drinking Styles

The second study (Kilty, 1990) differed in several important ways from the previous one. First, it included a broader range of "normal" drinking behaviors, extending the original inventory from 37 to 55. Second, part of the focus of this research was on "problem" as well as "normal" drinking, and a second set of 18 "problem" behaviors was developed from the National Council on Alcoholism criteria for the diagnosis of alcoholism (Ringer et al., 1977). Finally, the sample was also quite different, consisting of adolescents and young adults (N=237) and located in a large urban area in another part of the United States.

Interestingly enough, the results were quite similar to those from the previous study. A factor analysis of the "normal" drinking behaviors identified six types of drinking. The first four types were nearly identical to those found before. The two new drinking types clearly related to the drinking activities of younger people. One represented "familial and ceremonial drinking" (e.g., drinking with relatives, with parents, or during religious ceremonies). The other was labeled "drinking to be part of the group" (e.g., drinking to feel accepted by the group and drinking to be independent). These latter drinking styles suggest that younger people drink as a way of demonstrating attachment to their peers and independence from their families. To drink with the family reflected participation in ceremonial drinking.

The differences that emerged between the two studies were mainly due to the larger list of drinking behaviors included in the second. These findings imply that drinking by adolescents and young adults is no better or worse—in essence, *no different*—than drinking by adults (Finn, 1979). They also imply that young people *learn* to drink and, more importantly, learn how to feel and act after they have been drinking. As Christiansen et al. (1982) and Miller et al. (1990) have shown, expectancies about the effects of alcohol develop prior to actual use of alcoholic beverages. Furthermore, the expectancies of adolescents are quite similar to those of adults. Barnes (1981), for example, demonstrated strong similarities between young people and their parents, in terms of frequency of drinking, type of setting, and reasons for drinking.

In addition to concerns about "normal" drinking, this study also focused on "problem" drinking. A factor analysis of the "problem" drinking variables separated them into two clusters, one consisting of serious but relatively uncommon experiences, and the second consisting of less serious but more common experiences. These categories seemed rather simplistic and were probably related to the nature of the sample and to the kinds of behaviors included. The age range of the sample (from 17 to 24) limited the extent of their drinking experiences (whether positive or negative). In addition, some of the variables that were included were rather extreme, and it was unlikely that anyone who was not a long-term, chronic problem drinker or alcoholic would have experienced them.

Interestingly, several of the "normal" drinking factors were found to be important predictors of the "problem" drinking scores, suggesting that certain styles of drinking are more likely than others to lead to later problems. Certain normal drinking factors, such as "convivial drinking" and "altering one's mood," were substantially better predictors of some problems (the less serious but more common problems) than were traditional predictors of drinking problems (e.g., social and demographic characteristics).

Drinking Styles and Drinking Problems

The major limitations for the first two studies were the nature and the size of the samples; both were small, and their representativeness was open to question. In contrast, the third study (Kilty et al., 1987) was a secondary analysis of a survey that used a national probability sample (N = 1,772) representing the adult population of the United States (Clark et al., 1981). Although the data did not cover as extensive a range of behavior as was the case in the previous research, there was enough similarity to allow for reasonable comparison. The data were most limited in terms of normal drinking activities. A distinct advantage of this study was its emphasis on problem drinking. The wide range of these variables meant that the analysis could focus in detail on the relationships among problem drinking indicators, as well as the associations among normal and problem drinking behaviors.

Analyses of the limited range of "normal" variables produced findings that were generally consistent with the previous results. The "convivial drinking" and the "alcohol and lifestyle" types of drinking were replicated. A factor similar to the "alcohol as a thirst quencher" type was also identified, although too few behaviors were common to this study and the other two, for the replication to be considered entirely successful. Finally, the "changing one's mood" drinking type was reproduced.

This data set also contained a group of variables that concerned comportment (or "proper" behavior). The 11 behaviors included in this set yielded three types: "drinking behavior was embarrassing" (e.g., drinking behavior was embarrassing, tried to cut down); "drinking caused problems" (e.g., people I know were getting into trouble, became worried about health effects); and "more social interaction" (e.g., went to more parties, drank more with a group of friends).

There were 35 indicators of problem drinking included in this survey. A factor analysis identified five distinct types. The first was "traditional alcohol abuse" (e.g., not remembering what happened, drinking to get quick effect, losing temper, staying away from work). The second was "lost control over drinking" (e.g., drinking in morning, staying intoxicated for several days, taking quick drink when no one was looking, finding it difficult to stop until intoxicated). The third was "other people complaining" (e.g., people at work, friends, and physician suggesting cutting down, feeling that drinking becoming serious threat to health). The fourth was "legal problems and accidents" (e.g., being arrested for driving after drinking, having contact with police, drinking contributing to accident). The last was "job problem" (e.g., losing job because of drinking, quitting job because of drinking, losing promotion because of drinking).

Including a broader sampling of problem behaviors, which represented a wide variety of problems as well as the "classic" symptoms of alcoholism, led to an important finding: "problem" drinking, just like "normal" drinking, consists of more than one type. In fact, five distinct types were found. Any given individual could be having problems in any one (or more) of these areas, *independent* of the others. It is also significant that these results were based only on responses from "current drinkers" (N = 1,169), who had had problems at one time or another but not necessarily now. Furthermore, only 22 of these respondents had ever been in any form of "treatment," whether formal or informal.

Findings similar to those of the study on adolescents and young adults were obtained when the normal drinking factors were used as predictors of the problem behavior types. However, the significant predictors were quite different for this sample, and there were also differences in the direction of some of the relationships. The single most powerful predictor was the "drinking behavior was embarrassing" factor. Yet, with the exception of the "alcohol as a thirst quencher" factor, all of the other variables had substantial influences on the various types of problem drinking. In fact, "convivial drinking" and "alcohol and lifestyle" seemed to have inoculating effects, since they were *negatively* associated with the problem drinking variables. That is, individuals who engaged in those particular activities were *less* likely than others to display some types of problem behaviors.

Conclusions

If we are to come to grips with the problems associated with alcohol in our society, we must also come to an understanding of the place of drinking in everyday life. Most drinking is not pathological, and there is even some evidence that certain types of "normal" drinking may help prevent the development of drinking problems. Traditional explanations of drinking behavior and alcoholism need to be re-examined. The medical or disease model of alcoholism still holds precedence in the field of alcohol studies, even in light of conflicting evidence. Not only are there styles or types of "normal" drinking, but there are also different kinds of problem drinking. Actually, that is not a new idea; some important theorists, such as Jellinek (1960), have suggested much the same in the past.

Unfortunately, little research has been focused on different kinds of problem drinking, even though the empirical literature has long included evidence that not all people with a drinking problem have exactly the same condition (Pattison et al., 1977; Sobell & Sobell, 1987). Seldom is there any discussion of the possibility that there might be different kinds of drinking problems, requiring different kinds of treatment methods. In fact, treatment methods have changed very little for several decades, and one might even question whether different treatment methods exist (Kilty, 1982). That is, most treatment is based on the disease model, which does not distinguish alcohol problems from alcoholism. All persons are seen as having essentially the same problem, which is permanent and irreversible as well as progressive (Pattison et al., 1977). When these principles are translated into practice, we find that treatment consists of inpatient detoxification and then outpatient counseling, either in an individual or group format, with little variation from one program to another. Even where differences among programs can be documented, not much difference has been found in treatment effectiveness (Armor et al., 1978).

What is more significant, though, in terms of theory building, is the relationship that was found between the types of problem drinking and some of the types of normal drinking. As Denzin (1989) notes, a taxonomy should provide information about interdependencies among the different categories. Efforts to develop a taxonomy of drinking behavior produced measures of normal drinking activities and comportment that were accurate predictors of problem behaviors. Certain results even implied that some individuals could be "inoculated" against drinking problems. Those findings should come as no surprise, since that is hardly a novel idea. For quite some time, advocates of prevention programs have argued that drinking problems can be forestalled by teaching "appropriate" drinking practices (Wilkinson, 1970). The drinking practices of certain ethnic groups (such as Jews) have been used to document this idea. In other words, drinking habits may be a crucial issue in the prevention and treatment of drinking problems, especially if drinking behavior and behavior after consuming alcohol are *learned* phenomena (MacAndrew & Edgerton, 1969). Habits that are learned can be modified by new learning.

Developing a taxonomy of drinking behavior could help to improve treatment interventions. A typology that organizes specific behaviors into syndromes could bring greater focus to the diagnosis and treatment planning processes, since it would make possible the identification of specific behaviors requiring intervention. Developing a classification system for drinking problems is necessary in order to have a reliable and valid diagnostic method. This would allow treatment to be focused on the specific problem or problems of given individuals, rather than being broad-based and general, as it typically is now (Sobell & Sobell, 1987). For example, one of the problem drinking factors identified in the third study (Kilty et al., 1987) centered around "legal problems and accidents." While drinking certainly contributes to auto accidents, it is not necessarily the only or even the most significant factor in many cases (Gusfield, 1981). The condition of the auto and the driving abilities of the individual, among other elements, may be just as important. In this situation, a treatment intervention might deal with more than just the way alcohol affects driving. It could also focus on improving driving ability or personal responsibility for maintaining a safe car.

Using a behaviorally-oriented typology of drinking also has implications for evaluating treatment interventions, particularly with regard to establishing conceptually distinct outcome goals. This orientation focuses on observable behaviors, which may be related to the consumption of alcohol, or to consumption patterns, or to situational contexts, or to types of behaviors while consuming alcoholic beverages or afterward (e.g., a socially embarrassing action "under the influence"), or to performance of other behaviors (e.g., job-related activities or driving behavior), etc. The particular behaviors would be derived from an assessment of what type (or types) of problems the individual has, and relevant behaviors would not need to be exclusively related to alcohol. That is, some individuals' low job performance may be due to poor work habits, with alcohol consumption a secondary problem. Therefore, treatment "effectiveness" could be defined in a *multidimensional* way and assessed along a continuum of improvement, rather than seen as "either/or," usually sober or not (Marlatt & Nathan, 1978; Pattison et al., 1977). In other words, effectiveness would be defined in terms of specific behavioral conditions (including physical conditions, if appropriate). More than one criterion for establishing effectiveness would be involved, and degrees of improvement could be assessed.

While the typology of drinking behavior described in this research shows a great deal of promise, more work remains to be done. The next step would be to combine the best elements of the three studies already completed. That is, future research needs to cover a broader range of behavior, including both normal and problem indicators. It also needs to include a large and representative sample. However, more is needed than just a general population sample, in which one would be unlikely to find many individuals with serious problems. Including a large sample of clients representing a wide variety of treatment programs would provide data more useful in establishing a true taxonomy of drinking behavior and drinking problems.

References

Armor, D. J., & Polich, M. M., & Stambul, H. B. (1978). *Alcoholism and treatment.* New York: Wiley.

Bales, R. F. (1946). Cultural differences in rates of alcoholism. *Quarterly Journal of Studies on Alcohol 6,* 480–499.

Barnes, G. M. (1981). Drinking among adolescents: A subcultural phenomenon or a model of adult behaviors. *Adolescence, 16,* 211–219.

Brecher, E. M. (1972). *Licit and illicit drugs.* Boston, MA: Little, Brown.

Cahalan, D., Cisin, I. H., & Crossley, H. M. (1969). *American drinking practices.* New Brunswick, NJ: Rutgers Center of Alcohol Studies.

Chafetz, J. S. (1978). *A primer on the construction and testing of theories in sociology.* Itasca, IL: Peacock.

Christiansen, B. A., Goldman, M. S., & Inn, A. (1982). Development of alcohol-related expectancies in adolescents: Separating pharmacological from social learning influences. *Journal of Consulting & Clinical Psychology, 50,* 336–344.

Clark, W. B., Midanik, L., & Knupfer, G. (1981). *Report on the 1979 National Survey.* Berkeley, CA: Social Research Group, School of Public Health, University of California.

Denzin, N. K. (1989). *The research act* (3rd ed.). Englewood Cliffs, NJ: Prentice-Hall.

Fallding, H., & Miles, C. (1974). *Drinking, community and civilization.* New Brunswick, NJ: Rutgers Center of Alcohol Studies.

Finn, P. (1979). Teenage drunkenness: Warning signal, transient boisterousness, or symptom of social change? *Adolescence, 14,* 819–834.

Fishbein, M., & Ajzen, I. (1974). Attitudes toward objects as predictors of single and multiple behavioral criteria. *Psychological Review, 81,* 59–74.

Gusfield, J. R. (1981). *The culture of public problems: Drinking-driving and the symbolic order.* Chicago, IL: University of Chicago Press.

Heath, D. B. (1986a). Drinking and drunkenness in transcultural perspective: Part I. *Transcultural Psychiatric Research Review, 23,* 7–41.

Heath, D. B. (1986b). Drinking and drunkenness in transcultural perspective: Part II. *Transcultural Psychiatric Research Review, 23,* 103–112.

Jellinek, E. M. (1960). *The disease concept of alcoholism.* Highland Park, NJ: Hillhouse Press.

Kilty, K. M. (1978). Attitudinal and normative variables as predictors of drinking behavior. *Journal of Studies on Alcohol, 39,* 1778–1194.

Kilty, K. M. (1980). Situational context and the meaning of drinking. *International Journal of the Addictions, 15,* 1021–1033.

Kilty, K. M. (1982). Scientific ideologies and conceptions of drinking behavior and alcoholism. *Journal of Sociology and Social Welfare, 9,* 755–765.

Kilty, K. M. (1983). Styles of drinking and types of drinkers. *Journal of Studies on Alcohol, 44,* 797–816.

Kilty, K. M. (1990). Drinking styles of adolescents and young adults. *Journal of Studies on Alcohol, 51,* 556–564.

Kilty, K. M., Leung, P., & Cheung, K. M. (1987). Drinking styles and drinking problems. *International Journal of the Addictions 22,* 389–412.

Knupfer, G., & Room, R. (1967). Drinking patterns and attitudes of Irish, Jewish, and white Protestant American men. *Quarterly Journal of Studies on Alcohol, 28,* 676–699.

MacAndrew, C., & Edgerton, R. B. (1969). *Drunken comportment.* Chicago, IL: Aldine.

Marlatt, G. A., & Nathan, P. E. (1978). *Behavioral approaches to alcoholism.* New Brunswick, NJ: Rutgers Center of Alcohol Studies.

Miller, P. M., Smith, G. T., & Goldman, M. S. (1990). Emergence of alcohol expectancies in childhood: A possible critical period. *Journal of Studies on Alcohol, 51,* 343–349.

Mulford, H. A., & Miller, D. E. (1959). Drinking behavior related to definitions of alcohol. *American Sociological Review, 24,* 385–389.

Pattison, E. M., Sobell, M. B., & Sobell, L. C. (1977). *Emerging concepts of alcohol dependence.* New York: Springer.

Peele, S. (1989). *Diseasing of America.* Boston: Houghton Mifflin.

Pittman, D. J. (1967). *Alcoholism.* New York: Harper & Row.

Pittman, D. J., & Snyder, C. R. (1962). *Society, culture, and drinking patterns.* New York: Wiley.

Ringer, C., Kufner, H., Antons, K., & Feuerlein, W. (1977). The N.C.A. criteria for the diagnosis of alcoholism: An empirical evaluation study. *Journal of Studies on Alcohol, 38,* 1259–1273.

Robinson, D. (1976). *From drinking to alcoholism.* New York: Wiley.

Royce, J. E. (1989). *Alcohol problems and alcoholism: A comprehensive survey* (rev. ed.). New York: Free Press.

Rudy, D. R. (1986). *Becoming alcoholic.* Carbondale, IL: Southern Illinois University Press.

Sanders, W. B., & Pinkney, T. K. (1983). *The conduct of social research.* New York: Holt, Rinehart, & Winston.

Skinner, H. A. (1987). A model for the assessment of alcohol use and related problems. *Drugs & Society, 2,* 19–30.

Sobell, M. B., & Sobell, L. C. (1987). Conceptual issues regarding goals in the treatment of alcohol problems. *Drugs & Society, 1,* 1–38.

Strug, D. L., Priyadarsini, S., & Hyman, M. M. (1986). *Alcohol interventions: Historical and sociocultural approaches.* New York: Haworth.

Vaillant, G. E. (1983). *The natural history of alcoholism.* Cambridge, MA: Harvard University Press.

Wilkinson, R. (1970). *The prevention of drinking problems.* New York: Oxford University Press.

Zinberg, N. E. (1984). *Drug, set, and setting.* New Haven, CT: Yale University Press.

Discussion Questions

1. How would you define "normal" drinking? Is it the same as "social" drinking?
2. How would you characterize problem drinking? Is it the same as "alcoholism"?
3. What is meant by the "disease model" of alcoholism?
4. Can you identify different kinds of normal drinking? Problem drinking? Alcoholism?

II

Part II—Youth and Drug Use

Few will disagree with the belief that a society's future is vested in its youth. Yet, many parents, teachers, counselors, health care providers, social workers, law enforcement agents, and religious leaders are fully aware that drugs are a threat to our nation's youth. Further, nationwide illicit drug abuse remains a very serious problem facing our nation's future.

Part I was devoted to alcohol and alcoholism because of the overwhelming percentage of users and its costly repercussions. Premature deaths, reduced productivity, treatment costs, traffic accidents, suicides and homicides are some of society's costs (Wodarski, 1990). Part II is equally important because our future is at risk when drug abuse is widespread throughout the new generation.

How serious is the problem of drug use among our youth? From 1979 to 1990, 48 percent of youths aged 12–17 and a shocking 88 percent of young adults aged 18–25 used alcohol (NIDA, 1990). The estimated 25 percent of adolescents who currently use alcohol and other drugs experience school failures, early unwanted pregnancy, and delinquency (U.S. Dept. of Health and Human Services: Public Health Services, 1992). "Adolescents who use alcohol and other drugs are much more likely than their non using peers to experience other serious problems" (Clayton, 1981; U.S. Dept. of Health and Human Services: Public Health Services, 1992). Wodarski (1990) found that of the 1,289,443 drivers arrested for DUI (drinking under the influence) offenses in 1980, " . . . 29,957 were drivers under the age of 18, and 696 were under 15" (p. 668). Further, over 10,000 teenagers became traffic fatalities in alcohol-related cases (Allen, 1983). Another study shows that in 1987 the percentage of fatalities in alcohol-related motor vehicle crashes was approximately 22 percent per 100,000, for people aged 15–24 (U.S. Department of Health and Human Services: Public Health Services, 1992). As these statistics show, youth who often use drugs are frequently involved in DUI offenses both as victims and perpetrators of fatal traffic accidents (NIAAA, 1990).

Some disguised effects of drug abuse by youth are worth noting. Drug abuse exacts a toll on both mind and body. Physiologically, when alcohol is abused for a sustained length of time, bodily organs are irreversibly damaged and life expectancy is considerably shortened (Blake et al., 1988). Chronic drug use retards physical maturation and mental development (Coombs, 1988). Finally, there is a great likelihood that adolescents who abuse drugs and who are from dysfunctional families will make poor role models for their own children and will perpetuate their own dysfunctional families later in the life cycle (Jacob, Seilhammer & Rushe, 1989; Kandel, 1974; Rees & Wilborn, 1983; and Worobec, Turner, O'Farrell et al., 1990).

We need not be reminded that dysfunctional families are highly efficient in the sense that they replenish and sustain our nation's high rates of divorce, child abuse, high school dropouts, juvenile delinquency, and crime. The abuse of drugs among our nation's youth is serious for two reasons: First, substance abuse is physically, emotionally, and materially damaging. Teenagers who abuse drugs are at a higher risk of not finishing school, suffering physically, and experiencing delinquent behavior (Humm-Delgado & Delgado, 1983). Second, from a macroscopic position, youth who become seriously addicted to drugs disrupt and threaten their own cycles of adolescence, adulthood, and old age. Marriage and family, neighborhood and community stability, and the continuity of our society are jeopardized when drug use is imparted to the next generation.

In addressing the use and abuse of drugs, the first article, "Understanding Adolescent Alcohol Use and Abuse," by Fagan, highlights the fact that adolescent alcohol use has become a major social, psychological, and medical concern in American society today. The article addresses the issue of adolescent alcohol use by raising such questions as: How many adolescents drink? How many are problem drinkers? Is there an adolescent problem drinker profile? Do educational and prevention programs work? Fagan's article concludes by making seven policy recommendations about the prevention, control, and treatment of adolescent alcohol use.

The second article, "Why Adolescents Use Drugs: An Application of Three Deviance Theories," by Raskin White, Johnson, and Horwitz tests the ability of several central concepts from three theories of deviance—namely, differential association, control, and strain theories—to explain drug and alcohol use and abuse among a group of 12-, 15-, and 18-year-olds. Regression analyses are conducted separately on each theory as well as on a general model combining aspects of all three perspectives. Results show that differential association theory is a stronger and more powerful predictor of adolescent drug and alcohol use than either the control or strain theory. Briefly stated, differential association theory predicates that deviant behavior is learned from friends. Control theory emphasizes that society keeps people from becoming deviant through the many bonds they maintain with family members, conforming peers, and others who function as positive role models. Finally, strain theory states that people are prone to deviant behavior when they are unable to achieve respect, status, or wealth. In this article the authors show that friends who use drugs and friends who tolerate drug use are the best predictors of whether adolescents will try various substances, and how often and how much they will use these substances. Gender is not a significant predictor of substance use, while age is. Thus, while Fagan begins Part II with an overview, Raskin White, Johnson, and Horwitz provide theoretical insights from statistically significant findings to explain why adolescents use drugs.

In the third article, "Changes in Sensation-seeking Needs and Drug Use," Bates, LaBouvie and Raskin White study the relationship between adolescent substance use and the personality characteristic of sensation seeking. The authors examine a form of sensation seeking termed disinhibition needs (defined as the desire to experience novel and varied sensations despite substantial risks that may be involved), during adolescence, and the way in which changes in such personality needs are related to changes in patterns of alcohol and other drug use over time. The relationship between personality and substance use patterns is discussed within a developmental perspective, and implications for the treatment of youthful drug abusers are discussed. Interestingly, the results suggest that the desires for novel and stimulating experiences are a significant motivation for drug use during adolescent development.

What characteristics distinguish the users of different types of drugs? An attempt to answer this question is found in the fourth article, "A Comparative Study of Marijuana and Psychedelic Mushroom Users," by Hirsch, Conforti, and Pearsall. To understand the patterns of drug use, the authors draw on 50 users of marijuana and 50 users of psychedelic mushrooms. Specifically, Hirsch, Conforti, and Pearsall focus on understanding the motivations involved in the use of illicit drugs and on deciphering the patterns of drug use.

The authors use a *symbolic interactionist* theoretical framework. Implied in this theoretical view is the belief that all meaning arises from the interpretation of experiences through social interaction. In comparing the two samples, similarities and differences in motivation, patterns of use, and expectations of future use are discussed. The research concludes with a summary statement regarding the use of illicit drugs and some suggestions for future research.

Is it generally true, as often claimed by policy makers, that providing leisure/recreation opportunities will reduce drug use? For example, does involvement in sports reduce drug use? Answers to such questions are found in Part II's fifth and final article, "Adolescent Drug Use and Leisure Activity," by Agnew and Petersen. The authors use data from a survey of 600 adolescents in a major metropolitan area.

Interestingly, Agnew and Petersen discover that the determining factor is not leisure activity *per se,* but the *amount of time spent* in organized leisure activity supervised by adults. The findings suggest that such organized leisure activities as sports and other club memberships occupy only a small proportion of the adolescent's time. The total amount of time spent engaged in such activities is small, and thus does not curtail drug use. This finding is based on the fact that the largest proportion of adolescent leisure time is spent on *passive unsupervised activities,* such as watching television and movies, or attending rock concerts—activities that are more likely to be accompanied by drug use.

References

Allen, T. J. (1983). The school as a family support system. *U. S. Journal of Drug & Alcohol Dependence, 6*(3), 4–14.

Blake, J. E., Compton, K. V., Schmidt, W., & Orrego, H. (1988). Accuracy of death certificates in the diagnosis of alcoholic liver cirrhosis. *Alcoholism, 12,* 168–172.

Clayton, R. R. (1981). The delinquency and drug use relationship among adolescents: A critical review [Monograph]. NIDA Research 31. In D. J. Letieri, & J. Ludford (Eds.), *Drug abuse & the American adolescent.* U. S. Dept. of Health & Human Services.

Coombs, R. H. (Ed.). (1988). *The family context of adolescent drug use.* New York: Haworth.

Humm-Delgado, D., & Delgado, M. (1983). Hispanic adolescents and substance abuse: Issues for the 1980s. *Child and Youth Services 6,* 71–87

Jacob, T; Seilhammer, R. A., & Rushe, R. H. (1989). Assessing life stressors and social resources: Applications to alcoholic patients. *Journal of Substance Abuse, 1,* 135–152.

Kandel, D. (1974). Inter- and intragenerational influences on adolescent marijuana use. *Journal of Social Issues, 30*(2), 107–135.

National Institute on Alcohol Abuse & Alcoholism (NIAAA). (1990). *Seventh special report to the U. S. Congress on alcohol and health.* Rockville, MD: NIAAA.

National Institute on Drug Abuse (NIDA). (1990). Overview of the 1990 National Household Survey on Drug Abuse, *NIDA Capsules.*

Rees, C. D., & Wilborn, B. L. (1983). Correlates of drug abuse in adolescents: A comparison of families of drug abusers with families of non-drug abusers. *Journal of Youth and Adolescence, 12*(1), 55–63.

U. S. Dept. of Health & Human Services: Public Health Services. (1992). *Healthy people 2000, National health promotion and disease prevention objectives.* Boston, MA: Jones & Bartlett Publishers, Inc.

Wodarski, J. S. (1990). Adolescent substance abuse. *Adolescence XXV, 99,* 667–688.

Worobec, T. G., Turner, W. M., O'Farrell, T. J. , Cutter, H. S., Bayog, R. D., & Tsuang, M. T. (1990). Alcohol use by alcoholics with and without a history of parental alcoholism. *Alcoholism: Clinical & Experimental Research, 14,* 887–892.

Understanding Adolescent Alcohol Use and Abuse

Ronald W. Fagan

Ron Fagan is Professor of Sociology and Chairperson of the Social Science Division at Pepperdine University. He received his Ph.D. in sociology from Washington State University. His primary research interests are in the area of alcoholism especially as it relates to spouse abuse, homelessness, adolescents, and legal control. He also has published works on the criminal justice system, non-profit organizations and volunteerism, and religion. His works have appeared in such journals as *Social Problems, Journal of Studies on Alcohol, Journal of Drug Abuse, American Journal of Drug Abuse and Alcoholism, Journal of Alcohol and Drug Education, Journal of Police Science and Administration, Journal of Criminal Justice, Criminal Justice Review* and *Journal of Youth and Adolescence.*

Introduction

Adolescent alcohol use has become a major social concern in American society today. There are numerous reasons for the increased concern. With the decline of adolescent use of other chemical substances during the early-to-middle 1970s, interest in adolescent alcohol use was rekindled. The interest was heightened by concerns about alcohol-related problems, especially drunk driving, antisocial or delinquent behavior, implications for psychosocial development, and the relationship between alcohol use and the use of other chemical substances (Filstead & Mayer, 1980). It was hoped that an understanding of adolescent alcohol use would shed light on "... later and often more severe consequences of alcohol misuses in adulthood, and toward the earlier actions that might be required for a comprehensive effort in primary prevention" (Donovan & Jessor, 1980).

The use of alcohol and other drugs cannot be understood without examining the role that chemical substances play in American society. As a society we send mixed messages to young people about the use of chemical substances. On the one hand, we are constantly bombarded with messages that various drugs will provide us with instant relief from the boredom or stresses of everyday life. The use of these drugs is often associated with various personality or lifestyle characteristics such as being more beautiful, adventuresome, or grown-up. On the other hand, we spend millions of dollars every year encouraging young people to say no to drugs, or to use legal drugs responsibly.

The purpose of this paper is to explore the key issues surrounding adolescent alcohol use by examining the following questions: How many adolescents drink? How many adolescents are problem drinkers? Is there an adolescent problem drinker profile? Do education and prevention programs work? Finally, various policy recommendations are presented and discussed.

Contrary to popular opinion, most contemporary survey research studies show that adolescent alcohol use is either leveling off or showing a gradual decline for at least the past five years. Alcohol continues to be the drug most widely used by teenagers. The most popular drink continues to be beer, followed by wine.

Eighty percent of American youth in grades seven through 12 have had a drink at least once in their lives, with 50 percent of seventh graders and over 90 percent of high school seniors having used alcohol at least once during their lifetime. Over half of adolescents report some alcohol use prior to high school. The average age at which an adolescent begins to drink is 13 years. Approximately 25 percent of high school students are abstainers, and approximately five percent of adolescents are daily users.

Drinking tends to increase as adolescents get older, but there is often a plateau in the prevalence of drinking by the age of 15 or 16, with a further "maturing out" as they reach young adulthood and take on increased responsibilities. Adolescent males continue to drink more than females, with rates of heavy drinking two to three times higher than those of females. But recently there has been some slight diminishing of the sex differences in drinking patterns (Johnston et al., 1985, 1986; Rachael et al., 1982; Wechsler & McFadden, 1976).

Most adolescent drinking is done in unsupervised settings, usually away from home, often in cars (NIAAA, 1981/1982; Smart & Grey, 1979). Especially significant is the relationship between adolescent alcohol use and traffic injuries. In the 1980s, motor vehicle accidents were the leading cause of death among persons 15 to 24 years of age (NIAAA, 1981/1982).

Over three-quarters of the adolescents surveyed said they had friends who were regular users of alcohol (Gallup, 1984). Approximately one-third of older adolescents reported that most or all of their friends drank regularly. But the great majority of adolescents said that they would face the disapproval of their friends if they engaged in heavy daily drinking (Johnston, O'Malley, & Bachman, 1985).

Researchers have found a strong association between adolescent alcohol use and use of other psychoactive drugs among senior high-school students. The most frequently used drugs are marijuana, stimulants, cocaine, hallucinogens, and inhalants. While over 90 percent of high school seniors reported using alcohol at least once in their life, survey research shows that over 50 percent of adolescents reported using marijuana, and 40 percent reported using some other type of illicit or hard drugs. Just as with alcohol use, research shows similar declines in marijuana and other drug use since the mid-1970s (Johnston et al., 1986 & 1987; NIAAA, 1981/1982).

How Many Adolescents Are Problem Drinkers?

Estimates of the number of adolescent problem drinkers vary widely depending upon a number of factors, including how problem drinking is defined. Traditional measures of alcoholism have not been adequate for adolescents, because of the unique characteristics of young people (Mayer & Felstead, 1980; Blane & Hewitt, 1977; Schuckit, 1978). There have been estimates ranging from two percent to over 50 percent of adolescents as problem drinkers. Some commentators would label all adolescents who drink as problem drinkers because almost all adolescent alcohol use is illegal, and because of potential alcohol-related problems (Marden & Kolodner, 1977).

The generally accepted adult standard of alcoholism is physical dependence with associated physiological damage (i.e., delirium tremens, neurological damage, and liver cirrhosis). Research does show that youth who misuse alcohol tend to begin drinking at an earlier age (Rachael et al., 1982). Early initiation to alcohol use is associated with later alcohol and drug abuse and antisocial behavior (Lewis, Rice, & Helzer, 1983; Hesselbrock, Hesselbrock, & Stabenau, 1985; Cadonet, Troughton, & Widmer, 1984). While adolescent alcohol misusers do often exhibit some immediate physical consequences, they are typically not of a serious nature. Very rarely do adolescents show physical dependence on alcohol. It usually takes 15 to 20 years of chronic, heavy drinking to develop physical dependency symptoms (Penning & Barnes, 1982). In addition, the negative social consequences that frequently accompany adult alcoholism, such as marital or job problems, are not typically relevant to the adolescent population.

One common definition of adolescent problem drinking is being drunk (usually defined as having five or more drinks) six or more times in the previous year, or experiencing negative consequences from drinking, on two or more occasions in the past year, in at least three problem areas such as drinking and driving, or trouble with the police, school officials, friends, or a date. Using this definition, approximately 30 percent of 10th through 12th grade students could be classified as problem drinkers (Johnston et al., 1987; Rachael et al., 1980).

A commonly adopted definition of a problem or heavy drinker is an adolescent who drinks five or more drinks at least once a week. About 15 percent of high-school students meet this criterion. Almost one-third of high-school seniors reported this level of drinking during the preceding two weeks.

Another way to define teenage alcohol use is to focus on the more age-appropriate negative consequences, such as trouble with police, drinking and driving, problems with family, friends, or school personnel. Using this criterion, prevalence rates of greater than 30 percent have been reported (Rachael et al., 1980).

No matter what definition of problem drinking is accepted, most experts would agree that alcohol intoxication poses some significant physical, psychological, and social risks for adolescents because, first, adolescents often do their drinking in unsupervised settings away from home—frequently in, or while driving, automobiles. Second, heavy alcohol use frequently disrupts nutritional and metabolic cycles, which can be critical during adolescent growth and, if left unchecked, this disruption can lead to serious health problems in later life. And finally, heavy alcohol use can retard the development of adequate coping, learning, and problem-solving skills necessary for proper life functioning.

Is There an Adolescent Problem Drinker Profile?

Problem drinking among adolescents is part of a complex behavioral syndrome. It is both a cause and an effect of growing up as a teenager in American society. It is important to remember that the overwhelming reason adolescents drink is that they aspire to be like adults—a status that typically includes alcohol use. As Keller (1980) observes:

> Youngsters drink because they see that adults drink. Youngsters drink to get drunk, in part because they perceive that adults around them drink to get drunk. Youngsters will drink moderately and avoid getting drunk when they perceive that the adults around them drink moderately and avoid getting drunk. Youngsters will even abstain if the adults around them abstain. (p. 255)

For most adolescents, drinking has few negative consequences. Drinking and its consequences are dependent on such factors as genetics, expectancy, dose, setting, adult and peer modeling, gender, life functioning, and motivation for drinking. A common set of generally nonpathological, psychosocial variables can describe both problem and nonproblem drinkers. It is merely a matter of degree (Donovan & Jessor, 1980; Jessor & Jessor, 1975). The relationship between alcohol consumption and alcohol problems is complex. Cohen (1981) notes:

> At times it is difficult to determine whether certain personality features cause or are the results of drinking excessively. Diminished personal controls, impulsivity, and antisocial trends are supposed to be predisposing personality factors. It may be so, but it should be remembered that alcohol intoxication also releases such behavior. (p. 86)

While the study results are not uniform, the personality factors most commonly associated with adolescent drug and alcohol abuse are deficits in psychological adjustments and psychological competency. Studies indicate that, as a group, adolescent alcohol abusers often show signs of lower self-esteem, depression, anxiety, restlessness, rebellion, impulsivity, less conformity to established institutions (especially school and religion), and involvement in other delinquent activities such as lying, stealing, vandalism, aggression, and other drug use (Lettieri, 1985; Hawkins et al., 1986; Jessor et al., 1980). They are more apt to weigh the positive aspects of drinking more heavily than the negative aspects (Braucht, 1980, 1982; Gullotta & Adams, 1982; Barnes, 1982; Donovan & Jessor, 1980).

Two variables that are consistently reported to be related to adolescent alcohol use are the behaviors of parents and peers (Marden & Kolodner, 1977). There is a strong association between parental drinking and attitudes toward drinking and the drinking behavior of children (Walker, Jasinska, & Carnes, 1978). It has been well documented that children of alcoholic parents are at very high risk of becoming alcoholics (Goodwin, 1985).

Studies show that adolescents who drink heavily are less likely to feel very close to their families. They reported tensions, poor communication, and lack of involvement by their parents (Barnes, 1982; Kandel, 1985). The worst parental combination is when parents drink or use drugs and fail to provide an adequate nurturing and supportive environment for the children (Kimmel & Weiner, 1985; McDermott, 1984; Kandel, 1985). As adolescents drink more, they become increasingly influenced by their own needs and feelings and by their friends, and less by their families and school (Mayer & Filstead, 1980; Biddle et al., 1980).

Kumpfer and DeMarsh (1986) identify the following family risk factors in the development of adolescent alcohol and drug abuse: age of children when parent(s) become(s) involved with substance abuse; degree of involvement in substance abuse of the primary caretaker and nonfulfillment of parental responsibilities; severity of emotional, physical, educational, and spiritual neglect or abuse; temperament of the child and the role the child assumes in the family; degree of family stress due to inconsistencies in child raising practices; degree of family conflict; and degree of open modeling of drug or alcohol abuse by the parent and siblings.

The behavior of the adolescent's peers is a very important element in the development of a problem drinking behavior. Studies show that adolescent drinking becomes heavier and more problematic as the extent of drinking among friends increases (Harford & Speiger, 1982). Alcohol use can be both a cause and a consequence of peer relationships. Peers can pressure adolescents to drink, but some researchers feel it is more likely that friends are chosen simply because of similar attitudes and behavioral patterns in their use of alcohol (Jessor & Jessor, 1975; Barnes, 1982).

Therefore, it appears that adolescent alcohol use and misuse is a result of the interaction among numerous genetic, social, psychological, and situational factors. Rice (1984) classifies drug use into five motivational patterns. Experimental drug use involves the short-term, low-frequency use of drugs and alcohol. The primary motivations are curiosity, novelty, and excitement, in a spirit of adventure-seeking and mild rebellion. In the social-recreational use of drugs and alcohol, the motives are peer-oriented, to share a pleasurable experience with friends. In the circumstantial-situational use of drugs and alcohol, the motive is a need to achieve a mood or mental effect in a specific situation, e.g., using alcohol to relax or to be cool at a party. Intensified drug and alcohol use involves long-term use to escape from perceived daily stresses and problems of living. Use becomes a habitual part of the adolescent's lifestyle. Finally, compulsive drug use is high-frequency use of long-term duration. The adolescent's lifestyle revolves around drugs and alcohol. Withdrawal from drugs is likely to be accompanied by physical and psychological withdrawal.

In conclusion, the etiologies of initial alcohol use, occasional alcohol use, regular alcohol use, and alcohol abuse may very well be quite different (Robins & Przybeck, 1985; Hawkins, et al., 1986). Prevention and treatment need to vary depending upon the individual and the developmental stage.

Do Education and Prevention Programs Work?

In America, we have a strong tradition of turning to the school system to solve our social problems. This is no less true for the problems of adolescent drug and alcohol use. Alcohol education began in the late 1800s as a product of the temperance movement, and by 1902, virtually all states mandated some instruction about alcohol use in the public school curriculum.

A variety of alcohol and drug abuse prevention programs has been initiated by the schools. Rather than focus on identified high-risk adolescents, most of the programs are aimed at the general elementary, junior or senior high-school populations. Rarely do such programs systematically include parents or siblings as an integral part of the instruction. Prevention programs range from one-time activities to semester- or year-long formal instruction; programs are either integrated into an existing class or form the foundation of a new curriculum.

Bukoski (1986) identified five educational domains upon which most contemporary school-based prevention and treatment programs typically focus. The cognitive domain focuses on increasing student knowledge about the pharmacological effects and physical, psychological, and social hazards of substance and alcohol abuse. The affective and interpersonal domains focus prevention activities on improving the student's social and psychological development and adjustment. The behavioral domain focuses on training youth in socially relevant and appropriate responses to social pressure to use alcohol and other drugs. The environmental domain includes preventive strategies and school management activities implemented by school administrators to deal with student drug problems. Finally, the therapeutic domain includes preventative interventions for those children already experiencing adjustment problems with school, family, and the community.

Most school-based prevention programs are based on the knowledge/attitudes model that assumes that increased knowledge about the consequences of alcohol misuse will produce more negative attitudes toward misuse, which, in turn, will reduce the likelihood of misuse. Research results of this model are, at best, inconsistent. Some studies show that such programs can be mildly successful at increasing knowledge about, and, to a lesser extent, negative attitudes toward alcohol use, but that they are generally not successful at changing levels of consumption or alcohol-related problem behavior. If consumption levels are reduced, the effect is usually short-lived (usually less than six months). Some programs, in fact, appear to facilitate student experimentation with alcohol and other drugs (Goodstadt, 1981; Hanson, 1980; Kinder, Pope, & Walfish, 1980; Williams, Ward, & Gray, 1985).

Other school-based programs use a values/decision-making or social competency model (Moskowitz, 1989). These models focus not just on alcohol use, but on the adolescent's values and psychological functioning skills. The assumption is made that:

> ...if an adolescent knows something about alcohol and alcoholism, holds attitudes tolerant of moderate use and abstinence but intolerant of excessive use, has high self-esteem and has well developed skills in decision-making and coping, then the adolescent will be unlikely to abuse alcohol. (Mauss et al., 1988)

The studies that have been done generally do not support these models (Hopkins et al., 1988; Moskowitz, 1989; Kinder, Pope, & Walfish, 1980; Sheppard, Wright, & Goodstadt, 1985). Mauss and Associates (1988) conclude that such school-based programs fail because they are limited in the variables they can potentially manipulate to influence drinking. Programs will succeed to the extent that they are part of a comprehensive, community-wide prevention effort that addresses the major social, psychological, legal, and situational variables that influence drinking (Perry, 1986; Holder & Wallach, 1986).

In the United States, one of the most often-used strategies to deal with alcohol use has been to control physical, economic, and social availability of alcohol (Room, 1984). Physical availability factors most relevant for adolescents are minimum legal drinking age, type of alcoholic beverage, and type and number of retail outlets. Economic availability is concerned with the price, while social availability is primarily concerned with the promotion of alcoholic beverages.

The evidence suggests that raising the minimum drinking age has an effect on adolescent beer consumption, while the effect on liquor consumption is mixed. The research on the effects of advertising on adolescent drinking is inconclusive, but there is some evidence of a positive relationship between exposure to advertising and drinking (Atkins, Hocking, & Block, 1984; Atkin, Neuendorf, & McDermott, 1983; Strickland, 1983). Studies suggest that mass media prevention campaigns, while they are most likely to influence knowledge and least likely to influence behavior, may be effective in building public support for sound prevention policies and programs (especially drinking and driving programs) (Room, 1980). Studies do show that increasing the minimum legal drinking age can reduce alcohol-related automobile crash and fatality rates for the affected age group and, in some cases, for other young drivers as well (Arnold, 1985; Williams, et al., 1985; DuMouchel, Williams, & Zador, 1987; Saffer & Grossman, 1986). It has been estimated that alcohol-related crashes and fatalities could be reduced by approximately one-fourth by raising the minimum legal drinking age in all states to 21 (Wagenaar, 1983; Arnold, 1985). There is some research to show that increasing the price of liquor and beer can decrease alcohol-related traffic crashes and fatalities (Saffer & Grossman, 1986).

Human service professionals have found that it is difficult to reach and treat the adolescent population. The major reason is that young people often do not see themselves as having an alcohol problem. Drinking alcohol is seen by them as a regular part of their lives, supported by their peers, and useful in relieving stress, boredom, and the developmental problems inherent in growing up. Even when adolescents are aware that they have a problem with alcohol, they still may not receive adequate help because (1) they may be unaware of the available services and how to use them, (2) they fear reprisals from school officials, parents, or law enforcement personnel, (3) they are embarrassed by the problem, or (4) they lack the necessary financial resources (Turanski, 1985/1986).

Even when an adolescent is referred to a treatment facility, it does not necessarily mean that he/she is an alcoholic. Many adolescents encounter problems with alcohol because of a single incident such as drunk driving, assaultive behavior, or underage buying, rather than as a result of a chronic condition (White & Labouvie, 1989). A variety of treatment facilities and programs is available, including hospitals, schools, churches, mental health clinics, halfway houses, youth homes, private programs, and Alcoholics Anonymous. Programs are either inpatient, outpatient, or residential. There is a need for more programs that are designed specifically to serve adolescents.

Recommendations

1. The minimum legal drinking age should be raised to 21. There is a large body of evidence that indicates that this measure would be an effective means of reducing alcohol-related injuries. In addition, there must be effective mass media campaigns against drinking and driving, and strict enforcement and severe penalties for drinking and driving, especially for young drivers.
2. Continued restrictions must be placed on the physical and economic availability of alcoholic beverages. While the research is limited, there is evidence that increasing the excise tax on liquor and beer can effectively reduce alcohol problems, especially alcohol-related automobile crashes where youth are involved. As Moskowitz (1989) notes: "It seems reasonable that drinkers should underwrite more of the cost to our society of alcohol-related problems by paying higher excise taxes on alcoholic beverages" (p. 79). There needs to be strict enforcement of laws prohibiting the selling and serving of alcoholic beverages to minors.
3. The research is not encouraging on the effectiveness of mass media education and prevention campaigns at changing drinking behavior. But mass media campaigns will likely be most effective when they reinforce existing attitudes (such as opposition to drinking and driving) and are combined with other community and school-based prevention and intervention strategies. Just as we argue that alcoholic beverage consumers should be made economically responsible for alcohol-related problems, by taxation, so too should alcoholic beverage manufacturers and producers be held to a higher standard by being required to produce socially responsible advertisements promoting their products, as well as make significant economic contributions to support adolescent prevention and treatment efforts (Flay & Sobel, 1983).
4. Americans have long believed that education is not only valuable in itself, but that it can also serve a wide variety of social goals. Students bring their personal and social problems to school with them. It is simply unrealistic to expect schools to solve these problems in isolation. School-based programs have not proven to be very successful, especially at changing behavior. Other social and psychological factors, particularly parents and peers, not so amenable to school-based intervention, have more significant effects on alcohol use. Adolescent alcohol problems belong to everyone in the community. We need multifaceted programs that can have a school-based component, but that also work with these other factors.
5. Cultures with the most ambiguous norms about drinking typically experience the greatest problems (Room, 1980). Today's adolescents live in a society that tolerates, if not glamorizes, drinking. Adolescents drink because they see adults drinking. Before we solve the alcohol problems of our youth, we have to address the alcohol problems of the adults. It is interesting to note that anti-smoking school-based programs have produced results largely because they occur in the context of an adult community that has been increasingly turning against smoking. There have been some similar successes with the campaigns against drinking and driving. There have been some very promising findings from programs that teach parenting skills that will help in the prevention of risk factors associated with alcohol and drug abuse

and other forms of delinquency (Hawkins, Lishner, & Catalano, 1985).

6. Adolescents themselves, both those adolescents with alcohol programs and those without, need to be integrally involved in the planning, execution, and promotion of all education, prevention, and treatment efforts. Programs such as SADD are models for such an effort.
7. More treatment programs need to be developed that are specifically designed for adolescent alcohol abusers. We need to better assist parents, school officials, and the adolescents themselves in identifying the signs of adolescent alcohol problems, and we must develop more effective means of getting problem youth into treatment.

References

Arnold, R. (1985). *Effect of raising the legal drinking age on drivers' involvement in fatal crashes: The experience of thirteen states.* National Highway Traffic Safety Administration (Pub. No. DOT HS806-9021). Washington, DC: U. S. Government Printing Office.

Atkin, C., Hocking, J., & Block, M. (1984). Teenage drinking: Does advertising make a difference. *Journal of Communication, 34,* 157–167.

Atkin, C. K., Neundorf, K., & McDermott, S. (1983). The role of alcohol advertising in excessive and hazardous drinking. *Journal of Drug Education. 13,* 313–325.

Bell, C., & Battljes, B. (Eds.). (1985). *Prevention research: Deterring drug abuse among children and adolescents.* (DHHS Pub. No. ADM 85–1334). Washington, DC: U. S. Government Printing Office.

Beschner, G. (1986). Treatment for childhood chemical abuse. *Journal of Children in Contemporary Society, 18,* 231–248.

Biddle, B. J., Bank, B. J., & Marlen, M. M. (1980). Social determinants of adolescent drinking: What they think, what they do, and what I think and do. *Journal of Studies on Alcohol, 41,* 215–241.

Blane, H. T., & Hewitt, L. (1977). *Alcohol and youth: An analysis of the literature 1960–1975* (NTIS No. PB 268698). Rockville, MO: NIAAA.

Braucht, G. N. (1980). Psychosocial research on teenage drinking: Past and future. In F. R. Scarpitti, & S. K. Datesman (Eds.), *Drugs and the Youth Culture* (pp. 109–143). Beverly Hills, CA: Sage Publishers.

Braucht, G. N. (1982). Problem drinking among adolescents: A review and analysis of psychosocial research [Monograph]. In NIAAA, *Special Population Issues.* Alcohol & Health No. 4. DHHS Pub. No. (ADM) 82-1193 (pp. 143–164). Washington, DC: U. S. Government Printing Office.

Bruvold, W., & Rundall, T. (1988). A meta-analysis and theoretical review of school-based tobacco and alcohol intervention programs. *Psychology and Health, 2,* 53–78.

Bukoski, W. J. (1986). School-based substance abuse prevention: A review of program research. *Journal of Children in Contemporary Society, 18,* 95–116.

Cadonet, R., Troughton, E., & Widmer, R. (1984). Clinical differences between anti-social and primary alcoholics. *Comprehensive Psychiatry, 25,* 1–8.

Coate, D., & Grossman, M. (1986). *Effects of alcoholic beverage prices and legal drinking ages on youth alcohol use: Results from the second national health and nutrition examination survey.* (NBER Working Paper No. 1852), Cambridge, MA: National Bureau of Economic Research.

Cohen, S. J. (1981). *The substance abuse problems.* New York: Haworth Press.

Donovan, J. E., & Jessor, R. (1980). Adolescent problem drinking: Psychological correlates in a national sample study. *Journal of Studies on Alcohol, 39,* 1506–1524.

Donovan, J. E., Jessor, R., & Jessor, L. (1983). Problem drinking in adolescence and young adulthood: A follow up study. *Journal of Studies on Alcohol, 44,* 109–137.

DuMochel, W., William, A., & Zador, P. (1987). Raising the alcohol purchase age: Its effect on fatal motor vehicle crashes in 26 states. *Journal of Legal Studies, 16,* 249–266.

Fillmore, K. M., Bacon, S. D., & Hyman, M. (1979). *The 27 year longitudinal panel study of drinking by students in college, 1949–1976.* Final Report to NIAAA (Contract No. ADM 281-7600015).

Filstead, W. J., & Mayer, J. E. (1980). Adolescence and alcohol: An overview and introduction. In J. E. Mayer, & W. J. Filstead (Eds.), *Adolescence and alcohol* (pp. 1–6). Cambridge, MA: Ballinger.

Gallup, G. Jr. (1984, Sept. 6–7.) *Most teens have friends who drink or use drugs. Teen drinking up sharply in two years.* Gallup Poll.

Goodstadt, M. S. (1981). Planning and evaluation of alcohol education programs. *Journal of Alcohol & Drug Education, 26,* 1–10.

Goodstadt, M. S. (1985). Shaping drinking practices through education. In J. P. Von Wartburg, P. Magnenat, R. Mullen, & S. Wyss (Eds.), *Currents in alcohol research & the prevention of alcohol problems* (pp. 85–106). Toronto: Hans Haber.

Goodwin, D. W. (1985). Alcoholism and genetics. *Archives of General Psychiatry, 42,* 171–174.

Grossman, M., Coate, D., & Arluck, G. M. (1987). Price sensitivity of alcoholic beverages in the United States: Youth alcohol consumption. In H. D. Holder (Ed.), *Control issues in alcohol abuse prevention: Strategies for states and communities.* Advances in Substance Abuse, Supplement No. 1 (pp. 169–198). Greenwich, CT: JAI Press.

Gullotta, T. P., & Adams, G. R. (1982). Substance abuse minimization: Conceptualizing prevention in adolescent and youth programs. *Journal of Youth and Adolescence, 11,* 409–424.

Hawkins, J. D., Lishner, D. M., & Catalano, R. F. (1985). Childhood predictors and the prevention of adolescent abuse [Monograph]. In C. L. Jones, & R. J. Battjes (Eds.), *Etiology of drug abuse: Implications for prevention.* National Institute on Drug Abuse Research S6, DHHS Pub. No. ADM 85-1335 (pp. 75–126). Washington, DC: U. S. Government Printing Office.

Hawkins, J. D., Lishner, D. M., Catalano, R. F., & Howard, M. O. (1986). Childhood predictors and the prevention of adolescent substance abuse: Toward an empirically grounded theory. *Journal of Children in Contemporary Society, 18,* 11–48.

Hesselbrock, V. N., Hesselbrock, M. D., & Stabenau, J. R. (1985). Alcoholism in men patients subtyped by family history and antisocial personality. *Journal of Studies on Alcohol, 46,* 59–64.

Hirschi, T. (1969). *Causes of delinquency.* Berkeley, CA: University of California Press.

Holder, H. D., & Wallach, L. (1986). Contemporary perspectives for preventing alcohol problems: An empirically divided model. *Journal of Public Health Policy, 7,* 329–339.

Hopkins, R. H., Mauss, A. L., Kearney, K. A., & Weishiet, R. A. (1988). Comprehensive evaluation of a model alcohol education curriculum. *Journal of Studies on Alcohol, 49,* 62–73.

Jessor, R., & Jessor S. L. (1975). Adolescent development and the onset of drinking: A longitudinal study. *Journal of Studies on Alcohol, 36,* 27–51.

Johnston, L. D., O'Malley, P. M., & Bachman, J. G. (1985). *The use of licit and illicit drugs by America's high school students, 1975–1984.* DHHS Pub. No. (ADM) 85-1394. Rockvlle, MD: Alcohol, Drug Abuse, & Mental Health Administration.

Johnston, L. D., O'Malley, P. M., & Bachman, J. G. (1986). *The use of licit and illicit drugs by America's high school students, 1975–1984.* Ann Arbor, MI: University of Michigan Survey Research Institute.

Johnston, L. D., O'Malley, P. M., & Bachman, J. G. (1987) *National trends in drug use and related factors among American high school students and young adults, 1975–1986.* (DHHS Pub. No. (ADM) 87-1535). Washington, DC: Government Printing Office.

Kandel, D. B. (1985). On process of peer influence and adolescent drug use: A developmental perspective. *Advances in Alcohol and Substance Abuse, 4,* 139–164.

Keller, M. (1980). Alcohol and youth. In J. E. Mayer, & W. J. Filstead (Eds.), *Adolescence and Alcohol* (pp. 245–256). Cambridge, MA: Ballinger.

Kimmel, D. C., & Weiner, I. B. (1985). *Adolescence: A developmental transition.* Hillsdale, NJ: Lawrence Erlbaum Associates.

Kinder, B. N., Pope, N. E., & Walfish, S. (1980). Drug and alcohol education programs: A review of outcome studies. *International Journal of Addiction, 15,* 1035–1054.

Kumpfer, K. L., & De Marsh, J. (1986). Family environmental and genetic influences on children's future chemical dependency. *Journal of Children in Contemporary Society, 18,* 49–91.

Lettieri, D. J. (1985). Drug abuse: A review of explanations and models of explanation. *Advances in Alcohol & Substance Abuse, 4,* 9–40.

Lewis, C. E., Rice, J., & Helzer, J. E. (1983). Diagnostic interactions: Alcoholism and antisocial personality. *Journal of Nervous & Mental Disease, 171,* 105–113.

Maddox, P. G., & McCall, B. C. (1964). *Drinking among teenagers.* New Brunswick, NJ: Rutgers Center of Alcohol Studies.

Manson, D. J. (1980). Drug education: Does it work? In F. R. Scarpitti, & S. K. Datesman (Eds.), *Drugs and the youth culture* (pp. 251–282). Beverly Hills, CA: Sage Publishers.

Marden, P. G., & Kolodner, K. (1977). *Alcohol use and abuse among adolescents.* NCALI report NCA 1026533. Rockville, MD: NIAAA.

Mauss, A. L., Hopkins, R. H., Wesheit, R. A., & Kearney, K. A. (1988). The problematic prospects for prevention in the classroom: Should alcohol education programs be expected to reduce drinking by youths? *Journal of Studies on Alcohol, 49,* 51–61.

Mayer, J. E., & Filstead, W. J. (1980). Adolescence and alcohol: A theoretical model. In J. E. Mayer, & W. J. Filstead (Eds.), *Adolescence and alcohol* (pp 151–164). Cambridge, MA: Ballinger.

McDermott, D. (1984). The relationship of parental drug use and parents' attitude concerning adolescent drug use to adolescent drug use. *Adolescence, 19,* 89–97.

Moskowitz, J. M. (1989). The primary prevention of alcohol problems: A critical view of the research literature. *Journal of Studies on Alcohol, 50,* 54–88.

National Institute on Alcohol Abuse & Alcoholism (NIAAA). (1981, 1982). *Alcohol and youth: Facts in planning.* National Clearing House for Alcohol Information.

Penning, M., & Barnes, G. E. (1982). Adolescent marijuana use: A review. *International Journal of Addiction, 17,* 749–791.

Perry, C. L. (1986). Community programs for drug abuse prevention. *Journal of School Health, 56,* pp. 359–363.

Polich, J. M., Ellickson, P. L., Reuter, P., & Kahan, J. P. (1984). *Strategies for controlling adolescent drug use.* Santa Monica, CA: Rand Corporation.

Prendergast, T. J., & Schafer, E. S. (1974). Correlates of drinking and drunkenness among high school students. *Quarterly Journal of Studies on Alcohol, 35,* 232–242.

Rachael, J. V., Guess, L. L., Hubbard, R. L., Maisto, S. A., Cavanaugh, E. R., Waddell, R., & Benrud, C. H. (1980). *Adolescent drinking behavior, vol. 1: The extent and nature of adolescent alcohol and drug abuse: The 1974 and 1978 national sample studies.* Research Triangle Park: Research Triangle Institute.

Rachael, J. V., Guess, L. L., Hubbard, R. L., Maisto, S. A., Cavanagh, E. R., Waddell, R., & Benrud, C. H. (1982). Facts for planning No. 4: Alcohol misuse by adolescents. *Alcohol Health & Research World, 3,* 61–68.

Rice, F. P. (1984). *The adolescent: Development, relationships, and culture* (4th ed.). Boston, MA: Allyn & Bacon.

Robins, L. N., & Przybeck, T. R. (1985). *Age of onset of drug use as a factor in drug use and other disorders* [Monograph]. NIDA Research No. 56, U.S.D.H.H.S. Pub. No. 1415. Washington, DC: U. S. Government Printing Office.

Room, R. (1980). Concepts and strategies in the prevention of alcohol-related problems. *Contemporary Drug Problems, 9,* 9–48.

Room, R. (1984). Alcohol control and public health. *Annual Review of Public Health, 5,* 293–317.

Room, R. (1985). Alcohol as a cause: Empirical links and social definitions. In J. P. Von Wartburg, R. Magnenat, Muller, & S. Wyss (Eds.), *Currents in Alcohol Research & the Prevention of Alcohol Problems* (pp. 11–19). Toronto: Hans Huber Publishers.

Saffer, H., & Grossman, M. (1986). *Beer taxes, the legal drinking age, and youth motor vehicle fatalities* Working paper No. 1914. Cambridge, MA: National Bureau of Economic Research.

Schuckit, M. A. (1978). *Alcohol patterns and problems in youth.* Unpublished paper presented at the Alcohol and Drug Abuse Institute Conference, University of Washington, Alcoholism and Drug Abuse Institute.

Sheppard, M. A., Wright, D., & Goodstadt, M. S. (1985). Peer pressure and drug use—exploding the myth. *Adolescence, 20,* 949–958.

Smart, R. G. (1976). *The new drinkers: Teenage use and abuse of alcohol,* vol. 4. Toronto: Addiction Research Foundation.

Smart, R. G., & Grey, G. (1979). Parental and peer influences on correlates of problem drinking among high school students. *International Journal of Addictions, 14,* 905–917.

Strickland, D. E. (1983). Advertising exposure, alcohol consumption and misuse of alcohol. In M. Grant, M., Plant, & A. Williams (Eds.), *Economics & Alcohol: Consumption & Controls* (pp. 201–222). New York: Gardner Press.

Tobler, N. S. (1986). Meta-analysis of 143 adolescent drug prevention programs: Quantitative outcome results of program participants compared to a control or a comparison group. *Journal of Drug Issues, 16*, 537–567.

Turanski, J. J. (1985/1986). Reaching and treating youth with alcohol related problems: A comprehensive approach. *Alcohol Health & Research World, 10*, 3–5.

Wagenaar, A. C. (1983). Preventing highway crashes by raising the legal minimum age for drinking: The Michigan experience six years later. *Journal of Safety Research, 17*, 101–109.

Walker, B. A., Jasinska, M. D., & Carnes, E. F. (1978). Adolescent alcohol abuse: A review of the literature. *Journal of Alcohol and Drug Education, 23*, 51–65.

Wechsler, R. M., & McFadden, M. (1976). Sex differences in adolescent alcohol and drug abuse: A disappearing phenomenon. *Journal of Studies on Alcohol, 37*, 1291–1301.

Weiskeit, R. A. (1983). Contemporary issues in the prevention of adolescent alcohol abuse. In D. A. Ward (Ed.), *Alcoholism: Introduction to theory and treatment* (pp. 253–263). Dubuque, IA: Kendall Hunt.

White, H. R., & Labouvie, E. W. (1989). Towards the assessment of adolescent problem drinking. *Journal of Studies on Alcohol, 50*, 30–37.

White, J. L. (1989). *The troubled adolescent.* New York: Pergamon.

Williams, R. E., Ward, D. A., & Gray, L. N. (1985). The persistence of experimentally induced cognitive change: A neglected dimension in the assessment of drug prevention programs. *Journal of Drug Education, 15*, 33–42.

Wittman, F. D. (1982). Current status of research demonstration programs in the primary preventions of alcohol problems. In NIAAA, *Prevention, Intervention and Treatment: Concerns and Models* [Monograph]. Alcohol & Health No. 3, DHHS Pub. No. (ADM) 82-1192. Washington, DC: Government Printing Office.

Discussion Questions

1. What were Fagan's major findings with regard to youth and alcohol consumption?
2. What main reasons does Fagan give for adolescents becoming problem drinkers? Do you agree with his contention? Support your opinion with other research findings.
3. Fagan recommends that the minimum legal drinking age remain at 21. Do you agree or disagree with this age limit? If you agree, support your argument; if you disagree, support your argument.
4. Do you think that an increase in the excise tax on alcohol and cigarettes would decrease the use of these drugs? How would a very large tax increase affect the use of these drugs? For example, would a 50 percent increase in the selling price decrease the use of these legal drugs?

Why Adolescents Use Drugs
An Application of Three Deviance Theories

Helene Raskin White Valerie Johnson Allan Horwitz

Helene Raskin White is an Associate Professor of Sociology at the Center of Alcohol Studies and Sociology Department, Rutgers University. She received here B.A. from Douglass College and her M.Phil. and Ph.D. degrees from Rutgers University. Since joining the Center of Alcohol Studies, Dr. White has been involved primarily in longitudinal research on the antecedents, correlates, and consequences of alcohol and other drug use in clinical and nonclinical populations. She is the co-editor (with Edith L. Gomberg and John A. Carpenter) of *Alcohol, Science and Society Revisited* and (with David J. Pittman) of *Society, Culture and Drinking Patterns Reexamined,* both readers in the field of alcohol studies, and the author of more than 50 articles, chapters, and reports on drug use and other forms of deviance.

Valerie Johnson is an Assistant Professor at the Rutgers University Center of Alcohol Studies. She is currently investigating factors influencing the transition from moderate to excessive use of alcohol and the vulnerabilities to the consequences of drug and alcohol use in a longitudinal sample of young adults. She has published the results from her research in a variety of journals and presented papers at sociology, psychology, public health, and alcohol/drug conferences. Dr. Johnson's other areas of interest include treatment outcome research, substance abuse prevention programs for college students, and employee assistance programs.

Allan V. Horwitz is a Professor of Sociology in the Department of Sociology and the Institute for Health, Health Care Policy, and Aging Research at Rutgers University. His primary areas of interest lie in the social response to deviant behavior and the determinants of psychological well-being. He is the author of two books, *The Social Control of Mental Illness* and *The Logic of Social Control.* His articles appear in a number of journals.

Introduction

For many years, research on the study of the causes of drug use was largely limited to descriptive reports that ignored theoretical questions. During the last two decades, however, research in this area has become more theoretically sophisticated. A number of theories, including social learning (Akers, 1985), socialization (Kandel, 1978), problem behavior (Jessor & Jessor, 1977), self-derogation (Kaplan, 1980), and integrated models (e.g., Elliott, Huizinga, & Ageton, 1985) have successfully explained various aspects of drug-using behavior. Most of these works examine the extent to which a single theoretical perspective fits the data at hand (Akers, 1985; Kaplan, 1980), while others incorporate elements of several theories into one overarching model (Elliott et al., 1985). Rarely has the comparative power of different theoretical perspectives been tested.

This article is reprinted with the permission of Marcel Dekker, Inc. A version of this article was published in the *International Journal of the Addictions, 21*(3), 347–366 (1986). Preparation of this manuscript was supported in part by grants from the National Institute on Drug Abuse (#DA-03395) and the National Institute of Alcohol Abuse and Alcoholism (#AA-05823).

The purpose of this study is to compare the ability of several central concepts of three major sociological theories of deviant behavior—differential association, social control, and strain—to explain drug and alcohol use among adolescents.

Differential association theory postulates that deviant behavior is learned through associations and definitions that either encourage (reinforce) or discourage (punish) such behavior (Sutherland, 1942). People engage in acts defined as deviant because of the values of their reference groups, not because of any abnormal processes. Since people presumably learn to deviate in the same way and through the same mechanisms in which they learn to conform, recent work in the differential association tradition has come to incorporate the assumptions of social learning theory. Akers and his colleagues (Akers, Krohn, Lanza-Kaduce, & Radosevich, 1979), for example, have combined elements of Sutherland's differential association theory with Skinner's (1953) behaviorism and Bandura's (1977) social learning theory to explain differential substance use. Akers et al. (1979) test the hypotheses that the balance of rewards and punishments determines substance use and that the peer and family groups are the major contexts in which these rewards and punishments are administered. Their data demonstrate that the differential association variables explain the most variation in both alcohol and drug use among adolescents. In agreement with other research (Kandel, 1978; Kaplan, Martin, & Robbins, 1984; Marcos, Bahr, & Johnson, 1986), their strongest predictor of substance use was having friends who use drugs and alcohol.

Social control theory posits that deviance arises when young people lack sufficient bonds to conventional social groups, such as families, schools, and churches (Hirschi, 1969). When individuals lack social integration, there is little control to be exercised over their behavior, and nothing in their environment prevents them from engaging in deviance. From this point of view, youth deviate not through frustrated desires or actions in accordance with their own reference groups but through broken or underdeveloped ties to conventional groups. Not only has social control theory amassed substantial support in the delinquency literature (e.g., Agnew, 1985; LaGrange & White, 1985; Matsueda, 1982; Wiatrowski, Griswold, & Roberts, 1981), but recent applications suggest that control theory has relevance to explaining substance use (Elliott et al., 1985; Massey & Krohn, 1986; Marcos et al., 1986). It has also become common in the delinquency literature to test both control and differential association theories simultaneously (e.g., Dull, 1984; Elliott et al., 1985; LaGrange & White, 1985; Massey & Krohn, 1986; Marcos et al., 1986; Matsueda, 1982; White & LaGrange, 1987).

Finally, strain theory emphasizes entirely different processes than either differential association or control theory. Its central thesis is that people become prone to deviate when society is unable to satisfy their fundamental needs; that is, deviance is a response to actual or anticipated failure to achieve socially induced needs or goals, such as status, wealth, or social acceptance (Elliott, et al., 1985). One version of strain theory emphasizes how deviance arises when expectations for success fall short of aspirations (Merton, 1938; Short & Strodbeck, 1965). A broader version of strain theory views various forms of deviance as mechanisms that allow people to cope with the stresses of everyday life (Agnew, 1992; Dohrenwend & Dohrenwend, 1981; Pearlin, 1981). If strain theory is correct, substance use might be especially prevalent among adolescents who are experiencing the greatest amount of strain. While strain theory has not had much success in explaining delinquent behavior (Elliott et al., 1985; Hirschi, 1969; Kornhauser, 1978), a recent test of General Strain Theory suggests that it holds promise for explaining both delinquency and drug use among adolescents (Agnew & White, 1992). This study will explore the comparative power of several central concepts of differential association, social control, and strain theories in explaining alcohol and drug use among adolescents.

A second task of this research is to view the various theories of deviance in a developmental context. While the types and dynamics of substance use are related to the age of users (see, for example, Kandel, 1978), only recently have theories of deviance explored age differences (LaGrange & White, 1985). Most empirical studies either sample only one age group, such as high-school or college students, or have not stratified their samples by age groups. Therefore, researchers have not determined, for example, if peers are more important influences on substance use during high school, while imitation or lack of parental control is more salient among younger adolescents. Similarly, despite interest about gender roles and deviant behavior (Adler, 1976; Simon, 1975; White & LaGrange, 1987), most studies fail to test for differential facilitators of substance use between males and females. Here we examine whether any single theory can explain substance use among varying age and gender groups, or whether different mechanisms apply in various groups.

Methods

Sample

Data for this study were collected as part of the Rutgers Health and Human Development Project, a longitudinal study that examines the development of alcohol- and drug-using behaviors. Each year for three years (1979–1981) subjects within three selected age groups (12-, 15-, and 18-year-old individuals), living in the state of New Jersey, were selected by a random telephone survey. After the initial telephone survey, field staff interviewed interested subjects and their parent(s) in their homes. Following this contact, subjects came to the test site for testing. Self-selection does not appear to seriously threaten the sample's representativeness in terms of the variables of interest. Comparisons of demographic characteristics and drinking behaviors of eligible households who agree to participate to those of households who refuse indicate high comparability. (See Lester, Pandina, White & Labouvie, 1984 and Pandina, Labouvie, & White, 1984, for greater detail on subject selection, research design and measures.)

The sample consists of 1,381 New Jersey adolescents grouped into three age groups: 458 18 year olds (Males=230, Females=228); 475 15 year olds (M=238, F=237); and 448 12 year olds (M=231, F=217). The sample is predominately white (89%), a somewhat higher proportion than the 83 percent of whites in New Jersey. About half of the subjects are Catholic (50%); the others are as follows: Protestant (29%), Jewish (10%) and another or no religion (11%), analogous to the religious breakdown of New Jersey. The median family income of the sample, between $20,000 and $29,000, is also comparable to that of the entire state ($24,510) (U.S. Bureau of Census, 1981).

Data Collection and Instruments

Self-report questionnaires provide the data utilized in this study. Other authors have addressed the issue of bias in self-reported alcohol and drug use. In general, however, self-reports have been accepted as reliable indicators of use behaviors (Single, Kandel, & Johnson, 1975).

The data on the prevalence of alcohol and drug use in our sample are comparable to national surveys at the time using other methods of data collection (Johnston, Bachman, & O'Malley, 1982). The prevalence of substance use exhibits developmental trends by age. Alcohol is the most extensively tried substance, ranging from about one third of the 12 year olds to 80 percent of the 15 year olds to greater than 90 percent of the 18 year olds. Almost no 12 year olds have tried marijuana, while about one half of the 15 year olds and between 70 percent and 80 percent of the 18 year olds report some use of marijuana. Virtually no 12 year olds and less than 10 percent of the 15 year olds have tried any other drugs. However, among 18 year olds, especially males, somewhere between 10 percent and 25 percent have tried all other drugs except heroin and PCP.

Dependent Variables

The dependent variables are several measures of substance use. First, we examine the use/nonuse dichotomy of all substances together in a scale called Stage. Stage is a variable consisting of: (1) no use of alcohol or drugs, (2) use of alcohol only, (3) use of alcohol and marijuana, and (4) use of alcohol, marijuana and at least one other drug.[1] This variable reflects the level of alcohol and drug involvement of the subject.

Intensity of use is measured by multiplying the value for frequency of use by the value for quantity of use. For alcohol, this quantity-frequency (AQF) measure combines quantity and frequency of beer, wine, and distilled spirits. For marijuana (MQF), it is simply quantity times frequency. For other drugs we use the Substance Use Index (SUI) as an alternative procedure to measure intensity of use. The SUI represents a composite score reflecting overall substance use involvement relative to the other subjects in the sample. The SUI combines weighted values for extent (number of times), frequency, recency (last time), and quantity of use of alcohol, marijuana, PCP, inhalants, psychedelics, cocaine, heroin, and non-medical use of analgesics, stimulants, sedatives, and tranquilizers. (See Pandina, White, & Yorke, 1981.) In addition to the SUI, a Drug Use Index (DUI) is constructed, which represents the composite use of all substances in the SUI except alcohol and marijuana. The quantity-frequency indices (AQF and MQF) and the DUI are constructed only for users of a particular substance. Hence, they measure intensity of use among those who use. The SUI measures the intensity of substance use involvement for the total sample regardless of user/nonuser status.

Independent Variables

Differential association theory is operationalized by using variables concerning both significant others' substance use and their attitudes about use. Peer involvement in substance use is measured by the respondent's reports of the proportion (none to all) of friends who use. Scales of parental alcohol use for this analysis are based on respondents' perception of frequency of parental alcohol use. Respondents' perceptions of parental and peer attitudes toward alcohol, marijuana, and other drug use are included in a tolerance of substance use scale (whether parents and peers would approve, not care, or disapprove of subjects' drinking alcohol, smoking marijuana, or using other drugs). Parents' attitudes are also measured by whether they permit their child to drink alcohol in the home, outside the home, both, or neither.

We use several commonly used indicators of variables central to social control theory. Parental attachments are indicated by a Love-Nurturance Scale containing 17 items (e.g., parents comfort you when you are afraid) and a four-item Control Scale (e.g., parents tell you how to spend your free time) (Streit, 1978). Measures of commitment to conventional behavior include a three-item indicator of religiosity (e.g., church attendance), two items tapping commitment to educational achievement (e.g., how often do you try to get the best grade) (Moos & Tricket, 1974) and grade point average (GPA).

Several indicators are used to measure strain theory. The first is a common indicator of psychological distress, the Global Severity Index (GSI) of the SCL-90-R, a 90-item, self-report symptom inventory (Derogatis, 1977). The second indicator is a 16-item scale about stressful life events (e.g., death of a parent) (Dohrenwend & Dohrenwend, 1981). Finally, we use a 26-item scale about other bothersome life conditions (e.g., I feel that I am not in control of my life), compiled from a list of typical adolescent worries found in the literature (Conger, 1973) and from adaptations of selected items from Rotter's Locus of Control Scale (1966). Initially, Merton's (1938) version of strain theory was measured by questions tapping the discrepancy between aspirations and expectations of educational and occupational achievement, which is a generally used operationalization (Hirschi, 1969; Short & Strodtbeck, 1965). However, this variable proved to be unusable since virtually all sample members reported no discrepancy. Therefore, as operationalized in this study, strain theory refers only to the broader psychological notion of strain found in the stress literature (Agnew, 1992; Dohrenwend & Dohrenwend, 1981).

Results

Table 1 presents a summary of the associations (zero-order correlations) between the independent and dependent variables. The differential association variables show by far the highest correlations with substance use. Friends' use of alcohol, marijuana, and drugs is consistently strongly related to subjects' use. In addition, friends' tolerance of use is strongly related to the various dependent variables. In contrast to the friend variables, the only variable tapping parental attitudes and behavior strongly related to substance use is respondents' perception of parental permission to drink. Parents' tolerance of drinking and parental alcohol use are weakly correlated with subject use.

The five variables that measure control theory also often have statistically significant relationships to the dependent variables, although their relationships to substance use are not as strong as the differential association variables. Similarly, two measures of strain theory, the number of stressful life events and the degree to which respondents are bothered by life conditions, have significant relationships with the dependent variables, although the size of the correlations is small.

We next performed a series of multiple regressions on each dependent variable. Multiple regression is a

Table 1
Zero Order Correlations Between Independent and Dependent Variables

	Dependent Variables				
	STAGE	SUI	AQF	MQF	DUI
Independent Variables	N=1345	N=1381	N=1006	N=494	N=224
Differential Association Variables					
Parental Permission to Drink	.46‡	.51‡	.30‡	.10*	.21†
Friend Alcohol Use	.63‡	.59‡	.42‡	.09*	.15*
Friend Marijuana Use	.80‡	.71‡	.57‡	.31‡	.32‡
Friend Drug Use	.58‡	.64‡	.48‡	.37‡	.58‡
Parental Alcohol Use	.22‡	.26‡	.18‡	–.01	.11
Friend Tolerance	–.63‡	–.63‡	–.54‡	–.41‡	–.32‡
Parental Tolerance	–.23‡	–.24‡	–.18‡	–.09	–.09
Control Variables					
School Commitment	–.35‡	–.32‡	–.29‡	–.15†	–.13
Religiosity	–.25‡	–.23‡	–.16‡	–.16‡	–.09
Grade Average	.21‡	.21‡	.19‡	.26‡	–.19†
Parental Control	–.11‡	–.10†	–.01	–.03	.02
Parental Nurturance	–.19‡	–.18‡	–.16†	–.07	–.12
Strain Variables					
Life Events	.22‡	.25‡	.16‡	.12†	.22‡
Botherscore	.17‡	.14‡	.07*	.06	.08
GSI	.06*	.06*	.06	.03	.12

*p ≤ .05
†p ≤ .01
‡p ≤ .001

method by which we attempt to predict the occurrence or magnitude of a single dependent variable (e.g., SUI) from a number of independent variables (e.g., friends' use, parents' use, etc.). We then can look at how much variation in each dependent variable is explained by different sets of predictor variables. Table 2 presents a summary of the total and unique variance (R^2) explained when we partition the variance (i.e., divide up the amount of variation accounted for) among the separate theoretical clusters (Mood, 1971).[2] The total variance for each theoretical cluster is the amount of variation in the dependent variable that is explained by that set of theoretical predictor variables. The unique variance is the amount of variation in the dependent variable that is explained by a set of theoretical predictor variables after controlling for the other two sets of variables.

The three theories together (D+C+S) account for a sizable proportion of the variance in Stage (R^2= .70, i.e., the three theories together explain 70% of the variance), SUI (67%), DUI (45%), and alcohol use (41%), and a smaller proportion in marijuana use (23%). Differential association variables, as compared to strain and control variables, account for the greatest amount of total variance in all the dependent variables: over two-thirds in Stage and SUI, over one-third in alcohol use and DUI, and one-fifth in marijuana use. More importantly, they account for a much greater amount of the unique variance (ranging from 13% to 46% of the variance) than the variables in the other two theoretical models.

The control variables account for between eight percent and 19 percent of the total variance in the dependent variables. Yet, when the unique variance is partitioned, they account for virtually none of the variance in Stage and SUI and two to three percent in alcohol use, marijuana use, and DUI. Thus, in the presence of the differential association variables, the control variables lose their unique predictive ability. A similar effect is observed for the strain variables. They account for a small proportion of the total variance in the dependent variables ranging from two percent for marijuana use to seven percent for SUI. However, the unique variance explained by these variables is virtually nil for Stage, SUI and marijuana use, one percent for alcohol use and six percent for DUI. The strain and control variables uniquely remove more of the variance in DUI than they do in any other dependent variable. None of the theoretical models uniquely explains much variance in marijuana use.

The standardized regression coefficients (beta weights) are also presented in Table 2. These coefficients were derived by regressing each theoretical model separately on each of the dependent variables. Regression coefficients represent the amount of change in a dependent variable (e.g., SUI) that can be associated with a given change in an independent (predictor) variable (e.g., friends' use) when all the other independent variables are held constant.

In order to compare the power of predictors within each theory, we examine the standardized regression coefficients. For each dependent variable, the friend variables are far more powerful predictors than any of the other differential association variables: friend marijuana use for Stage and SUI; friend alcohol use for intensity of alcohol use; friend drug use for SUI and DUI; and friend tolerance of use for intensity of all substance use, alcohol use, and marijuana use. Parental permission to drink is the most powerful parental predictor, although its beta weight is never very large. The parental use and tolerance variables are negligible.

Within the control model analyses, commitment to school, religiosity, and GPA are the strongest predictor variables. Commitment to school is especially important in terms of both initiation and intensity of total substance use, as well as intensity of alcohol use, yet it is negligible in the intensity of marijuana and other drug use analyses. On the other hand, GPA, an alternate measure of school commitment, is a more important predictor for these latter two dependent variables. The parental control and nurturance variables are more important for predicting Stage of use than for the other dependent variables; however, parental nurturance is also relatively important for predicting intensity of drug use. With one nonsignificant exception, all coefficients are in the predicted direction. By far the strongest predictor among the strain variables is life stress.

When all variables from the three theories are entered into the regression analyses together, the friend use variables are far more powerful predictors than any other variables (not shown here but available from the authors). In fact, they were the only predictor variables with even moderately sized beta weights (e.g., above .20). In the presence of all the variables, friends' marijuana use is the strongest predictor of Stage; friends' marijuana use, friends' drug use, and friends' tolerance of use are the strongest predictors of SUI; friends' alcohol use and tolerance of substance use are the strongest predictors of alcohol use; friends' tolerance of use is the strongest predictor of marijuana use; and friends' other drug use is the strongest predictor of DUI.

These regression analyses conducted on the total sample suggest that differential association variables are far more powerful than control and strain variables in predicting both whether adolescents will try various substances and how much and how often they will use these substances. Specifically, the proportion of friends who use and friends' tolerance of use are the most important predictor variables.

We next included age and gender in the models to test their independent predictive powers. (These data are not presented here but are available from the authors upon request.) These analyses suggested that age alone is a significant predictor of initiation and intensity of substance use (besides marijuana use), except in the presence of certain differential association variables. On the other hand, gender did not appear to be a significant predictor at all. Since the differential

Table 2
Standardized Coefficients and R²s[a] for Regressions of Differential Association (D), Control (C), and Strain (S) Variables on Measures of Substance Use

Differential Association Variables	STAGE N=1345	SUI N=1381	AQF N=1006	MQF N=494	DUI N=224
Parental Permission to Drink	.10‡	.18‡	.14‡	c	.17†
Friend Alcohol Use	.12‡	.10‡	.26‡	b	b
Friend Marijuana Use	.49‡	.25‡	b	.19‡	b
Friend Drug Use	.15‡	.31‡	b	b	.51‡
Parental Alcohol Use	.02	.07‡	.09†	–.07	.05
Friend Tolerance	–.16‡	–.22‡	–.43‡	–.35‡	–.21‡
Parental Tolerance	c	.01	.03	.02	.04
Total Variance	.69 (.69)	.67 (.67)	.37 (.37)	.20 (.19)	.39 (.37)
Unique Variance	.46	.45	.27	.13	.26
Control Variables					
School Commitment	–.27‡	–.24‡	–.21‡	–.04	–.01
Religiosity	–.18‡	–.17‡	–.12‡	–.13†	–.11
Grade Average	.10*	.11‡	.09*	.19†	.20*
Parental Control	–.10*	–.09‡	–.02	–.06	.01
Parental Nurturance	–.10†	–.09†	–.08*	–.07	–.11
Total Variance	.19 (.19)	.16 (.16)	.11 (.11)	.08 (.07)	.08 (.05)
Unique Variance	c	0	.02	.02	.03
Strain Variables					
Life Events	.20‡	.24‡	.16‡	.11†	.21‡
Botherscore	.11†	.08†	.01	.03	c
GSI	c	c	.03	c	.10
Total Variance	.06	.07	.03	.02	.06
Unique Variance	0	c	.01	0	.06
D+C+S Variance	.70 (.69)	.67 (.67)	.41 (.40)	.23 (.20)	.45 (.38)

*p < .05
†p < .01
‡p < .001
[a]In order to partition the variance the standardized R^2s are used, the adjusted R^2s are found in the parentheses.
[b]This variable not entered into the regression equation.
[c]Beta weight less than .01.

association variables are more interrelated with age (e.g., friends' use is dependent upon age of friends), the addition of age does not have as much of an impact on this model as on the other two theoretical models. Based upon these results, the model is tested below separately for each age group, but not by gender of the respondent.

Table 3 presents the total adjusted R^2s for each theoretical model and the combined model for the three age groups. In general, there are few clear patterns for the various age and use categories. For Stage of use the model accounts for about half of the variance for the 18 and the 15 year olds and less than one-third for the 12 year olds. The smaller percentage for the 12 year olds could be due to the lack of variation in the dependent variable, which for 12 year olds is virtually a dichotomy of abstainer vs. alcohol only user. Friends' tolerance of use and friends' substance use have the highest beta weights for each age group as well as in the total sample. (These beta weights are not presented here, but are available from the authors.) School commitment is also significant for Stage of use among 15 year olds, although not for the other age groups.

There is little difference in the ability of the total model to predict SUI among the age groups; it explains about one half of the variance for each age group. Again, friends' tolerance and friends' substance use are among those variables having significant beta weights. In addition, parental permission to drink is significant for the 12 and 15 year olds, and parental use is significant for the 12 year olds.

Among all alcohol users, the model predicts quantity and frequency of use better for 18 and 15 year olds than for the 12 year olds. Again, friend variables (use of alcohol and tolerance) have significant beta weights. In addition, parental use has a significant beta weight for 18 year olds. For marijuana users, the model accounts for about one-fifth of the variance in use for the 18 year olds and one-fourth for the 15 year olds. Friends' tolerance exhibits the highest beta weight in this analysis. Among the 18-year-old drug users, the model accounts for almost one-third of the variance in intensity of use. Friends' drug use and friends' tolerance have significant beta weights for drug use among 18 year olds.

Thus, when all three theories are analyzed together, the friend variables (use and tolerance) consistently obtain the highest beta weights. Some parental variables (use and permission to drink) and school variables (commitment and grade average) are also significant in a few analyses. When the three theoretical models are examined separately for each age group, we find that, regardless of the type of drug, level of use, or age group, the differential association variables have the strongest impact in this sample of adolescents.

Discussion and Conclusion

The results strongly support the major tenets of differential association theory. By far the best predictors of adolescents' substance use are the proportion of their friends who use and their friends' tolerance of use. These findings suggest that adolescent alcohol and drug use conforms to the behavioral and value structure of the peer influence groups. Peers are the reference group that provides the rewards and punishments for substance use, since parental behaviors and attitudes add little explanatory power to the peer variables. Hence, the associative and learning processes involved in the initiation and maintenance of substance use have little to do with the family context, but are mostly limited to the adolescent culture. The fact that adolescent alcohol and drug use is a social activity, engaged in by the peer group, may further suggest why friend variables have such a strong influence on adolescent use.

Control and strain theories add little explained variance beyond the contribution of the differential association variables. Adolescents with weak ties to school and religion are only slightly more likely than those with stronger ties to engage in various forms of substance use. In addition, drug and alcohol use are clearly not related to strain among this representative sample of adolescents, with the sole exception that, when only strain variables are considered, adolescents who are somewhat more involved with substance use experience a greater number of stressful life events. Scales of psychological distress and bothersome life conditions have no significant relation to substance use.

Another interesting finding is the lack of major gender differences in substance use. This finding is in contrast to gender role explanations of deviance. Harris (1977), for example, claims that gender is the most

Table 3

R^2s[a] for Regressions of Differential Association (D), Control (C), and Strain (S) Variables on Measures of Substance Use for Each Age Group

AGE GROUP	STAGE	SUI	AQF	MGF	DUI
18	N=451	N=458	N=444	N=295	N=162
D	.45	.55	.29	.15	.40
C	.16	.12	.04	.13	.02
S	.03	.04	b	b	.02
D+C+S	.47	.54	.36	.16	.35
15	N=450	N=475	N=388	N=190	N=59
D	.53	.52	.25	.26	c
C	.13	.11	.10	.01	c
S	.04	.06	.04	.04	c
D+C+S	.55	.54	.30	.26	c
12	N=444	N=448	N=174	N=9	N=3
D	.27	.42	.12	c	c
C	.03	b	b	c	c
S	.01	b	b	c	c
D+C+S	.29	.43	.10	c	c

[a]Adjusted R^2s

[b]R^2 less than .01

[c]There were very few marijuana and/or drug users in this age group; thus, analyses were not performed for this dependent variable.

powerful predictor of deviant behavior in general, and several theories have been developed to explain gender differences in rates of deviance (Adler, 1976; Cernkovich & Giordano, 1979; Hagan, Gillis, & Simpson, 1985; Simon, 1975; White & LaGrange, 1987). If the finding here is representative of substance use, such explanations of substance use are superfluous since the same variables predict substance use for both males and females. This may reflect a convergence of peer cultures for males and females that has occurred over the past decade, which renders some gender role explanations of deviance obsolete.

While there is a lack of gender differences in predicting substance use, age differences are apparent. There is a progression from alcohol use among the 12 year olds to marijuana use among 15 year olds to a wider range of drug and alcohol use among 18 year olds. However, as with the findings regarding gender, the same variables predict substance use across all age groups. While we had expected that the effect of a peer using culture might be more important in the older age groups, and that a lack of control might be more important in the youngest age group, the dynamics of use are not greatly different among the age groups. For all three age groups, the differential association variables are most powerful, while most control and strain variables have little or no effect.

In general, our findings are not surprising from the perspective of the drug use literature. The central concepts derived from differential association theory are clearly the most powerful predictors of drug use. We cannot, however, claim that these processes are causal factors leading to use, since we do not know whether association with substance-using peers preceded or followed a motivational disposition to use drugs. Because of the general prevalence of substance use in the sample and the fact that users differed from nonusers only in the extent and tolerance of substance use among their friends, it seems unlikely that users have any special motivation that distinguishes them from nonusers. However, it is possible that cross-sectional data suppresses possible strain effects. If highly strained youth use alcohol and drugs heavily and these substances are effective in reducing strain, cross-sectional data would mask this effect. We do not believe the cross-sectional data would mask any effects of control theory because drug use among weakly controlled adolescents should serve to weaken controls further (Agnew, 1985).

Another potential limitation of our cross-sectional data concerns the inability to specify the changes in measures as youth move through adolescence. We can only determine the strength of various mechanisms as they impact upon youth of different ages at the same point in time. We should be able to deal more adequately with these questions of causality with the longitudinal data from this study. For the present, it appears that the emphasis on refining the specific learning mechanisms involved in the initiation to and use of substances is a promising direction for research (Akers et al., 1979; Strickland, 1982; Stafford & Eckland-Olson, 1982).

Future theoretical work on the etiology of deviance should explain why certain theories, such as control theory, are powerful predictors of delinquency while others, such as differential association, can better explain drug and alcohol use. It will be particularly interesting to learn what types of behaviors are transmitted through contact with adults (e.g., some forms of sexual deviance), emerge because of a failure of adults to properly control behavior (e.g., juvenile delinquency) or develop through the presence of life strain (e.g., psychological distress), and what other types of behaviors, such as those considered here, are shaped within the confines of the adolescent peer group. Some of the deviance theories may be inapplicable to most adolescent substance use, since this behavior is often viewed as conventional rather than deviant, from the perspective of the adolescent culture. Hence, it is learned in the same way as other behaviors, through the mechanisms stressed by social learning theory (White, Bates, & Johnson, 1991). Before more adequate general theoretical models of deviant etiology can be developed, researchers must be sensitive to the differences, as well as to the similarities, among behaviors conventionally viewed as deviant.

Notes

1. Stage is a Guttman Scale (coefficient of reproducibility = .98). Other authors (e.g., Kandel, 1975) have also applied this developmental stage approach to substance use. Drug use forms a Guttman Scale from no use to multiple drug use. Although there are a few subjects who use marijuana but have never tried alcohol, their frequency is so small that we believe that a stage model can validly be applied to these analyses.
2. In order to partition the variance, first each theoretical cluster is regressed separately on the dependent variables. Then each pair of clusters is entered together and regressed separately on each dependent variable. Finally, all three clusters are combined and regressed on the dependent variables. The unique variance of a cluster (e.g. differential association) is computed by subtracting the total variance for the other two clusters combined (e.g., control and strain) from the total variance explained when all three clusters are entered into the regression together. Using an alternative method to determine the amount of variance explained by each cluster (Cohen & Cohen, 1983), we obtained results similar to those reported below.

References

Adler, F. (1976). *Sisters in crime: The rise of the new female criminal.* New York: McGraw-Hill.

Agnew, R. (1985). Social control theory and delinquency: A longitudinal test. *Criminology, 23,* 47–61.

Agnew, R. (1992). Foundation for a general strain theory of crime and delinquency. *Criminology, 30,* 47–87.

Agnew, R., & White, H. R. (1992). An empirical test of general strain theory. *Criminology, 30,* 475–499.

Akers, R. L. (1985). *Deviant behavior: A social learning approach.* Belmont, CA: Wadsworth.

Akers, R. L., Krohn, M. D., Lanza-Kaduce, L., & Radosevich, M. (1979). Social learning and deviant behavior: A specific test of a general theory. *American Sociological Review, 44,* 636–655.

Bandura, A. (1977). *Social learning theory.* Englewood Cliffs: Prentice Hall.

Cernkovich, S. A., & Giordano, P. C. (1979). A comparative analysis of male and female delinquency. *Sociological Quarterly, 20,* 131–45.

Cohen, J., & Cohen, P. (1983). *Applied multiple regression correlation analysis for the behavioral sciences* (2nd ed.). Hillsdale, NJ: Erlbaum.

Conger, J. J. (1973). *Adolescence and youth: Psychological development in a changing world.* New York: Harper & Row.

Derogatis, L. R. (1977). *SCL-90R Manual 1 (rev. ed.).* Baltimore: Johns Hopkins University School of Medicine.

Dohrenwend, B. S., & Dohrenwend, B. P. (1981). *Stress life events and their contexts.* Reseda, CA: Watson.

Dull, R. T. (1984). An empirical examination of the social bond theory of drug use. *International Journal of the Addictions, 19,* 265–286.

Elliott, D. S., Huizinga, D. H., & Ageton, S. S. (1985). *Explaining delinquency and drug use.* Beverly Hills, CA: Sage.

Hagan, J., Gillis, A. R., & Simpson, J. H. (1985). The class structure of gender and delinquency: Toward a power-control theory of common delinquent behavior. *American Journal of Sociology, 90,* 151–78.

Harris, A. R. (1977). Sex and theories of deviance: Toward a functional theory of deviant type-scripts. *American Sociological Review, 42,* 1–16.

Hirschi, T. (1969). *Causes of delinquency.* Berkeley: University of California Press.

Jessor, R., & Jessor, S. (1977). *Problem behavior and psychosocial development—A longitudinal study of youth.* New York: Academic Press.

Johnston, L. D., Bachman, J. G., & O'Malley, P. M. (1982). *Highlights from student drug use in America 1975–1981.* Rockville, MD: National Institute on Drug Abuse.

Kandel, D. (1975). Stages in adolescent involvement in drug use. *Science, 190,* 912–914.

Kandel, D. (1978). *Longitudinal research on drug use: Empirical findings and methodological issues.* New York: Hemisphere-Halsted.

Kaplan, H. B. (1980). *Deviant behavior in defense of self.* New York: Academic Press.

Kaplan, H. B., Martin, S. S., & Robbins, C. (1984). Pathways to adolescent drug use: Self-derogation, peer influence, weakening of social controls, and early substance use. *Journal of Health and Social Behavior, 25,* 270–289.

Kornhauser, R. R. (1978). *Social sources of delinquency: An appraisal of analytic models.* Chicago, IL: University of Chicago Press.

LaGrange, R. L., & White, H. R. (1985). Age differences in delinquency: A test of theory. *Criminology, 23,* 19–47.

Lester, D., Pandina, R. J., White, H. R., & Labouvie, E. W. (1984). The Rutgers health and human development project: A longitudinal study of alcohol and drug use. In S. A. Mednick, M. Harway, & K. M. Finello (Eds.), *Longitudinal studies in the United States.* New York: Praeger Press.

Marcos, A. C., Bahr, S. J., & Johnson, R. E. (1986). Test of a bonding/association theory of adolescent drug use. *Social Forces, 65,* 135–161.

Massey, J. L., & Krohn, M. D. (1986). A longitudinal examination of an integrated social process model of deviant behavior. *Social Forces, 65,* 106–134.

Matsueda, R. L. (1982). Testing control theory and differential association theory: A causal modeling approach. *American Sociological Review, 47*(4), 489–504.

Merton, R. K. (1938). Social structure and anomie. *American Sociological Review, 3,* 672–82.

Mood, A. M. (1971). Partitioning the variance in multiple regression analyses as a tool for developing learning models. *American Educational Research Journal, 8*(2), 191–200.

Moos, R. H., & Tricket, E. J. (1974). *Classroom environment scale.* Palo Alto, CA: Consulting Psychologists Press, Inc.

Pandina, R. J., Labouvie, E. W., & White, H. R. (1984). Potential contributions of the life span developmental approach to the study of adolescent alcohol and drug use: The Rutgers health and human development project, a working model. *Journal of Drug Issues, 14,* 253–268.

Pandina, R. J., White, H. R., & Yorke, J. (1981). Estimation of substance use involvement: Theoretical considerations and empirical findings. *International Journal of Addictions, 16,* 1–24.

Pearlin, L. (1981). The stress process. *Journal of Health and Social Behavior, 22,* 337–356.

Rotter, J. B. (1966). Generalized expectancies for internal versus external control of reinforcement. *Psychological Monographs, 609,* 80, 1–28.

Short, J. F. Jr., & Strodtbeck, F. L. (1965). *Group process and gang delinquency.* Chicago, IL: University of Chicago Press.

Simon, R. J. (1975). *The contemporary woman and crime.* Washington, DC: Center for Studies of Crime & Delinquency, National Institute of Mental Health.

Single, E., Kandel, D., & Johnson, B. (1975). The reliability and validity of drug use responses in a large scale longitudinal survey. *Journal of Drug Issues, 5,* 426–433.

Skinner, B. F. (1953). *Science and human behavior.* New York: Macmillan.

Stafford, M. C., & Eckland-Olson, S. (1982). On social learning and deviant behavior: A reappraisal of the findings. *American Sociological Review, 47*(1), 167–169.

Streit, F. (1978). *Technical manual: Youth perception inventory.* Highland Park, NJ: Essence Publication.

Strickland, D. E. (1982). Social learning and deviant behavior: A special test of a general theory: A comment and critique. *American Sociological Review, 47*(1), 162–167.

Sutherland, E. H. (1942). *Principles of criminology.* Chicago, IL: Lippincott.

U. S. Bureau of the Census. (1981). Current population survey: Money income and poverty status of families and persons in the United States: 1980. *Current Population Reports,* Series P-60, No. 127.

Voss, H. L. (1964). Differential association and report delinquent behavior: A replication. *Social Problems, 12,* 78–85.

White, H. R., Bates, M. E., & Johnson, V. (1991). Learning to drink: Familial, peer, and media influences. In D J. Pittman, & H. R. White (Eds.), *Society, culture, and drinking patterns reexamined.* New Brunswick, NJ: Rutgers Center of Alcohol Studies.

White, H. R., & LaGrange, R. L. (1987). An assessment of gender effects in self report delinquency. *Sociological Focus, 20*(3), 195–213.

Wiatrowski, M. D., Griswold, D. B., & Roberts, M. K. (1981). Social control theory and delinquency. *American Sociological Review 46,* 525–541.

Discussion Questions

1. How can differential association theory be applied to explain adolescent drug use?
2. How can social control theory be applied to explain adolescent drug use?
3. How can strain theory be applied to explain adolescent drug use?
4. According to the findings from this study, which variables were the best predictors of adolescent drug use? How do you explain this finding?

Changes in Sensation-seeking Needs and Drug Use

Marsha E. Bates   Helene Raskin White   Erich Labouvie

Marsha E. Bates is an Assistant Research Professor in Psychology at the Rutgers Center of Alcohol Studies. She received her Ph. D. from Rutgers University in cognitive psychology and then, as a postdoctoral research fellow, completed three years of advanced studies in alcohol and other drug effects. Dr. Bates's current research centers around the assessment of alcohol and drug use behaviors in relation to personality, psychopathology, and neurocognitive functioning. With her colleagues at the Center of Alcohol Studies, she is currently conducting a longitudinal study of the development of substance use behavior of New Jersey adolescents and young adults, investigating short- and long-term intoxification effects on social drinkers' cognitive abilities, and studying the relationship between neuropsychological deficit and treatment outcome in chronic alcoholics.

Helene Raskin White is an Associate Professor of Sociology at the Center of Alcohol Studies and Sociology Department, Rutgers University. She received her B. A. from Douglass College and her M. Phil. and Ph. D. degrees from Rutgers University. Since joining the Center of Alcohol Studies, Dr. White has been involved primarily in longitudinal research on the antecedents, correlates, and consequences of alcohol and other drug use in clinical and nonclinical populations. She is the co-editor (with Edith L. Gomberg and John A. Carpenter) of *Alcohol, Science and Society Revisited* and (with David J. Pittman) of *Society, Culture and Drinking Patterns Reexamined,* both readers in the field of alcohol studies, and the author of more than 50 articles, chapters, and reports on drug use and other forms of deviance.

Erich Labouvie is an Associate Professor of Psychology at the Rutgers Center of Alcohol Studies. He received his Ph. D. from West Virginia University in developmental psychology. Before coming to Rutgers University, he taught for six years at the University of Wisconsin-Madison. Dr. Labouvie's research centers around the role of alcohol and drug use in relation to coping and the self-regulation of internal events. In collaboration with several of his colleagues, he is currently conducting a prospective longitudinal study of the development of alcohol and drug use from adolescence into adulthood.

This chapter is a condensed version of a research report available, in its entirety, from the ERIC Document Reproduction Service No. ED 236456. This research was supported by the National Institute on Alcohol Abuse and Alcoholism, the National Institute on Drug Abuse, and the Alcoholic Beverage Medical Research Foundation.

An important question when studying the relationship between personality and substance use is whether certain personality traits lead to early experimentation with drugs, or place an individual at risk for heavy alcohol and other drug use. This question is of special relevance early in the life span because of the need to identify adolescents at high risk for drug abuse. Past research has shown that personality needs such as sensation seeking, impulsivity, and exhibitionism tend to be relatively high in youth who are more involved in substance use than their peers (Bates, 1993) and contribute to a lifestyle characterized by a low concern for societal expectations (Segal, Huba, & Singer, 1980).

Little remains known, however, about how *changes* in personality may relate to *changes* in drug use behaviors. A developmental perspective is essential to answer this question, because personality needs are less stable over time during adolescence than later in adulthood (Schuerger, Tait, & Tavernelli, 1982). There are also large differences between adolescents in how much their personalities change. Adolescence appears to be a time of major personality reorganization for some youth, while others show consistency and stability in personality needs and other areas of functioning (Bates & Pandina, 1989, 1991; Block, 1971; Offer & Sabshin, 1984). Further, personality instability, especially when certain high-risk personality characteristics are involved, has been related to alcohol and other drug use intensity, level of stress, and the use of drugs to cope with life problems in youth between the ages of 12 and 21 years (Bates & Pandina, 1989, 1991).

In this study we focus on initial level and changes over three years in sensation-seeking needs and substance use. Research on why people consume alcohol and other drugs has shown that they often do so to regulate internal emotional states, for example, to relieve stress or enhance pleasure (Bates, 1993). During youths' initial experimentation with substance use, emotionally uplifting reasons for use appear quite strong (Segal, et al., 1980). An important dimension of the tendency to seek out or enhance positive emotional experiences is tapped by Zuckerman's (1979) construct of sensation seeking. This trait is defined by the need for, and value placed on, varied new and complex sensations and experiences, and the willingness to take physical and social risks for the sake of such experiences. Disinhibition needs appear to be especially related to the tendency to use psychoactive drugs by encouraging nonconformity and pleasure seeking. Nonconformity is displayed through rebellion against norms that prescribe acceptable social behavior, and pleasure seeking is accomplished through extroverted behaviors such as drug taking, sexual activity, and partying (Zuckerman, 1979). Disinhibition has been consistently related to drinking intensity and other drug use in young adults (Bates, 1993).

In this study, we extend this line of research by exploring whether stability or change in disinhibition needs over three years in adolescence can predict changes in alcohol and other drug use during the same time period. Specifically, this study provides information about: (a) The extent to which disinhibition needs tend to remain at stable levels or change (increase or decrease) as adolescents age from 15 to 18 years and 18 to 21 years and (b) whether, and how, changes in disinhibition needs over three years are related to simultaneous changes in an adolescent's pattern of substance use.

The answers to these questions may provide information relevant to certain ideas regarding individualized treatment plans for young drug misusers. That is, a number of researchers (Ratliff & Burkhart, 1984; Segal, et al, 1980; Zuckerman, 1979, 1983) have proposed that information about underlying motivations for substance use may be used to help select an effective, individualized treatment regimen for those adolescents who misuse drugs. For example, youth whose reasons for drug use involve high sensation-seeking needs may be poor candidates for traditional counseling (Segal, et al., 1980). Instead, an effective treatment alternative may involve changing behavior through substitution. Substitution would involve providing more socially acceptable sensation-fulfilling activities or experiences as an alternative to drug use. Zuckerman (1979) also writes of a California drug treatment community where sensation-seeking needs giving rise to drug use were shifted through a program of parachute jumping. Participants claimed "that it provided the 'highest high' of them all, and they compared the period prior to the opening of the parachute to the 'rush' produced by heroin" (p. 293). Less extreme behavioral examples of displacement of disinhibition needs might include substituting downhill skiing, wind surfing, or mountain climbing as alternatives to drug use. The current findings will be discussed in terms of their implications for these suggestions.

Methods

Subjects

The population from which this sample was drawn consisted of New Jersey households having telephones. Randomly generated telephone numbers were weighted by population density and used to contact and identify eligible adolescents. Eligibility was based upon year of birth, and the absence of serious physical or mental handicap, or language difficulty. Participants were generally comparable to eligible non-participants on a number of demographic characteristics (Pandina, et al., 1984). During 1979 and 1980, 933 adolescents were initially tested at the ages of 12, 15 and 18 (Time 1, T1). Ninety-four percent (882) of these subjects were tested three years later at the ages of 15, 18 and 21, respectively (Time 2, T2). Because the items of the Sensation-seeking Scale are not easily understood by individuals below the age of about 14 (Zuckerman, 1979), the present study includes only those subjects (N = 584) who were 15 or 18 years old at the first test time.

Measures

Sensation-seeking Needs

Disinhibition subscale from Form V of the Sensation-seeking Scale (Zuckerman, 1979) was administered at T1 and T2. The subscale items are shown in Table 1. Subjects are asked to choose the statement, A or B, that most describes their likes or the way they feel. In cases where subjects find they like both or neither response, they are asked to choose the one closest to their feelings. Subjects' disinhibition scores from T1 were correlated with their scores at T2. This correlation is referred to as a "stability coefficient" and indicates the extent to which individuals' scores remained stable versus changed across the three years between tests. The three-year stability coefficient we obtained was moderate in magnitude, . 54, suggesting that some subjects maintained relatively similar levels of disinhibition needs at T1 and T2, while others' disinhibition needs changed (increased or decreased) quite a bit over three years.

Alcohol and Other Drug Use

The frequency of beer, wine, hard liquor, and marijuana use in the past year was obtained from self-report ratings on a l0-point scale ranging from no use in the past year to using more than once per day. The quantity of each substance consumed on a typical occasion of use was rated on a nine-point response scale ranging from no use to more than six drinks or 15 "joints" of marijuana per occasion. The frequency of getting "drunk" when drinking and of getting "high" when smoking marijuana was rated on a six-point scale ranging from never to always. Overall experience with illicit drugs is the number (range 0–10) of the following drugs ever used: marijuana, cocaine, heroin, psychedelics, inhalants, PCP, and the non-medical use of analgesics, stimulants, sedatives, and tranquilizers.

Sample Drug Use Characteristics

Like Jessor and Jessor (1977) and Segal et al. (1980), we find that experimentation with alcohol and other drugs is a normative behavior engaged in by the majority of adolescents in this sample. At T1, 15 percent of the female subjects and 14 percent of the male subjects reported that they abstained from alcohol and all drugs. These proportions dropped to four percent and three percent, respectively for females and males, by T2. Approximately 22 percent of the sample indicated at each testing occasion that they used alcohol but no other drug. The remainder of the subjects reported having used alcohol and at least one other illicit drug. Females' and males' initial (T1) levels of illicit drug use and the extent to which their use changed over time were similar. In this sample, the traditional view that alcohol use is more prevalent among males than females is supported only in terms of males' larger average quantity and frequency of beer use at T1 and larger increase in frequency of beer drinking by T2. Female subjects' alcohol use surpassed that of males in terms of a larger total increase from T1 to T2 in frequency of wine consumption. The drug use characteristics of our subjects are quite similar to those found in several large-scale surveys of adolescents in the

Table I
Disinhibition Items from Form V of the Sensation-seeking Scales (Zuckerman, 1979).

1. A. I like "wild" uninhibited parties.
   B. I prefer quiet parties with good conversation.
2. A. I dislike "swingers."
   B. I enjoy the company of real "swingers."
3. A. I find that stimulants make me uncomfortable.
   B. I often like to get high (drinking liquor or smoking marijuana).
4. A. I am not interested in experience for its own sake.
   B. I like to have new and exciting experiences and sensations even if they are a little frightening, unconventional, or illegal.
5. A. I like to date members of the opposite sex who are physically exciting.
   B. I like to date members of the opposite sex who share my values.
6. A. Heavy drinking usually ruins a party because some people get loud and boisterous.
   B. Keeping the drinks full is the key to a good party.
7. A. A person should have considerable sexual experience before marriage.
   B. It's better if two married persons begin their sexual experience with each other.
8. A. Even if I had the money I would not care to associate with flighty persons like those in the "jet set."
   B. I could conceive of myself seeking pleasure around the world with the "jet set."
9. A. There is altogether too much portrayal of sex in movies.
   B. I enjoy watching many of the "sexy" scenes in movies.
10. A. I feel best after taking a couple of drinks.
    B. Something is wrong with people who need liquor to feel good.

Adapted from M. Zuckerman, *Sensation-seeking.* Hillsdale, NJ: Erlbaum Associates, 1979.

same geographical region (Fishburne, Abelson, & Cisin, 1982; Johnston, Bachman, & O'Malley, 1982).

Analyses

It is a well-established fact that differences in behavioral change (e. g., increases or decreases in drug use from T1 to T2) over a given time period can, to some extent, be predicted from differences between individuals in their initial level of the behavior at T1. This phenomenon has been referred to as *regression to the mean.* Individuals who score well below average at T1 tend to increase and to score closer to the average at T2. In comparison, individuals who score well above average at T1 tend to decrease and score closer to the average at T2. While this regression to the mean effect holds for the sample as a whole, *individuals* will actually deviate from this predicted pattern to varying degrees. We compared predicted changes (based upon regression to the mean) and actual changes (the real difference between a subject's score at T1 and T2) in disinhibition in order to assign subjects to one of four disinhibition groups. In the first group, subjects scored low in disinhibition at T1 and remained low (increased less than expected) by T2 (Low–Low); in the second group, subjects also scored low in disinhibition at T1 but increased to a higher level (increased more than expected) by T2 (Low–High). In the third group, subjects scored high in disinhibition at T1 and remained high (decreased less than expected) by T2 (High–High); and in the fourth group, subjects scored high in disinhibition at T1 but subsequently decreased to a lower level (decreased more than expected) by T2 (High–Low).

We examined the effects of age and disinhibition groups on alcohol and other drug use at T1 as well as changes in use by T2. Of particular interest were changes in use not predictable from T1 use levels, termed *residual changes*. A measure of residual change is obtained by subtracting the predicted change score from the actual change score. We hypothesized that individual differences in sensation seeking would help explain changes in substance use at T2 that could not be predicted on the basis of differences in use at T1. All analyses were performed separately for females and males based on past reports that the relation of drug use to sensation-seeking needs may be different for the two sexes (Ratliff & Burkhart, 1984; Zuckerman, 1979).

Results

As expected (Farley & Cox, 1971), average levels of disinhibition needs in our sample did not tend to increase or decrease significantly as subjects got older. Also, as expected, rather large increases in the use of alcohol and drugs from 15 to 18 years of age were followed by somewhat smaller increases, or even some declines in use, from 18 to 21 years of age.

Disinhibition Group Differences in Alcohol and Other Drug Use

For females, disinhibition group membership significantly affected quantity and frequency of substance use at T1 and also affected changes in use over time. For males, disinhibition group primarily affected T1 levels and later increases in the frequency and quantity of marijuana smoking, frequency of hard liquor use, and the quantity of beer consumed per occasion. The total number of illicit drugs ever tried by both sexes also varied significantly by disinhibition group membership.

Figure 1 illustrates the differences between the four disinhibition groups at T1 in terms of the typical quantity of beer consumed per occasion, the frequency of marijuana use, and the number of illicit drugs ever tried. Figure 2 shows residual change (change not predicted from level of use at T1) patterns for the same substances. Subjects in group Low–Low, who were initially low and remained low in disinhibition needs, reported the lowest frequency and quantity of alcohol and drug use at T1. Increases in substance use from T1 to T2 in this group also tended to be smaller than expected on the basis of their T1 levels of use (see data points below the horizontal line showing zero change in Figure 2). In comparison, those in Group High–High, who maintained high–stable disinhibition needs over time, typically exhibited high use levels at T1 and larger than expected increases by T2 (data points above the zero change line in Figure 2). This shows that initially high levels of use were maintained over time and sometimes increased in continuously high-level sensation seekers.

In group Low–High, where an initially low level of disinhibition needs was followed by a strong increase in these needs, moderate levels of use at T1 often gave way to substantial increases in use at T2. Finally, in group High–Low, where an initially high level of disinhibition needs was followed by a strong decrease in needs, relatively high levels of use at T1 were followed by moderate changes or a leveling off in intensity of use.

We also examined the frequency of getting drunk or high, when subjects used alcohol or marijuana. These analyses include those subjects who were users of alcohol (N = 501) or marijuana (N = 272) at both T1 and T2 (not shown). In general, both of the groups that were high in sensation-seeking needs at T1 (High–High and High–Low) reported drinking and smoking until intoxication equally often, and significantly more often than group Low–Low at T1. Only subjects whose disinhibition needs remained low or decreased from T1 to T2 (groups Low–Low and High–Low) showed little or no increase in the likelihood of becoming intoxicated when drinking or smoking marijuana over the three years. Disinhibition needs thus also seem to be related to the level of intoxication desired by the adolescent, that is, the intensity of the drug experience that he or she desires to achieve when using psychoactive substances.

Discussion

The present results extend the previous finding that disinhibition needs are related to the intensity of substance use engaged in by adolescents and young adults. Our cross-sectional (T1) data generalize this relationship to a younger sample of adolescents than has previously been tested, and suggest that the desire or need for novel and stimulating experiences may be a significant motivation of drug use during adolescent development.

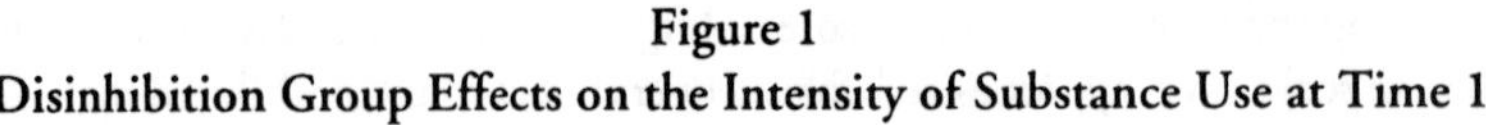

Figure 1
Disinhibition Group Effects on the Intensity of Substance Use at Time 1

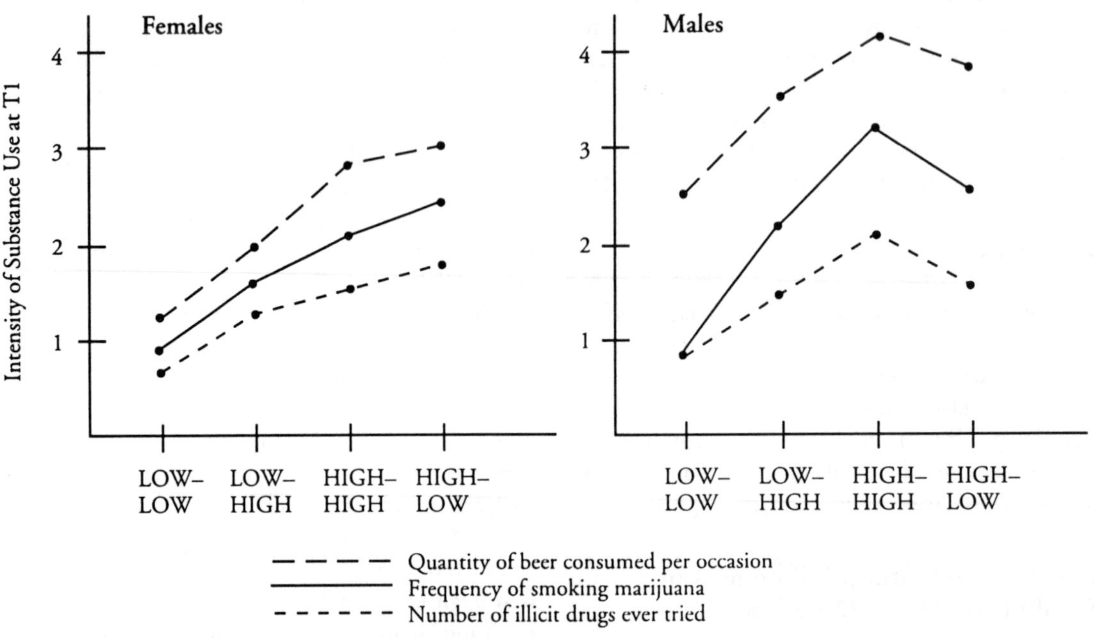

The results of the longitudinal change analyses further suggest that developmental stability versus change in disinhibition needs may be related to whether alcohol and other drug-taking behaviors will tend to increase or decrease over time. Recall that the 3-year stability coefficient (.54, see Methods) between disinhibition scores at T1 and T2 indicates that there was considerable variability in the extent to which different subjects' level of disinhibition needs changed over time. Some subjects showed stable disinhibition needs, while others showed substantial increases or decreases in disinhibition needs across three years. The present results show that this stability versus change distinction accounts for differences in the development of a number of alcohol and drug use behaviors. For those subjects who change in disinhibition needs during adolescence, knowledge of their level of needs at one age does not provide enough information to predict whether their overall level of alcohol and other drug use will remain the same, decrease, or increase in the future.

There were significant disinhibition group effects on both sexes' frequency of beer and marijuana use, and females' frequency of hard liquor use (not shown) at T1. Note that for these substances, the average frequency of use in group Low–Low at T1 was already distinguishably lower than in all other groups. These findings suggest that those subjects who would in the future maintain low disinhibition needs as a stable personality characteristic were, at T1, already engaging in less frequent alcohol and marijuana use than all other subjects, including those who were also low in disinhibition needs at T1, but who would increase more than expected in these needs in the future. Only those subjects who maintained low, stable levels of disinhibition needs at T1 *and* T2 showed very low substance use habits from age 15 to 21 years.

Conversely, subjects in groups High–High and High–Low reported similar quantity and frequency of use at T1. However, by T2 these two groups of subjects, on the average, exhibited quite different patterns of change in drug use. Over time, decreases in previously high levels of disinhibition needs were associated with more conservative use patterns by T2, compared to the increases in use shown by peers in the high–stable disinhibition groups. At the same time, high disinhibition needs may be particularly critical in establishing initial use levels. Subjects whose sensation-seeking needs naturally decreased from T1 to T2 (group High–Low) did not tend to increase their drug use over time but also did not show strong decreases in drug use over time. This result supports Segal et al. 's (1980) and Zuckerman's (1983) suggestion that therapy with high sensation-seeking drug abusers might be better aimed at providing behavioral substitutes (i. e., high thrill and adventure-seeking activities) for drug taking than at facilitating personality change, because personality change may not prompt decreased use.

In terms of actual drug use levels, average differences in drug use between groups were not always large, and the average use rates even in disinhibition group High–High were far from excessive. However, there were consistent and reliable trends in large versus small increases in use that accompany differences in disinhibition needs. These patterns suggest that the development of sensation seeking as an aspect of personality may help determine future levels of use. With respect to the questions raised at the start of this study, these data suggest that there are meaningful differences between youth in their tendency to maintain relatively stable versus changing disinhibition needs between the ages of 15 and 18, and 18 and 21. It is also clear that these individual differences in personality are related to the level of, and changes in, substance use. It is important to note, however, that although the present findings are based on longitudinal observations, we cannot assume that changes in personality necessarily *cause* changes in drug use. An alternative explanation involves the possibility that drug taking may cause changes in the level of sensation seeking that youth exhibit. An important question for future research would include determining what fac-

Figure 2
Disinhibition Group Effects on Residual Changes in the Intensity of Substance Use from Time 1 to Time 2

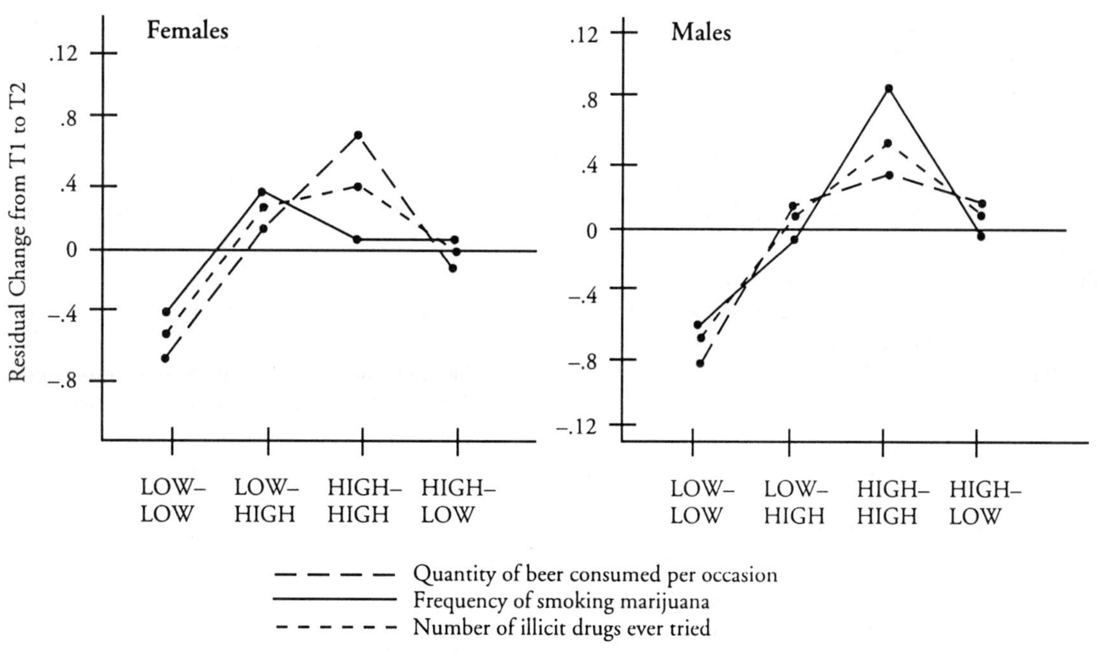

tors might influence the maintenance of stable low- or high-level need states, versus changing personality need states during development.

Conclusions

1. Some adolescents change in their levels of sensation-seeking needs over time, and others remain relatively stable.
2. These patterns of stability and change in sensation-seeking needs are related to initial levels and changes in substance use patterns.
3. Those adolescents who maintain low, stable levels of disinhibition needs across time report consistently low substance use across time.
4. Relative increases in sensation-seeking needs over time are often associated with increases in substance use, while relative decreases in sensation-seeking needs appear to forestall increases in drug use, but do not necessarily lead to decreases in use.
5. The extent to which substance use affects personality development during adolescence is unknown and warrants further study.

References

Bates, M. E. (1993). Recent developments in psychology and alcoholism: Personality and neurocognition. In M. Galanter (Ed.), *Recent developments in alcoholism (vol. 11).* New York: Plenum Press.

Bates, M. E., & Pandina, R. J. (1989). Individual differences in the stability of personality needs: Relations to stress and substance use during adolescence. *Personality and Individual Differences, 10,* 1151–1157.

Bates, M. E., & Pandina, R. J. (1991). Personality stability and adolescent substance use behaviors. *Alcoholism: Clinical & Experimental Research, 15,* 471–477.

Block, J. (1971). *Lives through time.* Berkeley, CA: Bancroft.

Farley, F. N., & Cox, S. O. (1971). Stimulus-seeking motivation in adolescents as a function of age and sex. *Adolescence, 6,* 207–218.

Fishburne, P. M., Abelson, N. I., & Cisin, I. (1982). *National survey on drug abuse: 1979 vol. 1.* Rockville, MD: National Institute on Drug Abuse.

Jessor, R., & Jessor, S. L. (1977). *Problem behavior and psychosocial development: A longitudinal study of youth.* New York: Academic Press.

Johnston, L. D., Bachman, J. C., & O'Malley, P. M. (1982). *Highlights from student drug use in America 1975–1981.* Rockville, MD: National Institute on Drug Abuse.

Offer, D., & Sabshin, M. (1984). Adolescence: Empirical perspectives. In D. Offer & M. Sabshin (Eds.), *Normalcy and the life cycle: A critical integration* (pp. 76–107). New York: Basic Books.

Pandina, R. J., Labouvie, E. W., & White, N. R. (1984). Potential contributions of the life span development approach to the study of adolescent alcohol and drug use: The Rutgers Health and Human Development Project, a working model. *Journal of Drug Issues, 14*(2), 253–268.

Ratliff, K. G., & Buckhart, B. R. (1984). Sex differences in motivations for and effects of drinking among college students. *Journal of Studies on Alcohol, 45*(1), 26–32.

Schuerger, J. M., Tait, E., & Tavernelli, M. (1982). Temporal stability of personality by questionnaire. *Journal of Personality and Social Psychology, 43,* 176–182.

Segal, B., Huba, G. J., & Singer, J. L. (1980). *Drugs, daydreaming and personality: A study of college youth.* Hillsdale, NJ: Lawrence Birnbaum.

Zuckerman, M. (1979). *Sensation-seeking.* Hillsdale, NJ: Erlbaum Associates.

Zuckerman, M. (1983). Sensation seeking. In E. L. Gottheil, A. T. McLellan, & K. A. Druly (Eds.), *Etiologic aspects of alcohol and drug abuse.* Springfield, IL: C. C. Thomas.

Discussion Questions

1. What personality needs other than sensation-seeking might possibly be related to adolescents' use of alcohol and other drugs? Explain why.
2. What factors in the environment might encourage stability versus change in personality needs for sensation-seeking, achievement, aggression, autonomy, and social support?
3. Can you explain some ways in which consistent or heavy alcohol or other drug use might affect an adolescent's personality needs?

4. If a researcher tested the relationship between sensation-seeking needs and drug use in a sample of 15-year-old boys and girls, what result would she be likely to find? What could she predict about future drug use (at age 18) in the sample? Would her predictions about drug use at 18 change if she had been able to test the same sample a second time? Would the relationship between sensation seeking and drug use be about the same for the girls and boys?
5. For adolescents with high sensation-seeking needs who are receiving treatment for drug misuse, what do you think about the notion of trying to substitute socially acceptable, yet highly stimulating activities for drug use? Can you think of any drawbacks for this strategy?

A Comparative Study of Marijuana and Psychedelic Mushroom Users

Michael L. Hirsch Randall W. Conforti Alexander Pearsall

Michael L. Hirsch received his M.A. from the University of Wisconsin at Milwaukee in 1984 and his Ph.D. from the University of Texas-Austin in 1990. His work includes *Democracy and Drama,* an ethnographic and dramaturgical analysis of his run for public office in 1988, and "The Use of Marijuana for Pleasure: A Replication of Howard Becker's Study of Marijuana Use," which was published in the *Journal of Social Behavior and Personality* in 1990. He is currently involved in a study of cocaine users. Dr. Hirsch is an Assistant Professor of Sociology at Central Methodist College.

Randall W. Conforti received his B.A. in Sociology in 1980 from the University of Wisconsin-Madison and has performed graduate work at the University of Wisconsin-Milwaukee in Sociology, concentrating in the study of revolution. Currently, Conforti is the Director of Human Resources at the Ranch Rehabilitation Service in Menomonee Falls, Wisconsin.

The Ranch, Inc. is a vocational and treatment facility for behaviorally-challenged adults with developmental disabilities. In his seven years of work at the Ranch, Conforti served as Director of Clinical Services. Since 1980, Conforti teaches sociology and has been professionally involved in community-based services dealing with runaway youths and adults with mental illness. In the past few years, Conforti has also published several articles on drug use with Dr. Michael Hirsch.

Alexander Pearsall graduated from Lawrence University in 1991 and is currently residing in San Francisco, California, before resuming his graduate studies.

The use of illicit drugs in the U.S. is viewed by policy makers as one of our pressing social issues. Though the use of illicit drugs has long been a part of our history (Blum, 1984), recent rhetoric has pushed the war against drugs to the top of the social agenda (Tonry & Wilson, 1990).

Responses to the use of illicit drugs range from an outright declaration of war on both users and traffickers of such substances to arguments for the decriminalization of drug use (Riding, 1989; Keer 1988). Regardless of one's position on the use of such drugs, it is generally recognized that there is much to learn about the motivations of drug users and the patterns of use through discussions with users themselves.

In what follows, data obtained from interviews with two samples of drug users (users of marijuana and users of psychedelic mushrooms) will be reviewed in an attempt to understand the motivations of drug users. The examination will include a review of first encounters with the drug, rites of initiation to the drug, and career patterns of use. In addition, comparisons between the samples will be made in an attempt to provide a clearer understanding of this phenomenon.

Theoretical Statement

The use of these drugs will be approached from the framework of symbolic interactionism. This perspective assumes that human beings are best understood as acting toward objects in their environment on the basis of the meanings objects hold for them. Interactionists assume that an object's meaning arises through a process of social interaction, i.e., interaction with others. In addition, those who are most significant in our lives, e.g., family members, peers and dating partners, are believed to have the greatest effect upon the formation of our orientation to our world (Meltzer et al., 1975; Mead, 1984). Rather than view those who use illegal drugs as being motivated by some personal defect, interactionists argue that such behavior should be seen as a result of interactions between individuals and "significant others."

Methods and Procedures

An open-ended survey questionnaire was used in each set of interviews. Questions were designed to draw a chronological history of respondents' relationships to marijuana or mushrooms. Initial questions centered on early preconceptions of marijuana or mushrooms and concluded with speculation on future use.

In the case histories, special attention was paid to the first encounters with the drug, initiation to its use, and perceptions of the drug's effects, as well as the reconstruction of subsequent use patterns. Subjects were also given the chance to volunteer information they believed to be important, regarding drug use, which had not been solicited by the other questions.

Snowball Sample Method

Samples were drawn for each set of interviews by using the snowball sample method. Snowball samples are drawn when a researcher makes contact with, and wins the confidence of, one or two subjects engaged in the activity of interest. These subjects in turn recommend others to participate in the study. Initial contacts for this research were solicited through word of mouth and newspaper ads. Each sample was limited to 50 respondents. Though this method is known to lack randomness (limiting the ability to generalize from the sample to wider populations), it has proven effective in penetrating populations normally closed to inspection from those outside the network or group (True, 1989).

Demographic Characteristics

Each sample was demographically mixed. In the marijuana study the group was composed of 32 men and 18 women. Respondents ranged in age from 18 to 44. Their occupations were varied; respondents included college students, mechanics, nurses, house-painters, teachers, social workers, middle managers, and lawyers. All respondents were white.

The mushroom users were similarly mixed. This sample included 30 men and 20 women. Ages ranged from 18 to 46. This group included college students, nurses, machinists, waitresses, mail carriers, small business owners, counselors, teachers, and managers. All subjects were white. The subjects in both samples were drawn from two geographic regions in Wisconsin, Milwaukee and the Fox River Valley.

Career Patterns of Marijuana Use

Because individuals act toward objects on the basis of the meanings objects have for them, insight into the preconceptions individuals hold about each drug provides insight into the way motivations and career patterns of drug use develop. The marijuana users' recollections of their preconceptions of the drug clustered around three evaluative positions.

Fifty percent of the respondents in this sample (Table 1) held negative preconceptions about marijuana. This group included some who associated marijuana with the socially undesirable, those who recounted antidrug instruction and those whose extended family included drug abusers (including abusers of alcohol and tobacco).

Thirty-seven percent of the respondents held neutral preconceptions. Members of this group included those with an intellectual curiosity about marijuana

Table 1
Preconceptions of Marijuana

Negative	Neutral	Positive
50%	37%	13%

(and other drugs) and those with no idea that it existed before their use of the drug. (One house-painter stated that the first time she used the drug, with her cousin, was also when she first learned that it existed). Others viewed marijuana as a relatively harmless drug, equating it with tobacco and/or alcohol.

Finally, 13 percent of the sample held positive preconceptions. This group included those who recalled exposure to others who were enjoying themselves while on the drug. It also included those who believed its use was "cool."

Preconceptions and Patterns of Experimentation

The willingness to experiment with a drug must be understood in relation to an individual's preconceptions. Those with a positive orientation to the drug were already willing to try it. What had been lacking before initial use of the drug was the right opportunity.

It is not clear that a willingness to use the drug had developed prior to its use by those with neutral orientations. Rather, these individuals found themselves confronted with an opportunity to try the drug (usually in the presence of peers) prior to any decision about it. The use of the drug in such situations is perhaps the clearest example of the strength of '"peer pressure." Such situations included small gatherings of friends where the drug was introduced unexpectedly and where the willingness of some to try the drug in turn persuaded others. In such settings, and at parties, alcohol was also consumed, resulting in lowered inhibitions. Some subjects reported trying the drug so as to maintain their status within the group, while others reported that they were guided by a "what the hell" party attitude.

Those reporting negative orientations experienced the most dramatic change in their opinions about the drug, before a willingness to experiment with it appeared. Among this group two processes of change were noted. For some, willingness to experiment with the drug was a result of encounters with persons they respected, who either spoke about their personal use of the drug or used the drug in their presence. Most often these individuals were family members or good friends. One teacher said that his future wife (a nurse) introduced him to the drug.

For many, such experiences shattered many of the stereotypes regarding marijuana users (e.g., that they were socially undesirable) or the effects of the drug (loss of control or memory, etc.). Such beliefs had checked the willingness of many to experiment with marijuana; the erosion of these beliefs resulted in a greater willingness to experiment with the drug.

The second process resulting in a willingness to use the drug was socially more broad-based. Here a rejection of the status quo (e.g., in reaction to the Vietnam War) led some respondents to reevaluate their stance toward the use of the drug. Two respondents reported going through such a process.

First Encounters and Initiations

It is important to note that, in all instances, initiation to the drug involved family members, friends, or dating partners. For many, initial encounters with the drug occurred in a private location with only one other present. Others recounted their experiences with a small group of friends. For some, initiation took place at a large gathering, such as a party, where both friends and strangers were present.

Initiation to the use of the drug often involved advice on how it should be smoked. Subjects were coached on inhaling the correct amount of the drug so as not to choke on the smoke, and on holding the drug in their lungs in order to maximize the dosage. Many heard that they might not feel the drug's effects if they smoked it incorrectly. Friends, dates, and family members were cited as filling this coaching role. For those who hadn't anticipated the drug's use at a party, the initiation was less formal and mainly consisted of modeling the behavior of others.

Patterns of Follow Up Experimentation

Seventeen (34%) of the 50 subjects reported experiencing the drug's effects following their initial encounter (Table 2). Of these 17, 13 evaluated the experience favorably, two had neutral reactions and two reported nausea and vomiting. Sixteen (32%) of the subjects reported not experiencing the drug's effects until their second or third attempt, and 15 (30%) after several additional attempts. The remaining two (4%) respondents did not experience the drug's effects until after

Table 2
Trials and the Perception of the Effects of Marijuana

After Initial Encounter	17 (34%)
2–3 Attempts	16 (32%)
Several Attempts	15 (30%)
20–30 Attempts	2 (4%)

approximately 20 to 30 additional attempts. Their continued use of the drug after their failed attempts to get high was based upon their continued exposure to the drug and a belief that they would eventually experience its effects.

The respondents' reasons for continued experimentation with the drug after initial use varied in relation to the results of their initial experience and their thoughts about the drug at the time of its first use. Those who had experienced the drug's effects after its first use, and positively evaluated the experience, attempted to recapture "pleasurable sensations," (euphoria, creativity, heightened perceptions) through the drug's continued use. Those who had come to their initiation with positive motivations to try the drug, but who did not experience its effects after its use, pursued further experimentation with some rigor. (One student said that he stole from his parents' supply as a means of furthering his experimentation.) For those with neutral attitudes about the drug's use, further experimentation was more haphazard. For this group, chance would determine further use, just as in initial attempts.

Patterns of Continuing Use

Regardless of preconceptions, or the results of initial experimentations with the drug, once an individual's experience with the drug resulted in pleasurable sensations, further use of the drug was predicated upon the attempt to create similar experiences. We don't mean to suggest that the "pleasurable sensations" experienced by different respondents were necessarily identical. Sociological, psychological and biological differences preclude such a possibility. Also, it should be recognized that continued experience with the drug was not always pleasurable. Several respondents spoke of being frightened while being high. One person reported a psychotic episode during his use of the drug. He told of finding himself naked under a streetlight at night talking with God. However, regardless of such subsequent experiences, most agreed that, after a favorable experience, the drug was used with the intent of recreating a pleasurable state.

Given the similarity in motivation, it is interesting to note that subsequent use patterns varied greatly. Eighteen subjects reported that subsequent use was sporadic and based upon chance encounters. Twenty-seven reported trying to procure supplies of the drug for private use. Those procuring personal supplies varied in use from rare recreational encounters of two to three uses/year to more chronic use patterns of seven to nine uses/day. The majority fell between these two extremes, limiting their use to small amounts after work and/or on weekends.

In addition to the variation in use patterns, use also varied in purpose. Among chronic users the drug was used in a manner which paralleled others' use of, or addiction to, tobacco or caffeine. Less frequent users reserved use for vacations or events such as concerts or festivals, experiences they hoped to enhance with its use. Some reported its use as a sexual stimulant. Others turned to it for inspiration or insight as they struggled with a project. Most viewed marijuana as a drug to be used instead of alcohol in various social situations.

Speculation on Future Use Patterns

All but five respondents reported a willingness to continue its use, with several noting that they were likely to modify use patterns as family and job responsibilities shifted. In one case a professional couple had eliminated their use of the drug after their children began to question the smell of smoke (Yamaguchi, 1985). While most recognized potential legal consequences of being caught with the drug, all took precautions in its use and expressed little fear of the law.

Several individuals said they had made a conscious choice between the use of alcohol and marijuana, marijuana being their drug of choice. This group felt that marijuana should be legalized and that prejudices against its use were fed by those who had a financial stake in maintaining its illegality, e.g., tobacco and alcohol interests. Those who quit smoking marijuana cited their inability to enjoy its effects as their reason for discontinuing its use.

Users of Psychedelic Mushrooms

Preliminary analysis of the findings from the two studies alerted us to an important fact regarding the users of these two drugs. Though most of those in the marijuana study had used tobacco and/or alcohol illegally prior to trying marijuana, illegal drug use among this group was primarily confined to status offenses. This contrasts sharply with the histories of mushroom users, who, with only one exception, had tried other illegal drugs prior to experimentation with mushrooms. This prior drug experience greatly influenced their responses to our questions.

Respondents' Preconceptions

Preconceptions of this drug varied among those studied. As was true of marijuana users, mushroom users reported neutral, positive, and negative predispositions to the drug prior to its initial use (Table 3). Thirty-eight percent reported positive preconceptions of the drug. Eleven of these reported positive encounters with LSD (a synthetic drug with similar effects) prior to their use of mushrooms. They expected that mushrooms would provide a milder LSD experience. Five respondents, with no LSD experience, still had positive preconceptions and expected their experience to include feelings of euphoria and laughter. Such expectations were drawn from discussions with family members, close friends, and dating or marital partners. Three respondents experimented with the drug with hopes of gaining spiritual enlightenment.

Forty percent of those studied reported neutral preconceptions of the drug. This included those who thought of mushrooms as a "hippie drug," those who equated its properties with those of marijuana and those who were somewhat curious about the drug but did not feel compelled to use it. Nine of the 20 in this category had no real knowledge of the drug prior to its use. As mushrooms seem more obscure than marijuana, cocaine, or LSD, this last finding should come as no surprise.

Table 3
Preconceptions of Mushrooms

Negative	Neutral	Positive
22%	40%	38%

The final 22 percent of the sample held negative preconceptions of the drug. Here, fear of having an uncontrollable experience was most often cited as the reason for the negative evaluation. Those who held negative conceptions of LSD and equated mushrooms with LSD, generalized their negative evaluations to mushrooms. Others, who felt it was reasonable to use marijuana, thought of mushrooms as a harder drug and thus avoided their use. Given the strength of the fears reported, it is important to note that these respondents went on to experiment with the drug.

Preconceptions and Patterns of Experimentation

As was true of those in the marijuana sample, the willingness to experiment with the use of mushrooms is best understood in relation to initial preconceptions. Among those who had a positive orientation, a willingness to try it already existed. For this group, first attempts to use mushrooms were related to use opportunities.

Among those with neutral preconceptions of the drug (including those who had no knowledge of its existence before its use), it is again unclear that a willingness to use the drug developed before its use. It could be suggested that the use of the drug was a sign of a willingness to try it. However, as one reviews responses to questions regarding initial use, it is clear that many found themselves using the drug with no forethought regarding its use. Many had found themselves in situations similar to those discussed in conjunction with early marijuana use. These are situations wherein subjects reportedly drank alcohol and/or smoked marijuana before mushrooms were passed out. In such situations many acted on assurances from friends, dating partners, and acquaintances that the drug was safe and would also provide them with an enjoyable experience.

One teacher, with no prior knowledge of the drug before its use, told of entering a room at a party when the drug was being distributed among a small group of friends. He waited until all but one person had left the room before asking about the drug. He received a brief introduction to it before trying it himself. Two respondents were told, after the fact, that the drug was mixed in the punch they had been drinking. Here there was no forethought regarding its use.

As was true of those with negative preconceptions of marijuana, those with negative preconceptions of mushrooms went through dramatic changes in their orientation to the drug prior to its use. Here a slow process of reorientation seemed to take place as encounters with the drug and its users gradually convinced them that the drug was safe to use. Though some expressed apprehension about the drug's effects before its use, they had been put at ease by respected friends or by others with whom they had intimate, kindly relationships. Two women, a waitress and a self-employed businesswoman, spoke of using the drug after extensive discussions with their husbands. Only one respondent expressed the belief that her initial use of the drug went against her better judgment.

First Encounters and Initiations

Initiation into the use of mushrooms involved persons of some significance to those trying the drug. Though gatherings of friends were most often cited as the setting in which experimentation took place, some reported using the drug with only one other present, while others were at public functions such as festivals or concerts. Only one person reported experimenting with the drug by herself.

The use of marijuana involved some mastery of technique, but mushrooms are ingested, and little ritual accompanied their use. Many pointed to the importance the setting played in their being comfortable with the drug's effects. Initial use included creating a situation or attending an event that would allow them to be relaxed. Such planning, however, was true of only a small number.

Patterns of Follow Up Experimentation

While 66 percent of those in the marijuana sample reported no effects from the drug after their initial encounter, only four percent (two people) of this sample (Table 4) reported a similar inability to feel effects. One social worker concluded that she had taken too little of the drug to feel its effects, while the other respondent, a public administrator, was convinced that his use of alcohol and marijuana had masked the effects of the mushrooms.

Of the 48 who reported feeling the effects of the drug, two reported negative experiences; one (a cashier) was frightened by the drug's actual effects, the other (a machinist) was uncomfortable with the situation she was in while under its influence. The remaining 46 reported positive experiences with the drug, ranging from those who had found the experience to be intellectually interesting to those who reported euphoria and prolonged laughter. These subjects, and the two who reported no effects, continued or wished to continue their use of the drug.

Patterns of Continuing Use

Current use patterns varied as greatly as the use patterns noted among the sample of marijuana users. Most reported that they did not have any regular use patterns. Use among this group is almost entirely dependent upon the chance appearance of the drug. The range of use reported varied from those whose chance encounters translate into use once every one to three years to those whose chance encounters allow for three to seven uses per year. Those who actively seek the drug do so with wide variation of effort. Those who use the drug most frequently reported using the drug up to 25 times per year. Those with the least frequent self-procuring patterns reported using the drug as little as once or twice per year.

In addition to variation in use patterns, mushroom use also varied in purpose. For a minority (three of the 50), mushroom use was associated with spirituality

Table 4
Trials and the Perception of the Effects of Psychedelic Mushrooms

After Initial Encounter	48 (96%)
Never Perceived Effects	2 (4%)

and introspection. For this group the drug's use was connected with profound and lasting revelations regarding life and its meaning. Two found inspiration for their art and music while using the drug. Here the transformation of perception was seen as revealing underlying structures, forms, and textures which were overlooked in their normal state. For both of these groups the use of the drug was a serious matter, as they hoped to gain insight that would carry beyond the period of intoxication.

The majority of users saw mushrooms as another recreational drug to be added to the list of drugs used for this purpose. Though the drug-induced experience from mushrooms is reported to be of a deeper or more profound nature than that of other drugs, such as alcohol and marijuana, their motivation for using this drug was no different. In such cases, relaxation from responsibilities was a primary concern. All subjects agreed that the actual physical effects of mushrooms were more draining than those of alcohol or marijuana. Given this, the use of this drug, with few exceptions, was limited to weekends (Fridays or Saturdays) or vacations. Such timed use of the drug was said to allow one to recover from its physical effects before resuming responsible activities.

Speculation on Future Use of the Drug

Unlike the marijuana sample, nearly 33 percent of those in this sample predicted that their use of the drug would be of short duration (several had already discontinued its use). Though most stated that they enjoyed the drug's effects and/or learned something as a result of its use, there was general concern that long-term use would be detrimental to their health. Some speculated that they might use the drug two or three more times before they discontinued its use (several students said they would not continue its use beyond graduation). Others were unsure as to whether or not they had already stopped using it.

Another 33 percent believed that continued use would most likely be determined by chance. Though they had positive feelings about its use at the time of the interviews, they also shared reservations about the physical effects of extended use. Such concerns served to check active procurement activities.

The remaining 33 percent believed that they would use the drug from time to time through the course of their lives. Though it was not the drug of choice for any, many viewed it as valuable either as a recreational option or for the insights its use could provide.

Discussion

In the following discussion the career patterns of each sample of drug users will be compared to one another. It is hoped that this comparison may provide insight into the social phenomenon of drug use. The comparison will include a search for similarities as well as differences. This search will be conducted in the order of career patterns.

Similarities and Differences in Career Use Patterns

Preconceptual Positions

Similarities and differences between the samples can be noted at the beginning of the career patterns in statements of preconceptions (Table 5). The two samples were similar in the reporting of divergent preconceptual positions. Similarities were also found in the categories themselves. For example, each sample's positively oriented group included respondents who reported observations of others enjoying themselves on the drug prior to their own use. Each neutral group included those who reported an intellectual curiosity about the drug, as well as some reporting no knowledge of the drug prior to its use. Both groups reporting negative preconceptions included those reporting an overarching antidrug position.

Differences in the preconceptions of the groups are also important. Though each sample had individuals in each of the preconceptual categories, distribution within the categories varied greatly between samples.

Table 5
A Comparison of Preconceptions

	Negative	Neutral	Positive
Marijuana	50%	37%	13%
Mushrooms	22%	40%	38%

While recognizing the limits in our ability to generalize, given the nature of the samples, it does seem that differences in the number of illegal drugs used, i.e., drug sophistication, among respondents in each sample were related to preconceptual distributions (with more respondents in the mushroom sample stating a positive orientation). It also seems that the greater drug sophistication among members of the mushroom sample created a considerable state of fear among those reporting negative preconceptions. A possible explanation for this may be that greater experience in the drug culture provided evidence for and/or an understanding of bad trips.

Movement toward Initial Use

Respondents in the samples seemed to follow similar paths toward initial use of each drug. Those who began with positive preconceptions seemed only to wait for an opportunity for experimentation. Those with negative preconceptions went through a reprogramming period that was heavily influenced by friends, dating/marital partners and family members. Those with neutral orientations found themselves in situations where the drug was being used and where they tried the drug as a matter of course, or as a way of maintaining their status in the group. In general, patterns of movement toward experimentation seem to be identical for each group.

One major difference between the samples is related to the way in which each of the drugs is taken. As marijuana is most often smoked, a majority of the respondents in this sample reported receiving coaching on appropriate techniques. Here, initiation to the drug was somewhat ritualistic, including many unsuccessful attempts at getting high. Because mushrooms are ingested, there was little coaching regarding their use and an overwhelming rate of success in achieving a drug-induced state.

Motivations for Continued Use

Individuals from both samples reported that the continued use of each drug was predicated upon attempts to re-experience pleasurable sensations. For some, the sensations included feelings of euphoria and laughter. For others, the sensations included a heightening of perceptual experience. A minority in each group thought of the drug-induced state as an opportunity for introspection and/or spiritual enlightenment. A majority in each group thought of the drug in strictly recreational terms. One major difference between the two groups was the number of marijuana users who cited it as their drug of choice. No one chose mushrooms as his or her favorite drug.

Subsequent Use Patterns

In both samples a wide variance in subsequent use patterns emerged after initial experimentation. Use patterns among marijuana users varied from one use per three years to seven to nine uses per day. Use patterns among mushroom users were more episodic, with lows of one use per three years to highs of 25 times per year. While a majority of marijuana users reported regular use patterns, fewer than 50 percent of mushroom users reported such patterns. It is important to note that each sample reported a wide variance of use patterns. It is also important to note both the greater frequency of regular use patterns among marijuana users and the higher rate of actual use.

Differences in use patterns and the intensity of drug use are most easily explained by the nature of the drugs being used. Remember that a majority of those who used mushrooms reported concerns about the long-term effects of extended use. Such concerns were not as evident among the marijuana users.

Speculations Regarding Future Use

Speculations regarding future use also varied from one sample to the next. Whereas 90 percent of marijuana users indicated that they believed their use of the drug would continue at some level, only 66 percent of the mushroom users predicted future use. One half of this 66 percent indicated that future use would be limited to a short period of time, leaving only 33 percent of the sample open to long-term use. Clearly the physical demands of this drug, combined with fears about its long-term effects, influenced projections of future use.

Conclusions

The use of illicit drugs, long a part of our heritage, has again come forward as a point of conflict within society. The government has declared a war on drugs, hoping to destroy the infrastructure that supplies users and to discourage real and/or potential users. In spite of these efforts, the use of illicit drugs remains. By studying 100 drug users from within the interactionist framework, we have attempted to understand how individuals come to use drugs in the face of public prohibitions.

One of the most notable lessons to be drawn from our work is that the pattern of learning associated with the use of illegal substances is identical to the general pattern of learning normally associated with the process of socialization. Just as individuals are not born with predispositions to a type of music, neither are individuals born with a predisposition to use drugs. In recounting their preconceptions of the drugs and their movement toward their use, individuals in both samples continually pointed to the way in which significant others, family members, close friends, and dating/marriage partners influenced their willingness to use drugs. The role that peer pressure played in convincing individuals to experiment with illicit drugs also seems to be identical to the role that peer pressure plays in such things as the wearing of specific styles of clothing or the piercing of one's ear(s). It should be kept in mind that only one of the 100 subjects reported feeling somewhat coerced into using the drug against her better judgment.

In making such observations, we do not suggest that the use of illicit drugs is to be equated with such things as musical preference. It is the opinion of the authors that the use of all drugs, legal or illegal, is fraught with numerous dangers. One must note, however, that decisions to do so are guided by the actions and opinions of others whom individuals look up to and respect, and/or by whom they wish to be accepted. This symbolic interactionist vision of becoming a user of illicit drugs is in sharp contrast to the stereotypical vision of the impersonal drug pusher who is able to convince individuals to experiment with such substances.

The review of the data obtained from our interviews also points to the complexity of the use of such substances. The statement "not all drug users are alike" underscores the differences that exist between users. Respondents came from all walks of life, differed in political and religious beliefs, and had varying educational backgrounds. The one thing they all had in common was their willingness to use illicit drugs. Whatever other conclusions may be drawn from the information gained in this study, perhaps none is more important than the recognition that drug use is as complex as other aspects of human life. Such complexity must be recognized by those who attempt to deal with the "drug problem."

References

Blum, K. (1984). *Handbook of abusable drugs.* New York: Gardner Press, Inc.

Hirsch, M. L., & Conforti, R. W., & Graney, C. J. (1990). The use of marijuana for pleasure: A replication of Howard S. Becker's study of marijuana use. *The Journal of Social Behavior and Personality, 4,* 497–510.

Keer, P. (1988, May 15). The unspeakable is debated: Should drugs be legalized? *The New York Times,* pp.1, 12.

Mead, G. H. (1934). *Mind, self and society.* Chicago: University of Chicago Press

Meltzer, B. N., et. al. (1984). *Symbolic interactionism: Genesis, varieties and criticisms.* Boston. Routledge & Kegan Paul.

Riding, A. (1989, April 2). Western panel is asking end to all curbs on drug traffic. *The New York Times,* p. 6.

Tonry, M., & Wilson, J. Q. (1990). *Drugs and crime.* Chicago, IL: The University of Chicago Press.

True, J. A. H. (1989). *Finding out: Conducting and evaluating social research.* Belmont, CA: Wadsworth Publishing Company.

Yamaguchi, K., & Kandel, D. B. (1985). On the resolution of role incompatibility: A live event history analysis of family roles and marijuana use. *American Journal of Sociology, 90,* 1284–1293

Discussion Questions

1. What problems do law enforcement agencies face as they try to convince the public to turn in individuals who are known to use or traffic in drugs?
2. Why do antidrug programs meet with limited success?

3. Do individuals' antidrug beliefs guarantee that they will not become drug users themselves? Why or why not?
4. How is the nature of the drug used related to use patterns?
5. Given the process of socialization involved in becoming a drug user, what can you do to protect yourself from becoming a user of illicit drugs?

Adolescent Drug Use and Leisure Activity

Robert Agnew

David M. Petersen

Robert Agnew is an Associate Professor of Sociology at Emory University in Atlanta. His research focuses on the causes of delinquency, with a special focus on strain and social control theories. Recent publications include "The Interactive Effect on Peer Variables on Delinquency" (1991) in *Criminology, 29,* 42–72 and "A Longitudinal Test of Social Control Theory and Delinquency" (1991) in *Journal of Research in Crime and Delinquency 28,* 126–156.

David M. Petersen is a Professor of Sociology at Georgia State University. He received his Ph.D. from the University of Kentucky in 1968. He is a frequent contributor to the professional literature on the administration of justice, drug addiction, and penology. Recent publications include *Social Issues: Conflicting Opinions* and "Leisure and Delinquency" (1989) (with Robert Agnew) in *Social Problems, 36,* 332–350.

Drug use has increased dramatically since the late 1960s and is now widespread among adolescents. In a recent survey of high-school seniors, for example, 82.7 percent reported alcohol use in the last 12 months, 29.6 percent marijuana use, and 6.5 percent cocaine use (Flanagan & Maguire, 1990). Much attention has focused on the causes of this drug use, with the bulk of research focusing on family, school, peer, and economic variables (for summaries see Abadinsky, 1989; Akers, 1992). This research, however, has largely ignored the impact of leisure on drug use (although see Johnston, 1973; Kamali & Steer, 1976; Osgood & Yong-Min, 1988). This neglect is surprising for several reasons. Leisure has come to play a central role in the lives of modern adolescents, a role perhaps more important than the family and school for many adolescents. Patterns of leisure activity have long been used to explain closely related forms of deviance—including delinquent behaviors such as property crime and violence (see Agnew & Petersen, 1989)—and many of the proposed solutions to the drug problem have as a central focus the provision of leisure/recreation opportunities. It is not uncommon to hear local politicians, for example, suggest that we should attack the drug problem by providing more recreational opportunities for young people. In this paper, we try to determine whether there really is a relationship between leisure/recreation and drug use.

Leisure and Drugs

There are several reasons to expect a relationship between leisure and drug use, with the most popular being listed below.

Involvement

Perhaps the most common reason for expecting a relationship between leisure and drug use is that involvement in conventional leisure activities leaves the adolescent with little time for, or interest in, drug use (Hirschi, 1969, discussion on the bond of involvement). This argument is often summarized in the adage that "the devil finds work for idle hands." Adolescents who are not involved in conventional leisure activities will have more free time on their hands, and so have more opportunity to get involved with drugs. Further, the boredom often associated with ample free time may make drugs more appealing to such adolescents.

Supervision

Organized leisure activities—that is, structured activities supervised by conventional adults—are said to prevent drug use because at least part of the adolescent's time is spent under the supervision of an adult. Such activities include organized sports at school or in the community, Boy and Girl Scouts, participation in YMCA and YWCA programs, organized church activities, clubs and organizations at school, etc.

Strengthening the Bond to Family and School

Certain types of leisure activities are also said to strengthen the adolescent's bond to parents and school. Leisure activities with parents have been said to strengthen ties to parents and prevent deviance for that reason (Nye, 1958; Glueck & Glueck, 1950). Adolescents who like their parents are less likely to use drugs, because they do not want to do anything to hurt their parents or cause their parents to have a bad opinion of them (see Hirschi's 1969 discussion of the bond of attachment). Also, parents are able to exercise more influence over adolescents when ties are strong (Hirschi, 1983). Likewise, activities such as interscholastic sports at school and participation in school clubs may increase the adolescent's attachment and commitment to school. For example, certain studies suggest that participation in athletics/extracurricular activities is associated with higher grades, placement in college preparatory programs, higher expectations, and higher levels of educational attainment (Landers & Landers, 1978; Loy et al., 1978; Segrave, 1980). Adolescents who like school and are doing well in school are said to be less likely to engage in deviance such as drug use. They do not want to do anything to jeopardize their position in school or their chances for future success (see Hirschi's 1969 discussion of the bond of commitment).

Fostering Conventional Beliefs

Certain types of leisure activity may prevent delinquency by fostering conventional (antidrug) beliefs. Organized leisure activities, supervised by adults, may foster conventional beliefs by exposing adolescents to conventional role models and increasing their attachment to such models. Also, certain individuals have argued that leisure activities such as sports teach such values as sportsmanship, persistence, good manners, the delay of gratification, and cooperation (Landers & Landers, 1978).

Exposure to Peers Who Foster Drug Use

Certain types of leisure activity may increase the adolescent's exposure to peers who encourage drug use or provide access to drugs. Numerous researchers, for example, warn of the dangers of leisure time spent hanging out on street corners, in pool halls and arcades, and cruising city streets (Arnold & Brungardt, 1983; Glueck & Glueck, 1950; Kvaraceus, 1954). Such activities are thought to put the adolescent in contact with delinquents who may provide drugs and encourage drug use. At a general level, activities such as "hanging out" and unsupervised peer-oriented social activities, such as parties, are thought to be dangerous because they increase the likelihood of exposure to peers who may encourage or provide opportunities for drug use.

Reducing Frustration

Finally, several researchers have argued that leisure may prevent deviance—including drug use—by relieving tension and frustration. Drug use is often said to be a reaction to the tension and frustration caused by such factors as the failure to achieve one's goals. Leisure, however, may provide a socially acceptable outlet for such frustration (Roberts, 1983).

Also, some researchers have argued that adolescents have a need for leisure (Nye, 1958; Anson, 1976), or more generally for thrills and excitement (Schafer, 1969; Segrave, 1983). If adolescents are unable to satisfy this need through socially accepted channels, they may become frustrated and try to satisfy it through delinquent channels—including drug use. Both these arguments suggest that increased participation in leisure activities should reduce frustration and therefore prevent drug use.

Kvaraceus (1954), however, notes that forcing adolescents to participate in disliked leisure activities may increase tension and frustration, and for that reason contribute to deviance (piano and dancing lessons are used as examples). The reduction of tension and frustration, then, is only likely to result from participation in pleasurable leisure activities.

There are, then, several reasons for expecting a relationship between leisure and drug use. Certain of these explanations focus on the *type of leisure activity.* Certain types of leisure, such as sports and organized activities, are said to reduce drug use. Other types of leisure, such as hanging out and unsupervised social activities, are said to increase drug use. Other explanations focus on *with whom the adolescent spends his or her leisure time.* In this area, leisure activities with parents are said to reduce drug use. Finally, certain explanations focus on whether the adolescent *likes or dislikes leisure activities.* Liked activities are said to reduce drug use, and disliked activities are said to increase it. We will examine these arguments below.

The Study

Our data are from a random sample of 600 high school students in suburban DeKalb County, located in the greater metropolitan Atlanta, Georgia area. This sample was selected from the larger group of 23,289 white students attending grades 9–12 in the 21 public high schools in the county. The sample is representative of that group, and the adolescents in the sample were interviewed during the summer and fall of 1974. It is important to note that the sample was drawn from the white population of a relatively prosperous metropolitan county. The respondents tend to come from families that are well educated and relatively affluent (see Elifson et al., 1983, for further information on the sample). The results of this study are not necessarily generalizable to other populations, such as crack users in the inner city.

The respondents in the sample were asked a series of questions about their leisure activities and the extent of their drug use. The drug questions focused on the illicit use of alcohol, marijuana, and seven other drugs (amphetamines or uppers, barbiturates or downers, heroin, cocaine, inhalants such as glue, LSD, and other hallucinogens such as PCP and peyote). The frequency of drug use in this sample is comparable to the frequencies reported in nationally representative samples of adolescents. For example, one of the best national surveys of delinquency and drug use among adolescents is the National Youth Survey (Elliott et al., 1985). According to the National Youth Survey (NYS), 67 percent of all 14–17 year olds used alcohol in 1976. According to our survey, 62.8 percent of the adolescents in DeKalb County used alcohol in 1974. The NYS estimates that 28 percent of adolescents used marijuana, while our estimate is 33.8 percent. Figures for the other drugs are likewise comparable. The NYS, for example, estimates that 2.4 percent of the 14–17 year olds used cocaine, while our estimate is 2.7 percent. The extent of drug use in this sample, then, is not very different from that of the United States as a whole.

Alcohol and marijuana are by far the most frequently used drugs. The percentage of adolescents using other drugs is low, and for that reason we will combine these other drugs into a single category called "other drugs" in all subsequent analyses. The analyses that follow, then, will focus on the illicit use of alcohol, marijuana, and "other drugs."

Is Participation in Certain Types of Leisure Activity Associated with Drug Use?

As discussed earlier, some individuals claim that certain types of leisure activity—such as sports and organized activities—reduce drug use. Other types of leisure activity—such as hanging out and unsupervised peer-oriented social activities—are said to increase drug use. We investigated these assertions by examining the relationship between type of leisure activity and drug use. The adolescents in the survey were asked to list their most and least favorite ways of spending free time. They could list up to five most favorite leisure activities and up to three least favorite leisure activities. Close to 300 different leisure activities were listed, ranging from football and watching TV to kyacking and decoupage. We classified these leisure activities into the nine categories shown in Table 1. These categories reflect the distinctions made in the first part of the paper (e.g., organized activities, sports, hanging out, unsupervised social activities) and also reflect the typologies of leisure developed in the sociology of leisure research.

After the adolescents listed their leisure activities, they were asked "How frequently do you do these leisure activities?" Based on their responses, we calculated the number of times per year that the adolescents engaged in each of the nine types of leisure. Table 1 shows the *average* number of times each leisure activity is performed per year. The most frequent leisure activity is passive entertainment, followed closely by noncompetitive sports and housework. The least frequent leisure activity is music/art.

Table 1

A Typology of Leisure Activities

1. *Organized Activities* (e.g., drill team, band, school newspaper, cheerleading, scouts, church activities, school homework). (80.7)
2. *Social Activities* (e.g., dating, parties, telephone conversations, visiting friends, playing with friends). The *focus* of such activity is clearly social interaction with another person or persons. (48.0)
3. *Hanging Out/Loafing* (e.g., doing nothing, sitting around loafing, pleasure driving, hanging around house). Hanging out may occur alone or with others. Such activity is distinguished by the fact that it *lacks* a clear focus or purpose. (43.9)
4. *Passive Entertainment* (e.g., listening to records or radio, reading, watching TV, attending movies, concerts, sporting events). Such activity may occur alone or with others. If it occurs with others, however, the focus is not on social interaction. Rather, it is on an external source of entertainment, such as music or TV. (170.7)
5. *Housework Activities* (e.g., baby-sitting, cleaning, mowing lawn, doing housework, yardwork). (143.3)
6. *Sport—Competitive* (e.g., baseball, football, basketball, tennis). Includes both supervised (e.g., school sports, Little League) and unsupervised competitive sports activities. (97.1)
7. *Sports—Noncompetitive* (e.g., bike riding, horseback riding, roller skating, swimming, jogging, boating). Includes both supervised and unsupervised noncompetitive sports activities. (159.0)
8. *Games/Crafts/Hobbies* (e.g., embroidering, sewing, model building, chess, cooking). (40.9)
9. *Music/Art* (as a performer or active participant—includes dancing, playing guitar, playing piano, drawing, painting, and photography). (35.1)

Is the amount of time spent in these leisure activities related to drug use? Table 2 shows the *correlation coefficients* between drug use and the nine types of leisure activities. The correlation coefficients tell us the extent to which an increase in leisure activity is related to an increase (positive coefficient) or decrease (negative coefficient) in drug use. A coefficient at or near zero means that the leisure activity and drug use are unrelated, while a coefficient in the +/–.10 to .20 range indicates a weak relationship (see Blalock, 1979, for more information on the correlation coefficient).

An examination of the data reveals some support for the arguments presented earlier. First, hanging out is weakly correlated with all three forms of drug use. Thus, adolescents who report that they spend a lot of time hanging out or loafing are slightly more likely to engage in drug use. Second, adolescents who report that they spend a lot of time engaged in social activities are moderately more likely to consume alcohol. This finding is not surprising, since alcohol is frequently found at social functions such as parties. Time spent in social activities, however, is large unrelated to marijuana and other drug use. Finally, adolescents who spend a lot of time in sports activities are slightly less likely to use marijuana and other drugs. Other types of leisure activity, *including organized activities*, are largely unrelated to drug use.

(Note: Largely the same results were obtained in a multiple regression analysis. Multiple regression allows one to examine the *unique* contribution of each type of leisure to drug use. See Blalock, 1979, for a description of this technique.)

Does It Matter with Whom the Adolescent Performs the Leisure Activity?

As we discussed, some theories suggest that leisure activities performed with parents may reduce drug use. After the adolescents in our study listed each of their leisure activities, they were asked with whom they engaged in these activities. Based on their responses, we calculated the number of times respondents engaged in leisure activities with parents, with peers, and alone. On average, respondents engaged in 52 leisure activities with parents during the previous year—or one leisure activity with parents per week. They engaged in 398 leisure activities with peers during that time, and 366 leisure activities alone.

We then calculated the correlations between the various types of drug use and the number of times respondents engaged in leisure activities with parents, with peers, and alone. Adolescents who spend a lot of leisure time with parents are slightly less likely to use marijuana (the correlation coefficient = –.08). Time spent in leisure activities with parents, however, is unrelated to alcohol use and the use of other drugs. Time spent in leisure activities with peers and alone is unrelated to all types of drug use.

Does It Matter Whether the Adolescent Likes the Leisure Activity?

The above data focus on the amount of time the adolescent spends in various types of leisure activity, and with whom the activity is performed—regardless of whether the adolescent likes the leisure activity. As discussed above, however, it may be important to consider whether adolescents like the leisure activities in which they participate. Liked leisure activities may reduce drug use, since these activities reduce frustration and tension. Disliked activities, however, may increase frustration and perhaps foster drug use. The distinction between liked and disliked activities also has important policy implications. While it is relatively easy to get adolescents to participate in a leisure activity, it is more difficult to ensure that they will like the activity. Several authors, for example, note that delinquents often dislike the organized leisure activities in which they are forced to participate (Arnold & Brungardt, 1983; Glueck & Glueck, 1950; Segrave, 1983). A crucial question, then, is whether it makes a difference whether adolescents like or dislike the leisure activities in which they are involved.

As noted above, the adolescents in the sample were asked to list their five most favorite and three least favorite leisure activities. We decided to test the above arguments by analyzing most favorite leisure activities separately from least favorite leisure activities. It should be noted, however, that respondents do not necessarily *dislike* their least favorite leisure activities—they may merely *like these activities less* than their most favorite activities. The most common "least favorite" activities are housework and organized activities. The most common "most favorite" leisure activities, by way of contrast, are noncompetitive sports, passive entertainment, and competitive sports.

If the above arguments are correct, the relationship between drugs and most favorite activities should be

Table 2
The Correlations Between Drug Use and the Nine Types of Leisure Activities

	Alcohol Use	Marijuana Use	Other Drugs
Organized Activities	–.07	–.05	–.03
Social Activities	.19**	.08	.05
Hanging Out/Loafing	.13**	.11**	.08
Sports—Competitive	–.01	–.10**	–.05
Sports—Noncompetitive	–.06	–.09*	–.10*
Passive Entertainment	–.03	–.09	–.06
Housework Activities	.01	.04	.08*
Games/Crafts/Hobbies	.07	.04	.04
Music/Art	–.05	.01	.03

**Statistically significant with $p < .01$.
*$p < .05$.

different from the relationship between drugs and least favorite activities. For example, adolescents who spend a lot of time in most favorite activities with parents should be lower in drug use. Spending a lot of time in least favorite activities with parents, however, should have no effect on drug use, or should even be associated with higher levels of drug use.

The data suggest that, in most cases, distinguishing most from least favorite leisure activities does not make a difference. This is because most leisure activities—whether liked or disliked—are unrelated to drug use. If we focus on those leisure activities that are related to drug use, however, we find that distinguishing most from least favorite activities often makes a difference. For example, we earlier found that adolescents who frequently engaged in social activities were more likely to drink. The data in Table 3, however, indicate that only the amount of time spent in *liked* (or most favorite) social activities is related to drinking. Time spent in *disliked* social activities is unrelated to drinking. Further, Table 3 indicates that time spent in *liked* social activities is related to marijuana use. To give another example, we earlier stated that adolescents who spent a lot of time in noncompetitive sports were less likely to use other drugs. Table 3, however, indicates that only adolescents who spend a lot of time in *liked* noncompetitive sports are less likely to use other drugs. Time spent in *disliked* noncompetitive sports is unrelated to the use of other drugs. Table 3 shows all those cases where distinguishing most favorite from least favorite leisure activities makes a significant difference. It is sometimes important, then, to take account of the extent to which adolescents like their leisure pursuits. These data are important because they suggest that simply requiring adolescents to engage in certain leisure pursuits may not prevent drug use. It is sometimes also necessary to ensure that the adolescents *like* these leisure pursuits.

Does the Relationship between Leisure and Drug Use Mean That Leisure Causes Drug Use?

We have found that certain leisure activities—especially liked activities—are related to drug use. In particular, leisure pursuits such as hanging out and social activities seem to be associated with slightly higher levels of drug use, while sports and occasionally certain other leisure activities seem to be associated with slightly lower levels of drug use. The relationship between leisure and drug use, however, does not necessarily mean that leisure *causes* drug use.

First, leisure may be associated with drug use because both *are caused by the same third variable.* For example, we found that people who frequently engage in social activities consume more alcohol. This relationship may be due to the fact that both alcohol consumption and frequency of attending social activities are caused by the same third variable. The variable of gender, for example, may cause alcohol consumption on the one hand (with males drinking more than females) and may cause social activities on the other (with males attending more social activities than females). The fact that gender causes both alcohol consumption and social activities may explain why these latter two variables are related. This argument can be tested by examining the relationship between social activities and alcohol use while "controlling for" gender or holding gender constant. That is, we examine the relationship between social activities and alcohol consumption among males only. We then do the same for females. If social activities are still related to alcohol consumption when we conduct these separate examinations, we conclude that the relationship is not due to gender. We examined the relationship between leisure and drug use while controlling for gender, age, parents' education, and size of community. For the most part, the leisure variables were still related to drug use.

The fact that these variables are still related to drug use, however, still does not mean that they cause drug use. The relationship between leisure and drug may be due to the fact that *drug use causes leisure.* For example, perhaps the release of inhibition that often accompanies alcohol use leads to greater socializing by adolescents. Therefore, before we can say that leisure causes drug use, we must first establish the correct *causal order.* Does leisure cause drug use, does drug use cause leisure, or is it some combination of the two? It is not possible to give a definitive answer to this question with data from just one point in time. Such data do not allow us to determine whether the leisure activities in question precede the use of drugs. Nevertheless, in most cases there seems just as much, if not more, reason to argue that leisure causes drug use as there is to argue that drug use causes leisure.

Table 3
The Correlations Between Drug Use and Most and Least Favorite Leisure Activities

	Alcohol Use	Marijuana Use	Other Drugs
Social Activities			
Most Liked	.20**	.08*	—
Least Liked	–.01	–.01	—
Hanging out/Loafing			
Most Liked	—	—	.11**
Least Liked	—	—	–.01
Sports—Competitive			
Most Liked	—	–.11**	—
Least Liked	—	.00	—
Sports—Noncompetitive			
Most Liked	—	—	–.11**
Least Liked	—	—	.02
Housework Activities			
Most Liked	—	—	–.01
Least Liked	—	—	.09*
Games/Crafts/Hobbies			
Most Liked	.03	—	—
Least Liked	.16**	—	—

Differences between most and least liked activities are only shown when they are significant at the .05 level or better.

**p < .01
*p < .05

Summary

At the start of this research, we stated that policy makers often claim that the provision of leisure/recreation opportunities will reduce drug use. We also reviewed several reasons for expecting a relationship between drug use and leisure. We may summarize the major findings of this study as follows.

1. "Hanging out" and unsupervised peer oriented activities—especially liked activities—have a slight to moderate positive effect on drug use. Other studies have also provided some support for this finding (Osgood & Yong-Min, 1988).
2. Sports have a small negative effect on drug use—with people active in sports being slightly less likely to use drugs (also see Kamali & Steer, 1976).
3. Organized leisure activities are largely unrelated to drug use. Certain other studies have also found that selected types of organized activities are unrelated or weakly related to drug use (Johnston, 1973; Osgood & Yong-Min, 1988; Kamali & Steer, 1976).
4. Other types of leisure activity, including passive entertainment, housework, games, and music/art, are also largely unrelated to drug use.
5. Leisure activities with parents have, at best, a very weak relationship to drug use.

6. Leisure activities that are liked often have a different effect on delinquency than leisure activities that are disliked.

Taken as a whole, these data suggest that the provision of leisure/recreation opportunities would have, at best, only a minor effect on drug use. Further, they suggest that any antidrug program with a leisure component should be carefully constructed. While certain types of leisure activity are associated with lower levels of drug use, other types are associated with higher levels of use. Also, it is often the case that the adolescent must *like* the leisure activity if it is to have an impact. Simply participating in the activity is often not enough.

How can we explain the generally weak relationship between leisure and drug use? In the first section of this research, we offered several reasons for expecting a relationship between leisure and delinquency. Let us reevaluate those reasons in light of the data. First, we said that leisure may reduce drug use since it leaves the adolescent with little time for or interest in drugs. In retrospect, however, it may be that few adolescents are so heavily involved in leisure activities that they do not have time to use drugs if they so desire. Hirschi (1969) came to a similar conclusion when he examined the relationship between involvement in conventional activities and delinquency. Also, drugs can be used during many leisure activities, such as passive entertainment. It is not uncommon, for example, to consume drugs before a concert or while watching TV. Second, we said that organized leisure activities may prevent drug use because such activities are supervised by conventional adults. In most cases, however, such activities occupy only a small portion of the adolescent's time—once again leaving the adolescent with ample time for drug use.

Third, we said that certain leisure activities may prevent drug use by strengthening the bond to family and school, and by fostering conventional beliefs. The data, however, suggest that most adolescents spend only a small amount of time in leisure activities with parents—perhaps too little time to strengthen ties to parents significantly. The same is true for many adolescents involved in school-related activities. Further, the adolescent's level of involvement in many school-related activities may be marginal. Fourth, we stated that involvement in peer-oriented social activities may increase drug use, since peers may provide the adolescent with drugs and encourage drug use. The amount of time spent in social activities with peers, however, may be less important than the nature of one's peers. Time spent with drug-using peers may significantly increase drug use, while time spent with conventional peers may have little effect on, or reduce, drug use.

Fifth, we stated that leisure activity may reduce drug use by reducing frustration and tension. Many leisure activities, however, may not occur frequently enough to have a meaningful impact on frustration/tension. Further, certain leisure activities—such as dating and competitive sports—may sometimes function as sources of tension in and of themselves. Finally, it must be remembered that drug use is influenced by many factors besides leisure, including a host of variables related to such institutions as the family, school, peer group, religion, and mass media. All these reasons, then, may explain the weak relationship between leisure and drug use. At the same time, it is important to note that certain categories of leisure do bear a weak to moderate relationship to drug use, and that leisure may play a limited role in reducing drug use in carefully constructed programs.

References

Abadinsky, H. (1989). *Drug abuse: An introduction.* Chicago, IL: Nelson-Hall.

Agnew, R., & Petersen, D. M. (1989). Leisure and delinquency. *Social Problems, 36,* 332–350.

Akers, R. L. (1992). *Drugs, alcohol, and society.* Belmont, CA: Wadsworth.

Anson, R. H. (1976). Recreation deviance: Some mainline hypotheses. *Journal of Leisure Research, 8,* 177–80.

Arnold, W. R., & Brungardt, T. M. (1983). *Juvenile misconduct and delinquency.* Boston, MA: Houghton Mifflin.

Blalock, H. J. Jr. (1979). *Social statistics.* New York: McGraw-Hill.

Elifson, K. W., Petersen, D. M., & Hadaway, C. K. (1983). Religiosity and delinquency,. *Criminology, 21,* 505–27.

Elliott, D. S., Huizinga, D., & Ageton, S. S. (1985). *Explaining delinquency and drug use.* Beverly Hills, CA: Sage.

Flanagan, T. J., & Maguire, K. (1990). *Sourcebook of criminal justice statistics—1989.* U. S. Department of Justice, Bureau of Justice Statistics. Washington, DC: USGPO.

Glueck, S., & Glueck, E. (1950). *Unraveling juvenile delinquency.* New York: Commonwealth Fund.

Hirschi, T. (1969). *Causes of delinquency.* Berkeley: University of California Press.

Hirschi, T. (1983). Crime and the family. In J. Q. Wilson (Ed.), *Crime and public policy* (pp. 53–68). San Francisco, CA: Institute for Contemporary Studies.

Johnston, L. (1973). *Drugs and American youth.* Ann Arbor, MI: Institute for Social Research.

Kamali, K., & Steer, R. A. (1976). Polydrug use by high-school students: Involvement and correlates. *International Journal of the Addictions, 11,* 337–343.

Kvaraceus, W. C. (1954). *The community and the delinquent.* Yonkers-on-Hudson, NY: World Book Company.

Landers, D. M., & Landers, D. M. (1978). Socialization via interscholastic athletics: Its effects on delinquency. *Sociology of Education, 51,* 299–303.

Loy, J. W., McPherson, B. D., & Kenyon, G. S. (1978). *Sport and social systems.* Reading, MA: Addison-Wesley.

Nye, I. (1958). *Family relationships and delinquent behavior.* New York: Wiley.

Osgood, D. W., & Yong-Min, S. (1988). *Mundane activities and deviant behavior during late adolescence and early adulthood.* Paper presented at the annual meeting of the Midwest Sociological Society, Minneapolis, MN.

Roberts, K. (1983). *Youth and leisure.* London: George Allen and Unwin.

Schafer, W. E. (1969). Participation in interscholastic athletics and delinquency: A preliminary study. *Social Problems, 17,* 40–47.

Segrave, J. O. (1980). Delinquency and athletics: Review and reformulation. *Journal of Sport Psychology, 2,* 82–89.

Segrave, J. O. (1983). Sport and juvenile delinquency. In R. L. Terjung (Ed.), *Exercise and sport sciences reviews, vol. 11* (pp. 181–209) Philadelphia, PA: Franklin Institute.

Discussion Questions

1. Why would we expect a relationship between drug use and leisure activity?
2. What types of leisure activities do you think would increase drug use, and what types do you think would decrease drug use?
3. Suppose you find that people who participate in sports have lower levels of drug use. Does it *prove* that sports prevent drug use? If not, why not?
4. What advice would you give to a politician who claims that providing more recreational facilities for young people will decrease drug use?

Part III—Race, Ethnicity, and Drug Use

What is the relationship between drug use and ethnic identity? How does ethnic identity affect the consumption of both licit and illicit drugs? How do different racial and ethnic groups respond to drug use? Part III reviews existing current research findings that account for numerous relationships between race, ethnicity and drug use.

We begin by presenting findings that suggest that the amount of drugs used by certain racial and ethnic groups may be linked to physiological features. Following this brief discussion, the following issues are presented in this introductory chapter: (1) the effect of the processes of assimilation and acculturation (culture contact) on drug use within particular ethnic groups, (2) views of drug use by different ethnic groups and how treatment outcomes are affected by these personally held views, (3) racial and ethnic gender differences in the use and abuse of drugs, (4) some of the more consistent research findings regarding ethnic groups that are more likely to use and abuse illicit drugs, and (5) the relationship of minority group members to the use of particular drugs. In summary, this review of the research literature outlines how certain minority group members have greater contact with certain drugs. The final section of this introduction presents the four articles that follow.

Some researchers have found that the physiological responses to drug use vary along racial and ethnic lines. Chan (1986) believes that alcohol sensitivity may be racially linked, and Chi, Kitano et al. (1988) say that when Orientals consume alcohol they are more likely to experience the "flushing response." This response is characterized by sudden and temporary reddening of the face and upper body following consumption of lighter amounts of alcohol. Would this in part explain why Chi, Kitano, et al. (1988) found that Chinese-Americans are more likely to abstain from alcohol than whites?

How do the processes of ethnic acculturation and assimilation affect drug use? The findings show that as immigrants assimilate into our culture, they develop more liberalized attitudes about drinking (Caetano, 1987). In other words, our permissive alcohol-drinking culture affects assimilating immigrants who, prior to their arrival, maintained traditional and restrictive views regarding alcohol consumption.

What effect does the extent of acculturation have on adolescent drug abuse? Humm-Delgado and Delgado (1983) report that when Hispanic parents refuse to modify their ethnic heritage by accepting assimilation, a gap often develops between the "Old World" ethnic parents and their "New World" assimilating offspring. The researchers point out that such adolescents compensate for the gap by abusing drugs. Similarly, Japanese men who retain their native language as their primary language and refuse to assimilate linguistically are more likely to be heavy drinkers (Kitano, 1988). In these examples, the process of either accepting or refusing absorption into the new culture affects drug use. Further, even conflict between the ethnic values of the Old World and the newly formed attitudes of the New World has an impact on drug use.

How do different ethnic groups view alcohol use? The use of alcohol by Mexican-Americans often correlates with the intensity of their attitudes toward *machismo.* These attitudes dictate that it is natural for men to drink and that extensive amounts of alcohol consumption further manhood (Arrendondo, Weddige, et al., 1987). For Mexican-Americans, as well as other ethnic groups who adhere to these values, the positive attitudes surrounding alcohol consumption are culturally ingrained. In effect, such culturally prescribed behavior is often perceived as normal activity.

Cultural support for alcohol ingestion is found at most ethnic festive occasions. For example, it is not unusual to witness an extensive amount of alcohol consumption at weddings and baptisms, and during national holidays. Such practices often contribute to the groups' alcohol problems.

The extent of assimilation often determines whether alcoholism is viewed as an illness or as an uncontrollable habit. For example, lesser assimilated Mexican-Americans may believe that alcohol addiction is either a punishment from God or a destiny dictated by one's fate in life (Arrendondo, Weddige, et al., 1987). Similarly, the more Mexican-Americans are assimilated, the greater the likelihood that they will accept the disease concept of alcoholism.

Why are these beliefs regarding the causes of alcoholism important? Particular beliefs determine attitudes toward rehabilitation. For example, if alcoholism is perceived as an outgrowth of immorality, or a punishment from God, rather than a psychological and physiological addiction, why bother with treatment programs? According to such mystical beliefs, atonement for wrong deeds, not an innovative treatment program, is the cure for alcoholism.

Some evidence for this may be found in the research by Arrendondo, Weddige, et al. (1987), who report that most Mexican-American men enter alcohol treatment involuntarily, often through court orders. In comparing Hispanics with African Americans and whites, Gilchrist, Schinke, et al. (1987) found that Hispanics were less likely to use any voluntary treatment facilities. These findings are supported by Gilbert and Cervantes (1986). Their research shows that Alcoholics Anonymous has had very little success with Mexican-American alcoholics.

How do gender differences affect treatment? Interestingly, one study indicates that maternal drives compel Mexican-American women to seek methadone treatment. Anglin, Hser et al. (1987) report that Mexican-American women often cite pregnancy as a reason for starting treatment. Further, Mexican-American women are more likely to encourage their spouses to seek treatment than Anglo women. While Mexican-American men avoid alcohol treatment because of Old World beliefs and attitudes, Mexican-American women apply these same Old World attitudes differently by seeking methadone treatment to protect their unborn children. Thus, even within the same ethnic group, cultural traits are applied differently and result in very different outcomes across gender lines.

Gender differences in the extent of drug use are also found among whites. Harvey (1985) found that white single women under age 40 are more likely to be heavy drinkers than other women. African American women are more likely than white women to abstain from alcohol use. Further, Herd (1988) found that African American women were more likely to abstain despite socioeconomic standing (SES), age, and marital status. However, the small percentage of African American women who drink heavily begin their heavy drinking at a younger age, and are more likely to drink heavily than women in other groups (Anglin & Booth, 1987; Amaro, Beckman et al., 1987).

Certain ethnic groups have more problems with alcohol than other ethnic groups. Caetano (1987) reports that among Hispanics heavy drinking and alcohol problems occur more often than in the general population, and Caetano reports that these two problems do not decrease with age.

Concerning marijuana use, Cockerham and Alster (1983) report that in comparison to other ethnic groups, the Mexican-American ethnic group they studied was more likely to have tried marijuana. The Mexican-American youth in their study had more favorable attitudes toward marijuana and other drugs and were generally more likely to use drugs. Another study comparing Hispanics with Anglo counterparts showed that the Hispanic youth in a small town had higher rates of having tried marijuana, cigarettes, stimulants, and tranquilizing drugs (Chavez, Beauvais, & Oetting, 1986).

Finally, does membership in a *minority group* increase the chance that drugs will be abused? Lex (1987) found that "Blacks, Hispanics, and American Indians comprise about 20 percent of the U.S. population and are believed to have high rates of alcohol problems." With regard to the drug PCP, Bailey (1987) found that the more typical user is of African American or Hispanic ancestry. American Indian youths also have a greater likelihood of abusing marijuana, inhalants, and stimulants (Beauvais & La Boueff, 1985). Further, although current illicit drug use has been decreasing, more than half of American Indian youths are at risk for drug use (Beauvais, Oetting et al., 1985). Castaneda and Galanter (1988) discovered that Puerto Rican patients had more severe alcohol problems than patients who were of other ethnic stock.

The findings here point to the fact that high levels of addiction and related drug problems are much greater for minority members who experience consistent discrimination. In support of this is a study by Benjamin and Benjamin (1981), who discovered that race was a significant factor with regard to treatment. For example, their research showed that African Americans were "underrepresented in all treatment programs, and the quality of treatment received was not comparable to that received by whites." Finally, it is important to remain aware that the effects of social class have to be taken into account when minority group status and economic deprivation coincide (see Beauvais, Oetting, et al., 1989 for more specific research findings regarding social class and minority group status).

The foregoing research shows that there definitely is a strong relationship between drug use and abuse and race and ethnicity. The four articles comprising Part III will present and discuss additional evidence in support of this interesting relationship. The research in these articles discusses how the relationships among race, ethnicity and drug use are interrelated in unique and interesting ways.

The first article, "Alcohol Consumption Patterns among American Indian and White College Students," by Hughes and Dodder, presents available data on drug use among two cultural groups. The authors administered a questionnaire to 431 white students and 58 American Indian students to compare the drinking behaviors of the two groups. Hughes and Dodder discovered interesting findings. Some of these findings include: how both groups perceive their drinking behavior; their preferred type of drink; places whites, in contrast to American Indians, prefer to drink; reasons why they drink; which group reports more drinking-related problems, and the types of problems reported. One group for example experiences more arrests and disruptions of social relationships and school work, while the other group cites very different problems. The article concludes with a noteworthy finding regarding American Indian women and their drinking patterns.

While this first article compares alcohol use by Native Americans and Caucasians, the next three articles discuss and analyze aspects of drug use in two other minority groups, Chicanos and Mexican Americans. The second article, "Men, Women, and Heroin Use in Two Chicano Gangs," by Moore, looks at gender differences among heroin users. In our discussion above, we found that recent research literature has started reporting on the gender differences that exist with regard to drug use. Moore's timely article focuses on the gender differences among men and women who are addicted to heroin. Throughout her article she includes very interesting excerpts of life histories from women heroin addicts.

Earlier in her research, before she authored this article, Moore and several collaborators did a probability survey study of men and women who had been active gang members during the 1950s and 1970s. Their research showed that during this time, heroin was the "climax" drug in two Los Angeles Chicano gangs. To their surprise, male heroin users and nonusers did not differ much in the characteristics of their families of origin, but among women, the users came from families of origin who had notably more serious problems than those of nonusers. In other words, gang women tended to come from more troubled families than gang men. Similarly, there were few significant differences between male users and nonusers in their roles in the gang, while women users were notably more drug-oriented in the gang than were nonusers. Finally, though there were many similarities between men and women heroin users as they described their lives on heroin, there were also strong differences. Men's heroin use was more peer-oriented, and women's more family-focused: men were more likely to go to prison. Women also were involved with heroin more deeply, and longer, than men. They were more likely to live with an addict and to accelerate their involvement with the heroin lifestyle as they grew older, whereas men on the average, seemed to extricate themselves earlier. Moore points out that it is highly likely that the double standard of morality operative in these communities has an influence on these gender differences in the fate of heroin users.

Why are some of the most severe addiction problems found within minority youth groups? In our review of the literature and discussion above, we found that membership in a disfavored minority group increased the chances of illicit drug use and abuse. In response to this issue, the third article, "Black Male Youth and Drugs: How Racial Prejudice, Parents and Peers Affect Vulnerability," by Ferguson and Jackson, presents three propositions concerning the factors responsible for contributing to the use of drugs by African American male youths.

The first proposition the authors advance is that biased messages and unfair treatment, based on stereotypes of African American male youth as dangerous, dishonest and ignorant, induce some African American youth to become alienated and discouraged about social acceptance and material success in mainstream society. The second proposition is that by weakening bonds to mainstream society, this alienation and discouragement tend to increase the vulnerability of some youth to corrupting peer pressures that encourage involvement with drugs. The third proposition is that to minimize the degree to which race-sex bias and corrupting peer pressures interfere with their healthy development, young African American males need trusting adults. These adults can serve as effective advocates, interpreters, and supervisors in helping them to manage their exposure to and interpretation of race-biased messages, and can help them control their responses to peer pressures that feed on alienation and discouragement—including pressures to use and sell drugs. Ferguson and Jackson also believe that society needs to monitor and modify the discouraging messages that young African American males receive.

Ending Part III with some fireworks is the fourth article, "African American Perspectives on Mobilizing Organizational Responses to Drugs," by Quimby. In a sense, the author reanalyzes the problems of drug use by African American male youth discussed in the article by Ferguson and Jackson, from a broader, macrosociological perspective. Quimby contrasts African American perspectives with official and social science conceptions of substance abuse, drug dealing, and other drug-related crime and violence. A major theme in this research is that both the definition of and the response to "problems" are linked to the larger social structures, culture and power.

Quimby's stimulating article begins by discussing conceptual issues regarding the definitions of substance abuse, followed by epidemiologic data compiled mainly from the National Institute of Drug Abuse on the use of marijuana, cocaine, and other illegal drugs by African Americans. Next, the author identifies and describes competing and contradictory theoretical and ideological descriptions of drug abuse. The author concludes his discussion with the policy implications that are raised by controversies within African American communities over causes of and solutions to drug abuse. This final article raises many questions about what is often referred to as "African American" drug problems. After reading Quimby's article, the reader can easily begin to question whether African American drug problems should more accurately be entitled *American* drug problems.

References

Amaro, H., Beckman, L. J., & Mays, V. M. (1987). A comparison of black and white women entering alcoholism treatment. *Journal of Studies on Alcohol, 48,* 220–228.

Anglin, M. D., Hser Y., & Booth, M. W. (1987). Sex differences in addict careers: Treatment. *American Journal of Drug & Alcohol Abuse, 13,* 253–280.

Arrendondo, R., Weddige, W. L., Justice, C. L., & Fitz, J. (1987). Alcoholism in Mexican-Americans: Intervention and treatment. *Hospital and Community Psychiatry, 38,* 180–183.

Bailey, D. N. (1987). Phencyclidine detection during toxicology testing at a university medical center. *Clinical Toxicology, 25,* 517–526.

Beauvais, F., Oetting, E. R., Wolf, W., & Edward, R. W. (1989). American Indian youth and drugs, 1976–87: A continuing problem. *American Journal of Public Health, 79,* 634–636.

Beauvais, F., & La Boueff, S. (1985). Drug and alcohol abuse intervention in American Indian communities. *The International Journal of Addictions, 20,* 139–171.

Beauvais, F., Oetting, E. R., & Edwards, R. W. (1985). Trends in drug use of Indian adolescents living on reservations: 1975–1983. *American Journal of Drug & Alcohol Abuse, 11,* 209–229.

Benjamin, R., & Benjamin, M. (1981). Sociocultural correlates of black drinking. *Journal of Studies on Alcohol. Supplement #9*(9), 241–245.

Caetano, R. (1987). Acculturation and attitudes toward appropriate drinking among U. S. Hispanics. *Alcohol and Alcoholism, 22,* 427–435.

Caetano, R. (1984). Ethnicity and drinking in Northern California: A comparison among whites, blacks, and hispanics. *Alcohol and Alcoholism, 19,* 31–44.

Castaneda, R., & Galanter, M. (1988). Ethnic differences in drinking practices and cognitive impairment among detoxifying alcoholics. *Journal of Studies on Alcohol, 49,* 335–339.

Chan, A. W. K. (1986). Racial differences in alcohol sensitivity. *Alcohol and Alcoholism 21,* 93–104.

Chavez, E., Beauvais, F., & Oetting, E. R. (1986). Drug use by small town Mexican American youth: A pilot study. *Hispanic Journal of Behavioral Science, 8,* 243–258.

Chi, I., Kitano, H. H. L., & Lubben, J. E. (1988). Male Chinese drinking behavior in Los Angeles. *Journal of Studies on Alcohol, 49,* 21–25.

Cockerham, W. C., & Alster, J. M. (1983). A comparison of marijuana use among Mexican-American and Anglo rural youth utilizing a matched set analysis. *International Journal of the Addictions, 18,* 759–767.

Gilbert, M. J., & Cervantes, R. C. (1986). Alcohol services for Mexican-Americans: A review of utilization patterns, treatment considerations, and prevention activities. *Hispanic Journal of Behavioral Sciences, 8,* 191–223.

Gilchrist, L. D., Schinke, S. P., Trimble, J. B., & Cvetkovich, G. T. (1987). Skills enhancement to prevent substance abuse among American Indian adolescents. *International Journal of Addictions, 22,* 869–879.

Harvey, W. B. (1985). Alcohol abuse and the black community: A contemporary analysis. *Journal of Drug Issues, 5,* 81–91.

Herd, D. (1988). Drinking by black and white women: Results from a national survey. *Social Problems, 35,* 493–505.

Humn-Delgado, D., & Delgado, M. (1983). Hispanic adolescents and substance abuse: Issues for the 1980s. *Child and Youth Services, 6,* 71–87.

Kitano, H. H. L., Lubben, J. E., & Chi, I. (1988). Predicting Japanese-American drinking behavior. *International Journal of the Addictions, 23,* 417–428.

Lex, B. W. (1987). Review of alcohol problems in ethnic minority groups. *Journal of Consulting and Clinical Psychology, 55,* 293–300.

Alcohol Consumption Patterns Among American Indian and White College Students

Stella P. Hughes   Richard A. Dodder

Stella P. Hughes is Professor of Sociology at the South Dakota School of Mines and Technology, Rapid City, South Dakota. She has been involved in funded research projects dealing with cultural and ethnic drinking patterns, minimum drinking-age laws, juvenile justice and juvenile delinquency, victim-offender mediation, science and engineering career opportunities for American Indian children, and lowering the infant mortality rate among American Indian children.

Richard A. Dodder received his Ph.D. from the University of Kansas and is now a Professor of Sociology and of Statistics at Oklahoma State University. He has recently been involved in funded research examining the impact of legislation changing the age from 18 to 21 for the purchase and consumption of alcoholic beverages, evaluating the impact of a community-wide alcohol education program, and examining the process of deinstitutionalization of the developmentally disabled. In addition, his research interests include international comparative research, particularly in Central Europe, sociology of sport, crime, and delinquency, and the quality of research methodology.

North American Indians have received a great deal of attention in relation to how they perceive and use alcoholic beverages. From the earliest stages of the white man's settlement, historians have described Indians as having a craving for alcohol, being ill-equipped to handle it, and being inclined toward violent, destructive, and antisocial behavior when drinking (MacAndrew & Edgerton, 1969). The literature seems to indicate that alcohol-related problems among Indians are becoming even more widespread. In 1960, for example, federal crime statistics showed that a greater proportion of Indians than of other ethnic groups were arrested for all alcohol-related offenses (Steward, 1964). In 1972, 21.3 percent of white arrests, but 61.8 percent of Indian arrests, were for drunkenness (Cockerham, 1977).

It has been suggested that statistics of this nature could be influenced by differential arrest rates. Forslund and Meyers (1974), for example, found the delinquency rate among reservation youth to be nearly five times the national average, but a majority of court appearances were for "relatively minor offenses," and a large proportion were alcohol-related. On the other hand, Indian health statistics paint a somewhat different picture. The death rate from cirrhosis of the liver increased from 14.2 deaths per 100,000 population in 1955 to 42.5 deaths per 100,000 in 1975 and was the fourth leading cause of death among Indians in that year (U.S. Health Services Administration, 1978). In 1975, accidents were the leading cause of Indian deaths (156.4 per 100,000 population); the majority of these were motor-vehicle-related, many involving alcohol.

Reprinted with permission from the *Journal of Studies on Alcohol,* vol. 45, pp. 433–39, 1984.

Several theoretical explanations for Indian drinking behavior have been proposed, some of them substantiated by research. Early interpretations suggested that physiological differences made this group less tolerant of alcohol; in recent years, research along this line has been revived. Some investigators (Farris & Jones, 1978; Fenna et al., 1971) reported that Indians metabolized alcohol more slowly than whites. Bennion and Li (1976), however, found no differences between the metabolic rates of the two groups. Wolff (1972) examined facial flushing as a result of drinking and concluded that some Indians exhibited vasomotor characteristics not found among whites.

The psychological aspects of Indian drinking have also been investigated. Using the Minnesota Multiphasic Personality Inventory (MMPI), Kline et al. (1973) compared Indian and white alcoholics and found the Indians to have higher personality disturbance scores. Uecker et al. (1980), however, reported no differences in MMPI scores between Indians and whites. Social variables such as stress, anomie, or anxiety have also been implicated. For example, Maynard (1969) identified stress as a factor in Indian drinking, and Littman (1970) suggested that Indian alcoholism could be the result of anomie, or of conflicts arising from rural-urban transition. Lemert (1956) concluded that Indian drinking could be an expression of anxiety.

A third group of researchers has studied the cultural aspects of Indian drinking behavior. Some authors (DuToit, 1964; Lemert, 1956) have indicated that Indian drinking may have positive functions in that it helps integrate individuals into intimate groups or replaces lost social institutions. Lurie (1971) postulated Indian drinking to be a means of protesting against the white culture and of validating Indian-ness. Price (1975), however, related problem drinking among Indians to a breakdown of traditional cultural controls. Stratton et al. (1978) reported eastern Oklahoma tribes to have lower rates of both alcohol-related arrests and deaths than did those from western Oklahoma. They attributed this to differences in tribal culture and to the fact that eastern Indians had become farmers and merchants at an earlier stage in their history than western tribes, which more recently had experienced the culture shock of entering the white world. These authors maintained that drinking among western tribes could be a "retreatist or escapist response to acculturational stress" (p. 1171).

A great deal of variation in drinking incidence has been cited among American collegians. The initial study of Straus and Bacon (1953) found a range of from 20 percent among some women to 98 percent among some men. In a survey of 37 colleges across the U.S., Hanson (1977) reported an average drinking incidence of 83.5 percent. Wechsler and McFadden (1979) indicated that abstainers comprised less than five percent of their sample from 34 New England schools. Since methodologies often differed, comparisons must be viewed with caution, but it can be noted that some variables, such as region of the country or population density, appear to have an impact on drinking incidence.

Although many of the seminal studies on alcohol use (e.g., Straus & Bacon, 1953) have been with college populations, little research has been conducted on Indian students in this context. No known studies have examined only those Indian collegians who identify culturally with their native heritage and tend to practice its traditions. Strimbu et al. (1973) analyzed drug use among over 20,000 southeastern college students, 74 of whom were Indians, and found Indian students to report a high incidence of both drug and alcohol use. The degree of cultural identity among this group, however, was not known.

The literature concerning Indian drinking behavior has been inconsistent and does not lend itself to predictive hypotheses. Explanations of Indian drinking have been varied, and have dealt with such topics as Indian youth, Indians on reservations, or those in alcoholism treatment programs. Few studies have examined Indian collegians, and the drinking patterns of Indian students who are involved in their native culture have been neglected. The purpose of this research, therefore, is to compare drinking behavior of culturally active Indian collegians with the activities of white students in the same environment.

Method

Data were collected from the student body of Oklahoma State University during the spring semester of 1981. The on-campus enrollment at the university was

20,739 (58.2% men and 41.8% women), and Indian enrollment was 329 (59.1% men and 40.9% women). The state of Oklahoma has one of the largest Indian populations in the U.S. (Bahr et al., 1979), but the proportion who identify with their native culture is not known. Indian students were identified for the present survey by an Indian who was able to separate the "cultural" Indians (those who considered themselves to be Indian, attended Indian tribal or cultural functions, and associated with other Indians) from those who identified primarily with the majority society. Sixty students were so designated and completed self-administered questionnaires. It was estimated that this group comprised nearly the entire known population of "cultural" Indian students at the university.

The tribes represented were largely from central Oklahoma (Pawnee, Ponca, Kaw, Tonkawa, and Otoe-Missouria). All respondents were at least one-quarter Indian, and the majority had one-half or more Indian heritage. These tribes originated in the central part of the U.S. and in cultural orientation were considered Prairie Indians. They lived in areas in which a sedentary living pattern was possible, but would seasonally assume the lifestyle of the Plains Indians and follow the buffalo. In acculturation to the white society, they more closely resemble the Plains Indians from the western part of Oklahoma than tribes from the eastern part of the state (Howard, 1978).

The sample of white students (N = 500) was obtained from self-administered questionnaires completed in a random selection of 14 introductory sociology classes. The original sample included 46 non-white and foreign students but they were eliminated from the data analysis. Seven of the 46 were Indian students, and they were also excluded since it could not be determined whether they identified with the white or Indian culture.

The white cohort tended to be fairly young, with a mean age of 19.2 and was largely freshman. There were slightly more women (59.6%) than men. Most (96.8%) were single, almost half (46.9%) came from communities with populations of over 50,000, and 72.2 percent reported higher parental occupational prestige. The mean age for Indians was 23.4, and they indicated a more bell-shaped distribution over year in school. More than half (56.7%) of the Indians were men, 30 percent were married, 61.7 percent came from communities with populations of under 50,000, and 78.3 percent reported lower parental occupational prestige.

Approximately three-fourths of both samples declared either business or arts and sciences as a major. Somewhat more Indian students than whites were in agriculture and education and fewer were in engineering and home economics. In grade-point average, Indians were more inclined to be average students, a smaller number reporting both higher and lower grades. Descriptions of the sample apply to both drinkers and abstainers, but data analysis was conducted on drinkers only—431 white and 58 Indian students.

Since these Indians probably constituted most of the population of "cultural" Indians, it was concluded that some of the demographic differences, particularly those of age, were due not so much to sampling procedures, but to the fact that this group was essentially different from the more typical college student population. Indians tends to be rural in background and as a group are economically deprived (Brinker & Klos, 1976). Indian collegians enter college at a later age for a variety of reasons, perhaps for financial or family considerations.

Results

Quantity and Frequency of Drinking

Quantity and frequency information was elicited from a slightly modified form of the questionnaire used by Jessor et al. (1968). Students were asked six questions regarding their alcohol consumption—how often, on the average, they usually drank beer, wine, and distilled spirits, and how many drinks of beer, wine, and distilled spirits they usually had at any one time. Answers for quantity ranged from "none" to "over six drinks at any one time" and for frequency, from "never" to "daily." These were dichotomized at the 50 percent mark to obtain a chi-square statistic. With abstainers identified as those who answered "none" or "never" to all six questions, 86.2 percent of white and 96.7 percent of Indian students were classified as drinkers ($\chi^2 = 5.30$, 1 df, $p = .02$). For men, 89.6 percent of whites, and all Indians were classified as drinkers ($\chi^2 = 3.88$, 1 df, $p = .05$), and for women these figures were 83.9 percent of whites and 92.3 percent of Indians. The mean age for beginning to drink was 16.0 for whites and 17.5 for Indians.

White and Indian students, as a whole, were not strikingly different in quantity and frequency of alcohol consumption, although in most cases, whites reported drinking more alcohol and doing so more often than Indians (Table 1). The only exception to this trend was in both quantity and frequency of beer consumption, in which the percentage of Indians in the high categories exceeded those of whites. Whites, however, had a significantly higher quantity and frequency of distilled spirits consumption.

When whites and Indians together were examined by sex, several differences were noted, four of these significant: Although women drank wine more often than did men, men exceeded women by a significant margin in quantity and frequency of beer consumption and quantity of distilled spirits consumption. This seems to indicate that the whites and Indians in this sample were similar to samples from other studies, both collegiate and nationwide, since almost all researchers have reported a higher rate of drinking among men (Cahalan & Cisin, 1968; Engs, 1977; Gallup, 1980; Straus & Bacon, 1953).

Comparisons between white and Indian men as well as between white and Indian women showed similar trends. In all but beer drinking, white students of both sexes indicated a higher quantity and frequency of consumption than Indians, the differences for distilled spirits being significant for quantity in both sexes and for frequency in men. A comparison of the percentages of students in the high categories indicated that beer was the most popular drink for both whites and Indians and for both men and women; relatively few reported drinking wine.

Drinking Locations

Frequencies of drinking in each of eight locations are shown in Table 2. Since these variables were dichotomized at the midpoint (ranging from "never" to "very often"), percentages do not reflect the number of times that respondents drank in the given location but the frequency with which they drank there more often. In general, a somewhat greater difference between white and Indian students was found when drinking locations were considered but, again, a higher percentage of white students reported drinking in most places. White students drank significantly more often in nightclubs or bars, in restaurants and in parked cars.

Again, drinking was more frequent among men and, when men and women were examined by ethnicity, some interesting differences emerged. White men drank more often than Indian men in all locations, four of which were significant — nightclubs or bars, restau-

Table 1
Drinking Quantity and Frequency by Ethnicity and Sex, in Percent, with Percentages Given Only for the High Categories of Each Variable

		Ethnicity			Sex			Men only			Women only		
	Total (N=439)	Whites (431)	Indians (58)	x^2	Men (215)	Women (274)	x^2	Whites (181)	Indians (34)	x^2	Whites (250)	Indians (24)	x^2
Quantity													
Beer	66.9	65.9	74.1	1.57	79.5	56.9	21.78*	79.6	79.4	0.00	56.0	66.7	1.02
Wine	25.6	26.9	15.5	3.49	27.0	24.5	0.40	29.3	14.7	3.09	25.2	16.7	0.86
Distilled Spirits	48.4	51.8	22.8	16.88*	55.1	43.0	7.05*	61.1	23.5	16.33*	45.0	21.7	4.64*
Frequency													
Beer	55.2	53.8	65.5	2.83	69.3	44.2	30.80*	68.5	73.5	0.34	43.2	54.2	1.07
Wine	18.8	20.0	10.3	3.09	14.4	22.3	4.85*	16.0	5.9	2.39	22.8	16.7	0.48
Distilled Spirits	32.6	35.1	13.8	10.58*	32.1	33.0	0.04	35.9	11.8	7.66*	34.5	16.7	3.16

*$P < .05$.

Table 2
Frequency of Drinking Locations by Ethnicity and Sex, in Percent, with Percentages Given Only for the High Categories of Each Variable

		Ethnicity			Sex			Men only			Women only		
	Total	Whites	Indians	x^2	Men	Women	x^2	Whites	Indians	x^2	Whites	Indians	x^2
Residence halls	48.1	49.8	36.2	3.76	51.4	45.6	1.62	53.4	41.2	1.70	47.2	29.2	2.86
Own home	41.4	40.0	51.8	2.85	52.7	32.6	19.37*	53.2	50.0	0.12	30.6	54.6	5.26*
Night clubs, bars, etc.	45.4	48.7	20.7	16.18*	49.3	42.3	2.37	55.9	14.7	19.37*	43.6	29.2	1.86
Restaurants	65.8	67.7	51.7	5.78*	68.5	63.6	1.30	73.2	44.1	11.20*	63.7	62.5	0.01
Friend's home	60.6	59.7	67.2	1.21	65.7	56.6	4.15*	65.9	64.7	0.02	55.2	70.8	2.17
City parks	37.8	38.3	34.5	0.31	52.4	26.5	33.96*	54.5	41.2	2.03	26.6	25.0	0.03
City streets	27.3	28.4	19.0	2.29	39.2	18.0	26.83*	42.1	23.5	4.15*	18.6	12.5	0.54
Parked cars	54.0	56.7	34.5	10.15*	65.4	45.2	19.49*	70.6	38.2	13.22*	46.8	29.2	2.74

*$P < .05$.

rants, city streets, and parked cars. Indian women drank significantly more often than white women in their own homes. In total reported frequencies, Indian women were closer to Indian men than white women were to white men. In no instance did white women report a higher frequency than white men, but Indian women drank more often than Indian men in three locations—at home, in restaurants, and in the homes of friends.

Reasons for Drinking

Questions on reasons for drinking followed Cahalan and Cisin's (1968) model and were divided into three response areas: social reasons, hedonistic reasons, and escapist reasons (Table 3). Cahalan and Cisin reported that the escapist reasons constituted a Guttman scale with a reproducibility of 0.96. A prior factor analysis with this questionnaire had indicated the same divisions, and all items were found to load well on the three distinct orthogonal factors. A twelfth item, drinking to "get high," was included in the questionnaire but not in the scales. These responses also ranged from "never" to "very often" and were dichotomized at the 50 percent point. The trend for white students to surpass Indians was considerably less apparent in reasons for drinking; for half of the reasons, a larger percentage of Indians appeared in the high categories. Whites reported drinking more often for hedonistic reasons, whereas Indians tended to cite social and escapist reasons. Whites reported drinking significantly more often to celebrate special occasions, for enjoyment of taste, and for a sense of well-being or to feel good, whereas Indians reported drinking more often to improve appetite for food and to "get high."

Men reported drinking more often than women for every reason, significantly so for seven of the 12 reasons. The effects of ethnicity by sex remained somewhat similar to the effects of ethnicity in the sample. That is, white men reported drinking significantly more often than Indian men to celebrate special occasions, for enjoyment of taste, to feel good, to relax, and to be sociable. Indian men, on the other hand, drank significantly more than white men to "get high."

Although white men reported more frequent drinking than Indian men for most reasons, the opposite was true of women. Indian women indicated significantly more drinking than did white women only to improve appetite for food and to "get high."

Problem Drinking

Questions regarding problem drinking were taken from research by Engs (1977), and responses again ranged from "never" to "very often." Respondents were asked how often their drinking had led to the 12

Table 3
Reasons for Drinking by Ethnicity and Sex, in Percent, with Percentages Given Only for the High Categories of Each Variable

		Ethnicity			Sex			Men only			Women only		
	Total	Whites	Indians	x^2	Men	Women	x^2	Whites	Indians	x^2	Whites	Indians	x^2
SOCIAL REASONS													
Get along better on dates or other social occasions	54.3	54.2	55.2	0.02	65.0	46.0	17.42*	66.1	58.8	0.67	45.6	50.0	0.17
Be sociable	49.0	50.0	41.4	1.52	53.7	45.2	3.48	57.2	35.3	5.53*	44.8	50.0	0.24
Friends drink	61.7	61.0	67.2	0.85	65.4	58.8	2.21	66.1	61.8	0.24	57.3	75.0	2.84
Adult thing to do	22.7	21.8	29.8	1.87	34.9	13.3	31.50*	35.2	33.3	0.04	12.2	25.0	3.14
HEDONISTIC REASONS													
Celebrate	54.5	57.2	34.5	10.67*	54.7	54.4	0.00	60.6	23.5	15.82*	54.8	50.0	0.21
Enjoyment of taste	38.5	41.2	19.0	10.63*	47.9	31.3	13.86*	53.1	20.6	12.09*	32.7	16.7	2.61
Feel good	48.7	50.8	32.8	6.67*	53.6	44.9	3.60	57.6	32.4	7.33*	46.0	33.3	1.41
Get drunk	58.1	59.1	50.9	1.38	67.1	51.1	12.52*	69.5	54.2	2.82	51.6	45.8	0.29
ESCAPIST REASONS													
Help relax	61.7	63.1	51.7	2.79	65.4	58.8	2.21	68.9	47.1	6.02*	58.9	58.3	0.00
Relieve aches, pains or fatigue	30.0	29.2	36.2	1.19	38.3	23.5	12.46*	38.9	35.3	0.16	22.2	37.5	2.86
Improve appetite	21.4	19.7	34.5	6.65*	33.2	12.2	31.31*	32.2	38.2	0.47	10.5	29.2	7.11*
GET HIGH	47.2	44.0	70.7	14.59*	61.1	36.4	29.18*	57.6	79.4	5.70*	34.3	58.3	5.47*

*$P < .05$.

problems listed in Table 4. Variables were dichotomized into those who reported that they had never experienced the problem and those who reported that they had. Therefore, the percentages reflect frequencies with which the particular behaviors were actually reported.

In many areas of problem behavior, white and Indian students indicated quite similar responses, but a somewhat greater percentage of Indians appeared in the high categories of seven of the 12 problems. The significant differences, though, were more often in areas in which whites reported greater difficulties. Whites significantly more often reported nausea or vomiting, drinking and driving, and behavior that was later regretted. Indians significantly more often reported being arrested and thinking that they had a drinking problem.

Men indicated a higher frequency of problem behavior than did women, most differences being significant. White men generally reported more problem behavior than Indian men. Only in arrests and in being criticized by a date did Indian men indicate more problems than white men, and these differences were not significant. Reported significantly more often by white men were the problems of nausea or vomiting, interference with school or work, drinking and driving, damaging property, and behavior that was later regretted.

Differences between white and Indian women, however, were mostly in the opposite direction. With the exception of nausea or vomiting, and drinking and driving, Indian women indicated higher frequencies than did white women. Two of these were significant: interference with school or work and concern about a drinking problem. White women reported fewer problems than white men in every area, but Indian women exceeded Indian men in over half of the problem areas. In total incidence of reported problems, white men indicated a mean of 47.7 percent, Indian women 39.9 percent, Indian men 36.3 percent and white women 31.4 percent.

Discussion

The present study was exploratory in nature and involved a limited number of Indian tribes in only one state. Therefore, caution must be used in generalizing beyond these data.

The historical description presented by MacAndrew and Edgerton (1969) of Indians craving alcohol, being unable to handle it and exhibiting destructive behavior while drinking did not appear to fit these Indian collegians; in many respects, they reported drinking patterns quite similar to those of the white students.

Table 4
Problem Drinking by Ethnicity and Sex, in Percent

	Ethnicity				Sex			Men only			Women only		
	Total	Whites	Indians	x^2	Men	Women	x^2	Whites	Indians	x^2	Whites	Indians	x^2
Hangover	68.5	68.9	65.5	0.27	72.4	65.4	2.64	75.0	58.8	3.73	64.5	75.0	1.06
Nausea or vomiting	62.6	64.4	50.0	4.51*	66.7	59.6	2.56	71.0	44.1	9.28*	59.7	58.3	0.02
Blacking out	31.3	30.7	36.2	0.73	34.3	20.0	1.51	34.7	32.4	0.07	27.8	41.7	2.04
Interference with school or work	35.1	34.9	36.2	0.04	44.8	27.6	15.38*	48.3	26.5	5.49*	25.4	50.0	6.63*
Human relations	39.6	39.2	43.1	0.33	42.9	37.1	1.62	44.3	35.3	0.95	35.5	54.2	3.27
Drinking and driving	55.2	57.1	41.4	5.08*	67.6	45.6	23.26*	71.6	47.1	7.38*	46.8	33.3	1.59
Arrested for drunken driving or public intoxication	5.2	4.3	12.1	6.35*	10.5	1.1	21.17*	9.1	17.7	2.22	0.8	4.2	2.27
Criticized by date	24.3	23.1	32.8	2.58	32.9	17.7	14.92*	31.8	38.2	0.53	16.9	25.0	0.98
Fighting	31.0	30.3	36.2	0.84	40.0	24.0	14.19*	40.3	38.2	0.05	23.1	33.3	1.26
Damaging property	21.2	21.9	15.5	1.26	38.6	7.7	67.61*	42.1	20.6	5.54*	7.7	8.3	0.01
Regretting behavior	62.0	63.6	50.0	4.00*	67.9	57.4	5.62*	72.6	44.1	10.58*	57.3	58.3	0.01
Drinking problem	21.5	19.7	34.5	6.64*	32.1	13.3	24.68*	32.0	32.4	0.00	10.9	37.5	13.41*

$^*P < .05$.

Some interesting differences, however, can be noted. A higher percentage of Indian students were classified as drinkers but they tended to begin drinking at a later age. In quantity and frequency of drinking, whites drank more wine and distilled spirits, but Indians more beer. This was particularly surprising given the mean age of the two samples. At the time of this survey, the legal age in Oklahoma for drinking wine and distilled spirits was 21, but 18 year olds could purchase and drink beer containing 3.2 percent alcohol. In this study, however, the Indian students drank more beer even though the majority of them were of legal age to purchase wine and distilled spirits, and the white students drank more wine and distilled spirits even though they were largely under the legal age for purchasing these beverages.

White students tended to drink more in public places, but Indians in homes or restaurants. Whites reported drinking more often for hedonistic reasons, but Indians cited more social and escapist reasons. Indian students drank most often to "get high." The incidences of problem behavior for whites and Indians were fairly high and of about equal value. White men indicated the highest mean percentage of problems, followed by Indian women, Indian men and white women. It is not too surprising that over half experienced some of the behaviors (e.g., having a hangover), but the percentages of both whites and Indians who reported blacking out from drinking appear excessive in light of the contention that this phenomenon could be indicative of future alcoholism (Straus & Bacon, 1953). This could only lend emphasis to recent concern over drinking patterns of our nation's youth.

The commonly held stereotype of the American Indian drinking in city parks was not upheld by this research, since these Indian students appeared to be considerably less visible than whites in their drinking locations. The Indian students were also less inclined to report drinking and driving, fighting after drinking, or damaging property—all highly visible and socially censured behaviors. A surprising finding in this context, therefore, was the relatively high arrest rate for Indian students. Forslund and Meyers (1974) reported a disproportionate arrest rate among reservation youth, and our research supported these findings among culturally active Indian collegians. This might suggest that law enforcement has not been uniformly applied and that the mere fact of being an Indian, particularly a male Indian, is influential in the decision to arrest.

Cahalan and Cisin (1968) previously suggested that individuals who drink for escapist reasons are more inclined toward problems associated with drinking, and Stratton et al. (1978) indicated that these reasons could be important in Indian drinking patterns, contentions somewhat substantiated by the present study. The incidence of escapist drinking for the Oklahoma Indian collegians somewhat paralleled the mean problem percentage; i.e., white men reported the highest rate of escapist drinking, followed by Indian men, Indian women, and white women. Drinking to "get high" could also be a reflection of escapist drinking, and Indian students in the present study, both men and women, reported this reason significantly more often than whites.

Another surprising finding was the relatively high frequency of problem drinking in Indian women and the fact that many of the drinking patterns reported by this group are not those normally associated with problematic behavior. Indian women drank somewhat more beer than white women but less than either white or Indian men, and the differences were not significant. They drank more often in homes or restaurants and less often in bars, parks, or other areas that are commonly associated with less moderate drinking. They cited escapist reasons for drinking more often than white women but less often than white or Indian men. Nevertheless, this group indicated the highest response rate in four of the 12 problem areas and exceeded Indian men in three other areas. Of particular significance were the problems of blacking out, interference with school or work, and difficulties in human relations—areas often considered more serious and more suggestive of future alcoholism. These Indian women students may also have had some perception of this trend since they expressed the most concern of all the subjects that they might have a drinking problem.

Clearly, additional research is needed to explain some of these differences, particularly in regard to Indian women. The effects of changing women's roles, variables such as anomie or powerlessness, perceptions of job discrimination, or differing approaches to family socialization could be investigated in relation to alcohol consumption patterns. Also, further examination of the reasons behind the Indian affinity for drinking to "get high" might shed some light on problem drinking in this context.

Acknowledgment

We thank Mildred Hudson of the Otoe-Missouria Tribal Agency, Red Rock, Oklahoma, for her invaluable assistance in polling the American Indian student sample.

References

Bahr, H. M., Chadwick, B. A., & Stauss, J. H. (1979). *American ethnicity.* Lexington, MA: D.C. Heath Co.

Bennion, L. J., & Li, T. K. (1976). Alcohol metabolism in American Indians and whites: Lack of racial differences in metabolic rate and liver alcohol dehydrogenase. *New England Journal of Medicine, 294,* 9–13.

Brinker, P. A., & Klos, J. J. (1976). *Poverty, manpower, and social security.* Austin, TX: Lone Star Publications, Inc.

Cahalan, D., & Cisin, I. H. (1968). American drinking practices: Summary of findings from a national probability sample. 1. Extent of drinking by population subgroups. *Quarterly Journal of Studies on Alcohol, 29,* 130–151.

Cockerham, W. C. (1977). Patterns of alcohol and multiple drug use among rural white and American Indian adolescents. *International Journal of Addictions, 12,* 271–285.

DuToit, B. M. (1964). Substitution: A process in cultural change. *Human Organization, 23,* 16–23.

Engs, R. C. (1977). Drinking patterns and drinking problems of college students. *Journal of Studies on Alcohol, 38,* 2144–2156.

Farris, J. J., & Jones, B. M. (1978). Ethanol metabolism and memory impairment in American Indian and white women social drinkers. *Journal of Studies on Alcohol, 39,* 1975–1979.

Fenna, D., Mix, L., Schaefer, O., & Gilbert, J. A. L. (1971). Ethanol metabolism in various racial groups. *Canadian Medical Association Journal, 105,* 472–475.

Forslund, M. A., & Meyers, R. E. (1974). Delinquency among Wind River Indian Reservation youth. *Criminology, 12,* 97–106.

Gallup, G. H. (1980). *The Gallup Poll.* Wilmington, DE: Scholarly Resources, Inc.

Hanson, D. J. (1977). Trends in drinking attitudes and behaviors among college students. *Journal of Alcohol and Drug Education. 22,* 17–22.

Howard, J. (1978). *North American Indian cultures independent & correspondent study,* Stillwater, OK: Oklahoma State University.

Jessor, R., Graves, T. D., Hanson, R. C., & Jessor, S. L. (1968). *Society, personality and deviant behavior.* New York: Holt, Rinehart & Winston, Inc.

Kline, J. A., Rozynko, V. V., Flint, G., & Roberts, A. C. (1973). Personality characteristics of male Native American alcoholic patients. *International Journal of Addictions, 8,* 729–732.

Lemert, E. M. (1956). Alcoholism: Theory, problem and challenge. III. Alcoholism and the sociocultural situation. *Quarterly Journal of Studies on Alcohol, 17,* 306–317.

Littman, G. (1970). Alcoholism, illness, and social pathology among American Indians in transition. *American Journal of Public Health, 60,* 1769–1778.

Lurie, N. O. (1971). The world's oldest on-going protest demonstration: North American Indian drinking patterns. *Pacific Historical Review, 40,* 311–332.

MacAndrew, C., & Edgerton, R. B. (1969). *Drunken comportment: A social explanation.* Chicago, IL: Aldine Publishing Co., Inc.

Maynard, E. (1969). Drinking as a part of an adjustment syndrome among the Oglala Sioux. *Pine Ridge Research Bulletin. S.D., 9,* 35–51.

Price, J. A. (1975). An applied analysis of North American Indian drinking patterns. *Human Organization 34,* 17–26.

Steward, C. (1964). Questions regarding American Indian criminality. *Human Organization, 23,* 61–66.

Stratton, R., Zeiner, A., & Paredes, A. (1978). Tribal affiliation and prevalence of alcohol problems. *Journal of Studies on Alcohol, 39,* 1166–1177.

Straus, R., & Bacon, S. D. (1953). *Drinking in college.* New Haven, CT: Yale University Press.

Strimbu, J. L., Schoenfeldt, L. F., & Sims, O. S. Jr. (1973). Drug usage in college students as a function of racial classification and minority group status. *Research in Higher Education, 1,* 263–272.

Uecker, A. E., Boutilier, L. R., & Richardson, E. H. (1980). Indianism and MMPI scores of men alcoholics. *Journal of Studies on Alcohol, 41,* 357–362.

U. S. Health Services Administration. (1978). *Indian health trends and services*. Washington, DC: U. S. Government Printing Office.

Wechsler, H., & McFadden, M. (1979). Drinking among college students in New England: Extent, social correlates and consequences of alcohol use. *Journal of Studies on Alcohol, 40,* 96–996.

Wolff, P. H. (1972). Ethnic differences in alcohol sensitivity. *Science, 175,* 449–450.

Discussion Questions:

1. What type of methodology was used in gathering information for this study? Was the selection of respondents strictly random? If not, how might this have influenced the results?
2. What social or cultural factors might account for the finding that there were more abstainers among white than Indian students?
3. What factors might account for the higher rate of arrests for drinking-related activities among Indian students in this study?
4. Why do you think Indian students reported drinking more for escape reasons, and white students for hedonistic reasons?

Men, Women, and Heroin Use in Two Chicano Gangs

Joan Moore

Joan Moore, Professor of Sociology at the University of Wisconsin-Milwaukee, has done research and published on poverty in minority communities—especially Chicano—and on gangs and drug use. She is the author of *Homeboys: Gangs, Drugs and Prison in the Barrios of Los Angeles* (1987), and of *Going Down to the Barrio: Homeboys and Homegirls in Change* (1992), and co-editor of volumes on drugs in Hispanic communities, on the effect of immigration on American minorities, and on the extent to which the underclass paradigm applies to poor Latino communities.

In the 1980s, gangs again became a major focus of media and public policy attention. They seemed to show up in all kinds of "new" cities, and one might reasonably think that they were, in fact, new on the national scene (Needle & Stapleton, 1983). But in some places, as for example in many Chicano neighborhoods in East Los Angeles, gangs have been institutionalized for more than 45 years. When the gangs first appeared there, shortly before World War II, they were composed of young people from conventional—even traditional—Mexican families. Although some of their families may have had problems, this was by no means true for all of them. The gangs fought and used drugs at parties; some members were involved in delinquent acts. Police harassed them, and some members went into juvenile facilities.

As the members aged, the original cliques splintered into yet other sub-cliques. Some members got married and settled down, while others remained involved in a street lifestyle which centered on heroin and prison. Those *veteranos* who were enmeshed in the street lifestyle, with periodic time in prison, almost always perpetuated the old gang ties, which are of prime value both in prison and in the marginal life of the streets. Thus, as the gangs evolved, many of their members turned to heroin and to what has been called a *cholo* lifestyle that could well be described as deviant. Gangs have been in existence for so long that they have developed a subculture. There are special values. For example, members are supposed to be *loco,* or wild. This wildness may be expressed in willingness to use drugs, in willingness to fight fiercely, or in "being game for anything," accepting any challenge. Members are supposed to be completely committed to the gang: "all for their barrio." There are also symbolic markers of *cholismo;* gang members often dress in special ways, and use a special English-Spanish slang called *calo* (Vigil, 1988).

In any community, whether they are institutionalized or not, youth gangs represent the rowdiest of the adolescent peer groups—most likely to fight, to use drugs, and to be sexually active. As such, they are classic loci for the study of drug use, since adolescence and peer groups are generally considered to be of prime importance in initiating drug use (Elliott et al., 1985; Jessor et al., 1980; Kandel, 1985). In fact, drugs, including hard drugs, have been endemic in these gangs for a long time.

In the late 1980s, cocaine and crack were the publicized drug plagues of poor communities. However, Chicanos in the gangs we studied had been faithful to heroin as a "climax" drug ever since its introduction in the 1950s, and continued to focus on the drug even into the 1990s. In fact, in the Southwest there was a little-publicized but serious heroin epidemic in the late 1980s, with heroin-related deaths escalating dramatically during the decade (Crider et al., 1989). And, not surprisingly, heroin continued to be by far the most serious drug for our respondents when they were interviewed in the late 1980s.

However, not all people in these gangs use drugs. The stereotype of a coercive gang drug culture is not valid. In particular, not all members use hard drugs, such as heroin or cocaine. It is important, then, to see how drug users are different from non-drug-using gang members when both groups function inside a strongly drug-oriented subculture.

We will look at three sets of factors. The first relates to family of origin. Gangs, according to the stereotype, are composed primarily of youth escaping particularly serious family problems. Are the hard drug users the ones from the most disturbed families?

Our second question relates to the peer group: In this rowdiest of local adolescent peer groups, is it the rowdiest members who wind up using hard drugs?

But drug use is more than an adolescent phenomenon in these gangs. Drugs—particularly heroin—have been the historical focus of street life for gang members after they grow into young adulthood. Street involvement often precludes normal adult life, families, and children. Thus we asked a third set of questions: When it comes to setting up families, how do heroin users compare with those who did not use? One would expect drug users to be more likely to have unstable marriages, and not to raise their children.

To anticipate, we found that heroin users in these gangs do not differ much from non-heroin users. However, there are sharp differences between men and women in (1) family background, (2) roles in the gang, and (3) relationship to their family of procreation. These rowdiest of adolescent groups appear to function differently for men and for women. In developing this evidence, we will discuss each of these three topics separately.

Data

Sample

In 1986 my colleagues and I obtained funding for a study that may be unique in its sample. We had been doing research with two Chicano gangs in East Los Angeles for more than a decade, and our staff—all former gang members—had developed rosters of members of the gangs' age-graded cliques going as far back as the 1950s. In our 1986 study we interviewed probability samples from the rosters of eight male and associated female cliques. Half of the cliques had been active in the 1950s and half in the 1970s. Through their networks of friends and former gang buddies, our staff was able to locate most of the sample. The final group of respondents, 106 men and 51 women, comprised roughly 25 percent of the original membership of these cliques. More important, of course, is that this is *not* a convenience sample, and not one which depends on the criminal justice system. We can, therefore, actually generalize from this sample to the gangs as a whole. Interviewers in this study, as in our previous studies, were members of these gangs during their youth, and helped develop the interview schedule and interpret the data as the study progressed. We have termed this a "collaborative methodology" (Moore, 1977, 1978). Obviously, without the efforts of such insiders it would have been impossible either to locate or to interview such individuals. (See Moore, 1991, for a full report of the study.)

Measure of Heroin Use

As indicated, heroin has been the historic "climax" drug in these gangs. In the late 1980s and early 1990s, cocaine became equally significant, but our interviews were conducted during the epoch when heroin was unrivaled. The measure of heroin use in this report is based on year-by-year recollections of drug use. In most of the analyses below, the measure is whether or not they *ever* used heroin.[1] Seventy-six percent of the men and 44 percent of the women had used heroin at some time in their lives. During their teens, half of the male respondents and a quarter of the female respondents had used heroin. Most young adults who continued to hang around with their homeboys and homegirls after the peak years of gang activity were involved with heroin, and it became the focus of the adult street lifestyle in these two gangs.

Family of Origin: Were Users Different in Family Climate?

We asked a series of questions about the climate in the family of origin. These included questions about who reared the respondent, the parents' normal mood states, abusiveness both between the parents and toward the respondent, and the presence of various problems in the household.[2]

The first, and perhaps most important, finding is that among the men we found almost no significant differences between heroin users and nonusers. But among the women there were significant differences between users and nonusers. Here are some details.

On only one relatively unimportant variable—whether or not the father was perceived as grouchy all the time—were male heroin users different from men who never used; users were less likely to report that their fathers were grouchy.

Women heroin users, by contrast, were more likely than nonusing women to have lived in families with serious problems. They saw their fathers beat their mothers (48% of the users compared with 24% of the nonusers); they were less likely to be afraid of their mothers' anger, were more likely to have grown up in a household where somebody else was addicted to heroin—often a brother (60% of the users as compared with 34% of the nonusers), and less likely to have grown up with somebody who was chronically ill. They were also more likely than nonusers to have run away from home.

A second noteworthy finding is that when we looked just at gender differences, without regard to heroin use, we found more statistically significant differences between men and women in our sample than between heroin users and non-heroin users. Almost all of the variables on which heroin users differed significantly from nonusers were ones in which men and women also differed significantly.

Thus gang women in general were from more troubled families. Though more men than women were raised by someone other than parents, and although more men reported that their fathers were usually grouchy, women were far more likely to report a range of other problems. Irrespective of their heroin use, gang women were more likely to have seen their fathers beat their mothers. More women were afraid of their mothers when they were angry. More women lived in homes where someone was chronically sick, died, had been arrested, and/or been addicted to heroin. Women were far more likely to have had a family member make sexual advances to them. (However, contrary to much speculation in the literature, incest was no more common for women heroin users than for nonusers.) More women ran away from home when they were children (75% compared with 30% of the men) and they ran away more frequently.

What do these findings imply? For the men, heroin users were really not much more likely than nonusers to have come from seriously disturbed families. But women heroin users were. This implies that gang membership and ensuing hard drug use may mean something quite different for males than for females from these communities. For males, gangs started out as rowdier versions of traditional barrio groups that assume tolerance for youthful masculine activities outside the home. But this is not true for girls. Girls are not allowed such tolerance in youthful activities outside the home. In fact, women were much more likely to conceal their gang membership from their parents. Though men's parents varied in their reactions to the gang—and many disapproved—at least most of their parents knew of the boys' membership.

Women differed most sharply from men in family problems that imply a combination of weakened family controls, family deviance, and/or stronger incentives for girls to escape distressing conditions at home. Girls in the gang—and especially those who later became heroin users—were more likely to be from troubled homes (Dembo et al., 1989). It is particularly notable that women gang members and subsequent heroin users were much more likely to have run away. This implies that the gang is a refuge as well as a resource for women.

In the Gang: Were the Users Rowdier?

Our questions about the gang included 24 specific items. There were inquiries relating to significant others and the gang, the general position of drugs and drug users in the clique, and special gang values.

How do heroin users and nonusers differ in these respects? Our special interest is in whether those members who ultimately used heroin were especially likely to be drug-oriented or "wilder" in general. It is important to note at the outset that users did not join the gang at earlier ages than nonusers, nor were they more likely to have had relatives in the gang. Thus they had no special relationship to the gang.

First, drugs in the gang: There were only a few differences either between men and women or between heroin users and abstainers on our (nine) questions about drugs. Men reported that more of their fellow clique members were dealing drugs, and, among women, heroin users reported seeing more dealers among their homies than did nonusers. These differences probably reflect real differences in exposure: there *were* more dealers among the males, and women heroin users were more likely than their abstaining homegirls to be aware of them. The drug orientation of the women heroin users is also evident in more general ways: more heroin users than nonusers among them defined "partying" to mean drinking and getting high. And it was only the heroin users among the women who believed that heroin users stayed with the clique, rather than withdrawing to their own sub-cliques. In sum, it appears that heroin-using women, but not men, were more drug-oriented than their homies, even while they were active in the gang.

Were the heroin users among the rowdiest of the gang members? We tried to answer this by looking into the special values that prevail in the gang, or *cholo*, subculture. We asked about two values that are of particular relevance to the question of rowdiness or wildness. First, we asked straightforwardly whether the respondent considered him/herself to be *loco* (wild), *muy loco* (very wild), or "square" during his/her gang years. These terms are used widely within the gang subculture to refer to a member's willingness to act "crazy," including using drugs. Second, we asked whether s/he was "all for the barrio" then. This refers to the notion that gang members should go all out for their gang (or barrio), should be totally committed to the gang at all times.

There were very few differences either by gender or by heroin use in responses to these questions. Heroin users were *not* more likely to define themselves as *loco*, nor were they more likely to have seen themselves as "all for the barrio." Turning to gender differences, men's views of their *locura* (wildness) were distributed more widely than women's: more men declared themselves to have been *muy loco*—but more men also said they were "square." More women declared themselves *loca* when they talked about their self concepts during the gang years. Men and women were equally committed to the gang (were "all for their barrio").

In sum, among the men, there were few differences between heroin users and nonusers in their recollections of gang life. Among women, heroin users are significantly more likely to focus on certain aspects of drug using during the gang years—notably on their definition of "partying" and on their perceptions that heroin users stayed in the gang. These two perceptions—along with their report that more clique members were dealing—were probably genuinely selective. That is, women who became involved with heroin were selectively exposed to these features of the gang. Curiously, however, these patterns are not found among the men.

The Importance of Heroin

Beginning Heroin Use

When did the gang men and women start using heroin? Except for a handful of experimenters, most of the gang members who used heroin did not start until the late teens, usually in the gang context. Even then, it was primarily men, not women, who used heroin. (Almost half of the men, but less than a quarter of the women were using heroin by the age of 20.) But, as Long (1990) argues, by the age of 20, "many of these individuals had been labeled *tecatos*—heroin addicts," even within the gang. They tended to withdraw into their own sub-cliques even if they remained active in the gang.

It wasn't *just* labeling; those who became seriously involved with the drug became preoccupied with the hustling lifestyle that heroin dictated. This was a major life change. We asked "What do you think were the major changes in your life, the times when your life really saw a change, like when you were in your teens?" A full 39 percent of all of the men and 16 percent of the women named "heroin, drugs, narcotics" as the major happening of their teens. No matter how much heroin they were actually using during their teens, these men and women were acknowledging the fact that it was during their teens that they were initiated into the world of heroin and its usually disastrous life consequences. One man who started heroin when he was 17 said "The clock stopped for me then." Street life preoccupied him almost continuously for years to come.

Life Histories

The Chicano *tecato* (heroin user) lifestyle has been portrayed in several accounts (Casavantes, 1976; Jorquez, 1984), but it may help to give the bare bones of the life history of one man from an early clique, and later, of a woman heroin addict:

> HM56 was 50 years old when he was interviewed. His parents moved to the Hoyo Maravilla neighborhood when he was a baby, and he continued to live there—with his family—all his life. He joined the Hoyo Maravilla gang when he was 15 and began using heroin when he was 16, just chipping a couple of days a week, making money to score by doing odd jobs, and "stealing and dealing." He went to jail (California Youth Authority) that same year, on a heroin-related charge, served 13 months, and was released back to the barrio, where he rejoined his gang homies and began to use heroin more frequently. He began selling narcotics again, and went back to jail for a 14-month term. When he was released he again began a heroin run, and though he no longer dealt heroin, for several years he began a pattern of doing County jail time—three or four months to a year—for "marks."[3] The pattern was interrupted at the age of 23, when he went to prison for three years, was resumed when he came out three years later, and was interrupted again when he went to prison from the ages of 28 to 30 and again from the ages of 32 to 36. Every time he was released he went back to his heroin-using friends. But then he "stopped doing time." He never held a job until he was 39, when he worked a year for the County, as a custodian. His heroin use tapered off: he was "just chipping." He quit altogether when he was in his early 40s. He survived by doing odd jobs—gardening, painting. He lived with a woman, briefly, when he was 19, and fathered a daughter, but saw very little of her. Major turning points: In his teens? "Using drugs." In his 20s? "I started going to jail." In his 30s? "Just that I went to prison." In his 40s? "By staying out of jails and prison." His summary: "I wasted most of my life, behind them prisons, jails, kicking habits."

But beyond this kind of typical male life history, the literature on drugs gives virtually no information about how women may cope. And the few existing discussions of women's heroin use tend somewhat to ignore men (Rosenbaum, 1981; Moore, 1990), who are often a critical factor. (Binion, 1982, is an exception.) Indeed, as this condensed life history of a younger woman shows, the typical experiences are quite different. Very few of the women in the earlier cliques used heroin. A woman from a recent clique, born in 1960 and a member of the White Fence Lil Termites clique, exemplifies many women users:

> (WF101). Her father was a conventional, home-owning, working man until he was injured when she was 13, and the family became dependent on welfare. She was one of 13 siblings; several of her brothers were gang members and one was dealing marijuana when she was a teenager. One was a heroin addict, and was "in and out, in and out" of prison, and one brother died of an overdose of heroin. She joined the gang when she was 14, was arrested for forgery but only served three months' time. She had her first child when she was 17, and also started using heroin at the same time—with her boyfriend. The relationship lasted only a year, but he continued to supply her with heroin, even after they broke up. She had two more children with another boyfriend, moved out of her parents' house and continued to use heroin, going on a long run for four years up to and including the time she was interviewed. She was never imprisoned, even though she and her current boyfriend were dealing heroin. She held a job only once, when she was 16, just before she dropped out of school. The major turning point in her teens was the birth of her daughter, and in her 20s:—"Drugs. That changed everything." Her lifestyle began to revolve around the need to get money for heroin.

These two brief life histories capture some characteristic differences between men and women *tecatos.* Men tended to start heroin and to continue the lifestyle largely within the peer group. Men were also much more likely to go to prison, and to spend their lives "in and out, in and out." Women tended to be preoccupied with their children, even when they didn't stay with their husbands or rear the children (Moore & Devitt, 1989), while men tended to lose contact with their children when they left their wives. It was rare, but by no means unknown, for *tecatos* of either sex to be fully involved in the world of work.

Men's heroin use tends to have been peer-oriented, but women's tended to be family-focused. As indicated above, women were more likely to grow up in a household with an addicted brother or father. Women were also much more likely to have their heroin use bracketed by a mate: they tended more to start heroin use with a boyfriend or husband, and, even though each liaison might be short-lived, the street world almost dictates that a *tecata*'s next boyfriend will also be a heroin user. To some extent, then, women's heroin use is enacted in a familial context. This represents a twisted version of the usual Mexican emphasis on family roles for women. (See also Moore with Devitt, 1989 and Moore, 1990, for an analysis of family background among Chicana addicts.)

The Role of the Gang for the Heroin User

Have the heroin users outgrown their gang loyalties? To find out, we asked if they were "all for their barrio *now*?" It should really come as no surprise that both men and women heroin users were more likely to answer "yes," while those who had grown out of the gang and avoided the street life answered "no." This gang value is preserved among people who are still involved in the drug-oriented street lifestyle. Obviously, the difference lies in the fact that the *tecatos* were still relying on their homeboys both on the streets and in prison. For some, like this 52-year-old *tecato*, such reliance was a total way of life:

> The barrio, you get away from the barrio it's different, you know. It'd be different because, you know, when you're away from your barrio you're not comfortable. I got to be in my barrio to feel comfortable, good. But if I go out of my barrio I don't feel right, you know. HM 43.

For others, it is more a matter of convenience, and these selfish motivations are masked by sentimentalism. They retain a convenient "gang loyalty" long past the age when other loyalties usually supersede. As one of my colleagues remarked, these are the dinosaurs, roaming the streets long after their time has passed.

Family of Procreation

Typically, the family life of former gang members is precarious. Most of these men and women—addicts and non-addicts alike—had been married at least once. Notably more women married a gang member (45% of the women compared with 26% of the men), but heroin users were no more likely to have done so. Men were more likely to enter common-law rather than formal marriages (and several, at that); among the women, heroin users were significantly less likely to have married formally and significantly more likely to have entered into common-law arrangements. These patterns reflect a greater *chola* lifestyle among women addicts than among male addicts: women heroin users were less likely to get married in a conventional fashion.

Marriages of gang members tended not to last. At the time of the interview, married life was not the norm for our respondents. Even the nonusers tended to have been divorced or separated—often more than once.

Most of these men and women also had children—82 percent of the men and 94 percent of the women. Women who used heroin had significantly fewer children than those who did not, an average of 2.7 children, compared with 3.6 for nonusers. And, though women were notably more likely to have raised their own children than were men, women heroin users were significantly more likely to have given their children to relatives to raise.

Women (especially the heroin users) were more likely than men (even the heroin users) to live with an addict. These figures once again illustrate the greater vulnerability of women gang members to long-range problems. In their teens, half of the men were using heroin, but by the time of the interview only 24 percent were doing so. By contrast, in their teens, only a quarter of the women were using heroin, but by the time of the interview 43 percent were involved in some way in the heroin lifestyle, either addicted themselves or living with an addict.

The figures on arrest patterns are also very telling. Arrests are often heroin-related, of course. When we asked if any member of the household had ever been arrested, 49 percent of the men and 33 percent of the women said "Yes." All of the men referred to themselves: they all had been arrested. By contrast, only half of these women had been arrested. In almost all cases, it was the husband in the household who had been arrested.

Discussion

It was quite surprising to find that differences between heroin users and nonusers were less substantial than differences between men and women. This generalization holds at every life stage: First, women who were gang members came from families with greater problems, and the problems in their families or origin were exaggerated among women who used heroin. Second, in their gang years, women heroin users were more exposed than nonusers to the drug life while they were still active in the gang. Finally, on our few variables about the family of procreation, women—and especially women with a history of heroin use—were less conventional in marriage patterns, and had more problems than men.

What this limited analysis does *not* show is a direct link between "deviant" aspects of gang membership and later heroin use. Among the men, heroin users are not particularly different from nonusers, except for a rather clear indication of the "dinosaur" syndrome—the continuing attachment to gang values and gang relationships. But what the analysis *does* indicate is that gang women should be looked at more seriously, both because the gang girls apparently have more problems than gang boys throughout their lives, and because the women may play more of a role in perpetuating the *cholo* value system among their children than do the men.

The gang as an institution may well attract girls from more problem-filled families, and may occupy a greater portion of their adolescent life-space. It clearly has greater implications for problems in adult life among women—and particularly for the small minority of women heroin users. There is an obvious difference between men and women when it comes to problems in adulthood, with or without heroin use. Men less frequently date—or marry—girls from the gang, and more frequently date conventional women. Thus, women are not only more immersed in the gang during adolescence, but they also have a greater chance of carrying the *cholo* lifestyle into adulthood and of passing it on. Few gang men raise their own children; gang women, by contrast, have more to do with their children, even if they may periodically leave them with relatives (Moore & Devitt, 1989).

There is a substantial literature in the drug prevention field that emphasizes the role of "deviant" adolescent peer groups in the onset and development of drug use. Our data suggest strongly that we need much more understanding of how these peer groups operate. The gender-based double standard of morality remains important and may be oppressive, especially in somewhat traditional populations such as the Mexican-American. For boys, gang membership and drug use appear not to be seen as quite so deviant—boys, after all, will be boys. On the other hand, there are strong community norms against girls' becoming involved either in gangs or in drugs. Thus gang girls tend to come from more problem-filled families, and to have greater incentives than boys both to join and to remain with the gangs. Once girls are involved, their fates are much more closely linked to the gang than are boys. The implications for drug prevention with so-called "high risk" peer groups are important.

Notes

1. Twenty-two percent of the men and four percent of the women used heroin only during their teen (or gang) years; 16 percent of the men and 20 percent of the women used only during their adult years, while the remainder (38% of the men and 20% of the women) used during both gang years and later.
2. Seventeen variables were included in this part of the analysis.
3. This charge stems from arguments that needle track marks are indications that the individual has been using heroin. In recent years, the charge has fallen into disfavor, and heroin addicts are now arrested for being "under the influence."

References

Binion, V. J. (1982). Sex differences in socialization and family dynamics of female and male heroin users. *Journal of Social Issues, 36,* 43–58.

Casavantes, E. J. (1976). *El Tecato: Cultural and sociologic factors affecting drug use among chicanos.* Washington, DC: National Coalition of Spanish Speaking Mental Health Organizations.

Crider, R., Groerer, J., & Blanken, A. (1989). *Black tar heroin field investigation.* Rockville, MD: National Institute on Drug Abuse: Unpublished manuscript.

Dembo, R., Williams, L., La Voie, L., Berry, E., Getreu, A., Wish, E., Schmeidler, J., & Washburn, M. (1989). Physical abuse, sexual victimization, and illicit drug use: Replication of a structural analysis among a new sample of high-risk youths. *Violence and Victims, 4,* 121–138.

Elliott, D. S., Huizinga, D., & Ageton, S. S. (1985). *Explaining delinquency and drug use.* Beverly Hills, CA: Sage.

Jessor, R. J., Close, A., & Donovan, J. E. (1980). Psychological correlates of marijuana use and problem drinking in a national sample of adolescents. *American Journal of Public Health, 70,* 604–613.

Jorquez, J. (1984). Heroin use in the barrio: Solving the problem of relapse, or keeping the *tecato gusano* asleep. *The American Journal of Drug and Alcohol Abuse 10,* 63–75.

Kandel, D. (1985). On processes of peer influence in adolescent drug use: A developmental perspective. *Alcohol and Substance Abuse in Adolescence, 4,* 139–163.

Long, J. (1990). Drug use patterns in two Los Angeles barrio gangs. In R. Glick, & J. Moore (Eds.), *Drugs in Hispanic communities* (pp. 155–166). New Brunswick, NJ: Rutgers University Press.

Moore, J. (1977). The Chicano Pinto Research Project: A case study in collaboration. *Journal of Social Issues, 33,* 144–150.

Moore, J. (1990). Mexican American women addicts: The influence of family background. In R. Glick, & J. Moore (Eds.), *Drug use in Hispanic communities* (pp. 127–154). New Brunswick, NJ: Rutgers University Press. Forthcoming.

Moore, J. (1991). *Going down to the barrio: Homeboys and homegirls in change.* Philadelphia: Temple University Press.

Moore, J., Garcia, R., Garcia, C., Cerda, L., & Valencia, F. (1978). *Homeboys: Gangs, drugs and prison in the barrios of Los Angeles.* Philadelphia, PA: Temple University Press.

Moore, J. & Devitt, M. (1989). The paradox of deviance in addicted Mexican-American mothers. *Gender & Society, 3,* 53–70.

Needle, J., & Stapleton, W. (1983). *Police handling of youth gangs.* Washington, DC: National Institute for Juvenile Justice and Delinquency Prevention.

Rosenbaum, M. (1981). *Women on heroin.* New Brunswick, NJ: Rutgers University Press.

Vigil, J. D. (1988). *Barrio gangs: Street life and identity in Southern California.* Austin, TX: University of Texas Press.

Discussion Questions

1. This chapter demonstrates that family problems are major source of hard drug use. Discuss.
2. What are the major differences in the careers of male and female heroin users from these Chicano gangs?
3. Why do you think these differences exist?
4. Would you expect to find the same differences in white gangs or in African American gangs? Why, or why not?
5. Do your answers to #4 have any implications for understanding race and ethnic differences in drug use in general, or just for drug use among so-called street people?

12

Black Male Youth and Drugs

How Racial Prejudice, Parents, and Peers Affect Vulnerability

Ronald F. Ferguson **Mary S. Jackson**

Ronald F. Ferguson is Associate Professor of Public Policy at the John F. Kennedy School of Government at Harvard University. His research covers topics that fit generally under the heading of social and economic development. His publications include studies of the fiscal health of cities, youth employment, public education, drug problems, and state and local economic development policy. His current research addresses the effects of teacher quality on school achievement, the determinants of child support payment by non-custodial fathers, initiatives to improve the quality of life for teenagers and young adults in low-income black neighborhoods, and various topics concerning African American males. Professor Ferguson received his graduate training in economics at MIT, but much of his recent work is interdisciplinary.

Dr. Mary S. Jackson is an Assistant Professor of Criminal Justice in the Department of Social Work at Cleveland State University. The focus of her research and teaching is drugs, gangs, and African American adolescents. In addition to teaching and research, Professor Jackson practices psychotherapy and substance abuse counseling. She received her Ph.D. from the Case Western Reserve University School of Applied Social Sciences.

Introduction

In 1987, one of the authors of this article administered a survey to black male teenagers at a juvenile detention facility in Ohio (Jackson, 1988). Among this group of 243 boys, more than 90 percent reported regular use of either alcohol or illicit drugs: 203 used illicit drugs, 209 used alcohol, and 186 used both. A question on the survey asked, "What would it take for you to stop getting high?" Poignantly, the most frequent choice from among 10 possible responses was, "If I could just be myself." Almost 35 percent gave this answer. The second most frequent was, "Stop trying to please my friends," followed by, "If I would leave the gang." Fewer than 10 percent responded, "I would stop if I wanted to." These youth are not a random sample of African American boys. They occupy one end of a continuum. Their behaviors and perspectives represent the worst consequences of forces that distort the development of far too many black male youth.

This article suggests that being feared by strangers, followed in stores by suspicious clerks, disparaged by teachers, and generally disrespected—all experiences that black males report more than other groups—can confuse and alienate African American youth and discourage them from, for example, "just being themselves." Data in the paper establish plausibility for the proposition that these experiences are common for virtually all young black males. The perpetrators, often well meaning, represent all races and ethnic groups, including African Americans themselves. Consequences for any given youth depend on situational factors and on the availability and power of messages that are countervailing to those based on negative stereotypes.

Data in the article, both quantitative and qualitative, come from small surveys and interviews that the authors have conducted over the past few years. They include African American and Latin American students at Harvard and Carnegie Mellon Universities during the summer of 1989, a small group of black males in an unwed fathers' program in Cleveland during the same summer, and two groups of black males incarcerated in Ohio during 1987 and in Kentucky during 1990.

The article argues that credible and reliable adult guidance, usually from parents, helps some youth to anticipate and understand messages based on race-sex stereotypes. In this way, parents help youth to avoid the "strain" of alienation and of discouragement regarding prospects for conventional success that some theories suggest as an explanation for social deviance—including excessive involvement with illicit drugs (Cloward & Ohlin, 1960; Cohen, 1962; Sutherland & Cressey, 1970). Simultaneously, effective parents can exert controls that mediate the possible corruptions of peer pressure (Hirschi, 1969; Clark, 1983; Spencer, 1990). Young black males who lack adult guidance to reduce strain, and supervision to impose control, are more at risk for becoming alienated and discouraged about finding happiness and acceptance in society's mainstream. They are more vulnerable to mischievous peers and self-destructive social learning (Bandura, 1977), including the learning that accompanies regular engagement in using and selling drugs.

The first half of the article reviews some standard discouraging messages that black male youth receive from society, and some corrupting messages that are present in black youth culture. We document that even youth at elite universities tend to receive these messages. At the end of the first half, we suggest briefly how the latter youth manage to avoid discouragement and excessive mischief.

The second half of the article concerns the youth in the article's opening paragraph—those who do become discouraged and who resort to excessive involvement with using or selling drugs. It suggests that in the absence of high quality adult guidance and supervision, being feared, mistrusted, disrespected, and underestimated are both causes and consequences of misbehavior, including involvement with drugs.

Nurturing Environments and Human Motivation

Drawing most directly on the work of motivational psychologists, (e.g., McClelland, 1987), we assume that behavior has both rational and impulsive elements that adapt over time in a search for supportive responses from the social environment. Supportive responses produce basic forms of satisfaction associated with such natural motives as desires for friendship, achievement, influence, stimulation, security, freedom from hunger, and material comfort. The adaptive process of searching to have one's basic human needs met includes selecting (or rejecting) particular friends and associates and conforming (or not conforming) to various social norms.

Youth search to have their basic needs met in social ecologies that this paper calls "nurturing environments." The ideal nurturing environment sets rewards and penalties that support its core values; it transmits important knowledge, fosters physical health, cultivates skills and talents, and responds to basic psychological needs. Rooted most strongly in the family, it also includes other social structures in the community that specialize in various care-giving, provisioning, teaching, and regulatory functions. Collectively, these structures generate experiences and shape the messages that people receive about themselves, the groups with which they identify, and the general environment. Included are not only churches, schools, and social service agencies, but also businesses, the news media, medical centers, and law enforcement agencies.

Black male youth occupy a continuum, from those who have learned to expect success in mainstream society to those who have learned to expect rejection and failure. Those expecting rejection and failure are most likely to take personally messages based on negative racial stereotypes. Perceiving rejection in conventional settings, and hungry to experience friendship, influence. achievement, and some semblance of security, such youth are more at risk for drifting into settings where using and selling drugs are the norm. They use and sell drugs even while claiming a preference for a different lifestyle—one where they could just be themselves.

Discouraging and Corrupting Messages

When people are unfamiliar with one another but nevertheless need to make judgments, they make guesses. Relying mostly on stereotypes, they use characteristics that they observe (e.g., race, ethnicity, sex, age, weight, dress, speech, demeanor) to guess about traits that are invisible (e.g., diligence, honesty, aptitude). Using such guesses as the basis for making decisions is what social scientists call statistical discrimination. (For a detailed explanation, see Campbell and Stanley, 1985.) Employers, for example, use signals such as race, demeanor, and education to guess how productive and reliable an applicant will be. Individuals from groups with less negative stereotypes have an automatic advantage in getting the benefit of the doubt (Kirschenman & Neckerman, 1991). This phenomenon applies in a variety of different settings.

Young African American males who benefit from the wise counsel of responsible adults are more likely than others to learn signals—dress, speech, demeanor—to identify themselves as exceptions to negative stereotypes (Jenkins, 1982). Because of the hope and positive self-images that parents and others instill in them, and because adults give them specific advice concerning racial biases, they know not to take personally many of the discouraging messages that they receive. They expect conventional success in life, work for it, and tend to avoid risky behaviors, such as excessive involvement with drugs, that might harm their life chances.

Many others, however, do not recognize that discouraging treatment and biased messages are the results of stereotypes. These youth take the messages seriously and personally. In this section, we review some of the negative assumptions that people make about black males, particularly about adolescents and young adults, and the ways that such assumptions affect communication, both implicit and explicit, within and across races and social strata. The text reviews ways that biased assumptions distort the messages that society delivers to black males, and ways that such messages warp the black male's understanding of himself and his potential, when credible countervailing messages are absent. Data in this section, some of which are in tables constructed from very small samples, establish the plausibility of empirical regularities that some readers may find surprising.

Message: We Fear and Distrust You

One of the authors recently surveyed a small group of academically talented college juniors and seniors, aged 20–25. All were attending graduate school preparatory programs at Carnegie Mellon University and Harvard University in the summer of 1989. A group of young fathers, aged 15–23, in a community-based parenting program in inner-city Cleveland, responded to the same survey. Three of the seven young fathers were high school dropouts, one was in high school, two had finished high school, and one was attending a community college. All seven were African American.

Tables 1 through 8 show some of the answers to the survey. The pattern of answers for the African American males at Harvard and Carnegie Mellon is remarkably similar to that for the young fathers. The only noticeable difference among the tables is that most of the young fathers (none of the college group were fathers) have friends who sell drugs (Table 8). The tables suggest that black males receive messages that they are dangerous (Table 1), dishonest (Table 4), and stupid (Tables 5 and 6). They report receiving these messages more than either the black females in the sample or the students of Latin/Mexican descent. Note the mix of anger and sympathy in Tables 2 and 3.

The young fathers were unaware that most black males receive these messages. The question, "What is it about you that makes people react this way?" followed the question about being feared or expected to steal. All members of the college sample mentioned race in their replies. In contrast, only one of the seven young fathers mentioned race. The other six mentioned various combinations of "the way I look," "the way I act," "I don't know," and "nothing." Similar patterns emerged in interviews with other teenagers. As one member of the Mayor's Youth Leadership Council in Pittsburgh said, "What I learned is that I don't have to feel different about myself: everybody (in the discussion group of six black teenaged males) seems to be saying the same things." Differences among the Pittsburgh group in the level of awareness about stereotypes and prejudice were remarkable; youth with greater understanding seemed generally more sophisticated and articulate.

It is important to emphasize here that the destructive messages come not only from whites but from other African Americans as well. They constitute distorted and confusing feedback to black males and, if taken personally, probably influence several dimensions of self-concept. They may reduce self-estimated intellectual potential, distort assumptions about natural roles in society (e.g., being "bad"), and make youth feel unliked and unwelcome in mainstream social settings.

Responses from Graduate-School-Bound College Juniors and Seniors and Young Men in a Teen Parenting Program

Table 1

People who do not know me _____ act afraid of me.

	Always	Usually	Sometimes	Almost Never	Never	Total Reply
African American Female	0	1	4	8	2	15
African American Male	0	2	8	3	0	13
Latin/Mexican Female	0	0	1	3	2	6
Latin/Mexican Male	0	0	0	5	0	5
African American Teen Fathers (Cleveland)	1	0	5	1	0	7

Table 2

When people who do not know me act afraid of me I feel angry.

	Always	Usually	Sometimes	Almost Never	Never	Total Reply
African American Female	0	0	6	3	2	11
African American Male	1	1	5	1	3	11
Latin/Mexican Female	0	0	3	0	1	4
Latin/Mexican Male	0	1	1	0	3	5
African American Teen Fathers (Cleveland)	1	2	0	0	3	6

Table 3

When people who do not know me act afraid of me I feel sorry for them.

	Always	Usually	Sometimes	Almost Never	Never	Total Reply
African American Female	3	2	5	0	1	11
African American Male	4	2	1	2	1	10
Latin/Mexican Female	1	1	2	0	0	4
Latin/Mexican Male	1	0	1	1	1	4
African American Teen Fathers (Cleveland)	2	0	0	2	1	5

Table 4

In stores, people _____ act like they expect me to steal something.

	Always	Usually	Sometimes	Almost Never	Never	Total Reply
African American Female	0	3	7	4	1	15
African American Male	2	4	4	2	0	12
Latin/Mexican Female	0	0	4	1	1	6
Latin/Mexican Male	0	1	1	0	2	4
African American Teen Fathers (Cleveland)	3	0	3	1	0	7

Responses from Graduate-School-Bound College Juniors and Seniors and Young Men in a Teen Parenting Program

Table 5

Teachers who are not from my race _____ expect students from my race to be as smart as other students.

	Always	Usually	Sometimes	Almost Never	Never	Total Reply
African American Female	5	3	4	4	0	16
African American Male	1	4	2	6	0	13
Latin/Mexican Female	0	2	2	1	1	6
Latin/Mexican Male	1	1	1	2	0	5
African American Teen Fathers (Cleveland)	3	1	1	0	2	7

Table 6

Teachers who are from my race _____ expect students from my race to be as smart as other students.

	Always	Usually	Sometimes	Almost Never	Never	Total Reply
African American Female	9	4	0	3	0	16
African American Male	4	7	2	0	0	13
Latin/Mexican Female	1	4	1	0	0	6
Latin/Mexican Male	4	1	0	0	0	5
African American Teen Fathers (Cleveland)	0	2	3	0	2	7

Table 7

People say I _____ act white.

	Always	Usually	Sometimes	Almost Never	Never	Total Reply
African American Female	3	0	4	2	7	16
African American Male	0	1	2	5	5	13
Latin/Mexican Female	0	1	2	1	2	6
Latin/Mexican Male	0	0	2	2	1	5

Table 8

My friends _____ sell drugs.

	Always	Usually	Sometimes	Almost Never	Never	Total Reply
African American Female	0	0	3	0	10	13
African American Male	0	0	1	1	9	11
Latin/Mexican Female	0	0	1	3	2	6
Latin/Mexican Male	0	0	0	5	0	5
African American Teen Fathers (Cleveland)	3	2	0	0	2	7

Message: Society Has Low Expectations of You

Teachers

A large number of studies over many years have documented the self-fulfilling prophecy of low teacher expectations (Jussim, 1986; Palardy, 1969; Rosenthal & Jacobson, 1968; Rosenthal, 1971, 1973; Marsh et al., 1984). If teachers expect black students to do poorly most of the time, these studies suggest, we should not be surprised when performance is poor.

In an elaborate study of disciplinary procedures conducted around 1980 in a midwestern school district, researchers asked teachers in an anonymous survey what they thought about black and white students. A number of questions asked for comparisons of black with white students. While only 1.6 percent of the teachers said black males read better than white males, 55 percent suggested that white males needed more of their help (Harris & Bennett, 1982). Perhaps the teachers expected that white males wanted more help, or that helping black males was relatively hopeless.

Whatever the reason, students' answers to a survey in a related study by the same authors demonstrated that black students clearly perceived a difference in teachers' attitudes about white versus black students (Harris, Pugh & Heid, 1983). White students were much less likely to perceive a difference in teachers' treatment of the two races. In answering the question of whether teachers were nicer to white students, 18 percent of white students and 60 percent of black students answered yes. This pattern was the same across all grade levels, 2 through 10. Only 77 percent of white students and 55 percent of black students believed that the teachers wanted the black students in their school. Across grade levels, this percent varied from a high of 89 for white fourth graders to a low of 35 for black ninth graders (Harris, et al., 1983).

Tables 5 and 6 in the present paper summarize respondents' perceptions concerning teacher expectations related to race. The majority of students perceived racial bias. The college students perceived it more among white than among black teachers. Note, however, that while three of the seven inner-city fathers answered that white teachers always expect black students to be as smart as white students, none of them said the same for black teachers. Though based on a very small sample, this underscores the fact that negative messages to black male youth come from African Americans and whites alike.

Teachers' racially differentiated attitudes can penalize both strong and weak black students. Rubovits and Maehr (1973), working at the University of Illinois in the early 1970s with seventh and eighth graders, assigned each of 66 student teachers to teach a math concept to four pupils: two black and two white. The student teachers were told that they were testing a part of a new math curriculum. The children all had average IQs, but the student teachers were told that one of the black pupils and one of the white pupils were highly intelligent, while the two other students in the group were average.

Experimenters watched the student teachers through a one-way glass and noted the numbers of positive and negative reinforcements the teachers gave the pupils. The "superior" white pupils got two positive reinforcements for every negative, and the "average" white students got one. The "average" black students got one positive for every 1.5 negatives. And the "superior" black students got one positive response for every 3.5 negative ones. One possible explanation for this pattern is that the student teachers subconsciously may have experienced psychological dissonance at the thought that a black student was academically superior (Festinger, 1980). The study was done carefully, and the results were statistically very significant.

Evidence collected by Jawanza Kunjufu (1983) suggests that, over time, some of the most able black males turn off to school. Kunjufu collected data for 20 black males randomly selected from among students who had been in the same school for five consecutive years. For each child, he compared the child's national percentile rating on the Iowa Reading Test at the beginning of the third grade with the child's rating at the end of the seventh grade. Most fell backward. Students who had scored at the 98th, 97th, 92nd, and 91st percentiles at the beginning of the third grade had dropped to the 35th, 54th, 24th, and 68th percentiles, respectively, by the end of the seventh grade; two who had scored at the 63rd percentile dropped to the 7th and 4th.

This pattern shows that children who do poorly in school after the fourth grade are not necessarily the least intellectually gifted.

News and Entertainment Media

Another source of skewed and demeaning messages to and about black males is the news and entertainment media. A blatant example aired on the Friday night situation comedy *Family Matters* in October, 1989. The context was a conversation between two high-school-aged males, one white and the other black. The white male, clearly a smart but mischievous student, had made fake copies of report cards for all of his friends, including the black youth, and had sent the cards to his friends' home addresses. The black youth's parents had opened the report card and were proud of his accomplishment. He did not know that the report was a fake, and his confidence rose. When his white friend told him about the scheme, the black youth was clearly disappointed, saying, "For a minute there, I thought I was smart." The white youth replied, "You? (pause) Thought you were smart?! (pause) What are you? Stupid?!!"

A few moments later, in an unrelated scene, the black youth's younger sister remarked that she had to do her homework because she did not want to end up at "Bubba University."

Message: Don't Conform

In response to negative messages and experiences over many years, a face-saving defensive posture has become an aspect of black male culture (Majors & Billson, 1992; Wilson, 1990). The degree to which a young black male adopts this posture seems to increase with the degree to which his own experience has caused him to feel discouraged and alienated, but most black male youth appear to accept it to some degree. Those who openly resist often pay a price in social acceptance. Majors and Billson call this posture "cool pose":

> . . . cool pose . . . is a strategy that many black males use in making sense of their everyday lives. We believe that coolness as a strength may be linked to pride, self-respect, and masculinity. . . . As a response to a history of oppression and social isolation in this country, coolness may be a survival strategy that has cost the black male—and society—an enormous price. (p. xi)

In this posture, black males implicitly declare an unwillingness to take certain values of mainstream society too seriously. Black youth face peer pressure to adopt this posture as early as the middle elementary school years. To resist it, youth need substantial will-power and social support from adults and like-minded peers.

Message: Resist Low-Wage Work

Some of the most influential messages that peers communicate to one another concern the acceptability of particular types of employment. Low-wage work is considered demeaning. For example, four of the seven young fathers from Cleveland (recall Tables 1–8) report that their friends sometimes, usually, or always make fun of people who work for low wages. All of the young gang members whom Carl Taylor surveyed in Detroit expressed their unwillingness to accept minimum wage jobs (Taylor, 1989). This does not mean that black youth have unreasonable job expectations. For example, Holzer (1986) finds that black youth do not hold out for higher wages than do white youth. However, their opportunities are such that the gap between the wages that they are willing to accept and the wages that are available is often greater for black youth. This helps to explain why it takes black youth longer to find jobs.

Message: Don't Work Too Hard in School

Ironically, striving to do more than get by academically is often construed as a sign of trying to act white. Many black youths assert their blackness by rejecting the value that society places on academic achievement (Fordham, 1988; Fordham & Ogbu, 1986; Fisher, 1987; Shervington, 1986). Hence, students who work hard for good grades without clearly and regularly expressing their non-white identity risk being accused of "acting white." (Despite being called white, all but one of the African Americans represented in Table 7, both male and female, checked the answer indicating that they are "always" proud to be members of their race. The one exception answered "never.") Signithia Fordham (1988) writes about the tendency for some black youth to become "raceless" when they decide to excel academically. This is partially because achievers reject the anti-achievement ethic of their peers, and partially because their peers reject them. Fordham notes that black girls are more prone to become raceless than black boys. Academically ambitious boys make more of an effort to compensate through athletics or other activities, such as dancing, that peers regard positively.

At the other end of the spectrum, the anti-achievement ethic offers no consolation to youth who struggle unsuccessfully. The minority of black youth, disproportionately males, who for various reasons are viewed as the least intellectually endowed, are the most demeaned and have the greatest psychological burden to carry. Adults insinuate to these youths, and their peers often tell them directly, that they are stupid. We have interviewed young men who say that they dropped out of school because they were tired of classmates making fun of their academic deficiencies.

The primary harm in this anti-achievement culture is not what it does to the youth who excel. Similarly, it does not encourage failure. Instead, it encourages mediocrity. The primary harm that it poses is the wasting of potential of those who choose not to excel. Also, it provides spurious validation for the stereotype of racial inferiority that generates the discouraging messages.

The previous few pages give examples of discouraging messages that most young black males receive from strangers, teachers, peers, and others. With the help of parents and other adults, many youth learn to discount such messages and to cope. They sustain belief in the possibility of conventional success and focus their efforts on achieving it. For example, when asked why they keep striving, the students from Harvard and Carnegie Mellon represented in Tables 1–8 gave answers that fell into three broad categories: (1) support from family and friends, (2) a sense of purpose, and (3) a belief that they are doing God's will and that He will support their efforts.

Some young African American males are much less fortunate. They experience the same types of discouraging messages as other black males, but have little or no informed adult support and encouragement, no sense of purpose in their lives, and no religious faith to fall back on. The separate messages come together into one big message: "You will not find much satisfaction in conventional settings pursuing conventional goals."

* * * * *

The next few pages rely largely on the testimony of the incarcerated teenagers in Ohio whose survey responses we addressed in the opening paragraph of the article. The discussion is about their relationships with both service providers and parents. These youth were aged 12 through 20 when interviewed in 1987. They found it surprising that anyone respectable thought that they were worth talking to.

Messages for Delinquents

A recent survey of 387 adolescent black males in Washington, D.C., found that those who reported both using and selling drugs had a distinctive profile:

> Most aberrant was the group that both sold and used drugs who . . . viewed as poorest their chances of conventional success, and felt most isolated/alienated . . . .These are the same youth who reported high levels of peer support for their use and sales behavior. (Brounstein et al., 1989, p. 114)

No one explanation can completely explain these patterns. The discussion above and that which follows emphasize a narrow class of risk factors: negatively biased treatment that confuses and alienates black male adolescents who lack effective parenting. Often, youth who carry the label "bad" or "delinquent" receive the most disparaging messages and suffer the least effective relationships with adults. (On labeling, see Gove, 1975).

Most discussions of "youth at risk" emphasize the importance of providing services and breaking their isolation from community institutions. A problem that such discussions often fail to address, however, is the way that community institutions treat youth once they earn the label "bad" and become the black sheep of the black community. Often, these young people are not isolated. Instead, they are very well connected to schools, churches, and social service agencies. But the connections reinforce discouragement and alienation. Testimony of youth, social workers, and parents says that few of the adults in the lives of "bad" black male youth give positive reinforcements or have enough credibility to be relied upon for advice and affection, and the few who might be both positive and credible are too busy.

Message: Your Parents Are Powerless

The quality of parenting, including parental interaction with the rest of the nurturing environment, seems central in determining whether offspring suffer the kinds of discouragement and disorientation that lead to drugs and delinquency. Some parents are not sufficiently well informed and self-confident to be effective guides, brokers, and advocates outside of the home (Clark, 1983; Spencer, 1990; Gibbs, 1988). These parents are not likely to intervene effectively with teachers and other authority figures, or to provide children with informed discipline and credible guidance for aligning behavior with the requirements of local institutions. The children of such parents are at greater risk for poor academic performance, delinquency, and drug abuse, and for intensive interaction with often ill-equipped professional service providers, especially police and social workers.

Many of the teenagers in the Ohio sample claim to believe that only their mothers and siblings really care about them. They express love and protectiveness toward their families. But they show little confidence in their mothers' ability to help in the external environment. Also, though they love their mothers, some suggest that even this relationship is often strained as mothers attempt to impose structure and discipline. For example, church attendance, for those who attend, is simply to placate mothers: attending church is to "keep our mothers off our backs." One young man states: "Yeah, I went to church . . . my mother got me up, and I went, but I went to church high." Nearly without exception, religious beliefs played no major role in these youths' lives even though many attended church regularly.

Relationships with fathers are filled with ambivalence. Identification with fathers is often associated with negative dimensions of self-concept: "My mother don't get high. My father drinks. He's like me—drinks and gets high." Few have positive things to say about fathers. Those who do not know their fathers express curiosity about what characteristics they might have in common. Those who know their fathers strain to understand why their fathers are not more responsible or more understanding. Still others wonder, "What if . . . ?": "If I had a father, instead of a stepfather who turns me on, then maybe I would not be in a place like this. But my mother don't believe me when I tell her about him."

As a signal that even their parents have given up trying to influence their behaviors outside of the home, several make claims that: "My parents never said don't use drugs . . . they said don't you bring drugs into my house." Some claim to regard this ambiguity in the parental message as a license to use drugs away from home.

Message: Don't Trust Service Providers

A view that we have encountered frequently in field interviews is that professionals in the nurturing environment—including teachers, social workers, police, and others—often send mixed and discouraging signals to youth who are slow to conform to mainstream behavioral norms. As a result, relationships between youth and service providers often fester with mutual disrespect and produce self-fulfilling prophecies of negative outcomes. Incarcerated teenagers in Ohio express unequivocal distrust of most professionals in the nurturing environment—teachers, ministers, social workers—who they say are "just in it for the pay check" and do not really care.

The interviewer in Ohio had to assure young men that she had not been sent by their social workers. When given a negative response to the question, "Did my social worker tell you to talk to me?" the subjects would become less apprehensive and respond more warmly, "Well, that's cool, you're straight then." Most of the subjects said that the two things that had secured their cooperation was her race (African American) and her apparent effort to be honest with them, for example by answering, "Nothing but a conversation," when asked, "What's in this for me?"

Security workers in the facility behaved as though they were in competition with the adolescents for attention: "I don't know why you are wasting your time with them. They are just going to end up in Mansfield (an adult prison)." "You need to talk to us to see how we feel, not to them—they committed the crime, we didn't. Everybody is always wanting to know how we treat them, but they don't ask how they treat us." "They committed the crime. These kids have received just too many breaks—and not enough punishment." The adolescents are resentful of both the security and counseling staffs whom they view as being there "just for the paycheck." These are the primary adults with whom the youth interact while incarcerated, and the youth are distressed that most of the staff seem to hold them in such low regard. Staff members remind them, they say, of some public school teachers—many of whom, they say, have given up teaching and simply need the income. They talk about teachers who are positive exceptions, such as one who showed his caring by being a strict disciplinarian, but in general they believe that teachers are afraid and not very useful.

Youths consider some staff members in the correctional institution to be exceptions to the rule that nobody cares. When interviewed, these exceptional people express frustration. They talk of wanting to introduce more programmatic activities but being short on staff, or not getting cooperation from superiors who have long since given up hope. One staffer was willing to talk about his ideas, but unwilling to have his name used: "You know, I don't mind if you write about some of this, but please do not use my name. I don't want to lose my job." Social workers at the institution admit the need for more social services but lament bureaucratic constraints and their own lack of training for the job.

One young man viewed the lack of attention as just more of the same. He directly connected his substance abuse to the need for someone to listen: "Sometimes no one wants to listen to you, so the hurt just stays there until you do something about it, by getting high." Following his comment, another in the group added: "I know how he feels. It's no fun getting the shit beat out of you by your old man. I cried so much until I can't cry anymore. But I guess he had his reasons, and I can't blame my mother because she needed him."

When these youth are released from jail they go back to the public schools where the teachers fear them, to the gangs who are the only friends they have, to families to whom they are a disappointment, to a peer culture built around drugs and violence, and, generally, to a community where most people do not welcome them but wish instead that they could be kept off the streets indefinitely.

Involvement with Drugs

Using or selling drugs is not necessarily a sign that a youth is alienated, discouraged, confused, or heavily invested in unconventional values. Some level of experimentation with alcohol and drugs is normal. Experimentation does not suggest that a youth lacks sophistication of the type that would protect him from being wounded and discouraged by messages based on racial stereotypes. Selling drugs may be simply a means to more conventional ends. However, the more deeply involved a youth becomes in using and selling drugs, the greater is the potential cost he faces in missed conventional opportunities. Accordingly, young people who perceive more and better opportunities for finding fulfillment in society's mainstream tend on average, though not uniformly, to take fewer chances with drugs—particularly with drug use (Boufides et al., 1987; Brounstein et al., 1989).

Drug Sales

The fact that selling drugs can be a "job" means that a young person's reason for selling drugs may be unrelated to his use of drugs. Though the precise numbers vary across studies, young black males who sell illicit drugs but claim not to use them represent a non-trivial percentage of sellers (Taylor, 1989; Brounstein et al., 1989; Reuter et al., 1989; Johnson et al., 1987). For example, the Urban Institute's survey (Brounstein et al., 1989) showed that of the boys who admitted either selling or using drugs, 44 percent said that they only sold, 37 percent said that they only used, and 19 percent admitted doing both. A theme of the report is that sellers who do not use are more similar to those who neither use nor sell than they are to those who do both. Though sellers who were nonusers did worse in school than youth who neither used nor sold, they were not more likely to come from single-parent households, or from households where the head was unemployed or had little education. They felt no more alienated or isolated from their family and peers than the average student who was not involved with drugs.

Taylor (1989) studied a black drug gang in Detroit that absolutely prohibited drug use by its members. Taylor calls this gang a "corporate gang" and distinguishes it from what he calls "scavenger gangs." Scavenger gangs may also sell drugs, but their members are much more prone to use drugs and to have less control over their lives. Interestingly, 37 of 57 corporate gang members in a survey that Taylor conducted claim to be close to their parents; the number for scavenger gang members is only two out of 40. Many of the corporate gang members claim that their parents support their lifestyles.

Selling an illicit substance is a form of deviant behavior, and youths who sell drugs frequently perform poorly academically. But, like running numbers, selling drugs can be an expression of entrepreneurial drive, self-efficacy, and self-discipline for those who have the self-control not to use the product. The act of selling drugs shows disrespect for the law and disregard for the welfare of customers, and is evidence that superior income-generating alternatives are scarce. Also, it is evidence that parental influence strong enough and conventional enough to successfully dissuade a young person from such activity is missing. But it does not appear to be as strong a sign of discouragement and alienation as is use of hard drugs or heavy use of alcohol or marijuana.

Drug Use

Drug and alcohol use occupies a continuum from no use at all, to frequent use of multiple and dangerous substances administered via the most dangerous methods. Researchers have not found that initial use per se signals any particular form of social alienation or emotional distress (Jessor & Jessor, 1977). Instead, youngsters experimenting with drugs and alcohol for the first time tend to be responding to a fairly standard list of home and social influences, few of which would typically be considered pathological. The primary inducements that studies identify with early use are curiosity, peer and family influences, the desire to act grown up, rebelliousness, and the desire to feel good, all mediated by values, availability, opportunity costs of time, and perceptions of potential consequences (e.g., studies reviewed in Polich et al., 1984). Addiction and other problems that produce significant harms are omnipresent risks, but seldom the expected consequences for youthful experimenters. Many young people experiment at some time with alcohol or drugs.

However, a standard research finding is that problem use among adolescents is typically associated with academic difficulties and delinquency (Brunswick, 1989; Fagan, 1990). The same factors that predispose a young person to delinquency may propel him and his peer group to early experimentation with alcohol, cigarettes, and marijuana, and eventually to heavier substances. Researchers call the lighter drugs (e.g., tobacco, alcohol, marijuana) "gateway drugs" (Kandel, 1980; Clayton & Voss, 1981; Stephens, 1991). These are the first drugs in a hierarchical sequence; few people who have used heavier drugs such as cocaine, heroin, and psychedelics have not used the gateway drugs, though most people who try the gateways do not progress further. A consistent finding is that the earlier the onset of use, the greater is the likelihood of progressing from "lighter" to "heavier" substances. Again, however, most youth who experiment seem predisposed neither to delinquency nor to more dangerous involvement with drugs.

The relationships between delinquency, various nurturing deficits, and drugs are clearly evident in the comments of the incarcerated youths in Ohio whose perspectives we discussed above. Fully 45 percent admitted everyday use of alcohol, and 30 percent reported everyday use of illicit drugs. Similar to the most alienated youth in the Urban Institute's Washington, D.C., study, many of these adolescents admitted selling drugs for money to buy drugs, though most were incarcerated for other than drug offenses. When asked in unstructured interviews why they used drugs, they frequently answered "boredom" and "to escape from pain." Several talked about not knowing what to do with idle time: "I do it 'cause it's there. Most of us do drugs 'cause it's there. There's not much else for us to do. If I can get it, I'm gonna." They rationalized use as a way of concealing pain, fear, and anxiety—as a means for escaping reality.

Recall from the introduction their answers to the question, "What would it take to get you to stop getting high?" The most frequently chosen response was, "If I could just be myself," which accounted for almost 35 percent of the replies. The second most frequent reply, "Stop trying to please my friends," was the choice of 12.4 percent, and "If I would leave the gang" accounted for another 8.4 percent (following "I don't know," at 9.7%) of the replies.

These answers are not what might be expected from the stereotypically self-assured street-hardened black male delinquent. Were it not for the time that the interviewer spent developing rapport, the answers would not likely have been so revealing. The answers show vulnerability, dissatisfaction with peer relations, and a wish for alternatives. They portray much about why these youths abuse drugs. They feel trapped. In interviews, they say that their delinquent friends are the only people on whom they can count. "Most of us get into gangs and do drugs because we can't get along with our families."

The fact that so many of the youngsters in Ohio answered, "If I could just be myself" suggests the pervasiveness of the feeling that neither society at large nor even their peers are willing to accept them for who they are (or would be). Drug use is among their responses to this unfortunate condition.

Conclusion

The stereotype that young African American males are dangerous, dishonest, and lacking in intelligence causes people in society's mainstream—African Americans and whites alike—to fear, mistrust, and disrespect young black males. This can cause the stereotype to become a self-fulfilling prophecy for youth who lack the sophistication not to take such treatment personally. Under the best of circumstances, sophistication about such matters comes from the wise counsel of parents. Many of the same parents who provide such counsel typically also provide the supervision and peer resistance training that protect youth from corrupting influences. In other cases, however, parents and peers may operate in ways that simply reinforce discouragement, alienation, and irresponsibility. In these cases, youth can become mired in mischief as they search for opportunities to experience friendship, achievement, influence, and security. This mischief often includes using and selling drugs.

Communities need to monitor and modify what they communicate to and about young African American males. This article argues that reducing the fear, mistrust, and disrespect that people communicate to black male youth, and improving supervision can, over a period of time, reduce levels of deviance and self-destructive behavior—including involvement with drugs—by this segment of our population. The challenge is finding ways to sensitize adults (1) to be more conscious of the messages that their words and behaviors send, (2) to understand how young people interpret and react to those messages, and (3) to send clear messages of hope, encouragement, and support for conventionality, even to youth whose reputations would seem to warrant other treatment.

An alternative to the list of alienating and corrupting messages that the paper discusses is easy to imagine: teachers and employers encourage every student or employee, keep open minds about people's potentials, and provide constructive feedback on behavior and performance. Strangers offer friendly and respectful greetings and, on occasion, express interest in establishing friendship; peers offer support and encouragement for any constructive effort toward self-improvement; parents are well informed, listen and communicate well, exercise appropriate levels of supervision, and do all that they can to facilitate their children's happiness and success in life. While easy to imagine, these things will be difficult to achieve for youth who are currently facing the opposite circumstances.

Acknowledgments

The authors wish to thank Mark A. R. Kleiman for helpful comments on an earlier draft. Also, Professor Ferguson would like to acknowledge the support of the Rockefeller Foundation for some of the work on which this paper draws.

References

Bandura, A. (1977). *Social learning theory.* Englewood Cliffs, NJ: Prentice-Hall.

Boufides, D., Crnkovich, P., Finnerty, K., Lawrence, J., & Madoff, N. (1987). *Anti-drug marketing study for the mayor's policy office of the City of Boston.* Harvard Business School Creative Marketing Study.

Brounstein, P. J., Hatry, H. P., Altschuler, D. M., & Blair, L. H. (1989). *Patterns of substance use and delinquency among inner city adolescents* Washington, DC: The Urban Institute.

Brunswick, A. (1989). Health stability and change: A study of urban black youth. *American Journal of Public Health, 76,* 504–513.

Campbell, D., & Stanley, J. (1985). *Experimental and quasi-experimental designs for research.* Chicago, IL: Rand & McNally.

Clark, R. M. (1983). *Family life and school achievement: Why poor black children succeed or fail.* Chicago, IL: University of Chicago Press.

Clayton, R. R., & Voss, H. L. (1981). *Young men and drugs in Manhattan: A causal analysis* [Monograph]. National Institute on Drug Abuse Research 39. U. S. Department of Health & Human Services.

Cloward, R. A., & Ohlin L. E. (1960). *Delinquency and opportunity: A theory of delinquent gangs.* New York: The Free Press.

Cohen, Albert K. (1962). Multiple factor approaches. In M. E. Wolfgang, L. Savitz, & N. Johnston (Eds.), *The sociology of crime and delinquency.* New York: Wiley.

Fagan, J. & Pabon, E. (1990). Contributions of delinquency and substance use to school dropout among inner-city youths. *Youth and Society, 21*(3).

Schachter, S., & Gazzaniga, M. & Festinger, L. (Eds.). (1989). *Extending psychological frontiers: Selected works of Leon Festinger.* New York: Russell Sage Foundation.

Festinger, L. (1980). *Retrospection on social psychology.* New York: Oxford Press.

Fisher, M. (1987, March 14). Peers inhibit black achievers. *Washington Post,* p. 1.

Fordham, S. (1988). Racelessness as a factor in black students' school success: Pragmatic strategy or pyrrhic victory? *Harvard Educational Review, 58*(1), 54–84.

Fordham, S., & Ogbu, J. U. (1986). Black students' school success: Coping with the burden of "acting white." *The Urban Review,* 18, 176–206.

Gibbs, J. (1988). *Young, black, male: An endangered species.* New York: Auburn Press.

Gove, W. R. (Ed.). (1975). *The labeling of deviance: Evaluating a perspective.* New York: Halsted.

Hale-Benson, J. E. (1982). *Black children: Their roots, culture, and learning styles.* Baltimore, MD: The Johns Hopkins University Press.

Harris, J. J. III, & Bennett, C. (1982). *Student discipline: Legal, empirical and educational perspectives.* Bloomington, IN: Center for Urban and Multicultural Education, Indiana University.

Harris, J. J. III, Pugh, R. C., & Heid, C. A. (1983). *Beyond school desegregation: A study of student perceptions and needs.* Bloomington, IN: Center for Urban and Multicultural Education, Indiana University.

Hirschi, T. (1969). *Causes of delinquency.* Berkeley, CA: University of California Press.

Holzer, H. J. (1986). Black youth nonemployment: Duration and job search. In R. B. Freeman, & H. J. Holzer (Eds.), *The black youth employment crisis.* Chicago, IL: The University of Chicago Press.

Jackson, M. S. (1988). *Drug use and delinquency in the black male adolescent: A descriptive study.* Unpublished dissertation, Case Western Reserve University School of Applied Social Sciences.

Jenkins, A. H. (1982). *The psychology of the Afro-American: A humanistic approach.* Elmsford, New York: Pergamon.

Jessor, R., & Jessor, S. (1977). *Problem behavior and psychosocial development: A longitudinal study of youth.* New York: Academic Press.

Johnson, B., Hamid, A., Morales, E., Sanabria, H. (1987, November 12). *Critical dimensions of crack distribution.* Paper presented at the American Society of Criminology in Montreal, Canada.

Jussim, L. (1986). Self-fulfilling prophecies: A theoretical and integrative review. *Psychological Review, 93*(4), 1–18.

Kandel, D. B. (1980). Drugs and drinking behavior among youth. *Annual Review of Sociology, 6,* 235–85.

Kerlinger, F. (1986). *Foundations of behavioral research* (3rd ed.). New York: Holt, Rhinehart & Winston.

Kirschenman, J., & Neckerman, K. M. (1991). We'd love to hire them but . . .: The meaning of race for employers. In C. Jencks, & P. Peterson (Eds.), *The urban underclass.* Washington, DC: The Brookings Institution.

Kunjufu, J. (1983). *Countering the conspiracy to destroy black boys.* Chicago, IL: Afro-Am Publishing Co.

Majors, R., & Billson, J. M. (1992). *Cool pose: The dilemmas of black manhood in America.* New York: Lexington Books.

Marsh, H. W., Cairns, L., Relich, J. Barnes, J., & Debus, R. L. (1984). The relationship between dimensions of self-attribution and dimensions of self-concept. *Journal of Educational Psychology, 76*(1), 3–32.

McClelland, D. C. (1987). *Human motivation.* New York: Macmillan.

Ohlin, L. & Miller, A.(1985). *Delinquency and community: Creating opportunities and controls.* Beverly Hills, CA: Sage.

Palardy, J. M. (1969). What teachers believe—what

children achieve. *Elementary School Journal, 69,* 370–374.

Polich, J. M., Ellickson, P., Reuter, P., & Kahan, J. (1984). *Strategies for controlling adolescent drug use.* Santa Monica, CA: The RAND Corporation.

Reuter, P., Maccoun, R., Murphy, P., Abrahamsen, A., & Simon, B. (1989). *Fruits of crime: Drug dealing and poverty (WD No. WD-4608-RF.).* Santa Monica, CA: The RAND Corporation, Rockefeller Foundation

Rosenthal, R. (1971). Teacher expectations and their effects upon children. In G. S. Lesser (Ed.), *Psychology and educational practice.* Glenview, IL: Scott Foresman.

Rosenthal, R. (1973). On the social psychology of the self-fulfilling prophecy: Further evidence for pygmalion effects and their mediating mechanisms. *Module, 53,* 1–25.

Rosenthal, R., & Jacobson, L. (1968). *Pygmalion in the classroom: Teacher expectation and pupil intellectual development.* New York: Holt, Rhinehart, & Winston.

Rowe, M. B. (1986). Wait time: Slowing down may be a way of speeding up! *Journal of Teacher Education, 37*(1), *43–50.*

Rubovits, P. C., & Maehr, M. L. (1973). Pygmalion black and white, *Journal of Personality and Social Psychology, 25*(2), 210.

Shervinton, W. (1986). The black family: Clinical overview. *The American Journal of Social Psychology, 6*(1), 6–10.

Spencer, M. B. (1990). Parental values transmission: Implications for the development of African-American children. In H. E. Cheatham & J. B. Steward (Eds.), *Black families: Interdisciplinary perspectives.* New Brunswick, NJ: Transaction Publishers.

Stephens, R. (1991). *The street addict role: A theory of heroin addiction.* Albany, NY: State University of New York Press.

Sutherland, E., Cressey, D. (1970). *Criminology* (8th ed.). Philadelphia, PA: Lippincott.

Taylor, C. S. (1989). *Dangerous society.* East Lansing, MI: Michigan State University Press.

Ward, L., & Wilson, J. P. (1980). Motivation and moral judgment as determinants of behavioral acquiescence and moral action. *Journal of Social Psychology, 1122*(2), 271–286.

Wilson, A. (1990). *Black on black violence.* New York: Africana Research Publications.

Discussion Questions

1. What is the main argument of this research?
2. According to Ferguson and Jackson, what are nurturing environments? What role do these environments play in the fulfillment of basic needs, and the development of self-esteem and ethnic identification? How important are these environments?
3. Interpret Tables 1–8. What main findings can be derived from these tables? Why are the findings important with regard to basic needs, self-esteem, and ethnic identification?
4. What effects can teachers exert on culturally diverse students? Do you think the influence is long-term? If so, how and in what ways are the teachers' effects long-lasting? If not, explain why the effects are not long-lasting.
5. Of all the skewed and demeaning messages given to black youth, as presented by Ferguson and Jackson, which are the most damaging? Why are the messages you selected more damaging than the others?
6. What do the authors believe is the main cause for drug use by black males? Do you agree or disagree with their findings? Why or why not?

African American Perspectives on Mobilizing Organizational Responses to Drugs

Ernest Quimby

Ernest Quimby is an Associate Graduate Professor of Sociology and Criminal Justice in the Department of Sociology and Anthropology at Howard University. His continuing research on substance abuse and AIDS/HIV mobilization and evaluation issues was commenced as a National Institute on Drug Abuse Post-Doctoral Research Fellowship in the late 1980s. Dr. Quimby is a Co-Principal Investigator and Director of Ethnography of a study funded by the National Institute on Alcohol Abuse and Alcoholism of homeless persons in Washington, D.C., who are dually diagnosed with substance abuse and mental illnesses. His publications include: "Dynamics of Black Mobilization Against AIDS in New York City" (with Samuel Friedman, *Social Problems,* 1989), "Dilemmas of Drugs—AIDS Research Among African Americans" (in *Drug Abuse Research Issues at Historically Black Colleges and Universities,* Tuskegee Institute, 1991), "Drug Trafficking and the Caribbean Connection: Survival Mechanisms and Social Symptoms" (in *The Urban League Review,* 1991), and "Anthropological Witnessing for African Americans: Power, Responsibility, and Choice in the Age of AIDS" (in *Social Analysis in the Time of AIDS: Theory, Method and Action,* Sage Publications, 1992).

Defining Substance Abuse

Cultural attitudes about drugs affect how we define problems and act on them. In turn, definitions affect policies. There is a tendency to refer to licit and illicit substances. These perceptions can obscure issues. There are no good versus bad drugs. A drug is a substance whose chemical action changes an organism's structure or functioning.

History, socialization, ideology, politics, and economics affect science and law. Thus, although 50,000 individuals may smoke a pack and a half of cigarettes each day, tobacco usage in the United States is not seen by many as drug addiction. Major causes of death are linked to alcohol and tobacco. An estimated 30–40 percent of yearly mortality figures are due to these—which may be twenty times more than those caused by illegal drugs. Some 50–60 percent of homicides and fatal accidents are related to alcohol.

Substance abuse is a major health problem. The issue is not a drug's legal status, but its specific effects. How a problem or question is viewed or framed affects how it is addressed. Understanding drug use requires consideration of who defines the subject matter, and according to whose and what criteria. Who identifies and formulates the scientific problems is a socio-political issue that impacts on public policies and scientific investigations. Empirical data and conceptual models are needed. Otherwise, politics may wind up driving the science.

Psychoactive chemicals can cause dependence. When people stop prolonged coffee use, certain reactions may take place. There are also physiological symptoms of withdrawal, such as irritability and headaches. Are these individuals drug abusers? Does the terminology get in the way of understanding the behavior? Again, a drug is a chemical substance that causes physiological and/or emotional and/or social behavioral change. Cultural images influence what we call illicit substances. As a result, only certain chemicals are seen as drugs.

Definitions are problematic. For instance, a narcotic is an analgesic dod. However, although cocaine and marijuana are not pharmacologically narcotics, legally they are classified as such. Substance abuse is deviation from approved medical, legal, and social patterns within a culture. Sometimes, legality and power override scientific reasoning.

African American Concerns

Although the majority of drug users and reported cases of acquired immune deficiency syndrome (AIDS) in the U.S. are white, epidemiologic data show that ingesting drugs has created special problems for African Americans (NIDA, 1992). However, African American substance abuse professionals have articulated particular issues that have not been heeded. According to one review of the drug abuse literature, "Overall, the response of the field to the concerns expressed years earlier by minority drug abuse specialists has been minimal" (Tucker, 1985, p. 1022). It concluded with an agenda of critical needs. Recommendations included: comprehensive substantive reviews of empirical and clinical literature on minority drug use; regular, systematic, and broad assessments of chemical use and dependency among people of color; etiological studies that explain racial/ethnic variations of use; studies that have applied relevance for service delivery, instead of just racial/ethnic comparisons; drug use/abuse theories specifically applicable to unique circumstances of minorities; development of empirical literature to organize and guide intervention methods specific to minorities; and official support for culturally sensitive efforts of service delivery specialists, especially those who belong to racial/ethnic minorities.

Policies and research take place within a socio-political context. But there is resistance (active and passive) to this reality. Denial of political economy by some professionals and lay people prevents them from including socio-political factors in their analyses of and approaches to drug trafficking, chemical dependency, and AIDS (Quimby 1991a, 1992). Confounding the matter is a virtual mystification of bio-medical models.

Presentation of the problem is critical. Organizations and individuals are critical of a siege mentality created by media, politicians, and law enforcement officials. African American males are projected as urban menaces who imperil white society's social order and stability. Policy makers need to acknowledge and confront the consequences of equating "drug kingpins" with African Americans, while avoiding documentation of white suppliers and controllers of drug trafficking.

Polarized constructions of reality depict criminals as poor, violent, and pathological. They are supposedly raised by emotionally crippled women in families living in chaotic neighborhoods. Disturbed, overwhelmed, disorganized, hopeless, without positive self-esteem, directionless, and bitter, they seemingly turn to drugs for social mobility and visible recognition. According to this assessment, they must be protected from themselves if possible, but certainly society must be guarded. According to the illogic of fear, threats must be isolated, contained, quarantined and eliminated. Thus a metaphoric virus of contamination is seemingly spread by particular groups.

However, this popular scenario overlooks structural issues of equality, schooling, justice and empowerment. Some within the research community may be adding to the confusion by promoting socio-biological views to the exclusion of alternative theories. One danger is that accumulating the same types of data in the same ways can become self-fulfilling.

Traditional theoretical concepts, assumptions and data seem to operationally confirm and reinforce one another. But do they? Are the computer-generated models and studies by predominantly white investigators and their African American apprentices illuminating our understanding, or merely displaying the same historical equations with a new cast? For instance, is it accurate to conclude—based on what data, collected by whom, and in what ways?—that drug dependency is caused by poverty, or that any particular racial category is a high-risk group?

Are ever increasingly sophisticated data collection techniques doing anything more than confirming and circulating old anecdotes and incomplete observations? Where are the theories, hypotheses, and data that show relationships between higher socio-economic, social, and psychological pathology? In the U.S., why are racial minorities associated with drug dependency, crime, and disruptive or unhealthy environments? Researchers refer to risk factors, predependent or high-risk groups, diagnostic probabilities, and other concepts that project certain ethnic groups as both the problem and symptom of America's drug problem. However, official data on drug abuse (as well as other public health problems) are incomplete and can be conflicting. Research methods classes have often taught that "there are lies, damned lies, and statistics." Hence, it is necessary to be careful about issues of reliability, validity, generalization, and applicability. At best, epidemiologic data are selective approximations of constructed reality, mere indicators of the range of social experience. Nevertheless, when cautiously approached they can become powerful assets in helping to shape, implement, and evaluate public policies (USDHHS, 1985) .

Historically, public policies have reflected inconsistent perceptions of drug dependency (Musto, 1973): as a crime, a sickness, and as both. Many addicts lack health insurance, even if facilities were made available. This is a critical problem for those trying to utilize nontraditional or new methods such as acupuncture or replacing amino acids depleted by cocaine usage. However, permitting Medicaid and Medicare to pay for such health care may require special legislation. Hence, elected officials and policy makers have to be educated and sensitized, which in turn requires that chemically dependent people be seen as ill constituents rather than social threats.

Drug addicts have been variously regarded, and responded to in conflicting ways: as criminals, patients, and pathological misfits. The presumed causes have generally been either emotional defects, sociological deficits, biological flaws, or combinations thereof. But to date, there is too little recognition or support for the development of theory and empirical research by African Americans to explain, describe, or document the presumed social or individual disorders (whether genetic, physiological or emotional) .

There is a tendency to link drugs and anti-social behavior with politically marginal peoples and classes. In an effort to reverse this negative association, the prevalence and incidence of homicides among African Americans are now recognized as public health issues (USCDC, 1985) .

Understanding drug abuse requires an appreciation of the dynamic relationships between particular users, specific drugs, and the particular contexts of their use. The drug treatment and research fields need different ways to collect and interpret new kinds of data. African American researchers and service providers may be uniquely suited to provide specialized insights.

Dominant Theoretical Perspectives on Drug Dealing and Drug Abuse

The concepts most frequently used to explain causes of juvenile drug dealing include anomie, blocked opportunity, containment, differential association, labeling, psychosis, social control and bonding, social disorganization, cultural deviance, strain, structured inequality, and subculture. Drug use and abuse theories are numerous. A summary monograph issued by the National Institute on Drug Abuse contains 43 perspectives on "one's relationship to" self, others, society, and nature (Lettieri et al., 1980). They center on initiation, continuation, transition (use to abuse), cessation, and relapse. There are overlapping types: socio-biological, sociological, and psychological. Deviance is a common theme. Each can be subdivided. The more influential sociological perspectives center around structural functionalist, conflict, and symbolic interactionist explanations. What they reveal is the absence of any one adequately comprehensive theory of drug use and abuse. There can be as many theories as there are users, abusers, and dealers. However, one lay tendency is to overgeneralize, referring to the "problem of drug abuse."

Overview of African American Perspectives

A contentious issue is whether drug abuse is essentially a criminal justice or a health issue. Despite—or along with—neighborhood and political support for increased penalization and get tough policies, there is also an emerging consensus that law enforcement per se will not solve the problem. Although generally not in favor of decriminalization, African American proponents of the health orientation argue that the tendency to portray use or abuse as criminal activity has had major negative consequences. Profits from distributing illegal drugs have increased. Dealing has led to the organization of complex neighborhood, regional, national, and international networks. The allure and monetary rewards from street sales have seduced youths into becoming entrepreneurs and employees in the drug business. A selective, biased war on drugs targets working-class African Americans and Latinos. The criminal justice system has become overloaded and nearly unmanageable. Desperately needed governmental resources are being drained from health, housing, education, and infrastructural development.

According to this perspective, policy solutions need to regard illegal drug use and dealing as symptoms both of general structural defects and cultural malaise, as well as of dysfunctional communities, families, and individuals. Drug abuse and dealing are thus examples of health risk behavior, not simply criminal activity. The social contexts of political and economic underdevelopment, class inequality, racism, and other dynamics of social relations must be addressed. Otherwise, there may be continued alienation, more violence, intensified scapegoating, and misguided but intensified clamor for killing the marginal victims of a society. Being born in the wrong place and time should not be a chargeable offense.

African Americans express diverse views about AIDS and drug-related issues (Quimby, 1989, 1991b). No consensus has yet formed (Quimby, 1993). However, there is an emerging discussion of the viability of Afrocentric programs (Nobles et al., 1989). Moreover, researchers are adding new contextual perspectives and data on family, gender, and youth dynamics (Rodgers-Rose, 1980; McAdoo & McAdoo, 1985; Gibbs, 1988; McAdoo, 1988) .

Two conflicting assumptions about illegal drug acts exist. They are generally viewed either as racist manipulation or as so-called "Black on Black" crime. There is no singular stance, other than the perception that African American perspectives on problems directly affecting their survival and development are not sufficiently known, appreciated, or circulated.

African American Policy Perceptions

Community participation is necessary for success. The traditional approach is a top-down model. It should be upwards. Community-based organizations are in touch with daily realities and family problems. They could be instrumental in helping to train parents and siblings. This must be part of a comprehensive approach, including job training.

There is a need for more coordination and communication between the criminal justice system and community organizations. Some neighborhoods and groups complain of inefficient concentration and deployment of police forces. A common perception is that sometimes elected political leadership reacts not to objective need, but to political clout. The belief is that politicians are more concerned with getting elected and staying in office than with actually leading, or mobilizing around critical issues. Coordinated municipal and federal government actions are necessary to assist neighborhood activities.

Tolerance of drug violence frustrates solutions and limits antidrug participation efforts. Condoning may be at one or several levels and sectors: individual, family, community, media, corporate, and government. Some factors contributing to local drug problems are insulation, unawareness, apathy, complacency, and denial by community organizations and political groups. Their members may live in the area, but may not feel part of it. Mobilizers feel frustrated by responses of residents and traditional leadership. Part of the struggle is how to develop a sense of community. Each area has unique conditions that affect community consciousness and mobilization.

Success is relative. Dealing in one neighborhood may be a result of displacement from another area. Measuring effectiveness is controversial and complicated because problems and resolutions are sometimes framed quite narrowly. The overwhelming criterion is "not on my block." New detention and treatment centers are generally rejected by neighborhood boards.

Spontaneous neighborhood activity usually becomes dissipated or bureaucratized. Certain questions arise. Will an institutionalized community approach become less empowering? Will it allow for individualized expression and energizing of neighborhoods or will it permit greater organizational effectiveness? Research is needed to answer these questions.

Different institutional players (e.g., police and tenant associations) may have conflicting conceptions about the limits of "taking back" the block. Consensus is necessary on the role and authority of each. For example, antagonistic thoughts on the role of churches may reduce their effectiveness. A highly vocalized position is that low self-esteem is a process of cultural oppression by some churches and schools. How then can they help correct distorted self-imagery when they have been willing partners in deforming the imaginations of African Americans? This controversial view asserts that Westernized churches cannot motivate actual or would-be users or dealers towards different attitudes and behaviors. They allegedly de-motivate youths from developing positive identities.

However, critics disagree and cite progressive activism by churches. There is also grassroots sentiment for the Nation of Islam's "dope busting" activities in Washington, DC. A belief exists that the Muslims are not valued by or incorporated into official or traditional efforts.

Policy Recommendations by African Americans

The following is a compilation of recommendations advanced by policy makers, researchers, educators, activists, and intervention specialists. Systematic opportunities must be provided for developing positive self-images. Avoid one-dimensional answers. The urban situation is complicated. There is no one cause or solution. Thus, reduction of the problems cannot be just a criminal justice approach. Informed dialogue and ideological debate would be useful for clarifying the role of schooling and dominant institutions in instilling healthy values, goals, and skills. Such discussion could help build consensus as to how churches, mosques and other spiritual organizations could inculcate wholesome lifestyles. Information and a willingness to struggle collectively are needed in order to answer the questions: whose values, whose morality, and for what purposes?

Structured individual and group chances to avoid initiation into drug use are required. People need decision-making skills, so as to learn how to refuse. Techniques can be theater, music, dance, and other performing arts. One must feel safe and able to share personal feelings. Experiences can be structured to help people become empowered and accomplish positive goals. In addition, although males are conspicuously endangered, specific programs are needed for females.

Workable proposals require securing political protection of turf by individuals, groups, and agencies. If participants feel that their interests are jeopardized, then cooperation may be reduced. Neighborhood political factors need to be identified and appreciated, such as structure, organization, competing agenda, methods of groping for ideas, strategies, and techniques. Who claims to lead and on what basis? Who articulates the questions and to whom? What are the effects of competing ideologies? For some activists the cause of drug problems is not racial exploitation per se, but class inequality. For others, ultimately the reason is racism.

There is a recognition that neighborhood social control mechanisms are lacking. Discipline is regarded as being either slack or nonexistent. Current youths are looked at as seeking more intense excitement and different experiences, compared to past generations. Drug use and other activities are seemingly immediately rewarding, profitable, and exciting.

One argument is that solutions start with the parents and family. Other role models help to reinforce positive attitudes and behaviors. Another perspective is that solutions start with the government, whose policies affect parental and familial efforts.

A critical position is that "the system" provides middle-income whites with jobs, rehabilitation, and alternatives to jails, but ensures that others will not get opportunities for employment, treatment, or access to a responsive criminal justice bureaucracy. Yet, some whites view certain reforms as "reverse racism." To them, justice is lenient and social services are going to African Americans at the expense of whites.

Policies need to be sensitive to fears of selective enforcement or loss of civil liberties. Fear, anger and frustration are fueling calls for throwing youths into jail, rather than focusing on prevention, education, and rehabilitation. According to some people, addiction and dealing are irrational but deliberate choices, whose consequences must be accepted by addicts and dealers.

Another unresolved controversy is what model(s) should be used (e.g., punishment vs. treatment approach) to address problems of addiction and dependency. For instance, what should be the position towards chemically dependent pregnant women? Is a punitive approach more effective than treatment? Are jail sentences racist and anti-working class? What are reproductive rights, and under what circumstances, if any, should they be curtailed? Do the "unborn" have rights? Is drug dependency fundamentally a public health or a criminal justice issue?

According to one perspective, racism is being used as an excuse to avoid making choices, and as a crutch for not making correct ones. Hence, because some parents have not prepared their children for the realities of racism and inequality, whites should not be blamed. Racial naiveté is regarded as the fault of African Americans. Some are tired of hearing about racism. They do not believe that discrimination is at fault. Others argue that it is not enough to talk about the system without challenging it. They maintain that "the struggle" is primarily and initially a personal responsibility, which later gets transformed into collective action.

There is concern about media "hype." One fear is that political fallout from antidrug strategies may make leaders reluctant to take stances. Weak or nonexistent political leadership is also considered part of the problem. Mechanisms of accountability are necessary. Moreover, because drug problems seem to be periodically sensationalized, there is anxiety that no consistent efforts will be forthcoming.

An increasing perception is that economic investments in chemical therapies for emotional and physical health, medicating for personal problems, and encouraging substance use for social acceptance promote dealing of legal and illegal drugs. Thus there is resentment and concern over advertising aimed specifically at African Americans that hails cigarette smoking and alcohol use. In some cities, local activists tear down or paint over billboards that celebrate tobacco and liquor.

Another critical view is that the inner city's economic instability erodes the self-worth and compassion of its young residents—as opposed to middle-class youths, who are presumed to be nurtured, self-fulfilled, and emotionally intact. However, it is also possible to have high self-esteem and still use or deal drugs. Even so, the argument is for leaders to develop strategies to stop the flight of capital from low-income areas.

Political and financial investments in communities are projected by some as interrelated solutions. The hardship of youths needs addressing through jobs and alternative forms of education. But a problematic aspect of leadership responsiveness and accountability is that new policies may require money—thus new taxes—which may make politicians uneasy about proposing programs. Skeptics of the economic empowerment model insist that "Black capitalism" in itself will not resolve civil liberties and human rights problems. They assert that creating African American-owned businesses will not decrease racism. Thus, dependency on entrepreneurship allegedly amounts to denial and avoidance of the real problems: spiritual and economic impoverishment, and lack of affordable health care for treatment and counseling. This view claims that business ownership is no insurance that African Americans will have the right to walk the streets freely and safely.

In some urban areas, police are seen almost as an occupying force protecting the property interests of whites. A more controversial position is that oppressed people are forced to take advantage of whatever opportunities they can create. Trafficking is symptomatic of injustice. The belief is that the dominant Euro-American society relates to African America as a stigmatized, problematic blemish. This view also maintains that responsibility is a result of perceived choices, consciousness, and possibilities of understanding one's condition. Therefore, political and cultural awareness demand that a people should not self-destruct. Drug abuse is depicted as a form of slavery.

Drug-related Crime and Violence

When does drug use become a problem? A classic answer is when it interferes with psychological, physiological, or social functioning. But definitions of problems are frequently related to the interests of dominant groups. There is suspicion that drug-related crime and violence only became issues when the syndrome of white denial could no longer be sustained.

In any case, there are no apparent, clear-cut reasons for or explanations of the relationships between drugs and violence. Evidence (NIDA, 1989) points to a variety of factors ranging from the drugs themselves to conditions of their usage, and characteristics of the users. The causes of violence vary. They include pharmacological effects of chemicals, physiological condition of users, and developmental and social factors. Different specialists highlight different causes. Social scientists connect the effects of drugs with social psychological variables and physiological factors such as genetic traits, organically induced or aggravated psychiatric problems, central nervous system infections, head traumas, and neurochemical complications of intoxication or ingestion.

Clearer profiles of users and the range of consequent violent behaviors are needed. It is becoming evident that some chemicals may induce violent behavior. Psychoactive barbiturates may lead to aggression. Social scientists develop explanatory and interventionist models that highlight social and psychological components. Intervention for drug-related violence has to account for a chain of interactions.

A variety of explanations has been offered to explain relationships between drugs and inner-city violence (Tonry & Wilson, 1990). All are understandably limited. One attempt to categorize unapproved aggressive behavior is the violence-prone syndrome perspective. This psycho-pathological model assumes that acute antisocial personality disorders are related to early socialization, poverty, substance use, and violence. It suggests that school children be identified, diagnosed, and targeted for special forms of intervention and social control. This model holds that it is psychological disorder, not the drug or social context, which causes violence. Hence, criminal justice needs programs aimed at persons with antisocial pathologies.

An opposite contention is the structural strain model. It hypothesizes that there is a disparity between opportunity and economic gain. Therefore, violence is not essentially a pharmacological, socio-biological, or personality issue. Drugs are chosen not so much because of effects, but for their availability, price, acceptance, and contexts of use. From this perspective, drug-associated violence is structurally, culturally, and socio-psychologically propelled.

Another perspective is that public health in working-class locales reflects structural underdevelopment, institutional insufficiency and marginality (Quimby & Friedman, 1989). What drives the problems is the inability of communities to mobilize adequately. A major difficulty confronting organizations is the lack of sustained participation by members. In many cases, communities are unable to mobilize effectively because of competing priorities. Potential activists are torn between organizing around AIDS, alcohol, crack-cocaine, housing, education, sanitation, and a host of other critical issues. Specific patterns of violence depend on the particular characteristics of each city and neighborhood. However, the concepts of disabled and enabled communities remain to be operationally clarified. Moreover, the factors and processes of community disabling and enabling have not yet been specified as they directly pertain to drug-related crime and violence.

Summary

No one concept or perspective adequately explains reasons for drug use or related criminality. Causes and patterns exist within a variety of contexts: pharmacologic, social, political, historical, cultural, psychological, and economic. Drug-related problems are associated with structural circumstances, social experiences, symbolic meanings, and pharmacology.

Responses to drug-related problems incorporate ideological assumptions, political attitudes, and conceptions of reality. Effective prevention is preferable to correction. Prevention, treatment, and corrections policies are counterproductive, if they do not address structural realities, cultural relativity, and individual needs. Otherwise, programs may create revolving doors and become instruments of confusion and perceived repression. Structures, experiences, and learning opportunities must be implemented that help to enhance social status and self-esteem.

Some drug-related activities reflect a perceived lack of self and social actualization, empowerment, and purpose. Understanding the barriers to community development and empowerment helps to clarify intervention issues. Policies have to be culturally appropriate and aimed at changing social institutions, not just at punishing individuals. Prevention needs community support and participation. Local effectiveness requires neighborhood infrastructural development.

References

Gibbs, J. T. (Ed.). (1988). *Young, black, and male in America: An endangered species.* Dover, MA: Auburn House.

Inciardi, J. A. (1992). *The war on drugs II: The continuing epic of heroin, cocaine, crack, crime, AIDS, and public policy.* Mountain View, CA: Mayfield Publishing Company.

Lettieri, D. J., Sayers, M., & Pearson, H. W. (Eds.). (1980). *Theories on drug abuse: Selected contemporary perspectives* [Monograph]. (NIDA Research

30). Washington, DC: U. S. Government Printing Office.

McAdoo, H. A. (Ed.). (1988). *Black families* (2nd ed.). Newbury Park, CA: Sage Publications.

McAdoo, H. A., & McAdoo, J. L. (Ed.). (1985). *Black children: social, educational, and parental environments.* Newbury Park, CA: Sage Publications.

Musto, D. (1973). *The American disease: Origins of narcotic control.* New Haven, CT: Yale University Press.

National Institute on Drug Abuse. (1992). *NIDA Capsules* fact sheet. Rockville, MD: NIDA

National Institute on Drug Abuse. (1989, September 18–19, 25–26.). *Technical review of longitudinal studies, Washington, DC, Technical review of drugs and violence, Rockville, MD.*

Nobles, W. W., Goddard, L. L., & George, P. Y. (1989). *The culture of drugs in the black community.* Oakland, CA: The Institute for the Advanced Study of Black Life, and Culture.

Quimby, E. (1989). Precarious dilemmas: Mobilizing blacks against AIDS. In L. S. Harris (Ed.), *Problems of drug dependence* [Monograph]. National Institute on Drug Abuse Research 95, pp. 473–474. Washington, DC: U. S. Government Printing Office.

Quimby, E. (1991a). Drug trafficking and the Caribbean connection: Survival mechanisms, entrepreneurship and social symptoms. *The Urban League Review, 14*(2), 61–70.

Quimby, E. (1991b). Dilemmas of drugs—AIDS research among African Americans. In *Substance abuse research issues facing historically black colleges and universities.* Clark Atlanta University and National Institute on Drug Abuse Research [Monograph]. (pp. 170–192). Tuskeegee Institute Press.

Quimby, E. (1992). Anthropological witnessing for African Americans: Power, responsibility, and choice in the age of AIDS. In G. Herdt, & S. Lindenbaum (Eds.), *The time of AIDS: Social analysis, theory, and method* (pp. 159–184). Newbury Park, London, & New Delhi: SAGE Publications.

Quimby, E. (1993). Obstacles to reducing AIDS among African Americans. *The Journal of Black Psychology, 19*(2), 215–222.

Quimby, E., & Friedman, S. R. (1989). Dynamics of black mobilization against AIDS in New York City. *Social Problems, 36*(4), 403–415.

Rodgers-Rose, L. F. (Ed.). (1980). *The black woman.* Newbury Park, CA: Sage Publications.

Tonry, M., & Wilson, J. Q. (Eds.). (1990). *Drugs and crime.* Chicago, IL: University of Chicago Press.

Tucker, B. M. (1985). U. S. ethnic minorities and drug abuse: An assessment of the science and practice. *The International Journal of the Addictions, 20*(6, 7), 1021–1047.

U. S. Centers for Disease Control. (1985,October 18). Homicide among young black males (United States, 1970–1982). *Morbidity & Mortality Weekly Report, 34,* 629–533.

U. S. Department of Health & Human Services. (1985). *Report of the Secretary's Task Force on black & minority health.* Washington, DC: U. S. Government Printing Office.

Discussion Questions

Give reasons and examples for your responses to the following questions.

1. Are the concerns and perspectives of African Americans about drugs fundamentally different from those of white Americans?
2. What major obstacles limit effective mobilization against drug abuse in your community? Do you personally feel sufficiently empowered to regulate your own drug use and/or that of your peers?
3. What are the similarities and differences between those issues in your neighborhood and those raised in the author's paper?
4. Which theoretical perspective about drug dealing and drug abuse seems to be the most plausible?
5. List and discuss the national and local public policy implications of the paper.

Part IV—Drug Abuse Prevention

IV

We begin this introductory chapter by asking the following questions: What is prevention, and does it differ from treatment? What does prevention entail? What types of prevention exist? Given the enormity of the problem, what types of prevention are more successful?

The need for prevention becomes increasingly important when we consider that over 23 million Americans use drugs monthly (Senate Task Force for a Drug Free America, 1990). Besides the estimated millions of addicts, we also have to include the millions who use illicit drugs mainly for recreational purposes. The millions of recreational users easily disguise their use and are often indistinguishable from nonusers.

Prevention refers to programs or procedures that are used to reduce the extent of drug use. Prevention differs from treatment in that it includes delaying or preventing the drug use. While treatment presumes that drugs are being used, prevention may or may not involve drug use. Two types of prevention exist, primary and secondary. *Primary prevention* techniques are aimed at nonusers and early experimenters. *Secondary prevention* techniques are directed at more experienced users, and often the goal is to prevent further use of a particular drug or increased involvement with other types of drugs.

Nearly all primary programs use educational approaches and are taught in elementary and secondary schools. Three approaches are generally employed in these primary prevention educational programs. The first is the *information/knowledge education* approach. The primary goal in using this approach is to relay information about particular drugs and drug use. This method assumes that drug use results from a lack of information about the harmful effects and consequences of drug use. Providing drug use information informs potential adolescent users, in the hope that they will either refrain from use or become responsible users.

Affective education is the second approach. The goal of this approach is to penetrate the students' attitudes and emotions about drug use. The assumption is that drug use results from an inadequate personality, and that the user's values, attitudes and self-esteem need redefinition and enhancement. The third approach is *social influence/skills education.* Unlike the affective education approach, which emphasizes psychological inadequacies, the social influence and skills education approach addresses more sociological factors that cause drug use. Such factors as: drug resistance strategies, and positive interaction with family, school, and peers are emphasized. Students are often involved in role playing, socio-drama, and other positive modeling techniques that promote drug-free behavior.

In evaluating the primary prevention approach, we find that the information/knowledge based method does increase the knowledge about drugs and drug use, but it has very little effect on stopping or curtailing drug use behavior (Polich, Ellickson et al., 1984; Botvin, 1990). This approach equips adolescents with drug use knowledge but does not change their drug use behavior.

The second type, the affective education approach, has been more successful in penetrating attitudes, but has demonstrated very mixed results regarding drug use (Huba, 1980). The main weakness is that peer pressure often overwhelms newly formed values and attitudes against drug use. Any affective education approach that does not include techniques and skills for resisting peer influences is not very effective.

The third type, the social influence approach, is more successful than the other two approaches (Botvin, 1990; Akers, 1992). Key reasons for the success of this approach are that refusal or resistance is emphasized, and self-esteem coupled with interpersonal skills are taught. Social influence entails learning to effectively express feelings, attitudes and beliefs. In addition to enhancing self-esteem, effective communication inoculates the student against succumbing to peer pressure and fosters enough self-confidence so that, when confronted by drug using peers, the student has the tenacity to voice contradictory or opposing views concerning drug use. Similarly, resistance techniques provide alternate responses whenever drug use is suggested by peers.

Why is the social influence prevention approach more successful than other preventative approaches? Specifically, what aspects of this approach result in equipping the student to resist drug use when peers exert pressure? How do more effective communication skills strengthen resistance to drug use? Social influence begins from the premise that drug use results from numerous personality inadequacies and shortcomings. Shortcomings include an unstable personality, insecurity, a lack of trusting relationships, inability to take other people's perspectives, lack of direction in life, and a lack of meaningful interdependence with other people (Johnson, 1984). Lack of trusting relationships often results from a dysfunctional family structure. Children who have not had the chance to develop trust with parent(s) or guardians often experience anxiety, fear, and apprehension when relating to others. Through interaction, *perspective-taking* involves assuming the role(s) of significant others from other people's perspectives during conversation. This process involves the ability to relate to others in a meaningful manner. Direction in life refers to the ability to set goals and priorities and act on them. Becoming actively involved in meaning and purpose is part of having direction in life. Finally, meaningful interdependence with others involves sharing with others and cooperating in joint efforts. Relying on others is subsumed under interdependence. In turn, interdependence demands trust, perspective taking, and direction in life.

Notice that all these qualities involve the ability to relate meaningfully to others and instilling these qualities means drawing the individual out of himself or herself into a communicative life. When this is done, anxiety, fear, apprehension, low self-awareness and self-esteem, rigidity, and lack of commitment are confronted and minimized by meaningful and effective interaction.

Beyond the primary and secondary prevention methods, there are other techniques that have had some measure of success. Some of these other methods include: (1) reducing the number of alcohol retail outlets in given areas (Macdonald & Whitehead, 1983; Frankel & Whitehead, 1985); (2) increasing the price of alcoholic beverages through federal, state, and local tax increases (Babor, 1985); (3) banning of alcohol advertising (Frankena, Cohen et al., 1985); and (4) increasing the minimum drinking age. As shown above, numerous studies have introduced a large quantity of different factors associated with drug use and abuse. These studies have in common limited success, and they often lack follow-up validation research.

The pandemic use of illicit drugs affects all social classes in our society.[1] The extensive abuse of drugs that has been documented throughout this volume, and its accompanying medical, psychological, social and criminal outcomes, serve as the central justification for the "War on Drugs." The current strategies of this war may be related to a small decrease in the use of *gateway drugs*. In criticizing the massive funding and efforts expanded to reduce supply and prosecute offenders, many social scientists argue that there has been an insignificant emphasis on prevention, education, and treatment. The articles in Part IV address the lack of emphasis on prevention by focusing on key concepts, strategies and techniques, and model programs for lessening and preventing drug abuse.

Is prevention possible, and what types of prevention strategies exist? To answer this question, Part IV has eight articles arranged into three categories. The three articles in the first category serve as metaperspectives on drug prevention. Pittman and Staudenmeier's "Twentieth Century Wars on Alcohol and Other Drugs in the United States" asserts that the present convergence of restrictive drug and alcohol social movements is not unique; in fact, throughout the twentieth century, both alcohol and drug control movements have been in close temporal proximity. But while the social control goals and tactics of each movement can be quite similar, the actors are different. This article explores: (1) the similarities and differences between these movements and (2) the influences leading to the simultaneous emergence of drug and alcohol social control movements.

Pittman and Staudenmeier use three cases of parallel efforts at drug and alcohol social control to explore these issues. The first case examines the period leading to the passage of the Harrison Anti-Narcotic Act in 1914 and the enactment of the Eighteenth Amendment to the United States Constitution in 1919 (National Alcohol Prohibition). The second case focuses on the activities leading to the passage of the Hughes-

Javits Act (PL91-616) in 1970 and the "First War on Drugs" of the Nixon Years (1969–1974). The third case investigates the recent "social control" movements directed at alcohol, as reflected in the new temperance movement, and at other drugs, as represented in the "Second War on Drugs" of the recent Reagan era.

The second article, "Advertising Against Drugs: Themes from a Televised Anti-Drug Campaign," by Baumann and Waterston, analyzes the largest coordinated voluntary mass media campaign in advertising history. In 1986, the advertising community of the United States formally joined the nation's "War on Drugs." The Media-Advertising Partnership for a Drug-Free America produces and distributes over two hundred public service advertisements for television, radio, newspapers and magazines. Their aim is to show, in very graphic terms, that the use of drugs is not normal, and to reverse the allure of drug use. The Partnership for a Drug-Free America works to "unsell" or "denormalize" drug use through the creation, production and distribution of advertising focused on discouraging the purchase and consumption of illegal drugs. Their goals include the formation and development of attitudes and behavior against drug use.

The research is a case study exploring the *social construction* of the drug problem. Baumann and Waterston examine the Partnership's televised public service advertisements in order to identify the themes and images of the drug problem as they construct it. Particular attention is paid to the following concerns: the substances identified as problematic, the identity of the drug abusers, and the nature of the drug-taking experience.

The third article, "Drinking Behavior: Taking Personal Responsibility," by Hanson and Engs, begins by reviewing the background of collegiate drinking and describes efforts to solve a perceived social problem through legislation. The failure of such efforts is detailed along with a possible explanation; potential unintended negative consequences are also identified.

Hanson and Engs argue that the failure of a legislative solution suggests the need for greatly increased self-responsibility. To inform the reader in this regard, the article provides guidelines for low-risk drinking, gives hints for being a responsible host, identifies characteristics that increase one's risk of being alcoholic, and includes a checklist to determine if one might have a drinking problem. Sources of information and help are also listed. The article concludes by emphasizing the necessity for taking personal responsibility for decisions and actions.

In the second category, two articles specifically focus on drinking and driving. In "Do Friends Let Friends Drive Drunk?: Decreasing Drunk Driving through Informal Peer Intervention," Monto, Rabow, Newcomb and Hernández look at the efforts made to deter drunk driving in the U.S. The emphasis has been on strengthening penalties and educating drivers, but neither effort has proven very effective. Monto, et al. examine informal intervention by one's peers as a method of decreasing drunk driving. The authors see peer intervention as a naturally occurring form of helping behavior, and they use helping behavior theories to explain the complexity of the phenomenon. Monto et al. view the decision to intervene as involving four steps: (l) noticing the potential drunk driving situation, (2) deciding it is an emergency, (3) deciding that one is able to intervene, and (4) intervening. The authors explore characteristics of the situation, the potential helper, and the relationship between the driver and the potential helper that predict whether someone will intervene. Finally, what is shown is that when intervention occurs, it is usually done either passively or assertively, and often this is tried before intervention is successful.

The next article in the category of drinking and driving, "Protecting our Future: Options for Preventing Alcohol-impaired Driving Among Youth," by Wagenaar, begins by discussing the fact that alcohol-impaired driving and resulting casualties are a leading cause of death and disability among teenagers and young adults. The research in this article shows that the major reasons for the overrepresentation of youth in motor vehicle crashes include: driving in more hazardous times and places, a drinking pattern that involves frequent occasions where large quantities of alcohol are consumed, and relatively high sensitivity to the impairing effects of alcohol.

Most efforts to reduce youth alcohol-related traffic crashes are based on three traditional approaches: (1) deterring young people from drinking/driving through arrest and punishment of offenders, (2) educating, treating, and rehabilitating apprehended drinking drivers, and (3) informing and educating the general population of young people about the dangers of alcohol-impaired driving, and attempting to persuade them to reduce or eliminate their driving after drinking. Wagenaar finds that these approaches have had only limited success. Challenging some findings reported in the introduction of this chapter, the author asserts that other policies and programs designed to reduce youth drinking and driving have shown greater preventive effects. Such efforts include: raising the legal age for alcohol consumption, increasing the price of alcoholic beverages, raising the driving age, and limiting nighttime driving with curfew laws. Suggestions for further research on promising prevention avenues are offered.

In the third and final category of Part IV are three complementary articles on general and specific model prevention strategies. The first article, "Prevention of Drug Abuse among Children and Youth," by Froehle, takes a historical, theoretical, and research-based approach, to describe the various efforts at education and prevention of drug use among children and adolescents. Froehle looks at various prevention approaches that have been tried for preventing alcohol and drug abuse among America's children and youth and the research evidence that is supportive and non-supportive of drug use by school age youth. While the author explores and discusses a variety of exemplary programs, he gives special consideration to one theoretically driven and empirically refined community-based model of prevention regarded as especially superior and exemplary. Froehle voices concern regarding the possibility that the public's commitment to prevention may wane now that prevalence use rates of gateway drugs have reached a plateau and in some cases have decreased. The author also asserts that early prevention efforts may not have sufficient impact on children and youth who are more likely to be at risk for drug abuse problems. Froehle concludes his article with a consideration of the issues that surface in designing, implementing, and evaluating drug abuse prevention programs.

The next article, "Drugs, Suds, and College: Drug Use Prevention and Intervention," by Cooper, extends Froehle's research to include the college population. Cooper's research relies on an explication of the biopsychosocial model of addiction as a framework for developing interventions targeted at individuals, their behavior, and their environment. The author's research concludes with an analysis of three successful campus demonstration projects that use the biopsychosocial approach to reduce alcohol and drug abuse on campus.

The final article, "Understanding Strategic Planning as an Emerging Drug Abuse Prevention Model," is authored by Rozecki and Kurpius. The authors assert that the language and required focus of strategic planning improve our understanding of prevention. Strategic planning does this by proposing a more concrete framework for the proactive establishment of community needs and actions in addressing mental health concerns or future directions for health care. Also included in this article by Rozecki and Kurpius are the following: a definition and outline of all the strategic planning steps, a discussion of other prevention models, an explanation of prevention in relation to strategic planning, and a sample case analysis.

Notes

1. I wish to acknowledge Stewart Cooper's advice regarding the arrangement of the eight articles and assistance in writing the remainder of this chapter.

References

Akers, R. L. (1992). *Drugs, alcohol and society: Social structure, process, and policy.* Belmont, CA: Wadsworth Publishing Company.

Babor, T. F. (1985). Alcohol, economics and ecological fallacy: Toward an integration of experimental and quasi-experimental research. In E. Single & T. Storm (Eds.), *Public drinking & public policy. Proceedings of a Symposium on Observation Studies, Banff, Alberta* (pp. 161–189). Toronto, Canada: Addiction Research Foundation.

Bennett, W. J. (1990). Drugs damage American society. In N. Bernards (Ed.), *War on drugs: Opposing viewpoints* (pp. 16–28). San Diego, CA: Greenhaven Press.

Botvin, G. T. (1990). Substance abuse prevention: Theory, practice, and effectiveness. In M. Tonry & J. Q. Wllson (Eds.), *Drugs & crime* (pp. 461–561). Chicago, IL: University of Chicago Press.

Frankel B., & Whitehead, P. (1985). *Effective strategies for prevention: Alcohol problems and public health policy.* London, Ontario: University of Western Ontario.

Frankena, M., Cohen, M. D., Ehrlich, T. L., Greenspun, N., & Kelman, D. (1985). Alcohol advertising, consumption and abuse. In Staff (Ed.), *Recommendations of the staff of the federal trade commission: Omnibus petition for regulation of unfair and deceptive alcoholic beverage marketing practices.* Docket No. 290-46, Washington, DC: Federal Trade Commission.

Huba, G. J., Wingard, J. A., & Bentler, P. M. (1980). Aplication of a theory of drug use to prevention programs. *Journal of Drug Education, 10,* 25–38.

Johnson, D. W. (1984). Constructive peer relationships, social development, and cooperative learning experiences: Implications for the prevention of drug abuse. In S. Eiseman, J. A. Wingard, & G. J. Huba (Eds.), *Drug abuse: Foundation for a psychosocial approach* (pp. 24–42). Farmingdale, NY: Baywood Publishing Company, Inc.

Macdonald, S., & Whitehead, P. M. (1983). Availability of outlets and consumption of alcoholic beverages. *Journal of Drug Issues, 13,* 477–486.

Polich, J. M., Ellickson, P. L, Reuter, P., & Kahn, J. P. (1984). *Strategies for controlling adolescent drug use.* Santa Monica, CA: Rand Corporation.

Senate Task Force for a Drug Free America. (1990). The war on drugs is necessary. In N. Bernards (Ed.), *War on drugs: Opposing viewpoints* (pp. 16–28.) San Diego, CA: Greenhaven Press, Inc.

Tovares, R. (1990). Drugs damage American society. In N. Bernards (Ed.), *War on drugs: Opposing viewpoints* (pp. 41–53). San Diego, CA: Greenhaven Press, Inc.

Twentieth Century Wars on Alcohol and Other Drugs in the United States

14

David J. Pittman

William J. Staudenmeier, Jr.

David J. Pittman is a professor emeritus in psychology at Washington University, St. Louis, Missouri. He received his B.A. and M.A. degrees from the University of North Carolina-Chapel Hill. His Ph.D. degree was conferred by the University of Chicago. Dr. Pittman has been concerned with alcohol use, alcohol problems, and alcohol policy for many years. He is the author with C.W. Gordon of *Revolving Door: A Study of the Chronic Police Case Inebriate* and is the author of more than 200 published scientific articles, reports, and essays in the areas of alcoholism, drug addiction, criminology, and mass media. Dr. Pittman served as chairman of the 28th International Congress on Alcohol and Alcoholism in 1968; he is a former president of the North American Association of Alcoholism Programs; and he received the Silver Key Award from the National Council on Alcoholism (NCA) in 1978 for his "excellent and devoted service to NCA over the years." He is currently researching the economic effects of alcohol use and misuse and is working on a monograph focused on alcohol control measures.

William J. Staudenmeier has 20 years of experience in the drug/alcohol field. His first full-time work in this area, starting in 1972, involved the development of workplace drug/alcohol programs in the United States and overseas for the U. S. Air Force. Following this, he received his Ph.D. from Washington University in St. Louis in 1985, teaching the university course on Alcohol, Alcoholism and Society and helping develop and teach workshops on Employee Assistance Programs and Alcohol Rehabilitation while he was a graduate student. Currently Dr. Staudenmeier is an Associate Professor of Sociology at Eureka College in Eureka, Illinois and holds the position of Chair of the Social Science and Business Division. His recent publications focus on alcohol and other drug policies across American institutions; he maintains a special interest in workplace policies.

Introduction

For the third time in the twentieth century, the United States has witnessed simultaneous "wars" on alcohol and other drugs. The results of the most recent war have ranged from widespread drug testing of employees to warning labels on alcoholic beverages. The present convergence of restrictive drug and alcohol social movements, however, is not unique. In this century these movements have been in close temporal proximity. But while the social control goals and tactics of each movement can be quite similar, the actors, for the most part, are different. This article explores two major issues: (1) the sociocultural influences leading to the emergence of drug and alcohol social control movements in the United States in the twentieth century and (2) the similarities and differences between these two movements.

Three cases of parallel efforts at drug and alcohol social control are used to explore these issues. The first case, or the first war on alcohol and other drugs, examines the time period leading to the passage of the Harrison Anti-Narcotic Act in 1914 and the enactment of the Eighteenth Amendment to the U.S. Constitution in 1919. The second case, or the second war on drugs, focuses on activities leading to the passage of the Hughes-Javits Act (PL91-616) in 1970 and the Nixon administration's concern with the diffusion of illicit drugs throughout American society (1969–1974). The third case, or the third war on drugs, investigates the recent social control movements directed at alcoholic beverages, as reflected in the new temperance movement, and at other drugs, as represented by the Reagan/Bush administration's War on Drugs.

The First War on Drugs

For more than 200 years after the settlement of the United States, the attitude towards the use of alcohol and other drugs was generally a permissive one. But in the nineteenth century the alcohol temperance movement diffused beliefs about the harmful nature of alcoholic beverages and led the call for prohibitory alcohol legislation. Efforts at passing state-level alcohol prohibition were successful as early as the 1850s, but the call was not answered on a national level until the early twentieth century. For analytic purposes we arbitrarily define the first war on alcohol as beginning in 1913, when the Anti-Saloon League adopted the goal of national prohibition (the manufacture, distribution, and sale of alcoholic beverages would be ended) (Odegard, 1928). This war on alcohol was successful, as the Eighteenth Amendment to the U.S. Constitution was ratified in 1919 and the implementing legislation, the Volstead Act, was passed in 1920. Some of the major influences that led to this success include: (1) the century-long temperance movement and its influence on redefining the nature of alcohol, (2) the successful political organization of temperance supporters into an effective lobbying and voting force, (3) the increasing role of the federal government in addressing social problems in the Progressive Era, and (4) the crisis atmosphere of World War I.

The permissive attitude toward other drugs such as morphine started to wane later, in the last quarter of the nineteenth century, with spreading media attention and public awareness of drug abuse among Americans (Morgan, 1974). But the negative stereotypes of other drugs that spread in this period did not lead immediately to a movement for prohibitory legislation. That was not to come until the beginning of the next century (Morgan, 1981). The first war on other drugs had its origin in the cauldron of domestic reform at the beginning of the twentieth century, which was in response to the factors of industrialization, urbanization, immigration, and the division of labor. Social conditions were deplorable, as reflected in the distribution of adulterated foods and drugs, children working in unsafe situations, unsanitary living quarters, etc. One of the social responses to these conditions was the passage of the Pure Food and Drug Act in 1906, which prohibited the interstate transportation of adulterated or mislabeled drugs and food, and required that patent medicines have ingredient labels noting their content of alcohol and other drugs; above all, it gave the new organization, the Food and Drug Agency (FDA), regulatory powers. Yet, to those reformers who were concerned about "checking the formation of the drug habit" this law seemed inadequate.

The other pillar on which the first war on other drugs was built was the Harrison Anti-Narcotic Act of 1914. Antidrug reformers were concerned about the failure of state and local laws passed in the early 1900s to effectively reduce drug abuse. Domestic national antidrug legislation also had unusual leadership from the State Department. This leadership role, strongly influenced by the State Department reformer Hamilton Wright, was strengthened when America became a signatory to the Hague Opium Convention in 1912, which obligated its members to curtail domestic production of opium and its derivatives, and to restrict consumption to strictly regulated channels (Taylor, 1969). But because of the necessities of coalition politics and the need for the support of the medical and pharmaceutical lobbies, the Harrison Act failed to emerge as the strong antidrug law many reformers desired (Musto, 1973). Its purpose was that individuals who imported, manufactured, sold, or distributed opiate drugs and cocaine were to register with the Department of Treasury, pay special taxes and keep records of all transactions. However, as later events, especially interpretations of the laws by the Supreme Court, occurred, the Act became one by which drug users and those who treated them were vigorously prosecuted by law enforcement authorities. Thus, in the 1920s both alcohol and other drugs, except under special circumstances, had become for most intents and purposes illegal, as the Department of Treasury was interpreting the enforcement of the Harrison Act to be the prohibition of drugs.

Thus, the first war on alcohol and other drugs had resulted in victory for those moral and bureaucratic entrepreneurs whose goal was the eradication of these substances. There were a number of convergences in the ideology of these social movements. Both were built on the desire to make American society one in which social problems related to the use of alcohol and other drugs would be eradicated. Both drew on the symbols of widespread public fears, such as the imagery of drug and alcohol enslavement of good Americans, the fear of cocaine- or alcohol-intoxicated African Americans raping and murdering, the xenophobic fear of intoxicated immigrants, and the concern with war productivity and sober soldiers. Specifically, for instance, both movements were associated with American xenophobia—especially toward the Germans during World War I. Many of the major brewers were of German origin, and there were rumors that the "enemy" was giving drugs to school children. Opium smoking had been associated with the Chinese immigrants, who were viewed as second-class citizens at the time. Repression of the alcohol and drug traffic were both initially delegated to the Prohibition Unit within the Department of the Treasury. Thus, the alcohol movement in fact fueled the law enforcement direction of the tax aspects of the Harrison Act, and subsequently led to the systematic closing of all treatment clinics for narcotic addicts. This event, coupled with the decline of the treatment orientation towards alcoholics, squarely placed the social control of both alcohol and other drugs in the area of law enforcement. Since both substances were now the property of the legal institution, the medical profession was effectively removed from the treatment of alcoholics and drug dependent individuals. The goal convergence that police authorities were to be final arbiters of drug and alcohol problems became firmly embedded in the American value structure. The result of the first war on drugs was the criminalization of the drug user and the stigmatization of the alcoholic as a moral derelict, which reinforced the existing primitive and punitive policy of incarcerating chronic drunkenness offenders whose only crime was being intoxicated in public (King, 1972).

Although the first war on drugs created by legislative action in the 1920s a drug-free America, the situations in reference to obtaining supplies were radically different for alcohol and drug users. Since significant numbers of Americans throughout the class structure drank alcoholic beverages, a widespread black market developed, with supplies smuggled from Canada and Mexico and illicitly produced in this country. Violations of the prohibition law became so pervasive that efforts to repeal the law were successful by 1933. Thus, the social control of repression of alcohol use failed because it was not widely supported by powerful economic and social groups in our society, and because the drinking of alcohol for religious, ceremonial, and recreational purposes was accepted by many groups. A drug-free society confronted users of other drugs with a different problem to solve. The only major source for obtaining them was the medical profession, which was under constant siege by federal authorities not to supply drug users, throughout the 1920s. Interestingly enough, as one other indicator of the difference between the implementation of prohibition for alcohol and other drugs, the prescription of alcohol by physicians went up significantly in the same time period (Sinclair, 1962). In contrast to alcohol prohibition, no major social movements developed to evade or curb law enforcement authorities, probably because there was no mainstream, culturally integrated historical tradition of using drugs for recreational purposes. While a black market did develop among drug addicts, they remained a stigmatized, criminal minority in stark contrast to the widespread acceptance and of collusion with the black market in alcohol.

In fact, public attitudes towards the use of other drugs became more severe, as reflected in the "reefer madness" era of the 1930s, culminating in the passage of the Marijuana Tax Act in 1937, which classified this weed as a narcotic. Alcohol prohibition ended in 1933 with alcohol becoming a legal beverage to be purchased if the state regulated it and the user was not perceived as a criminal. However, the other drugs continued to be prohibited with vigorous law enforcement activities. Clearly, this divergence had been made easier by the establishment three years earlier of the Federal Bureau of Narcotics, which separated federal alcohol control from the control of other drugs and consolidated the control of other drugs in one federal agency under the direction of the first Commissioner of Narcotics, Harry J. Anslinger (Musto, 1973). This fundamental distinction, developed in the first war on drugs, that recreational use of alcohol was proper, whereas the same for other drugs such as heroin, marijuana, cocaine, etc., was not, is essential for understanding American social control policies toward alcohol and other drugs throughout the rest of the twentieth century.

The Second War on Drugs

The second war on drugs was a consequence of the convulsions in America's social structure in the 1960s, when traditional values underwent intense scrutiny. The norms and laws that regulated relationships between African Americans and whites were the focus of the civil right movement; African Americans were no longer willing to be deprived of their rights as human beings. The emergence of the women's movement questioned the traditional subservient roles assigned to females. Liberation from the chains that imprisoned groups in stigmatized positions by virtue of their economic circumstances, sexual orientation, gender, age, political beliefs, physical condition including alcoholism and drug addictions, etc., was the goal of various social movements in the 1960s. From the new organizations that these movements spawned were constructed the drug revolution, especially by sons and daughters of the veterans of World War II, and the new orientations to alcohol control policies and alcoholics.

The antecedents of the second war on drugs were developed in the case of alcohol use and misuse by those pioneers who labored to counter the stigma, low esteem and status, and rejection attached to the alcoholic. Eschewing involvement in a controversy about the role of alcohol use in society, i.e., the "wet vs. dry" conflict, the leaders concentrated on developing scientific knowledge about alcoholism and disseminating the concept that "alcoholism is a disease." The scientific anchor for the disease concept rested originally with the Yale University Center of Alcohol Studies and with the dissemination of empirical studies through the *Quarterly Journal of Studies on Alcohol*, located at the same institution (both founded in 1940). The disease concept of alcoholism, originally promulgated in America by Dr. Benjamin Rush in 1784 and others too numerous to mention, reemerged in the late 1930s. Instrumental in the public diffusion of the medical orientation to alcoholism were: (1) the founders of Alcoholics Anonymous in 1935, one of whom was a physician, who conceptualized alcoholism partially as being an allergy to alcohol, (2) the founders, especially Marty Mann, of the National Council on Alcoholism (NCA) in 1945, which emphasized that "alcoholism was a treatable and beatable" disease, and (3) scientists such as E. M. Jellinek, whose research was published in 1960 in his book *The Disease Concept of Alcoholism*, which outlined the empirical basis for considering alcoholism a disease.

Thus, the social construction of the alcohol problem in the second war on drugs was based on the disease model. Leaders of the various social movements to change the status of the alcoholic were cognizant that in Western society the victims of a disease are the primary responsibility of medical and social helping professions—not of police, courts, and correctional institutions. But to implement this ideology into social policy involved political action which found a receptive climate in the 1960s.

The experience of American government bodies with prohibition had made them reluctant to confront issues involving alcohol and alcoholism. From the repeal of prohibition in 1933 until the enactment of the Hughes-Javits Act (PL91-616), "The Comprehensive Alcohol Abuse and Alcoholism Prevention, Treatment, and Rehabilitation Act," by the United States Congress in 1970, only one significant piece of alcoholism legislation had been enacted by the Congress. In 1947 the Alcoholism Treatment Act for the District of Columbia was passed by the Congress, which defined alcoholism as an illness and provided for medical, psychiatric, and social treatment instead of jail sentences for alcoholics. However, neither the District of Columbia nor the Congress initially appropriated funds to implement this legislation.

In the second war on drugs, the alcohol-oriented organizations had emphasized the concept of alcoholism as a disease and the need for a national program for alcoholism control. This is documented in David J. Pittman's (1966) presidential address to the Seventeenth Annual Meeting of the North American Association of Alcoholism Programs in 1966, in which he stated:

> . . . there is no national program for alcoholism control in America.... The time for educational pieces of literature, films and 'pats on the back' for us is over. The time for mounting a systematic program of national alcoholism control is at hand. (p. 5)

By medicalizing the condition of alcoholism and emphasizing alcoholism control, the social movement not only neutralized any opposition that might have occurred from the alcoholic beverage industry if the movement had claimed that alcohol was the cause of alcoholism, as in the first war on drugs, but it also reassured non-problematic drinkers that a new prohibition had not been created. The issue of alcohol-related problems, such as drunk driving and other socially irresponsible behaviors by non-alcoholic individuals, had been finessed by the social movement leaders by their almost exclusive concern with alcoholism and the policy of jailing public alcoholics.

It was not only the changing social conditions in American society in the 1960s that affected social control policies towards other drugs, but also the emergence of a drug subculture among the youth population, especially those under 25 years of age. Both old and new drugs became widely used, e.g., marijuana, LSD, amphetamines, quaaludes, various sedatives, etc. Illustrative of the increasing drug use is the estimate that from the early 1960s to 1970, the number of Americans who had used marijuana increased from a few hundred thousand to around eight million (Inciardi, 1986).

The recreational use of drugs played a major role in the development of the counterculture of the 1960s, personified in the emergence of the Hippies. This group, characterized by distinctive styles of dress, language, and protests against the status quo, represented a threat to the established American value structure. The 1960s were a decade of violence—the assassinations of John Kennedy, Lee Harvey Oswald, Malcolm X, Martin Luther King, Robert Kennedy; the domestic riots of ghetto African Americans against deplorable social conditions; rioting by university students and others against America's involvement in the Viet Nam War and the military draft; the police riot at the Chicago Democratic Convention in 1968. Domestic crimes against both persons and property increased in the 1960s, leading to President Johnson's War on Crime and President Nixon's emphasis on "law and order" in the latter part of the decade.

Social control policies toward other drugs were reexamined by various government commissions and conferences throughout the 1960s. In 1962 the White House Conference on Narcotic and Drug Abuse concluded that more research was needed, as the current information on drugs was incorrect and based on insufficient data. This was followed by President Kennedy's Advisory Commission on Narcotics and Drug Abuse in 1963, which, although not deviating from the law enforcement perspective on drug use, did concede the need for treatment of drug addicts—but under the jurisdiction of the Department of Justice. The nation's concern about crime led to the creation of President Johnson's Commission on Law Enforcement and Administration of Justice in 1965 with Task Forces on Narcotics and Drug Abuse and Drunkenness. In 1967 the Narcotics and Drug Abuse Task Force both recommended that the law enforcement aspects of drug control be strengthened and simultaneously endorsed research on marijuana, but it did not recommend any specific treatment plans for drug users.

The widespread diffusion of various illicit drugs had occurred throughout America by the late 1960s, and their use was perceived by many people as associated with those groups opposing the Viet Nam War, the law and order policies of the Nixon administration, and the traditional arrangements of the American social structure. Thus, the use of drugs was painted by Nixon and his Attorney General, John Mitchell, as a threat to the American way of life. This danger was to be ameliorated by the enactment of the Comprehensive Drug Abuse Prevention and Control Act of 1970, which returned the ownership of the drug franchise to the law enforcement profession. The discovery in the early 1970s that American troops in Viet Nam were using heroin, and that some had become addicted, alarmed the federal government and the nation. Nixon responded by creating in 1971 the Special Action Office for Drug Abuse Prevention under his jurisdiction (King, 1972) and by mounting a new worldwide offensive against drugs.

Unlike alcoholics, who could secure treatment for their condition from medical personnel, abusers of illicit drugs were required to go through criminal justice diversion programs for treatment. This was especially true for opiate addicts, who were treated in methadone maintenance programs, which proliferated in the early 1970s. Arbitrarily, we note the second war on drugs ending with the resignation of Nixon in 1974 and the cessation of direct involvement of American troops in Viet Nam in 1973.

At the end of the second war on drugs, the social control policies toward alcohol were ones in which access to alcoholic beverages became more liberalized, with many states lowering their legal purchase age to 18 or 19 years of age and also removing other restrictions relating to time of day, day of week, and point of purchase. Alcoholism became fully medicalized. Social policy towards other drugs still remained firmly entrenched in the hands of police authorities. Although the penalties for the possession of small amounts of marijuana were reduced in some states, and decriminalized in others, the attitudes toward the opiates, especially heroin, remained as negative as ever. And policies toward alcohol and illicit drugs diverged most radically in access to treatment facilities. Typically, drug addicts came to them through criminal diversion programs, whereas alcoholics entered under the auspices of a physician. In conclusion, while the widespread experimentation with other drugs in the 1960s had increased the tolerance of significant segments of society for recreational drug use, the gap between the social response to alcohol and other drugs had widened as the second war on drugs led to the medicalization of alcohol abuse in contrast to the continued law enforcement jurisdiction over other drugs.

The Third War on Drugs

In 1986 President Reagan and the Congress rediscovered the drug problem. Their attention was drawn to the area by public opinion polls that reported concern about drugs as being a high priority issue, by the deaths of sports celebrities from cocaine, and by media stories on the dangers of a cheap form of cocaine known as "crack," which was diffusing widely throughout the country. However, the empirical evidence actually indicated that, with the exception of cocaine use, the use of illicit drugs (such as heroin and marijuana) had peaked in the early 1980s (Johnston, O'Malley, & Bachman, 1986). Despite this, the Anti-Drug Abuse Act of 1986 was passed by the Congress and signed by President Reagan in October 1986. This legislation, called by some the "Drug-Free America Act," placed the greatest emphasis on reducing supplies by increased law enforcement activities both on the national and international level and increasing criminal penalties for drug offenders. This type of drug policy, although a failure in both the first and second wars on drugs, has once again been resurrected. Only one-fourth of the funds in the 1986 Act were devoted to demand reduction, which includes prevention, rehabilitation, and research. Whether the Clinton and future administrations and the Congress will have the resolve to provide the funds over the long term to implement this legislation, especially the demand reduction aspects, is questionable. Interestingly, the Bush administration emphasized in this war on other drugs the role of private employers in drug demand reduction by encouraging explicit antidrug policies with the Drug-Free Workplace Act and encouraging the use of innovative drug detection technology such as employee urine testing (Staudenmeier, 1989).

Since 1977 a major new temperance movement has emerged in the United States, built on a control of consumption orientation. Simply stated, this approach, developed from the seminal works of S. Ledermann (1956), states that a reduction in the per capita consumption of alcoholic beverages in a population will result in a decrease of alcohol-related damage. To achieve this, the following measures have been proposed by these new temperance advocates: (1) television advertising restrictions on alcoholic beverages, especially wine and beer, (2) health warning labels on containers of alcoholic beverages, (3) disallowing tax deductions for alcohol beverage advertising, (4) increasing the tax on alcoholic beverages, (5) increasing the minimum legal purchase and possession age to 21 years of age, (6) basing the tax on alcoholic beverages on alcohol content, and (7) restricting the availability of alcoholic beverages through limitations on number of sales and outlets in low-income areas (Pittman, 1980).

However, this agenda in reference to alcoholic beverages cannot be successful in totality unless there is a frontal attack on the use of product per se. The fact that alcohol is a legal drug places it in a different perceptual and legal category from other illicit drugs. Furthermore, the American public is issue specific, and its attention span for any problem is short. Therefore, the greatest successes in the war on alcohol have occurred when activists have focused on drunk driving, the fetal alcohol syndrome, and raising the legal purchase age. Consistent with this view, the following goals of the movement have been accomplished: (1) federal legislation requires health warning labels on alcoholic beverage containers, (2) all states have raised the legal purchase age to 21, and (3) alcoholic beverage taxes have been increased.

This third war on alcohol and other drugs has led to a narrowing in the gap, a movement toward convergence in American's social control approach to alcohol and other drugs. The focus on alcoholism as a disease, present in the last war, has been expanded to include other problems related to alcohol and social control efforts, such as taxation and warning labels that affect all drinkers. A major change in other drug policy is to emphasize the role of private sector employers in dealing with these problems through urine testing and other federally encouraged initiatives. This follows the effort in the last war to expand employers' funding of health insurance for alcohol treatment and their adoption of Employee Assistance Programs to identify and rehabilitate employees with alcoholism and other problems.

Conclusion

Public and official concern with alcohol and other drugs in America waxes and wanes, reflecting the persistence of alcohol and other drug-related problems, conflicting views on these substances and their social control, and the relatively short political and public attention span that seems part of our national character. We have identified three periods in the twentieth century when there was widespread American concern at the national level with both alcohol and other drugs. During these three periods, these social problems ranked among the greatest concerns facing the American people.

For historical and cultural reasons, alcohol control is treated differently from other drug control. For these same reasons, while there is some overlap, it is primarily the case that the social movements fighting the contemporaneous wars on alcohol and other drugs are separate. Yet, in many ways these movements provide ideological, tactical, political, and human resources for each other by raising the general concern over insobriety and its effects in our society. And for any message used by the other drug forces, the alcohol movement can add, "And alcohol remains our number one drug," a prominent message during the second war on drugs.

The divergences of the wars against alcohol from the wars against other drug problems of our society reflect the very different history and cultural integration of these two subjective classes of mood-altering substances. The convergences reflect similarities in the problems caused by these substances, and the social and cultural changes that affect our attitudes toward these problems and our social control behavior. For in our society these matters are not settled. And the morally charged debate over what to do about our alcohol and other drug problems is part of the fundamental shifting American debate over the extent of personal liberty to be allowed in a free society (Bakalar & Grinspoon, 1984). The battles being fought, therefore, are not just over questions of vice, disease, and effective control strategies; the fight is also over the nature of a just society.

Notes

1. This article is a revised version of a plenary session lecture presented at the 33rd International Institute on the Prevention and Treatment of Alcoholism, Lausanne, Switzerland, May 31–June 5, 1987.

References

Bakalar, J. B., & Grinspoon, L. (1984) *Drug control in a free society.* New York: Cambridge University Press.

Inciardi, J. A. (1986) *The war on drugs.* Palo Alto, CA: Mayfield.

Johnston, L. D., O'Malley, P. M., & Bachman, G. J. (1986) *Drug use among American high school students, college students, and other young adults.* Rockville, MD: National Institute on Drug Abuse.

King, R. (1972) *The drug hang-up.* Springfield, IL: Charles C. Thomas.

Ledermann, S. (1956) *Alcool, alcoolisme, alcoolisation, données scientifiques de caractère physiologique, economique et social,* Institute Nationale d'Etudes Démographique, Travaux et Documents, Cah. No. 29. Paris: Presses Universitaires de France.

Morgan, H. W. (1974) *Yesterday's addicts, American society and drug abuse, 1965-1920.* Norman, OK: University of Oklahoma Press.

Morgan, H. W. (1981) *Drugs in America: A social history, 1800-1980.* Syracuse, NY: Syracuse University Press.

Musto, D. F. (1973) *The American disease, origins of narcotic control.* New Haven, CT: Yale University Press.

Odegard, P. H. (1928) *Pressure politics, the story of the anti-saloon league.* New York: Columbia University Press.

Pittman, D. J. (1966) *The monumental year for alcoholism.* Paper presented at the 17th annual meeting of the North American Association of Alcoholism Programs, Albuquerque, NM.

Pittman, D. J. (1980) *Primary prevention of alcohol abuse and alcoholism: An evaluation of the control of consumption policy.* St. Louis, MO: Social Science Institute, Washington University.

Sinclair, A. (1962) *Prohibition, the era of excess.* Boston, MA: Little, Brown and Company.

Staudenmeier, W. J. Jr. (1989) Urine testing: The battle for privatized social control during the 1986 war on drugs. In J. Best (Ed.), *Images of issues* (pp. 207-221). New York: Aldine DeGruyter.

Taylor, A. H. (1969) *American diplomacy and the narcotics traffic, 1900-1939.* Durham, NC: Duke University Press.

Discussion Questions

1. Briefly, what are the three wars on alcohol and other drugs that the authors discuss?
2. What are some of the influences on the emergence of social movements during each of the three wars?
3. What were the similarities and/or differences in the handling of alcohol versus other drugs in each war?
4. What were the social control outcomes (for example, new laws) of each war?
5. Looking across the three cases, what are the authors' major conclusions?

15

Advertising against Drugs

Themes from a Televised Antidrug Campaign

John R. Baumann
Alisse Waterston

John Baumann is presently an Assistant Project Director for Grant and Proposal Development at National Development and Research Institutes, Inc. (NDRI—formerly Narcotic and Drug Research, Inc.). In this capacity he has assisted in the development of research projects involving drug and alcohol use, abuse, and treatment among a variety of populations. His specific research interests revolve around issues in the social construction of social problems by the mass media and the culture of drug and alcohol use, particularly in the workplace. He is also an adjunct faculty member of Hofstra University.

Alisse Waterston is an urban anthropologist and author of *Street Addicts in the Political Economy* (Temple University Press, 1993). Dr. Waterston has recently completed a Postdoctoral Research Fellowship at Narcotic and Drug Research, Inc. in New York, and teaches cultural anthropology at Fordham University. She is president of Surveys Unlimited, a cultural research and consulting company serving social service agencies and private industry. Dr. Waterston received her doctorate from the Graduate Center of the City University of New York in 1990.

The television commercial opens with a shot of a robust, middle-aged man leaning against a set of kitchen cabinets and addressing his audience sternly, with a degree of barely tolerant patience.

"Fried Egg/Fried Brain"[1]

> Is there anyone out there who still isn't clear about what "doing drugs" does? Okay. Last time. This is your brain. This is drugs. This is your brain on drugs. Any questions?

These words are accompanied by a set of equally unambiguous, no-nonsense images. During the monologue, the speaker picks up an egg and points to a frying pan sizzling with burning butter. While speaking the words "This is your brain on drugs," he breaks the shell and drops the egg into the hot frying pan. The screen blackens, and across the lower portion appears the credit: "Partnership for a Drug-Free America."

In 1986, the "war on drugs" was formally joined by the nation's advertising community. The Media-Advertising Partnership for a Drug-Free America, operating under the umbrella of the American Association of Advertising Agencies, has emerged as the largest coordinated voluntary mass media campaign in advertising history. Since its founding, the Partnership for a Drug-Free America has created, produced and distributed over two hundred public service advertisements for newspapers, magazines, radio and television. The various mass media outlets have run the ads on a pro bono basis—donating advertising space estimated at $310 million (AAAA, 1990). The goals of the Partnership have been stated repeatedly and succinctly:

> The Partnership for a Drug-Free America has an ambitious mission: the objective of reducing demand by *unselling any illegal drug use* in the United States. Unlike most advertising, which is directed at *selling* a product or service, the Partnership is directed at discouraging the purchase and consumption of its three target products—marijuana, cocaine, and crack. The Partnership's task is to marshall the resources of the advertising and media industries to produce advertising

> that encourages non-users not to start and encourages users to decrease or terminate their use. (Black, 1987, p. 1)

Their aim is to help "unsell" or "de-normalize" drug use through the creation, production and distribution of advertising that "discourages the purchase and consumption of illegal drugs and encourages the formation and growth of attitudes and behavior antagonistic toward consumption" (Black, 1988, p. 1; AAAA, 1990.) These messages are directed towards target populations defined according to two sets of criteria: basic demographic characteristics and relationship to drug use or users. With regard to the former, messages are targeted to: pre-teens, teens, college students and adults. With regard to the latter, messages are targeted to: "non- and occasional users to convince them that any perceived usage benefits are far outweighed by negatives" and "'influencers'—parents, healthcare professionals and management—to encourage them to bring their influence to bear on the problem of illegal drugs" (AAAA, 1990, p. 5).

This article investigates the advertisements through which the Partnership goes about this process of "unselling" and "de-normalizing" drugs. We understand it as a case study exploration in the social construction of the "drug problem." Our research is intended neither as a historical review nor as an effectiveness evaluation of the Partnership and its media campaign. Our intention, rather, is to identify the themes and images of the drug problem as constructed by the Partnership in their televised public service advertisements. These representations will, in turn, be discussed within the context of the social science literature on the "drug problem." Thus the purpose in this research is to investigate the degree to which this representation is consistent with or matches the "reality" of the "drug problem."

We are, therefore, concerned with the selection of images and representations by the Partnership and with the emergence of themes that collectively shape and foster a particular understanding of the drug problem. Thus, the Partnership's media campaign contributes to the formation of a particular ideology or set of beliefs concerning the nation's drug problem and "war on drugs." Particular attention is paid to the representation of the following concerns: the substances identified as problematic; those who are recognized as drug abusers; and the nature of the drug-taking experience.

Data and Methodology

The analysis of the processes of mass communications has a long and rich tradition in the social sciences. Moreover, the thematic analysis of mass media content, in particular, is well represented by an extensive body of literature. It is from this tradition of social science research that this paper emerges. Treating the ads as "text," the analysis developed herein is based on a thematic reading of the advertisements created, produced and distributed for television broadcast by the Partnership for a Drug-Free America.[2]

Our data are comprised of the entire collection of the Partnership's television ads during its first three years of operation—from its founding in 1986 till the summer of 1989.[3] The sample consists of 42 separate television advertisements.[4] The selection of television advertisements rather than those prepared for radio or print distribution reflects the primary role of television as a mass medium of communication in our society.

Once collected, the advertisements were examined in order to identify the recurring organizing themes and dominant narratives that collectively shaped the boundaries and depictions of the "drug problem." The specific steps involved in our analysis were as follows: (1) the transcription of the advertisements, accomplished by the literal recording of the words and detailed description of the images utilized, (2) the identification of themes or categories corresponding to general issues of concern, and (3) the matching of content to themes or categories. While neither an exercise in literary criticism nor traditional content analysis, our methodology grew from an appreciation of these approaches to data. Additionally, the insights of standard forms of qualitative research proved useful. Our methodology, then, is a form of ethnographic content analysis or ethnography of material culture, which might be described as "applying observational methods to prepared cultural products" or documentary evidence (Room, 1989, p. 370; see also Altheide, 1986; Johnson, 1989).

Textual Analysis and Commentary

Drug-Free from What?

The first step in our effort to decipher the Partnership's construction of America's drug problem involves the examination of the particular substances pictured in the advertising campaign: in other words, "drug-free" from what "drugs"? Some drugs are portrayed and others ignored—and it is necessary to ask both "Which substances are included?" and "Which are excluded?" As Andrew Tudor (1979) notes:

> Thus, in research, as well as establishing what the media DO say, we must also ask about what they DON'T say, about what is simply absent from the reservoir of conceptions they provide. For instance, a great deal can be learned about media representations of women by asking about the many ways in which they are NOT portrayed, itself a reflection of the restrictions on how they actually are portrayed. (1979, p. 11)

By representing some drugs and ignoring others, assumptions are being made about which drugs are at the center of the substance abuse threat.

In our review of the Partnership's campaign, it is clear that the focus is on marijuana, cocaine and crack as the specific drugs of disrepute, while reference to drugs in general is directed at any substance that is not legal. When mention is made of a specific drug, the majority of these advertisements in our sample present illustrations of crack and cocaine, with a somewhat smaller number depicting marijuana. At no point in any of the advertisements are tobacco, alcohol, over-the-counter drugs, or prescription drugs identified as playing a part in the "drug problem"—either directly or indirectly.

That the overall focus of the campaign is on illegal substances, and these three in particular, is not in and of itself surprising. These same substances seem to constitute the general target of most mass media discussions about the problem of drugs in society (Reinarman & Levine, 1989a, 1989b). Further, the Partnership for a Drug-Free America has stated repeatedly and specifically that these substances constitute their "target products" (Black, 1987, 1988; AAAA, 1990). This narrow focus, though certainly not unexpected, is nonetheless somewhat problematic when examined both in light of the "actual" prevalence of substance use and abuse in the United States and in terms of the processes of initiation into the world of illegal drug use.

The emphasis by the Partnership's campaign on these three particular drugs does not reflect official government research findings and statistics on the prevalence of drug use in this country.[4] Several national studies have identified tobacco and alcohol as the nation's primary drugs of use and abuse, particularly among young people. Use of these substances far exceeds the consumption of marijuana, cocaine and crack. (Barron, 1988). Among these studies, the National Institute on Drug Abuse's (NIDA) National Household Survey shows that tobacco and alcohol consumption continue to be the most prevalent substance abuse activities of early adolescence (1986). In contrast, the same study indicates that by 1982, cocaine use had already reached a plateau of steady levels and begun to show signs of decline. The NIDA survey also shows that while drinking and smoking account for 56 percent and 45 percent of adolescent drug use, respectively, cocaine accounts for only five percent of drug use among this population.

Another important government-sponsored study reports annually on drug use among high school seniors (Johnston et al., 1987). Among the significant recent findings of this research are that 15 percent of seniors have tried cocaine and six percent have tried crack. The data also indicate that alcohol use is extensive among high school seniors, with 92 percent having used it at least once and 66 percent having used it in the last month (Johnston). These findings lead the authors to conclude that "use of many illicit drugs has declined or is declining and current users are using less" (Johnston, p. 12). It is important to note that the evidence from the high school survey points to significant regional differences in rates and patterns of substance use. Considerable increases in drug use are noted for urban areas, particularly the Northeast (Johnston). The apparent lack of concern in this campaign for adolescent abuse of cigarettes and alcohol is surprising, considering both the prevalence of and the dangers associated with these substances (Eckardt et al., 1981; Giesbrecht et al., 1983; Newcomb & Bentler, 1989; OSAP, 1990). Indeed, as a recent poster sponsored by the New York City Department of Health announces, in a takeoff of the Marlboro advertisements: "COME TO WHERE THE CANCER IS. Smoking kills more Americans each year than alcohol, cocaine, crack, heroin, homicide, suicide, car accidents, fires and AIDS COMBINED."

The absence of concern over substances such as tobacco and alcohol is problematic even given the Partnership's stated goals of "de-normalizing" and "unselling" the use of marijuana, cocaine and crack specifically. This is due to the key role of tobacco and alcohol in introducing young people to illegal substance use. Research that charts the processes by which individuals discover and enter the world of illegal drug use has documented a path marked by a series of steps or "gateways" (DeJong & Winsten, 1989; Yamaguchi & Kandel, 1984; Kandel & Logan, 1984). Prior to trying illegal substances such as marijuana, cocaine and crack, youths often experiment with and use such "gateway" substances as tobacco and alcohol. Typically, consumption of tobacco and alcohol occurs prior to, and in connection with, illicit drug use. By ignoring tobacco and alcohol use, an antidrug campaign may in effect be undermining its own efforts, as attention is directed away from an appreciation of the actual stages of initiation into drug use. Moreover, a potentially useful strategy of prevention may be blocked.

Who Are the Users?

The vast majority of Partnership advertisements in our sample depict white individuals who are portrayed as either using drugs or suffering the negative consequences of drug use, or both. While a sprinkling of ethnic minorities appears in the ads, very few play a central role in the narrative.[6] Moreover, most of the characters, including the minorities, seem to be from upper-middle-class to upper-working-class backgrounds. Only two of the commercials depict clearly inner-city street youth. In one, a white teenage girl appears to have suffered extreme downward mobility as crack led her into a life of street prostitution. In the other, a young Latino boy describes his brother's fall from grace as he succumbed to the lure of street drugs. The predominant age groups portrayed in the advertisements range from young children and teenagers to adults no older than their late thirties.

There is a complete absence of black females in the advertisements. The only spot to portray a black male as protagonist tells the brief, poignant tale of a cocaine-abusing basketball star. We witness his travels from college and professional basketball courts to the trash-filled gutters and, ultimately, to arrest and imprisonment. The star athlete with potential for greatness takes a gamble with coke and finds himself down and out—visibly a disappointment to himself, his family and the youngsters for whom he has been a role model.

The question now is: How consistent are these demographic images with what is known about the social distribution of substance use and abuse? The demographic profiles and images presented in the advertisements are generally rather inconsistent with findings on the social distribution of substance use and abuse. There is a certain lack of fit between the advertisements' representations of "who" is at risk for abusing "what" substances and the findings of social science research. With regard to the age groupings, the portrayals in the ads are fairly consistent with research on at-risk age groups. However, the fit is poor with regard to other demographic characteristics. In terms of race and social class, there are significant differences between the representations in the Partnership's ads and the research findings. Research on illicit drug use and abuse points to the particular vulnerability of low-income, ethnic minority populations in urban areas (see for instance, Johnson et al., 1990; Waterston, 1990; Williams, 1989; Goode, 1989; Johnston et al., 1987; Friedman et al., 1987).

Indeed, the Partnership's own sponsored research, conducted during the planning stage of the media campaign, offers a picture of the distribution of substance abuse similarly at odds with the commercial portrayal. Their findings can be summarized as follows:

> Blacks and Hispanics are more likely to be drug abusers than the general public. Drug abuse is more common among the very affluent and the very poor, and is significantly less common among middle income groups . . . . In every sample but the adults, Blacks show a pattern of greater vulnerability to drug use than Whites . . . . By any standard, Blacks are at greater risk for the use of marijuana and cocaine than Whites. (Black, 1987, pp. 36–38)

The gap between these findings and the portrayals in the Partnership's antidrug campaign is substantial. This is certainly not to claim that the images of the user presented in the ads are "false." These portrayals may, in fact, represent possible or even actual occurrences. These kernels of truth, however, have been exaggerated and overstated to the point of distortion as the "exception becomes the rule." This practice has been variously defined. Reinarman and Levine refer to it as "'the routinization of caricature'—[whereby] worst cases [are] framed as typical cases, the episodic rhetorically recrafted into the epidemic" (1989b, p. 543). Cohen (1980), in his discussion of moral panics, describes this symbolization through extreme cases as the "sharpening up process":

> Another highly effective technique of symbolization was the use of dramatized and ritualistic interviews with [so-called] "representative" members of either group. Through symbolization, plus the other types of exaggeration and distortion, images are made much sharper than reality. There is no reason to assume that photographs or television reports are any more "objective." (pp. 42–43)

We now turn to an examination of how the drug-using experience is represented in the Partnership's campaign while bearing in mind these processes of the "routinization of caricature" or "sharpening up."

The Nature of the Drug Experience

In this section we are concerned with identifying the themes emerging from the Partnership's advertisements that typify the experience of illicit drug usage. In their effort to "unsell" and "de-normalize" the use of drugs, the advertisements present a series of powerful, negative representations of the nature of the drug-using experience. Nothing good can be said of the experience—despite the fact that, historically, human beings throughout the world have sought artificial means to enhance the senses or arrive at altered states of consciousness (DuToit, 1977; Morales, 1989; Reinarman, 1983; Weil, 1977, 1972). Moreover, scholars note that in American culture, attitudes and beliefs about drug use change radically and often correspond to the political climate of particular times. (See, for instance, Goode, 1989; Hannerz, 1980; Helmer, 1975; Inciardi, 1986; Musto, 1987; Schlossman, 1984.) At this time, the "war on drugs" is hot copy for both politicians and the media. The advertisements, reflecting the current mood, emphasize the relationship between drug use and danger, death and personal and social disintegration.

The Consequences of Drug Use: Risk, Danger and Death

The portrayals of drug use explicitly predict devastating consequences resulting from their consumption. Variations occur based upon the target product: illegal drugs in general, cocaine and crack, or marijuana. Generally, the more specific the target product, the more specific the dangers portrayed.

Ads that are aimed at discouraging illicit drug use in general—that is, those that lack a reference to a specific drug—tend to offer vague, undefined images of danger. The "Fried Egg/Fried Brain" ad that opened this paper is a good illustration of this point. So too is the following ad:

> "The Plunge"
>
> An attractive, young, white woman is seen climbing up to the high diving board of a swimming pool. As we watch the woman climb the ladder, a narrator says: "Doing drugs is like being on top of the world. Everyone says so. Everyone seems to be having one dandy old time. Part of growing up—or is it? Just think about this: before you go and do something you've never done before, you just better know what you're jumping into."

As the narrator speaks, we see the young woman dive off the board—plunging down into an empty pool.

In contrast, the ads that speak about particular drugs tend to link them with more specific accompanying dangers or problems. Marijuana, for example, is shown to cause carelessness, silliness, memory loss, early senility and, as illustrated below, infertility.

> "Reefer Sadness"
>
> A young, white couple is sitting at a desk. We see the sullen expression on their faces as a doctor delivers the bad news: "I'm very sorry to have to tell you this. It's not an easy thing. The test came

back and I'm afraid the results are the same. Well, um, it's going to be difficult for the two of you to have your own children."

At this, we see the following words written across the screen: "Studies show smoking marijuana can dramatically decrease sperm count. Marijuana: It's time you knew the whole truth."

The risks and dangers associated with cocaine and crack use, on the other hand, are presented as more immediate, more intense and more devastating than those accompanying marijuana consumption. As depicted in the media campaign, users of these substances are virtually guaranteed to suffer consequences ranging from seizures to comas to death. Indeed, in nearly every ad targeting cocaine or crack, we witness these recurring tragedies. The following examples outline the range of risks directly associated with cocaine or crack consumption.

"Brother Dearest"

A nice-looking young teenager is sitting in a room, talking sadly about his brother's birthday two years ago.

"My brother's friend Rick wanted to do something special for his birthday—bought him some crack. Maybe it was bad stuff. Maybe he just couldn't handle it. That was two years ago today. Sometimes I think Rick was the lucky one. He died. Happy birthday, buddy."

At this, the camera pans to the brother, lying in a coma with tubes in his nose and arms, surrounded by various medical equipment. We hear only the ominous sound of a respirator.

"Heartbreaker"

Snow is falling on an urban street scene. We see ambulance lights and hear the sound of its siren penetrating the night. A bearded, white man appearing to be in his mid-forties is being treated by the emergency medical technicians. The camera withdraws to show the interior of the ambulance as the medics attempt to resuscitate the patient with an electronic heart stimulator. As the medics work on the man, their facial expressions show a lack of hope for a good outcome.

As we watch this scene, the narrator says: "You know, it's true what they say about crack and cocaine. This year over 15,000 people who try it are in for a real ride.

Appearing across the screen is the admonition:

Face the Facts
Drugs are A Dead End.

Consider, additionally, the untimely death of a suburban teenager from freebasing or smoking crack in her lovely home.

"Susie's Tale"

The camera pans to a teenage girl's perfect bedroom—beautifully decorated and furnished with dolls and feminine toys, trinkets on the shelves, bureaus and tables. There are numerous family photographs, and everyone looks happy. One shows a cute little girl on a bike, another a teenager with mom, a third shows her with her dad and another shows her playing tennis. There is a goldfish tank, a telescope, a teddy bear and tennis trophies. Ballet slippers hang on the wall. While the background music suggests a sad, tragic story, the narrator says:

"When she was six, after a few scrapes and tumbles, her dad taught her how to ride a two-wheeler. When she was nine, he helped her build a telescope that could see the moons of Jupiter. When she was 14, after a lot of giggling and giving up, her mom finally taught her how to hit a wicked two-handed backhand. All through her growing up, Susie's parents taught her well. But for all their love and attention, there was one lesson left untaught."

At this, the camera pans to a fallen pipe, broken into pieces. We see a long hallway with a door at its end, slightly ajar. As we hear an ambulance siren, the camera points out the bedroom window to an ambulance as it pulls away into the night.

Accompanying these visuals, the narrator says: "Susie's parents never taught her about drugs. They never told her that drugs maim, drugs kill. So Susie learned one final lesson on her own."

He then warns: "When you don't say no to your kids about drugs, it's the same as saying yes."

The Consequences of Drug Use: Character Transformation

Another theme that emerges from the Partnership's portrayal of the experience of drug use revolves around the relationship between drug use and the transformation of the user's personality or character. Users of a variety of substances display a wide range of personality and character flaws. The overall message in the commercial below is that marijuana inhibits ambition, motivation, progress and success:

> "Eddie and the MJs"
>
> Two white, working-class men, who appear to be in their late twenties, are in a bedroom, smoking marijuana. In the background we hear a radio from which an announcer is reporting the latest findings that link paranoia and marijuana use. The main character, Eddie, tokes on a joint and says to his friend:
>
> "I'm tired of hearing that marijuana can mess you up. We've been smoking for 15 years, nothing ever happened to me. I didn't get into other drugs. I didn't start stealing, mugging people. It didn't make me do anything different. In fact, I'd say I'm exactly the same as when I smoked my first joint."
>
> From the background we hear Eddie's mother yell out: "Eddie, did you even look for a job today?"
>
> Eddie replies, "No, ma, I called them this morning . . . "
>
> A narrator states: "Marijuana can make nothing happen to you, too."
>
> The camera opens to include the entire bedroom, where Eddie is waving the smoke from his marijuana cigarette, as he asks his buddy, "Do me a favor, crack one of the windows for me."
>
> In the final shot, we see printed across the screen: "Nothing Happens with Marijuana."

In regard to this discussion of the psycho-social consequences of marijuana use, it is noteworthy to mention the recent findings of Shedler and Block concerning the relationship between adolescent mental health and the use of this illegal drug: teenagers who experimented with marijuana tended to be better adjusted than those who abstained or used drugs frequently.

> On the basis of the drug use information collected at age 18, subjects were divided into nonoverlapping groups made up of frequent users, experimenters, and abstainers. At age 18, frequent users were observed to be alienated, deficient in impulse control, and manifestly distressed, compared with experimenters. At age 18, abstainers were observed to be anxious, emotionally constricted, and lacking in social skills, compared with experimenters . . .
>
> When the psychological findings are considered as a set, it is difficult to escape the inference that experimenters are the psychologically healthiest subjects, healthier than either abstainers or frequent users. (Shedler & Block, 1990, pp. 624–625)

The *New York Times* (1990) reported that other drug researchers assert that experimentation does not always lead to addiction, and that experimentation was "often part of having a healthy personality." The *Times* article also quotes Brian Flay, director of drug prevention research at the University of Illinois, on another national drug effort: "The 'Just Say No' campaign has always been off the mark. [It] is extremely simplistic. It should be, 'learn how to moderate your behavior, learn how to resist the pressures to go overboard'" ("Drug Study Cites Behavior Traits").

Following the pattern identified in the above discussion of risk, danger and death, ads targeting cocaine or crack offer a more intense and dramatic portrayal of their consequences. Cocaine and crack use is pictured as responsible for major shifts in personality, lifestyle and individual morality. Commercials that illustrate these patterns include the story of the fallen basketball star previously described. In this advertisement, cocaine use is directly responsible for the abandonment of family, friends, work, and a promising future. This theme is also illustrated in other commercials in which character transformation and marginalization are attributed singularly to cocaine use. Specifically, cocaine use is dramatized as causing social isolation, abandonment of goals and the general feeling that life is futile.

> "Bottoming Out"
>
> As we hear background sounds of a deep, pounding, driving rhythm, the following words are written boldly on the darkened screen:

> If . . .
> You don't care . . .
> What your family is feeling . . .
> Or that your friends are avoiding you . . .
> Or that the money's running out . . .
> Or that you don't
> or can't
> have sex anymore . . .
> Or that life is losing its meaning . . .
> You got more out of cocaine than you bargained for.
> Cocaine. It's not for anybody.

Even more telling is the ad featuring the story of drug use leading to prostitution.

> "Street Pro"
>
> A young, white teenage girl is putting on make-up, combing her hair and getting dressed. We see her go out to the streets, stopping cars in the hopes of soliciting a customer. As we watch, the girl tells her story to the camera:
>
> "I'll tell you one thing—it's tough being 14, you know what I mean? I've been around and tried everything. Been on my own for over a year now. One thing I really don't know about—is tomorrow."
>
> As the young girl is speaking, a narrator intersperses the following comments.
>
> "There's a lot of tough things out on the streets today. There's a new drug called crack out there. Crack's made from cocaine, but it's more addicting than cocaine. Some girls who get hooked on crack will walk a long way to get it."

All of the commercials in the campaign depict the dangers associated with drug use in a similarly dramatic and extreme fashion. A summary of the consequences caused by the use of illicit drugs includes: brain damage, ruination, failure, coma, addiction, despair, loss of both self-respect and the respect of others, personal deterioration, death, infertility, paranoia, loss of self-control and autonomy, accidents, family strife, financial loss, incompetency, lack of seriousness, lack of incentive, laziness, shiftlessness and stupidity.

The representation of both the physical and psychosocial consequences of drug use raises a number of concerns. First and foremost, the presentation of both drug use and its consequences is abstracted out of the social context within which it occurs; or, to put it another way, it is decontextualized. No distinction is made between first-time, occasional, regular or compulsive use patterns. The identified consequences are, further, attributed directly and exclusively to the experience of drug use and abuse. Missing from this representation is an appreciation of the social, psychological and economic conditions and difficulties that provide an understanding of both drug use and the experience of negative consequences. In other words, the antidrug advertisements tend to ignore the adage that "Drug abuse is a symptom of a problem, not the problem itself" (Tortu, 1990). The commercials mistakenly identify the use and abuse of drugs as the independent variable, when, in fact, it can be best understood as a dependent variable.

There is, secondly, the question of "facts." A number of commercials end on the note "Face the Facts." But to what extent are these "facts" presented in a clear and usable fashion? The claims made in the "Face the Facts" ads include: "Over 15,000 people who try it [crack and cocaine] are in for a real ride," from the "Heartbreak" advertisement described above. Or the following: "While the popularity of cocaine has been on the rise over the last 5 years, so have other things: cocaine related emergency room treatments up 300 percent, cocaine related deaths up 323 percent." These are certainly impressively strong "facts." Unfortunately, they are also remarkable ambiguous—quite apart from the question of accuracy and the use of percentages without any baseline reported. Does the statistic presented mean that, as a result of cocaine and crack use, 15,000 people are dead? Are rushed to the hospital emergency room? Have heart failure? Are cocaine and crack alone responsible for these 15,000 "rides"? Do the 15,000 people include occasional users, or are they drug abusers or addicts? Let us further make note of Reinarman and Levine's discussion of the mass media's accounts of cocaine deaths as an illustration of the complexities and distortions of such statistical "reporting."

> In 1986 medical examiners coded 1092 deaths as "cocaine related." Yet cocaine ALONE was mentioned in only about one in five of these deaths (18.9%). In three fourths of these cases

> cocaine had been used with other drugs, again, most often alcohol. Although any death is tragic, cocaine's role in these fatalities is ambiguous. "Cocaine-related" is not the same as "cocaine-caused," and "cocaine-related deaths" does not mean "deaths DUE TO cocaine." These uncertainties and ambiguities are lost in media accounts and political rhetoric. Finally, it is worth keeping in mind the comparison to other drugs when evaluating the claims made about cocaine's devastation. For every ONE cocaine-related death in the U.S. in 1987 there were approximately 300 tobacco-related deaths and 100-alcohol related deaths. Seen in this light cocaine's impact is somewhat less dramatic than media and political accounts suggest. (Reinarman & Levine, 1989a, pp. 119–120)

These are important aspects of the "facts" that are not to be found in the advertisements.

The dramatic depictions of these extreme consequences, on the other hand, place the antidrug advertisements squarely within the historical tradition of relying on "fear messages."

> Campaigns against drugs in the United States date back at least to the nineteenth century and have employed a variety of interpersonal and mass-mediated efforts. From the earliest efforts of the Women's Christian Temperance Union through the first radio broadcast defining drugs as a social "problem" ("The Struggle of Mankind Against Its Deadliest Foe"), fear has been the central theme of antidrug campaigns. The use of fear appeals is obvious from the titles of anti-marijuana movies in the 1930s, e.g., REEFER MADNESS, ASSASSIN OF YOUTH, and MARIJUANA, THE WEED WITH ROOTS IN HELL. (Salmon, 1989, p. 23)

The widespread reliance on fear messages, however, has generated significant controversy. "Fear messages" are understood as those communications whose content dramatically illustrates in an extreme form the dire, possible consequences that may result from any particular action. While the actual viewing of fear-arousing advertisements has been found to be initially highly motivating and effective, researchers have consistently indicated their limitations to effect behavior change. There are several related explanations for these findings. First, there is the question of the nature and quantity of fear. How much of what kind of fear is most appropriate or effective?

> If the appeal is too mild, or if the threat seems too unlikely or remote in time, people will not be motivated by it. On the other hand, if the appeal is too strong, or if the behavioral prescription being offered is inadequate for alleviating the level of induced fear, people might tune out the message, deny its validity, derogate the source's credibility, or adopt a fatalistic attitude. Unfortunately, it is very difficult to anticipate and control the level of fear that will be generated by a campaign or to judge whether the prescribed action will be adequate to offset it. (DeJong & Winsten, 1989, p. 21)

Second, we need to be concerned about the bleakness of fear messages that fail to offer a way out. Reardon's research on AIDS prevention messages is instructive on this point.

> Fear research informs us not only that too much fear leads to denial, but that fear without information regarding ways to avoid the problems described or depicted in the message may also lead to denial. Adolescents lacking information and skills needed to resist pressure to engage in behavioral risks for AIDS may retreat into a state of irretrievable denial. To avoid this problem, media messages that include fear should be followed by face-to-face opportunities to discuss strategies for reducing risks for AIDS that in turn reduce fear as well as denial. (Reardon, 1989, p. 286)

A third limitation of "fear messages" is their tendency to be built around the depiction of the most negative set of consequences possible. They are, in other words, founded on the practice of the "routinization of caricature." This emphasis on the possible consequences, to the exclusion of the probable ones, has important implications. DeJong and Winsten's review of the mass media campaigns on behalf of the Harvard Alcohol Project is particularly informative on this aspect of "fear messages." In order to be most effective, they conclude, the advertisements should focus on "immediate, high-probability consequences" rather than on the more dramatic, but relatively low-probability ones. Several lessons on this matter have been drawn from the rather limited deterrent effects of the youth-directed, antismoking campaigns of the past decades.

> First, even when the credibility of factual information is accepted, young people might question its application to them. Most are in good health, and they may view the dire, long-term consequences of substance use as too distinct and too unlikely to be of concern to them. Second, their own observations may beget the conclusions that experimentation does not necessarily result in addiction, and that regular use does not necessarily result in severe health consequences. This uncertainty can be an opening for denial. Third, for most young people, substance use is occasional, not daily, and typically occurs in social situations. As a result, they might overestimate their own capacity to control the extent of their substance use, believing that they are fundamentally different from those who develop a drug dependency. (DeJong & Winsten, 1989, pp. 19–20)

"Fear messages" certainly make for dramatic and eye-catching advertising. The intricacies of "fear messages," however, raise a multitude of issues. These may inadvertently hinder their effectiveness in a campaign such as the Partnership's, which is aimed at complex attitudinal and behavioral changes. The Partnership's seemingly exclusive reliance upon this type of communication has implications in terms of both effectiveness and ideological manipulation.

The Threat of the "Pusher"

Another important question to be asked about the drug experience as it is portrayed in the campaign advertisements pertains to the sources of the drugs themselves. That is, how are the processes of learning about and acquiring the drugs illustrated? Who provides the drugs? How? And under what circumstances?

While most of the advertisements focus specifically on drug use and drug users, a few present narratives on the processes of drug distribution or dealing. The image that emerges from these portrayals is that of the stranger conspiring against the youth of our nation. In other words, there is a strong reliance on the image of the stereotypic "Evil Pusher." In one compelling commercial, the pusher is a street-wise teenager "teaching" a particularly naive and impressionable youngster how to lure his junior high schoolmates into drug use.

> "Be Cool"
>
> The scene takes place outside a school building. We see both a schoolyard and the pusher's car just outside the playground fence. The children in the schoolyard are mostly white, fresh-faced and innocent. As the teen pusher talks with his recruit, shots of them in conversation are interspersed with pictures of the children behind the schoolyard fence. The focus is on the dialogue between the pusher and his recruit. As they sit in a car talking, we see a container filled with vials, pills and drug paraphernalia.
>
> Teen Pusher: "Now kid, all ya gotta do is be cool. You just give the stuff to your best buddies. Take it to a party. Tell your friends it's a great high, they should just try it. Tell 'em it can't hurt 'em."
>
> Recruit: "I can do that."
>
> Teen Pusher: "Yeah it's easy. Those kids are gonna be a pushover cause they like you. You're a hot shot, right? [The recruit offers an embarrassed yet proud smirk.] They'll love you for it."
>
> Recruit: "So how much do I charge?"
>
> Teen Pusher: "Right now, nothin'."
>
> Recruit: "Nothin'?"
>
> Teen Pusher: "Just give it away: Go ahead and have a free taste. Then you watch—when you see who comes back for more . . . "
>
> Recruit: " . . . then I start charging!"
>
> Teen Pusher: "You're a smart kid. Have a good day at school, Billy Boy."
>
> The camera then cuts to the written words:
>
> Kids. It's You Against Them.

In a second example, the pusher is presented as a swarthy foreigner, perhaps the archetype of pure evil, willing to betray the trust of children and the honest citizens of his host neighborhood. Greed is his god, and our children his pass to wealth.

"Candy Man"

The commercial begins with a truck driving by a store in an inner-city neighborhood. We see some children walk up to the outside of a store that looks run-down, with barred windows—not much of a local "candy" shop.

Inside the store are two men. The one behind the counter is the store owner, dark, sinister and with a slight accent, in other words, "foreign." The other is his friend.

Friend: "This place is a dump, man. You ain't gonna make no money in here."

Owner: "You don't know nothin'."

Friend: "I don't know nothin'? I know that this is rotten [holding up a browned banana]. I know I don't see no people in here. Where's your gold mine?"

Owner: "It's down the street, man. It's the school."

Friend: "Oh, I see. You're gonna get rich on selling gum to school kids."

Owner: "Not gum, man. This [holding up a vial]. For ten dollars the little snot noses can blow their heads off. The little brats are dying to fry their brains. And I'm only too happy to help them."

At this, we begin to see young children peer through the window expectantly.

Friend: "So where they get the money?"

Owner: "Who cares where they get it, as long as they get it."

The first child then enters the store, followed by a crowd of other children. The commercial ends with the written words across the screen:

Kids. It's you against them.

The influences promoting and the sources for drug use and abuse, then, are represented as external or foreign to the dominant culture and way of life as experienced in our society. These are common themes in American popular culture. For example, the attempt to link "foreign elements" or "outsiders" with social breakdown, particularly in urban areas, has a long history in the political culture of the United States (Waterston, 1990; Klein, 1983; Reinarman, 1983; Kramer, 1976). As the combined source of our troubles, both drugs and strangers become easy scapegoats.

The problem with this representation, however, is that it contradicts much of our knowledge about the mechanisms of drug initiation and distribution. Rather than confirming the scenario of faceless, evil strangers "pushing" drugs onto naive and ill-defended innocents, research points to the conclusion that initiation into illegal drug use and much of the dealing activity occurs within rather well-defined social networks. Particularly central to these processes are family and friends. What Pearson found to be true of heroin users in England applies across boundaries of substance and nation:

> The first time that someone is offered heroin it will be by a friend. Or maybe by a brother or sister. But always by someone well known, liked, and even loved . . .
>
> There is no element of compulsion in these offers of heroin within a friendship network. It is simply that someone who has already tried the drug wishes to share what they have found to be an enjoyable experience with other friends, even though it may be an experience they may live to regret. (1987, pp. 9–12; Becker, 1953, 1963; Waldorf et al., 1977)

Thus this image of the "foreigner"—so powerfully displayed not only in the Partnership's ads but also in contemporary films, novels and television police dramas—appears to be both a largely inaccurate portrayal and a rather unhelpful one as well. For it diverts our attention away from some of the more fundamental cultural and interactional factors that are more central to the processes of initiation into the world of drugs.

Our sample, however, includes two ads that differ from the above and present a more accurate portrayal of these issues. In the first we see a young boy's initiation into illegal drug use being facilitated not by a "pusher," but rather by the culture and way of life of his parents. In the second ad, we witness drug dealing occurring within a social network of friendship.[7]

Drugs and Processes of Addiction

A small number of the advertisements in the Partnership's media campaign refer to the dangers of addiction, with specific reference to cocaine and crack addiction. The view presented in these commercials is that illicit drug use inevitably leads to abuse and, ultimately, to addiction. The implicit argument in these advertisements is that addiction flows from abuse, which in turns flows from use. Commercials with these messages range from the "scientific" to the interpretative.

> "The Trap"
>
> A white laboratory rat is in a cage. We see a small white cylinder drop into the cage. The rat runs to consume it voraciously. The rat stumbles. Scurrying around the cage, it moves more and more slowly. Its fur is wet, and finally the animal collapses and dies. In the background, we hear swirling, pounding, scratching sounds.
>
> While we watch the rat die, a narrator says: "Only one drug is so addictive, nine out of ten laboratory rats will use it, and use it, and use it, until dead. It's called cocaine, and it can happen to you."
>
> Across the screen appears the lettering:
>
> Face the Facts.
> Drugs are a Dead End.

In another such ad, a young girl is poignantly recounting her experience with drugs. Her life has turned tragic, and she despairs as she tells her story.

> "Crackpot"
>
> "I started on pot about a year ago, but crack really messed me up bad. I started on that, and, you know, I just wanted to see what it would, you know, be like. I said, 'Na, never to me, you know, I can handle it.' We tried some, and like a month later, I couldn't live without it. I mean, I didn't think one time was gonna hurt me. I'm sorry what I put my family through. I never thought this could happen—moved to crack about a month ago. Now, I can't live without it. I didn't want to hurt anyone."

Emerging from these presentations is an image of addiction that follows in a direct and linear fashion from either the pharmacology of the drug itself or from initial exposure and ingestion of the substance. Such a portrayal both simplifies and distorts the complex processes of addiction.

"Addiction" is a very complex process, involving the interplay of pharmacology, psychology, sociology, and culture. The term itself is used rather casually these days reflecting, perhaps, the disputes on its process and meaning in scientific circles (May, 1988; Peele, 1985). When a person is said to be "addicted," do we mean that there is only physical dependence on a particular substance? Or, does the concept include "psychic dependence" as well? Van Dyke and Byck (1982) report that the medically accepted definition of addiction

> . . . derives from the description of opiate effects. For a drug to be considered addictive a person must develop a tolerance for it, in the sense that repeating the same dose causes a diminishing response. Moreover, the drug must lead to physical dependence, so that repeated doses are required to prevent the onset of withdrawal. (p. 140)

They argue that, in keeping with this definition, cocaine cannot be considered "addictive." On the other hand, others adopt a broader, more flexible conceptualization that understands "addiction" to include psychological dependence and habituation (Wallace, 1989, 1987; Smith & Wesson, 1985).

It is surely beyond the capabilities and scope of the advertisements to address such intricacies. However, by glossing over the distinctions and complexities built into the concept of "addiction," the advertisements in the antidrug campaign may ultimately risk being counterproductive. Social or casual drug use does not automatically, or even usually, lead to abuse or "addiction." Thus, some viewers may well dismiss these advertisements as gross exaggerations or falsehoods, given the extent to which they diverge from their own drug-taking experiences. This is, of course, an inherent danger of "fear messages."

No Exit: The Absence of Recovery

". . . [W]e surely only have to be told that we are going to see a film about an alcoholic to know that it will be a tale of either sordid decline or of inspiring redemption" (Dyer, 1979, p. 18). Such was the resolution of the alcoholic drama in film.

The drug experience as depicted in the Partnership's advertising campaign, however, offers no such choice. In commercial after commercial, we witness "sordid decline" and the complete absence of "inspiring redemption." The protagonists in the commercials experience a wide range of physical, psychological, and social ailments—and they die. But they never stop using. Completely missing from the ads is the presentation of either images or information concerning both the realities and the possibilities of limiting or terminating drug use. The absence of such "recovery" from drug use and abuse is particularly glaring given both the stated aims of the commercials and the extensive research literature documenting "pathways from addiction."[8]

Discussion

A number of assumptions framed this research. We began with the recognition that there is, indeed, a social problem of drugs. The use and abuse of various chemical substances—including but not limited to cocaine, crack and marijuana—have very real and significant consequences on the social, psychological and physical health of our nation, our neighborhoods, our families and our citizens. We believed, further, that a mass-media-based public communication campaign may well be a useful and effective instrument in the struggle to confront this problem. The Media-Advertising Partnership for a Drug-Free America represents just such an effort at using the mass media to "unsell" and "de-normalize" the use and abuse of drugs.[9] Our intent in this examination of the Partnership's campaign against drugs was twofold. We sought, first, to identify the themes and images that constitute the "drug problem" as constructed by their television commercials. Second, we compared this representation to the nature of the drug problem as revealed by social science research.

Our analysis shows that the commercials created, produced and distributed by the Partnership present a particular representation of the "drug problem." This image of the "drug problem" emerges from the establishment of a particular set of answers to the questions: "What drugs constitute the 'drug problem'?", "Who are the users/abusers of these drugs?" and "What is the nature of the drug experience?" We have shown, further, that the representation constructed by the antidrug advertisements varies significantly from the knowledge about "drugs" and the "drug problem" available from a wide-ranging body of social science research. We understand this to be a result of the processes of "sharpening up" or "the normalization of caricature."

The demands and criteria for "good" or "effective" advertising may well be distinct from the development of a "truthful" or "accurate" portrayal of social reality. We question, however, the principle that what is appropriate for the selling of toothpaste, laundry detergent or automobiles is necessarily appropriate to a public communication campaign against drugs. The nature, seriousness and diversity of the problems associated with the use and abuse of drugs necessitate a more realistic, probable and balanced approach. The introduction of contemporary versions of such ideologically laden propaganda as "Reefer Madness," "Cocaine Fiends" or "Why Do You Think They Call It Dope?" in today's discourse on drugs is a disservice to the challenge of dealing with the social problem of drug abuse. The commendable goals and efforts of the Partnership would be better served by a greater appreciation of the "realities" of substance abuse—even at the cost of a reduction in their dramatics.

Notes

1. The titles of the ads described in this article are our own and not those of the Partnership for a Drug-Free America.
2. By referring to the advertisements as a "text," we are identifying them as a "unit of discourse, a sentence, a paragraph, a book, a television programme, which can be identified as an autonomous and clearly defined unit of communication organized and structured according to decipherable rules—rules of grammar, narrative, rhetoric" (Silverstone, 1985, p. 167). We, therefore, understand "texts" in the broadest sense of the term: "All structured systems of representation, no matter what the medium, can be construed as "texts" for the study of stereotypes. From advertising copy to medical illustration, from popular novels to classical drama, from the academic portrait to graffiti scratched on the walls of the prison—all are texts in that they function as structured expressions . . . " (Gilman, 1985, p. 26). They, further, offer a particularly useful and rich source of insight into the construction of social problems. Every society has "generated a seemingly endless series of texts as a means of fixing stereotypes within a world of

constant forms (whether aesthetic or scientific), and these texts provide a very good basis for analyzing the historical forces at work in the shaping of stereotypes" (Gilman, 1985, p. 11).

3. Copies of the ads were made available to us by the Media-Advertising Partnership for a Drug-Free America for use in classroom educational activities. We gratefully appreciate the Partnership's cooperation.
4. A number of the advertisements were distributed in a variety of versions. For instance, several ads in our sample appeared in both English and Spanish; others were edited so as to be available for broadcasting in shorter and longer versions. While we have a total of 42 prepared commercials in all, our sample includes 33 distinct "story lines."
5. For a discussion of the problematics of statistics in general, and government statistics, in particular, in social problems research, see Best, 1989; Reinarman and Levine, 1989a, 1989b.
6. This may well, in part, be a function of the nature of our sample. Beginning in the summer of 1989, the Partnership introduced a series of commercials specifically targeting Hispanic and African Americans. In no way, however, do these new efforts call into question either the validity or the importance of our findings on the visual demographics during the sample period of the Partnership's first three years of operation. In three regards they substantiate our findings. First, the introduction of these new advertisements indicates that the Partnership itself found something missing in their portrayals of "who are the users?" Second, despite the production of these new advertisements, our observations reveal a continued reliance on the commercials included in our sample. And, third, regardless of the changes in focus, direction, and emphasis, the Partnership makes in the future, our analysis of their first three years stands on its own.
7. We have seen several other advertisements that offer a similarly more accurate representation of these issues. They, however, were not included in our sample because they were both too recent and in another medium—they appeared in print advertisements beginning in 1990. See, additionally, note 5 above.
8. For research documenting the processes of terminating or controlling the use of a variety of drugs, see: Biernacki 1986; Pearson 1987; Shaffer and Jones 1989; Waldorf 1983; Waldorf and Biernacki 1977, 1981; Winick 1962.
9. For a more general discussion of media-based public communication campaigns see Rice and Atkin 1989; Rice and Paisley 1981; and Salmon 1989.

References

Altheide, D. L. (1986). Ethnographic content analysis. *Qualitative Sociology, 9,* 55–72.

American Association of Advertising Agencies (AAAA). (1990). *What we've learned about advertising.* New York: AAAA.

Barron, J. (1988, August 7). The teen drug of choice: Alcohol. *The New York Times,* pp. 41–44.

Becker, H. S. (1953). Becoming a marijuana user. *American Journal of Sociology, 59,* 235–242.

Becker, H. S. (1963). *Outsiders: Studies in the sociology of deviance.* Glencoe, IL: Free Press.

Best, J. (1989). Dark figures and child victims: Statistical claims about missing children. In J. Best (Ed.), *Images of issues: Typifying contemporary social problems.* New York: Aldine De Gruyter.

Biernacki, P. (1986). *Pathways from addiction: Recovery without treatment.* Philadelphia, PA: Temple University Press.

Black, G. S. (1987). *The attitudinal basis of drug use: A report from the Media-Advertising Partnership for a Drug-Free America, Inc.* Rochester, NY: The Gordon S. Black Corporation.

Black, G. S. (1988). *Changing attitudes toward drug use: The first year effort of the Media-Advertising Partnership for a Drug-Free America, Inc.* [Executive Summary]. Rochester, NY: The Gordon S. Black Corporation.

Cohen, S. (1980). *Folk devils and moral panics: The creation of the mods and rockers.* New York: St. Martin's Press.

DeJong, W., & Winsten, J. A. (1989). *Recommendations for future mass media campaigns to prevent preteen and adolescent substance abuse.* Boston, MA: Center for Health Communication, Harvard School of Public Health, Harvard University

Drug study cites behavior traits. (1990, May 5). *The New York Times,* p. C-1.

DuToit, B. M. (Ed.). (1977). *Drugs, rituals and altered states of consciousness.* Rotterdam: A. A. Balkema.

Dyer, R (1979). The role of stereotypes. In J. Cook, & M. Lewington (Eds.). *Images of alcoholism* (pp. 15–21). London: British Film Institute.

Eckardt, M. J., Harford, T. C., Kaelber, C. T., Parker, E. S., Rosenthal, L. S., Ryback, R. S., Salmoiraghi, G. C., Vanderveen, E., & Warren, K. R. (1981). Health hazards associated with alcohol consumption. *Journal of the American Medical Association, 246*(6), 648–666.

Friedman, S. R., Sotheran, J. L., Abdul-Quader, A., Primm, B. J., Des Jarlais, D. C., Kleinman, P., Mauge, C., Goldsmith, D. S., El-Sadr, W., & Maslansky, R. (1987). The AIDS epidemic among blacks and Hispanics. *The Milibank Quarterly, 65*(Suppl. 2), 455–499.

Giesbrecht, N.(Ed.). (1983). *Consequences of drinking: Trends in alcohol problem statistics in seven countries.* Toronto: Addiction Research Foundation.

Gilman, Sander L. (1985). *Difference and pathology: Stereotypes of sexuality, race, and madness.* Ithaca, NY: Cornell University Press.

Goode, E. (1989). *Drugs in American society* (3rd ed.) New York: McGraw-Hill.

Gusfield, J. R. 1986 (1963). *Symbolic crusades: Status politics and the American temperance movement.* Urbana, IL: University of Illinois Press.

Hannerz, U. (1980). *Exploring the city: Inquiries toward an urban anthropology.* New York: Columbia University Press.

Hawkins, J. D., Lishner, D. M., & Catalano, R. F. Jr. (1984). *Childhood predictors and the prevention of adolescent substance abuse.* Paper presented at the NIDA Research Analysis and Utilization System Meeting, Washington, DC.

Helmer, J (1975). *Drugs and minority oppression.* New York: The Seabury Press.

Inciardi, J. A. (1986). *The war on drugs: Heroin, cocaine, crime, and public policy.* Mountain View, CA: Mayfield Publishing Co.

Johnson, J. M. (1989). Horror stories and the construction of child abuse. In J. Best (Ed.), *Images of issues: Typifying contemporary social problems.* New York: Aldine De Gruyter.

Johnson, B., Williams, T., Dei, K. A., & Sanabria, H. (1990). Drug abuse in the inner city: Impact of hard-drug users and the community. In M. Tonry, & J. Q. Wilson (Eds.), *Drugs and crime.* Chicago, IL: University of Chicago Press.

Johnston, L. S., O'Malley, P. M., & Bachman, J. G. (1987). *National trends in drug use and related factors among American high school students and young adults, 1975–1986.* Rockville, MD: National Institute on Drug Abuse.

Kandel, D., & Logan, J. (1984). Patterns of drug use from adolescence to young adulthood: I. Periods of risk for initiation, continued use, and discontinuation. *American Journal of Public Health, 74,* 660–666.

Klein, D. (1983). Ill and against the law: The social and medical control of heroin users. *Journal of Drug Issues, 13*(1), 31–55.

Kramer, J. C. (1976). From demon to ally—how mythology has, and may yet, alter national drug policy. *Journal of Drug Issues, 6*(4),390–406.

May, G. G. (1988). *Addiction and grace.* San Francisco, CA: Harper and Row.

Morales, E. (1989). *Cocaine: White gold rush in Peru.* Tucson, AZ: University of Arizona Press.

Musto, D. F. (1987). *The American disease: Origins of narcotic control.* New York: Oxford University Press.

National Institute on Drug Abuse (NIDA). (1986). *National household survey on drug abuse, 1985.* Washington, DC: Division of Epidemiology and Statistical Analysis, NIDA.

Newcomb, M. D., & Bentler, P. M. (1989). Substance use and abuse among children and teenagers. *American Psychologist, 44*(2), 242–248.

OSAP. (1990). *Seventh special report to the U. S. Congress on alcohol and health.* Office of Substance Abuse Prevention. Rockville, MD:NCADI.

Peele, S. (1985). *The meaning of addiction.* Toronto: D. C. Heath.

Pearson, Geoffrey. (1987). *The new heroin users.* New York: Basil Blackwell.

Reardon, K. K. (1989). The potential role of persuasion in adolescent AIDS prevention. In R. E. Rice, & C. K. Atkin (Eds.), *Public communication campaigns* (2nd ed.). Newbury Park, CA: Sage Publications.

Reinarman, C. (1979). Moral crusades and political-economy: Historical and ethnographic notes on the construction of the cocaine menace. *Contemporary Crisis, 3*(3), 225–254.

Reinarman, C. (1983). Constraint, autonomy, and state policy: Notes toward a theory of controls on consciousness alteration. *Journal of Drug Issues, 13*(1), 9–30.

Reinarman, C., & Levine, H. G. (1989a). The crack attack: Politics and media in America's latest drug scare. In J. Best (Ed.). *Images of issues: Typifying contemporary social problems.* New York: Aldine De Gruyter.

Reinarman, C., & Levine, H. G. (1989b). Crack in context: Politics and media in the making of a drug scare. *Contemporary Drug Problems, 16*(4), 535–577.

Rice, R. E., & Atkin, C. K. (Eds.). (1989). *Public Communication Campaigns* (2nd ed.). Newbury Park, CA: Sage Publications.

Rice, R. E., & Paisley, W. J., (Eds.). (1981). *Public communication campaigns.* Newbury Park, CA: Sage Publications.

Room, Robin. (1989). Alcoholism and Alcoholics Anonymous in U. S. films, 1945–1962: The party ends for the wet generation. *Journal of Studies on Alcohol 50*(4), 368–383.

Salmon, C. T. (1989). Campaigns for social "improvement": An overview of values, rationales and impacts. In C. T. Salmon (Ed.), *Information campaigns: Balancing social values and social change.* Newbury Park CA: Sage Publications.

Schlossman, S. L. (1984). The "culture of poverty" in ante-bellum social thought. *Science and Society, 38,* 150–166.

Shaffer, H. J. & Jones, S. B. (1989). *Quitting cocaine: The struggle against impulse.* Lexington, MA: Lexington Books.

Shedler, J., & Block, J. (1990). Adolescent drug use and psychological health: A longitudinal inquiry. *American Psychologist, 45,* 612–630.

Silverstone, R. (1985). *Framing science: The making of a BBC documentary.* London: British Film Institute.

Smith, D. E., & Wesson, D. R. (1985). Cocaine abuse and treatment: An overview. In D. E. Smith, & D. R. Wesson (Eds.), *Treating the cocaine abuser.* Center City, MN: Hazeldon Foundation.

Tortu, S. (1990, October). *The utility of drug research.* Paper presented at Narcotic and Drug Research, Inc., New York.

Tudor, A. (1979). On alcohol and the mystique of media effects. In J. Cook, & M. Lewington (Eds.), *Images of alcoholism* (pp. 6–14). London: British Film Institute.

Van Dyke, C. & Byck, R. (1982). Cocaine. *Scientific American, 246*(3), 128–141.

Waldorf, D. (1983). Natural recovery from opiate addiction: Some socio-psychological processes of untreated recovery. *Journal of Drug Issues, 13*(2), 237–280.

Waldorf, D., & Biernacki, P. (1977). Natural recovery from opiate addiction: A review of the incidence literature. *Journal of Drug Issues, 9*(2), 281–290.

Waldorf, D., & Biernacki, P. (1981). Natural recovery from opiate addiction: Some preliminary findings. *Journal of Drug Issues, 11*(1), 61–74.

Waldorf, D., Murphy, S., Reinarman, C., & Joyce, B. (1977). *Doing coke: An ethnography of cocaine users and sellers.* Washington, DC: Drug Abuse Council.

Wallace, B. C. (1987). Cocaine dependence treatment on an inpatient detoxification unit. *Journal of Substance Abuse Treatment, 4,* 85–92.

Wallace, B. C. (1989). Psychological and environmental determinants of relapse in crack cocaine smokers. *Journal of Substance Abuse Treatment, 6,* 95–106.

Waterston, A. (1990). *Aspects of street addict life.* Doctoral dissertation, City University of New York.

Weil, A. (1972). *The natural mind.* Boston, MA: Houghton Mifflin.

Weil, A. (1977). Observations on consciousness alteration. *Journal of Psychedelic Drugs, 9*(1), 75–78.

Williams, T. (1989). *The cocaine kids.* New York: Addison-Wesley.

Winick, C. (1962). Maturing out of narcotic addiction. *Bulletin on Narcotics,* 14, pp. 1–7.

Yamaguchi, K. & Kandel, D. (1984). Patterns of drug use from adolescence to young adulthood: III. Predictors of progression. *American Journal of Public Health, 74,* 673–681.

Discussion Questions

1. What is the mission of The Media-Advertising Partnership for a Drug-Free America? What drugs does it particularly focus on?
2. According to the research by Baumann and Waterston, how does The Partnership for a Drug-Free America convey its message? What role models do they use? What role models do they leave out?
3. As you read through the scripts presented, comment on whether you believe the antidrug commercials are effective in curtailing drug use. Why are they effective, or not effective? Discuss.
4. At the conclusion of this article, to what extent do the authors find that The Partnership for a Drug-Free America is effective? Do you agree or disagree with the authors? Why or why not?

Discussion Questions

Drinking Behavior

Taking Personal Responsibility

David J. Hanson **Ruth C. Engs**

David J. Hanson is Professor of Sociology and Director of Assessment at the State University of New York at Potsdam. He is particularly interested in collegiate drinking behavior and has received grants supporting research on this subject from federal, state and foundation sources. Dr. Hanson has authored over 260 publications and conference papers and is president of the New York State Sociological Association. He is a recipient of that organization's Award for Excellence and of his institution's Award for Excellence in Research and Creative Endeavors.

Ruth Engs, Professor, Applied Health Science, Indiana University, Bloomington, has been doing research on college students for almost 20 years. She and David Hanson have been conducting a national trend study of college drinking patterns since the early 1980s. Dr. Engs has given numerous presentations and lectures both in the United States and abroad. She has been active as a consultant for government, industry and school and community programs helping to design education, intervention and prevention programs concerning youthful alcohol and other drug abuse. She has written numerous research and pedagogical articles and four books. Her latest books include *Alcohol and Other Drugs: Self-Responsibility, Controversies in the Addiction Field,* and *Women: Alcohol and Other Drugs,* of which she is editor. Engs and Hanson have co-authored over 30 articles during the past decade and are considered the top researchers in their field.

There is extensive evidence that the consumption of alcoholic beverages has occurred in most societies throughout the world. It has probably occurred since the Paleolithic Age, and certainly since the Neolithic Age (Knupfer, 1960). The records of all ancient civilizations refer to the use of alcoholic beverages. Such accounts are found in Egyptian carvings, Hebrew script, and Babylonian tablets (Patrick, 1952). The Code of Hammurabi (c. 2225 B.C.) devoted several sections to problems created by the abundance of alcohol, and in China, laws that forbade making wine were enacted and repealed forty-one times between 1100 B.C. and 1400 A.D. (Alcoholism and Drug Research Foundation of Ontario, 1961). These and other sources of evidence indicate that concern over alcohol use and abuse is not unique to present societies.

The place of alcohol in American society since the colonial period has clearly been ambivalent. "Drinking has been blessed and cursed, has been held the cause of economic catastrophe and the hope for prosperity, the major cause of crime, disease and military defeat, depravity and a sign of high prestige, mature personality, and a refined civilization" (Straus & Bacon, 1953).

Not surprisingly, college student drinking is not a recent occurrence in the United States. As far back as the early eighteenth century, alcohol was used by students, and there were admonitions and strict regulations on the part of authority figures regarding the practice. However, American students have been drinking for nearly three centuries, regardless of restrictions or prohibitions (Kuder & Madson, 1976).

Following the repeal of the Eighteenth Amendment in 1933, prohibition efforts have largely been age-specific. In 1970, Congress passed the Twenty-Sixth Amendment, which grants the right to vote in federal elections to citizens between the ages of 18 and 21. A movement then began to extend other rights and privileges of adulthood to those aged 18; between 1970 and 1975, 29 states reduced their minimum legal drinking age (Wagenaar, 1983). However, by the late 1970s, controversy over minimum drinking age laws became widespread, and this pattern was reversed. Much of the concern arose over the number of young people involved in auto accidents, many of which were alcohol-related (Wechsler & Sands, 1980).

A common response to the need to solve a perceived social problem has been to seek a legal solution through legislation, and it appears that alcohol laws in the United States are among the most stringent in the world (Mosher, 1980). Mosher has pointed out that minimum drinking age legislation and its enforcement contrast with actual drinking patterns: statistics show that underage persons increased their use of alcohol steadily from the 1930s to the 1960s, when legislation to curtail sales was most active. He stresses that "Ironically, a plateau was reached both in the prevalence of teenage drinking and in legislation action to restrict availability to teen-agers at approximately the same time" (p. 25). Both updating and corroborating these observations is the fact that following the reduction of drinking age laws in the 1970s, the proportion of collegians who drank trended downward (Engs & Hanson, 1988).

Research has shown that a large proportion of collegians currently drink (Engs & Hanson, 1988). Over the past three decades research has also indicated that the proportion of collegiate drinkers increases with age (Studinski, 1937; Dvorak, 1972; Hanson, 1974; Strange & Schmidt, 1979; Walfish et al., 1981). However, in July of 1987 the minimum purchase age became 21 in all states.

Researchers have found that telling persons not to do something often produces the opposite reaction. People value their sense of freedom and autonomy and like to project an image of self-control (Baer et al., 1980). *Reactance theory* suggests that whenever people believe their freedom either has or will be unjustly threatened, they enter into a reactance motivational state and act to regain control by not complying (Brehm, 1966). Coercion, in particular, leads to the arousal of reactance, which in turn tends to reduce compliance (Brehm & Brehm, 1981).

Because drinking has traditionally been part of the college experience, and because it is now illegal for students under 21 to purchase alcohol in any state, it was hypothesized that reactance motivation would be increased among underage students, leading them to exhibit greater and more frequent alcohol consumption than collegians of legal age to purchase alcohol. Because it is well established that younger students are less likely to drink than are older students, it was assumed that any abrupt change in that pattern would be a result of the legislation raising the drinking age.

Shortly after that legislation went into effect, a nationwide sample of 3,375 students at 56 colleges revealed that the number of students under 21 who drank was now significantly higher than the number of students 21 and older who were drinking. Additionally, a higher proportion of underage students were drinking heavily, compared to those of legal age (Engs & Hanson, 1989).

While sampling error always remains a possible explanation for these findings, other evidence supports the reactance explanation. The more important an eliminated freedom, the greater will be the reactance (Wortman & Brehm, 1975). Drinking is traditionally seen as important to college life, and many activities are focused around it. Also, more reactance is aroused when people expect to enjoy a freedom that is subsequently eliminated (Wortman & Brehm). Many students, even while still in high school, presumably expected to be able to purchase alcohol when they got to college. Finally, students who could legally purchase alcohol before the legislation lost that right (i.e., were not "grandfathered") after the law changed. This would be expected to generate high reactance. Thus, it appears that this legislation has not only been ineffective but actually counterproductive.

Underlying minimum age legislation are the assumptions of American prohibitionism: alcohol consumption is sinful and dangerous; it results in problem behaviors; and drinking in any degree is equally undesirable because moderate social drinking is the forerunner of chronic inebriation (Stern et al., 1967). Naturally, young people, if not everyone, should be protected from alcohol, according to this view.

Unfortunately, attempts to legislate drinking behavior often lead to unintended and undesirable consequences. For example, Australian laws closing bars at six o'clock got the working men out of the establishments and possibly home to their families in time for dinner. However, they also produced the undesirable custom known as the six o'clock swill, which involves consuming as much beer as possible between the end of work and the six o'clock closing time (Room, 1976). Sterne (1967) and her colleagues concluded that minimum age laws not only fail in their intent but also produce very questionable consequences, such as encouraging drinking in cars, creating disrespect for law, and encouraging the consumption of alcohol in undesirable environments (Sterne et al.). Anecdotal statements by college students in North Carolina regarding the increase in the drinking law revealed the belief of some that "it might be easier to hide a little pot in my room than a six pack of beer" (Lotterhos et al., 1988, p. 644).

It has been said that if there is one universal characteristic that pervades humanity, it may be the urge to manipulate and control the behavior of others (Cisin, 1978), and nowhere is this more apparent than in the effort to control drinking behavior through legislative edict. The minimum drinking age laws in the United States have undergone more than 100 modifications since their widespread introduction in the 1930s (Wechsler & Sands, 1980). The most recent series of increases in the minimum age have been no more successful than were those of the past.

This sad conclusion suggests the need for greatly increased individual responsibility. We are a nation composed largely of drinkers and about 80 percent of college-aged individuals reading this book drink at least once a year. Drinking, like eating or any other social activity, benefits from guidelines to help participants enjoy the activity with low risk. Gobbling down half a chocolate cake at a party would be neither responsible nor polite eating behavior. The same principle applies to drinking. Responsible, low-risk choices concerning alcohol may mean not drinking when a person is alcoholic, ill, taking medications, or serving as designated driver. For drinkers, responsible drinking means that you never have to feel sorry for what has happened while you were drinking. Basically, this means not becoming drunk. If you choose to drink, the following guidelines should help you do so with enjoyment and low risk (Engs, 1987).

1. *Know your limit.* If you do not already know how much alcohol you can handle without losing control, try it out one time at home, with your parents or roommate present. Explain to them what you are attempting to learn. Most people find that taking no more than a drink and a half per hour will keep them in control of the situation and avoid drunkenness.
2. *Eat food while you drink.* It is particularly good to eat high protein foods such as cheese and peanuts, which help to slow the absorption of alcohol into the circulatory system.
3. *Sip your drink.* If you gulp a drink for the effect that it produces, you are losing a pleasure of drinking, namely savoring the taste and aroma. This is particularly true for wine.
4. *Accept a drink only when you really want one.* If someone tries to force a drink on you, ask for an alternative beverage.
5. *Cultivate taste.* Choose quality rather than quantity. Learn the names of fine wines, whiskeys, and beers and learn which beverages taste best with various foods.
6. *Skip a drink occasionally.* At parties, have a nonalcoholic drink between alcoholic ones, to keep your blood alcohol concentration down. Also, space out your alcoholic drinks to maintain a low blood alcohol concentration.
7. *If you must drive home after drinking, have your drink(s) before or with dinner rather than afterward.* This permits time for the alcohol to be absorbed slowly into the circulatory system and burned up. Consume no more than one drink per hour.
8. *Beware of unfamiliar drinks.* Drinks such as zombies and other fruit and rum drinks can be deceiving because the degree of alcohol is not always detectable by taste.
9. *Make sure that alcohol improves social relationships rather than impairs them.* Serve alcohol as an adjunct to an activity rather than as the primary focus.
10. *Appoint a designated driver.* Have someone available who will not be drinking and will drive others home.

11. *Use alcohol cautiously in connection with prescription or over-the-counter drugs.* If in any doubt, consult your physician or pharmacist regarding possible negative drug interactions.
12. *Respect the rights of those who do not wish to drink.* It is inconsiderate and rude to attempt to get people to drink if they do not wish to do so. They may abstain for religious or medical reasons, because they are recovering alcoholics, or just because they don't like the taste of alcohol or the effect it has on them. In any case, the reason is their business and their choice not to drink should be respected.
13. *Avoid drinking alcohol (especially mixed drinks) on an empty stomach on hot days.* This can produce hypoglycemia, leading to dizziness, weakness, and mood changes.
14. *Avoid heavy drinking while pregnant.* Research appears to suggest that heavy drinking among pregnant women may cause fetal alcohol syndrome.

Most people enjoy going to parties and most also enjoy hosting them. The following are helpful tips for being a responsible host.

1. *Pass the drinks.* Serve drinks at regular, reasonable intervals along with plenty of nonalcoholic beverages. A schedule of one alcoholic drink per hour is a good guide.
2. *Have a responsible bartender.* If you plan to have a friend act as bartender, make sure that the person is not a drink pusher.
3. *Don't serve doubles.* Many people count and pace their drinks. If you serve doubles, they will be drinking twice as much as they intended.
4. *Push snacks.* Make sure that people are eating along with drinking.
5. *Don't push the drinks.* Let the glass become empty before you offer a refill.
6. *Be sure to serve nonalcoholic beverages also.* Remember that one out of five college students chooses not to drink. Make sure that you have a reasonable selection of appealing nonalcoholic drinks to serve.
7. *End the party properly.* Decide, in advance, when you want your party to end. Before that time, stop serving alcohol and offer coffee and a substantial snack. This provides some nondrinking time before your guests leave.

If you are at high risk for alcoholism, you might wish to consider abstaining from alcohol. Your risk of being alcoholic increases with the following characteristics.*

1. A member of your family is/was alcoholic.
2. There was teetotalism in your family with strong moral overtones.
3. There is a history of either alcoholism or teetotalism in your spouse or family of your spouse.
4. You come from a broken home or a home with parental discord.
5. You are one of the last children in a large family.
6. You are from an Irish or French Catholic background.
7. You have female relatives of more than one generation who have a high incidence of recurrent depression.
8. You are a heavy smoker.
9. You have no religious affiliation.
10. You are separated, single, or divorced.
11. You are a beer drinker rather than a hard liquor or wine drinker.
12. You are male.

If you answer "yes" to any two of the following questions, you may have a drinking problem: *

1. Do you gulp drinks for the effect that rapid drinking produces?
2. Do you start the day with a drink?
3. Do you drink alone to escape from reality, boredom, loneliness, or anger?
4. Do you frequently overdose on alcohol or get drunk?
5. Do you drink to relieve a hangover?
6. Do you lose time from school because of drinking?
7. Do you drink to lose shyness and build up your self-confidence?

---

*Adopted from the following reports: DHEW pub. no. ADM 74–68 (1974) and DHEW pub. no. 1 (1974) SM-77-90099 (1983).

8. Is drinking affecting your reputation?
9. Do you drink to escape from study or home worries?
10. Does it bother you if somebody says maybe you drink too much?
11. Do you have to take a drink to go out on a date?
12. Do you ever get into money trouble over buying liquor?
13. Have you lost friends since you've started drinking?
14. Do you hang out now with a crowd where alcohol is easy to get?
15. Do your friends drink less than you do?
16. Do you drink until the bottle is empty?
17. Have you ever had a loss of memory from drinking?
18. Has drunk driving ever put you into a hospital or a jail?
19. Do you get annoyed with classes or lectures on drinking?
20. Do you think you have a problem with alcohol?

Information and help are available through a number of organizations and hotlines, including those listed below.

Alcoholics Anonymous National Headquarters
Box 459
Grand Central Station
New York, NY 10163
(212) 686-1100
Local offices are located throughout the country. Consult telephone directory for local numbers.

Al-Anon Family Group Headquarters
Box 862
Midtown Station
New York, NY 10018-0862
24-hour answering service is (800) 356-9996
Local offices are located throughout the country. Consult telephone directory for local number.

Adult Children of Alcoholics
Suite 200
2522 West Sepulveda Boulevard
Torrance, CA 90505
(213) 534-1815

National Council on Alcoholism
7th floor
12 West 21st Street
New York, NY 10010
24-hour, seven-day hotline
(800) 622-2255

It should now be clear that efforts to eliminate drinking among young people by raising the legal drinking age have been unsuccessful, if not counterproductive. This should not be surprising; prohibition efforts around the world have been met with failure to achieve their intended results. Given the wide acceptability and availability of alcohol in our society, successful prohibition among young people is hard to imagine.

The failure of legislative solutions suggests the need for greatly increased self-responsibility. Abstinence is a wise decision for individuals who don't like the effects of alcohol, who prefer to be alcohol-free, who hold religious beliefs prohibiting alcohol, who have certain medical problems, who are at risk of being alcoholic, or who believe they may have a drinking problem. For those who choose to drink, this chapter provides guidelines for low-risk drinking as well as hints for being a responsible host.

Ultimately, the decision to abstain or to drink is yours. If you choose to drink, the decision regarding how to drink is also yours. Most importantly, the consequences of your decision, whatever they may be, are yours to face.

References

Alcoholism & Drug Addiction Foundation of Ontario. (1961). *It's best to know.* Toronto, Ontario: Alcoholism & Drug Addiction Foundation of Ontario.

*Questions 6 to 20 from *Young People and A.A.* Reprinted with permission of Alcoholics Anonymous World Services.

Baer, R., Hinkle, S., Smith, K., & Fenton, M. (1980). Reactance as a function of actual versus projected utility. *Journal of Personality and Social Psychology, 38,* 416–422.

Brehm, J. (1966). *A theory of psychological reactance.* New York: Academic Press.

Brehm, S., & Brehm, J. W. (1981). *Psychological reactance: A theory of freedom and control.* New York: Academic Press.

Cisin, I. H. (1978). Formal and informal social controls over drinking. In J. A. Ewing, & B. A. Rouse (Eds.), *Drinking: Alcohol in American society—issues and current research.* Chicago, IL: Nelson-Hall.

Dvorak, E. J. (1972). A longitudinal study of nonmedical drug use among university students—a brief summary. *Journal of American College Health Association, 20,* 212–215.

Engs, R. C. (1987). *Alcohol and other drugs: Self-responsibility.* Bloomington, IN: Tichenor.

Engs, R. C., & Hanson, D. J. (1988). University students' drinking patterns and problems: Examining the effects of raising the purchase age. *Public Health Reports, 103,* 667–673.

Engs, R. C., & Hanson, D. J. (1989). Reactance theory: A test with collegiate drinking, *Psychological Reports, 64,* 1086.

Hanson, D. J. (1974). Drinking attitudes and behaviors among college students. *Journal of Alcohol and Drug Education, 19,* 6–14.

Knupfer, G. (1960). Use of alcoholic beverages by society and its cultural implications. *California's Health, 18,* 17–21.

Kuder, J. M., & Madson, D. L. (1976). College student use of alcoholic beverages. *Journal of College Student Personnel, 17,* 142–144.

Lotterhos, J. F., Glover, E. D., Holbert, D., & Barnes, R. C. (1988). Intentionality of college students regarding North Carolina's 21-year drinking age law. *International Journal of Addiction, 23,* 629–647.

Mosher, J. F. (1980). The history of youthful-drinking laws: Implications for current policy. In H. Wechsler (Ed.), *Minimum-drinking-age laws.* Lexington, MA: Lexington Books.

Patrick, C. H. (1952). *Alcohol, culture and society.* Durham, NC: Duke University Press.

Room, R. (1976). Evaluating the effect of drinking laws on drinking. In J. A. Ewing, & B. A. Rouse (Eds.), *Drinking: Alcohol in American society—issues and current research.* Chicago, IL: Nelson-Hall.

Stern, M. W., Pittman, D. J., & Coe, T. (1967). Teenagers, drinking and the law: Study of arrest trends for alcohol-related offenses. In D. J. Pittman (Ed.), *Alcoholism.* New York: Harper & Row.

Strange, C C., & Schmidt, M. R. (1979). College student perceptions of alcohol use and differential drinking behaviors. *Journal of College Student Personnel, 20,* 73–79.

Strauss, R., & Bacon, S. D. (1953). *Drinking in college.* New Haven, CT: Yale University Press.

Studenski, P. (1937). Liquor consumption among the American youth: A study of the drinking habits of certain segments of the American youth. Report presented to the conference of the Social Study Committees of the National Conference of State Liquor Administrators, Mackinac Island, MI. In G. M. Barnes, & J. W. Welte (Eds.), Predictors of alcohol use among college students in New York State. *Journal of American College Health, 31,* 150–157.

Wagenaar, A. C. (1983). *Alcohol, young drivers, and traffic accidents.* Lexington, MA: Lexington Books.

Walfish, S.,Wentz, D., Benzing, P., Brenan, F., & Champ, S. (1981). Alcohol abuse on a college campus: A needs assessment. *Evaluation Program Planning, 4,* 163–168.

Wechsler, H., & Sands, E. S. (1980). Minimum-age laws and youthful drinking: An introduction. In H. Wechsler (Ed.), *Minimum-drinking-age laws.* Lexington, MA: Lexington Books.

Wortman, C., & Brehm, J. (1975). Response to uncontrollable outcomes: An investigation of reactance theory and the learned helplessness model. In L. Berkowits (Ed.), *Advances in experimental social psychology vol. 8.* (pp. 278–336). New York: Academic Press.

Discussion Questions

1. What evidence exists that American society tends to be ambivalent toward alcohol? What could be some consequences of that ambivalence?
2. Reactance theory was used to predict the increase in underage drinking after the legal age was raised.

To what other phenomena might the theory be applied? Under what conditions might the theory not explain behavior?

3. In what ways might higher legal drinking ages be counterproductive?
4. What are the pros and cons of lowering the drinking age?
5. The chapter provides guidelines for both responsible hosting and responsible consumption of alcoholic beverages. Can you think of any additional guidelines, hints, or suggestions?

Do Friends Let Friends Drive Drunk?

Decreasing Drunk Driving Through Informal Peer Intervention

Martin A. Monto
Michael D. Newcomb
Jerome Rabow
Anthony C.R. Hernández

Martin Monto received his B.A. in sociology from Kansas State University and his M.A. and Ph.D. in sociology from UCLA. He is currently an assistant professor of sociology at the University of Portland. His interests include social psychology, the sociology of education, socialization, gender, and helping behavior. His research focuses on the ways in which individuals (1) participate in the construction of social reality, (2) are themselves shaped by social processes, and (3) may challenge, resist, or participate in alternative conceptions of social reality. He has published several articles on peer intervention in drunk driving situations. His current research includes an exploration of women's understandings of childbirth and a study of adolescent sex offenders.

Jerome Rabow received his Bachelor's degree from Brooklyn College, where he majored in sociology and psychology. He subsequently worked with delinquent boys at the Highfields Residential Treatment Center in Hopewell, New Jersey, and was the group therapist at the Provo Experiment in Delinquency Rehabilitation in Utah. Professor Rabow did graduate work at Columbia University and received his Ph.D. from the University of Michigan. He is a professor of sociology at UCLA where he teaches courses in psychoanalytic sociology, social psychology, and the sociology of education. He is also a practicing therapist. His research interests lie in psychoanalytic sociology, peace attitudes, gender and money, and college students' drinking and driving. His published works include *Vital Problems for American Society; Sociology, Students, and Society; Cracks in the Classroom Wall;* and *Advances in Psychoanalytic Sociology.*

Michael D. Newcomb is a licensed clinical psychologist, a Professor of Counseling Psychology at the University of Southern California, and a research psychologist in the Psychology Department at the University of California, Los Angeles. He is principal investigator on several grants from the National Institute on Drug Abuse. He has published well over 100 papers and chapters and written two books on drug problems: *Consequences of Adolescent Drug Use* (with Bentler, published by Sage), and *Drug Use in the Workplace* (published by Auburn House). His interests include: etiology and consequences of adolescent drug abuse; structural equation modeling, methodology, and multivariate analysis; human sexuality; health psychology; attitudes and affect related to nuclear war; and cohabitation, marriage, and divorce.

Anthony C. R. Hernández is a Research Psychologist at the Chicano Studies Research Center at the University of California in Los Angeles. Dr. Hernández has co-authored several journal articles in the areas of nuclear war attitudes and drunk driving interventions. His research interests include: race relations, ethnic identity, Latino academic achievement, attitudes and affects related to nuclear war, drunk driving interventions, and uses of structural equation models. Dr. Hernández received his B.A. in Psychology/Chicano Studies from the University of California, Riverside, and his M.A. and Ph.D. in Developmental Psychology from the University of California, Los Angeles.

Imagine you are at a party on a cool autumn evening. People are drinking and laughing, loud music is playing, and some are dancing. Now think about the party winding down. People in various states of drunkenness are thinking about how to get home, or back to the dorm, or maybe to Swannies donut shop for a late night snack. Inevitably some will try to drive drunk. What happens now is critical. Will anyone notice a wasted friend heading for the car? Will anyone decide to take responsibility to stop the person from driving drunk? Maybe you yourself will decide to help. Whether you help, why you help, and how you help are interesting and important questions. Our research team has been studying the process of peer intervention to find out more about the individual, situational, and social factors that make helping the potential drunk driver more or less likely.

Alcohol abuse contributes to a number of problems in our society including unemployment, low productivity, health problems, property loss and crime (Moscowitz, 1989). One of the most tragic is drunken driving. According to Ravenholt (1984), driving under the influence of alcohol was responsible for 26,000 fatalities in 1980. Despite increasing attention to the problems of drunken driving in the last decade, the annual number of alcohol-related deaths has not decreased. Young drivers between the ages of 15 and 24 have the highest rate of drunk driving (Barnes & Welte, 1988). Additionally, motor vehicle accidents are the leading cause of death among persons of this age group (National Center for Health Statistics, 1981; National Safety Council, 1986), and many of these accidents are alcohol-related (Douglass, 1982; Lowman, 1986; Simpson, 1985).

Efforts at deterring drunk driving in the United States have focused primarily upon strengthening penalties (Hilton, 1984; Ross, 1983; Laurence, no date) and educating drivers (Cox, 1985), but neither approach has proven very effective. Strengthening penalties appears to decrease drunk driving temporarily (Moscowitz, 1989), but drivers soon discover that the likelihood of getting caught is small and that they can still get away with driving while intoxicated (Ross, 1984). Raising the drinking age also appears to decrease drunk driving temporarily (Moscowitz, 1989), but its long-term effectiveness is not clear. Educating young drivers, one of the most popular new ways of combating the problem, improves knowledge about alcohol (Lund & Williams, 1984) but appears to have no effect on drunk driving behavior (McKnight, Preusser, Psotka, Katz, & Edwards, 1979).

Another less explored avenue for preventing drunk driving is informal intervention to prevent one's peers from driving under the influence—in other words, individuals stopping their intoxicated friends, acquaintances, and fellow drinkers from driving drunk. In studies from 1975 through 1982, between 37 and 43 percent of adults report that they have tried to stop someone from driving drunk during the past year (Davis, 1982; Berger & Persinger, 1980). Intervention by others may be helpful in the prevention of DUI (driving under the influence) because it may depend on a sober individual, rather than on the potential drunk driver whose judgment has been impaired by alcohol (McKnight, 1986). Additionally, while laws about drunken driving may not seem relevant to the intoxicated person deciding to drive, intervention by his or her peers is something that the drunken driver cannot ignore.

We see peer intervention as a naturally occurring form of helping behavior or altruism, which is "behavior carried out to benefit another without anticipation of rewards from external sources" (Macauley & Berkowitz, 1970, p. 3). You may think of helping behavior as rescuing a drowning victim, giving someone first aid, or helping a handicapped person board the bus. Researchers who study helping behavior usually set up a controlled experiment, such as a secretary in another room (apparently) falling and hurting herself, or a convenience store holdup, to see if bystanders will do something to help. This research has resulted in a rich body of theories and findings about the conditions in which people will try to help others. However, until recently, researchers have not applied theories of helping behavior to drunk driving intervention. Our research team has been applying social psychological theories of helping behavior to the process of drunk driving intervention by looking at situations in which people try to stop others from driving drunk. We believe that helping behavior theories can give us a basis for understanding drunk driving intervention. Most studies on helping behavior are done in experimental settings, but our research looks at the theories and findings of previous studies in real situations.

We believe that increasing drunk driving intervention can reduce the number of deaths and injuries due to drunk driving. We have been surveying college students about the drunk driving situations they have experienced, in an effort to find out how, when, and why people intervene to prevent a drunken peer from driving. Fifty-one percent of the students we have surveyed report that they have tried to stop someone from driving drunk during the past year (Rabow, Newcomb, Monto, & Hernández, 1990). Our research has focused on four areas: (1) the decision-making process that individuals go through in deciding whether or not to intervene, (2) the personal, situational, and social characteristics that make intervention more or less likely, (3) whether social status differences or similarities between the potential driver and the potential helper make intervention more or less likely, and (4) what people do when they intervene, and which methods of intervention are most effective. This research will be organized according to these topics. In each following section we introduce you to some of the relevant helping behavior theories and research, and describe how we applied them to drunken driving situations.

To Intervene or Not to Intervene: A Model of the Decision-Making Process

"Friends don't let friends drive drunk." You've heard the statement from the media, but the process of deciding whether or not to intervene is much more complicated than this. Deciding to intervene in a drunk driving situation seems to involve a series of decision-making steps. Latane and Darley's (1970) laboratory experiments on helping in emergencies suggest that in order to help you must: (1) notice the situation, (2) decide that it is an emergency, (3) decide that you are responsible, (4) select a course of action, and (5) intervene.

When applied to the DUI situation, the model would suggest that in order to decide to intervene to prevent a person from driving drunk, you must go through five steps. (1) You have to notice the DUI situation. Perhaps you are not paying attention, or perhaps you are too drunk to notice. If you do notice, you can move on to the next step. (2) You have to decide if the DUI situation is dangerous. Maybe the driver is only driving a few blocks, or maybe the driver is only moderately drunk. If you decide that the situation is dangerous, you move on to the third step. (3) You have to decide if you are responsible for the potential drunk driver. Perhaps the driver is not a friend or even an acquaintance, and you feel that his or her friends should help. Or perhaps the potential driver is obnoxious and aggressive, and intervening might get you hurt. Maybe you are intoxicated yourself and you want to leave the worrying to someone who is in better condition to help. If you decide that you are responsible and able to help, you move on to the fourth step. (4) You must decide what to do. Even if you have noticed the situation, decided that it is dangerous, and decided that you are responsible, you still may not know what to do. If you are able to select an appropriate course of action, then you move on to the next step. (5) You intervene.

To test this model we asked UCLA undergraduates whether they had been in any DUI situations in the last year, then asked them a number of questions about the most recent situation. In testing the model, we modified some of the steps to better reflect the DUI situation (see Figure 1). For the third step of the model, instead of asking whether they felt responsible, we asked them whether they felt able to intervene. We did this because a respondent's sense of responsibility depends largely upon whether he or she feels able to intervene (Latane & Darley, 1970). Not everyone can or should intervene, and the potential helper must decide if he or she is the most able and qualified to intervene, or whether others should be responsible. Also, ability to intervene is extremely important in the DUI situation because potential helpers may also be intoxicated. We chose not to use the fourth step of the model. We felt that if they were unable to select a course of action, this would be reflected in their perceived ability to intervene (step 3).

The results of our study are consistent with the modified decision-making model shown in Figure 1 (Rabow et al., 1990). We found that the steps occurred in the order that we predicted.[1] We also found that passing through each step significantly increased the likelihood that a student would intervene.[2] Of all students interviewed, 51 percent reported having in-

Figure 1
A Conceptual Model of Drunk Driving Intervention

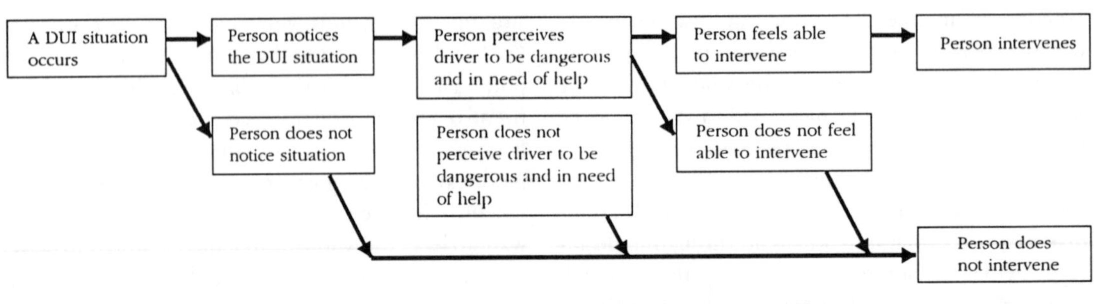

tervened at least once in the past year. When we limited analysis to those who reported that they had been in (noticed) a DUI situation, 65 percent reported intervening. Among those who also perceived the situation as dangerous, 73 percent reported intervening. And finally, when we looked at only those who noticed a DUI situation, perceived it as dangerous, and felt able to intervene, 82 percent reported intervening.

Although our tests supported the modified decision-making model, we also wanted to know if any other aspects of the situation influenced the steps. We found that both the number of people present and the number of people known by the student affected the student's perception of danger, with larger numbers increasing feelings of danger. We also found that when students knew and liked the driver, they felt more able to intervene and were more likely to intervene.

To summarize, our study found that drunk driving intervention tends to conform to a modified model similar to the one described by Latane and Darley. Before intervening, potential helpers must notice the situation, decide that it is dangerous, decide that they are able to intervene, and finally intervene. In large gatherings and situations in which potential helpers know many people, helpers are likely to perceive more danger. Additionally, when potential helpers know and like the driver, they are more likely to feel able to intervene and are more likely to intervene.

Characteristics of Individuals, Situations, and Relationships that Affect the Likelihood of Intervention

Although we believe that the decision-making model described above is a good way to understand drunk driving intervention, there are many other variables that affect whether someone will try to stop another person from driving drunk. All research on helping behavior indicates that the relationship between the helper and the recipient is important. When one feels similar to the person in need of help, one is more likely to feel empathy for that person and is more likely to help. We asked questions about how well the students knew and liked the potential driver, and what type of relationship (boyfriend, brother, etc.) they had with the potential driver.

Helping behavior research also shows that the presence of others who are not helping decreases the likelihood that a given person will help (Latane & Nida, 1981). Evidently, individuals assume that if others don't feel concerned about the situation, then they shouldn't either. However, if others do intervene or talk about intervening, it makes individuals more likely to be concerned and help. We asked students about whether others in the situation intervened or talked about intervening.

Helping behavior research has also given us other findings to explore. Previous experience at helping increases the likelihood that a given individual will help, since it indicates a disposition to help and the capability to help. Emotions, especially feelings of alarm, warmth, and compassion, may contribute to helping behavior (Batson, Duncan, Ackerman, Buckly, & Birch, 1981). When these feelings are strong, this intensity leads to personal distress that must be acted upon and makes intervention more likely. We asked UCLA undergraduates 33 questions on these and other personal, situational, and relationship issues, to find out what variables influenced the likelihood of drunk driving intervention.

We analyzed the responses separately for each sex, since we thought that intervention might be different for males than for females (Gusfield, Kotarba, & Rasmussen, 1981; Eagly & Crowley, 1986). We did two different types of statistical analysis—correlations and regression. Correlations show us whether two variables are related significantly. They let us know for example, that the more prior interventions by the student, the more likely that the student intervened in the given DUI situation. Regression lets us know which variables uniquely predict intervention.[3] It can show us, for example, that the amount the student thought about intervening was more important than how well the respondent liked the driver.

Our results show that twelve variables were significantly correlated with intervention for women. Five *relationship* variables were significantly correlated with intervention for females: (1) closeness of the relationship to the potential driver, (2) how well they knew the potential driver, (3) believing that the driver needed help, (4) how badly the potential driver needed help, and (5) how well they liked the driver. Six *situational* variables were significantly related to intervention: (1) another person intervened, (2) how much they thought about intervening, (3) having a conversation that encouraged them to intervene, (4) feeling stressed about the situation, (5) feeling able to intervene, and (6) a more intimate environment. Only one *individual* variable, more prior interventions, was significant. The regression revealed five variables that significantly predicted intervention for females: (1) how well they knew the potential driver, (2) how much they thought about intervening, (3) a more intimate environment, (4) having a conversation that encouraged them to intervene, and (5) the student's weight.

For males there were four *relationship* variables that were significantly correlated with intervention: (1) closeness of the relationship with the potential driver (brother, girlfriend, etc.), (2) how well they knew the potential driver, (3) believing that the driver was in need of help, and (4) how badly the potential driver needed help. Six *situational* variables were significantly correlated with intervention: (1) another person intervened, (2) how much they thought about intervening, (3) having a conversation that encouraged them to intervene, (4) feeling stressed about the situation, (5) feeling able to intervene, and (6) knowing more persons in the situation. Two *individual* variables, frequency of beer consumption and feeling that intervention reflected their self-image, were significant. The regression showed that three variables were significant predictors of intervention for males: (1) how well they knew the potential driver, (2) how badly the potential driver needed help, and (3) having a conversation that encouraged them to intervene.

Our research supports some of the helping behavior findings discussed at the beginning of this section. The relationship between the helper and the recipient, especially how well the respondent knew the potential drunk driver, was crucial for both males and females. Liking and having a close relationship with the potential driver were also significant for females. Others' actions and responses to the situation proved to be important as well. Conversations about intervening were significant for all analyses for both males and females, while others' intervention was significant for the correlation analysis for both sexes. Our findings only partially support the research that suggests previous experience with helping will increase the likelihood of helping. Prior interventions increased the likelihood that women would help (correlation only), but not men.

Social Status and Drunk Driving Intervention: A Look at Race, Sex, and Age

This section explores the effect of the race, sex, and relative age of the student and the potential drunk driver, on the likelihood of intervention. These variables have been shown to be important in helping behavior research and drunk driving research. Studies show that whether the helper and the recipient are of the same race can affect whether help is offered; however, the results seem contradictory. Some studies find that whites are more likely to help whites than to help African Americans (Bryan & Test, 1967; Dovidio & Gaertner, 1981; Gaertner, 1973), while others find that whites are equally willing to help African Americans (Gaertner & Dovidio, 1977). This latter article suggests that whites may help minority group members in order to compensate for the guilt they feel because of their dominant social status. Helping behavior research suggests that persons are most likely to help others who are like themselves (Dovidio, 1984; Karabenick, Lerner, & Beecher, 1972; Krebs, 1975; Piliavin, Dovidio, Gaertner, & Clark, 1981). This would predict that people would be most likely to help others who are of the same racial or ethnic group.

The sex of the potential helper and the potential drunk driver also affects intervention. Studies show that men may not accept help because it challenges their competence as drinkers (Gusfield et al., 1981). Women however, are not expected to demonstrate the same degree of self-control and competence in regard to drinking, so they are more likely to receive help. Helping behavior research indicates that males tend to help females more than they help males, and that females help females more often than they help males (Isen, 1970; West, Whitney, & Schnedler, 1975).

Finally, age is a crucial variable in both intervention research and helping behavior research. Studies indicate that people of all ages intervene in drunk driving situations (Berger & Persinger, 1980; Davis, 1982; Hernández & Rabow, 1986), although intervention tends to become less frequent with age. Additionally, older people tend to receive help more than younger people. This latter research deals with people whose advanced age makes them seem dependent. Differences of only a few years may have the opposite effect, especially among younger populations. For example, we would expect that college seniors would feel obliged to take care of their younger, less experienced peers.

The brief review of the studies above indicates that there are two competing perspectives for understanding the relationship of race, sex, and relative age to intervention. The first, which we can call the *status difference hypothesis,* suggests that people tend to help others who have lower social status than they do themselves. This perspective views helping as reinforcing existing status differences and demonstrating the superiority and competence of the helper. The second perspective can be called the *similarity hypothesis.* This perspective suggests that people feel more sympathy for others whom they perceive to be like themselves, and that they are consequently more likely to help them.

The status difference hypothesis would predict that intervention is more likely when: (1) the potential helper is white and the potential drunk driver nonwhite, than vice versa, (2) the potential helper is male and the potential driver female, than vice versa, and (3) the potential helper is older than the potential drunk driver, than vice versa. The similarity hypothesis, on the other hand, would predict that intervention is more likely when the helper and the potential drunk driver, are of the same race, sex, or age, than if they are different.

To test these hypotheses, we again asked UCLA undergraduates to describe their most recent experience in which someone was too drunk to drive (Monto, Newcomb, Rabow, & Hernández, 1992). Interestingly, neither perspective was supported. In a given DUI situation, intervention was no more likely if the potential helper was white and the potential drunk driver black than if the potential helper was black and the potential driver white. Intervention was no more likely if both were of the same race than if they were of different races. Similarly, intervention was no more likely if the driver was female and the helper male, than vice versa. In other words, both men and women were as likely to help members of the opposite sex as members of the same sex. The relative age of the potential helper and the potential drunk driver also had no significant effect on the likelihood of intervention.

We did learn some interesting things about drunk driving situations. People were more likely to find themselves in a DUI situation with others of the same race and sex than with others who were different in terms of these characteristics. In other words, although people are more likely to find themselves in DUI situations in which the driver is similar in terms of race and sex, in a given DUI situation intervention is no more likely if the two are similar than if they are different.

The situation for relative age is more complex. Again, neither status differences nor similarity affected the likelihood of intervention in a given DUI situation. For further analysis, we looked at sex and relative age at the same time. We found that in situations in which the potential driver was older than the potential helper, helpers were more likely to be females. In situations in which they were of the same age, the potential helper was about three times more likely to be male than female. In situations in which the potential driver was younger, the potential helper was about three times more likely to be female than male.

In summary, we found no indication that social status differences in age, sex, or race come into play in determining whether intervention takes place in a given DUI situation. Similarity in terms of race, sex, or age does not seem to affect the likelihood of intervention either. People more frequently encounter DUI situations in which the potential drunk driver is of the same race and sex.

Forms of Intervention: How Do People Help and What Works Best?

So far we have been talking about drunk driving intervention as if deciding to intervene is the end of the story. But the decision to intervene is more than a simple "yes they do, no they don't" question. How one intervenes and whether one is successful may be an entirely different story. This is also a neglected area of helping behavior research. Most studies simply focus on whether someone offers help rather than looking at what they do when they help. One of our most recent goals has been to learn more about what it means to intervene.

Preliminary results (Monto, Newcomb, Rabow, & Hernández, 1992) show that intervention is not usually a single action, but a series of behaviors. We asked students who had intervened what they did to prevent the inebriated person from driving drunk. We found that most students tried not one form of intervention, but a variety of interventions. The average student who intervened tried between three and four different forms of intervention. For example, a student might *ask* the person not to drive, and if that didn't work, *tell* the person not to drive, and if that still didn't work, *take* the person's keys. We also found that students who did intervene were successful in stopping the intoxicated person from driving drunk 96 percent of the time. Even though a number of attempts to stop the person from driving often failed, the students kept trying until they were successful. These results demonstrate that when students decide to intervene, they will do almost everything in their power to stop the person from driving drunk. For whatever reason, students do not always intervene, but when they do, they take their responsibility to stop drunk driving very seriously.

We also wanted to see what sorts of things influenced how a student would intervene and whether the student's intervention would be successful. Preliminary results suggest that there is a distinction between passive, nonconfrontational methods of intervention (such as asking for the person's key or asking the person not to drive) and assertive intervention (such as taking the person's key or telling the person not to drive). Different variables influenced whether a student would favor one form of intervention or another. We looked at the number of passive and assertive interventions, and the success of passive and assertive interventions separately.

Generally, passive interventions were less common and less successful. People who felt anxious were likely to try more passive interventions. Females were more likely to succeed with passive interventions than males. Having more friends present also increased the success of passive interventions.

The amount of danger the students perceived and two other variables related to danger—the chance of accident and how much the driver needed help—increased the number of assertive interventions that students tried. Prior experience intervening and being a light drinker also increased the number of assertive interventions. Assertive interventions were more likely to be successful if the student perceived danger. The greater the perceived chance of accident and the more the driver needed help also increased the success of assertive intervention. Three other variables—being a light drinker, being older than the potential driver, and being calm—also increased the success of assertive interventions.

To summarize, we found that intervention does not usually consist of a single behavior, but a number of repeated attempts to stop the intoxicated person from driving. Fortunately, once a student decides to intervene, he or she will continue trying and will usually succeed. Passive interventions are less common and less successful than assertive interventions, although having friends present and being female increases the success of passive interventions. Assertive interventions and their success are strongly related to the danger of the situation. Being calm and being a light drinker also lead to success with assertive interventions.

Discussion

Our studies give us reason to be optimistic about the potential for decreasing drunk driving through informal peer intervention. We know from the decision-making model that when students are present in DUI situations, feel they are dangerous, and feel able to intervene, they do intervene at extremely high rates (82 percent). The application of our findings to educational programs or media campaigns is also a possibility. Other programs aimed at encouraging people to intervene have increased reported rates of intervention (McKnight & McPherson, 1986). Our research indicates that instead of saying "friends don't let friends drive drunk," educational programs should help students to recognize DUI situations and evaluate their seriousness, and teach them techniques for intervention so that they will feel capable of intervening.

Our study of the individual, situational, and relationship variables that influence intervention can help us identify the reasons people fail to intervene in drunk driving situations. By recognizing the barriers to intervention, perhaps we can begin to remove them.

Our findings about the effects of age, sex, and race help us understand the social situations in which college students drink. We can begin to better understand who is in a position to help whom. The fact that neither status differences nor similarity in terms of age, sex, and race affect the likelihood of intervention also gives us reason to feel optimistic. Policies and educational programs can have little effect on age, sex, and race.

Finally, knowing which forms of intervention are most common and most successful can help us teach people to feel more capable and be more successful at stopping inebriated persons from driving.

Of course, our discussion here has only touched upon the potential applications of our research. We hope that our findings will be useful in many other ways as well. We feel that the research does point out the potential of this less explored avenue for preventing drunk driving. Additionally, we feel that our findings lend support to the idea that drunk driving can be productively studied using helping behavior theory.

One unanswered question is how accurately our studies reflect the actual behavior of the students we questioned. Since we are asking students to report their own behavior, we know that there may be biases. For example, people my tend to report and remember the situations that make them look good, and forget the times when they didn't intervene. Further research is needed to gather additional kinds of information. Observational research (watching behavior first hand) is one possible avenue for further study, and in-depth interviews may also help. One thing that you can do to help is to let us know about your experiences with drunk driving and drunk driving intervention. You may reach us care of Professor Jerome Rabow, Sociology Department, UCLA, Haines Hall, Room 264, Los Angeles, CA 90024

Notes

1. The test we used is called a Guttman analysis of scalability. It tells us whether passing through one step indicates that a person has passed through the prior steps.
2. For each step, we used a Chi-squared test of independence to compare the group that passed through the step with the group that did not.
3. Regression looks at the effect of a particular variable while holding other variables constant. Not all variables that correlate significantly with intervention are critical in determining whether intervention will take place. For example, how well the student liked the potential driver was significantly correlated with intervention, but probably only because it was related to how well the student knew the potential driver. To give a totally unrelated example, gray hair is correlated to heart disease, but only because age is correlated to heart disease, and older people are more likely to have gray hair. Because regression looks at the unique

effects of each variable, it shows fewer significant variables related to intervention.

References

Barnes, G. M., & Welte, J. W. (1988). Predictors of driving while intoxicated among teenagers. *Journal of Drug Issues, 18,* 367–84.

Batson, C. D., Duncan, B., Ackerman, P., Buckley, T., & Birch, K. (1981). Is empathic emotion a source of altruistic motivation? *Journal of Personality and Social Psychology, 40,* 290–302.

Berger, R. J., & Persinger, G. (1980). *1980 Survey of public perceptions on highway safety.* Report prepared for the Department of Transportation, National Highway Traffic Safety Administration. McLean, VA: Automated Services, Inc.

Bryan, J. H., & Test, M. A. (1967). Models and helping. *Journal of Personality and Social Psychology, 6,* 400–407.

Cox, C. H. (1985). *Influences that impact on the effectiveness of mandated adult education.* Thesis, North Carolina State University at Raleigh.

Davis, S. (1982). Driving under the influence: California public opinion. *Abstracts and Reviews in Alcohol & Driving, 3,* 3–8.

Douglass, R. L. (1982). Youth, alcohol, and traffic accidents [Monograph]. In United States Department of Health & Human Services, *Alcohol & Health, No. 4, Special Population Issues,* 197–223. DHHS Publication No. (ADM) 82–1193. Washington, DC: United States Government Printing Office.

Dovidio, J. F. (1984). Helping behavior and altruism: An empirical and conceptual overview. In L. Berkowitz (Ed.), *Advances in Experimental Social Psychology, vol. 17* (pp. 362–427). New York: Academic Press.

Dovidio, J. F., & Gaertner, S. I. (1981). The effects of race, status, and ability on helping behavior. *Social Psychology Quarterly, 44,* 192–203.

Eagly, A. H., & Crowley, M. (1986). Gender and helping behavior: A meta-analytic review of the social psychological literature. *Psychological Bulletin, 100*(3), 283–308.

Gaertner, S. I. (1973). Helping behavior and racial discrimination among liberals and conservatives. *Journal of Personality and Social Psychology, 25,* 335–341.

Gaertner, S. I., & Dovidio, J. F. (1977). The subtlety of white racism, arousal, and helping behavior. *Journal of Personality and Social Psychology, 35,* 691–707.

Gusfield, J., Kotarba, J., & Rasmussen, P. (1981). The public society of intimates: Friends, wives, lovers and others in the drinking-driving drama. *Research in the Interweave of Social Roles: Friendship, 2,* 237–257.

Hernández, A. C. R., & Rabow, J. (1986). College students do intervene in drunk driving situations. *Sociology and Social Research, 70,* 224–225.

Hilton, M. E. (1984). The impact of recent changes in California drinking-driving laws on fatal accident levels during the first postintervention year: An interrupted time series analysis. *Law and Society Review, 18,* 605–627.

Isen, A. M. (1970). Success, failure, attention and reaction to others: The warm glow of success. *Journal of Personality and Social Psychology, 15,* 294–301.

Karabenick, S. A., Lerner, R. M., & Beecher, M. D. (1972). Relation of political affiliation to helping behavior on election day, November 7,1972. *Journal of Social Psychology, 91,* 223–227.

Krebs, D. (1975). Empathy and altruism. *Journal of Personality and Social Psychology, 32,* 1134–1146.

Latane, B., & Darley, J. M.(1970). *The unresponsive bystander: Why doesn't he help?* New York: Appleton-Century-Crofts.

Latane, B., & Nida, S. (1981). Ten years of research on group size and helping. *Psychological Bulletin, 89,* 308–324.

Laurence, M. (no date). *The origins and development of penalties for drunk drivers in California.* Bureau Criminal Statistics Forum, State of California.

Lowman, C. (1986). Drinking and driving among youth. In C. Felsted (Ed.), *Youth and alcohol abuse: Readings and resources* (pp. 141–157). Phoenix, AZ: The Oryx Press.

Lund, A., & Williams, A. (1984). *The effect of post-licensure driver training: A review of DDC literature.* Washington, DC: Insurance Institute for Highway Safety.

Macaulay, J. R., & Berkowitz, L. (1970). *Altruism and helping behavior.* New York: Academic Press.

McKnight, A. J. (1986). Intervention in teenage drunk driving. *Alcohol, Drugs and Driving—Abstracts and Reviews, 2,* 17–28.

McKnight, A. J., & McPherson, K. (1986). Evaluation of peer intervention training for high school alcohol safety education. *Accident Analysis & Prevention, 8*(4), 339–347.

McKnight, A. J., Preusser, D. F., Psotka, J., Katz, D. B., & Edwards, J. M. (1979). *Youth alcohol safety education criteria development.* (NTIS Publication No. PB80-17894-O.) Washington, DC: U. S. Department of Transportation.

Monto, M. A., Newcomb, M., Rabow, J., & Hernández, A. C. R. (1992). Social status and drunk driving intervention. *Journal of Studies on Alcohol, 53,* 63–68.

Monto, M. A., Newcomb, M., Rabow, J., & Hernández, A. C. R. (no date). *How friends stop friends from driving drunk: Passive and assertive forms of helping.* Unpublished paper.

Moscowitz, J. M. (1989). The primary prevention of alcohol problems: A critical review of the research literature. *Journal of Studies on Alcohol, 50,* 54–88.

National Center for Health Statistics. (1980). Annual summary of births, deaths, marriages, and divorces: United States (1981). *Monthly Vital Statistics Report, 29*(13).

National Safety Council. (1986). *Traffic safety.* Washington, DC: National Highway Traffic Safety Administration.

Piliavin, J. A., Dovidio, J. F., Gaertner, S. L., & Clark, R. D. III. (1981). *Emergency intervention.* New York: Academic Press.

Rabow, J., Newcomb, M. D., Monto, M. A., & Hernández, A. C. R. (1990). Altruism in drunk driving situations: Personal and social factors in intervention. *Social Psychology Quarterly, 53,* 199–213.

Ravenholt, R. T. (1984). Addiction mortality in the United States, 1980: Tobacco, alcohol, and other substances. *Population Development Review, 10,* 697–724.

Ross, H. L. (1983). *Deterring the drinking driver: Legal policy and social control.* Lexington, MA: Lexington Books.

Ross, H. L. (1984). *Deterring the drinking driver: Legal policy and social control* (rev. ed.). Lexington, MA.: Lexington Books.

Simpson, H. (1985). Polydrug effects and traffic safety. In H. Moskowitz (Ed.). *Alcohol, drugs, and driving* (pp. 17–44). Los Angeles, CA: Alcohol Information Service, University of California.

West, S. G., Whitney, G., & Schnedler, R. (1975). Helping a motorist in distress: The effects of sex, race, and neighborhood. *Journal of Personality and Social Psychology, 31,* 691–698.

Discussion Questions

1. Have you ever been too drunk to drive safely? What would someone have had to do to prevent you from driving drunk?
2. Have you ever noticed someone who was too drunk to drive? What did you do? Why?
3. Under what circumstances would you try to stop someone from driving drunk? What might prevent you from intervening?
4. What do you think could be done to encourage individuals to stop their drunken peers from driving?

Protecting Our Future

Options for Preventing Alcohol-Impaired Driving Among Youth

Alexander C. Wagenaar

Alexander C. Wagenaar is an Associate Professor of Epidemiology at the University of Minnesota School of Public Health, where he is director of the Alcohol/Tobacco/Drug Epidemiology Program. He has published a book, several book chapters, and 40 journal articles in the alcohol studies and injury control fields. He has a longstanding interest in using public policy, community interventions, and socio-environmental strategies for health promotion and disease and injury prevention. Specific studies in recent years have focused on randomized community trials, adolescent drinking-driving, effects of macroeconomic conditions, pediatric injuries, effects of speed limits on traffic fatalities, natural experiments with alternative alcohol policies, and public opinion surveys. Dr. Wagenaar has served in several leadership positions in the American Public Health Association, and is an editorial referee for a dozen medical, public health, and social science journals.

There is now little question that consumption of alcoholic beverages is a major contributor to motor vehicle crashes and the casualties that result. The exact magnitude of the contribution of alcohol continues to be debated, and considerable underreporting of alcohol involvement continues in most jurisdictions. Despite this, there is general agreement, based on controlled studies using the best available data, that: (1) about 10 percent of drivers involved in minor property damage crashes have elevated blood alcohol concentrations (BACs; i.e., over .05mg/100ml); (2) about 15 percent of drivers involved in extensive property damage crashes have elevated blood alcohol concentrations; (3) approximately 25 percent of drivers involved in serious injury crashes are intoxicated (i.e., BAC .10 g/100ml or more); and (4) about 40 percent of all drivers involved in fatal crashes are intoxicated.(Jones & Jocelyn, 1978; Fell, 1982; USNHTSA, 1987). In short, as the damage and injury severity of crashes increases, so does the probability of alcohol involvement. Driver intoxication rates for certain crash categories, such as single-vehicle fatal crashes occurring on weekend nights, approach 70 percent.(USNHTSA)

Injuries resulting from alcohol-impaired driving are a particularly severe problem among teenagers and young adults. Of all crash-involved drinking drivers in the U.S., over 40 percent are between 16 and 24 years old (Baker et al., 1984). About a quarter of all deaths among 16–24 year olds are associated with alcohol-impaired driving. Reasons for such high rates of alcohol-related crash injuries and deaths are related both to the drinking patterns and driving patterns among young people.

Youth Drinking Patterns

Most young people in the United States regularly drink alcoholic beverages. Blane and Hewitt (1977) reviewed 120 surveys of adolescent (ages 13 to 18) drinking practices conducted since 1941. They concluded that the prevalence of young drinkers (that is, "have you ever had a drink?") was increasing before the mid-1960s and that about 70 percent of junior- and senior-high-school students were consistently identified as drinkers over the period from 1966 through 1975. A similar pattern was revealed for lifetime prevalence of intoxication (that is, "have you ever been drunk?"), which increased from 19 percent prior to 1966 to 45 percent during the period from 1966 to 1975, and remained stable during the latter ten-year period.

Prevalence of self-reported monthly intoxication ("how often do you become drunk?") similarly increased from 10 percent before 1966 to about 19 percent during the period from 1966 to 1975.

The ongoing nationwide probability surveys conducted by Johnston, O'Malley, and Bachman (1991) provide the most recent information concerning drinking practices among young people. They reported that 90 percent of high-school seniors surveyed in 1990 had at least tried beverage alcohol, 57 percent reported use within the past month, and 32 percent reported binge drinking, that is, consuming five or more drinks on at least one occasion in the previous two weeks. Furthermore, similar surveys conducted each year since 1975 revealed that, while the prevalence of drinkers ("ever used alcohol") has remained stable in recent years, the prevalence of high-school seniors who frequently become intoxicated increased from 37 percent in 1975 to 41 percent in 1979, declining to 32 percent in 1990. The figures for college students are higher, with 41 percent reporting consumption of five or more drinks on at least one occasion in the previous two weeks.

The prevalence of drinkers among older adolescents and young adults has apparently reached a plateau, with about 90 percent of this group identifying themselves as drinkers. Until the past few years, however, the prevalence of young people who frequently become intoxicated had been increasing, though it now appears to be stabilizing with about one-third of the young people in the United States becoming intoxicated at least once every 14 days. It is clear that the drinking pattern of youthful Americans involves frequent intoxication, with alcohol consumption sufficient to cause serious performance impairment.[1] This creates the strong potential for serious injury and mortality consequences when young drinkers operate motor vehicles while in an alcohol-impaired state. A result is their overrepresentation among crash-involved drivers.

Youth Driving and Crash-Involvement Patterns

Significantly more young people are involved in automobile crashes than would be expected, based on the total number of young people in the population, the number of young people licensed to drive, or the amount of automobile travel among youth. For example, U.S. youth aged 15 to 24 have a motor-vehicle-crash death rate of about 37 per 100,000, twice the rate for those aged 25 and over (NSC, 1985). Similarly, the total (fatal and nonfatal) crash rate per licensed driver is almost twice as high for those under age 25 as it is for drivers aged 25 and over (NSC). The overrepresentation of youth in automobile crashes is even more pronounced when amount of automobile travel is taken into account. The fatality rate per 100 million miles traveled (as driver or passenger) among women aged 18 to 24 is three times the rate for women aged 30 to 60; the corresponding rate for young men is six times the rate for older men (Casrsten, 1981)

Many exposure variables have been suggested as explanations for the overrepresentation of youth among crash-involved drivers, especially involvement in the more serious injury-producing collisions. Exposure factors include: (1) driving at more hazardous times and locations, for example, driving at night and on weekends, (2) more frequently driving with passengers present, which increases the probability of distraction, (3) driving vehicles that are in poor condition, which increases the probability of vehicle malfunction, and (4) more frequent use of two-wheeled vehicles. Although much research needs to be done on the effects of differential exposure, studies to date indicate that, after allowing for higher exposure, young drivers are clearly overrepresented in the crash-involved population (OECD, 1975; Preusser et al., 1975)

Comparisons of the proportion of crashes among young drivers that involve alcohol with the corresponding proportion for older drivers provide further insight into the role of alcohol in youth crashes. Several studies conducted in the 1960s and early 1970s found that among young drivers a lower proportion of crashes involved alcohol than among older drivers (Farris et al., 1976; Borkenstein et al., 1964; Waller et al., 1970; Perrine et al., 1971). Waller, for example, examined a sample of fatal crashes in California and found that 49 percent of the 15- to 19-year-old drivers had been drinking, compared with 61 percent of the drivers aged 20 and over. However, none of these early studies examined youth residing in a state with a legal-drinking age below 21. Flora and others (1978) examined fatal-crash involvement in a state that had lowered its minimum drinking age to 18. Although the ratio of alcohol-related to nonalcohol-related crashes among youth under 21 years old increased when the drinking age was lowered, the ratio was not consistently higher for drivers under the age of 21 than for drivers aged 21 and over.

One might conclude from the above data that young drivers involved in crashes are less likely to have been drinking than older drivers. Is this difference a result of less driving after drinking among youth, or more careful driving after drinking? Recent research indicates that the answer is clearly the former. Roadside breath-test surveys have revealed that the proportion of all young drivers on the road with elevated BACs is the same as, or lower than, the proportion of drivers in their thirties or forties who have elevated BACs (Farris et al., 1976; Preusser et al., 1975; Perrine et al., 1971; Wolfe, 1975). Again, most of the 18- to 20-year-old drivers studied did not have legal access to alcohol. Differences in the amount of impaired driving appear to have narrowed for youth who gained legal access to alcohol in the 1970s (Wagenaar, 1983). In the late 1970s and 1980s, however, the legal drinking age returned to 21 in all states, with consequent reductions in consumption of alcohol (O'Malley & Wagenaar, 1991).

Clearly, youth do not drive more carefully than adults after consumption of alcoholic beverages. Just the opposite is true. The risk of crash involvement at various BACs is higher for youth than it is for middle-aged drivers. A young driver with a given BAC is more likely to be involved in a crash than is an older driver at the same level, and the risk of a crash increases more sharply with increasing BACs for youth than for drivers of other ages (Farris et al., 1976; Perrine et al., 1971; Zylman, 1972).

The particularly high susceptibility to traffic crashes of youth, compared with older drivers at identical BACs, may be the result of a lack of extensive experience with drinking and with driving after drinking. Such an explanation is supported by the work of Hurst (1973), who found that, among drinkers of all ages, those who drink infrequently have a higher risk of crash involvement at a given BAC than do frequent drinkers. For those young people recently initiated into patterns of regular drinking, time may not have allowed them sufficient experience with the effects of drinking and with driving after drinking to develop compensatory behaviors that may reduce the risk of an alcohol-related collision. Finally, driving simulation studies have found that drivers who believed they had consumed a moderate amount of alcohol exhibited greater risk taking than those who believed they had consumed no alcohol or a large amount of alcohol (McMillen & Wells-Parker, 1987).

A second explanation for the particularly serious effect of an elevated BAC on the risk of crash involvement among young drivers is that alcohol exacerbates the pre-existing impulsiveness and propensity toward risk-taking behavior that are characteristic of adolescents and young adults (Klein, 1971; Pelz & Schuman, 1971; Makela, 1978). Both these explanations are probably valid, with the high risk of crash involvement of young drivers at relatively moderate BACs occurring as a result of their inexperience with alcohol and their higher threshold of acceptable risk.

In short, compared to older individuals, many young people have a drinking pattern that includes frequent intoxication, they have larger driving performance decrements with a given alcohol dose than older drivers, they are more likely to drive at hazardous times and places, and they have a higher propensity for risk taking than older drivers even when sober. As a result, they are overrepresented among those involved in motor vehicle crashes. A variety of policies and programs designed to reduce alcohol-related crashes among young drivers must be considered.

Enforcement and Increased Penalties

Several traditional approaches designed to reduce alcohol-impaired driving are currently being implemented with renewed vigor. The first major approach is general deterrence of alcohol-impaired driving by increasing penalties for violations of drinking/driving statutes and increasing the probability of detection through additional enforcement efforts. The first component of such a deterrence program, more severe penalties for drinking/driving, is unlikely to have a significant permanent effect in the absence of a reasonable probability of apprehension for violating the law (Ross, 1992). Estimates of the probability of being arrested for driving under the influence of alcohol range from 1 in 500 to 1 in 2,000 (NHTSA, 1980). No matter how severe the penalty, its effect on drinking/driving behavior of young people is likely to be minimal if the perceived probability of experiencing the penalty after violating drinking/driving statues is extremely low. Severe penalties also can be counterproductive deterrence policy if the result is: (1) increased reluctance on the part of police officers to arrest those marginally over the legal limit for BAC, and (2) increased plea bargaining, diversions of offenders into alternate programs, and requests for long, drawn-out jury trials, all of which further reduce the numbers of violators experiencing the statutory penalties for impaired driving.

Ross (1992) recently reviewed scientific evidence concerning the effectiveness of increasing the probability of apprehension for impaired driving. New laws and enhanced enforcement can increase arrest rates and effectively reduce alcohol-related motor vehicle crashes. Following a deterrence model, the most important component of such programs is increasing the perceived probability of detection among the driving population. As a result, a critical factor in past successful programs has been public controversy surrounding new laws and enforcement crackdowns, resulting in media coverage and enhanced public awareness. However, crash reductions associated with such programs have usually been temporary, lasting from a few months to a few years. Controversy, public awareness, and media coverage associated with major new drinking/driving deterrence efforts typically subside over time, and young drivers realize that even with the stepped-up enforcement activities, their probability of apprehension for driving while impaired remains extremely low. It appears that achievement of a permanent alcohol-related crash reduction through deterrence will require a major permanent increase in resources devoted to enforcement.

Current efforts by many states to streamline enforcement procedures and increase the numbers of impaired drivers punished for their violations are to be applauded. However, a realistic view of the potential of drinking/driving deterrence must consider the relative value of such efforts. Typically, these legal and procedural innovations include: (1) making driving with a blood alcohol concentration greater than .08 or .10g/100ml a *per se* offense, removing the need to prove in court that the individual's ability to drive was significantly impaired by alcohol, (2) permitting police officers to use portable breath-testing equipment, facilitating the identification of drivers who should be detained for a series of tests, the results of which can be used in court, (3) using sobriety checklanes to gain enforcement visibility and to increase the perceived probability of detection, and (4) using swift administrative measures to suspend the driving licenses of those driving under the influence, rather than limiting punishment to the results of court cases, typically characterized by plea bargaining and frequent reduction of charges to nonalcohol-related offenses. Such refinements in law and procedure are important steps toward the goal of increasing the probability that impaired drivers will experience punishment for their violations. Such measures should be continually evaluated, to ensure that they are having their intended effects, with few negative side effects. However, even with such innovations, very few occasions of impaired driving result in detection and punishment. Efforts to increase deterrence, therefore, should be seen as only one component of an overall strategy to reduce alcohol-impaired driving and the casualties that result.

Punishment for alcohol-impaired driving also serves a specific deterrence function; that is, it serves to deter the individual experiencing the punishment from repeating the offense. The effect of specific deterrence on the overall alcohol-related crash problem is limited for three reasons. First, only a small proportion of drinking drivers are punished for their offense. Second, in spite of prior apprehension and punishment for drinking/driving, a substantial fraction repeat the offense. Third, the population of those at high risk for alcohol-related crashes changes over time, with the addition of new individuals at high risk and the deletion of individuals who are no longer at high risk. For these reasons, specific deterrence effects of laws prohibiting driving while intoxicated are not likely to significantly reduce the aggregate frequency of alcohol-related crashes.

Education, Treatment, and Rehabilitation

A second major conventional alcohol-related prevention approach is education, treatment, and rehabilitation of individuals arrested for drinking/driving. Addicted drinkers clearly are overrepresented among apprehended drinking drivers, and changing their drinking patterns will reduce subsequent drinking/driving. In a humane society, adequate recovery services for such individuals should be available. However, most youth who are driving while intoxicated would not be identified by treatment professionals as problem or addicted drinkers (Vinglis, 1983). For drinking drivers who are considered dependent on alcohol, treatment success rates are low, even with the best programs (Saxe et al., 1983), and many will therefore be re-arrested for impaired driving (Hagen, 1985).

Limited treatment success is not the main reason treatment of arrested drivers will not substantially reduce the number of casualties caused by alcohol-impaired driving. Assume for a moment that all drivers arrested this year for driving under the influence never again consume alcohol. The result would be only a very small reduction in the incidence of traffic crashes next year. The National Highway Traffic Safety Administration estimates that this year's arrestees account for less than one percent of next year's serious and fatal crashes (NHTSA, 1980). Current treatment efforts cannot significantly reduce the alcohol-related crash problem, for the same reasons that specific deterrence is ineffective. Only a very small fraction of those who drive while impaired by alcohol are ever detected or treated, and many individuals who are not now problem drinkers, and do not drive while impaired, may do so in the future. The point is that the problem drinking driver group is not a stable group that can be identified and "cured," solving the alcohol-related crash problem. It is rather a dynamic group, with new members constantly joining and old members leaving. Recognition of this "moving target" problem and the low rates of detection discussed earlier makes it obvious that massive resources are required to treat all drinkers at risk for alcohol-related crash involvement. Therefore, even if completely successful treatment modalities were ever identified, the resources required to apply them to all drinking drivers would not be available.

Public Information and Education

The third approach for the amelioration of the alcohol-related crash problem is implementation of public information and education (PI/E) programs. Themes of past campaigns have included the effects of beverage alcohol on driving skills, exhortations not to drink and drive, and ways to prevent intoxicated friends and associates from driving. While some PI/E efforts have been found to increase knowledge among those exposed to the information, demonstrable effects on drinking/driving or alcohol-related crash involvement are rarely seen (NHTSA, 1990). Programs that have produced reductions in drinking/driving are usually associated with new laws that increase penalties for drinking/driving, along with major increases in enforcement efforts such as sobriety checkpoints. In such cases the PI/E programs appear to play a major role in enhancing public awareness of a drinking/driving "crackdown," increasing the perceived risk of punishment for impaired driving. Even successful PI/E campaigns, however, usually have temporary effects. The limited success of past PI/E programs does not mean that they should be abandoned. While the alcohol-related crash problem is unlikely to be significantly reduced through PI/E campaigns alone, such programs can play an important supporting role in: (1) disseminating information, (2) making the public aware of new policies and programs, and (3) encouraging public support for new laws, regulations, and programs needed to effectively reduce the toll associated with youth drinking and driving.

This brief overview of traditional countermeasures for drinking/driving illustrates their limited effectiveness in reducing the incidence of alcohol-related crashes. Improved implementation and evaluation of programs based on these approaches, along with substantially increased resources, are likely to have a beneficial effect. However, given past experience and the limited resources available, it is unreasonable to expect these approaches alone to be adequate for a comprehensive effort designed to substantially reduce health and safety problems resulting from alcohol-impaired driving.

Alternative Prevention Approaches

There are several areas in which alternative countermeasure strategies can be identified. First, traditional approaches have focused on reducing alcohol-impaired driving, which is only one variable along the causal chain that culminates in motor vehicle injury and death. Efforts might be focused on reducing crashes, independent of the amount of drinking/driving, through improved design of roadways (e.g., wider lanes, clearer lane and road edge markings, removal of trees and other objects at roadsides). An improved system of roads would be more forgiving of errors made by both impaired and nonimpaired drivers. Alternatively, the emphasis might be placed on reducing the probability of serious injury once a crash has occurred, through improved vehicle design (air bags are an obvious example). Requiring by law that drivers and passengers use seat belts results in a substantial increase in belt use, protecting a larger proportion of motorists from injury (Wagenaar, 1986).

A reduction in vehicle availability or driving opportunities also might reduce alcohol-related crashes. Such a strategy is most likely to be used for young drivers, through restricted licenses, curfew laws prohibiting nighttime driving, requirements that an adult accompany young drivers, limitations on the numbers and/or ages of passengers with a young driver, lengthening the duration of a learner's permit (to delay full licensure and provide for additional supervised driving), and raising the legal age for driving (Mayhew et al., 1983).

Research on the effects of such policy changes is limited. A few recent studies, however, indicate the potential public health benefits of stronger controls on youth driving. Williams and others (Williams et al., 1983) report that 65–85 percent fewer 16 year olds are involved in crashes when the legal driving age is 17, instead of 16. A 25–29 percent reduction in nighttime crash involvement among 16 year olds is associated with curfew laws that prohibit nighttime driving (Preusser, 1983). Even without police enforcement, nighttime curfew laws are likely to have a significant effect in reducing teenage nighttime driving, if parents restrict teenage driving as a result of the law.

There are other ways to reduce motor vehicle crashes, however, that are based specifically on the contribution of alcohol. Youth drinking/driving and its sequelae might be reduced by modifying the availability of beverage alcohol. Modifications in alcohol availability, and associated public health benefits, can be achieved through policies and programs that affect the marketing and distribution of alcoholic beverages. One such policy that has received much attention in the past decade is the minimum legal age for purchase and consumption of alcoholic beverages. In the early 1970s, 29 states reduced their legal drinking age, under the assumption that increasing the accessibility of alcohol would have little effect on youth drinking habits, since many young people had been consuming alcohol beverages in spite of legal prohibitions. Many studies over the subsequent decade, however, revealed that higher rates of youthful alcohol-related motor vehicle crashes frequently followed reductions in the legal age. Conversely, recent increases in the legal age have resulted in lower rates of alcohol-related crashes (Wagenaar, 1983; Wagenaar, in press). While few would argue that higher legal drinking ages solve the youth alcohol problem, recent research on legal drinking age changes provides evidence that reductions in the availability of beverage alcohol can significantly reduce alcohol-related problems such as injuries from crashes. Other dimensions of the distribution of alcoholic beverages should be examined for their utility in reducing alcohol-related traffic crashes among youth.

The price of alcoholic beverages has been found to influence the amount consumed and associated health and safety problems (Ornstein, 1980). Higher beverage alcohol prices reduce consumption even among those addicted to alcohol (Cook, 1982). Increasing alcohol prices has the largest effect on young people, who typically have lower levels of disposable income available. According to Grossman and associates, increasing the price by a nickel a beer would lead to an 11 percent reduction in the number of youth who drink, and a 15 percent reduction in the number of youth who consume three to five beers per occasion (Grossman et al., 1987). Periodic increases in beverage alcohol excise taxes should be implemented to arrest the continuing decline in the inflation-adjusted price of alcohol.

Regulations concerning the number and location of beverage alcohol outlets also might be examined for potential highway safety benefits. For example, should new bars and taverns be located where they are accessible only with personal automobiles, or should they be positioned along mass transit lines? While recognizing the limits to controls on beverage outlets, some have even suggested that on-premise outlets might be prohibited from providing parking for their customers, to discourage use of automobiles as a mode of transportation to/from such outlets (Ross, 1992). Bars and taverns might be a particular focus for regulation, because about half to two-thirds of alcohol-impaired drivers are traveling from such outlets (O'Donnell, 1985).

Another avenue for influencing the distribution of alcoholic beverages in an attempt to reduce impaired driving is the strengthening of "dram shop" liability laws (Mosher, 1979). Such laws make commercial providers of alcoholic beverages liable for damages caused by intoxicated customers who were served too much alcohol while patronizing a bar, restaurant, or tavern. Liability for extensive damages, including traffic crash injuries and deaths, on the part of commercial distributors of alcohol might cause proprietors to limit the amount of alcohol they sell to any single customer. Insurance coverage for such liability provides further opportunities to encourage safe serving practices. Lower insurance rates might be applied to establishments that implement employee training, limits on the number of alcoholic drinks a single customer may be sold, ready availability of nonalcoholic drinks, and so forth. Wagenaar and Holder (1991) found reduced traffic crashes after a sudden increase in legal liability exposure in Texas.

Liability for damage caused by intoxicated individuals has generally been limited to commercial servers of alcoholic beverages. However, some courts have ruled that social hosts are also liable if they provide alcoholic beverages to their guests in such quantities that intoxication is encouraged, in spite of the hosts' awareness that most guests will subsequently operate motor vehicles (Mosher, 1979). Implementation of social host liability might encourage individuals to prevent intoxicated friends and acquaintances from driving, causing a reduction in alcohol-related motor vehicle crashes. Liability might also extend to parents or other adults who provide alcohol to youth or do not adequately supervise social settings at which both alcohol and underage drinkers are present.

Conclusion

Available evidence indicates that the most fruitful avenues for efforts to prevent alcohol-related motor vehicle crashes among youth focus on changes in broader social and policy environments, not on attempts to modify the behavior of individual drinking drivers. Effective prevention tools reduce the number of people in the high-risk groups and reduce the number of occasions of high-risk activities. The number of young drivers can be reduced by increasing the driving age. The amount of youth driving can be reduced through curfew hours, requirements for adult supervision, or other restrictions on opportunities to drive. The amount of youth drinking can be reduced by increasing the legal age for purchase of alcohol and enforcing the law prohibiting alcohol outlets to sell to youth. All of these policies reduce aggregate exposure to risk of involvement in an alcohol-related crash. However, such policies reduce the privileges of a single age group only, while not directly affecting other age groups (such as those aged 21–24) who are also significantly overrepresented among alcohol-impaired crash-involved drivers.

An alternative policy that may have a large effect on youth drinking/driving is increasing the price of alcohol. A price policy would apply to all drinkers, and not be limited to a single age group. The effects of price changes on youth drinking have received little research attention, with the notable exception of Grossman and associates (Grossman et al., 1987). Examination of the effects of alcohol price changes at the state and local levels on youth drinking and driving patterns is needed. Do youth change their drinking patterns when the relative price of on-premise versus off-premise alcohol changes? How do changes in youth employment and disposable income interact with such alcohol price changes? Evidence to date indicates that price may be a key influence on youth drinking and alcohol-related problem patterns. Among the many factors that influence youth drinking/driving, the price of alcohol is one that is easily manipulable via public policy.

Finally, the many state and local changes in drinking age, driving age, curfew laws, belt law enforcement, alcohol outlet distribution, and other policies and programs must be continuously monitored and evaluated for their effect on youth drinking/driving. To do so, we need more detailed information on the physical and social environment that immediately precedes an alcohol-impaired driving event. Where did the drinking occur? With whom? Was transportation required? What alternative modes were available? Focus group and other qualitative methods can complement surveys and quantitative methods to address such questions (Wagenaar et al., in press).

We currently have only very limited self-report data on the number of youth driving at night, the purpose of those nighttime trips, the proportion of young nighttime drivers that had been drinking, the amount of alcohol consumed immediately prior to driving, and the proportion of drivers at various blood alcohol levels. Measurement of such items is required for an assessment of the effects of intended and unintended changes in the environment related to youth drinking/driving. These data should be collected on a regular basis, and should not be limited to retrospective self-reports. Such increased research efforts will not only provide information to guide policy development, but may also serve to identify new prevention options and to place them on the public agenda for debate, consideration, and testing.

Notes

1. A 160-pound person consuming five drinks in a two-hour period would have a blood alcohol concentration between .05 g/100ml and .10 g/100ml. At this level, a 16–24-year-old driver is four to eight times as likely to be involved in a fatal crash as a nondrinking driver.

References

Baker, S. P., O'Neill, B., Karpf, R. S., (1984). *The injury fact book.* Lexington, MA: DC Heath.

Blane, H. T., Hewitt, L. E. (1977). *Alcohol and youth: An analysis of the literature, 1960–1975.* Report prepared for the National Institute on Alcohol Abuse & Alcoholism. Pittsburgh, PA: University of Pennsylvania.

Borkenstein, R. F. (1964). *The role of the drinking driver in traffic accidents.* Bloomington, IN: Department of Police Administration, Indiana University.

Casrsten, O. (1981). *Use of the nationwide personal transportation study to calculate exposure.* HSRI Research Review, 11, 1–8.

Cook, P. J. (1982). Alcohol taxes as a public health measure. *British Journal of Addictions, 77,* 245–250.

Farris, R., Malone, T B., Lilliefors, H. (1976). *A comparison of alcohol involvement in exposed and injured drivers.* (Report HS-801-826). Washington, DC: National Highway Traffic Safety Administration.

Fell, J. C. (1982). *Alcohol involvement in traffic accidents: Recent estimates from the National Center for Statistics and Analysis.* Washington, DC: National Highway Traffic Safety Administration.

Flora, J. D., Filkins, L. D., Compton, C. P. (1978). *Alcohol involvement in Michigan fatal accidents: 1968–1976.* Ann Arbor, MI: Highway Safety Research Institute, University of Michigan.

Grossman, M., Coate, D., Arluck, & G. M. (1987). Price sensitivity of alcoholic beverages in the United States: Youth alcohol consumption. In H. D. Holder, & N. K. Mello (Eds.), *Advances in substance abuse: behavioral and biological research–Supplement 1–Control issues in alcohol abuse prevention: Strategies for states and communities* (pp. 169–198). Greenwich, CT: JAI Press, Inc.

Hagen, R. E. (1985). Evaluation of the effectiveness of educational and rehabilitation efforts: Opportunities for research. *Journal of Studies on Alcohol Supplement, 10,* 179–183.

Hurst, P. M. (1973). Epidemiological aspects of alcohol in driver crashes and citations. *Journal of Safety Research, 5,* 130–148.

Johnston, L. D., O'Malley, P. M., Bachman, J. G. (1991). *Drug use among American high school seniors, college students and young adults, 1975–1990.* Superintendent of Documents, USGPO, GPO Item No. 467-A-11, DHHS Pub No. (ADM) 91-1813. Washington, DC: National Institute on Drug Abuse.

Jones, R. K., & Joscelyn, K. B. (1978). *Alcohol and highway safety: A review of the state of knowledge.* Ann Arbor, MI: Highway Safety Research Institute, University of Michigan.

Klein, M. (1971). Adolescent driving as deviant behavior. In P. F. Waller (Ed.), *The young driver: Reckless or unprepared?* (pp. 2–19). Chapel Hill, NC: Highway Safety Research Center, University of North Carolina.

Makela, K. (1978). Level of consumption and social consequences of drinking. *Research advances in alcohol & drug problems, 4,* 303–348.

Mayhew, D. R., Simpson, H. M., & Donelson, A. C. (1983, November 2–5). *Young driver accidents: In search of solutions.* Proceedings of the International Symposium Conducted by the Traffic Injury Research Foundation of Canada, Alberta, Canada.

McMillen, D. L., & Wells-Parkers, E. (1987). The effect of alcohol consumption on risk-taking while driving. *Addictive Behaviors, 12*(3), 241–247.

Mosher, J. F. (1979). Dramshop liability and the prevention of alcohol-related problems. *Journal of Studies on Alcohol, 40,* 773–798.

National Highway Traffic Safety Administration. (1980). *Alcohol & highway safety workbook, 1980–81.* Workshop Series on Alcohol & Occupant Restraint. Washington, DC.

National Highway Traffic Safety Administration. (1990). *Alcohol and highway safety 1989: A review of the state of knowledge* (Report HS 807-557). Washington, DC: U. S. Department of Transportation.

National Safety Council. (1985). *Accident facts* (1985 ed.). Chicago, IL: NSC.

O'Donnell, M. A. (1985). Research on drinking locations of alcohol-impaired drivers: Implications for prevention policies. *Journal of Public Health Policy, 6*(4), 510–525.

O'Malley, P., & Wagenaar, A. C. (1991). Effects of minimum drinking age laws on alcohol use, related behaviors, and traffic crash involvement among American youth 1976–1987. *Journal of Studies on Alcohol, 52*(5), 478–1491.

Organisation for Economic Cooperation and Development. (1975). *Road research: Young driver accidents.* Paris, France: OECD.

Ornstein, S. I. (1980). Control of alcohol consumption through price increases. *Journal of Studies on Alcohol, 41,* 807–818.

Pelz, D. C., & Schuman, S. H. (1971, October 13). *Motivational factors in crashes and violations of young drivers.* Presented at the American Public Health Association Annual Meeting, Minneapolis, MN.

Perrine, M. W, Waller, J. A, & Harris, L. S. (1971). *Alcohol and highway safety: Behavioral and medical aspects.* Burlington, VT: University of Vermont.

Preusser, D. F., Oates, F. J. Jr., & Orban, M. S. (1975). *Identification of countermeasures for the youth crash problem related to alcohol: Review of existing literature and preliminary hypotheses.* Darien, CT: Dunlap and Associates.

Preusser, D. F., Williams, A. F., Zador, P. L., & Blomberg, R. D. (1983). The effect of curfew laws on motor vehicle crashes. *Law Policy Quarterly.*

Ross, H. L. (1992). *Confronting drunk driving: Social policy for saving lives.* New Haven, CT: Yale University Press.

Saxe, L., Dougherty, D., Esty, K., Fine, M. (1983). *Health Technology Case Study 22: The effectiveness and costs of alcoholism treatment.* Washington, DC: Office of Technology Assessment, U. S. Congress.

U. S. National Highway Traffic Safety Administration. (1987). *Fatal accident reporting system 1985* (Report H-807-071). Washington, DC: U. S. Department of Transportation.

Vingilis, E. (1983). Drinking drivers and alcoholics: Are they from the same population? *Research advances in alcohol & drug problems, 7,* 299–342.

Wagenaar, A. C. (1983). *Alcohol, young drivers, and traffic accidents: Effects of minimum-age laws.* Lexington, MA: D. C. Heath.

Wagenaar, A. C. (in press.). *Minimum drinking age and alcohol availability to youth: Issues and research needs* [Monograph]. Alcohol & health: Economic & socioeconomic issues in the prevention of alcohol-related problems. National Institute on Alcohol Abuse and Alcoholism.

Wagenaar, A. C., & Holder, H. D. (1991). Effects of alcoholic beverage server liability on traffic crash injuries. *Alcoholism: Clinical and Experimental Research, 15*(6), 942–947.

Wagenaar, A. C., Finnegan, J. R., Wolfson, M., & Anstine, P. S., Williams, C. L., & Perry, C. L. (1993). Where and how adolescents obtain alcoholic beverages. *Public Health Reports, 108* (4):459 464.

Wagenaar, W., (1986). Effects of mandatory seatbelt use: A series of surveys on compliance in Michigan. *Public Health Report, 101*(5), 505–513.

Waller, J. A., King, E. M. Nielson, G., & Turkel, H. W. (1970). *Alcohol and other factors in California highway fatalities.* Proceedings of the 11th Annual Meeting of the American Association for Automotive Medicine, Springfield, IL.

Williams, A. F., Karpf, R. S., & Zador, P. L. (1983). Variations in minimum licensing age and fatal motor vehicle crashes. *American Journal of Public Health, 73,* 1401–1404.

Wolfe, A. C. (1975, October 13–17). *Characteristics of alcohol-impaired drivers.* Presented at the Society of Automotive Engineers, Automobile Engineering Meeting, Detroit, MI.

Zylman, R. (1972). Age is more important than alcohol in the collision involvement of young and old drivers. *Journal of Traffic Safety, 20,* 7–8, 34.

Discussion Questions

1. Why have we traditionally focused on criminal justice deterrence of drinking-driving, treatment and rehabilitation of offenders, and education of the public?
2. What barriers do you see to changing the current social and political environment, which frequently encourages youth drinking and drinking-driving?
3. Why do efforts targeted at "high-risk" or "problem" youth have only modest beneficial effects?
4. What do you think is the most important thing we can do collectively to lower the rate of young people being killed or injured in alcohol-related traffic crashes?

Prevention of Drug Abuse among Children and Youth

Thomas C. Froehle

Thomas C. Froehle is a licensed psychologist and a professor in the Department of Counseling and Educational Psychology, Indiana University. He is probably best known for his theoretic and research contributions in counselor training, where he has developed a special interest in prevention programming for "high risk youth." He has been an invited lecturer in Bermuda and Canada, teaching courses in alcohol and drug abuse prevention and research and evaluation. His applied research efforts have been funded by the Kempf Foundation, Proffitt Endowment, Indiana University Lab for Educational Development, Midwest Center for Planned Change, and the U.S. Department of Education. Most recently he held a part-time appointment as a senior research specialist at the Indiana Prevention Resource Center. In a somewhat similar role, he worked as a research consultant with Project I-STAR 1987–1991. Currently, Dr. Froehle is serving as principal investigator and project director of a school counselor in-service training grant funded by Drug Free Schools and Communities.

Introduction

In the 1970s and early 1980s, we saw steadily increasing prevalence rates for the gateway drugs—cigarettes, alcohol, and marijuana. Concurrently, year-to-year surveys indicated that youth of this country were experimenting with these drugs at younger ages. During the mid 1980s, we began to see a leveling off and some slight declines in the prevalence of use rates for some gateway drugs. Most recent national surveys have shown that marijuana, cocaine, and crack use have declined since 1987 (Johnston, O'Malley & Bachman, 1988). Equivalent decreases in the prevalence of alcohol and cigarette use and abuse have not been reported, however.

While these declines were being reported, we were also seeing in this country a widespread proliferation of school-based prevention programs designed to discourage experimentation and regular use from ever occurring. The October 29, 1990, copy of *Education Daily* reported that only eight out of the nation's 23,200 school districts and post-secondary institutions did not meet the October 1, 1990, certification deadline for having a school-based prevention program in place.

Despite this gradual and steady decline in experimental use of certain drugs by adolescents, and the commensurate increase in prevention programming, major concerns continue to be voiced. On the one hand, there is the concern that the downward trends in experimental use and progress in arresting the downward trend in the age of first use of various substances may have served to create a false sense of confidence among the American public. These concerned parties argue that in order to maintain the declines in substance abuse, continued support for implementing successful prevention programs must be made top priority by federal, state, and local drug control agencies (Johnson, Pentz, Weber, Dwyer, Baer, MacKinnon, Hansen, & Flay, 1990).

A second concern centers on the focus that characterizes a majority of school-based programs. A statement by Newcomb and Bentler (1989) is representative of this concern. They write:

> Prevention and intervention should focus on the misuse, abuse, problem use, and heavy use of drugs to meet internal needs, cope with distress, and avoid responsibility and important life decisions and difficulties. The youngsters facing these tasks are in need of help, education, and intervention. It is misleading to bask in the success of some peer programs that have reduced the number of youngsters who experiment with drugs (but would probably never have become regular users, let alone abusers) and ignore the tougher problems of those youngsters who are at high risk for drug abuse as well as other serious difficulties. (p. 246)

Decisions regarding prevention programming are influenced by our beliefs about what causes individuals to experiment with drugs and eventually to become victims of drug abuse. The gateway theories assert that experimentation with one drug inclines the individual to use stronger drugs "either because of greater familiarity with drug use and those who use drugs or [because of the] addictive effects of the drugs first used" (Johnson, et al., 1990). Researchers who have studied factors that contribute to high risk for drug abuse have found that the same social influences that predict drug use onset also predict drug abuse (Johnson, et al., 1990). Research has consistently demonstrated that the best or strongest predictor of drug use is past use, while age and gender are the most consistent demographic predictors of substance use (Newcomb & Bentler, 1989). With respect to prevention, research has shown that programs targeted at late childhood or early adolescence are most effective, because this transition point is the first risk period for drug use onset.

Programming for Prevention: Where Have We Been and Where Are We Going?

Historically, prevention programming has focused on the agent (the drugs themselves), the host or demand (user of drugs), and the environment (social milieu relative to drug use) (Newcomb & Bentler, 1989). For years the federal government focused its efforts on supply reduction. Because drug use is clearly related to availability, this perspective on the problem and its solution seemed to make sense. However, efforts to control or limit availability, whether through law enforcement, technology, or social controls, have not been particularly effective (Schinke & Gilchrist, 1985). More recently the focus has shifted more in the direction of the host or demand (user of drugs).

Most contemporary prevention efforts focus jointly on environmental and host (i.e., demand) factors. Implicit in this practice is the assumption that drugs are available and that public access to them can never be totally controlled or eliminated. This redirection of focus also assumes that "personal desire (host) and social facilitation (environment)" are the most realistically amenable elements in the equation (Newcomb & Bentler, 1989, p. 245).

Given the success/failure statistics that previous research has associated with various prevention strategies, whether implemented singly or in combination with other strategies, it behooves us to know something about what prevention programs have been tried before, what outcomes have been observed, and where prevention programming with children and youth appears to be heading.

Prevention efforts vary also with regard to the directness of their attack on the problem of drug use and abuse. While some programs directly confront drug problems in the curriculum or in the environment, others indirectly address the problem by aiming at reducing the correlates of drug use and abuse. As we will see later, the knowledge or information approach and the peer programs that focus on refusal skills and social life skills are examples of direct approaches. Affective enhancement and alternatives programs are examples of indirect approaches. In both cases, however, the focus remains on the host or possible user. Law enforcement that restricts youth access to drugs is an example of a direct prevention strategy with an agent/environmental focus. The specific approaches are described in more detail in the following pages.

Direct Prevention Strategies: Host or User Focused

Knowledge or Information Approach

The knowledge/information approach assumes that a person's knowledge about drugs affects his/her attitudes, which affect his/her behavior. While drug information approaches emphasize the transmission of information, drug education approaches focus on the use of information. The earliest drug education efforts focused on values, attitudes, and decision-making skills that would enable young persons to avoid pressures to use drugs.

The knowledge or information approach has not been found to be effective when offered in isolation. In some early studies it was shown that prevention programs that focused only on information proved to be iatrogenic, i.e., they led to increased drug use. Apparently the provision of reliable information about drugs reduced fears and increased curiosity about drugs and their effects. Concurrent with this increase in the incidence of drug experimentation there was developing at the time a decrease in available resources needed to deal with the increased use. At one point the costly backfire effect prompted the federal government to place a ban on funding for certain marijuana prevention programs.

Peer Programs

Peer programs build on the now common knowledge that adolescents are particularly susceptible to peer influence and peer pressure. Children and youth with negative self-images are especially vulnerable to negative peer influence. Research has shown that peer approval of pro-drug attitudes and deviant patterns of behavior increases the probability of convergence upon what is seen as acceptable and normative. Included in this category are the simplistic tactics of "Just Say No" as well as the more comprehensive and more promising approaches that focus on peer interaction, social skills and competency, and enhancement of self-esteem.

"Say No" Programs. "Say No" programs were initiated in most instances by well-meaning individuals who had little sensitivity to or understanding of the complexity of the problem that they set out to address. Slogans, posters, bumper stickers, and other fanfare were major features of first generation "Just Say No" programs. More informed advocates of this naive and simplistic perspective, along with field implementers, soon discovered that at best such efforts served only to raise consciousness at the individual, family, school, and community levels.

Peer Resistance Strategies. The peer resistance and/or refusal skills approach concentrates more specifically on the student's ability to "Say No" when pressured to use drugs. The social competence skills training approach (Botvin, Eng, & Williams, 1980; Flay, 1985; Johnson, 1986) emphasizes systematic instruction and practice with specific resistance skills that youth can use in future situations. Reductions of 30 percent to 70 percent in adolescent smoking rates have been demonstrated using social competence skill training procedures. More moderate success in reducing alcohol and marijuana have also been reported (Botvin, 1986; Pentz, Dwyer, MacKinnon, Flay, Hansen, Wang, & Johnson, 1989). Prevention programs that include specific components for teaching youth peer pressure resistance have been especially effective (Hansen, Johnson, Flay, Graham, & Sobel, 1988; Killen, 1985; Tobler, 1986). Three components are embedded in the more sophisticated refusal skills programs: a competence component (refusal skill), a motivation component (the belief that the skill will be useful), and a confidence or refusal self-efficacy component (the belief that I will be successful in using the refusal skill).

Social and Life Skills Training

Prevention interventions included in this grouping have in common a focus on the enhancement of general, personal, and social competence. Gilbert Botvin, a prevention researcher at Cornell University, has been the most dominant contributor to the development and evaluation of the social and life skills approach to prevention. His Basic Life Skills component is designed to enhance the general competence level of individual students. Botvin's model builds on the assumption that drug use is a complex interplay of peer-imposed pressure to gain popularity and acceptance, along with self-imposed pressures that are created by the youngster himself/herself.

The social competency approach is the most recent one to have been introduced. This model assumes that persons who can relate to others, who can control their interpersonal environment and maintain their personal integrity, are less likely to engage in harmful behavior such as drug abuse. Two variations to the social competency approach have been shown to be effective: (1) the health promotion approach, and (2) the social skills approach. The *health promotion model* promotes behaviors that are conducive to good physical and psychological health, and avoids potentially harmful behaviors. The *social skills training* approach currently enjoys greater popularity than any of the other approaches. This approach emphasizes effective interpersonal relationships. Particular emphasis is given to skills that are needed to resist those social influences that compromise personal integrity.

Indirect Prevention Strategies: Host or User Focused

Affective Enhancement

Affective enhancement programs focus on values and decision making. These programs were first offered as an alternative to the didactic scare tactics, and were most often conducted with little or no reference to drugs. Aimed at promoting self-understanding, responsible decision making, intrapersonal growth and interpersonal relationships, the affective enhancement programs measure success in terms of their influence on the correlates of drug use.

Alternatives Programs

The alternatives programs approach concentrates even more directly on the correlates of drug use and abuse. Alternatives programs differ according to the individuals who are targeted in the prevention effort. Programs designed for the average student highlight community activities with opportunities for recognition and non-drug leisure activities. Alternatives programs that are targeted at youth regarded to be "at risk" place greater emphasis on special remedial tutoring, one-on-one relationships, job skills, and physical adventure (e.g., outward bound programs). Implicit in these offerings is the assumption that making these activities available to "at risk" youngsters serves to compensate for the many deficits that have operated in their lives, and that the resulting compensations will promote changes in drug use and drug abuse behavior.

Direct Prevention Strategies: Environment Focused

Advertising and Mass Media

Inoculation against mass media messages has been shown to be an effective prevention intervention (Hurd et al., 1980). Mass media drug prevention programs can be especially effective in increasing awareness and knowledge of prevention skills. These programs appear to be less effective in influencing individuals' motivation to change behavior, and they show even less promise for effecting actual behavior change (Flay, 1985).

Closely related, perceptions of social norms (i.e., use by others similar to ourselves and belief in social sanctions from using drugs) have been shown to influence our attitudes toward those norms and our own behavior. Several studies have actually shown that induced changes in one's perception of prevalence of use by peers, as well as one's perceptions of probable sanctions from friends following one's own use, better predict decreased drug use than do other prevention interventions, including resistance skills training.

Public Policy Explication and Implementation

One approach to drug use prevention that is only now beginning to receive systematic attention is the public policy approach. It stands to reason that public policy regarding drug use and abuse has been and remains significantly related to prevalence of use. Witness what has happened with respect to tobacco use. Only recently, however, have the effects of public policy received the researchers' attention. Several studies have shown that school, worksite, and community policies regulating smoking, for example, can decrease the amount of smoking in the short term (Moskowitz & Jones, 1988; Pentz et al., 1989; Rosenstock, Stergachis, & Haeney, 1987). Policies that serve to reinforce non-smoking, rather than punish smoking, appear to be especially promising.

Indirect Prevention Strategies: Environment Focused

It has been suggested that any measure that serves to promote the general level of social justice also serves indirectly as a drug abuse prevention intervention. George Albee has been one of the most articulate spokespersons for this position (Albee, 1986). The increasing popularity of this point of view is evidenced in the recent formation of the American Association for Applied Psychology and Prevention (AAAPP) and the appointment of George Albee as the first president of that organization. Because of space restrictions and the sheer scope of activities that warrant consideration here, there is no way that this chapter can consider the wide range of actions that are properly classified as indirect environmental focused approaches to prevention.

Research-Based Conclusions Regarding Effective Ingredients in Prevention Programming

Numerous reviews of the drug prevention research literature have been conducted in the interest of identifying programs and program components that serve to prevent and/or alter drug use behaviors. The professional journals in the areas of public health, drug abuse, preventive medicine, and drug education have been the major outlets for these reviews.

As with most traditions of prevention and intervention, the research findings on drug abuse prevention efforts have not always been positive. As a matter of fact, some of the strategies tried in the 1970s actually served to exacerbate the problem. A case in point is the scare tactics strategy (e.g., the old movie *Reefer Madness*). As mentioned earlier, the discouraging and sometimes opposite results from these and some other informational approaches tried in the late 1960s and early 1970s prompted the National Commission on Marijuana Use to recommend a ban on prevention programming.

In all too many situations, prevention programming success has been argued on the basis of *subjective gut feelings.* When quantitative measures have been introduced, some of the *gut feeling evaluations* have proven to be invalid. Recall the previously mentioned inconsistency that surfaced with the dissemination of evaluation data associated with the scare tactics that characterized the information approaches that were so popular during the early 1970s.

Data-based models stand in marked contrast to the theory-driven models of intervention and prevention programming. Systematic inquiry into the etiology of drug use and abuse is a central emphasis with the former approach to prevention programming. This process begins with investigations into the correlates of tobacco, alcohol, and other drug use and abuse. Knowing something about the etiology of problem use and the psychosocial and ecological concomitants of problem use suggests targets for change. For example, if easy access is highly correlated with early onset of first use, and with prevalence of use generally, then prevention programming designed to restrict access makes sense as one dimension of prevention.

Most of the published reviews are integrative, refereed reviews in which the final determination of worth and effectiveness is left to the subjective judgment of the reviewer. In addition, several meta-analytic reviews have been published (Bangert-Drowns, 1988; Tobler, 1986). Using meta-analytic procedures, the reviewer's conclusions are based on a statistical analysis of the effects that are reported in the studies. Because of its particular relevance to this chapter the Tobler meta-analysis of 143 drug prevention studies is singled out for special consideration in the pages that follow.

Tobler classified impact studies on the basis of the (1) outcome measures that were used to evaluate effectiveness and (2) type or modality that was given emphasis in the prevention effort. Five major classifications of outcome were used: (1) knowledge, (2) attitudes, (3) use, (4) skills, and (5) behavior. Based upon the nature and the combination of treatment components that were emphasized in the studies that met the a priori established criteria for inclusion in her meta-analysis, prevention interventions were reduced to a five-part system of classification: (1) knowledge only emphasis, (2) affective only emphasis, (3) peer programming emphasis (either refusal skills or social and life skills), (4) knowledge plus affective emphasis, and (5) alternatives emphasis (either activities or competencies).

Findings from her meta-analysis led Tobler (1986) to conclude that peer programs that emphasized the enhancement of refusal skills and other social skills were most effective in reducing drug *use* and preventing the initiation of drug use for the typical teenager. The alternatives programs, on the other hand, were shown to be "highly successful for the *'at risk'* adolescents such as drug abusers, juvenile delinquents, or students having school problems" (Tobler, 1986, p. 538). These findings suggest that youth most at risk for *abusing* drugs are best served by prevention efforts that promote alternative activities and broadening experiences designed to build confidence and social competence in youth.

Common Ingredients in Effective Drug Prevention Programming

A majority of the primary prevention programs that have been systematically evaluated have focused on a single channel or a single site for prevention delivery. The school, family, community, and mass media have each served as the primary site for prevention programs. Most commonplace are school-based prevention programs in which a prevention curriculum is delivered by teachers or specially trained school personnel. School-based drug prevention programs that have been most successful in preventing the onset of drug use are those that offer multiple components (e.g., peer resistance training, social skills development, inoculation against mass media messages). Some primary prevention programs are more general in their attack on the problem. Rather than focus only on problem behaviors, these models emphasize the promotion of healthy living behaviors, including diet, exercise, and stress reduction, in order to create a mutual reinforcement and synergy among various health behaviors (Perry, 1986).

The ideal for community-based approaches to drug prevention is to institute a comprehensive community-based program that is responsive not only to the developmental needs of youth in general but to the needs of various high-risk groups as well (Orlandi, 1986). Most social influences prevention programs are focused on the needs of adolescents at large, with very little prescriptive programming targeted at specific high risk groups.

Johnson et al. (1990) have pointed out that much has yet to be learned through research concerning "the conditions under which community-based programs are effective, the populations that benefit most and particularly any populations that may fail to benefit" and the question as to whether or not programs are similarly effective with those who are at high risk to use drugs as well as those who are at low risk. In this regard, a point that we will pick up on later, Newcomb and Bentler (1989) have suggested that too many prevention programs reach only low-risk adolescents and therefore are of limited value.

With respect to timing, research strongly suggests that the most promising prevention efforts are those that are targeted at early adolescents, particularly during the transition years to middle or junior high school (sixth or seventh grade). These programs tend to focus on delaying the onset of use of tobacco, alcohol, and marijuana, generally regarded as "gateway drugs" to the use of illicit substances such as cocaine or crack.

There is a growing consensus that prevention, if it is to have long-term effects on adolescent drug use, must be multifaceted. Programs that combine interventions for the individual and the environment realize greater success than do host-only or agent approaches.

What is sought after in school-based prevention is programming that is well suited to the general population of students. This includes both adolescents at high risk and those at low risk equally. This sought after ideal recognizes the impracticality of separating out low-risk and high-risk adolescents for prescriptive prevention programming. What is not clear at this time is whether or not this ideal can be reached. It is entirely conceivable that the accumulated research, coupled with cost-benefit analysis, will illustrate the desirability of situation specific programming that takes into consideration risk factors of the youth involved, as well as the risk factors associated with the overall context in which the individual attends school and resides when out of school.

Tobler (1986) found that different modalities have different effects on drug use and drug abuse behavior. This finding makes a lot of sense when we recognize that abuse of drugs occurs for different reasons than does experimental or occasional use of drugs. According to Newcomb and Bentler (1989), etiological findings indicate that "benign or non-problem use of drugs occurs in social or peer settings (addressed in the peer program models) but that problem use of drugs is generated by internal distress, limited life opportunities, and unhappiness (not ameliorated by the peer programs, but addressed somewhat by the alternative programs)." One of Tobler's firmest conclusions was that effect size (i.e., the difference found between treated and non-treated groups) was highly related to the inclusion of peers in the prevention process. However, while peer approaches have been shown to be effective in reducing the use of drugs, they appear to have less impact on abuse of drugs.

Considerations in Prevention Programming

Any prevention effort must be based on sound answers to three basic questions: What is to be prevented? What is the target population? What techniques are to be used?

What Is To Be Prevented?

Four subquestions fall under this general question: Is the program of prevention designed to focus on *use* or misuse of drugs? Is the program intended to *prevent* or to *delay* drug use? On *what drugs* will the program focus? How *specific* will the objectives be? Agreement on the answers to these questions is not likely; nor is it important that everyone agree. What is important is that these questions be addressed and some consensus reached prior to the initiation of any prevention effort. The considerations raised in the following section are just some of the issues that will likely surface in any serious discussion of the four subquestions.

Regarding the Question of Which Drugs.

"Gateway drugs," namely cigarettes, alcohol, and marijuana, are the usual targets for prevention programming. The term "gateway" is used to describe this group of drugs because, according to stage theories of drug abuse, these three drugs are generally used prior to harder drugs, such as heroin, LSD, or cocaine/crack. Implicit in this practice of targeting these three drugs is the assumption that preventing and/or delaying the use of the gateway drugs will preclude or at least delay the use of drugs that are higher in the sequence.

While the "gateway" rubric and its three-part makeup has some merit (e.g., its common language feature facilities communication), in some contexts it may serve to diminish the sense of urgency to change use behavior with respect to these specific substances. Johnson et al. (1990) argue that this is certainly the case with respect to cigarette smoking, a point that is touched on again when we consider the "use" vs. "misuse" question.

Regarding the Question of Use or Abuse

It has been argued that the introduction of prevention programs into the early grades has had its greatest effect on those individuals who were at risk as experimental users only (Newcomb & Bentler, 1989). Postponing the age of first use has caused the prevalence of experimental users to decrease steadily over the past several years. Despite these successes, there are those who criticize school-based prevention programs on the grounds that too large a portion of available resources is being earmarked to delay the age of first use of alcohol and other drugs. This practice leaves few resources for the prevention of frequent use and abuse of drugs. While there is growing evidence of a continuing decline in prevalence of experimental users of various substances, especially for marijuana, the same measure of progress has not been made in the area of frequent use and abuse.

It could be argued that the *use* vs. *abuse* question with respect to tobacco use by children and adolescents conveys an erroneous message. For example, albeit they were writing in a different context, Johnson et al. (1990) have convincingly argued that any level of cigarette smoking, especially by youth, is abusive because the amount of exposure to tobacco smoke is related linearly to heart disease and lung cancer. Perhaps the same cannot be said of alcohol and marijuana, but " . . . for tobacco, any level of use is problem use" (p. 454).

A research report published recently in the *Journal of Drug Issues* (Shedler & Block, 1990) points to some empirical evidence that supports the criticism that the American public may be distracted from the real prevention issue. Shedler and Block have been studying a group of individuals for a couple of decades. Their investigation was initiated in 1967 when they carefully studied 107 young children, the child-rearing practices that these individuals experienced in childhood, and the interactions they had with their parents. Frequent follow-ups have been conducted since 1967. The most recent follow-up was conducted when the majority of the subjects were 18 years old. The picture of the frequent user that emerges from this research is one of a "troubled adolescent, an adolescent who is interpersonally alienated, emotionally withdrawn, and manifestly unhappy, and who expresses his or her maladjustment through undercontrolled, overtly antisocial behavior" (p. 617).

The conclusions spelled out by Shedler and Block (1990) have particular relevance. They write: " . . . Problem drug use is a symptom, not a cause, of personal and social maladjustment . . . the meaning of drug use can be understood only in the context of an individual's personality structure and developmental history . . . current efforts at drug prevention are misguided to the extent that they focus on symptoms, rather than on the psychological syndrome underlying drug abuse." (p. 612).

In many published impact evaluations, salient distinctions between experimental users and frequent users have not been made. In many such situations a program's commitment to a *non-use* as opposed to a *responsible* or *controlled use* posture partially accounts for this state of affairs. Although this commitment is reflected in various ways, nowhere has this philosophy been more apparent than in the preferred practice of defining prevalence of use as "having used a substance one or more times during the past 30 days." Dividing participant pools into those who have used a drug during the past 30 days and those who have not serves to obscure the variance that exists within that portion of the population that reported use.

What Is the Target Population?

The timing of prevention interventions has become an increasingly critical consideration in light of recent empirical findings. With respect to delaying the onset of regular use of the gateway drugs, research clearly points to the transition years (i.e., first year in middle school or junior high school) as the critical periods for introducing school-based prevention programming. While it makes sense that prevention of use be given center stage during pre-adolescence, some have argued that a continued focus on use may not be as appropriate with adolescents, however. Newcomb and Bentler (1989) have this to say about prevention programming during adolescence.

> Adolescence is a period of experimentation, exploration, and curiosity. In this society, drug use has become one aspect of this natural process to the extent that a teenager is deviant (from the normative perspective) if he or she has not tried alcohol, cigarettes, or marijuana by the completion of high school. Although it is important to delay the onset of regular drug use as long as possible, to allow time for the development of adaptive and effective personal and interpersonal skills, it may be less important to prevent the use of drugs than the abuse, misuse, and problem use of drugs (which places a tremendous burden on the individual and society). It is in this area that prevention programs have been less successful and are in need of continued development. The typical teenager who experiments with beer or shares a joint at a party is unlikely to be the one who will have severe problems with drugs later in life. Labeling this person as a "druggy," sick, screwed up, or in need of treatment is liable to be more destructive than the use of the drug itself. (p. 246)

What Techniques Are To Be Used?

Regardless of the circumstances, it is always important that prevention programming decisions be informed and guided by past and ongoing research. This is especially critical in those situations where costs preclude ongoing impact evaluation. Several bodies have come into existence whose mission includes promoting and supporting research and dissemination of information regarding effective prevention programming. The National Prevention Network, an arm of the National Association of State Alcohol and Drug Abuse Directors (NASADAD), is one such body. For the past several years, this group has selected and disseminated project summaries regarding exemplary programs in the area of prevention. Two of their most recent publications were titled: *Helping Communities to Help Themselves; Twenty 1989 Exemplary Prevention Programs* and *Communities Christen Change: Exemplary Alcohol and Other Prevention Programs 1990.*

The Project Advisory Criteria Procedures used to select exemplary prevention programs focus on twelve program attributes. They are:

- Show evidence of a sound planning process
- Written measurable goals and objectives
- Multiple activities are used to achieve program goals and objectives
- Prevention program serves multiple targets/populations
- Prevention program has a strong evaluation base
- Prevention program is sensitive to the needs of all
- Prevention program is an integral part of an overall-health prevention and health care system

- Community involvement and ownership is likely
- Prevention program is long-term
- Prevention program collaborates with multiple social systems and levels within the community
- Prevention program includes a marketing approach for evaluation and showcasing positive effects
- Program documentation allows for evaluation and replication in other settings

The Midwest Prevention Project: A Case Study

One of the most comprehensive and carefully conceptualized models for organizing an entire community in a drug prevention program has been developed and implemented by a group of researchers once gathered at the Department of Preventive Medicine at the University of Southern California. This group, headed up by C. Anderson Johnson and Mary Ann Pentz, has been testing their model in two midwestern communities, Kansas City, Missouri, and Indianapolis, Indiana. This program of research and development has come to be known as the Midwest Prevention Project (MPP).

The MPP model and the prevention programming developed from that model are based on social learning, attitude/behavior change, communication, organizational development, and Person X Situation X Environment transactional theories of individual and community level change. Included in the program are five components: school, parent, community organization, health policy change, and mass media programming.

The MPP model takes into consideration many of the research findings that have been reported regarding individual, situational, and environmental variables that have been shown to be associated with drug use behavior. In the next few pages, the specific program features of the Indianapolis component of the Midwest Prevention Project are highlighted to serve as an example of a soundly conceptualized, rigorously implemented, and carefully evaluated multifaceted school/community-based drug prevention program for children and youth.

I-STAR Student Curriculum

At the core of Project I-STAR (Indiana Students Taught Awareness and Resistance) lies a two-part curriculum designed to prevent alcohol and other drug use among young people. Specially trained classroom teachers deliver the curriculum during regularly scheduled I-STAR sessions. Part I of the curriculum is designed to be offered to students during the first year of their transition into middle or junior high school. Part II is a booster curriculum. It is shorter and is designed for use during the student's second year under the program. Both Parts I and II are designed to help students become aware of the social pressures to use drugs and equip them with skills to resist those pressures. Included in the two-part curriculum are the following session titles: Consequences; Techniques to say "No"; Peer Pressure Resistance; To Tell the Truth/Prevention Baseline; Normative Expectations; Appropriate or Inappropriate Use of Alcohol; Advertising Influences; Developing Friendships; Question Box; Standing up for Myself; Reputations; Problem Solving; Refusing Requests; Proactive Skills Building.

I-STAR Teacher Corps

The major responsibility for training I-STAR teachers falls upon the curriculum training coordinator. This individual is assisted by several curriculum/training facilitators and a dozen or so I-STAR Teacher Corps members. This latter group is made up of individually selected teachers who have demonstrated particularly effective competencies in offering the I-STAR curriculum. "Selected for their excellent classroom implementation of the curriculum and willingness to help, these experienced I-STAR teachers assist the curriculum/training facilitators in training teachers new to I-STAR Part I or II. To prepare the Teacher Corps for training new I-STAR teachers, the Corps members participate in a special training of trainers session conducted by the curriculum/training facilitators" (*I-STAR Reporter*, 1990, p. 5).

I-STAR Parent Skills Training

The I-STAR Parent Training is offered by experienced I-STAR parents with assistance from I-STAR staff. After receiving their training in prevention strategies and communication skills, parent committees return to their schools and host I-STAR Parent Skills Program sessions where they train other parents at their schools in the same skills. Session topics include but are not limited to the following: identifying school and community needs, reinforcing resistance skills, developing positive friendships, knowing your child's friends, enhancing communication skills, increasing attentive listening, communicating expectations, encouraging parent-child communication, and setting and enforcing rules.

I-STAR Community Advisory Council

The I-STAR Community Advisory Council consists of 45 community leaders representing a variety of segments of the Indianapolis community. This council leads the community component of Project I-STAR. Members of the council work in subcommittees called action committees with specific goals. Included on the council are the following action committees: government action committee, parent/family action committee, medical/treatment action committee, media action committee, religious action committee, worksite action committee, schools/ education action committee, and youth agencies action committee.

MMP Impact Evaluation

The MMP Community Program Intervention Model has been subjected to careful and exhaustive empirical investigation over the past several years. Preliminary effects of the STAR program in Kansas City were published in 1989 in the *Journal of the American Medical Association* (Pentz et al., 1989). The longitudinal design of Midwest Prevention Project was crafted to permit (1) tests of the cost effectiveness of the various program components and (2) replication of the program in multiple, diverse communities. When Pentz et al. reported their preliminary findings, effects of the 10-session school program component, parent involvement in homework, and mass media coverage had been evaluated across 42 diverse schools in Kansas City-area communities 1.5 years after intervention was initiated. Findings from subsequent follow-ups have also been published (Johnson et al., 1990).

The impact evaluation based on data collected four years following the introduction of the comprehensive prevention program clearly shows that students who took part in the program were significantly less likely to be drinking alcohol and smoking cigarettes and marijuana than their peers who did not participate (Johnson et al., 1990). Unlike what has proven to be the case with so many drug prevention programs, effects of the STAR Project in Kansas city have held up or increased across time. This is clearly illustrated in the fact that prevalence of use differences between intervention and control participants gradually increased over the first three years and then remained constant through year four. Beginning in grades six and seven, controls and intervention students were near equivalent in the proportion of alcohol users to nonusers (6.6% for intervention students; 7.5% for controls). Four years later when these same students were enrolled in grades 10 and 11, 14 percentage points separated the two groups, with 50.1 percent of controls and only 36 percent of program students reporting that they had taken two or more alcoholic drinks during the 30 days prior to taking the survey. Although the differential in cigarette use during the past month was not as dramatic, the difference between the 24.1 percent prevalence rate for students who took part in the study and the 32 percent prevalence rate for teens who did not receive the prevention measures was statistically significant. The differential in prevalence rates for marijuana was similarly significant, with 14.2 percent of the program students and 20.2 percent of the nonparticipating students reporting that they had used marijuana during the last 30 days.

Assessment of Prevalence and Prevention Impact

It is generally agreed that the first step in prevention and intervention is to alter the state of denial. School corporations and local communities, like individuals, are prone to deny that a drug problem exists. While it is easy to recognize problems in other communities, problems "close to home" often go unnoticed. Assessment at a very minimum can serve as a consciousness-raising intervention. What most communities discover through a prevalence of use study is that they share much in common with other communities.

Funding support for research into the efficacy and impact of prevention programs has come from the federal, state, and private sectors. At the national level, the National Institute of Drug Abuse (NIDA) has been a long-time and steady source of research support for these programs. More recently, some support has been made available through other agencies of federal and state government. Several large foundations have also been major sponsors of prevention efforts and have seen fit to earmark substantial amounts of dollars to research the effectiveness of the programs that they underwrite. Two foundations, the Marion Foundation (Marion Laboratories) headquartered in Kansas City, Missouri and the Lilly Foundation (Eli Lilly) of Indianapolis have been particularly generous in supporting the Midwest Prevention Project discussed earlier.

Recognizing that the need for prevention consultation exists within most local communities, the federal government has put forth several initiatives to mobilize and energize prevention expertise at the local level. One such initiative is the establishment of a National Prevention Resource Center and federally disbursed state support for establishing State and Regional Prevention Resource Centers. A second initiative is the dissemination of materials that serve to guide prevention efforts at the local level. Particularly useful is a NIDA Publication titled *Handbook for Evaluating Drug and Alcohol Prevention Programs: Staff/Team Evaluation of Prevention Programs (STEPP)* (Hawkins, Lishner, & Catalano, 1985). This monograph carefully walks the reader through the various processes that accountable performance requires. The monograph opens with a hands-on unit on needs assessment, and concludes with considerations of both formative and summative evaluation. The STEPP program offers training in a six-step process for evaluating prevention programs. The steps are: (1) choosing an evaluation question, (2) designing an evaluation, (3) designing measurement instruments, (4) building a data collection plan, (5) analyzing the data, and (6) reporting the findings.

One of the problems that has plagued researchers and prevention program evaluators is the fact that there exist no standardized materials and/or procedures for the assessment of incidence and prevalence of use of the various substances. Typically, and much to the chagrin of researchers, prevalence surveys have not collected very precise data. This lack of standardization has made it difficult to compare results from study to study or from community to community. The most useful surveys pose questions of use during the individual's entire life, during the last month (30 days), and during the last week (seven days). The rates of drug usage reported in most studies are given as percentages of students who used each substance. For cigarettes, alcohol, marijuana, and smokeless tobacco, rates are often reported separately for students who have ever tried the substance *in their lifetime*, used the substance one or more times *in the last month*, and used the substance *in the last week*. ("Last month" is defined as the 30 days prior to taking the survey, and "last week" as the last seven days prior to the survey.) For cocaine, rates are typically reported for students who have ever tried the substance *in their lifetime* and those who used the substance one or more times *in the last month*. For other illicit drugs, including heroin, L.S.D., "uppers," "downers," and inhalants, rates are usually reported as the percentage of students who have ever tried the substance *in their lifeline*. Each of the three frequency of use criteria is of value and has relevance to drug prevention programming. Among the advantages of the "lifetime" criterion is its potential to differentiate at the early grade levels and with substances of lower prevalence, such as cocaine or crack. In the upper grades, interest tends to focus more on "habits of use" that are reflected best in the "last 30 days" and "last seven days" criteria. Use during the "last 30 days" seems to be the best single compromise measure.

Variation also exists with respect to the criteria that are used to classify students as users and nonusers. Binary classification is required in research efforts that compare the proportions of users to nonusers observed among students and/or schools assigned to control conditions (i.e., no intervention conditions) and students and/or schools assigned to the treatment(s) being investigated. In controlled studies like these, it is expected that significantly lower proportions of students who experienced the treatment condition will be classified as users. We are left with the question: "What should the cutoff point be for such classification?" The STAR and I-STAR projects, for example, classify youth as last month and/or last week users if they report having used two or more alcoholic drinks during the last 30 days or last seven days respectively. These procedures for classifying users and nonusers are not possible with the kind of survey data that are sometimes collected, showing more general frequency of drug use.

Another threat to the validity of impact studies exists when drug use behavior is assessed solely through self-report by a study's participants. Some researchers collect psychological samples as a validity check on participant self-report. For example, in the Midwest Prevention Project, students who respond to the Health Behavior Survey are also given a CO breath analyzer test as a cross validation on the level of use that they report on their surveys. Further, to encourage accurate reporting of use, surveys and the CO analysis are administered by trained personnel from Project STAR and/or I-STAR. Students are assured that school officials will not be given individual results or in any way be able to associate a survey form with a specific student.

Summary and Conclusions

If there is a major advance that has derived from research into the etiology and prevention of drug use and abuse, it is the realization that drug use and its prevention are very complicated. There are no simple or easy solutions, regardless of when, where, or how prevention efforts are introduced during the life span. The fact that there were brief moments during the 1980s when large segments of the American public were persuaded to think otherwise attests to the frustration level of a public searching out answers to the drug problem.

Simple solutions will continue to attract the public's attention. While there are no simple solutions to this very complicated problem, there will be those who want to convince us otherwise. New curriculum materials will be crafted, packaged, and marketed to a consumer public that is predictably attracted to whatever has common sense appeal. History presents many examples of perpetrated illusions that have lured the American public into a false sense of progress and current well-being. Unfortunately, resources allotted for primary prevention are the first to be redirected during times of seeming well-being. What's at stake is too critical to be left in the hands of the perpetrators of illusion.

References

Albee, G. (1986). Toward a just society. *American Psychologist, 41,* 891–898.

Bangert-Drowns, R. L. (1988). The effects of school-based substance abuse education: A meta-analysis. *Journal of Drug Education, 18,* 243–264.

Botvin, G. J. (1986). Substance abuse prevention research: Recent developments and future directions. *Journal of School Health, 56,* 369–374.

Botvin, G. J., Eng, A., & Williams, C. L. (1980). Preventing the onset of cigarette smoking through life skills training. *Preventive Medicine, 9,* 135–143.

Flay, B. R. (1985). Psychosocial approaches to smoking prevention: A review of findings. *Health Psychology, 4,* 449–488.

Hansen, W. B., Johnson, C. A., Flay, B. R., Graham, J. W., & Sobel, J. (1988). Affective and social influences approaches to the prevention of multiple substance abuse among seventh grade students: Results from Project SMART. *Preventative Medicine, 17,* 1–20.

Hawkins, J. D., Lishner, D. M., & Catalano, R. F. (1985). Childhood predictors and the prevention of adolescent substance abuse. In C. L. Jones, & R. J. Battejes (Eds.), Etiology of drug abuse: Implications for prevention. *NIDA Research Monographs 56,* 75–126.

Hurd, P., Johnson, C. A., Pechacek, T., Bast, L. P., Jacobs, D. R., & Luepker, R. V. (1980). Prevention of cigarette smoking in seventh grade students. *Journal of School Health, 52,* 295–300.

I. Star Reporter. (1990). Volume 4, p. 5.

Johnson, C. A. (1986). Prevention and control of drug abuse. In J. M. Last (Ed.), *Maxcy-Rosenau public health and preventive medicine* (pp. 1075–1087). Norwalk, CT: Appleton-Century-Crofts.

Johnson, C. A., Pentz, M. A., Weber, M. D., Dwyer, J. H., Baer, N., MacKinnon, D. P., Hansen, W. B., & Flay, B. R. (1990). Relative effectiveness of comprehensive community programming for drug use prevention with high-risk and low-risk adolescents. *Journal of Consulting and Clinical Psychology, 58,* 447–456.

Johnston, L. D., O'Malley, P. M., & Bachman, J. G. (1988). *Illicit drug use, smoking, and drinking by America's high school students, college students, and young adults.* National Institute on Drug Abuse. Rockville, MD: U.S. Dept. of Health and Human Services.

Kessler, M., & Goldsten, S.E., (Eds.). (1986). *A decade of progress in primary prevention.* Hanover, VT: University Press of New England.

Killen, J. D. (1985). Prevention of adolescent tobacco smoking: The social pressure resistance training approach. *Journal of Child Psychology and Psychiatry and Allied Disciplines, 26,* 7–15.

Moskowitz, J. M., & Jones, R. (1988). Alcohol and drug problems in the schools: Results of a national survey of school administrators. *Journal of Studies on Alcohol, 49,* 299–305.

Newcomb, M. D., & Bentler, P. M. (1989). Substance use and abuse among children and teenagers. *American Psychologist, 44,* 242–248.

Newcomb, M. D., Chou, C., Bentler, P. M., & Huba, G. J. (1988). Cognitive motivations for drug use among adolescents: Longitudinal tests of gender differences and predictors of change in drug use. *Journal of Counseling Psychology, 35,* 426–438.

Orlandi, M. A. (1986). Community-based substance abuse prevention: A multicultural perspective. *Journal of School Health, 56,* 394–401.

Pentz, M. A., Dwyer, J. H., MacKinnon, D. P., Flay, B. R., Hansen, W. B., Wang, E., Yu, I., & Johnson, A. (1989). A multi-community trial for primary prevention of adolescent drug abuse: Effects on drug use prevalence. *Journal of the American Medical Association, 261,* 3259–3266.

Perry, C. L. (1986). Community-wide health promotion and drug abuse prevention. *Journal of School Health, 56,* 359–363.

Rosenstock, I. M., Stergachis, A., & Heaney, C. (1987). Evaluation of a smoking prohibition policy in a health maintenance organization. *American Journal of Public Health, 76,* 1014–1015.

Schinke, S. P., & Gilchrist, L. D. (1985). Preventing substance abuse with children and adolescence. *Journal of Consulting and Clinical Psychology, 55,* 596–602.

Shedler, J., & Block, J. (1990). Adolescent drug use and psychological health: A longitudinal inquiry. *American Psychologist, 45,* 612–630.

Tobler, N. W. (1986). Meta-analysis of 143 adolescent drug prevention programs: Quantitative outcome results of program participants compared to a control or comparison group. *Journal of Drug Issues, 16,* 537–568.

Discussion Questions

1. How serious was the problem of alcohol and drug use/abuse in the community in which you grew up as a child and adolescent? Was the community aware of the problem that existed? What prevention strategies were tried to deal with the problem? What seemed to work in your opinion?
2. What are your thoughts about the "supply/demand" controversy? Is it realistic to expect that prevention efforts will be successful in changing demand? What about supply—is it likely that interdiction and law enforcement will eventually be successful?
3. Scare tactics have not proven effective either in changing motivation to use substances or in altering substance use behavior by adolescents. What might be some of the reasons why scare tactics do not work?
4. Peers and peer pressure, both positive and negative, appear to have a strong influence on substance use/abuse behavior. Why is this the case, particularly among adolescents?
5. There is a Native American saying that goes something like this: "It takes a village to raise a child." How does this adage apply to the idea of comprehensive alcohol and drug abuse prevention programming? Be specific in your considerations.

20

Drugs, Suds, and College

Drug Use Prevention and Intervention

Stewart E. Cooper

Stewart Cooper received his doctorate from Indiana University in 1981 with a double major in the areas of counseling psychology and research methodology. His B.A. in Psychology was previously completed at Indiana University in 1975. Dr. Cooper is a licensed psychologist in Indiana and Missouri, and currently serves as Director of the Student Counseling and Development Center, and as Associate Professor with the Psychology Department, at Valparaiso University. Professor Cooper has authored over thirty articles in the areas of psychotherapy models, gender studies, eating disorders, substance abuse, and group counseling.

I recently saw a cartoon that depicted inebriated college students. The caption read, "Why do we go to college?" The answer declared, "To drink from the fountain of knowledge." For innumerable college students, this cartoon bears more than a grain of truth. The society itself contributes to tacit approval of college student substance abuse, as parents recall with nostalgia their college drinking days, movies portray campus parties where everyone has a good tine and no one is hurt, and professors jokingly allude to late night get-togethers and hangovers. For the purposes of this chapter, alcohol abuse will be considered as one facet of the overall drug abuse problem affecting college students.

Drug Abuse among College Students

Johnson et al. (1989) recently completed a major longitudinal study of drug use, drinking, and smoking among the college population. The investigation concluded that the level of drug use among this group has continued to decline since 1975. While approximately one-third of all college students smoked marijuana in the past year, Johnson and his coworkers found a substantial increase (up to 77 percent) of this population who believed that heavy use of marijuana is a great health risk. Similarly, cocaine experimentation fell from 17 percent in 1986 to 10 percent in 1988. Use of crack-cocaine (a more potent and potentially more lethal dry combination of cocaine and baking soda, which can be smoked) fell from 2.0 percent to 1.4 percent. The data showed similar reductions in the use of other types of drugs, including psychedelics, amphetamines, PCP, quaaludes, and inhalants. Concomitantly, disapproval of others' occasional use of these latter drugs substantially increased.

About these reductions, Johnson et al. (1989) commented that "The declines in use have occurred in spite of a continuing increase in availability. . . In other words, these important successes have been achieved not through supply reduction: they are due almost entirely to a reduction in demand" (p. 3). While alcohol abuse has also declined slightly, it clearly remains a greater problem than all other drug abuse combined. For example, some researchers (e.g., Klein, 1989) report that as many as 80 percent of all college students drink abusively at some point during the year. Other research on drug abuse among college students has extended these findings. Smith (1989) summarized the results of several investigations showing a positive correlation between drug abuse and campus crime, while Maney (1990) found evidence to suggest that level of drug experimentation and use increases from freshman through senior years. When Goodwin (1989) studied moderate and severe abusers, he found that one sub-group of these was aware of negative effects, while the other sub-group was not. The latter group, he believed, was particularly at high risk for developing future problems. Concomitantly, the courts are substantially increasing the level of legal liability for higher educational institutions concerning accidents related to alcohol and drug use (Smith, 1989). Viewed collectively, this information suggests that drug use (especially when alcohol is included) is at high levels among today's college populations and that colleges and universities are increasingly being held accountable for it.

Shedler and Block (1990) completed a major longitudinal study on adolescent drug use and psychological health to uncover differences between experimenters (users) and abusers, and to determine whether these differences were pre- or post-college matriculation. Specifically, they investigated a group of west coast 18 year olds whom they had followed since age three, and who were now categorized as abstainers, experimenters, or abusers. Their data suggest that drug experimenters had better psychological health than either abstainers or abusers. As compared to experimenters, the abusers evidenced the negative triumvirate of interpersonal alienation, poor impulse control, and manifest emotional distress, while the abstainers tended to be more anxious, emotionally constricted, and lacking in social skills. Interestingly, these differences in psychological health were evident by age nine (and preceded the use of drugs). "Current theories tend to emphasize the role of peers in influencing drug use. The importance of peers in providing an encouraging surrounding for experimentation cannot be denied, but 'peer-centered' or 'environmental' explanations of problem drug abuse seem inadequate, given the present longitudinal findings" (Shedler & Block, 1990).

Shedler and Block strongly emphasize that they are not advocating drug experimentation, nor anything other than complete abstinence for addicted persons. Rather, they are suggesting that the U-shaped relationship between abstinence, experimentation, abuse and psychological health is primarily a product of the current adolescent/young adult culture, which values utilization of the mood-altering substances. They also agree with Tobler (1986) that our existing antidrug educational approach is off-base and ineffective. Specifically, productive prevention and intervention efforts must focus on addressing psychological factors and changing perspectives of the youth culture *in addition to* providing them information on drugs and their effects.

Theoretical Perspectives

Our understanding of the experience and process of drug addiction has greatly increased in sophistication and comprehensiveness in the last five years (Cooper, 1990). The current perspective espouses what is called a biopsychosocial, or interactional approach to the etiology, diagnosis, and remediation of abuse and addiction problems. Specifically, the biopsychosocial viewpoint maintains that drug abuse is the product of a reciprocal interaction of physiological, psychological, and environmental factors (Bandura, 1977). In elaboration, Donovan (1988) defines an addiction as:

> . . . a complex, progressive behavior pattern having biological, psychological, sociological, and behavioral components. What sets this behavioral pattern apart from others is the individual's overwhelmingly pathological involvement in or attachment to it, subjective compulsion to continue it, and reduced ability to exert personal control over it. Consistent with this perspective, addiction is seen as a total experience involving physiological changes in individuals (many of whom may be genetically and/or psychologically predisposed) as these are interpreted and given meaning by the individual within the sociocultural context in which the addictive behavior occurs. (pp. 5–6, 12–13)

Two points emerge from this definition. First, it advances the radically different notion that the core of any addiction is its pathological processes rather than the overt behavioral level of abuse of the specific object(s) of dependency. Thus, questions about the physical, emotional, social, and attitudinal experiences regarding the object of dependency are more important than the survey of frequency, intensity, and duration of abuse. Secondly, the definition holds that those addicted to different drug substances have much in common, such that productive research findings in one area can be adapted to another. For example, Cue Response Therapy, which was developed to help cocaine abusers successfully cope with a cocaine supply-rich environment, has now been utilized with clients having many other types of drug dependencies.

Elaborating on the above, Donovan, and Marlatt (1988) have outlined the five most common addiction processes according to the perspective of the biopsychosocial paradigm. They are as follows:

1. The addictive experience leads to a rapid change in one's mood and sensations as a result of both physiological experience and learned expectations.
2. Physiological and emotional disequilibrium is related to engagement in the addictive experience.
3. Previously neutral external and internal states become instrumentally conditioned to craving the addictive experience.
4. Engagement in the addictive experience, which brings short-term control, is experienced as out of control.
5. The likelihood of relapse is high, particularly when behaviors, thoughts, or situations that have a strong association with the addictive experience are involved.

A substantial and growing body of research on the assessment of and intervention in addictive disorders supports the biopsychosocial paradigm (Cooper, 1990), with each of the five most common addiction processes receiving considerable backing (Orford, 1985; Peele & Alexander, 1985; Donegan, Rodin, O'Brien, & Solomon, 1983; Marlatt & Gordon, 1985; Abrams, Niaura, Carey, Monti, & Binkoff, 1986). Compared to the earlier and well-known moral and disease models, the biopsychosocial viewpoint more closely parallels the "real world" experience of those with substance abuse problems (Cooper, 1989). Furthermore, failure to attend to the complexity of the biological, psychological, and sociological interactions involved in all substance abuse problems has probably led to reduced effectiveness of interventions (Donovan, Kivlahan, & Walker, 1986). Including genetic, physiological, and sociocultural factors within the biopsychosocial paradigm appears to offer a very comprehensive assessment framework and a great range of treatment options for those who work with addictive disorder clients (Cooper, 1989).

Commonalities of Addictions Recovery

The biopsychosocial perspective is applicable to the recovery process. Specifically, Prochaska and DiClemente (1983) have advanced a key theory in this area. The process of recovery is conceptualized as a sequence of four relatively discrete stages: precontemplation, contemplation, action, and maintenance.

The Precontemplation Stage

During the precontemplation stage, persons with addictive disorders do not yet recognize the need for any change. If a therapist were to conduct a biopsychosocially-based assessment at this point, he or she would uncover most or all of the five common addiction processes within the person and also would likely find an intrapersonal and interpersonal system both "struck" in the addiction and marked by significant denial of associated problems and consequences.

This precontemplation stage may last from months to years and sometimes parallels what Jellinek (1952) referred to as the "chronic" phase of addiction. This stage is not uncommon among a significant minority of the university population, i.e., those experiencing adverse effects of alcohol or drug abuse, yet believing that they don't have a problem. External pressures from authoritative sources such as student personnel deans or judicial boards, or "caring confrontations" from family and friends are often necessary to move the college student beyond the first phase.

The Contemplation Stage

The contemplation stage follows precontemplation. It is marked by an experience of ambivalence of motivation and commitment to change. Rosen and Leitenberg (1984) found evidence that this stage is also common among the anorectic and bulimic populations (which are concomitantly prevalent among college females). Biopsychosocially-based assessments conducted during this phase usually discover alternative periods of use and non-use and a greater willingness to be aware of consequences of the addictive behavior. Most college-age clients in this phase need help in resolving their motivational issues and in recognizing the extent of their addiction-related vulnerabilities and problems.

The Action Stage

Prochaska and DiClemente (1983) described the next step in the recovery process as an action stage, characterized by the person's attempts, either with or without external help, to deal with the addiction. The majority of research on addictions has been conducted on persons in this stage, as they are the ones most likely to have entered treatment (Marlatt, 1988). Intervention tools for this stage include the full range of biological, psychological, and sociological approaches. In the past few years, substance abuse service providers in university counseling services have witnessed a large increase in the number of students voluntarily seeking help for their problems with drugs and alcohol. These persons seem quite willing to accept abstinence as a necessary goal, and to work hard in addressing their therapeutic issues.

The Maintenance Stage

Although the final stage, maintenance, has previously been underinvestigated, it is now receiving considerable attention. Maintenance studies consistently demonstrate a high rate of relapse across most addictions (Abrams et al., 1986). The term "abstinence violation effect" was coined by Marlatt and Gordon (1985) to connote that an individual's likely return to full-scale addiction after a lapse is much higher if he or she attributes this slip to personal characteristics rather than to situational factors. In addition, research with several separate addictions, such as cocaine and heroin, has shown that the specific physiological, psychological, social, and situational factors that contribute to a client's initial addiction are the ones most likely to lead to a lapse that, when accompanied by negative cognitions, becomes a relapse (Washton, Stone, & Hendrikson, 1988; Brownell, Marlatt, Lichtenstein, & Wilson, 1986).

Some interventions seek to confront this pattern directly. For example, the new Cue Response Therapy mentioned earlier in this chapter is an attempt to apply extinction procedures to stimuli previously associated with use of and craving for cocaine. This method has the client repeatedly handle cocaine paraphernalia and deal with cocaine-intensive situations without using, until such time as these cues no longer elicit a craving for the drug.

With the biopsychosocial perspective, the use of ongoing assessment of and intervention in the personal, behavioral, social, and environmental worlds of the client provides the counselor or psychologist with multiple conceptual and pragmatic tools for dealing with the maintenance stage. The biopsychosocial viewpoint goes beyond the other psychological approaches with its emphasis on expanding the effects of treatment by working with the client's social and environmental networks.

Clinical Emphases

At each phase, the biopsychosocial view can be utilized to change the person and his or her behavior or immediate culture (Cooper, 1982). The biopsychosocial model explicitly calls for this, and for utilizing the reciprocal influences of person, environment, and treatment (Schwartz, 1982). Table 1 summarizes the relevant biopsychosocially-based techniques for each of the four stages of recovery.

A Multilevel Framework for Intervention

To better understand the biopsychosocially focused prevention and treatment effects at the college level, it would be helpful to the reader to have a general framework for treatment assignment and for integrating the importance of the special characteristics of each addiction. The following method has been labeled "differential intervention" (Cooper, 1989) or the "graded-intensity approach" (Marlatt, 1988).

Paul (1967) stated that the problem of psychotherapy is to find which approach works for which specific client in which specific situation. Although research has shown that some people (probably those who are more highly motivated and are in the action stage) overcome their addiction without outside assistance, most need some help. The first treatment level relies upon outpatient education and counseling, with an emphasis on dealing with the underlying psychological, social, and physiological issues. It works well for clients who exhibit mild addictive processes, i.e., those with only a light abuse problem. About more intensive treatment, Cooper (1989) stated:

Table 1
Educational and Counseling Implications of the Stages of Recovery

Stage	Clinical Emphasis
Precontemplation	External pressure, caring confrontation
Contemplation	Focus on enhancing motivation for change
Action	Behavioral, cognitive, and situational change
Maintenance	Prevention of abstinence violation effect

Adapted from "Stages and Processes of Self-Change of Smoking: Toward an Integrative Model of Change," by J.O. Prochaska and C.C. DiClemente, 1983, *Journal of Consulting and Clinical Psychology, 51,* 390–395.

> The second level of treatment is much more probable for a client who is referred by family or friends for a problem. Specifically, Level 2 treatment involves intensive individual outpatient work with group support and family counseling if it seems appropriate, i.e., as other family members are also involved in the disorder. This second level of treatment is usually necessary for those with moderate problematic abuse or disorder because of the intensity of the compulsiveness that persons with each of these problem areas experience. Level 2 treatment can also be used in a contract fashion for a client who is motivated to work hard and does not want inpatient treatment. Continuation of intensive outpatient interventions should continue as long as gains are made, but hospitalization becomes necessary if a client continues to decline in spite of treatment. The contract approach makes it more likely that resistant clients will accept and benefit from an inpatient program, if that becomes necessary. (p. 11)

Concerning the most intensive treatment, hospitalization, Cooper (1989) added:

> The third level of treatment is usually necessary for those with either severe or chronic [addiction] patterns. It consists of an inpatient program of stabilization, a forced breakage of negative behavioral patterns and preparation for the work to be done after hospitalization. When it is most productive, it prepares the client for Level 2 type interventions and for the adjustment of leaving a structured, secure environment. Education for possible lapses may be very important in preventing a relapse. (p. 11)

However, the goal of differential intervention is not to place clients with differing addictions together. Rather, the biopsychosocial perspective provides a general framework to develop and implement treatment applications and to conduct research on the effectiveness of programs. It offers a unifying model of understanding, equally useful to scientists and practitioners who are working on specific aspects of different addictions and dependencies.

Prevention and Intervention

Given the preceding discussion, it is obvious that different strategies, with some directed at persons, others at behavior, and others at the cultural environment, will be differentially effective for various individuals and sub-groups in the college population. What follows is a presentation of the prevention and intervention techniques that have received the most empirical research support in the college setting. While the target for each of these differs, there is an overall contiguity given by the biopsychosocial model. Table 2 outlines the principal activities involved in the discussion.

Person as Target

The study by Shedler and Block (1990) identified the negative emotional triumvirate of interpersonal alienation, poor impulse control, and manifest emotional distress among drug abusers. Maney (1990) similarly found that college students with low self-esteem and a low sense of well-being were much more likely to develop an abusive relationship with chemicals. Psychological maladjustment appears to be common

Table 2
Approaches to Drug Abuse Prevention and Intervention Based on a Biopsychosocial Perspective

Focus	Action Steps
Person	Educate about personal vulnerability to substance abuse effects.
	Promote attitudinal change about the drug experience.
	Teach environmental coping skills.
	Develop high self-efficacy beliefs.
Behavior	Set up a quick assessment referral system.
	Involve peers in monitoring use and abuse.
	Develop institutional policies and procedures.
Culture	Form support groups for abstinence or moderation.
	Create viable substance-free alternatives.
	Hold campus-wide antidrug activities.

among abusers. It seems apparent that prevention and intervention strategies that exclusively focus on information about drugs and their effects, without addressing these underlying psychological factors, would be less effective than those that also incorporate dimensions aimed at increasing self-esteem, social skills, assertiveness, and decision-making skills.

The integrated model of drug use prevention on campus by Gonzales (1989) suggests that abusing individuals only change when four processes occur. The abusers must: (1) see themselves as vulnerable to experiencing use or abuse related problems, (2) experience a change in attitudes and expectations of the drug, (3) have behavioral skills to deal with the college drug supply-rich environment, and (4) develop a sense of self-efficacy (i.e., the feeling that one can cope and have personal power). To meet these goals, colleges and universities employ substance abuse specialists to provide education diagnosis, treatment, and referrals when necessary. Extensive use of peer educators and counselors is also warranted, as the research has demonstrated their effectiveness. Regarding this point, Goodwin (1989) emphasizes the importance of utilizing the sizable group of mild to moderately using students who express high levels of concern about the effects of alcohol and drug abuse on their friends. Recruiting peer counselor-educators from this group would be a natural step, with creation of formalized Student Assistance Programs (modeled after industry's Employee Assistance Programs) being one service delivery possibility (Maney, 1990). Evidence of success in this area could be determined by a repeated assessment (pre- and post-treatment) of selected personal characteristics, such as self-esteem or assertiveness.

Behavior as Target

The settings where alcohol and drugs can or cannot be used may, to a limited degree, be influenced by institutional policies. For example, virtually all colleges have elaborate formal regulations in their student handbooks with prohibitions against substance use, plus sanctions for violations. Further, the courts are now holding institutions of higher education and smaller units, such as a specific fraternity, liable for accidents and damages related to substance abuse (Smith, 1989). Consistency in following these policies is important. Greater consistency in following restriction policies is warranted.

However, even the most effectively written and well-supported policies are generally inadequate in controlling addictive behavior. Utilizing peers as monitors is more productive. For example, there is a student organized and run committee at the author's institution that controls entrance into parties where alcohol is served and monitors infractions of the campus alcohol and drug use policies. This student committee has been given the authority and administrative backing to impose sanctions for violations. The results of its three-year history have shown good promise. Perhaps use of peers to moderate behavior eliminates the "us-them" mentality created when an administration seeks to exercise the same control.

Substance abuse behavior can also be reduced when students are sent for substance abuse assessments upon a first or second rule infraction rather than waiting for them to develop a chronic abuse pattern. Research has clearly demonstrated that the earlier the intervention, the easier and more effective it is (Cooper, 1989).

Developing this early referral system requires extensive coordination of substance abuse specialists with judicial boards, deans, and Residence Life staff. Evidence for success in this area would be available through student surveys and campus disciplinary reports.

System as Target.

Treating individuals without altering the environment is a very poor use of (usually very sparse) resources when dealing with substance abuse (Gonzalez, 1989). The use of alcohol and other drugs is heavily embedded in the campus culture. Only by focusing on facilitating changes in the culture can large numbers of people be affected. As an example, the unacceptability of drunk driving, with the consequent increase in legal penalties, is beginning to have a significant impact on reducing alcohol-related driving fatalities.

The primary mechanisms to alter the campus environment surrounding drug abuse include the following: (1) a vigorous campus-wide education program, (2) creation of viable and enjoyable substance-use-free social alternatives, and (3) provision of peer support groups for abstinence or moderation (as appropriate to the needs of the individual) (Gonzales, 1989). The social component of the biopsychosocial model would view these latter two suggestions as essential aspects of prevention and intervention. Effectiveness could be measured by recording activities and by comparing changes in student perspectives of the environment and of attitudes and behavior surrounding substance use and abuse.

Three Demonstration Programs

Three programs from the author's institution will highlight how colleges and universities can focus on person, behavior, and environment.

The At-Risk Program

The operational components of this program consist of eleven curriculum modules for workshops and presentations on alcohol/drug abuse information and coping skills strategies. All entering freshmen are tested with a brief 25-item questionnaire assessing the level of their substance use and experienced consequences. Those who score "at-risk," and who indicate consent to be contacted, are invited to an organizational seminar that combines information about the program, talks by other college students who are ex-abusers, and small group discussions. Participants are then free to select which of the eleven modules are appropriate for them. Consultation to make these selections is given at the time and made easily available afterwards. Evaluation of the "At-Risk" program consists of measuring changes in the individual student's behavior and attitudes before and after the program.

The Greek Social Responsibility Committee

As is true of most college and university campuses, the author's institution has a set of well-defined substance abuse rules and regulations. Also, like those of most other settings of higher education, these rules and regulations do not have a huge effect on reducing substance use and abuse. Utilizing the naturally occurring group of peers concerned about this issue offers an important opportunity for attitude and behavioral change.

The Greek Social Responsibility Committee (GSRC) is in charge of monitoring social functions at fraternities/sororities. Specifically, the GSRC works by controlling who enters these functions and who can be served alcohol. The goal of the program is compliance with state law (age 21 drinking minimum), campus policy, and fraternity guidelines. The GSRC, in conjunction with the Division of Student Affairs, has the power and authority to determine consequences for violations of the GSRC code. The committee was created and is governed by students. Since its inception, problematic use of substances, particularly alcohol, has been reduced at the monitored functions.

Wellness Program's Focus on Substance Abuse

The Office for Wellness Programs provides services for students, faculty, and staff of the university, and coordinates campus-wide activities in the area of wellness. Efforts to educate and change the campus culture vis-a-vis substance use and abuse are part of this campus-wide activity and are implemented in connection with the Office of Alcohol and Drug Education. In specific, the Office of Wellness Programs does the following: (1) sponsors Alcohol Awareness Week in the fall, (2) sponsors Drug Abuse Awareness Week in the spring, (3) coordinates Red Ribbon Day ("say no to drugs"),

(4) serves as co-advisor for BACCHUS, (5) sets up peer counselor-educator training sessions, (6) coordinates community service time for students arrested for minor consumption or DUI, and (7) serves as campus co-representative to the State Drug Abuse Prevention network. Partial feedback about the effectiveness of the campus-wide approach is obtained by examining changes in the drug section of the Lifestyle Assessment Questionnaire, which is administered to students in each fall term, and by examining the changes in abuse-related crime and disciplinary cases on campus.

Summary

This article has shown that drug abuse, particularly when including alcohol, is a major problem in colleges and universities today. Most institutions of higher education attempt to deal with college student abuse problems by implementing a range of solutions from formally-worded policy statements to the provision of extensive substance abuse educational, diagnostic, treatment, and referral services. Those programs that are most successful are based on the biopsychosocial perspective, viewing drug abuse as the product of a complex interaction of biological susceptibility, psychological factors, and sociocultural determinants. Concomitantly, successful collegiate antidrug programs have a balance of prevention and intervention efforts that equally emphasizes persons, their behavior, and the campus culture.

References

Abrams, D. B., Niaura, R. S., Carey, K. B., Monti, P. M., & Binkoff, J. A. (1986). Understanding relapse and recovery in alcohol abuse. *Annals of Behavioral Medicine, 8,* 27–32.

Bandura, A. (1977). Self-efficacy: Toward a unifying theory of behavior change. *Psychological Review, 84,* 191–215.

Brownell, K. D., Marlatt, G. A., Lichtenstein, E., & Wilson, G. T. (1986). Understanding and preventing relapse. *American Psychologist, 41,* 765–782.

Carroll, J. F. X. (1986). Treating multiple substance abuse clients. In M. Galanter (Ed.), *Recent developments in alcoholism* vol. 4 (pp. 85–103). New York: Plenum Press.

Cooper, S. E. (1982). Research into counseling and psychotherapy: A systems approach. *Counseling Psychologist, 10,* 62–72.

Cooper, S. E. (1983). Survey of studies on alcoholism. *International Journal of the Addictions, 18,* 971–985.

Cooper, S. E. (1989). Eating disorders and chemical dependency: Are they really so different? *Journal of Counseling & Development, 68,* 102–105.

Cooper, S. E. (1990). Biopsychosocial approaches to assessment of and intervention in addictive disorders. *Counseling and Human Development, 7,* 1–11.

Donegan, D. H., Rodin, J., O'Brien, C. P., & Solomon, R. L. (1983). A learning-theory approach to commonalities. In P. K. Levison, D. R. Gerstein, & D. R. Maloff (Eds.), *Commonalities in substance abuse and habitual behavior* (pp. 111–156). Lexington, MA: Lexington Books.

Donovan, D. M. (1988). Assessment of addictive behaviors: Implications of an emerging biopsychosocial model. In D. M. Donovan & G. A. Marlatt (Eds.), *Assessment of addictive behaviors* (pp. 3–50). New York: Guilford Press.

Donovan, D. M., Kivlahan, D. R., & Walker, R. D. (1986). Alcoholic subtypes based on multiple assessment domains: Validation against treatment outcome. In M. Galanter (Ed.), *Recent developments in alcoholism* vol. 4 (pp. 207–222). New York: Plenum Press.

Gonzales, G. (1989). An integrated theoretical model for alcohol and other drug abuse prevention on the college campus. *Journal of College Student Development, 30,* 492–503.

Goodwin, L. G. (1989). Explaining alcohol consumption and related experiences among fraternity and sorority members. *Journal of Counseling and Development, 30,* 448–458.

Jellinek, E. M. (1952). Phases of alcohol addiction. *Quarterly Journal of Studies on Alcohol, 13,* 673–684.

Johnson, L., O'Malley, P., & Bachman, J. (1989). Drug use, drinking, and smoking: National Survey Results from high school, college, and young adult populations, 1975–1988. *National Institute on Drug Abuse.* Washington, D. C.

Klein, H. (1989). Helping the college student problem drinker. *Journal of College Student Development, 30,* 323–331.

Maney, D. W. (1990). Predicting university students' use of alcoholic beverages. *Journal of Counseling and Development, 31,* 23–32.

Marlatt, G. A. (1988). Matching clients to treatment: Treatment models and stages of change. In D. M. Donovan, & G. A. Marlatt (Eds.), *Assessment of addictive behaviors* (pp. 474–484). New York: Guilford Press.

Marlatt, G. A., & Gordon, J. R. (Eds.). (1985). *Relapse prevention: Maintenance strategies in the treatment of addictive behaviors.* New York: Guilford Press.

Orford, J. (1985). *Excessive appetites: A psychological view of addictions.* New York: Wiley.

Paul, G. L. (1967). Strategy in outcome research in psychotherapy. *Journal of Counseling Psychology, 31,* 109–118.

Peele, S., & Alexander, B. K. (1985). Theories of addiction. In S. Peele (Ed.), *The meaning of addiction: Compulsive meaning and its interpretation* (pp. 47–72). Lexington, MA: Lexington Books.

Prochaska, J. O., & DiClemente, C. C. (1983). Stages and processes of self-change of smoking: Toward an integrative model of change. *Journal of Consulting and Clinical Psychology, 51,* 390–395.

Rosen, J., & Leitenberg, H. (1984). Exposure plus response prevention treatment of bulimia. In D. M. Garner & P. E. Garfinkel (Eds.), *A handbook of psychotherapy for anorexia and bulimia.* New York: Guilford Press.

Schwartz, G. E. (1982). Testing the biopsychosocial model: The ultimate challenge facing behavioral medicine. *Journal of Consulting & Clinical Psychology, 50,* 1040–1053.

Shedler, J., & Block, J. (1990). Adolescent drug use and psychological health. *American Psychologist, 45, 612–630.*

Smith, M. C. (1989). Students, suds, and summonses: Strategies for coping with campus alcohol abuse. *Journal of College Student Development, 30,* 612–630.

Tobler, N. S. (1986). Meta-analysis of 143 adolescent drug prevention programs: Quantitative outcome results of program participants compared to a control or comparison group. *Journal of Drug Issues, 16,* 537–568.

Washton, A. M., Stone, N. S., & Hendrikson, E. C. (1988). Cocaine abuse. In D. M. Donovan & G. A. Marlatt (Eds.), *Assessment of addictive behaviors* (pp. 364–389). New York: Guilford Press.

Discussion Questions

1. How serious is the alcohol and drug abuse problem on today's college campuses?
2. Who is involved in student substance abuse and dependency issues?
3. Why does drug abuse occur in some people, but not in others?
4. What is being done to eliminate or reduce drug use and to treat those with a dependency problem?
5. What are components of exemplary campus alcohol and drug abuse prevention and intervention programs?

Understanding Strategic Planning as an Emerging Drug Abuse Prevention Model

Thaddeus Rozccki

DeWayne J. Kurpius

Thaddeus Rozecki is a doctoral candidate in the Department of Counseling & Educational Psychology at Indiana University, Bloomington. Mr. Rozecki has worked in a variety of settings during the past ten years, most recently as the clinical director of a community mental health center specializing in the needs of the chemically dependent. He has published articles in the areas of drug use and prevention, strategic planning, counseling supervision, consultation, and ethics.

DeWayne J. Kurpius is a professor in the Department of Counseling & Educational Psychology at Indiana University, Bloomington. Dr. Kurpius has had a distinguished career in the field of Counseling Psychology, recently being named a Fellow of Division 17 (Counseling Psychology) and Division 13 (Consulting Psychology) at this year's American Psychological Convention in San Francisco. He is often sought out for his expertise in the areas of consultation, supervision, and systems. He has been widely published over the last twenty years in numerous professional journals and books.

Because of the enormity of the problems associated with drug use and abuse, the attention of many legislators, teachers, and mental health professionals has recently turned toward implementing prevention strategies for those who are in danger of becoming victims in the future. The hope is that through well defined and implemented prevention efforts this younger population can be steered away from involvement with drugs (Corry & Cimbolic, 1985; Bloom, 1984). Many of these prevention programs focus on educational methods that stress the dangers of drug use, the effects of drug use on the family unit, and the identification of healthy alternatives to drug use, which might collectively foster a new attitude for the youthful populations exposed to the program. Yet it is evident that strategies for designing and implementing such programs, while often well intentioned, are haphazard. For example, prevention strategies that stress the dangers of alcohol use can go unheeded in areas where the cultural norms stress the social benefits of drinking behavior. Many ethnic cultures that tolerate and even encourage some alcohol use have specific social remedies for dealing with those members of the population who become abusers, and these remedies are never mentioned in prevention programming (Pederson, 1988; Maloff, Becker, Fonaroff, & Rodin, 1985).

The numerous crises associated with the abuse of drugs in our country have reached enormous proportions during the last two decades. We have learned that drug use and abuse is a multifaceted issue that does not lend itself easily to short-term solutions. Any prevention or intervention initiative that specifically addresses only one area in the drug abuse arena is often hampered by its neglect of other areas (DuPont, 1982). Focusing on only one aspect of the problem more often leads only to short-term gains that are quickly eradicated by an emergence of other aspects of the larger problem.

Larger-scale attempts at intervention and prevention often suffer from the same fate. Although they use powerful and well-constructed strategies for dealing with the problem, they too often only redefine what the problem is and ultimately do little to solve it. Two current strategies that fit this mold are calls for the legalization of drugs and for legislation that increases penalties for drug abusers. If we only change the way that we deal with drugs in our legal system, it is obvious that the social, psychological, and political realities of drug use will be largely ignored.

In light of all these factors, how do we go about building a prevention or intervention program that is effective and still meets the needs of both the community and its individual members? What are the steps that have to be taken to ensure that all of the problems associated with drug abuse are defined and incorporated into the prevention model? Perhaps the best way to address these questions is by beginning to scrutinize more closely the strategies and programs that are currently in use.

Some Models of Prevention

Information Model

The information model that was prominent during the 1960s assumed that adolescents use drugs because they do not comprehend the negative effects resulting from the use of chemical substances, and that understanding the legal and medical consequences will keep them from becoming users. In fact, these programs frequently do increase students' knowledge about drugs, but they have been less successful at changing drug-using behavior (Goodstadt, 1981).

This failure might reflect the fact that knowledge alone rarely changes behavior. Many of the information programs also failed because they exaggerated the harmful effects of drugs. Predictably, such scare tactics undermined the credibility of the programs and the people who conducted them. (Ellikson & Bell, 1990).

The Affective (or General-Skills) Model

The affective model became popular during the 1970s. It assumes that adolescents use drugs to compensate for low self-esteem or because they have not developed effective communication and decision-making skills. This approach tries to bolster adolescents' self-esteem by helping them clarify their values and develop their skills. But it implicitly fails to recognize two important issues: (1) raising a young person's self-esteem is a complex task that is not likely to be accomplished by a short-term program; (2) it is not clear that adolescents readily make the connection between broad decision-making skills and their own actions in specific pressure situations. Moreover, many educators avoided any mention of drugs in the classroom because they did not want to be seen in the same light as those who subscribed to the information model for prevention (Ellikson & Bell, 1990).

The Social Influence Model

This model of prevention often falls under the more general category of psychosocial model and is currently very popular in dealing with drug abuse issues in the schools. Many of these types of programs have had success in anti-smoking campaigns and have reported significant results with pre-adolescent populations. (Flay, 1985; Maloff et al., 1985).

This model views initial experimentation with substances as a social phenomenon. Such programs present younger populations with ways to identify the pressures that are exerted on them by others to experiment with drugs, ways in which counterarguments can be used in refusing to participate, and simple techniques for refusing any offers ("just say no"). In providing relevant reasons why participants should refuse such offers, this type of programming stresses the immediate consequences of the decision and the way in which that decision will affect the participant in relation to his peers and environment.

The psychosocial models of prevention programming are typically fueled by social learning theorists such as Albert Bandura (1985), who stress that many behaviors are initiated and strengthened as a response to peer encouragement or approval and continue because of the desire to appear mature or independent.

Strategic Planning: What Is It and How Can It Be Used to Develop Prevention Programming?

Used correctly, strategic planning is a vehicle that can generate and guide prevention programming. In order to understand more about the strategic planning process, it is necessary to examine some of its key components and to examine the way it has been traditionally used in the business sector.

Strategy is used by organizational leaders to identify single actions covering a wide range of decisions, past and present, that result in shaping the image, culture, and performance of the organization. The strategy of an organization cannot be isolated to a single all-encompassing decision that provides purpose and direction over a long-term horizon. The organization develops a strategic design based on a series of significant decisions that relate and delineate the interdependence of the formulation, implementation, organization, and control phases of the policymaking process. Strategic plans form a linking device that connects categories of decisions at the various stages of the policy process. Each class of decisions has separate and distinct characteristics that permit the various classes to be analyzed and studied separately. Each successive set of strategic decisions is derived and flows from the preceding set. In terms of prevention programming, strategic planning would become the foundation on which the program would be built.

Experts propose that strategic planning is different from many other planning processes because it (1) is more process than product oriented, (2) utilizes visions as distinct from the steps needed to actualize those visions, (3) emphasizes involving as many stakeholders in the process as can be networked and included, (4) understands change as a significant force and not simply as an obstacle, (5) is fluid, long-term, and intuitive, and (6) is committed to the future survival of the people involved in the planning process (Gray, 1986; Davis, 1982; Bryson & Rearing, 1987).

Strategic planners are not necessarily decision makers, but they must raise issues and they must provide a process in search of solutions. The objective of strategic planners is to do everything they can to ensure that designated decision makers are making informed, conscious decisions. Strategic planners take the responsibility to see that the decision makers have whatever helps them to make those judgments in as informed a manner as possible, and that they are conscious of the potential consequences (Peter, 1986). The analytical processes involved in strategic planning are thus only as relevant as the real choices of action upon which they must focus.

Initially, both short- and long-range strategic planning shared three key assumptions: (1) environmental forecasting was believed to be sufficiently accurate to predict the future, (2) strategy formulation was viewed as a normative process by which objectives were formulated in hierarchical order, information was readily available, and alternatives could be neatly identified and optimized in the rational manner advocated by economic theory or management science, and (3) factors such as politics, self-serving interests, and psychological traits were seen as unimportant (Makridakis & Heau, 1987).

In general, the check list for strategic planning initiatives includes (1) Where are you (operationally, environmentally, and in terms of current capacity)? (2) Where do you want to go (assumptions and forecasts, possibilities, objectives)? (3) What opportunities or constraints can you identify that will affect movement toward desired ends (federal and state law, competition with other providers, and new technologies)? (4) How do you get there (policies, strategies, resources)? (5) Who is responsible (organization, staffing, delegation)? and (6) How do you monitor results (priorities, outputs, budgets, controls) (Fox, 1987)?

Thus, the multidimensional-dimensional nature of the strategic planning process stresses planning as (1) *a central control system* with explicit objectives, strategies, and review procedures, (2) *a framework for innovation* ensuring the regeneration of the enterprise, (3) *a social learning process* emphasizing cultural trust, confidence, and mutual direction in the methods for coping with unfamiliar problems in uncertain environments, and (4) *a political process* in which not only consensus but bargaining among interest groups is highlighted (Taylor, 1982). It provides the community with needed information, is sensitive to the psychological needs of the people, emphasizes social learning and trust, and stretches to encompass the political and cultural issues of the day. It is long-range but sensitive to the current environmental climate.

Who Are the Strategic Planners in a Community?

In developing prevention or intervention strategies the question of authority and control arises. In the strategic planning process, participation by the widest variety of parties is encouraged. Each community or school is unique in its orientation and environment, and the number of people involved in the planning process will vary, but it is important to remember that, generally, the greater the representation from the school or community the more powerful the plan. Many school planning sessions have included experts in mental health and chemical dependency, outside consultants, administrators, teachers, school counselors, parents, business leaders, and even students.

A Strategic Planning Model for Prevention

The strategic planning model that follows has been field tested and implemented in a variety of settings. Wherever the project has been implemented, it has been imperative for the leadership team to fully understand the dynamics of the process, paying particular attention to the consensus style of decision making practiced in the model. This would be essential in the formulation of a prevention or intervention plan. The steps that follow are common across most comprehensive planning models. The steps in the model are:

I. Articulating the Foundation
- Beliefs
- Creating a Vision
- Defining a Mission

II. Assessing the Forces
- Analyzing External and Internal Factors
- Generating and Assessing Essential Policies

III. Formulating the Plan
- Specifying Objectives
- Generating Strategies
- Implementing Action Plans
- Recycling

I. Articulating the Foundation

Sharing Beliefs

Planning models that focus primarily on technical and analytic tasks such as problem definition, analysis and diagnosis, monitoring, and outcomes may overlook factors that are crucial to planning and implementation (Brown, 1986). Participatory research and involvement in the strategic planning process begins with a shared definition of the group's beliefs.

There are many beliefs about the use of drugs in a school or community. Some believe that experimentation is acceptable or that alcohol use in the home with parental supervision is an appropriate social learning tool. Others believe that all substance use is intolerable and must be discouraged at all costs. In order to form an effective prevention program, these beliefs must be shared and eventually formed into a series of statements that clearly indicate what the school or community as a whole believes. This is certainly not an easy task, but is fundamentally imperative in beginning the prevention planning process.

An example of a consensus belief statement from a number of opposing parties might emerge as:

"We believe that the *promotion* of the use of drugs *cannot* in any way be the responsibility of the school or community. We further believe that the school and community must publicly be steadfast in their nonacceptance of drug use by those under the age of eighteen in any public circumstance. Although parents have the right to make decisions about substance use in the home, they should not allow any public display of drug use behavior that might influence other members of the community. In other words, parents should reinforce the notion that permission to experiment with legal substances such as alcohol in the home does not constitute acceptance of public displays of drug use by their children."

Many other belief statements will emerge from the group at this stage. It is important that each belief statement be analyzed and incorporated into a succinct whole that emphasizes the most important characteristics of the overall beliefs of the group.

Many communities will be encouraged to bring in drug experts at this point in the process. Michael (1973) states that if in-depth exploratory planning activities are not made available, then the expert's models will simply remain models. Expert and participant must share in the learning experience so that a joint reconceptualization of problems/goals can occur, and the possibilities for concerted action be discovered.

Simply put, beliefs serve two functions. They provide the value system on which the foundation of the plan will be built, and they become part of the published plan, serving as a public declaration of the organization's heart and soul. The beliefs are a formal and precise expression of the organization's values, code of ethics, and overall convictions. The focus is not on long, rambling, hazy philosophical statements.

The Visioning Process

Creating a vision of the future begins with a respect for cultural diversity and the differences in perspective, to which all planners can adhere. Ultimately, the vision should be tied to a set of explicit beliefs on which the key actors in the school or community have reached consensus.

In strategic planning, the vision of how the community would like to see things change is developed without the usual bias of investigation, which emphasizes what could go wrong. This differs from other forms of planning which begin by investigating those forces, both internal and external, that might impede or improve the chances for a certain goal's ultimate achievement. It is the portrait of a future that includes the purpose and hope of the entire culture. Without this vision statement, strategic planning would not have the power necessary to formulate changes within the community and could not hope to draw upon the combined intelligence and motivation of its members.

During the visioning process, consideration of the pragmatic boundaries that often limit other plans (e.g. insufficient funding, community apathy, peer promotion of substance use) should be temporarily curtailed. Vision statements do not include artificial boundaries. One example of such a statement is:

> We envision our community (or school) as a drug-free oasis. That is, a place where students and teachers can interact without the sale, distribution, or use of drugs, and where talk of drugs and the usual problems associated with drugs are only a subject of investigation in the classroom, and not a reality.

Developing the Mission Statement

The mission statement is a succinct expression of the community's vision that has been grounded in the beliefs. It represents the fundamental character of the members and purpose of the organization. The remainder of the prevention plan is guided by the unique qualities and purpose of the community or school as presented in the mission statement.

For internal members (such as teachers, community leaders, or students), the mission statement provides a focal point for the concentration of energy. The mission becomes the communal agenda for all organizational members. For the designated leadership of the organization, the mission statement provides the means to help organizational subdivisions or components find the underlying purpose and function toward which all must endeavor in order that the prevention plan function effectively and achieve success. The mission statement helps the prevention plan manager put into perspective the parts as they relate to the whole. For those stakeholders not employed by the organization (such as parents), the mission statement is clearly a means to bond them to the plan.

The components of a mission statement include audience, action, and aim. The direction of the mission statement is toward those persons, seen as an audience, who will benefit from the plan. The outcomes toward which the organization works are the expressed purpose or aim in the mission statement.

The mission statement, then, is an integration of beliefs and vision culminating in a clear and concise statement of distinct organizational purpose. It identifies the reasons why the organization exists. It provides focus and direction, and it allows the organization to advertise its unique mission. A sample mission statement such as the one below could become the rallying statement for the school or community plan:

> Sample Mission Statement
>
> To provide alternatives, activities, and support to all members of the school community who are opposed to the use of chemicals and who are seeking alternatives to their use. The school corporation in partnership with the community, is committed to serve all members of the community with programs that meet the highest standards of excellence.

II. Assessing the Forces

External and Internal Organizational Analysis

As prevention planners look toward the future, most agree that one of the first steps is the identification, definition, and prediction of events and conditions that will affect movement toward the mission. Understanding the meaning and subsequent impact of these events or circumstances is the second step in the analysis of external forces that impact the community or school mission. Preparation for these events or circumstances through effective anticipation and adaptation is the third step of conducting an external organizational analysis. In other words, the school officials or community members who are involved in the planning process must examine the events that they see as likely to come about (e.g., cuts in funding, increased school population), the overall effect those events will have on the prevention process (e.g., not enough money for data collection, less staff time, more children who might need to be involved in the training), and what steps can be taken in the present that can address those concerns (e.g., searching state or federal grants that can assist in the prevention process, fund raising within the community, more involvement from parents to help with prevention activities).

For any school or community, the trends and developments related to the prevention enterprise, as well as the surrounding environment's impact, require periodic examination. Specific external forces to be addressed in the external analysis include demographic, political, economic, social, and technical factors that affect movement toward the mission.

The internal analysis involves the identification of the internal context and culture of the prevention enterprise. This analysis includes a study of the human and structural factors that impact movement toward the mission. Internal analysis is the community's self-analysis and requires honesty and objectivity in order to be successful.

Analyzing the impact of these human and structural factors in terms of their directional strength requires determining their supporting or hindering movements or roles toward the mission. Lewin (1951) initially argued that "force field analysis," which describes the relationship between hindering and supporting forces, should be conducted in order to point out the existence or nonexistence of a dysfunctional equilibrium. Others suggest that the directional strength and malleability of hindering forces should be attacked first. Delimiting negative forces as well as accentuating positive forces demands the attention of strategic planners in the selection of organizational objectives and strategies.

Essential Policies.

Cook (1986) has stated that essential policies are the other side of the mission statement. In this strategic planning process, essential policies are the self-policing parameters by which community members agree to plan and work They are essential to the success of achieving the mission or goals in the strategic prevention plan.

Essential policies are central to the planning process in that they affect what organizational members will either do or will not do. They align community or school behavior with the mission. The essential policies provide the covenant that binds behavior to the public declaration of the community's heart and soul that is embodied in the mission statement. Without essential policies, the mission statement becomes a meaningless slogan. Finally, essential policies become a new set of cultural norms.

Some examples of policy statements best communicate what essential policies are. From the private sector, a well known essential policy is "We will sell no wine before its time," or, "We make money the old-fashioned way—we earn it." In human service organizations, examples of essential policies might include: "The prevention of chemical abuse in the community will not be undertaken simply as a lower-cost alternative to intervention and treatment."

III. Formulating the Plan

Objectives

The next step in the planning process is the development of a set of community or school commitments that will be used to obtain specific and measurable end results. These commitments are expressed as objectives, and they must be aligned with the mission statement described earlier. Generally, objectives are intended outcomes stated in such a way that their attainment (or lack of it) can be observed and measured. They can deal with the knowledge, comprehension, application, analysis, synthesis, and evaluation of goals that are implied by the broader mission statement. Objectives guide prevention planning members by describing, responding to, valuing, organizing, or characterizing specific actions that more completely emphasize the realization of the community's vision.

Writing and owning objectives create public commitment to priorities, resources, utilization, responsibility, time lines, and standards. It creates risk and accountability in a responsible way. Objectives should not become a millstone that can never be changed. Some objectives need to be refined, adjusted, or even disregarded when data suggest such a change.

Strategies

Strategies signify the deployment of resources toward programs or activities designed to improve the welfare of clients and/or patrons. In terms of prevention planning, strategies act as the flags signifying commitment for the community or school program. They efficiently deliver the message of prevention and emphasize the emotional side of the issue.

Strategies spring from stated objectives. They represent the general method by which the mission and objectives are translated into operational terms. They are not specific tactics. They should be stated in any way that will not reduce them into logistical plans. Rather, strategies are statements that describe the position and/or the type of intervention that the community or school will take in order to achieve its mission.

Action Plans

Action plans are the step-by-step directions for implementing all of the previous stages of the plan. They act as the road map for the implementation of both objectives and strategies, and clearly represent the way in which the mission will be accomplished, the analysis conducted, the policies put into force, and the vision realized.

Specific action plans and teams are developed for those school or community members whom the plan will most directly affect. They are those staff members closest to the direct delivery of services to the students. These staff member teams each select an objective and corresponding strategies meeting the objective, and then delineate specific tasks and guidelines that are necessary to establishing the changes desired. In addition, action plans outline the resources necessary for the accomplishment of the objectives. Action plans also mention those individuals who have the primary responsibility of carrying out the specific work plan indicated by each strategy, and the general strategy outlined by each objective. Action planners are required to describe how those individuals will be accountable for completing the task.

Recycling

Because strategic planning is not simply a linear or hierarchical process, it is essential that all steps in the process be constantly reexamined and evaluated. Not only is it important for the plan itself to be scrutinized, but for the specific actions taken as a result of the plan to be reviewed and recycled by all members of the community or school. In general recycling means monitoring the vital signs of each component of the planning process to guarantee that the organization's vision will be realized.

A School Case Using Strategic Planning as the Primary Prevention Strategy: Rosetown High School

Rosetown High School does not actually exist. But the strategic planning process that is demonstrated by this case is a combination of techniques and ideas taken from a variety of actual school corporations that have approached the prevention of chemical abuse at the high school level using a strategic planning perspective. This case illustrates the way in which the strategic plan is formed and the information that is often necessary for its implementation and evaluation. Although no two cases will ever appear exactly alike, prospective planners can gain from this case example insight into the possible successes and failures of prevention-oriented strategic planning.

Background Information

Rosetown is a small midwestern community with a population of about 15,000 people. It is generally a service-oriented community with little industry and few manufacturing centers. For the most part, the people of Rosetown are employed in a large urban industrial center about 30 miles from Rosetown, or support themselves by selling artisan crafts and other items. Rosetown is a popular tourist area in the spring, summer, and fall months, and all of the local businesses cater to the tourist trade. It is estimated that about 2,000 tourists a day visit the town between the months of May and November. Because of this influx of outsiders during these months many of the businesses hire high-school students to work in the shops or the restaurants. The high-school students who are not working do not have any particular place to gather in the town except for high-school sponsored activities which are generally sports events. Rosetown High School serves students from a multi-county area and houses academic as well as vocational programs. It graduates about 400 students per year, 30 percent of whom continue on to college. The remainder of the students either work in agriculture, attempt to find jobs in Rosetown, or seek employment in the larger urban area where many of their parents work. Many of the teachers in the school have already taught the second generation of students from a number of community families (i.e., sons and daughters of former Rosetown High School students).

Drug Abuse Problems in the School and Community and Past Strategies

Rosetown, like many of the neighboring towns in the area, has experienced problems with substance abuse during the last ten years. The use of alcohol has increased steadily as well as the use of marijuana, hallucinogens, tranquilizing agents, and cocaine. Recently, "crack" cocaine has begun to be used in the high-school population. Information regarding the use and accessibility of drugs has for the most part been a function of the police department, which has estimated usage based on the number of arrests in the community and the surrounding area. In the high-school, surveys have been used to try to estimate the size of the problem, but the results have been disappointing, with only 10 percent of the student population choosing to answer the surveys. Rumors have begun to circulate among the high-school staff that the primary school population is beginning to see signs of alcohol and marijuana use as well.

The local newspaper has recently rated drug abuse as the number two problem, only slightly behind other crimes that have been steadily increasing, such as robbery and vandalism. Some community officials have suggested that there is a connection between substance abuse and the increase of other crimes in the area.

The Culture of Rosetown

In order to assess the potential impact of the strategic planning initiative it is important for planners to understand the specific cultural context in which they will be working. In terms of the dimensions of culture presented earlier, Rosetown:

(a) values its individuals and believes generally that individuals are good.
(b) has generally operated from a hierarchical order both in the community and school system.
(c) is in harmony with the natural resources of the area.
(d) focuses on the past in general and discusses the "good old days" at some length.
(e) values success as most important.
(f) does not highly value individual differences except as they apply to artistic work.
(g) expects individual members to learn the culture independently.

Beginning the Planning Process

The principal and school board of Rosetown High School have begun to realize they have a problem that cannot be handled by the usual method. In the past, drug problems have been treated as isolated events that could be eliminated by specific remedies. This is how past drug policies took shape in the school. The principal would distribute posters to the teachers to post in the classroom, identifying the dangers of substance abuse. This, in effect, was the extent of prevention strategies. On an intervention level, strict school policies about drug and alcohol use on school ground were implemented. Although these policies reduced drug abuse violations within the school, many more students were suspended or expelled, causing increased anxiety in the community. Students began to realize that the use of illegal substances on school property could be avoided by gathering in the community at large in order to use and distribute drugs. Law enforcement officials blamed the school system and the parents, and school officials blamed the lack of effective law enforcement policies. School officials began to realize that although interventions might reduce the problem, without effective prevention strategies the next generation of high-school students would certainly be in danger.

Forming a Strategic Planning Team

The principal of Rosetown High School, in conjunction with the teachers' union representative, the superintendent of schools, the Parent-Teacher Organization leadership, the Rosetown student council, the director of the Rosetown chamber of commerce, support staff from the high school, a counselor from the county mental health center, law enforcement administration, a prominent town physician and the at-risk counselor from the school system, organized a town meeting. It was felt that the larger the group in attendance the better the chances of starting a planning process. From that meeting delegates were elected to participate in the strategic planning initiative whose initial aim was to reduce the amount of drug abuse in the high-school population and to promote a drug-free lifestyle for all the citizens of Rosetown during the next five to seven years. It was explained that the process of strategic planning would be the foundation for the collective approach to the drug abuse issue and that the responsibility for the success of the planning process and the plan itself would ultimately be the responsibility of all members of the school and community, and not just specific administrative officials. One member from each of the larger groups was selected as the contact person who would eventually be responsible for informing the other members of the groups, whether it be teachers, students, parents, business people, law enforcement officials or community mental health workers, about progress in achieving the aims of the plan. These members would meet twice per month for the next three months in order to formulate the initial plan.

Planning Meeting I: Understanding the Process and Listing Beliefs

The principal of Rosetown High School hired an outside consultant to review the strategic planning process with the designated planning team members, and to attend their first meeting so that an appropriate list of beliefs could be formulated and then distributed to the other members in the community for their comments. Some of the 30 belief statements about substance abuse that came out of that meeting were:

- The Rosetown High School should in no way promote the use of chemical substances in its classes or condone the socially conscious use of alcohol.
- The Rosetown community understands that there is a growing drug abuse problem in the community and that the responsibility for change rests with all members of the community.
- The Rosetown community believes that the effect of ignoring this issue would be an increase in drug use in the high school, intermediate school, and eventually elementary school populations.

Planning Meeting II: Establishing a Vision and Writing a Mission Statement

In this phase the edited belief statements were collected and used to form the foundation for the long-range vision of the community and subsequently the mission statement that would drive the rest of the plan. The Rosetown planning team published the mission statement in the local newspaper and distributed it at all school-sponsored events. In addition community businesses were asked to give this mission statement a place of prominence in their stores. The mission statement, as it emerged from the beliefs and the vision, was the most visible anchor for the community in its struggle to eliminate substance abuse related problems in the community:

> The Rosetown Community Mission
> Regarding Substance Use
>
> To provide for the entire Rosetown community a sense of unified action against all forms of alcohol and drug abuse, by actively promoting alternatives to substance use, encouraging creative displays of the dangers of substance use, seeking arenas where the youth of the community can actively participate in drug-free behaviors, and supporting school, community, and law enforcement officials in their active attempts to eliminate all chemical use.

Planning Meetings III and IV: Analyzing the Situation and Formulating Essential Policies

These meetings represented the planners' attempt to look at the community and the school objectively and to raise questions about the way in which the plan could eventually be implemented. It was important that all the planning members realized that they were part of a consensus-based change process and not simply delegates who steadfastly held to one opinion. Perhaps the greatest changes in the way that a school or community views the drug problem and subsequent prevention strategies appear during this assessment phase. Some of the issues that the Rosetown planners discussed were budgeting issues for prevention, leadership in the school and community, enforcement policies, enlisting outside aid and resources, tourist use of alcohol in the community, overall effects of prevention planning on community growth and income, and the relationship between substance abuse and other problems such as vandalism, family abuse, and teen pregnancy.

Essential policies that grew out of these meetings included: "We are not simply attempting to prevent drug abuse, but to promote knowledge, compassion, and a strong belief in the youth of our community," and "We will never sacrifice our youth to make a dollar."

Planning Meetings V & VI: Putting the Plan into Action

Having completed the more conceptual phases of the prevention planning process, the planning team set to work to establish those objectives, strategies, and action plans that would identify the individuals and groups in the school and community who would have primary responsibility for the plan's implementation and for the specific ways in which those groups would operate. Although the objectives and strategies are too numerous to list, some of the ideas are listed below.

Student Council: Members of the student council will be involved in three money-generating projects during the next year to help provide support for an artist workshop series that all students could attend. T-shirt sales that used slogans promoting drug-free creativity, dances in the town square, and parent-student competitive sports events have been suggested.

Parents: A parents' prevention group has been formed whose primary responsibility is to publicize the mission and essential policies of the plan and to offer assistance in the classroom on specific projects and Saturday sessions focusing on various topics.

Teachers: Teachers have elected delegates who will receive training from the community mental health center on techniques to foster positive lifestyle changes in the classroom and who will be responsible for training other staff members in the school during the upcoming 18 months.

Law Enforcement: Police officials have volunteered blocks of time during the next year to participate in youth events. They have also assumed the responsibility of publicizing drug-related arrests and are actively providing drug users with an alternative to incarceration through direct community service.

Other groups were made responsible for public relations, fund raising, material acquisition, and review of the strategic plan as it progressed and changed. Meetings to discuss the success or failure of the action plan were held quarterly in the school auditorium.

Some less positive events surfaced during the implementation of the plan, which should also be briefly mentioned:

> Teachers protested the anti-smoking policy set forth by the administration.
>
> Tavern and restaurant owners in the town were concerned at the plan's possible diminishment of alcohol sales.
>
> Parents who worked outside of town complained of time constraints, and some refused to participate in any prevention strategy that involved using free time.

The attitude of consensus and the broad support of the community in the formulation of the plan helped in the negotiation and remediation of these and other problems. The review procedure worked well in identifying those specific actions that were generally believed to be the most effective in achieving the mission and vision of Rosetown.

Some Final Notes on Rosetown

The strategic planning process that focused on prevention strategies helped Rosetown evaluate its own priorities. It is clear that without broad community support and a continuing effort on the part of all the planning participants, the end results would have been minimal. It is also clear that single prevention strategies that come about simply as a reaction to events in a school or community are usually too limited in their scope and fail to define the problem adequately.

Summary

Because of the immediacy that surrounds the question of drug abuse, there is a tendency to search for short-term strategies that will generate long-term positive results. Prevention strategies cannot be viewed in these terms if we hope for them to be successful. There is of course a desire to focus on the drugs themselves as the only culprit. The strategy that emanates from such a philosophy is that removal of the cause is the surest way of eliminating the problem. It is sometimes possible, however, to mistake the motive for the cause. For youth wishing to assert their independence, break tradition, gain power and control, or escape the abuses existent in some dysfunctional families, drug use can offer a powerful enticement. It is not clear in many of these cases what the alternative would be if drug use were totally eliminated. Positive alternatives to drug use as a solution to inadequate self-esteem and depression need to be modeled and encouraged in order to be effective. Self-help groups, although powerful, are formed only after the problem has surfaced and has manifested itself in a number of different behaviors. Prevention seems a long road, but one that is worthwhile in the end.

A strategic planning initiative that focuses on prevention can be the socially activating event that cements a school or community together. It is time to examine more closely its potential for success in combatting social problems.

References

Bandura, A. (1985). *Social foundations of thought and action.* Englewood Cliffs, NJ: Prentice-Hall.

Bloom, B. (1984). *Community mental health: A general introduction* (2nd ed.). Monterey, CA: Brooks/Cole.

Brown, D. (1986). Participatory research and community planning. In B. Checkoway (Ed.), *Strategic perspectives on planning practice* (pp. 123–138). Lexington, MA: Lexington Books.

Bryson, J., Freeman, R., & Rearing, W. (1986). Strategic planning In the private sector. In B. Checkoway (Ed.), *Strategic perspectives on planning* (pp. 65–86). Lexington, MA: Lexington Books.

Bryson, J., & Rearing, W. (1987). Applying private-sector strategic planning to the public sector. *American Planning Association Journal. 53*(1), 9–22.

Corry, J., & Cimbolic, P. (1985). *Drugs: Facts, alternatives, decisions.* Belmont, CA: Wadsworth Publishing.

Davis, S. (1982). Transforming organizations: The key to strategy is context. *Organizational Dynamics, 10*(3), 64–80.

Dupont, R. (1982). Drug abuse prevention comes of age in the '80s. In P. Carone, S. Yoles, S. Kieffer, & L. Krinsky (Eds.), *Addictive disorders update* (pp. 60–106). New York: Human Science Press, Inc.

Ellikson, P., & Bell, R. (1990). *Prospects for preventing drug use among young adolescents* (R-3896-CHF). Washington, DC: The RAND Corporation.

Ellikson, P., & Robyn, A. (1987). *Toward more effective drug prevention programs* (N-2666-CHF). Washington, DC: The RAND Corporation.

Fox, H. (1987). Strategic planning in small firms. In W. King, & D. Cleland (Eds.), *Strategic management and planning handbook.* New York: Van Nostrand Rheinhold Company.

Flay, B. (1985). Are social psychological smoking prevention programs effective? The Waterloo Study. *Journal of Behavioral Medicine, 8,* 37–59.

Goodstadt, M. (1981). Planning and evaluation of alcohol education programs. *Journal of Alcohol and Drug Education, 26,* 1–10.

Goodstadt, M. (1978). Alcohol and drug education: Models and outcomes. *Health Education Monographs, 6,* 263–279.

Gray, D. (1986, January, February). Uses and misuses of strategic planning. *Harvard Business Review,* pp. 89–97.

Ibrahim, F. (1985). Effective cross-cultural counseling and psychotherapy. A framework. *The Counseling Psychologist, 13,* 625–638.

Kluckhorn, F., & Strodtbeck, F. (1961). *Variations in value orientations.* New York: Harper & Row.

Kurpius, D., Burrello, L., & Rozecki, T. (1990). Strategic planning in human service organizations. *Counseling and Human Development, 22,* 1–9.

Lewin, Kurt. (1951). Field theory in social science. In

D. Cartwright (Ed.), *Field theory in social science: Selected theoretical papers.* New York: Harper.

Maloff, D., Becker, H., Fonaroff, A., & Rodin, J. (1985). Informal social controls and their influence on substance use. In N. Zinberg, & W. Harding (Eds.). *Control over intoxicant use* (pp. 53–76). New York: Human Science Press.

Makridakis, S., & Heau, D. (1987). The evolution of strategic planning and management. In W. King & D. Cleland (Eds.), *Strategic management and planning handbook.* New York: Van Nostrand Rheinhold Company.

Michael, D. (1973). *On learning to plan and planning to learn.* New York: Josey-Bass.

Moskowitz, J. M. (1989). The primary prevention of alcohol problems: A critical review of the research literature. *Journal of Studies on Alcohol, 50,* 54–88.

Pascale, R., & Ouchi, W. (1974, September, October). Made in America (under Japanese management). *Harvard Business Review,* 294–301.

Peter, M. (1986). Failures in strategic planning. In J. Gardner, R. Rachlin, & H. Sweeny (Eds.), *Handbook on strategic planning* (pp. 11.1–11.13). New York: John Wiley & Sons.

Pederson, P. (1988). *A handbook for developing multicultural awareness.* Alexandria, VA: American Association for Counseling and Development.

Shein, E. (1985). *Organizational culture and leadership.* San Francisco, CA: Jossey-Bass.

Shein, E. (1990). Organizational culture. *American Psychologist, 45,* 109–119.

Taylor, B. (1982). New dimensions in corporate planning. In B. Taylor, & D. Hussey (Eds.), *Realities of planning.* Oxford: Pergamon.

United States Department of Education (1986). *What works: Schools without drugs.* Washington, DC: United States Department of Education.

Zinsberg, N., & Harding, W. (1982). Control over intoxicant use: A theoretical and practical overview. In N. Zinberg, & W. Harding (Eds.). *Control over intoxicant use* (pp. 13–37). New York: Human Sciences Press.

Discussion Questions

1. List some earlier models of prevention and the ways in which they dealt with information about substance abuse.
2. What are the basic steps in a strategic planning model?
3. How does the future orientation of the strategic planning process allow for prevention strategies to be incorporated?
4. How do the culture and needs of the community become part of the planning process?

V

Part V—Drug Decriminalization

What major approaches can be used to decrease current drug consumption? Three models currently exist; they are: the *decriminalization* model, the *maintenance* model, and the *punitive* model. The decriminalization model wants to remove the criminal charges and penalties levied against drug users. Advocates of this approach differ regarding the extent to which they want to decriminalize drugs. Some people would prefer decriminalizing all drugs. Others want to remove criminal sanctions on only milder, less powerfully addictive drugs.

The main reasoning behind decriminalization is that: (1) it is illogical to allow one group of drugs, tobacco and alcohol, to remain legal and sold over the counter while a second group of drugs is banned and its use is a violation of law, (2) punishment for drug use stigmatizes and ostracizes large numbers of people, who, as a result, become even more committed to using drugs, (3) drug testing, surveillance, entrapment, and the like represent invasions of privacy, (4) the criminalization of illicit drug use focuses on punishment instead of treatment and rehabilitation, and (5) the punishment approach has not been effective and has overburdened our criminal justice system. Upholding laws against drug use compels the criminal justice system to concentrate large numbers of personnel and an extensive amount of human power and resources to fighting the consumption of illicit drugs. The effort to control drug use occurs at *the expense of* either alleviating or at least lessening other more serious crimes, such as murder, robbery, and fraud.

Maintenance, the next model, relates to decriminalization because it advocates that addicts—mainly narcotic addicts—should be supplied with the drug or substitute drug. Generally, the narcotic drug is methadone. Methadone is a substitute for heroin, and it is dispensed by government funded clinics. Reasoning behind this approach is that the addict will not be preoccupied with committing crime in order to momentarily support the addiction if a steady supply of the narcotic drug is available. Supporters of this model contend that if maintenance programs are implemented, crime will be cut at least in half!

Maintenance programs identify addicts who do not respond to rehabilitation and provide them with a steady supply of the much sought after drug. The assumption behind these programs is that if the state or some other type of government agency dispensed the drug, demand would drastically decrease. Curtailing demand eliminates the need for dealers and the organized crime that profits from supplying drugs to dealers.

Abadinsky (1989) further elaborates on three different models of legalization/decriminalization. The first model advocates that addictive types of drugs be dispensed "only through government-controlled clinics and only for short-term treatment purposes" (p. 273). Under this model, methadone is the only drug that is allowed to be dispensed on a long-time basis. The second model advocates that other powerfully addictive drugs can be prescribed by licensed physicians on a maintenance basis. Unauthorized use or marketing of addictive drugs would be a violation of law. The third model is the most inclusive, because it allows all powerfully addictive drugs to be sold to adults over the counter. Abadinsky reminds us that this was the case in the United States before the Harrison act was passed.

The punitive model is the last model we will be reviewing. This model has been used in the United States for over 75 years. It suggests that drug use is widespread because American society is too lenient with drug users and suppliers. The "war on drugs" declared by the Reagan administration was a manifestation of this model for preventing drug use. Another proponent of the spirit of the punitive model is William J. Bennett, the former "drug czar" under former President Bush who staunchly believed that we need " . . . a bigger criminal justice system as a form of drug *prevention*" (Bennett, 1989, p. 53).

The punitive model wants harsher sentencing, and a "zero tolerance" drug policy as outlined by Robert

DuPont (1984). Zero drug policy means "... no drug use in the schools, none in the workplace, none on the highways and none in the families. Sanctions need to be swift, effective, and broadly supported by all segments of our society." Although Dupont's stand on zero tolerance appears unrealistic, the U.S. Government in Washington continues to uphold the belief that the elimination of drug use is an achievable goal.

The debate for and against legalization or decriminalization is indeed a polemic issue. The main arguments and evidence *for* legalization or decriminalization are as follows:

1. Legalization would remove the drug trade from organized crime and children and reduce the crime and vice associated with illegal drug trade activity.
2. Legalization would allow our society to focus on preventive education. (As we did with educating the public about the harmful effects of nicotine drug use.)
3. We need to give decriminalization a chance, since punishment for drug use has not worked. After all, there has been greater success in diminishing the effects of legalized drugs than in diminishing the use of prohibited types of drugs. Several cases in point: regarding nicotine and alcohol, low tar and low nicotine cigarettes have nearly replaced the once standard filterless, high nicotine cigarettes. "Lite" beers and wine coolers are slowly gaining popularity and an increasing share of the market.
4. Failure of the current punitive model for restricting drug use is exemplified by the fact that the war on drugs has had its turn to succeed. During the 1980s the drug war reached all of its goals. Incarcerations increased—over one million drug arrests occurred in 1989. There have been record seizures and strongly funded antidrug publicity campaigns. Hundreds of thousands of urine tests have been conducted on employees. Yet, despite all the surveillance, arrests, confiscation and monitoring, before the "Reagan war," "war on drugs," "zero tolerance" and creation of the office of the "drug czar" we neither had the development of crack nor ice (Zeese, 1990, p. 6).
5. Legalization will allow the law to fulfill its purpose, that is to encourage civilized conduct, by driving a wedge between the drug user and the criminal (Riley, 1990).
6. Repeatedly, research shows that major drug busts increase demand by diminishing supply. When the supply diminishes, prices for drugs increase, which in turn entices more dealers to enter drug dealing (Tovares, 1989).
7. What about using the military for interdiction purposes as a method for stopping the amount of drugs entering the country, by militarizing the Mexican border? Has this been successful?

> Reagan's Miami Vice
>
> The [former] administration focused its interdiction efforts in South Florida. High-tech military surveillance aircraft were recruited in the war on drugs. Colombia's traffickers quickly realized that marijuana was too bulky to ship undetected. But they also discovered that cocaine could be transported in briefcases, suitcases, even within human bodies.
>
> These methods of moving coke easily penetrated the administration's hi-tech net. The upshot was that cocaine became cheaper. (Zeese, 1990, p. 38; Adler, 1985)[1]

8. Under the Reagan administration, our prison population went from 329,821 in 1980 to 677,402 at the end of 1988 (Trebach & Engelsman, 1989). Those incarcerated were " . . . serving a sentence of one year or more for drug related and other crimes" (p. 42). During this eight-year period, the prison population grew at the unprecedented rate of 90.2 percent. Trebach and Engelsman ask, how far do we want to run up the number before we realize our drug policy is ineffective? Will this solve the problem? How much expansion of the criminal justice system has to occur before legal sanctions against drug use become effective?
9. Trebach, a professor of criminal justice at American University in Washington, D.C. and Director of the Drug Policy Center states that,

> When we go over all the epidemiological data, we see that despite all the drug use, despite all we hear and despite the pockets of horror that we have, this is the healthiest generation of youth in our history. In 1983, for the first time

in our history, the death rate for youths 15–24 went below 100 per 100,000. Though there is a lot of contradictory data concerning the drug situation, one thing is clear: we are not losing our youth to anything, including drugs. (Trebach & Engelsman, 1989, p. 41)

10. Research shows that heroin and morphine addiction is a lifetime affliction that does not respond to the punitive model currently in effect (Schmoke, 1989).
11. The Maryland Drug and Alcohol Abuse Administration indicates that crime rates drop significantly when treatment, as it would result from decriminalization, is available (Schmoke, 1989). In one Baltimore study of the 6,910 residents admitted to drug-abuse treatment in 1987, 37 percent had not been arrested one or more times during the 24 months before admission to treatment. Out of 6,698 who were discharged during the same year, 91.8 percent were not arrested during the time spent in treatment.

The main arguments and evidence *against* legalization or decriminalization are:

1. While legalization would reduce the addicts' need to commit crime, it would increase the total number of addicts. The reality is that drug users cannot go to school or hold jobs. Therefore, Wilson, a Professor of Management and Public Policy at UCLA, contends that drug users would either commit crime or expect welfare benefits to survive on a daily basis, even if the daily "fix" were supported by the government.
2. Legalization is elitist, racist and immoral. It would have its most devastating effects on the economically deprived. We would be writing off hundreds of thousands of poor children to lifelong drug addiction.
3. Wilson believes that legalizing drugs would lead to a dramatic increase in use, further destruction of human personality, and a skyrocketing increase in accidents and violence (Wilson, 1990).
4. Former drug "czar" Bennett (who continued to influence the direction of national drug control policies in Washington, D.C.) concurs with Wilson. He says that when drugs are more readily available and when they drop in cost, drug use and especially addictions dramatically increase. "In opium and cocaine producing countries, addiction is rampant among the peasants involved in drug production" (Bennett, 1989, p. 23).
5. Further, Bennett believes that legalization could reduce the extent of drug gang and dealer types of crime, "... but unless you are willing to distribute drugs freely and widely, there will always be a black market to undercut the regulated one" (Bennett, 1989).
6. The proof that prohibition for the past seventy years is successful and drastically diminishes drug use is found in statistics. When the users of legitimated drugs such as tobacco and alcohol are combined there are 400,000 deaths per year. Compare this figure with "the death toll from the use of all illegal drugs which was only 3,562 in 1985" (Morganthau et al., 1988).[2]
7. Until the mid-1960s, physicians in Britain were allowed to prescribe heroin to certain classes of addicts. After the 1960s, Britain legalized methadone maintenance. In 1960 there were 68 heroin addicts and later in 1968 2,000 were in treatment. "At a minimum, the number of British addicts increased thirty fold in ten years" (Wilson, 1990, p. 23).

Up to this point we have looked at arguments and evidence regarding this issue from a pro/con perspective. Now in moving to the three articles comprising Part V we provide currently available additional research that will add to our understanding of the controversy surrounding drug decriminalization.

The first article, "The Futility of the War on Drugs," by McWilliams, begins Part V by providing a necessary historical review and analysis of the past 75 years, since the enactment of the Harrison Act. McWilliams finds evidence that the federal government's war on drugs has failed to eradicate or even substantially reduce drug use and abuse in the United States. On the contrary, the author asserts, efforts to eliminate the drug scourge have created a credibility gap, enabled bureaucrats and legislative leaders to exploit the drug issue for political gain, and produced inconsistent antidrug legislation. This essay is essentially a historical critique of America's drug war.

In the second article, "Between Legalization and War: A Reconsideration of American Drug Policy," Adler continues with the wide scope of analysis initiated by McWilliams, but in a different vein. In her analysis, Adler assesses both the merits and the problems of our current drug policy. Looking at the social psychology of drug use, the author begins by examining the problems coinciding with drug use in terms of individuals, crime, violence, and public health. Next, Adler assesses both the financial and social costs associated with current drug policies. Adler discusses how our current punitive drug policies are financially burdensome, require and promote an extensive amount of legal and social repression, create crimes, and cause deleterious and profound international effects. From a social control perspective, the author also looks at how the entire criminal justice system has become overwhelmed and preoccupied with drug offenses. This single concern with drug offenses has seriously affected such branches of the criminal justice system as our state prosecutors, the courts, and the prison system.

Adler believes that to continue the massive campaign against drugs will require an all-out societal investment that can only be accomplished by cutbacks in other areas, such as education and public health. The author cautions us that in the near future, important choices must he made regarding where our public efforts are best invested.

The outcome of Adler's findings, and her prognosis, is that we should begin considering alternative middle-range strategies of approaching drugs, somewhere between war and legalization, from the decriminalization policy of the 1970s to the normalization policy found in the Netherlands, to models based on harm assessment, harm reduction, and public health concerns. In summary, Adler advocates more moderation, *humaneness,* and *civility* in our efforts to understand and control drug use and abuse in our society. Her suggestion is not to be taken lightly when considering that the "war on drugs" has failed.

The last article, "The Sociology of Reefer Madness: The Criminalization of Marijuana in the United States," by Elsner, takes a more restricted focus than the two previous articles in Part IV. Instead of critiquing the entire drug war, as do the articles by McWilliams and Adler, Elsner concentrates on one very controversial drug that continues to be strongly debated. The crux of the marijuana debate is whether this drug, which is also perceived as a "gateway drug" like alcohol and nicotine,[3] should be legalized, and by extension, decriminalized. Marijuana is one of the mildest types of illicit drugs available, and users as well as many nonusers believe that it should be decriminalized.

Elsner begins by looking at the social origins of the Marihuana Tax Act of 1937, whereby federal legislation criminalized cannabis. The author reports that historians and sociologists have two competing theories about the factors that resulted in passage of the Act. The first theoretical explanation is the "Anslinger Hypothesis." This hypothesis says that the moral outrage against marijuana that one federal bureaucrat felt became manifested as a legislative crusade.

The second theoretical explanation, the "Mexican Hypothesis," asserts that the federal marijuana prohibition was enacted because of anti-Mexican pressure exerted by southwestern localities. While evidence for either theory is weak, Elsner provides a synthesis of the two views that he refers to as the "Social Control Hypothesis." In this article, Elsner also explores the anti-marijuana scare films of the 1930s, the notion of marijuana as a "stepping stone" to harder drugs, and the decriminalization of marijuana in the United States.

Notes

1. For an excellent in-depth case study analysis of how upper-level drug dealers prosper in their illegitimate business as suppliers despite the "war on drugs" and "zero tolerance," see Patricia A. Adler's *Wheeling and Dealing*: (1985).
2. Methadone is an addictive substitute drug that satisfies the need for heroin without providing the experience of a high, by blocking the withdrawal pains that occur during heroin abstinence.
3. "Gateway drug" refers to milder types of drugs that are believed to lead the way to other more addictive drugs, such as cocaine and heroin. The belief here is that the use of milder drugs directly leads to more serious drugs. While in part the evidence shows that most cocaine abusers started by using alcohol and nicotine, it is also true that most users of alcohol, nicotine and marijuana never progress beyond these drugs.

References

Abadinsky, H. (1989). *Drug abuse: An introduction.* Chicago, IL: Nelson Hall Publishers.

Adler, P. A. (1985). *Wheeling and dealing.* New York: Columbia University Press.

Bennett, W. J. (1989). A response to Milton Friedman. *The Wall Street Journal, 19,* A37.

DuPont, R. (1984, September 26). Two prongs in a winnable assault on drugs. *The New York Times,* p. A22.

Morganthau, T., Mc Killop, P., Cerio, G., & Sandza, R. (1988, May 30). Should drugs be legal? *Newsweek,* pp. 36–38.

Riley, N. (1990, May 5). Letters from readers: On the legalization of drugs. *Commentary, 88,* 4–12.

Schmoke, K. (1989, Summer). A war for the surgeon general, not the attorney general. *New Perspectives Quarterly, 6*(3).

Tovares, R. (1989, December 22). How to solve the drug problem: Legalize. *National Catholic Reporter,* p. 1–22.

Trebach, A., & Engelsman, E. (1989, Summer). Why not decriminalize? *New Perspectives Quarterly, 6*(3), 40–44.

Wilson, J. Q. (1990, February 2). Against the legalization of drugs. *Commentary, 89,* 21–28.

Wilson, J. Q. (1990, May 5). Letters from readers: On the legalization of drugs. *Commentary, 88,* 4–12.

Zeese, K. B. (1990). America has already lost the war on drugs. In N. Bernards (Ed.), *War on drugs: Opposing viewpoints,* (pp. 36–40). San Diego, CA: Greenhaven Press.

Zeese, K. B. (1990, May 5). Letters from readers: On the legalization of drugs. *Commentary, 88,* 4–12.

The Futility of the War on Drugs

John C. McWilliams

John C. McWilliams is Associate Professor of American History at the Penn State-DuBois Campus, where he teaches a course in federal drug policy. He has published *The Protectors: Harry J. Anslinger and the Federal Bureau of Narcotics, 1930–1962,* and several articles in academic journals. Currently, he is working on a manuscript-length historical analysis of federal drug control.

During a decade of prohibition in the 1920s, to eradicate the evils of alcohol as part of a "Noble Experiment," Congress passed the Volstead Act and appropriated just over $88 million to enforce the Eighteenth Amendment. When adjusted for inflation, that amount converts to roughly $500 million in 1992, when Congress appropriated $12.7 billion for the 1993 fiscal year alone, in yet another war on drugs. That figure represents a more than 100 percent increase since the Bush administration allocated $6.1 billion when it launched a war on drugs in 1989. Despite these fantastic increases in government expenditures, we have accumulated an abysmal record in trying to eradicate drug abuse.

In an attempt to improve on its past performance, Congress passed the Omnibus Anti-Drug Abuse Act in November 1988, which former President Ronald Reagan signed into law the following month. The most notable elements of this law are its provisions for tougher enforcement of drug statutes and stiffer penalties for drug offenders.[1] Less than a year later, in September 1989, then-President George Bush outlined his plan for fighting the drug scourge in a nationally televised address. Though the drug problem had become more intensified during the 1980s, neither the legislation nor the President's proposals contained any significantly innovative strategies for achieving a drug-free society, however realistic that goal may be. Rather, politicians seemed content to recycle strategies that were not effective in the past, and which offered little reason to suspect that they would be more effective in the 1990s.

During the Reagan-Bush war on drugs the federal government experimented with many diverse solutions intended to reduce or eliminate drug trafficking, unfortunately with little success. Crop eradication has not been effective and is probably unrealistic. It strains credibility to think that cutting off the supplies of coca leaves in South America, for example, will stop the flow of drugs into the United States or significantly reduce the demand among American users.

Military intervention, zero tolerance, interdiction, and demand-reduction are other techniques that have been tried—unsuccessfully—to solve the drug problem. A later strategy implemented by the Bush administration in a recent phase of its war on drugs, "Weed and Seed," was at least more innovative, in contrast to the strategies above. The objective of this program, which was adopted in Kansas City, Trenton, Philadelphia, and Omaha, is to "weed" drug dealers and gangs out of inner-city neighborhoods, then "seed" the community with social services such as health centers and public housing to prevent a reemergence of drugs. The initiative was commendable, but a $500 million allocation for all of our major cities was woefully insufficient. Recent proposed measures, both state and federal, were intended to send a "get tough" message to casual users, drug addicts, street dealers, and major traffickers. Finally, something new, it seemed. Actually, though, very little about such proposed measures was new.

The drug problem is serious, it is real, and though it may improve, it is not likely to disappear entirely, despite the last administration's goal of reducing drug abuse and achieving a drug-free society by 1995. Objectives of this sort reveal a naiveté about drug use that affects the public's perception about drugs and results in a credibility gap. Politicians, eager to convince constituents that they are serious about getting tough with drug offenders, and reluctant to risk losing their constituents' support, have failed to realize how firmly entrenched drugs have been in American society throughout our history, or to recognize the irresistible appeal drugs hold.

Simply put, people take drugs to feel good, not to feel bad. People take drugs to experience euphoria, to escape reality, even if only for half an hour on a rock of crack-cocaine. For many users, maintaining a drug habit is even more important than eating, at least according to journalist James Mills, who calculated that more money is spent on illegal drugs than on food, housing, or clothes. Estimates of how much Americans spend on illicit drugs range from $100 billion to $150 billion a year. Political scientist James Q. Wilson calculates that in the early 1990s we consumed perhaps as much as 60 percent of the world's illicit drugs. Representative Charles B. Rangel (D-NY), who chaired the House Select Committee on Narcotics (until Congress decided not to reauthorize it in January 1993), claims that the figure is over $100 billion. By contrast, the federal government spent $46 billion on all criminal justice programs in 1990.[2] It is painfully evident, as *Philadelphia Inquirer* columnist Claude Lewis argues, that "people believe more in drugs and alcohol than they do in themselves." Regrettably, our politicians, who have demonstrated a greater willingness to exploit the drug issue than to face harsh realities, have continued to enact the same kind of legislation that has been ineffective in the past. They have tended to ignore important facts and have perpetuated myths and misconceptions about drugs and about solutions. Political leaders who continue to endorse ineffective policies have also ignored history, and, in sounding like firebells in the night, they have compromised their veracity and have contributed to a sense of futility in the war on drugs.

Antidrug proposals also have been and continue to be enacted by policy-makers who have never seen a crack house, or a "shooting gallery," and who have never lived in a neighborhood plagued with drugs and drug-related crime. Journalist Jefferson Morley addressed this issue when he quoted ABC news anchor Peter Jennings, who said, "Using it [crack] even once can make a person crave cocaine for as long as they live." According to Morley, "When it comes to crack, politicians and pundits literally do not know what they are talking about." He is right. But it is not just crack that legislators are unfamiliar with, and this credibility problem did not emerge with the appearance of this powerful new form of cocaine.

In the 1930s, commissioner Harry J. Anslinger (1892–1975) and the Federal Bureau of Narcotics (reorganized as the Bureau of Dangerous Drugs in 1968 and again as the Drug Enforcement Administration in 1973) determined that a "new" drug, marijuana, was a dangerous substance that led to insanity and caused the user to commit heinous violent acts while under its influence. The government's pronouncements about drugs and their effects have been questioned ever since. By the mid-1930s, Anslinger, the nation's first drug czar, had generated enough publicity—hysteria would be more accurate—about this "killer weed" that Congress finally decided in the spring of 1937 to conduct hearings on the legality of the drug. In testimony before House and Senate committees, Anslinger reaffirmed his belief that marijuana was indeed a deadly drug and should be prohibited. To support his unfounded claims, he cited numerous cases, graphically describing acts of violence allegedly related to marijuana smoking.

Not once did a senator or congressperson challenge Anslinger to provide evidence substantiating the link between marijuana and such violent aggression. It mattered little that he did not have any. He did not need it, for the legislators inquiring about marijuana were not even certain what the drug was—one of them even confusing it with loco weed.[3] Only one voice of protest, that of Dr. William C. Woodward, who was the legal counsel for the American Medical Association, questioned the wisdom of outlawing marijuana without the benefit of testimony from expert witnesses who could support or refute claims that marijuana use had reached epidemic proportions in the nation's schoolyards. But the committee treated him contemptuously and cavalierly dismissed his testimony.

It was also in this milieu that Anslinger and the FBN enthusiastically endorsed the grade-B production *Reefer Madness* in 1938, just a year after the enactment of the Marihuana Tax Act. Essentially, the purpose of the 75-minute film was to deter school-aged youngsters from experimenting with a "drug more dangerous than heroin" by graphically demonstrating the effects one would experience after smoking a reefer of marijuana. In the opening scenes a stern, no-nonsense school official, addressing a group of alarmed parents, tells them that marijuana is more threatening than other "harder" drugs, that it produces violent behavior, and that the drug's permanent effects include insanity. This information, the speaker notes, was furnished and documented by agents from the Federal Bureau of Narcotics.

Throughout the sensationalistic movie there are numerous erroneous or highly exaggerated depictions of the use and effects of what Anslinger called the "assassin of youth."[4] In one scene, after a teenager smokes a joint he is overtaken by uncontrollable laughter and races his car through town, eventually running down an innocent bystander. In other situations even the smoking technique is inaccurate (when subjects handle and inhale a reefer in much the same manner they would a tobacco cigarette), and violent behavior is routinely anticipated as a consequence of smoking marijuana. The distortions of fact in *Reefer Madness*—approved by the Narcotics Bureau—only served to perpetuate myths about marijuana and to seriously hamper attempts to evaluate the drug's effects through controlled, scientific experimentation. By discouraging further research on the drug, the government laid the foundation for a credibility gap that has endured to the present.

More than a half century after Anslinger and the Treasury Department launched its crusade against the "killer weed," we must still exercise caution when the government issues reports about a drug epidemic. Certainly the drug menace permeates every strata of our society and touches virtually every community. But what is the real magnitude of the problem? President Bush told us that "the drug crisis reaches everywhere and is so dangerous it threatens government and its last bastion, the presidency itself." The drug problem is pervasive, but President Bush's penchant for exaggeration resembled that of Harry Anslinger when, during a nationally televised address in September 1989, to dramatize how easily crack could be obtained, even in the nation's capital, he held up a plastic bag that he said was "seized a few days ago by Drug Enforcement Administration agents in a park across the street from the White House." It was a bag of crack, he told the viewers, bought in Lafayette Park, directly opposite the White House on Pennsylvania Avenue. The president did not inform his audience, though, that drug deals in the park were virtually unknown. He also did not tell us that the sale was set up at his request by DEA agents who lured Keith Jackson to the park for a photo-opportunity bust. The hapless offender was a Washington, D.C. teenager who could not even identify the location of the White House.

Bush's proclaimed war on drugs, which he pledged would be waged "neighborhood by neighborhood, block by block, and child by child," did little to restore the government's credibility for at least two reasons. First, he failed to convince us that he was serious about a more consistent and comprehensive approach. While the Reagan administration, for example, declared war on drugs and admonished the young segment of the population to resist peer pressure, it drastically reduced DEA and Customs funds as well as numerous social programs, such as Head Start and CETA, that would make it easier for deprived young people to "just say no."

The second problem had to do with President Bush's proposed financial appropriation to fight a war against drugs. In his 1989 address, for example, he announced his total expenditure: $7.9 billion, the largest increase in history. Of this amount New York City would receive $30 million, or the equivalent of one half of one percent of its own current budget. As columnist Thomas Oliphant observed, "only amid the smoke and mirrors of Washington could a president be said to propose something he has already proposed," since his crime proposals earlier that year included more than $7.1 billion. In effect Bush was not asking for $7.1 billion, but only for an additional $717 million.

The former president used tough rhetoric when he talked about fighting drugs, but he was reluctant to make an all-out commitment. The $8 billion he proposed in 1989 and the $12.7 billion for 1993 seems like a lot of money, until one realizes that the Medellin cartel in Colombia may take in $16 billion a year in cocaine profits, in the United States alone. Put another way, Americans spend five times more annually to buy drugs than the government spends to eliminate them.[5] A close analysis of related drug expenditures also indicates that $8 billion dollars was not nearly enough. For international aid to cocaine-producing countries,

Bush asked for $449 million, which amounted to $2 billion over a three-year period, to wipe out the cocaine cartels in Colombia, Peru, and Bolivia. That figure, staggering as it is, does not equal the Medellin cartel's annual "income."

The government has seemingly condoned inconsistent messages that shape public and legislative perception toward licit and illicit drugs. The media are even more confusing. While one television commercial or magazine advertisement warns us about the problem of drug abuse, another promotes its drug product as a remedy for insomnia, an ache and pain reliever, or a tension reducer. Daily we are bombarded with the message that drugs—certain legal drugs—are acceptable. An adult is expected to understand the difference. A child, though—and many adults as well—may wonder why it is permissible to purchase one drug sold over the counter while possession of another drug could result in a fine and a prison term, especially when the child hears that both drugs produce similar results.

For a school-aged person this is no easy distinction. Simply put, marijuana, cocaine, heroin, and similar drugs are illegal because they are addictive, mind-altering, and physically harmful.[6] They are also illegal because of what Gary Trudeau once identified in his "Doonesbury" strip as "an accident of history."

Alcohol and tobacco, of course, are legal substances. But they, too, are addictive, mind-altering, and physically harmful. With the exception of a minimum age limit, no other restrictions apply to their purchase. They are easily accessible, for sale in pharmacies and grocery stores. Not only are they legal, much of the public does not even refer to them as drugs in conversation or in publications, as indicated in the use of the phrase "drugs and alcohol," implying that alcohol and tobacco are non-drugs and that they are somehow more permissible and less threatening to our mental and physical well-being.

As political scientist Ethan Nadelmann (1988) of Princeton University has concluded, "No illicit drug is as widely associated with violent behavior as alcohol." According to the Justice Department, slightly more than half of the violent offenders convicted in 1983 said they consumed alcohol before the offense. We are inundated with statistics linking alcohol to violent crimes, economic losses, and traffic deaths. Suffice it to say that our culture tolerates the social usage of a drug that is directly or indirectly responsible for 200,000 or more deaths each year.

Regrettably, Nadelmann's observation is consistent with a June 1992 study in the *Journal of the American Medical Association* that estimated that 40 percent of all college students are "binge" drinkers. This trend is also reflected in Bureau of Justice statistics indicating that nearly one-third (29.2%) of state prison inmates were under the influence of alcohol at the time of their arrest. Clearly, alcohol is one of our most serious substance abuse problems.

Tobacco is even more deadly. The number one preventable cause of illness and death in the United States, this drug is responsible for taking nearly 400,000 lives per year. This figure represents ten times the number who die from all illegal drugs combined. Tobacco kills more Americans—57 deaths every 79 minutes—every year than were killed during World War II. There is little consistency in our drug policies when more people die from legal drugs than from illegal drugs. There is no consistency in our policies when we export 100 billion cigarettes of tobacco—a drug some addicts say is more difficult to give up than heroin—to other countries every year. Nor is there congruity when our government uses tax dollars to fund cancer research while simultaneously subsidizing the tobacco industry.

We know that alcohol and tobacco, though legal, are harmful. What many of us do not realize, however, is how much more dangerous they are, and how many more lives they disrupt, than illicit drugs. According to federal estimates, 13 percent of the nation's adult population are plagued with alcohol-related problems, as compared to six percent of the same population who abuse legal drugs. Alcohol abuse is also a greater drain on our economy, costing $117 billion annually.

Tobacco and alcohol kill 35 times as many people as heroin and cocaine. Yet, too many of our politicians tell us that they are laboring to enact legislation that will enable us to achieve a drug-free society. A commendable and certainly desirable goal, but naive and unrealistic. Ours never has been a society without drugs, and there is no reason to expect that it will become one in the near future. Use of alcohol in our culture dates back to the Mayflower, morphine was in widespread use during the Civil War, and opium could easily be purchased in the form of pain killers and cough mixtures into the twentieth century. In fact, according to Edward M. Brecher (1972), "The United States of America during the nineteenth century could quite properly be described as a 'dope fiend's paradise.'" With many Americans taking advantage of an absence of government regulations, and physicians, drugstores, and general stores selling opiates without prescriptions or over the counter, it is easy to understand how extensive the drug problem was a century ago. The tragic but inescapable reality is that, to paraphrase H. Rap Brown, drugs are as American as cherry pie.

The philosopher George Santayana once observed that those who do not remember the past are condemned to repeat it. Regrettably, Congress and Presidents Reagan and Bush proved this exhortation by supporting and enacting legislation that is doomed to fail. Antidrug legislation enacted in 1984, 1986, and again in December 1988, the proposed $8 billion program outlined by Bush in September 1989, and a $127 billion allocation for 1993 were attempts to get serious about the drug problem and deal more harshly with drug dealers. To do this, these pieces of legislation contain provisions for longer prison terms and mandatory sentences; even the death penalty was proposed under certain conditions in the 1988 legislation. Few realize, though, that no evidence exists to suggest that this kind of "get tough" approach will work, and at least three prior instances suggest otherwise.

The first example was the Boggs Act, sponsored by Democratic Congressman Hale Boggs of Louisiana and passed in 1951. Responding to an anticipated increase in the number of postwar addicts, which commissioner Anslinger predicted would occur, this act escalated sentences for possession, first offense, to two to five years with possible probation. A second offense was punishable by a five-to-ten-year sentence, with no probation and no suspended sentence. A 10–20 year sentence was handed out for a third offense.[7] Anslinger was convinced that only long, mandatory sentences would deter drug offenders, and he argued that the increase in drug use was attributable to judges who were too lenient in sentencing violators. Presumably, the Boggs Act, with its stiffer penalties, would significantly reduce drug trafficking.

But even those draconian penalties did not satisfy the Narcotics Bureau. Just four years later, at Anslinger's prodding, Texas Democratic Senator Price M. Daniel, a member of the Senate Judiciary Committee, chaired subcommittee hearings for the express purpose of enacting even more severe sentences.[8] The legislation sailed through Congress with little opposition. When Senator Herman Welker (R-ID) asked Anslinger, as a witness, if the "Marijuana user has been responsible for many of our most sadistic, terrible crimes in the nation, such as sex slayings, sadistic slayings, and matters of that kind," the commissioner confirmed that in some instances that was true, and that the marijuana smoker was "completely irresponsible."

Not only did this kind of testimony exacerbate the credibility problem, it perpetuated the drug hysteria and reinforced the notion that if long, mandatory sentences were good, then longer, mandatory sentences were even better. The Narcotic Control Act of 1956 that came out of the Daniel hearings essentially doubled the Boggs penalties. The first possession offense carried a two-to-ten year sentence, second possession a mandatory five-to-ten years and no parole, third offense a mandatory 10–40 years with no parole, and for a person selling heroin to a minor (under 18 years old), the punishment was 10 years to life with no chance of parole, and imposition of the death penalty if recommended by a jury.

That Congressman Boggs and Senator Daniel were at that time preparing to launch gubernatorial campaigns in their respective home states is not insignificant. Politics and policymaking are virtually inseparable, certainly where drug legislation is concerned. Little changed in the ensuing thirty years; after the passage of the 1988 Anti-Drug Abuse Act, one congressional staffer sardonically concluded that the "primary purpose of this legislation is to re-elect members to Congress."

The third instance occurred nearly two decades after the Narcotic Control Act. When use of marijuana and the hallucinogenic LSD had "filtered up" into affluent white, middle-class communities, politicians again felt compelled to get tough. Responding to public pressure in 1973, New York Governor Nelson A. Rockefeller sponsored state legislation designed to deter drug dealers. Known as the "nation's toughest drug law," it contained three provisions designed to incapacitate heroin dealers. For Class A-I offenders, people who either sold one ounce or possessed two ounces, the law mandated a minimum prison term of 15 to 25 years and a maximum life sentence. Class A-II offenders, those who sold one-eighth of an ounce or possessed one to two ounces, received mandatory six to eight and one-third years and a maximum life sentence.

If spending time behind bars were sufficient to deter traffickers, enactment of the New York code should have resulted in a decrease in drug-related crimes. It did not. According to criminal justice historian Samuel Walker (1989), "The law had little if any effect on the crime rate." In fact, in 1976, after the new legislation had been in effect for three years, heroin use in New York City remained at about the same level. Worse, serious property crime—including, burglary, robbery, and assault—commonly linked to heroin users, actually increased 15 percent. Nor did the new law deter heroin use, which was as widespread in 1976 as it was prior to the enactment of the legislation. It also did not deter convicted felons from committing additional crimes or lower the recidivism rate, which remained about the same. What it did do was force dealers to begin using juveniles, who were not included in the Rockefeller law. As Walker observed, "The net effect on drug use and crime in New York was nonexistent."

Final Thoughts

Before we can develop more effective and more rational solutions to the drug problem, we must gain a better understanding of it. Our politicians should be more informed about the drug subculture. They should be more knowledgeable about the nature of addiction and the addict's desperate need to sustain his or her habit. They should realize that addicts who are capable of robbing or killing a person for $100 a day will show little reluctance to rob or kill for $1,000 a day. They should also know that these people are not likely to curtail their habit because they face the possibility of spending time in prison, even 10 years or more. They must also recognize the tremendous hypocrisy and inconsistency in the laws regarding the legal drugs alcohol and tobacco, as contrasted with illicit drugs.

Politicians have given too little consideration to the consequences of the "get tough" approach to the drug problem. Solutions are often hastily conceived and poorly formulated; they tend to be too visceral and unrealistic. Mandatory or minimum sentences, lengthy prison terms without the option of probation or parole do not sufficiently deter drug offenders, and, according to history, they will not work. What these policies will do, however, is place a tremendous and unrealistic burden on a prison system that is ill-equipped to handle the thousands of drug users who will enter the correctional system if such antidrug laws are strictly enforced. One immediate consequence of enforcing recent drug policies is a phenomenally large number of drug convictions and a burgeoning inmate population of about one million, for the first time in our history. That figure is expected to double in another seven years. An even more dubious result of these policies is that in 1992 the United States had the highest incarceration rate in the world, and black males were imprisoned at nearly five times the rate of South Africa.[9]

State prisons, which hold 85 percent of the drug convicts, cannot build cells fast enough. Also, few states can afford the projected $80 million it would take just to keep up. In 1989, Pennsylvania Commissioner of Corrections David S. Owens calculated that his state system was already 48 percent over capacity, and he predicted that the "current population of 20,000 inmates would double within nine years" under the Bush plan. In 1983, the inmate population at the Rockview State Correctional Institution, near State College, Pennsylvania, was approximately 900. In August 1992, the population had swollen to more than 2,000 inmates, of which 1,500 were double-celled.[10]

Pennsylvania is not unique. Officials in South Carolina have estimated that its 14,000 inmates will double by 1994 and that a new prison would have to be constructed every three months just to keep up with the increase. Paradoxically, while an increasing number of drug offenders are brought into the system, prison officials in 42 states are under court orders to reduce their populations. Little wonder that Connecticut Commissioner of Corrections Larry Meachum has become cynical about the drug war, arguing that "What we're doing today is making a mockery out of the entire process." Anthony Travisano, the Executive Director of the American Correctional Association, seemed to sum it up best, noting that "We have spent

$20 billion on correctional building since 1978 and the crime rate hasn't been affected."

Our prison system incapacitates drug offenders, and it does keep them off the streets. It does little, however, to rehabilitate them adequately or to prepare them for reintegration into society. Only the most exuberant idealist could imagine sentencing a pathetic drug addict to several years of incarceration—likely double celled—with the expectation that the offender will leave prison better adjusted and possessing social and vocational skills that he lacked when he began his period of incarceration. Yet this is precisely the assumption that many politicians naively convey to their constituents. Politicians also tell us that the way to win the war on drugs is to adopt inflexible and long mandatory sentences, even the death penalty in some cases. Though it is little wore than worn out rhetoric, it is also politically expedient.

In addition to being insufficiently informed about the nature of the drug problem and the solutions that have been attempted, politicians have ignored important lessons of the past. A "get tougher" policy with drug offenders is no anodyne; this has been demonstrated several times during the past three decades. If repressive penalties were the solution, the Boggs Act and the Narcotic Control Act would have eliminated the problem in the 1950s. If the mandatory sentences implemented by New York had been effective in 1973, certainly the other 49 states would have been quick to adopt similar legislation. They did not, because this approach did not and does not work, and history has demonstrated repeatedly the weaknesses of "getting tough." When considering possible solutions to the current drug problem, members of Congress, if they are sincere, should pay closer attention to the past rather than speculate about anticipated political benefits. Lessons from the past can be most instructive in developing strategies to overcome the present drug problem.

Policymakers must also stop or at least minimize the politicizing of drugs that began when Congress passed the Harrison Narcotic Act in 1914. This kind of shameful exploitation for political gain was repeated in Anslinger's anti-marijuana crusade in the 1930s, in the enactment of the Boggs Act and the Narcotic Control Act in the 1950s, in 1971 when President Richard M. Nixon officially initiated the first White House war on drugs, and in the Reagan-Bush war on drugs in the 1980s. We have not sufficiently learned from lessons of the past about drugs. Anslinger maintained throughout his 32-year tenure as Commissioner of the Narcotics Bureau that a punitive approach to drug abuse was the solution. But more than sixty years later, drugs still remain a viable issue for politicians and a major concern for much of the American public.

President Bush claimed to be waging a war on drugs. In 1992, he asked Congress for more than $13 billion to prove it. Despite the government's continued willingness to approve increased appropriations to fight drugs over the past decade, however, there has not been much progress in wiping out drug abuse. If perception of the drug issue matters, as it most certainly does, election-year public opinion was even more disappointing: Forty-eight percent of registered voters responding to an August 1992 *Newsweek* poll indicated that the drug problem had gotten worse during the Bush administration. Little wonder that many of those who are familiar with the history of drug use in the United States, as well as observers of contemporary drug policy, continue to be skeptical of government efforts to eradicate drug abuse. Perhaps we are deceiving ourselves and losing sight of reality when the goal is an unconditional victory in the drug war.

Drugs have been part of our culture since the beginning, and it is likely that they will continue to be. Crop eradication, military intervention, zero tolerance, interdiction, "Just Say No," and demand-reduction are examples of failed attempts to end the drug scourge. The sooner we accept the reality that there will be no total victory in the drug war, and that drugs—including alcohol and tobacco—have a long history and an irresistable allure, the sooner we can begin to make progress. Only then can we overcome an enduring sense of futility in the war on drugs.

Notes

1. In Pennsylvania, for example, State Representative Russell Fairchild recommended the death penalty for those convicted of dealing drugs to minors.
2. The federal government's estimate is $52 billion.
3. Democratic Congressman John D. Dingell from Michigan wondered if marijuana was "the same

weed that grows wild in some of our western states which is sometimes called the loco weed?" Anslinger also corrected Republican Congressman William C. Reed of Illinois, who thought the marijuana plant had "a very large flower."

4. Anslinger described marijuana as a "narcotic—as dangerous as a coiled rattlesnake." He also stated that "no one can predict its effect," and wondered "how many murders, suicides, robberies, criminal assaults, holdups, burglaries, and deeds of maniacal insanity it causes each year?"
5. According to Rosenberg, by comparison, coffee, Colombia's largest legal export, produced $1.7 billion in 1988. Coffee, unlike cocaine, is also susceptible to inflation and other economic fluctuations that affect prices.
6. According to Auth, the number of fatalities are: alcohol, 90,000; tobacco, 390,000; cocaine, 8,000; and heroin, 6,000.
7. Anslinger capitalized on contemporary social tensions and the pervasive sense of uncertainty stemming from McCarthyism, testimony to the Kefauver Committee about organized crime activities, and the FBN's own dire predictions of a drug epidemic among the nation's juvenile population.
8. The ABA also wanted Congress to review the Harrison Act and current enforcement policies, but Daniel introduced S. Res. 60 the same day "To conduct a full and complete study of the narcotics problem in the United States, including ways and means of improving the Federal Criminal Code and other laws and enforcement procedures dealing with possession, sale, and transportation of narcotics, marijuana and similar drugs."
9. The United States imprisons 455 people for every 100,000 in the population, putting it far ahead of the world's second most vigorous jailer, South Africa, which imprisons 311 for every 100,000. The rate in China, 111/100,000, is only one-fifth that of the U.S.
10. Penn State University sociologist John H. Kramer, Executive Director of Pennsylvania's Commission on Sentencing, encouraged the state to adopt more creative sentencing methods, such as electronic home surveillance, in-home detention, and treatment facilities, to reduce a predominant drug offender prison population. Rockview's facilities were designed to house 1,250; its current population pushes it to 60 percent over its capacity.

References

Allentuck, S. & Bowman, K. M. (1942). Psychiatric aspects of marihuana intoxication. *American Journal of Psychiatry, 99,* 48–50.

Anderson, P. (1991, June 20). Billions spent on illegal drugs. *Centre Daily Times,* p. 2A.

Anderson, P. (1992, January 28). Bush pledges to step up war against drugs. *Philadelphia Inquirer,* p. 24.

Anslinger, H. J., & Cooper, C. R. (1937). Marijuana: assassin of youth. *American Magazine, 18*(19), 150–53.

Associated Press. (1990, March 10). Military to widen drug net on border. *Centre Daily Times,* p. A8. State College, PA.

Auth, T. (1990, 4 May). Political cartoon. *Philadelphia Inquirer.*

Beamish, R. (1990, February 10). U. S. Money, military thrown into Latin drug war. *Centre Daily Times,* pp. A1, A8. State College, PA.

Blachman, M. J., & Sharpe, K. E. (1990, Spring). The war on drugs: American democracy under assault. *World Policy Journal,* 135–63.

Blakeslee, Sandra. (1988). Nicotine: Harder to kick...than heroin. *New York Times Sunday Magazine.*

Brecher, E.M. (1972). *Licit and illicit drugs.* Boston, MA: Boston, Little, Brown.

Buckley, W. F. (1988, May 19). *Enlisting military to fight drugs.* Associated Press.

Burck, J. (1990, April 19). Rockview employees protest overcrowding in state prison. *Centre Daily Times,* p. 1B.

Burck, J. (1990, August 5). Prison overcrowding resolutions vary among experts. *Centre Daily Times,* pp. 1B–2B.

Bush, G. (1989, September 5). Address to the nation on the national drug control strategy. *Weekly Compilation of Presidential Documents,* 1305.

Cassata, D. (1990, January 27). Defense increase planned by Bush. *Pittsburgh Post-Gazette,* p. A1.

Cohen, R. (1988, April 11). Decriminalize drugs: Let's think about it. *Washington Post,* p. A14.

Cohen, R. (1989, December 19) Bush's "crack dealer" tells another story. *Philadelphia Inquirer.*

Contreras, J. (1989, September 11). Anarchy in Colombia. *Time,* pp. 30–32.

Courtwright, D., Joseph, H., & Des Jarlais, D. (1989). *Addicts who survived: An oral history of narcotics use in America, 1923–1965.* Knoxville, TN: University of Tennessee Press.

Dinges, John. (1990). *Our man in Panama: How General Noriega used the U. S.—and made millions in drugs and arms.* New York: Random House.

Drugs, Lies & TV. (1989, October 16). *The Nation,* p. 408.

Ehrenreich, B. (1990, March/April). Drug frenzy: Why the war on drugs misses the real target that the most dangerous drugs in America are legal drugs. *Utne Reader,* pp. 7666–81.

Eldridge, W. B. (1967). *Narcotics and the law: A critique of the American experiment in narcotic control.* Chicago, IL: University of Chicago Press.

Epstein, E. J. (1977). *Agency of fear: Opiates and political power in America.* New York: Putnam.

Goodman, E. (1989, March 8). Uncle Sam should kick the habit. *New York Times Sunday Magazine.*

Goodman, E. (1992, February 11). U. S. jail rate still tops world. *Philadelphia Inquirer,* p. A3.

Grant, C. L. (1989, September 13). High school students say Bush misses point on drugs. *Centre-Daily Times, p. B1.*

Greve, F. (1990 February 9). Drug war may raise U. S. aid to Peru, *Philadelphia Inquirer,* pp. 1-A, 10-A.

Greve, F. (1990, April 26). Pentagon seeks radar network to track Colombian drug planes. *Philadelphia Inquirer,* p. 3A.

Greve, F. (1990, July 8). Costliest weapon may be unnecessary. *Philadelphia Inquirer,* p. 3A.

Hamowy, R. (Ed.). (1987). *Dealing with drugs: Consequences of government control.* Lexington, MA: Lexington Books.

House Committee on Ways and Means. (1937, 1st session). *Taxation of marihuana.* House of Representatives Hearings on M. R. 6385, 75th Cong., 19–29, 73–121.

Hufnagle, R. (1989, September 2). Lawmaker backs death penalty for certain drug sales. *Milton Standard Journal,* pp. 133–37.

Isikoff, M. (1992, February 27). Peru's leader hits U. S. Drug policies. *Washington Post,* p. A4.

Jehl, D. (1990, July 3). U. S. Military expanding role in Andean drug war. *Philadelphia Inquirer.* p. 1A, 10A.

King, R. (1972). *The drug hang-up: America's fifty-year folly.* New York: Norton.

Klien, J., & McDaniel, A. (1992 August 24). What went wrong. *Newsweek,* p. 23.

Kruger, H. (1980). *The great heroin coup: Drugs, intelligence, and international fascism.* Boston, MA: South End Press.

Lender, M. E., & Martin, J. E. (1987). *Drinking in America.* New York: Free Press; London: Collier Macmillan.

Lewis, C. (1990, March 2). Report shows record world drug production. *Philadelphia Inquirer,* p. A15.

Magnuson, E. (1990, January 22). More and more, a real war. *Time,* pp. 22–3.

Margasak, L. (1990, May 2). *Pentagon radar resurfaces in drug budget.* Associated Press.

Marshall, J. (1987). Drugs and United States foreign policy. In R. Hamowy (Ed.), *Dealing with drugs: Consequences of government control* (pp. 137–76). Lexington, MA: Lexington Books.

Mayor LaGuardia's Committee on Marihuana, 1944. (1973). *The marihuana problem in the city of New York* (reprint). Lancaster, PA: Metuchen, NJ.

McCormick, J. (1990, August 20). We can't catch what's coming. *Newsweek,* p. 45.

McWilliams, J. C. (1987). "Miller Time" in Antebellum America: A historical appraisal of the drinking habits among the working class. In R. L. Hogler (Ed.), *Substance abuse in the workplace: Readings in labor-management issues,* (pp. 3–21). University Park, PA: Penn State Press.

McWilliams, J. C. (1990). *The protectors: Harry J. Anslinger and the Federal Bureau of Narcotics, 1930–1962.* Newark, DE: University of Delaware Press.

Mezzacappa, D. (1989, October 13). What children know about drugs. *Philadelphia Inquirer,* p. 1-B.

Mills, J. (1986, August 25). Interview. *U. S. News & World Report,* p. 19.

Moore, A. (1989, September 7). After years of Reagan neglect on drugs, Bush has a Band-Aid. *Philadelphia Inquirer,* p. 12-A.

Morales, E. (1989). *Cocaine: White gold rush in Peru.* Tucson, AZ: University of Arizona Press.

Morgan, H. W. (1981). *Drugs in America: A social history, 1800–1980.* Syracuse, NY: Syracuse University Press.

Morganthau, T. (1989, September 18). Now it's Bush's war. *Newsweek,* p. 24.

Morganthau, T. (1989, September). The President whispers "Charge." *New York Times,* p. A26.

Morley, J. (1989, October 9). My (one) night on crack cocaine. *New Republic.*

Moyers, B. (1992, June. 24). *Listening to America.* PBS.

Musto, D. F. (1973). *The American disease: Origins of narcotics control.* New York: Oxford University Press.

Mutchler, T. (1990, July 9). Volatile prison situation considered "only option." Associated Press, *Centre Daily Times,* p. 1B.

Nadelmann, E. (1988, June 13). Shooting up. *The New Republic.*

National Drug Control Strategy: A nation responds to drug abuse (1992) p. 137. Washington, DC: Office of National Drug Control Policy.

Oliphant, T. (1989, September 10). A smoke-and-mirrors plan. *Boston Globe,* p. 18A.

Peirce, N. (21 June 1992). Weed and seed would work better if it were fed more green stuff. *Philadelphia Inquirer.*

Purdy, M. (1989, October 9). No place to hold drug war's prisoners. *Philadelphia Inquirer,* p. l-A.

Purdy, M. (1989, December 17). The other drug-use problem. *Philadelphia Inquirer,* p. 1-A.

Rorabaugh, W. J. (1979). *The alcoholic republic: An American tradition* New York: Oxford University Press.

Rosenberg, T. (1989, November 27). The kingdom of cocaine. *The New Republic,* pp. 26–28.

Sloman, L. (1983). *Reefer madness: Marijuana in America.* New York: Grove Press.

Sullivan, L. J. (1990, June 15). Stop peddling tobacco to kids. *Centre Daily Times,* p. A8.

Trudeau, G. (1990, October 17–21, November 7–11). *Doonesbury.*

U. S. Senate Committee on the Judiciary, 1st session, Part I. (1955). *Illicit narcotics traffic hearings.* Improvements in the Federal Criminal Code of the Committee of the Judiciary, on *S. Res, 67, 84th Cong., 18.*

Walker, S. (1989). *Sense and nonsense about crime: A policy guide.* Pacific Grove, CA: Brooks/Cole Publishing Co.

Waller, D. (1990, July 16). Risky business. *Newsweek* pp. 16–19.

Wechsler, H. & Isaac, N. (1992, June 3). "Binge" drinkers at Massachusetts colleges. *Journal of the American Medical Association, 267,* 2929–31.

Will, G. W. (1990, January 14). *Battling cigarettes.* Syndicated column.

Will, G. W. (1990, February 26). *Sundry facts about cigarette smoking, the first of which is death.* Syndicated column.

Wilson, J. Q. (1991). Drugs and crime. In M. Tonry & J.Q. Wilson (Eds.), *Crime & justice: A review of research* (p. 529). Chicago, IL: University of Chicago Press.

Wisotsky, S. (1990). *Beyond the war on drugs: Overcoming a failed public policy.* Buffalo, NY: Prometheus Books.

Woestendiek, J. (1990, August 3). Drug sweep: A fiasco or success? *Philadelphia Inquirer,* p. 1-A.

Discussion Questions

1. Summarize the major events that occurred during and after the decade of prohibition, leading to drug law legislation.
2. In reviewing McWilliams' history of the war on drugs, what three events do you find the most interesting, and why?
3. In what ways does this historical review increase your understanding of this topic?
4. After reading McWilliams' article, react to the statement: It is justifiably correct that alcohol and tobacco are legal, while other substances such as marijuana and cocaine are illegal. Make reference to this article as a basis of support for your argument, whether or not you agree with the statement above.

Between Legalization and War

A Reconsideration of American Drug Policy

Patricia A. Adler

Patricia A. Adler (Ph.D., University of California, San Diego) is Assistant Professor of Sociology at the University of Colorado. She has written and taught in the areas of deviance, white collar crime, women and crime, and juvenile delinquency. Her book, *Wheeling and Dealing* (Columbia University Press, 1985), a study of upper-level marijuana and cocaine smugglers, is currently being revised for an updated and expanded edition. Her other areas of interest include the sociology of children, sport, emotions, social theory, and qualitative methods. Together with her husband, Peter Adler, she edits the *Journal of Contemporary Ethnography* and has authored *Backboards and Blackboards: College Athletes and Role Engulfment* (Columbia University Press, 1991), and *Membership Roles in Field Research* (Sage Publications, 1987).

America has a socially-constructed drug crisis. Beginning in the spring of 1986, American news media and politicians began to seize on the drug issue with a frenzy, hyping public views of the situation into a perceived "epidemic" or "plague" (Reinarman & Levine, 1989). While the issue had not been of major concern before, public opinion polls conducted during the latter years of the 1980s showed a strong response to this "drug scare," so that the average citizen selected drug abuse, drug-related crime, and the government's inability to successfully deal with this situation as the most serious problem facing our nation as we enter the 1990s.[1] That drug issues received such widespread concern is especially remarkable given the host of other problems plaguing our society, including widespread homelessness, global warming, environmental pollution, flagging national educational achievement, loss of technological superiority, and a host of controversial moral and religious issues.

Ever since the passage of the Harrison Narcotics Act in 1914, which outlawed opiates and coca products and created the category of Class I illegal intoxicants,[2] and the subsequent criminalization of marijuana in 1937, we have witnessed the growth of both drug use and enforcement efforts to arrest it. Individual drugs have waxed and waned in popularity, yet the population of "problem" drug users has continued to grow, and with it our national uncertainty about a comprehensive and effective drug policy. Part of the confusion stems from the fact that the nature and the extent of the problems associated with drugs are not clear-cut, and neither are their solutions. Dilemmas exist both within the drug war approach and the drug legalization alternative.

Costs of Drug Use

Clearly, the social costs of drug use are great. Illegal drugs, like their legal counterparts, alcohol and tobacco, represent a major *public health problem*. Although marijuana was originally regarded as a fairly benign "natural organic product" (Grinspoon, 1971; Smith, 1970; Sloman, 1979), more recent research suggests that it combines the damaging effects of both alcohol and tobacco while lodging in fat-soluble molecules, thus ensuring longer retention in the body (the "persistence-of-residue" phenomenon) (Macdonald, 1988). Research on marijuana's behavioral effects suggests that although it is sometimes used to improve individuals' self-awareness and relationships with others (Hendin et al., 1987), it is also used by individuals to "buffer" them from dealing with difficult personal problems, especially those encountered during the stressful years of adolescence. This can lead to both the "motivational syndrome" and the problems associated with "arrested development" (DuPont, 1984).

Moderate use of inhaled cocaine may create feelings of euphoria, increase sexual endurance (although this varies both by and within gender, see Fagan, 1990a; Macdonald et al., 1988), diminish inhibitions, and contribute to social bonding, without the intravenous hazards of heroin or the lung cancer of marijuana (Adler, 1985). Approximately 90 percent of cocaine snorters successfully maintain themselves at this state of recreational consumption over long-term periods while suffering relatively few adverse effects (Murphy, Reinarman, & Waldorf, 1989; Newcomb & Bentler, 1988). Heavier use for a minority of individuals, however, can lead to "cocaine psychosis" (Weiss & Mirin, 1987), characterized by increased suspiciousness, compulsive behavior, fault finding, and eventually paranoia. Crack-cocaine, a form of cocaine base available in rock form for relatively low cost, can be similarly used on either a sporadic or episodic basis and governed by the social controls of group norms (Waldorf, Reinarman, & Murphy, 1991). Shifts from drug use to drug abuse are more prevalent among users with fewer outside "life investments" (Rosenbaum, 1989); however, with the drug's more intense effects leading to binge use, a swifter onset of dependence, and higher rates of addiction are prevalent (Inciardi & McBride, 1989).

Heroin can also be used moderately, especially when snorted, but when injected intravenously its addictive-potential is greater.[3] Direct physical deterioration beyond malnutrition and damage to veins is usually minimal, even among chronic users, and legalization proponents often cite this as one factor promoting heroin's inclusion in a legalization program. More problematic health effects associated with use and addiction include the HIV (human immunodeficiency virus) and hepatitis infections associated with needle-sharing,[4] and the potential for overdose-related deaths.

Using any of these illicit drugs (or their legal counterparts) to excess may further lead to undesirable *behavioral* and *developmental* consequences. Newcomb and Bentler's study (1988) of teenage drug use showed that the 10 percent of youths who moved beyond infrequent use of drugs at social gatherings and became frequent, committed consumers were less successful at developing the coping skills associated with interpersonal communication and maturation. They left school earlier, began working earlier, and formed families earlier.[5] As a consequence, a percentage of these individuals experienced family dissolutions, job instability, and ineffective relationships; some even moved into serious crime.

A third cost associated with illicit drug use is the *chronic criminal activity* associated with the lifestyle of addiction. Many addicts come from underclass populations where they are drawn into the informal economy and away from legitimate means of employment. Short-term illicit hustles such as burglary, robbery, prostitution, forgery, fraud, and drug dealing are thus a common means of addicts' earning the money necessary to support themselves (and their children) (Fiddle, 1967; Gould et al., 1974; Johnson et al., 1985; Lex, 1989; Miller, 1986; Rettig et al., 1977; Rosenbaum, 1981). Crack addicts are also less likely than the average population to hold legitimate jobs because most legitimate jobs available to them are both demeaning and unglamorous (Bourgois, 1989). In the inner-city areas, crack has become a more popular drug among women and children than heroin ever was, and its consequent destructive effects on the family are more profoundly devastating, including effects on unborn and newborn children.[6] Equally tragic is the fact that the depressed levels of legitimate opportunity in ghetto areas coupled with the status, money, and lack of humiliation or tedium associated with drug trafficking combine to continue attracting ghetto youth into illicit careers, making their future entry into legitimate jobs more difficult (Bourgois, 1989).

Finally, the levels of *drug-related violence* appear to have grown over the years. Violence, though not inevitable, may be associated with illicit drug use in three ways: psychopharmacologically (users become irritable, irrational, and finally aggressive), economically (users commit crimes to support their drug consumption), and systemically (violence is an integral component of illegal drug importation and distribution) (Goldstein et al., 1989; Inciardi & McBride, 1989). Psychopharmacological violence is rare for all drugs, including crack (Fagan, 1990a; Goldstein et al.,

1989). The strongest correlation between intoxication and aggression remains with alcohol, and that is heavily mediated by setting. Economic violence occurs most frequently with the most highly addictive drugs, heroin and crack, when people lose the ability to support themselves legally, and become so strung out that they have to resort to violence to get money. Systemic violence is more associated with the nature of the group involved in the dealing and the norms of the local dealing scene than with the actual substance involved (Adler, 1985). The highest levels of violence appear to be associated with drug trafficking by foreign nationals, inner-city gangs, and professional crime syndicates (Goldstein et al., 1989).

Costs of Current Drug Policies

Yet while the social costs of drug use are great, the social costs of the war on drugs have also been steadily rising. One of the greatest bankruptcies of the war on drugs is that it has been largely *unsuccessful.* It has failed on many fronts. Despite the massive infusion of money, manpower, and technology, the interdiction of drugs has been an avowed failure (Kraar, 1988; McBride et al., 1986; Rosenbaum, 1987; Trebach, 1987; Wisotsky, 1986). Drug enforcement agents acknowledge that their seizures represent no more than 10 percent of the flow of drugs coming into the country.[7] Reuter (1988) has argued that increased interdiction at the borders would have little or no effect on either the availability or price of street drugs because the producer nations are only yielding a small percentage of their actual capacity, prices are extremely low there, and most of the profits reflected in the price of street drugs are made by dealers on this side of the border. Thus despite interdiction efforts, prices, especially of cocaine, have failed to display a marked or consistent rise, especially since 1986 (Renfrey, 1988). Even if interdiction were successful, other drugs would arise to take the place of those kept out, either alone or in combination.[8] The war on drugs has also failed to deter potential users and dealers from involvement. The administration's major emphasis has been the application of criminal sanctions, with the recent addition of mandatory sentencing, designed to frighten individuals away from these potentially costly activities. However, there has been no shortage of willing consumers, and for every dealer or smuggler caught and removed from circulation there are scores of new recruits eager to take his place (Rosenbaum, 1989). Finally, and most abjectly, the war on drugs has failed to reduce demand. Despite government agencies explicitly focused on this task, the demand for illicit drugs has grown. These agencies have produced more hype and impression management than programs of actual substance (Clayton, 1989). Particularly underwhelming has been the array of "Just Say No" drug education programs based on an idealized and grossly unrealistic model of how adolescents think and act, and the routes by which drug consumption spreads among youth peer groups. The National Institute of Drug Abuse's annual survey of high school seniors, conducted each year by the University of Michigan, shows that some drugs, most notably marijuana and (powder) cocaine, have undergone a decline in usage patterns (Bachman et al., 1987; Johnston et al., 1986). Although proponents of the drug war cite this as a major success, there is no evidence linking their efforts with shifts in drug consumption behavior. It is more likely that this reduction has resulted from shifts in the popularity and availability of certain drugs than from a concerted effort to convince people to spurn the use of all drugs. Supporting this view is the rise in use of other newer and more available drugs or drug combinations, paralleling the reported decline in marijuana use. In fact there is a natural history to drug use that explains its recurring nature in American culture. The continual emergence of drug "epidemics" is based partly on this pent-up demand, leading to the incorporation of each new drug into the American intoxication landscape. As the failure of alcohol prohibition in the 1920s showed, people want to consume intoxicating substances, and legal sanctions will not deter them. Prohibition produced more lawlessness than the system could stand. Drugs, in contrast, produce enjoyment, pleasure, and relief from tension, and have been found in every known society since the beginning of recorded history (Rosenbaum, 1989; Siegel, 1989; Weil, 1972).

A second major problem plaguing the war on drugs is that it is perceived by many segments of the population as *hypocritical and discriminatory.* Its hypocrisy begins with the basic differentiation made between the licit and illicit drugs. Critics of the administration's drug policy question why alcohol and tobacco are legal and regulated while the other drugs are not. The division of drugs into separate legal categories is based more on historical and social usage patterns than on pharmacological merit (Reinarman, cited in Raymond, 1990). In this country, alcohol and tobacco are backed by huge manufacturing industries that aggressively lobby against any change in their legal status or regulation. Alcohol and tobacco are also the drugs of choice used by the middle classes and the establishment, giving them the weight of power and authority. While illegal drugs are used no more commonly by minority, poor, and youth populations, there is a disproportionate allocation of law enforcement resources in inner cities for drug control efforts. We are not targeting Wall Street, Madison Avenue, or the banking industries in Florida or California for "buy-busts" or the military-style enforcement pressure. As Reinarman (cited in Raymond, 1990) has noted, "It was only when crack moved to ghetto street corners that there was a call for crackdown on enforcement" (p. A10). Not only is enforcement more vigilantly directed against the poor and minority populations, but these groups have more limited access to the protections of the legal system, and they are discriminated against once again by the traditional biases inherent in the criminal justice system. Middle- and upper-class individuals have the resources to rescue themselves from the criminal justice system through admission into private treatment and rehabilitation programs, and by obtaining the efforts of private legal counsel. In many respects, then, our nation has a two-tiered punishment system. This creates feelings of discrimination, inequity, and societal division.

Pursuit of the current war on drugs has already had, and will continue to have, many significantly *deleterious consequences*. Internationally, our drug policies have had profoundly negative impacts on our relations with our Central and South American neighbors (Nadelmann, 1988a). We have bullied them into cooperating in joint law enforcement and military operations designed to eradicate cash-producing crops and processing operations in their countries, and to extradite their traffickers to our courts and jails. We have even waged war and overthrown governments for this purpose. This has led to feelings of mistrust and resentment. Moreover, resources allocated have been diverted by existing governments for their own purposes, not to eradicate drugs but to repress political opposition. Most South American countries regard the international drug problem as an American problem, and after the 1989–90 heavy war efforts against the Medellin cartel and other traffickers, the governments of Colombia, Peru, and Ecuador lost enthusiasm and political support at home for continued war efforts (Reiss et al., 1990).

Nationally, the war on drugs, especially in its most recent incarnation (since the release of the "zero-tolerance" armamentarium of 1988; see McBride and Inciardi, 1989; and the Bush plan in September, 1989), has had seriously injurious effects on our criminal justice system and national budget. It has overwhelmed the limited resources of our judges, prosecutors, and law enforcement agents, whose time could be better spent directed toward criminal activities that harm far more innocent victims than do violations of the drug laws. In fact, the drug war has skewed the sentencing patterns in the courts, so that robbers and burglars are punished more leniently than drug dealers (even when the dealers have shorter prior records) (Belenko, Fagan, & Chin, 1991; Fagan, in press). One estimate suggested that by 1988, drug law violators represented about 10 percent of the 800,000 people incarcerated in state and local jails, and more than one-third of the 44,000 individuals housed in federal prisons (Nadelmann, 1988b). The 1989 mandatory sentencing program, which offers few distinctions among the various Class I drugs (such as marijuana, heroin, cocaine, etc.), requires the courts to impose prison sentences on people involved even in low levels of drug trafficking, thus contributing to the vastly overcrowded conditions found there. This will shortly necessitate the allocation of even more huge sums for prison construction as the U.S. Sentencing Commission has estimated that, "largely as a consequence of the Anti-Drug Abuse Act passed by Congress in 1986, the proportion of federal inmates incarcerated for drug violations will rise from one-third of the 44,000 prisoners sentenced to federal-prison terms [in 1988] to one-half of the 100,000 to 150,000 federal prisoners anticipated in fifteen years" (Nadelmann, 1988b, p. 15). Federal expenditures for drug enforcement have also increased significantly between 1981 and 1988, going from one to three billion dollars a year: the Drug Enforcement Administration (DEA) and Coast Guard budgets rose from $220 million to roughly $500 million; the FBI drug enforcement allocations rose from $8 million to over $100 million; U.S. Marshalls' costs jumped from $26 million to $80 million; by 1988 U.S. Attorneys were spending $100 million compared to $20 million; State Department resources increased from $35 million to $100 million; U.S. Customs costs escalated from $180 million to over $400 million, and the Bureau of Prisons spent $300 million as compared to $77 million (Nadelmann, 1988b). Military expenditures from the Department of Defense for the counternarcotics budget grew to $450 million for 1990 and $1.2 billion in 1991, with an additional $191 million in 1991 to the Southern Command for military trainers to South America and $143 million more for new radar scanners across the northern rim of South America (Waller et al., 1990). This does not even begin to take into account intelligence costs, now that the intelligence agencies have been pressed into service in the drug war, nor expenditures at lower and more regional levels of government. These costs to the taxpayer are both direct and indirect, as they overtly cut into the federal and state budgets, and subtly and invisibly supersede other enforcement priorities, such as domestic violence.

A third deleterious consequence involves the creation of crime. The huge escalation of our enforcement effort has had significant consequences on the activities and social organization of drug smugglers and traffickers. Importation of drugs like marijuana and cocaine, which was once the domain of Mom-and-Pop operators, then became transformed into the entrepreneurial activities of individual and small rings of Americans, has now become the nearly exclusive province of huge syndicates of Colombian nationals (Adler, 1985; Morley, 1989). This escalation in the level of criminal organization and sophistication came in response to the growing pressure from law enforcement, and the need to stay technologically abreast of pursuers. The enormous profits earned by these criminal syndicates have enabled them to corrupt whole governments in our hemisphere, and to exert a significant amount of control over public officials even within our own nation (Nadelmann, 1988b). As a result, many of the European countries have retreated from formulating harder legal measures, feeling that any policy that drives users further underground will have the unintended effect of strengthening and unifying criminally controlled markets (Arnao, 1988; Kaplan, 1989).

Fourth, enforcement efforts in American ghettos have fostered a rise in gang activity. Once primarily social groups whose members drifted away from the group as they moved into adulthood, gangs became infused with purpose and resources once they began to get into the drug trade. The violence they once used to carve out and defend their territory has been turned toward protecting drug dealing markets, and has increased in severity. Enforcement efforts against them have driven these drug dealers to recruit ever-younger couriers as temporary and peripheral members to deliver and hold their contraband, so that their juvenile status will make them less vulnerable to law enforcement (Fagan, 1989, 1990b). Consequently, we now have adolescent youths as young as 14 and 15 "clocking" on corners, peddling small dosages of crack to customers by the hour (Williams, 1989).

Fifth, the increased emphasis on border interdiction has caused many smugglers to turn away from importing marijuana, which is bulky and odorous, to transporting cocaine, which is condensed and relatively odor-free (Adler, 1985). This has played a major part in the wane in the popularity and use of marijuana, pushed out by the ascension of cocaine, especially crack. Heavy emphasis on border interdiction has also encouraged the rise of a large domestic marijuana-producing industry throughout the country, to fill this void (DEA, 1988; Gettman, 1989; Weisheit, 1990b). But accompanying cocaine's drop in price has been an increase in the cost of marijuana. It is likely, therefore, that the 1990s will witness a new rise in the popularity of marijuana, as it once again becomes more profitable for importers to trade in this commodity.

Some Tough Choices

Ultimately, we as a nation have to ask ourselves if we are willing to support the drug war. This requires a reflection on what we have to pay and what we have to sacrifice to support it. Are we willing to live in a police state and sacrifice our civil liberties for the sake of zero tolerance? Are we willing to condone systematic drug testing, whereby people can be forced to incriminate themselves or lose their jobs? This shifts the burden of proof to citizens to prove that they do not use drugs, and raises the prospects of a new McCarthyism, which ostracizes and condemns those who refuse to submit to a drug test. Systematic drug testing threatens Fourth Amendment protections against unwarranted search and seizure, and Fifth Amendment protections against self-incrimination; it turns the presumption of innocence into the presumption of guilt. Drug testing, moreover (when not flawed by error), indicts people, not by their current state or condition (as reflex testing would do), but by their past behavior. Are we willing to morally support the invasion of people's bodies, the destruction of their civil liberties, the incursion into their private lives, and the accompanying widespread loss of trust between workers and managers incurred by mandatory drug testing as a precondition to employment, for the sake of social and corporate control?

Decisions by our policymakers have been overwhelmingly political ones, designed to make them look good to their constituents (Reinarman & Levine, 1989). Getting tough on crime is easy rhetoric to espouse and hard to oppose, but the costs have to be borne through the forfeit of other programs. The war on drugs has been almost wholly directed in law enforcement venues, with a decrease in funds for medical and social drug-treatment programs. Nearly nine out of 10 addicts in this country go without any form of treatment (Schmoke, 1989), and the waiting time to get into treatment programs can be as long as a year (Murphy & Rosenbaum, 1988; Rosenbaum et al., 1987). Yet once people get into treatment programs and successfully adapt to them (such as methadone maintenance), they may be forced by a new government policy either to leave the programs or to assume the (usually prohibitive) cost of sustaining them (Rosenbaum et al., 1987). Consequently, addicts who had been able to establish lives for themselves outside the realm of the illicit drug subculture are being driven back into it, with the associated costs that this incurs for society (Murphy & Rosenbaum, 1988; Rosenbaum et al., 1987).

The escalation of the drug war has also occurred at the expense of a variety of social service and social welfare programs. The Reagan and Bush administrations effected major cutbacks in a variety of areas. Education suffered through the slashing or reduction of school lunch programs, preschool programs such as Head Start, school supplement programs such as Upward Bound, and student loan programs. Community recreation programs designed to provide children with after-school activities were drastically reduced. Daycare, childcare, parental leave and numerous other family programs have lost support or funding. Community outreach and action programs designed to develop and support grassroots organizations within blocks and neighborhoods both to fight crime and strengthen the solidarity and voice of the local community have been canceled. Community clinics and community mental health services were closed or sharply curtailed, turning thousands of people out onto the streets, homeless. The most stigmatized and hardest hit, perhaps, were social welfare programs such as food stamps, Aid to Families with Dependent Children (AFDC), work-training programs (such as CETA and the job-training partnership act), and many others. Future costs, driven especially by the alarming need for new prison construction, will soon begin to come directly at the expense of social consciousness programs such as VISTA, agencies helping children such as the boys' clubs, big sisters and big brothers, and the mainstream budgets for community health programs and our children's public schools.

Do we as a nation feel that it is necessary to mandate this level of enforcement? Are the costs of the drug war becoming morally unacceptable to our sense of liberty and justice? Are they becoming socially unacceptable to our assessments of priorities? Further, are we entering the phase of the drug war where we are beginning to see that we are engaged in an unwinnable effort? This latest round of escalation is transforming the drug war into another Vietnam, with all of the accompanying impracticality, social divisiveness, and demoralization. It is at this point that the alternatives to the zero tolerance policy must be seriously considered.

A Middle Ground

What we need is a compromise between the extremes of legalizing all drugs and bearing the costs of the zero tolerance approach. In order to forge one, we must begin by differentiating drugs (both those currently legal and illegal) into categories of socially acceptable and unacceptable risk. It is both impractical and undesirable to treat all current Class I drugs with the same moral outrage and enforcement vigilance. While all drugs engender a variety of physical and/or social problems, there are some that our society has shown its willingness to tolerate and dispense in a regulated manner, either by prescription or over the counter. Thus, for example, we might want to differentiate between drugs with fewer social costs and greater potential medical benefits, and those engendering more alarming social costs with negligible medical benefits. Those deemed to carry a more socially acceptable risk could then be tolerated, reserving the more rigorous enforcement efforts for the drugs deemed unacceptable. Yet where do we draw the line?

Danish (1990) has suggested that we use alcohol as our yardstick. It is the intoxicant that most closely resembles illegal drugs in terms of both its effects and the consequences of its use. We have also had experience, moreover, in trying to regulate this drug both legally and illegally. After a period of time in which its free use was permitted (as with all drugs currently in the Class I category), we attempted to prohibit its manufacture, distribution, and consumption between 1920 and 1933. We terminated this unfortunate national "experiment" because we concluded that the addiction, violence, disease, and death associated with alcohol use were less disastrous than the consequences produced by prohibition. Therefore, if a drug carries roughly no worse consequences than alcohol, the principle of equal protection under law suggests that people should not be punished for using it.

Danish suggests that there are six criteria along which we should evaluate the harms of potential drugs compared with those of alcohol: (1) the ease of becoming addicted, (2) the ease of getting un-addicted, (3) the probability of use causing violent behavior, (4) the probability of suffering a fatal overdose, (5) the probability of death from chronic illness associated with over-consumption, and (6) the degree, nature, and duration of impairment. These were the six most commonly offered reasons for drug prohibition, but in the case of alcohol the American people concluded that these harms were more tolerable than the hypocrisy, violence, and corruption that resulted from criminalization. A middle ground might entail legalizing or relaxing enforcement against those drugs that pass the alcohol test. This might include such drugs as marijuana, which is no more socially destructive, and drugs such as MDMA and heroin in addition to marijuana, which have been identified by researchers as having valuable medical and psychological benefits[9] (Beck, 1990; Beck & Rosenbaum, 1990; Hilts, 1990; Peroutka, 1989; Rosenbaum et al., 1989; Young, 1988).

During the 1970s, Americans became cognizant of the widespread availability and use of marijuana without many of the horrors that had been predicted about it, and they relaxed their enforcement efforts against individuals possessing small quantities of the drug (Gettman, 1989). The Comprehensive Drug Abuse Prevention and Control Act of 1970 completely reconstructed the federal drug laws, allowing first-time users to receive probation, and significantly reducing many of the criminal penalties for users and dealers. During this decade, 11 American states passed some sort of decriminalization statutes (Slaughter, 1988). Decriminalization reforms a criminal justice system by removing an offense from its jurisdiction, while stopping short of changing the law. The forms of decriminalization varied from Alaska, Maine, Nebraska, and Oregon, which allocated civil fines for possessing small amounts of marijuana, to California, Colorado, Minnesota, Mississippi, New York, North Carolina, and Ohio, where the penalty for possession of small amounts was reduced to a small fine, to Alaska's abandoning all criminal penalties for personal marijuana cultivation (on the basis of the right to privacy guaranteed by the state constitution). Marijuana decriminalization bills during this period often stiffened penalties for heroin and cocaine distribution (Gettman, 1989), consistent with the principle of differentiation. The results of this differentiation have been largely positive. Both California and Maine have published studies showing law enforcement savings from their decriminalization efforts (Aldrich & Mikuriya, 1988; Maine Office of Alcoholism & Drug Abuse, 1979), and to date, none of the 11 states has rescinded its reforms, despite Reagan and Bush administration advocacy of a return to criminalization and zero tolerance.

While the American decriminalization approach showed a tolerance for the possession of small quantities of marijuana, this left users primarily reliant on illegal drug connections for obtaining their supply. This problem was taken into consideration by several European countries, such as Germany, Sweden, Norway, Spain, Italy, and the Netherlands, that also wrestled with the search for a middle ground between war and legalization (Kaplan, 1989; Reuband, 1988). Their populations have tended not to favor legalization, yet have wanted to relax legal sanctions against certain types of drug use. Most developed is the Dutch model of "normalization," whereby creative legal measures have been coupled with public health approaches to ameliorate the negative effects for individuals and society of both drug use and a repressive, prohibitive legal approach (Engelsman, 1989). The Dutch have tried to avoid a situation where consumers of marijuana suffered more damage from criminal proceedings than from the use of drugs. This approach has been characterized by practical (social and medical) rather than moral (political) considerations, and involves a de-dramatization of drug use and its effects, in contrast to the exaggerated media spectacle found in the United States. While the laws against marijuana have not been abolished, the drug is widely available in small quantities through the Amsterdam "coffeeshop" circuit, and its use is tolerated. The Dutch government's goal has been to contain the secondary problems associated with drug use by eliminating the harassment of casual users, sending realistic and credible messages to youth (avoiding double standards such as "your drugs are killers, but ours are pleasures") (Engelsman, 1989, p. 215), and preventing the labeling and stigmatization of drug abusers and their subsequent glamorization and mythologization by youth. The treatment approach has been pragmatic in its shift away from ending addiction toward helping abusers function within society. Rather than providing services only to abusers interested in abstinence (in clinic or hospital settings, which were not accessible to many addicts), the government has focused on shifting addicts' professions away from their drug use, and provided users with outreach workers, methadone maintenance, open-door medical support, material support, and social rehabilitation opportunities. Key to this approach have been the concepts of "low threshold facilities" and "accessible" help (Englesman, 1989, p. 216). The Dutch model of normalization went further than the American model of decriminalization because it not only limited the criminal prosection of marijuana users, it allowed the open sale of marijuana.

But these reforms still left many people with sources of anger and frustration: there was still a wide discrepancy between the written law and the official policy, and despite the fact that marijuana could be widely purchased and consumed, it generated no legal tax revenue. To solve this problem would require more than normalization, it would require legalization. A proposal for legalizing marijuana in this country has been advocated by the National Organization for the Reform of Marijuana Laws (NORML). This organization has suggested that: (1) adults be allowed to grow marijuana at home for personal use; (2) states determine the characteristics of statewide commercial sales, as with alcohol; (3) the federal government prepare guidelines regulating age limits and commercial advertising for alcohol, marijuana, and tobacco. They further recommend that the tax revenue produced from commercial marijuana sales be directed to anti-drug-abuse programs, especially for cocaine and heroin addicts (Gettman, 1989).

This approach combines the benefits of accepting common practice with relief to our overburdened criminal justice , law enforcement, and penal systems; it eliminates the hypocritical distinction between marijuana and alcohol, especially for our youth, removes the bulk of the criminal element from the manufacture and distribution of marijuana, and separates users of marijuana from the subculture of more risky drug use and dealing. Resources could be further saved and justice served, if these changes were made retroactive, so that people currently serving prison sentences for small possession offenses could be released, clearing room in our prisons for more serious offenders. Resources saved from the war against marijuana could then be used to combat the most organized criminal elements supplying other, harder, drugs.

While all of these models and proposals offer a middle ground through their differentiation among currently illegal drugs, some modifications would seem to be beneficial in our approach to *other drug* (such as crack or heroin) use as well. Just as the Netherlands adopted a less stigmatizing and more accepting approach to drug abusers, so too do we need to make our attitudes and policies more *humane.* People always have and always will abuse drugs. While we do not want to encourage abuse of the individually and societally most harmful drugs, we cannot abandon those individuals caught in the vise of drugs or those who have made the free choice to use drugs. Our current drug policies, by insisting on total abstinence, push drug users outside the margins of society, where we have no influence over them other than to punish them or exclude and alienate them more. This effectively ensures that they will use all the worst drugs in the worse possible ways and be subject to the least amount of moderating or normative influence (Zinberg, 1984). Such a policy of exclusion and abandonment was tolerated during the eighties and before, because it did not directly affect the wealthy and powerful segments of society. During this time we witnessed the growing disparity between the rich and poor segments of society. Along with the rich, the white, middle-class members of society, influenced by pervasive but underlying racism, turned their backs on the minority underclass, content that drug issues were minority issues and that the growing problems of this population were self-contained. But these dilemmas can no longer be regarded as self-contained. Urban America is reeling from the fear of roving bands of minority youth who advance into white neighborhoods to assault and rob. To reduce the worst social problems associated with drug abuse we need to ameliorate the poverty and lack of legitimate opportunity endemic among hard-core underclass populations. We need to restore and expand pre-natal health care and delivery assistance (instead of driving addicted mothers out onto the street to deliver their babies because they are afraid of being arrested), to fund daycare and early childhood education programs, to improve the quality of our inner-city schools, to strengthen affirmative action hiring programs so that more jobs for minorities become available. In short, we have to effect a sharing of the wealth and opportunity structure so that the most alienated groups develop the same kind of "investment" in leading legitimate lives that has led middle-class drug-users to moderate their use and keep the social problems they generate to a tolerable level.

In the area of drug policy,we need to focus less exclusively on the enforcement end of the drug war and devote more resources to treatment. Programs such as methadone maintenance should be expanded, not contracted, giving addicts willing to move away from the drug subculture a chance to reestablish more socially-integrated lives. Detoxification programs need to be expanded and made available to the underfunded populations. Community outreach programs, using indigenous workers, that supply health services, condom and bleach distribution, needle exchange, and counseling need to be enormously broadened. These programs must be most active in the hardest-core areas of the ghettos, where people are the most alienated from society and the most in need, and they should be much more "user friendly" than they are now.

We have been engaged in an enforcement battle against illegal drugs that has been lost at worst, maintained at best. Public cries that this should be handled as a public health problem (Bestemann, 1989) have been ignored. Yet the public health strategies designed to control smoking and drinking in the U.S., together with the development of informal social opprobriums against smokers and drunk drivers, have been effective in curtailing excessive use of these drugs. We need to turn away from law enforcement's destructive war on drugs to more informal, socially constructive approaches that unify and strengthen our society. As Weisheit (1990b) observed, "in a war against ourselves, even the victor emerges with battle scars" (p. 9). This, then, is the time to negotiate a peaceful settlement to the drug war, before it ignominiously bankrupts us in wholesale defeat.

Acknowledgments

I would like to gratefully acknowledge the assistance and support of Peter Adler, Jerome Beck, Russell Castro, Finn-Aage Esbensen, Jeffrey Fagan, Charles Gallmeier, Ben Heller, Charles Kaplan, Sheigla Murphy, Craig Reinarman, Marsha Rosenbaum, and Dan Waldorf.

Notes

1. The supremacy of the drug problem in the public opinion polls was only displaced, finally, in 1990 by the savings and loan crisis.
2. Illegal drugs categorized as Class I include heroin, cocaine, marijuana, PCP, the psychedelics, and a variety of other mind- and body-altering substances.
3. Studies have also shown, however, that heroin can be used intravenously in moderation as well (Zinberg, 1984).

4. Needle-sharing is a problem only because possession of hypodermics is illegal, a correlate of the prohibition against opiates. It is likely to diminish in importance once needles are made available at a reasonable price.
5. At the same time it should be noted that 90 percent of these youth did not go on to heavy drug use.
6. Crack's popularity among a wider population of underclass users, compared to heroin, may be due to several factors. First, their participation may be related to economic conditions. Changes in women's traditional gender roles may be moving them more actively into participation in the informal economy, of which drugs are a large, important part. Second, as more men in poor communities are imprisoned or die, women may be moving in to take their places in both using and dealing drugs. Third, cities have changed for the worse (Wilson, 1987), so the confluence of drugs and family problems may be related to the social structural devastation of inner cities, where the informal controls and social/economic networks that in the past sustained families have been decimated (Bourgois, 1989; Hamid, 1990).
7. Weisheit (1990a) has further remarked on the ineffectiveness of interdiction, noting that not only have we been unsuccessful at stopping the flow of drugs across our borders, but also at stopping their penetration into our prisons, stopping the flow of marijuana (a larger and bulkier drug than cocaine) from Hawaii to the mainland, or stopping the flow of illegal aliens (again larger and bulkier than drugs) into the country.
8. Treaster (1990) reports on the growing trend toward cocaine users' combining their crack use with heroin.
9. Marijuana has been found to offer important medical benefits as an treatment for asthma, nausea, convulsions, and pain. Heroin has long been noted for its effective pain relief. MDMA has been found effective in psychoanalysis as an "empathagen" for its anti-inhibitionary results, which enable patients to remove psychological blocks and introspect more successfully.

References

Adler, P. A. (1985). *Wheeling and dealing.* New York: Columbia University Press.

Aldrich, M., & Mikuriya, T. (1988). Savings in California marijuana law enforcement costs attributable to the Moscone Act of 1976. *Journal of Psychoactive Drugs, 20,* 1.

Arnao, G. (1988). Drug enforcement policy as a factor in trends of trafficking and use of different substances. *Journal of Psychoactive Drugs, 20,* 463–65.

Bachman, J. G., Johnston, L. D., & O'Malley, P. M. (1987). *Monitoring the future: Questionnaire responses from the nation's high school seniors.* Ann Arbor, MI: Institute for Social Research, The University of Michigan.

Beck, J. (1990). The public health implications for MDMA use. In S. J. Peroutka (Ed.), *Ecstasy* (pp. 77–103). Amsterdam: Kluwer Academic Publishers.

Beck, J., & Rosenbaum, M. (1990). The scheduling of MDMA ("Ecstasy"). In J. Inciardi (Ed.), *The handbook of drug control in the United States* (pp. 303–316). Westport, CT: Greenwood Press.

Belenko, S., Fagan, J. A., & Chin, K. (1991). Criminal justice response to crack. *Journal of Research in Crime and Delinquency, 28*(1), 55–74.

Besteman, K. J. (1989). War is not the answer. *The American Behavioral Scientist, 32*(3), 290–94.

Bourgois, P. (1989). In search of Horatio Alger: Culture and ideology in the crack economy. *Contemporary Drug Problems, 16,* 619–50.

Clayton, R. R. (1989). Legalization of drugs: An idea whose time has not come. *American Behavioral Scientist, 32,* 316–32.

Danish, P. (1990, June 8–11). The Danish plan. *Colorado Daily Weekend,* p. 16.

Drug Enforcement Administration. (1988). *1987 domestic cannabis eradication/suppression program—final report.* Washington DC: DEA.

DuPont, R. L. (1984). *Getting tough on gateway drugs.* Washington, DC: American Psychiatric Press.

Duster, T. (1970). *The legislation of morality.* New York: Free Press.

Engelsman, E. L. (1989). Dutch policy on the management of drug-related problems. *British Journal of Addiction, 84,* 211–28.

Fagan, J. A. (1989). The social organization of drug use and drug dealing among urban gangs. *Criminology, 27*(4), 633–667.

Fagan, J. A. (1990a). Intoxication and aggression. In J. Q. Wilson, & M. Tonry (Eds.), *Crime and justice: An annual review of research—vol. 13, drugs and crime* (pp. 134–143), Chicago, IL: University of Chicago Press.

Fagan, J. A. (1990b). Social processes of drug use and delinquency among gang and non-gang youths. In C. R. Huff (Ed.), *Gangs in America* (pp. 183–219) Newbury Park, CA: Sage.

Fagan, J. A. (In press). Do criminal sanctions deter crimes? In D. Mackenzie, & C. Uchida (Eds.), *Drugs and the criminal justice system: Evaluating public policy alternatives.* Newbury Park, CA: Sage Publications.

Fiddle, S. (1967). *Portraits from a shooting gallery.* New York: Harper and Row.

Gettman, J. (1989). Decriminalizing marijuana. *American Behavioral Scientist, 32,* 243–48.

Goldstein, P. J., Brownstein, H. H., Ryan, P. J., & Bellucci, P. A. (1989, Winter). Crack and homicide in New York City, 1988. *Contemporary Drug Problems,* pp. 651–87.

Gould, L., Walker, A. L., Crane, L. E., & Lidz, C. W. (1974). *Connections: Notes from the heroin world.* New Haven, CT: University Press.

Grinspoon, L. (1971). *Marijuana reconsidered.* Cambridge, MA: Harvard University Press.

Hamid, A. (1990). The political economy of crack-related violence. *Contemporary Drug Problems, 17*(1), 31–78.

Hendin, H., Hass, A. P., Singer, P., Ellner, M., & Ulman, R. (1987). *Living high: Daily marijuana use among adults.* New York: Human Sciences Press.

Hilts, P. J. (1990, July 21). How the brain is stimulated by marijuana is discovered. *The New York Times,* pp. 1, 9.

Inciardi, J. A., & McBride, D. C. (1989). Legalization: A high-risk alternative in the war on drugs. *American Behavioral Scientist, 32,* 259–289.

Johnson, B. D., Goldstein, P., Preble, E., Sehmeidler, J., Lipton, B., Spunt, B., & Miller, T. (1985). *Taking care of business: The economics of crime by heroin abusers.* Lexington, MA:Lexington Books.

Johnston, L. D., O'Malley, P. M., & Bachman, J. G. (1986). *Drug use among American high school students, college students, and other young adults, national trends through 1985.* Rockville, MD: National Institute on Drug Abuse.

Kaplan, C. D. (1989). *What works in drug abuse epidemiology in Europe.* Paper presented at What Works: An International Perspective on Drug Abuse Treatment and Prevention Research—A Conference to Set the Agenda for the 1990s, New York, New York.

Kraar, L. (1988, June 20). The drug trade. *Fortune*, pp. 27–38.

Lex, B. (1989). Narcotics addicts' hustling strategies: Creation and manipulation of ambiguity. *Journal of Contemporary Ethnography, 18,* 388–415.

MacDonald, D. I. (1988). Marijuana smoking worse for lungs. *Journal of the American Medical Association, 259,* 3384.

Macdonald, P. T., Waldorf, D., Reinarman, C., & Murphy, S. (1988). Heavy cocaine use and sexual behavior. *The Journal of Drug Issues, 18*(3), 437–55.

McBride, D. C., Burgman-Havermehl, C., Albert, J., & Chitwood, D. D. (1986). Drugs and homicide. *Bulletin of the New York Academy of Medicine, 62,* 497–508.

Maine Office of Alcoholism and Drug Abuse. (1979). *The decriminalization of marijuana and the Maine driminal justice system: A time cost analysis, 1979.* Augusta, ME: Author.

Miller, E. (1986). *Street woman.* Philadelphia, PA: Temple University Press.

Morley, J. (1989, October 2). Contradictions of cocaine capitalism. *The Nation* , pp. 341–47.

Murphy, S., Reinarman, C., & Waldorf, D. (1989). An 11-year follow-up of a network of cocaine users. *British Journal of Addiction, 84,* 427–36.

Murphy, S., & Rosenbaum, M. (1988). Money for methadone II: Unintended consequences of limited duration methadone maintenance. *Journal of Psychoactive Drugs, 20.*

Nadelmann, E. (1988a). U. S. drug policy: A bad export. *Foreign Policy. 70,* 83–108.

Nadelmann, E. (1988b). The case for legalization. *The Public Interest, 92,* 3–65.

Newcomb, M. D., & Bentler, P. M. (1988). *Consequences of adolescent drug use: Impact on the lives of young adults.* Newbury Park, CA: Sage.

Peroutka, S. J. (Ed.). (1989). *Ecstasy.* Amsterdam: Kluwer Academic Publishers.

Raymond, C. (1990, March 7). Researchers say debate over drug war and legalization is tied to Americans' cultural and religious values. *The Chronicle of Higher Education* , p. A6.

Reinarman, C., & Levine, G. (1989). Crack in context: Politics and media in the making of a drug scare. *Contemporary Drug Problems, 16,* 535–577.

Reiss, S., Miller, M., Farah, D., & Smith, M. (1990, September 10). Adios to the Andean strategy? *Newsweek* , p. 32.

Renfrey, M. (1988). *Cocaine price, purity, and trafficking trends.* Paper presented at the National Institute on Drug Abuse Technical Review meeting on the Epidemiology of Cocaine Use and Abuse, Rockville, MD.

Rettig, R. P., Torres, M. J., & Garrett, G. R. (1977). *Manny: A criminal addict's story.* Boston, MA: Houghton Mifflin.

Reuband, K. H. (1988). Haschisch im Urteil: Moralische Beurteilung, Gefahrenwahrenwahrnehmung und Sanktionsverlangen 1970–1987. *Neue Praxis, 6,* 480–95.

Reuter, P. (1988). Can the borders be sealed? In P. Reuter, G. Crawford, & J. Cave (Eds.), *Sealing the Borders* (pp. 1–36). Santa Monica, CA: The Rand Corporation.

Rosenbaum, M. (1981). *Women on heroin.* New Brunswick, NJ: Rutgers University Press.

Rosenbaum, M. (1989). *Just say what?* San Francisco, CA: National Council on Crime and Delinquency.

Rosenbaum, M., Morgan, P., Beck, J., Harlow, D., McDonnell, D., & Watson, L. (1989). *Exploring ecstasy: A descriptive study of MDMA users, final report.* Paper presented to the National Institute of Drug Abuse, Rockville, Maryland.

Rosenbaum, M., Murphy, S., & Beck. J., (1987). Money for methadone: Preliminary findings from a study of Alameda County's new maintenance policy. *Journal of Psychoactive Drugs, 10,* 397–402.

Rosenbaum, R. (1987, February 15). Crack murder: A detective story. *New York Times Magazine,* pp. 24–33, 57, 60.

Schmoke, K. L. (1989). Foreword. *American Behavioral Scientist, 32,* 231–32.

Siegel, R. K. (1989). *Intoxication: Life in pursuit of artificial paradise.* New York: Dutton.

Slaughter, J. B. (1988). Marijuana prohibition in the United States: History and analysis of a failed policy. *Columbia Journal of Law and Social Problems, 21*(4), 417–74.

Sloman, L. (1979). *Reefer madness: The history of marijuana in America.* Indianapolis, IN: Bobbs-Merrill.

Smith, D. E. (Ed.). (1970). *The new social drug: Cultural, medical, and legal perspectives on marijuana.* Englewood Cliffs, NJ: Prentice-Hall.

The decriminalization of marijuana and the Maine criminal justice system: A time cost analysis. (1979). Augusta, ME: Maine Office of Alcoholism and Drug Abuse.

Treaster, J. B. (1990, July 21). Cocaine users adding heroin to their menus. *The New York Times,* pp. 1, 26.

Trebach, A. (1987). *The great drug war.* New York: Macmillan.

Waldorf, D., Reinarman, C., & Murphy, S. (1991). *Cocaine changes.* Philadelphia, PA: Temple University Press.

Waller, D., Miller, M., Barry, J., & Reiss, S. (1990, July 16). Risky business. *Newsweek* , pp. 16–19.

Weil, A. (1972). *The natural mind.* Boston, MA: Houghton-Mifflin Company.

Weisheit, R. A. (1990a). Challenging the criminalizers. *The Criminologist, 15*(4), 1, 3–5.

Weisheit, R. A. (1990b). Declaring a civil war on drugs. In R. A. Weisheit (Ed.), *Drugs, crime, and the criminal justice system* (pp. 1–10). Cincinnati, OH: Anderson Publishing Co.

Weiss, R. D., & Mirin, S. M. (1987). *Cocaine.* Washington DC: American Psychiatric Press.

Williams, T. (1989). *The cocaine kids: The inside story of a teenage drug ring.* Reading, MA: Addison-Wesley.

Wilson, W. J. (1987). *The truly disadvantaged: The inner city.* Chicago, IL: University of Chicago Press.

Wisotsky, S. (1986). *Breaking the impasse in the war on drugs.* Westport, CT: Greenwood Press.

Young, F. (1988). *Opinion and recommended ruling, findings of fact, conclusions of law and decision of administrative law judge, docket No. 86-22.* Washington, DC: DEA.

Zinberg, N. E. (1984). *Drug set and setting: The basis of controlled intoxicant use.* New Haven, CT: Yale University Press.

Discussion Questions

1. What does Adler mean by a socially-constructed drug crisis?
2. In what ways does Adler *inform* your views about the use of certain drugs? Be specific.
3. What reasons does Adler give for the failure of the "war on drugs" campaign promoted by our federal government? Do you agree or disagree with her findings? Why?
4. What are some of the tough choices we as a nation have to make, with regard to supporting the costs of the drug war?
5. Do you agree or disagree with Adler's position in the section entitled "A Middle Ground"? Support your views. Do you have a better solution in mind?

The Sociology of Reefer Madness

The Criminalization of Marijuana in the United States

Michael C. Elsner

Michael C. Elsner, Ph.D., American University, teaches criminology, criminal justice and sociology courses within the Department of Sociology and Anthropology at Howard University in Washington, D.C. One of his special interests is the way in which drug laws have historically been enforced against ethnic minorities in the United States. His chapter in this book synthesizes a much larger thesis which he wrote as his doctoral dissertation: "The Sociology of Reefer Madness: the Criminalization of Marijuana in the United States." Prior to pursuing his doctorate, Elsner lived in Tucson, Arizona, where he worked in the civil and criminal justice systems for fifteen years. His writings reflect his concern for human rights on the local, national and international levels.

Introduction

The social origins of the Marihuana Tax Act of 1937, the federal legislation whereby cannabis became criminalized in the U.S., remain a mystery.[1] There is a lack of consensus and no clear, concise explanation of how and why marijuana came to be criminalized in the United States. Historians and sociologists have claimed that the passage of the Marihuana Tax Act of 1937 came about due to two competing theories, which Himmelstein (1983) refers to as the "Anslinger Hypothesis" and the "Mexican Hypothesis."

The "Anslinger Hypothesis" posits that a federal bureaucracy was responsible for the national prohibition against marijuana. This hypothesis holds that an individual's sense of moral outrage against marijuana became manifested as a bureaucratic crusade. Moreover, this crusade was driven by the pragmatic need of the bureaucracy (the Federal Bureau of Narcotics, forerunner of today's Drug Enforcement Administration) to expand and perpetuate itself.

The "Mexican Hypothesis" asserts that the Federal Bureau of Narcotics was prompted to support national anti-marijuana legislation due to local pressures exerted by western and southwestern communities in California, Colorado and Texas. Anti-Mexican sentiment in such communities as Alamosa, Colorado and El Paso Texas, was exacerbated by the fact that crime and violence attributed to Mexicans and Mexican-Americans there was causally linked to marijuana. The image of marijuana as "loco weed" ("loco" meaning "crazy" in Spanish) and "killer weed" thus emerged.

While scant evidence exists to support either the "Mexican hypothesis" or the "Anslinger Hypothesis," the two theories are synthesized herein as the "Social Control Hypothesis."

Historical Background

When John F. Kennedy assumed the presidency of the United States in 1961, he retained three holdovers from the Eisenhower Administration: Allen Dulles at the Central Intelligence Agency (CIA), J. Edgar Hoover at the Federal Bureau of Investigation (FBI), and Harry Anslinger at the Federal Bureau of Narcotics (FBN). While Dulles and Hoover are well-known historical figures whose deeds and exploits have been well chronicled, Anslinger in comparison is a relatively obscure entity.

Harry Anslinger was to the FBN what J. Edgar Hoover was to the FBI. Anslinger's World War I intelligence work paved the way for his federal career in Washington: he ascended to the number two position in the Prohibition Unit of the U.S. Treasury Department before being appointed by President Herbert Hoover in 1980 as the first Commissioner of the Federal Bureau of Narcotics. As the nation's first "drug czar,"[2] Anslinger shaped and directed the federal government's campaigns against the illicit substances of heroin, cocaine, and marijuana. More than any other person, Harry Anslinger was responsible for the development of U.S. drug control policies of the 1930s–1950s: policies which have carried over to the present day. Through his efforts, the United States has pursued a drug policy that is based not on a public health or a medical perspective, but rather on a crime and punishment approach.

Why, one may ask, would the Kennedy administration retain the old fossil Anslinger while shaping its image of the "New Frontier"? The answer, perhaps, can be found in the words of Harry himself, in which he describes his relationship with Attorney General Robert Kennedy.

> Bob called me right in after he took office. He said he got more help during that labor-rackets investigation of his from the Narcotics people than from anyone else in any department. . . . I've got a book on the Mafia. No a *secret* book. I gave a copy to Bob but I couldn't to anybody else. No, I couldn't give if to [J. Edgar] Hoover. I just couldn't risk it. (DeMott, 1962, p. 48)

Yet less than two years after gaining office, President Kennedy accepted Anslinger's resignation. According to Rufus King (1972), Anslinger was axed by the Kennedys as part of their ongoing political war with Richard Nixon.[3]

By September, 1962, when the White House Conference on Narcotic and Drug Abuse was held, a new FBN director had assumed office. It is clear that the once dominant star of yesteryear's drug czar, which had risen in 1930, was indeed setting by 1962. A virtually unknown era of U.S. history had passed.

The Anslinger Hypothesis

The "Anslinger Hypothesis," a term which was coined by Himmelstein (1983, p. 24), "argues that the FBN, acting on its own initiative, turned marihuana use into a public issue and secured passage of the Marihuana Tax Act." The first proponent of the Anslinger Hypothesis was Howard Becker (1963), who christened Anslinger a "moral entrepreneur." The activities of a "moral crusader," such as Anslinger, Becker argues, "can properly be called moral enterprise, for what [he is] enterprising about is the creation of a new fragment of the moral constitution of society, its code of right and wrong" (pp. 145–148). For years, Becker's moral entrepreneur analysis was accepted without question as the definitive sociological work that explained the Marihuana Tax Act of 1937. Yet Becker admittedly was not concerned with Anslinger's motives in seeking anti-marijuana legislation:

> While it is, of course, difficult to know what the motives of Bureau [FBN] officials were, we need assume no more than that they perceived an area of wrongdoing that properly belonged in their jurisdiction and moved to put it there. (p. 138)

Others who ascribed to the Anslinger Hypothesis, however, such as Lindesmith (1965), Solomon (1966), Kaplan (1970) and Grinspoon (1971), were concerned with the motives of Anslinger and the FBN. Dickson (1968) attempted to expand and improve Becker's notion of the "moral entrepreneur" by examining the FBN as an organizational bureaucracy. Dickson (1968), wrote: "What Becker ignores is that Anslinger was also a bureaucrat and thus responsive to bureaucratic pressures and demands as well. The distinction between these roles is difficult to make but it is fundamental in analyzing the legislation." (p. 152)

Evidence of Anslinger's bureaucratic acumen is provided to us by McWilliams (1990), who describes how Anslinger thwarted the Secret Service Reorganization Act of 1936. The plan was championed by Anslinger's boss, Secretary of the Treasury Robert Morgenthau, who sought to create a law enforcement "super agency" that would rival J. Edgar Hoover's FBI. Anslinger opposed the FBN's being absorbed by other agencies, and he mobilized his "army" to testify in Congress against the bill. Thereafter, President Roosevelt announced that he had abandoned the Treasury reorganization plan. Anslinger, the bureaucrat, had survived.

The two "entrepreneur" theories, Becker's "moral" and Dickson's "bureaucratic," may be viewed as two sides of the same coin. On each side of the coin, the image of Harry Anslinger is imprinted.

Whether the theory is that of Becker, Dickson, or other proponents of the Anslinger Hypothesis, in Himmelstein's view (1983) they all fall short of adequately explaining the passage of the Marihuana Tax Act of 1937: "The Anslinger Hypothesis . . . remains primarily a description of the FBN's actions; it offers no convincing explanations. Its assumptions, moreover, remain unexamined by most of its proponents" (pp. 25–27).

In formulating this position, Himmelstein drew upon the work of Galliher and Walker (1977), who critiqued previous sociological versions of the Anslinger Hypothesis:

> Becker, Lindesmith, and Reasons see a national marihuana panic created by FBN propaganda which propelled the legislation through Congress. Dickson finds this panic to be a result of a FBN propaganda effort designed to increase the scope and power of the Bureau after the bill's passage. Musto finds a marihuana crisis prior to the bill's passage but one localized in the Southwest and not a result of Bureau propaganda. Bonnie and Whitebread see evidence of FBN propaganda but no national marihuana crisis. (p. 369)

Galliher and Walker (1977, 1978) provide a convincing and excellent case for sociological "systematic research error" regarding the Marihuana Tax Act and the FBN. They have demonstrated how a fact (in this case the Anslinger Hypothesis) can remain unchallenged, be accepted as truth, and be perpetuated for years despite the lack of evidence to support the original claim. Galliher and Walker have revealed that Becker's notion of the moral entrepreneur, which was accepted without question for 15 years as *the* explanation of why the federal prohibition of marijuana came about, was a shallow and unsubstantiated argument. In essence, they revealed the nakedness of Becker's theory by stripping off its clothes. Yet the weakness in the work of Galliher and Walker is that they offered no alternate hypothesis of their own to account for the federal prohibition of marijuana. Although they successfully stood Becker's theory on its head, they failed to fill the theoretical void which they created. Instead, they pointed to the Mexican Hypothesis to suggest why the Marihuana Tax Act of 1937 was enacted.

The Mexican Hypothesis

Bonnie and Whitebread document (1974) that from 1914 to 1931, 29 states prohibited the use of marijuana for non-medical purposes. The battle cry to criminalize marijuana in the U.S. was first emitted in El Paso, Texas, and resulted in a recommendation that "loco weed" be included in the Harrison Narcotics Act of 1914. Federal legislation against marijuana was not instituted, however, until 1937—seven full years after Anslinger was appointed director of the FBN.

According to Himmelstein (1983), David Musto (1972, 1973) first put forth the notion that anti-marijuana legislation in the U.S. was enacted as a means of exerting social control over Mexican laborers and Mexican-Americans in the Southwest. Similarly. Helmer (1975) likens the plight of 1930s Mexican immigrants in Los Angeles to the earlier U.S. opium exclusion efforts waged against Chinese workers:

> Jail on drug or other charges, or repatriation by force or choice—these were the methods adopted for reducing the Mexican labor surplus in the city where surplus . . . was the fundamental economic threat. The situation was thus similar to the opium and Chinese exclusion campaign 50 years earlier. Then, as now, the use of a "narcotic" drug was one of many personal and social vices of the target group: Mexicans were lazy, dirty, promiscuous, violent, subintelligent, criminal, anarchistic, communistic—and intoxicated with marijuana. (p. 74)

Himmelstein (1983) has coined the term "the Mexican Hypothesis" to refer to the Musto/Helmer thesis that the FBN did not seek a national anti-marijuana law, but only responded to political pressure.

As exemplified by a 1936 letter from the city editor of an Alamosa, Colorado, newspaper, Musto (1972, 1973)[4] claims that Anslinger and the FBN were pushed into supporting the Marihuana Tax Act of 1937. However, Musto's evidence to support his claim—which essentially consists of a few letters, a few newspaper articles, and Anslinger's own statements—is quick thin.

Musto concludes (1972) his Marihuana Tax Act argument by stating:

> From the evidence examined, the FBN does not appear to have created the marihuana scare of the early 1930s nor can the law be simply ascribed to the Commissioner's determined will. Such scapegoating offers no more than it did in the era when marihuana was blamed for almost any vicious crime. (p. 107)

According to Musto, his explanation of the Marihuana Tax Act was shaped in large part by an interview he conducted with Anslinger in 1970 (1973). It is ironic that Musto's alternate theory to the Anslinger Hypothesis, which has gained popularity over the years, rests primarily on Anslinger's own word. It can thus be argued that the Mexican Hypothesis represents yet another case of systematic research error.

In refuting the "Mexican Hypothesis" of Musto and Helmer, Himmselstein states that an "important relationship" has been identified, but that its nature has been "misconstrued." Himmselstein argues that Musto and Helmer fall short on four points: (1) in demonstrating that the fear of marijuana was substantial in California of the early 1930s, (2) in documenting a rise in marijuana arrests at the time, (3) in documenting the emergency of a broad coalition of anti-Mexican forces as related to the marijuana issue, and (4) in providing significant direct evidence of local pressure on the federal government.

The Social Control Hypothesis

Himmelstein maintains that local pressure did not serve as the impetus that resulted in the passage of the Marihuana Tax Act. He instead posits, as exemplified by the following 1937 Anslinger quote (Walker, 1989), that the negative connotations associated with marijuana through the anti-Mexican campaign served to create an ideology that essentially equated the drug with the devil: "If the hideous monster Frankenstein came face to face with the monster Marihuana, he would drop dead of fright" (Walker, 1979, p. 106).

Two weeks later, at the Hearings on the Marihuana Taxing Bill before the House of Representatives' Committee on Ways and Means, Anslinger and Cooper (1937) compared marijuana to opium:

> In medical schools the physician-to-be is taught that without opium, medicine would be a one-armed man. This is true, because you cannot get along without opium. But here we have a drug that is not like opium. Opium has all of the good of Dr. Jekyll and all the evil of Mr. Hyde. This drug [marijuana] is entirely the monster Hyde, the harmful effect of which cannot be measured. (p. 19)

In explaining why marijuana became criminalized in the U.S., Himmelstein varies from those who preceded him in researching the record of the Marihuana Tax Act. His theory is unique in that it combines elements of both the Anslinger Hypothesis and the Mexican Hypothesis.

Himmelstein's (1983) premise is that Anslinger exploited prevalent anti-Mexican sentiment in the U.S. along with the image of "killer weed" to create an ideology (or a belief system) that served the FBN's own devices. Public discussion of marijuana was thereafter framed on the basis of its association with violence, madness, mayhem and murder:

> Because Mexican laborers and other lower-class groups were identified as typical marihuana users, the drug was believed to cause the kinds of anti-social behavior associated with these groups, especially violent crime. This led to a particular image of marihuana as a "killer weed," which was then used to justify . . . the Marihuana Tax Act. (p. 29)

Himmelstein (1983) considers his own explanation of why the Marihuana Tax Act came into existence to be a convergence of the two competing hypotheses:

> Since the proponents of the Anslinger Hypothesis have not developed an effective theory of *why* the bureau acted as and when it did and the advocates of the Mexican Hypothesis have failed to show that local pressure pushed the bureau into seeking a national law, the basic questions about the [origins of the] Marihuana Tax Act . . . remain unanswered . . . . *[A]lthough the Mexican Hypothesis was developed as a rebuttal to the Anslinger Hypothesis, the intellectual impulses underlying the two are not necessarily contradictory.* (Emphasis added.) (p. 30)

The synthesis of the Anslinger and the Mexican Hypotheses may be referred to as the "Social Control

Hypothesis."[5] The beauty of the Social Control Hypothesis is that it allows the Marihuana Tax Act of 1937 to be seen in the larger context of U.S. drug control policies.

In the aftermath of the prohibition era (1920–1933), in which alcohol was outlawed in the U.S., the Marihuana Tax Act did not represent an end in itself, but a beginning. The Marihuana Tax Act enabled the Federal Bureau of Narcotics to articulate and formulate U.S. drug control policies in a method that clearly defined the enemy. For decades to come, on the ideological foundation which was popularized through the Marihuana Tax Act, a war could be waged not only against the illicit substance of cannabis, but on the brother and sister evils of heroin and cocaine as well. Through the eyes of Anslinger, opium trafficking could be blamed on Communist ("Red") China, and domestic marijuana users, such as jazz musicians (Bonnie & Whitebread, 1974; Sloman, 1979), could be seen as subversives who were targeted for surveillance.

The Social Control Hypothesis appears to be supported by the contention of McWilliams and Block (1989, 1990) that the FBN was a counterintelligence agency that served as the prototype for the Office of Strategic Services (OSS), forerunner of the Central Intelligence Agency (CIA). They conclude their latter article by stating:

> What must be stressed is the discovery of the FBN as a secret intelligence agency participating in clandestine programs totally unrelated to narcotics enforcement . . . . An accurate understanding of the real nature and organization of the FBN reveals several policy-makers posing as law enforcers while engaging in classified and controversial activities affecting American foreign affairs. (p. 187)

Implicit in their theory is criticism of historians and criminologists for their:

> . . . disturbing tendency to concentrate on Anslinger solely as an anti-marijuana zealot, or as a "Neanderthal right-winger." . . . [S]cholars have neglected or misunderstood the Bureau's agents' full range of diverse activities, preferring instead to focus on the more obvious and traditional drug enforcement role. (pp. 354, 368)

Central to the role of FBN as a counterintelligence agency is Anslinger's connection, in the intervening years between World Wars I and II, with the "intelligence subculture": "a secret group of individuals who believed that peacetime intelligence was important" (1989, p. 356). Access to the "subculture" was provided to the first Commissioner of the FBN by his immediate superior, the powerful industrialist and Secretary of the Treasury, Andrew Mellon.[6]

Without labeling it as such, Walker (1989) summarizes the Social Control Hypothesis:

> These forces [which brought about the passage of the Marihuana Tax Act of 1937] resulted in a bureaucratic atmosphere which can only be described as one in which the Bureau of Narcotics under the direction of Harry J. Anslinger possessed hegemony [or political dominance] over the development and direction of domestic drug policy.
>
> . . . the presence of the Marihuana Tax Act served three general purposes: it perpetuated the existence of an already well-established federal drug law enforcement bureaucracy; it extended in the guise of liberal reform a continuing, repressive form of social control whose propriety would not soon be challenged; and it supported the formulation and execution of a foreign policy consistent with the domestic drug control objectives of the Federal Bureau of Narcotics. (pp. 107, 116–117)

The Du Pont Hypothesis

An extension of Becker's and Dickson's notions of the moral and the bureaucratic entrepreneur may be applied to the "Du Pont Hypothesis," which is simply entrepreneurship in its rawest form. Very little has been written of the Du Pont Hypothesis, which posits that the industrialist billionaire Du Pont family and its corporate interests worked behind the scenes to secure the passage of the Marihuana Tax Act of 1937.

According to Herer (1990), the Du Pont Corporation sought to outlaw hemp, or the entire marijuana plant (as opposed to its smokable leaves). For centuries, hemp had been used to create products such as clothing, paper and rope. Herer theorizes that by successfully prohibiting the use of hemp for industrial purposes in the U.S., the Du Pont Corporation created a situation whereby two of its new products could be marketed: a new sulfuric-acid process for wood pulp paper, which would replace paper made from hemp; and nylon, a new synthetic product referred to as "plastic fibers," which would replace hemp cloth and rope. The corporate body of the Du Pont family thus engaged in "a conspiracy to wipe out the natural competition" (1990, pp. 6, 22).

Herer alleges—with a minimum of research and documentation—that the conspiracy involved other influential players. They are: William Randolph Hearst, the powerful newspaper publisher; Andrew Mellon, the banker and financier of the billionaire Mellon family; and Harry Anslinger, director of the Federal Bureau of Narcotics.

Hearst stood to gain financially through utilizing timber acreage (as opposed to hemp) for his Hearst Paper Manufacturing Division. As Mellon and his Mellon Bank of Pittsburgh reportedly were Du Pont's chief financial backers, the Mellon fortune was tied to that of the Du Ponts.

Anslinger enters the picture not as a moral entrepreneur "enterprising about . . . the creation of a new fragment of the moral constitution of society, its code of right and wrong" (Becker, 1963, p. 145), but as the husband of Mellon's niece, the former Martha Denniston (Sloman, 1979). Uncle Andrew, who was Secretary of the Treasury from 1921–1932, appointed Anslinger as the director of the FBN in 1930.

The conspiracy comes full circle in light of the relationship between Hearst and Anslinger. The role Hearst played in Anslinger's appointment as FBN director is documented by Musto (1973), who obtained his information from an interview with Anslinger: "[Anslinger's] patriotism and his belief in the menace of certain foreign ideologies, such as Communism, gained . . . , in Anslinger's opinion, the crucial support of William Randolph Hearst" (p. 209).

Hearst was widely known for promoting racist views in his San Francisco-based newspaper chain. His anti-Chinese and anti-Asian sentiments were embodied by his newspapers' use of the term "the yellow peril." His tirades against Hispanic people in relation to the 1898 Spanish American War and the Mexican Revolution (1911–1914) are legendary, and he expanded that anti-Latino rhetoric to include Mexican and Mexican-American laborers in the U.S. The headlines of Hearst's publications linked vices and minorities: Chinese with opium, African Americans with cocaine, and Mexicans with marijuana.

Hearst used Anslinger and Anslinger used Hearst. Together they successfully framed the image of drug use within the U.S. in the context of violence, insanity and racial minorities. Thus, in 1937, when the Lawyers Legislative League of America "moved to end the deadly narcotic menace of marihuana cigarettes" by agreeing "to sponsor Federal legislation outlawing the weed," they also passed a unanimous resolution that commended William Randolph Hearst and the Hearst newspapers "for pioneering the national fight against dope" (Silver, 1979, p. 276).

Becker (1963) writes that "[w]henever rules are created and applied . . . we should expect to find people . . . using the available media of communication to develop a favorable climate of opinion" (pp. 145–146).

We can apply Becker's theorem not only to the Hearst/Anslinger newsprint relationship, but also to the motion picture industry. Specifically, we can examine how marijuana's "killer weed" image was promoted in the anti-marijuana films of the 1930s.

The Rise of Reefer Madness

Among the anti-marijuana "scare" films that were released prior to the passage of the Marihuana Tax Act of 1937 were *Marihuana: Weed With Roots In Hell* and *Assassin of Youth* (Starks, 1982; The Library of Congress Copyright Office, 1951). Starks writes (1982) that in the latter film, a high-school girl "is introduced to marijuana and is soon engulfed by wild parties, unleashed passions and the horrors of the criminal underworld" (p. 102).

Reefer Madness, the most famous of these films, was originally released as *Tell Your Children* (Sloman, 1979). Described as "one of the first sound films to expound the idea that marijuana leads to sex, madness and murder" (p. 166), the movie was independently produced without the sanction of Hollywood, because of the 1930 Motion Picture Code that outlawed references to drugs (Starks, 1982). In the 1930s, *Tell Your Children* was also released under the titles of *The*

Burning Question, Doped Youth, Dope Addict, and *Love Madness* (Victorek, 1972).[7] In the 1970s, when the film was first released in the U.S. as *Reefer Madness,* it enjoyed widespread popularity, particularly on college campuses, as a laughable "cult classic." In the film, writes Starks (1982):

> Four city slickers, two men and (by implication) their prostitutes, begin hanging out at a soda fountain frequented by high school students . . . . Bill smokes his first reefer [marijuana cigarette] and within minutes he is seduced by one of the loose women. Bill's innocent girl friend Mary comes looking for him and within minute[s] she is turned on and seduced by one of the pushers. Bill blunders on the scene and has a fight with the pusher who accidentally shoots Mary dead . . . (p. 102)

What kind of messages did these 1930s anti-marijuana films send to their audiences? The answer is clear: fear of youths becoming homicidal maniacs, fear of high-school girls losing their virginity, and fear of the criminal class in general. While the extent to which these films helped shape public opinion of the time has thus far been unexplored, it can be assumed that they played at least some kind of role in the passage of the Marihuana Tax Act of 1937.

Starks (1982) describes a scene from the film *Marihuana: Weed With Roots In Hell* in which a pusher's marijuana customers become "hooked on the stronger stuff such as H and C [Heroin and Cocaine]":

> One pusher to another with heavy Spanish accent: "This bunch sure uses up the joy weed don't they."
>
> "Well, that's one way of creating business. When they're that age they're not suspicious and easily hooked."(p. 102)

This notion that marijuana use leads to harder drugs, or the "stepping stone hypothesis," was flatly rejected by Anslinger in his testimony before Congress concerning the Marihuana Tax Act (House of Representatives Hearings before the Committee on Ways and Means, 1937, p. 24):

> Mr. Dingell. I am just wondering whether the marihuana addict graduates into a heroin, an opium, or a cocaine user.
>
> Mr. Anslinger. No, sir; I have not heard of a case of that kind. I think it is an entirely different class. The marihuana addict does not go in that direction.

Whereas Anslinger clearly stated in 1937 that marijuana use does not lead to the use of harder drugs, by 1951 the Commissioner of Narcotics had changed his tune (*U.S. News and World Report,* cited in Kaplan, 1970, p. 234):

> Q[uestion]: Is marijuana habit forming? Is it as dangerous as other narcotics?
>
> A[nslinger]: It is habit forming but not addiction forming. It is dangerous because it leads to a desire for a greater kick from narcotics that do make addicts.

In 1955, Anslinger articulated the stepping stone hypothesis in testimony before the U.S. Senate. However, the FBN director (Himmelstein, 1983) "omitted any reference to violent crime or any other danger tied directly to marihuana . . . . He gave no rendition of marihuana crimes and even de-emphasized the importance of the crime connection" (p. 87).

Clearly, the public image of marijuana that Anslinger and the FBN had promoted in the 1930s and 1940s had indeed changed. No longer was marijuana seen as the "killer weed," but it now was a "stepping stone" to harder drugs.

Testing the Stepping Stone Hypothesis

What was formerly called the "stepping stone hypothesis" is known today as the "escalation" or "gateway" theory, in which "medical experts seem to imply" (Trebach, 1987, p. 82) "that marijuana sucks many young occasional users through that gate and on to harder drugs and into the whole drug culture. Thus if that gate is kept closed to our youth, then that illegal culture is never entered."

The polar opposite of the gateway theory is the "filter theory" of the British psychiatrist Dale Beckett, who claims that the availability of marijuana "may actually filter off some adolescents who . . . [otherwise] would be likely to use narcotics" (Trebach, 1987, p. 84).

Similar to Beckett's drug control philosophy is that of the government of the Netherlands (Holland), which has established a drug control policy of "normalization."

The Dutch view their policy as a pragmatic and conservative one that is based on the realization that a nation surrounded by water, such as the Netherlands, cannot conquer the sea. Rather, by building dikes and locks, Holland has adapted and learned to live with the water in its midst. Just as the Dutch control the sea to the best of their ability, their social control policy of normalization is applied to illicit drug use and its consequences.

Frits Ruter (1988), a law professor at the University of Amsterdam, describes the drug control system of the Dutch as "a policy of encirclement, adaptation, integration and normalization, rather than a policy of social exclusion through criminalization, punishment and stigmatization."

While hemp products (i.e., cannabis or marijuana and hashish) remain illegal in the Netherlands, their use and small-scale sales are permitted. In other words, through the use of prosecutorial discretion, marijuana and hashish laws remain on the books but are not enforced by the Dutch authorities. In fact, cannabis may be purchased off menus in numerous coffeehouses throughout Holland, and it is additionally available through "youth centers."[8]

In developing their cannabis policy, the Dutch authorities have sought to create two markets: aboveground, where cannabis may be used by youths without fear; and underground, where the Dutch do not want their youth to venture. Separating the "hard" and "soft" drug markets is meant to prevent contact between cannabis-seeking Dutch youth and a "pusher." Thus, the goal of drug abuse prevention is achieved by the government of the Netherlands.

Table 1 provides us with convincing evidence that refutes the Stepping Stone Hypothesis. We can clearly see that the prevalence of cannabis use among students in the Netherlands is quite low, particularly when contrasted with similarly-aged students in the United States.[9]

Reefer Madness Revisited

The Dutch policy of normalization is but one form of decriminalization. Since the mid-1970s, 12 states in the United States have enacted marijuana decriminalization systems that operate similarly to the way traffic laws are enforced.[10]

The prefix "de" denotes a reversal or undoing, and decriminalization policies permit nations, states or localities to selectively enforce—or not enforce—cannabis laws. Under decriminalization, marijuana use or possession is not condoned, but is instead treated on a non-criminal basis. Legalization schemes for cannabis differ in that marijuana, like alcohol, cigarettes, coffee or tea, would be available to be purchased in the licit marketplace.

Opponents of marijuana legalization argue that drugs are the enemy of a civilized society, and that we

Table 1
Cannabis Use Among Students in Secondary Schools (13–18 Years)
in The Netherlands and The U.S.A.

	13–14 Years				15–16 Years				17–18 Years	
	Male		Female		Male		Female		Male and Female	
	USA	NL	USA	NL	USA	NL	USA	NL	USA	NL
Lifetime:	15%	3%	14%	2%	40%	12%	30%	9%	44%	18%
Last Mo.:	5%	2%	5%	1%	17%	7%	13%	4%	17%	5%

must not tolerate drug use. Marijuana, they argue, is a "stepping stone" whereby youths are led down the path of drug abuse.

Yet, the only drugs included in the category "Drugs the Enemy" are illicit substances. Not included as the Enemy are equally harmful but legal drugs that have been: (1) manufactured by factories on Main Street, (2) financed by institutions on Wall Street, and (3) packaged for consumption by public relation firms on Madison Avenue. A future question that may be before us is whether Wall Street and Madison Avenue can manipulate Main Street to produce, package and consume a new legal commodity: marijuana.

In the meantime, Drugs the Enemy tend to be viewed not as inert objects that people may or may not take, but as objects with actual life qualities of their own. In the true sociological sense, illicit drugs have become reified: people do not take drugs, but drugs take people.

Just as Reefer Madness reigned in the 1930s, it is alive and well today. Harry Anslinger's ghost smiles at us from above.

Notes

1. The word "marihuana," such as in the Marihuana Tax Act, is consistently used as it appears in the historical record. Otherwise, the use of the word "marijuana" (of Spanish origin and in which the "j" is pronounced as an "h" in English) is preferred. Cannabis is a term used to describe both marijuana and hashish.
2. Stanley Meisler's February 20, 1960 article in *The Nation,* "Federal Narcotics Czar, Zeal Without Insight," does a good job of chronicling Anslinger's career and demonstrating how his personal philosophy on drugs guided not only the FBN, but Congress and the nation as a whole.
3. In 1960, Nixon had been defeated in his bid for the presidency by John Kennedy. In 1962, Pat Brown, then the governor of California and a strong Kennedy supporter in the presidential election, was bracing for a gubernatorial challenge from Nixon. According to King, Brown convinced the White House to convene a conference on drugs that served to support Brown's California method of treating drug offenders through "lengthy and extensive parole supervision."
4. Also see p. 32 of the 1937 Taxation of Marihuana Hearings before the Committee on Ways and Means of the House of Representatives.
5. The term "Social Control Hypothesis" is the author's own creation, not that of Himmelstein.
6. The relationship between Anslinger and Mellon merits deeper analysis and is examined further in this text's next section: the "Du Pont Hypothesis." The "Du Pont Hypothesis" is the author's own term.
7. The source of this information is an obscure film review article located in the Motion Picture, Broadcasting and Recorded Sound Division of the Library of Congress in Washington, D.C.
8. In both instances, sales of cannabis to youths under the age of 16 are not condoned.
9. These data concerning cannabis use in the Netherlands and the U.S. were taken from a larger table entitled "Substance Use Among Students In Secondary Schools (13–18 Years) In The Netherlands And United States of America," which was provided to the author via a September 28, 1990, personal communication with Eddy Engelsman, who directs the Alcohol, Drugs and Tobacco Branch of the Ministry of Welfare, Health and Cultural Affairs for the Netherlands. Engelsman, who has been called the Dutch "drug czar," interpreted the table from Dutch to English as it originally appeared in a Dutch publication: *Roken, Alcohol-Endruggebruik Oncer Scholieren Vanaf 10 Jarr (Smoking, Alcohol and Drug Use Among School Students From 10 Years)* by Plomp, H.N.; Kuipers, H., and Van Oers, M. Stratified by age group and gender, the table lists "lifetime" and "last month" prevalence not only for cannabis, but also for tobacco, alcohol, inhalants, cocaine, heroin, stimulants, sleeping tablets and tranquilizers. For an unknown reason, the data provided are not stratified by gender for the 17–18 age group. The larger table has been published in *Drug Prohibition and the Conscience of Nations* edited by Arnold Trebach and Kevin Zeese (Washington, D.C.: Drug Policy Foundation, 1990).
10. Of the 12 U. S. states that have decriminalized marijuana, South Dakota's legislature and Alaska's

voters recriminalized marijuana possession for personal use. Despite the passage of the recriminalization ballot proposition by Alaska's voters in November, 1990, as of early 1993, marijuana possession for personal use by adults remains *legal* (as opposed to decriminalized) in the forty-ninth state. The fact that marijuana is legal in Alaska is due to an Alaska State Supreme Court 1975 ruling that the possession of marijuana for personal use within the privacy of the home is a protected right under Alaska's Constitution. The remaining 10 states that have decriminalized marijuana are: California, Colorado, Maine, Minnesota, Mississippi, Nebraska, New York, North Carolina, Ohio, and Oregon.

References

Anslinger, H. J., & Cooper, C. R. (1937). Marijuana: Assassin of youth. *American Magazine 18*(19), 150–53.

Becker, H. S. (1963). *Outsiders: Studies in the sociology of deviance.* New York: The Free Press of Glencoe.

Bonnie, R. J., & Whitebread, C. H. (1974). *The marijuana conviction: A history of marijuana prohibition in the United States.* Charlottesville, VA: University Press of Virginia.

Demott, B. (1962, March). The great narcotics muddle. *Harper's Magazine,* pp. 46–54.

Dickson, D. T. (1968). Bureaucracy and morality: An organizational perspective on a moral crusade. *Social Problems, 16,* 143–156.

Galliher, J. F., & Walker, A. (1977). The puzzle of the social origins of the marihuana tax act of 1937. *Social Problems, 24,* 367–376.

Galliher, J. F., & Walker, A. (1978). The politics of systematic research error: The case of the federal bureau of narcotics as a moral entrepreneur. *Crime & Social Justice, 10,* 29–33.

Grinspoon, L. (1971). *Marihuana reconsidered.* Cambridge, MA: Harvard University Press.

Helmer, J. (1975). *Drugs and minority oppression.* New York: The Seabury Press.

Herer, J. (1990). *The emperor wears no clothes: The authoritative historical record of the cannabis plant, hemp prohibition, and how marijuana can save the world.* Van Nuys, CA.: Hemp Publishing.

Himmelstein, J. L. (1983). *The strange career of marihuana: Politics and ideology of drug control in America.* Westport, CT: Greenwood Press.

Kaplan, J. (1970). *Marijuana—the new prohibition.* New York: The World Publishing Company.

King, R. (1972). *The drug hang-up: America's fifty year folly.* Springfield, IL: Charles C. Thomas.

Library of Congress Copyright Office. (1951). *Motion pictures: 1912–1939.* Catalog of Copyright Entries, Cumulative Series.

Lindesmith, A. (1965). *The addict and the law.* Bloomington: IN: University Press.

McWilliams, J. C. (1990). *The protectors: Harry J. Anslinger and the Federal Bureau of Narcotics, 1930–1962.* Newark, DE: University of Delaware Press.

McWilliams, J. C., & Block, A. A. (1989). On the origins of American counterintelligence: Building a clandestine network. *Journal of Policy History, 1,* 353–372.

McWilliams, J. C., & Block, A. A. (1990). All the commissioner's men: The Federal Bureau of Narcotics and the Dewey-Luciano affair, 1947–54. *Intelligence & National Security, 5,* 171–192.

Meisler, S. (1960, February 20). Federal narcotics czar, zeal without insight. *The Nation,* 159–162.

Morgan, P. A. (1976). John Helmer: Drugs and minority oppression. *Crime & Social Justice, 5,* 65–67.

Musto, D. F. (1972). The Marihuana Tax Act of 1937. *Archives of General Psychiatry, XXVI,* 101–108.

Musto, D. F. (1973). *The American disease.* New Haven, CT: Yale University Press.

Reasons, C. E. (1974). The "dope" on the Bureau of Narcotics in maintaining the criminal approach to the drug problem. In C. Reasons, (Ed.), *The criminologist: crime and the criminal* (pp. 144–155). Palisades, CA: Goodyear.

Ruter, F. (1988, on May 25). *The pragmatic Dutch approach to drug control: Does it work?* Paper presented at a forum of the Drug Policy Foundation in Washington, DC.

Silver, G. (Ed.). (1979). *The dope chronicles, 1850–1950.* San Francisco: Harper & Row.

Sloman, L. (1979). *Reefer madness.* New York: The Bobbs-Merrill Company.

Solomon, D (Ed.). (1966). *The marihuana papers.* New York: Signet Books.

Starks, M. (1982). *Cocaine fiends and reefer madness:*

An illustrated history of drugs in the movies. New York: Cornwall Books.

Trebach, A. S. (1987). *The great drug war.* New York: MacMillan.

Trebach, A. S., & Zeese, K. B. (Eds.). (1990). *Drug prohibition and the conscience of nations.* Washington, DC: Drug Policy Foundation.

United States House of Representatives, Committee on Ways and Means. (1937, April 27–30, May 4). *Taxation of marihuana, hearings on H.R. 6385,* 75th Congress, 1st session. Washington, DC: Government Printing Office.

Victorek, D. (1972, October). Dave O'Brien achieved his goals as a man with no pretensions as an actor, In C. P. Reilly (Ed.), *Films In Review* Vol. XXIII, No. 8, (p. 449). New York: National Board of Review of Motion Pictures, Inc.

Walker, W. O., III. (1989). *Drug control in the Americas* (2nd ed.). Albuquerque, NM: University of New Mexico Press.

White House Conference on Narcotic and Drug Abuse. (1962, September 27–28). *Proceedings.* Washington, DC: U. S. Government Printing Office.

Discussion Questions

1. What is the Social Control Hypothesis?
2. How can the domestic and foreign policy aspects of the "Social Control Hypothesis" be applied to the "war on drugs" of the 1980s and 1990s?
3. What are the components of the Dutch government's drug control policy known as "normalization"?
4. What does Table 1 reveal about cannabis use patterns by youth in the U.S.A. and the Netherlands?
5. How can the anti-marijuana films of the 1930s be compared with today's advertisements by the Partnership For A Drug-Free America?

VI

Part VI—Special Populations, Dilemmas, and Debates

Unlike Parts I through V, which dealt with drug use under clustered homogeneous topic headings, Part VI looks at drug use from a variety of problem areas.

The first article, "Impaired Health Care Professionals—An Overview," by Medora, raises the question: Are health care providers such as physicians, nurses, dentists and pharmacists, who have easy access to drugs, prone to drug addiction? In other words, are members of this occupational category more at risk than members of other occupational categories? Some research shows that among health care providers there is an estimated four percent to six percent who experience serious drug problems. Generally, the belief is that health care professionals double and triple the rates of dependence found in our general population (Moore & Lewis, 1989).

Another study shows that out of 500 physicians and 504 medical students in Massachusetts, 59 percent of the doctors and 78 percent of the students used psychoactive substances (Clark & Springen, 1986). Three factors that may be responsible for higher rates of drug use among health care professionals are: the availability of drugs, expected administration of drugs, and the fact that health care professionals can easily become desensitized and rationalize the negative effects of prolonged drug use. One other interesting study reports that compared to the general population, physicians are five times more likely to take mild opiates and benzodiazepine tranquilizers without medical supervision (Hughes, Brandenburg et al., 1992). Medora's research directly addresses this serious problem of drug abuse among health care professionals. In the research, he raises such possible reasons as long working hours, easy access to drugs, professional demands, and a tendency to self-treat for the drug abuse. Medora says that if addiction occurs in the health care practitioner, then logically, intervention strategies have to be created to protect the well-being of the public. Intervention is successful if the practitioner agrees to seek treatment. After the practitioner has been treated and is recovering, a reentry contract should be signed by the practitioner requiring him/her to observe specific behavioral codes in order to continue the practice of medicine. If intervention and treatment fail to rehabilitate a health care practitioner, then his/her license to practice can be revoked. Having realized the gravity of this problem, most health care organizations have established prevention, treatment and rehabilitation programs.

According to the second article of this part, "Sports and Clean Living: A Useful Myth?" by Rooney, the question "Why do people use drugs?" is a question that everyone asks, but the answer often goes begging.[1] In applying *control theory* to drug use, the explanation would revolve around the lack of social integration in society. Control theorists believe that drug use occurs whenever people lack (1) attachment to others, (2) commitment to goals, (3) involvement in conventional activity, and (4) belief in the common value system. Further, when individuals are not involved with either the family setting, the school or with non-delinquent peers, they tend to drift into drug use (Witters, Venturelli, & Hanson, 1992).

Application of control theory to Rooney's research should show that drug users are less likely than others to participate in social clubs and organizations and engage in team sport activities. Interestingly however, Rooney's research does not support this popular theory. Instead, the findings by Rooney support the research results by Agnew and Peterson in Part II. Rooney finds that except for diminishing cigarette use, the degree of participation in sports for both male and female seniors in high school has very little relationship to using mind-altering drugs. One would think that participation in sports would significantly diminish all forms of drug use.

Though Rooney's research does not support control theory, his study concurs with many research findings saying that an alarming amount of drug use is found in both professional sports and among the more "generic" athletes who are not in professional sports (Akers, 1992; Witters, Venturelli, & Hanson, 1992). In simply looking at high-school seniors, we find that an estimated 250,000 are using anabolic steroids (Kashkin & Kleber, 1989). Use of anabolic steroids by adolescent athletes is especially alarming because the latest research indicates that in comparison to older adolescents who first experiment with drugs, younger adolescents are increasingly less likely to cease drug use.

If such a high number use steroids mainly for muscle building, it is no surprise that illicit drug use among other athletes is likely to be rampant as well. Attesting to this is the extensive amount of drug use by athletes who are involved in nonprofessional as well as professional sports. Current estimates are that between 50 percent to 90 percent of athletes in baseball, basketball, and football use drugs (Akers, 1992).

Whether someone should use illicit drugs without legal repercussions remains very controversial and debatable. The question of drug use by pregnant women is equally debatable and perplexing. The crux of the concern is not the mother's use of drugs, but whether pregnant women should he held accountable for using an illicit drug while carrying a human fetus. Does this future mother have the right to inflict the consequences and effects of her drug use on the unborn infant? Should the fetus have legal rights apart from the mother? If so, should society have any role in this protection? Should the mother be liable to criminal prosecution? Should she he sentenced in a court of law if the infant born is addicted or suffers physical and mental retardation? What about a drug-addicted mother who delivers a normal baby—should she be made liable for risking the infant's life? In other words, should there be any intervention by a third party and if so, what amount of intervention should take place?

This issue has become increasingly debatable in light of research proving that there is widespread use of marijuana and cocaine by pregnant women (Zuckerman, Frank, Hingson, et al., 1989; Hatch, 1986; Tennes, Avitable et al., 1985; Gibson, Bayhurst, & Colley, 1983). Further, the issue becomes more tumultuous when many research findings clearly show that infants born to marijuana users weighed less (an average of 79 g less) and were on average shorter in length (0.5 cm shorter) than infants of nonusers. Similarly, infants born to cocaine-using mothers weighed even less at birth (93 g average). Infants were appreciably shorter (average of 0.7 cm shorter), and their head circumference was an average of .43 smaller than that of infants of nonusers (Zuckerman, Frank, Hingson et al., 1989). The general conclusion of many medical research studies on this topic is that the use of marijuana and cocaine during pregnancy has an independent effect on and is strongly associated with impaired fetal growth. Let us return to one of the original questions: Should society intervene in cases where pregnant women are using and abusing drugs? If so, how should society intervene? Should society intervene by punishing? Or, should it intervene by educating, treating and rehabilitating? What would be more satisfying to the public? What would be more humane? What would be the *most effective* solution for solving this problem?

Addressing this controversial and often unnerving issue are the third and fourth articles of Part VI. The third article, "Creating Fetal Rights and Protecting Pregnant Women's Constitutional Rights: An Analysis of Drug-Related Cases and Issues," by Viano, continues the discussion introduced thus far by systematically addressing the major issues involved.

Viano's research begins by looking at what modern medicine has defined as the negative impact that legal and illegal drugs have on the development of the fetus. Alcohol can cause the "fetal alcohol syndrome." Illegal drugs can impair the development of the fetus, cause the infant to become addicted, and result in baby abandonment by the addicted mother.

Several forces and issues in society that lead to increased involvement by the state in women's pregnancies are: protecting the developing fetus from harm, the abortion controversy, the drug epidemic (for example, 375,000 "drug babies" born each year in the U.S.), medical advances, and the responsibilities and costs our society has to bear in having so many drug babies.

Viano finds that the state's attempt to intervene is highly controversial. Some hail this intervention as necessary to save the children, who are perceived as the victims; others see such intervention as an unconstitutional intrusion into fertile women's lives, (here women are perceived as victims). Viano's article presents the major arguments advanced by each side, an examination of important related court cases, and the author's own perceptions and conclusions.

The fourth article, "Unintended Consequences: The Prosecution of Maternal Substance Abusers," by Maureen Norton Hawk takes a more deterministic position on the issue of punishing maternal substance abusers. The author believes that one casualty evolving from the current war on drugs has been the maternal substance abuser. Norton Hawk argues that punishing maternal substance abusers infringes on the rights of the mother, and that the methods used in punishing are counterproductive. The author uses Sieber's theory of unintended consequences as the analytical framework of her research. In applying Sieber's theory, Norton Hawk discerns that, in the end, the methods and practices of punishment are harmful to both the mother and child, and result in creating unintended effects.

To summarize these two articles: Viano clearly articulates and analyzes the more philosophical, social and political ramifications surrounding this problem, while Norton Hawk's research focuses on the consequences of applying punishment methods to maternal substance abusers. Not only are both articles instructive, but when taken together they leave the reader appreciably knowledgeable about this perplexing and controversial issue.

Shouldn't the federal government intervene to stop or at least substantially reduce the spread of AIDS? How serious has the AIDS epidemic become? An unexpected 22 percent of U.S. AIDS adult cases result from intravenous (I.V.) drug users who share needles; "another 52% of heterosexual AIDS cases; and 59% of nationwide pediatric cases are related to I.V. drug use" (Hagan, Des Jarlais, & Purchase et al., 1991). Considering these horrifying statistics, should our government intervene?

Most would spontaneously say yes and agree with at least some varying amount of government intervention. *However,* how many would continue to support this type of program when the intervention method consists of doling out sterilized syringes to drug addicts? In other words, many of us are supportive of curtailing the spread of AIDS, but how many would hesitate to support programs calling for any amount of indiscriminate distribution of syringes to heroin addicts? In fact, the image of our government distributing needles to drug addicts is so emotionally charged that many people lose sight of the long term ***humanistic goal*** of reducing the spread of AIDS—an unmistakably irreversible deadly disease.

Research clearly shows that needle exchange programs not only reduce the spread of AIDS, but also: (1) reduce the number of monthly injections, (2) increase the number of users who use *new* needles, and increase the percentage of users who *always* use bleach to disinfect their syringes, (3) encourage users to "hang out" in particular places other than shooting galleries and attend weekly meetings on risk reduction, and (4) identify, develop and work with community leaders advocating the cessation of drug dependence, to change risk behaviors within the needle-using subculture (Sufian, Friedman, Curtis et al., 1991; Becker, 1988; Friedman, Des Jarlais et al., 1987). In essence, the most important goals sought in needle exchange programs are to reduce sharing, halt the spread of AIDS that results from needle sharing, and establish successful educational intervention techniques that will *change the behavior of severely drug-addicted individuals.*

There is no question that needle exchange programs have very honorable intentions. However, as mentioned above, the success in implementing these programs is severely offset by negative public perception. The public's perception is that our government is supporting illicit drug abuse and helping a group of drug users who are not only perceived as supremely deviant, but who also carry the stigma of being poor and oppressed—and who are frequently minority members.

The fifth article in Part VI discusses this very controversial social problem of government-sponsored needle exchange programs. "The Politics of Needle Exchange in New York City" originated as a speech presented by Gillman, and was later revised as an essay for this volume. The essay represents a case study example illustrating how needle exchange programs are affected by outside forces, most often stemming from perception problems. Gillman's case study of one major city in the U.S. provides detailed information about how needle exchange programs can become affected by larger political ramifications and concerns.

Gillman begins by saying that two epidemics characterize our time—drugs and AIDS. The author believes that historically the two epidemics bifurcate our society into "us" and "them." Gillman suggests that our political heritage of rigid fundamentalism affects how science is used to inform public policy. Her aim is to offer some ". . . disquieting observations on how science is used to inform, here, health policy" (author's quotes).

It is conservatively estimated that 50 percent of New York City's 200,000 injecting drug users are infected with the AIDS virus. Gillman contends that the government's response to the AIDS epidemic is based on politics instead of epidemiological evidence and strategies. Politics has turned the issue into a choice between combating AIDS *or* addiction.

Concluding this anthology is the editor's postscript highlighting numerous extrapolations that can be derived from this collection of articles, and ending the postscript is an emphasis on the importance of *perceiving and understanding how drug use and abuse are inextricably connected with most major aspects of our daily lives.* Considering this view, and for the sake of beginning to curtail drug abuse, the editor advocates that we must cease blaming dependent factors erroneously perceived as the immediate causes responsible for the consumption of drugs. In essence, we must cease blaming the victims of drug abuse and their immediate social and cultural environments. Instead, we should effectively comprehend and deal with the more substantive and holistic causes of this problem.

Notes

1. Incidentally, this same question is responsible for driving many research studies.

References

Akers, R.L. (1992). *Drugs, alcohol, and society: Social structure, process, and policy.* Belmont, CA: Wadsworth Publishing Company.

Becker, M. H., & Joseph, J. (1988). AIDS and behavioral change to reduce risk: A review. *American Journal of Public Health, 78,* 394–440.

Clark, M., & Springen, K. (1986, October 6). Docs and drugs: Physicians heal thyself. *Newsweek,* p. 28.

Friedman, S. R., Des Jarlais, D., Sotheran, J. L., & Garber, J. (1987). AIDS and self organization among intravenous drug users. *International Journal of the Addictions, 22,* 201–219.

Gibson, G. T., Bayhurt, P. A., & Colley, D. P. (1983). Maternal alcohol, tobacco and cannabis consumption and the outcome of pregnancy. *Australian and New Zealand Journal of Obstetrics and Gynecology, 23,* 15–19.

Hagan, H., Des Jarlais, D. C., Purchase, D., Reid, T., & Friedman, S. R. (1991). The Tacoma syringe exchange. *Journal of Addictive Disease, 10,* 81–88.

Hatch, E. E., & Bracken,M. B. (1986). Effect of marijuana use in pregnancy on fetal growth. *American Journal of Epidemiology, 124,* 986–993.

Hughes, P. H., Brandenburg, K., Baldwin, D. C., Sterr, C. L., Williams, K. M., Anthony, J. C., & Sheehan, D. (1992). Prevalence of substance use among U. S. physicians. *Journal of the American Medical Association, 267,* 2333–2339.

Kashkin, K. B., & Kleber, D. H. (1989). Hooked on hormones? An anabolic steroid addiction hypothesis. *Journal of the American Medical Association, 262,* 8166–3170.

Moore, N. P, & Lewis, G. R. (1989). Substance abuse and the physician. In. G. W. Lawson (Ed.), *Alcohol and substance abuse in special populations.* Rockville, MD: Aspen Publishers.

Sufian, M., Friedman, S. R., Curtis, R., Neaigus, A., & Stepherson, B. (1991). Organizing as a new approach to AIDS reduction for intravenous drug users. *Journal of Addictive Diseases, 10,* 89–98.

Tennes, K., Avitable, N., Blackard, C., Boyles, C., Hasboun, B., Holmes, L., & Kreye, M. (1985). Marijuana: Prenatal and postnatal exposure in the human. In T. M. Pinkert (Ed.), Current research on the consequences of maternal drug abuse [Monograph]. *NIDA Research 59 (pp. 48–60)F. DHHS Publication No. (ADM) (85)1400.* Washington, DC: Government Printing Office.

Witters, W., Venturelli, P., & Hanson, G. (1992). *Drugs and society* (3rd ed.). Boston, MA: Jones & Bartlett Publishers, Inc.

Zuckerman, B., Frank, D. A., Hingson, R., Amaro, H., Levenson, S. M., Kayne, H., Parker, S., Vinci, R., Aboagye, K., Fried, L. E., Cabral, H., Timperi, R., & Bauchner, H. (1989). Effects of maternal marijuana and cocaine use on fetal growth. *The New England Journal of Medicine, 320,* 762–768.

Impaired Health Care Professionals

An Overview

Rustem S. Medora

Rustem S. Medora received his Bachelor of Pharmacy at the University of Gujarat in Ahmedabad, India, and subsequently received his Ph.D. in Pharmacognosy from the University of Rhode Island. Currently, he is Professor of Pharmaceutical Sciences at the University of Montana School of Pharmacy and Allied Health Sciences. Rustem Medora's area of expertise is the production of medicinal compounds from plant cell cultures. His research interests have resulted in more than 25 published articles and papers. He has been active on the University of Montana campus recruiting minorities into health care professional programs.

Problems associated with substance abuse and dependence on drugs are common to all health care professionals, and may even be higher in these special population groups, compared to the general population. When health care professionals work long hours, have demanding workloads, and experience stress as a normal component of their work, they may resort to drug and alcohol use as a means to escape from the realities of their jobs. Needless to say, an impaired health care professional is unable to provide quality care and jeopardizes the well-being of his patient.

Incidence

At the end of 1986 there were 569,160 registered allopathic physicians in the U.S. (Seventh report, 1990). A 1985 report indicated that at least 17,000 physicians had problems related to drug abuse, and estimated that about 100 died annually from drug and alcohol abuse (Smith, 1985). However, alcoholism among physicians is estimated to be two to five percent, the same as the general population (Niven et al., 1984). On the other hand, Talbott estimates that "lifetime occupational prevalence (the percentage of physicians who experience chemical dependency during their working careers) range from 13–14%, figures only slightly in excess of those found in the general population" (Talbot & Wright, 1987). In the past, there was general agreement that heavy drug use among physicians was greater than among comparable control groups and the population in general. According to Valliant's 1970 study, physicians used more tranquilizers, sedatives and stimulants than matched controls, and the incidence of heavy drug use was 1.6 times higher than in a comparable population (Valliant et al., 1972). In a more recent survey, carried out in 1984–85, McAuliffe et al. (1986) found that in the past year, 25 percent of the physicians had treated themselves with psychoactive drugs, while 10 percent had used them recreationally. Since substance abuse among physicians often begins in training years, then surfaces to clinical recognition a decade or two later (Westermeyer, 1991), surveys of drug use by students in the health professions as well as resident physicians and health care professionals alert us to future substance abuse patterns among these individuals.

Two recent surveys of medical students (Baldwin et al., 1991) and resident physicians (Hughes et al., 1991) indicate that, as a group, they have lower rates of use of illicit substances (i.e., amphetamines, cocaine, heroin, marijuana, and LSD) than their peers in the general population. However, these surveys note that self-prescribing is a problem early in their careers for the future practitioners and that the rate of use of drugs by women has risen closer to that of men. It is reassuring to note, however, that there is a decline in cocaine and marijuana use among medical students compared with an earlier study (Conrad et al., 1988). In another survey, at a private mid-Atlantic school, it was found that medical students were using less tobacco and marijuana than they did when they were pre-med students. This was not the case with cocaine, however, which was used by 17 percent of the respondents before and during medical school (Schwartz et al., 1990).

It is estimated that there are approximately 2,033,032 registered nurses in the U. S., five percent of whom are believed to be alcoholic, according to the general population figures used for females. While drug addiction among the general population is said to be one to two percent (Sullivan et al., 1988), The American Nurses' Association estimates that six to eight percent of nurses have a substance abuse problem (Green, 1989). In the disciplinary proceedings brought against nurses in 1980–81, 37 of the 58 member boards reporting indicated that 67 percent of the cases were related to some form of chemical abuse (Green, 1984). In spite of the gravity of the problem, it is unfortunate that a 1984 report indicated that most undergraduate nursing programs offered only two to four clock hours of instruction on addictions, while some provided none (Haack & Hartford, 1984). Although there is a high incidence of substance abuse among nurses, there is little information available on alcohol and drug use among the nursing student population. A recent study indicates that about one in four nursing students may have problems with alcohol abuse (Engs & Hanson, 1989).

There are an estimated 157,800 active pharmacists in the U.S. (Seventh report, 1990). Along with physicians and nurses, pharmacists represent another health care profession with a high potential for abuse of drugs (Smith, 1985). Nevertheless, there are almost no independent epidemiologic data on the extent of substance use or abuse among American pharmacists, although there is general consensus that drug addiction is a problem among pharmacists (McAuliffe et al., 1987). Moreover, it is interesting that relatively more physicians and medical students have used psychoactive drugs at some time in their life than comparable samples of pharmacists and pharmacy students (Valliant et al., 1972).

In recent drug use surveys of pharmacy students (McAuliffe et al., 1986; Tucker et al., 1988; Miller et al., 1990), the one carried out in eight southeastern schools by Miller et al. is the most extensive. When the results of this study are examined, it appears that pharmacy students were using significantly less alcohol and illicit drugs than the typical American college student, with the exception of tranquilizers (4% pharmacy vs 4.4% peers) and heroin (0.2% pharmacy vs 0.1% peers). There was significantly lower use among pharmacy students of alcohol, marijuana, amphetamines, cocaine, barbiturates, and LSD than among their peer group. The surveys also indicate that drug use among pharmacy students in the southeastern states is lower than in a mid-western state and in the New England area. These data seem to be in keeping with NIDA's national household survey that the south has a lower rate of drug use than the country as a whole (NIDA, 1987).

Factors Contributing to Substance Abuse by Health Professionals

- Easy access to controlled substances: Health care professionals work in an environment where drugs are easily available, and often they are in charge of prescribing or distributing them.
- Strenuous work schedules, stress and overwork: Many practitioners work more than 40 hours a week, respond to late night calls, and work rotating shifts, all of which may disrupt sleeping patterns and encourage the use of stimulants, sedatives and hypnotics.
- Professional demands: These include making "life and death" decisions, catering to demanding and difficult patients, and always facing the likelihood of malpractice suits. They are in a healing profession and so they put unreasonable demands on themselves to try to help or cure their clients. The glut of scientific knowledge and the new innovations in technology force them to attend continuing education classes and keep up-to-date with their knowledge and skills. Often their career demands compromise their family obligations.
- Tendency to self-treat: Most clinicians tend to self-diagnose and self-treat. The medication employed to treat a short-term problem may become an addiction.

- Lack of peer support and effective coping mechanisms: In the past there were no peer support groups, and the individual had to tackle his problems on his own. In recent years most professional groups have set up treatment programs to help their peers.

Identification of Impairment

The problem of deciding whether or not a health professional is impaired rests on how drug abuse is defined. Oakley and Ksir in their text define drug abuse as "patterns of drug use that impair the individual's ability to function optimally in his personal, social, and vocational life" (Ray & Ksir, 1990). Similarly, The American Society of Addiction Medicine, in part, defines a health professional as impaired "when one or more problems cause him or her to be dysfunctional in delivering patient care, in other professional activities, in educational or in private life" (NIDA, 1987).

Health care professionals who are addicted to alcohol and other drugs shy away from seeking help. The nature of the disease is such that the defense mechanisms of denial, rationalization, projection, and intellectualization tend to distance the affected health care practitioner from reality (Green, 1989). Factors that prevent these individuals from seeking help include embarrassment and shame, possible loss of licensure, financial loss, legal ramifications, and society's attitude that "health care providers should know better" (Talbot, 1990). Society has also placed them on a high pedestal, physicians are used as role models, pharmacists are considered the most trustworthy professionals, and nurses are the modern day Florence Nightingales.

The nature of addiction is such that the professional who has become addicted to alcohol and/or other drugs will do everything possible to conceal his habit. This is why it is important that health care practitioners be able to recognize the signs and symptoms of drug misuse in their impaired colleagues, bearing in mind that the drug problem is so complex that even experts have difficulty making accurate diagnoses (Micrograms, 1985). It is important to remember that signs which may appear to be drug abuse related may be due to myriad other reasons, and one could mistakenly accuse an innocent colleague. For example, a person carrying a syringe and needle may not be an addict but a diabetic, someone with constricted pupils may not be a junkie but be on medication, and a person with reddened eyes may have an infection and not be smoking pot.

Common signs and symptoms of drug abuse in a colleague include prolonged or continued deterioration in performance, not to be confused with the occasional negative moods and personal setbacks that everyone experiences (Green, 1989; Micrograms, 1985). The unbecoming behavior must become a trend, and this behavior must conflict with the colleague's own values and expectations. Whenever the practitioner begins to show declining work performance, poor interpersonal relationships, marked changes in attendance and work patterns, diminishing lifestyle, and defensive behavior such as withdrawal, blame, denial, hostility, and aggression, drug and alcohol involvement should be suspected and investigated. Always be aware that we all occasionally exhibit some of these life performance problems. It is a pattern of job performance problems over a period of time that one should note and document.

Intervention

Intervention is the next step to curb this disease process, but this relies on careful identification of impairment. Successful intervention depends on obtaining facts and establishing specific incidents and events that identify the health care practitioner as a true substance abuser or victim of chemical dependency. Such facts need to be accurate, specific and detailed in order to break through the chemically dependent person's denial system and act as a catalyst to motivate the individual to seek treatment (Talbot, 1990; Roth, 1987). Such data may be drawn from the changes in the quality of care provided by the professional, patterns of sociopsychological changes and behavior at work, and the changes occurring in his personal and family life.

Intervention is a structured method of presenting reality in a manner that will penetrate defenses and distorted perceptions. A successful intervention depends on the skillful collection and assessment of historical, physical, mental, and laboratory data. Also critical to success is the selection of an effective intervention strategy. There are many variations on the intervention strategy and the ways in which these can be implemented. The one first described by Vern Johnson in 1973 is summarized by Williams (Williams, 1989), and the one used at the Talbott-Marsh Recovery Campus is summarized by Talbott (Talbot, 1990). When intervention is implemented in a timely fashion, it will help the health care practitioner save his professional career. If intervention fails, then it may have to be tried again. Nonetheless, if intervention fails to result in recovery, then action to revoke the license of the practitioner and protect the clients and the profession is appropriate.

Treatment, Rehabilitation and Prevention

After a successful intervention, the health care professional is referred to facilities skilled in the treatment and management of chemical dependencies. It is recognized that professionals may need special treatment, but there is no general agreement about whether programs designed specifically for health care professionals are the best answer (Johnson, 1986). There are many options available for treatment, but it is important that the treatment plan for any individual include the option best suited for his or her needs. There are difficulties in treating health care professionals (Freudenberger, 1986; Talbot & Martin, 1984), and hence they may be referred to treatment facilities such as Merritt Peralta Institute in Oakland, CA, or Ridgeway in Smyma, GA, that cater to this select group of individuals.

Most treatment programs begin with detoxification, which involves helping the patient handle symptoms of withdrawal from the drug to which he is addicted. The protocol for detoxification will vary from drug to drug. Some symptoms such as malnutrition and insomnia are treated without drugs, while other symptoms such as seizures, depression, and hallucinations may require drug therapy. Depending on the patient's preference, he may select an outpatient or an inpatient treatment facility best suited to his needs. The outpatient facility costs less, allows the patient to work part-time, and helps him gradually adjust to a nonaddictive lifestyle while living in his own environment. Unfortunately, the outpatient treatment program leaves the individual with access to drugs and in an environment which may be the cause of his problem in the first place.

The inpatient programs are higher in cost, and they disrupt employment, family, and social life, but they provide 24-hour care and keep the patient from drugs and daily stress. Alcohol and drug dependence are complex behavioral and physiological disorders with multiple causes. Hence the treatments that work best are all-encompassing and include behavioral and pharmacological therapies. Addiction, however, remains a chronic relapsing condition usually requiring prolonged or repeated treatment (Shuckit, 1989).

Support from family, colleagues and friends is one of the few variables that is associated with long-term success in all programs. Often, codependence is a problem, and the family member (or significant other) needs as much help as the health care practitioner (Williams et al., 1991). Family participation is essential, because this gives the family a chance to begin healing the family pain. During the healing, education about the importance of resolving interpersonal conflicts must be stressed. Poor interpersonal relationships can hinder progress, and supportive relationships can help recovery. Support groups within one's discipline (e.g., Pharmacists Helping Pharmacists) are very useful in helping a professional's reentry into practice. These groups are not designed to replace 12-step programs such as Alcoholics Anonymous or Narcotics Anonymous, but to complement them.

Reentry is part and parcel of the rehabilitation of all health care professionals. According to Roth, reentry should involve a reentry contract that is valid for one to two years and includes a list of activities in which the health care professional is obligated to participate (Roth, 1987). The contract protects the employer and the professional. If a provision for random body fluid analysis is included, it will protect the innocent professional if controlled drugs are found to be missing. The contract could also include permission to monitor the individual, an agreement to maintain a drug-free lifestyle, specified attendance at support group meetings, counseling on a regular basis, use of medication such as Antabuse or naltrexone as prescribed, and action to be taken in case of relapse. Of course, most of the social and vocational reentry problems would be minimized if the practitioner's licensing board would allow the individual to practice throughout the treatment process.

If at all possible, preventing chemical dependency in health care professionals is the best solution to the prevalence of drug use among them. This can perhaps be best accomplished by education through high school, college and then the professional school. While most high schools and colleges in the U. S. have incorporated in their curricula some aspects of the use and abuse of drugs, most medical, dental, nursing and pharmacy schools are still trying to put together comprehensive curricula and programs designed to educate their own professional students in the area of chemical dependency, and in addition, to teach them how to tackle drug addiction problems in their own peers. In 1989, the National Institute of Alcohol Abuse and Alcoholism (NIAAA) and the National Institute on Drug Abuse (NIDA) jointly sponsored a program to develop and demonstrate twelve effective models for integrating alcohol and other drug abuse teaching into medical and nurse education curricula (Model curricula, 1989). Although NIAAA and NIDA funding is not available at the moment to develop similar curricula in the pharmacy schools, the American Association of Colleges of Pharmacy has provided some schools with modest funds to pursue this endeavor.

One way to prevent chemical dependency from occurring is to educate oneself by attending continuing education programs offered by professional organizations. The University of Utah School on Alcoholism and Other Drug Dependencies (UUSADD) also offers an intensive training program for faculty, students, and professionals in health care disciplines and their families. All health care professionals interested in the issues discussed above should make it a point to attend the UUSADD at least once every five years.

Ideally, every possible means must be employed to prevent chemical dependency from occurring in the health care professional. However, should the problem of chemical dependency occur in a professional, then the options discussed above under intervention, treatment, and rehabilitation may have to be pursued. Often even after extended periods of treatment the problem may recur, and individuals who suffer relapses must get all the support possible from their peers, family and friends. Some of the strategies suggested to prevent recurrence (Wartenberg, 1989) include:

- Maintaining an informal support system (e.g., with family and friends).
- Participating in a formalized support system (e.g., one designed for the health care professionals, their spouses, or one such as Alcoholics Anonymous).
- Teaching nonchemical coping skills (e.g., hobbies, exercise, meditation, etc.).
- Procuring balance in life so that work does not deprive one of social and family pleasures and obligations.
- Attempting to humanize working conditions so that the stress and strain of work is minimized.

Policy Statements by National Organizations

The American Medical Association (AMA) in 1956 endorsed the definition of alcoholism as a disease and adopted a resolution in 1987 that read as follows: "Resolved, that the AMA endorses the proposition that drug dependencies, including alcoholism, are diseases and that their treatment is a legitimate part of medical practice; and be it further resolved, that the AMA encourages individual physicians, other health professionals, medical and other health-related organizations, and government and other policymakers to become more well informed about drug dependencies, and to base their policies and activities on the recognition that drug dependencies are, in fact, diseases" (Green, 1989).

In 1982 the American Nurses Association (ANA) passed a resolution recommending the rehabilitation of impaired nurses and the establishment of programs for impaired nurses in every state nurses' association. The National Nurses Society on Addictions (NNSA) was started for nurses with interest and expertise in addictions nursing. The NNSA established a task force that developed into the Impaired Nurse Committee. This committee was assigned to oversee the activities of the state nurses' associations with regard to impaired nurses. NNSA is also responsible for organizing the national conference on the impaired nurse each year (15).

The American Pharmaceutical Association (APhA) in 1982 adopted a policy regarding impaired pharmacists. It recommended that programs be established for the prevention, treatment, and rehabilitation of impaired pharmacists, and that pharmacists should not practice while impaired (APhA, 1982). Subsequently, in 1985 the Student American Pharmaceutical Association adopted a similar resolution concerning pharmacy students. The National Association of Boards of Pharmacy (1983) and The American Society of Hospital Pharmacists have also adopted similar policies with regard to impaired pharmacists (ASHP, 1983; Talley, 1988).

Summary

Dependence on drugs is a problem common to all professionals, including health care professionals. In the past, the use of psychoactive agents among physicians was higher than among the general population, but the present trend in both medical students and physicians is towards less frequent use of all drugs except cocaine. It is estimated that substance abuse is also a major problem among six to 10 percent of nurses and that a very large percentage of nursing students have problems with alcohol abuse. On the other hand, although the potential for drug abuse among pharmacy students and pharmacists is high, as a general rule they tend to abuse drugs less frequently than their peers, medical students and physicians.

The major factors that may contribute to abuse of drugs in health care practitioners include: access to an environment in which drugs are prescribed, dispensed, and distributed; a demanding work schedule that causes stress and encourages self-diagnosis and self-treatment; unreasonable professional expectations that are demanding and difficult to cope with; and lack of training in how to handle stress or resolve problems of drug dependence if they happen to occur.

Proper identification of and intervention with an addicted practitioner is critical to the subsequent rehabilitating process. Rather than look for occasional lapse in job related performance, it is best to look for a trend in poor work performance, continued deterioration in interpersonal skills, and a counterproductive lifestyle. Intervention involves detailed documentation of unbecoming behavior and failure in professional competence such that the damaging evidence makes the practitioner seek treatment. Treatment is likely to be successful if the practitioner has support from his family, friends and professional associates.

The outpatient treatment programs, which are less expensive than the inpatient programs, allow the patient to keep a part-time job but leave him exposed to the stress and strain in his life that probably caused him to become addicted to drugs. The inpatient programs cost more but provide 24-hour care and protect a patient from exposure to daily stress and easy access to drugs. Reentry into professional practice is possible if a practitioner has recovered after treatment, maintains a drug-free lifestyle and agrees to disciplinary action in case of relapse.

Prevention is the best cure to the problem of drug dependence. In this regard, the professional organizations are playing an important role in offering educational programs and establishing rehabilitation programs for fellow professionals who are impaired.

References

American Pharmaceutical Association policy actions. (1982). *American Pharmacy, NS22,* 368.

American Society of Hospital Pharmacists. (1983). *American Journal of Hospital Pharmacy, 40,* 1368.

Baldwin, D. C. Jr., Hughes, P. H., Conrad, S. E., Storr, C. L., & Sheehan, D. V. (1991). Substance abuse among senior medical students. *Journal of the American Medical Association, 265,* 2074–2078.

Commonly used drugs, their uses, abuses, effects, and symptoms they produce. (1985, November). *Micrograms,* p.145–149. Washington, DC: U. S. Department of Justice, DEAXVIII.

Conrad, S., Hughes, P. H., Baldwin, D. C. Jr., Archenbark, K. B., & Sheehan, D. V. (1988). Substance use by fourth-year students at thirteen U. S. medical schools. *Journal of Medical Education, 63,* 747–758.

Engs, R. C., & Hanson, D. J. (1989). Alcohol knowledge and drinking patterns of nursing students over time. *College Student Journal, 23*(1), 82–88.

Freudenberger, H. J. (1986). The health professional in treatment: Symptoms, dynamics, and treatment issues. In C. D. Scott & J. H. Hawk (Eds.), *Healthy self: The health care of health care professionals* (pp. 185–193). New York: Brunner Mazel.

Green, P. (1984). The impaired nurse: Chemical dependency, *Journal of Emergency Nursing, 10,* 1

Green, P. (1989). The chemically dependent nurse. In J. Zerwekh (Ed.), *Nursing clinics of North America: Nursing interventions for addicted patients,* vol. 24, *No. 1* (pp. 81–94). Philadelphia, PA: W. B. Saunders Company.

Haack, M. R., & Hartford, T. C. (1984). Drinking patterns among student nurses. *The International Journal of the Addictions, 19,* 577.

Hughes, P. H., Conrad, S. E., Baldwin, D. C. Jr., Storr, C. L., & Sheehan, D. V. (1991). Resident physician substance use in the United States. *Journal of the American Medical Association, 265,* 2069–2073.

Johnson, V. (1986). *Interventions: How to help someone who doesn't want help.* Minneapolis, MN: Johnson Institute Books.

McAuliffe, W. E., Rohman, M., Santangelo, S., Feldman, B., Magnuson, E., & Weissman, J. (1986). Psychoactive drug use among practicing physicians and medical students. *New England Journal of Medicine, 315*(13), 805–826.

McAuliffe, W. E., Santangelo, S. L., Gingras, J., Rohman, M., Sobol, A., & Magnuson, E. (1987), Use and abuse of controlled substances by pharmacists and pharmacy students. *American Journal of Hospital Pharmacy, 44,* 311–317.

Micrograms, D. J. (1985). U.S. Dept. of Justice, DEA. Washington, D. C. November, XVIII, pp. 145–149.

Miller, C. J., Banahan, B. J., & Borne, R. F. (1990). A comparison of alcohol and illicit drug use between pharmacy students and the general college population. *American Journal of Pharmaceutical Education, 54,* 27–30.

Model curricula for alcohol and other drug abuse—physician and nurse education, national institute on alcohol abuse and alcoholism/national institute on drug abuse. (1989). Rockville, MD: U. S. Department of Health & Human Services.

National Association of Boards of Pharmacy. (1988). *Impaired Pharmacist Policy Statement* (84-15). Park Ridge, IL: NABP

National Institute on Drug Abuse. (1987). *National Household Survey on Drug Abuse 1985.* Washington, DC: Population Estimates.

Niven, R. G., Hurt, R. D., Morse, R. M., & Swenson, W. M. (1984). Alcoholism in physicians. *Mayo Clinic Proceedings, 59,* 12–16.

Policy atatement flier of the AMA. (No date). Chicago, IL: American Medical Association.

Ray, O., & Ksir, C. (1990). *Drugs society and human behavior.* St. Louis, MO: Time Mirror/Mosby.

Roth, L. H. (1987). Chemical dependency in the health professions, *Journal of Nurse-Midwifery, 32*(2), 91–97.

Schuckit, M. A. (1989). *Drug and alcohol abuse: A clinical guide to diagnosis and treatment* (3rd ed.). New York: Plenum.

Schwartz, R. H., Lewis, DC, Hoffmann, N. G., & Kyriazi, N. (1990). Cocaine and marijuana use by medical students before and during medical school. *Archives of Internal Medicine, 150,* 883–886.

Seventh report to the President and the Congress on the status of health personnel in the United States. (1990, March) U. S. Dept. of HHS, VI-1.

Seventh report to the President and the Congress on the status of health personnel in the United States. (1990, March). U. S. Dept. of HHS. VIII-8.

Seventh report to the President and the Congress on the status of health personnel in the United States. U. S. (1990, March). Dept. of HHS, XII-1.

Smith, D. E. (1985). A clinical approach to the impaired health care professional, *The International Journal of The Addictions, 20*(5), 713–722.

Sullivan, B., Bissell, L., & Williams, E. (1988). *Chemical dependency in nursing.* Menlo Park, CA: Addison-Wesley

Talbott, G. D. (1990). Intervention in the health professional—success and failure: The Georgia experience, In B.B. Wilford (Ed.), *Syllabus for the review course in addiction medicine* (pp. 565–572). Washington, DC: American Society of Addiction Medicine.

Talbott, G. D., & Wright, C. (1987). Chemical dependency in health care professionals. *Occupational Medicine, 2*(3), 581–591.

Talbott, G. E., & Martin, C. A. (1984). Relapse and recovery: Special issues for chemically dependent physicians. *Journal of the Medical Association of Georgia, 73* (11), 763–769.

Talley, C. R., (1988). Chemical impairment. *American Journal of Hospital Pharmacy, 45,* 2077.

Tucker, D. R., Gurnee, M. C., Sylvestri, M. F., Baldwin, J. N., & Roche, E. B. (1988). Psychoactive drug use and impairment markers in pharmacy students. *American Journal of Pharmaceutical Education, 52*, 42–47.

Valliant, G. E., Brighton, J. R., & McArthur, C. (1970). Physicians' use of mood-altering drugs: A 20-year follow-up report. *New England Journal of Medicine, 282*(7), 365–370.

Valliant, G. E., Sobowale, N. C., & McArthur, C., (1972). Some psychologic vulnerabilities of physicians. *New England Journal of Medicine, 287*, 372–375.

Wartenberg, A. A., Goldstein, M. G., & Dube, C. E. (1989). Health professional impairment. In C. D. Dube, M. G. Goldstein, D. C. Lewis,Dubé, C. E., Goldstein, M. G., Lewis, D. C., Myers, E. R., & Zwick, W. R. (Eds.), *Vol. II, Project ADEPT: Alcohol and drug education for physician training* (pp. H1-35). Providence, RI: Brown University.

Westermeyer, J. (1991). Substance use rates among medical students and resident physicians. *Journal of the American Medical Education, 265*(16), 2110–2111.

Williams, E. (1989). Strategies for intervention, In J. Zerwekh (Ed.), *The nursing clinics of North America: Nursing interventions for addicted patients, vol. 24, No. 1*. pp, 95–107. Philadelphia, PA: W. B. Saunders Company.

Williams, E., Bissel, L., & Sullivan, E. (1991). The effects of codepedence on physicians and nurses, *British Journal of Addiction, 86*, 37–42.

Discussion Questions

1. What is the incidence of drug use among physicians, nurses and pharmacists? To what extent does drug use among physicians and medical students differ from that of pharmacists and pharmacy students?
2. What factors, according to the author, contribute to substance abuse among health professionals? Can you think of other factors that may contribute to substance abuse among health professionals?
3. How does one go about determining the degree of impairment from substance abuse in a colleague?
4. Discuss the steps you would take to ensure a successful intervention in the case of a colleague who is chemically dependent.
5. What are the essential components of a good treatment and rehabilitation program for a chemically dependent professional?

Sports and Clean Living: A Useful Myth?

James F. Rooney

James F. Rooney is a professor of sociology at Penn State University at Harrisburg. He received his A.B. at Gonzaga University, his M.S.W. at the University of California at Berkeley, and his doctorate in sociology at the University of Pennsylvania. During his career, he has studied farm workers, skid row and migrant populations, and free-lance classical musicians, as well as drug use among youth in the United States and in Spain. In all instances, these populations were studied by utilizing both participant observation techniques and systematic surveys of the relevant populations.

Sports have traditionally been included in school curricula in Western culture as a desirable addendum to intellectually-oriented education. Sports are considered to possess a unique quality for promoting positive social behavior through instilling a sense of legitimacy for prevailing community norms as well as imparting ideal character traits such as a sense of cooperation and respect for others. In addition to molding morally healthy characters, participation in athletics is believed to build strong bodies and a concern for health.

A large number of researchers and educational administrators and athletes themselves have commented on the positive outcomes of sport participation. Leavitt and Price (1958) assert that athletics provides a positive social experience through building good sportsmanship, loyalty, cooperation and self-assurance. A former athletic director at the University of Southern California, Jess Hill (Edwards, 1973), asserts that organized athletics instills a desire to excel, guided by discipline and the knowledge that life must be lived by the rules. Friedenberg (1973) states that athletic skill is especially helpful to adolescents in establishing a sense of who they are. And the famous miler Roger Bannister (1973) likewise concurs and adds that intense participation facilitates the transition to adulthood. The Educational Policies Commission (1954) well summarizes the objectives of participation in school athletics as promoting the development of skill, self-reliance, emotional maturity, social growth and good sportsmanship. Good sportsmanship practices especially are seen as critical for the development of responsible civic values. Cozens and Stumpf (1953) concur regarding the instilling of civil values, pointing out that in common parlance, the designation of a "good sport" has supplanted that of "lady" and "gentleman" as the referent to the ideal person. Furthermore, they assert that values necessary for citizenship in a democracy are developed through participation and cooperation in team sports. The values fostered by the major sports are among those shared throughout all social classes, and thus constitute a great integrating factor in American society.

Implicit in these assertions is the thesis that organized athletics among youth contributes both to individual psychological growth and to the maintenance of a moral republic. The character-building function is especially emphasized in the multitude of sports programs sponsored by this nation's high-schools.

A second major function of organized sports programs includes the instilling of regard for one's health and of better health habits, resulting also in greater mental alertness (Leavitt & Price, 1958). This would

This is revised version of a paper presented at the annual meeting of the Society for the Study of Social Problems, Detroit, Michigan, August 1983. Data were gathered with funds provided by the Center For Study of Youth Development at the Catholic University of America. The article first appeared in *Drug and Alcohol Dependence, 13,* (1984) 75–87, published by Elsevier Scientific Publishers Ireland Ltd.

include learning habits of systematic exercise, health monitoring and maintenance as well as avoidance of all forms of behavior excess, including avoiding consumption of harmful substances.

This investigation deals with the relationship of participation in sports and the use or avoidance of mood-altering substances on the part of high-school seniors, both males and females. Use of certain drugs is officially illegal, and cigarette use is generally considered physically harmful. If participation in sports truly influences positive social behavior and concern for personal health, lower rates of drug use should be associated with increased sport participation.

There is no unanimity, however, regarding school sports and their consequences for the development of youth. Talamini et al. (1973) points out that educators are divided on the effects of sports. One faction asserts that sports are inherently beneficial to youth; another faction asserts that sports are inherently harmful; while a third faction stresses only their potential contribution for the betterment of youth if properly administered. In an investigation of the latter position, Talamini gives factual evidence of the contrast between policies advocated by the Educational Policies Commission and those practiced by a sample of high-school athletic directors. The Educational Policies Commission (1954) recommended that the major thrust of high-school athletics should be on intramural sports and on sports that can be continued into adulthood. The high-school athletic directors interviewed by Talamini, in contrast, placed overwhelming emphasis on winning teams in the major boys' sports because these gave public recognition to the school.

In the studies that relate sports to desirable or to deviant behaviors, the orientation toward sports has been measured in two manners: (1) behaviorally in terms of participation in athletics, and (2) psychologically in terms of attitudes, interest or self-conception. Athletic programs conducted under the policy of giving major emphasis to interscholastic team sports that attract a wide public following, although they do not teach athletic skills that can be used directly in later life, nevertheless appear to achieve some beneficial results. Outcomes do differ, however, according to whether the orientation toward sports is measured in terms of actual participation or in psychological terms.

In a comparison of juvenile court appearance rates of high-school male interscholastic athletes and non-athletes in a small city, one researcher found that athletes had a markedly lower court appearance rate; this same researcher cautions, however, that the association of athletics and lower delinquency rate may be the result of athletics attracting the more conforming boys. An important study confirms the opposition of conforming behaviors and drug use among adolescents. Based on a longitudinal study of youth from ages 12 to 18 years, Jessor and Jessor (1977) advance evidence that conventional behaviors such as religious participation and academic achievement have an inhibiting effect on drug use, while lower academic achievement and minor delinquent behavior are associated with heavier drug use. There is no mention of sports and their effect on curbing transgressions. A survey of drinking behavior among 10th and 12th grade students of both sexes conducted in 1977 found that those who participated in athletics more often were abstainers and less often were heavy drinkers than non-athletes.

Biener (1975) gathered very incisive data regarding the temporal sequence of sports, smoking and alcohol use through a four-year follow-up of Swiss youths exposed to a health education program at age 16 that also advocated participation in sports clubs. Measured again at age 20, the experimental group, in contrast to a matched control group, showed markedly lower rates of cigarette use (42% vs. 78%) and of alcohol use (53% vs. 92%). The main reason for abstinence from tobacco and alcohol was participation in sports. At follow-up, nearly all the experimental group members participated in at least one sport, while approximately only half the control group members did so. It is important to note that the success of the health education and sports participation program lay almost entirely in deterring its members from initiation use over the ensuing four years, not in inducing those who were already smokers at age 16 to become abstinent.

A study among college students regarding the relationship of sports to use of drugs other than alcohol was conducted by McCann et al. (1977). Although there were no differences in marijuana use between interscholastic athletes and non-athletes of either sex, interscholastic athletic participation was related to substantially lower rates of usage of stronger drugs among males, while consumption of strong drugs was unrelated to athletic participation among females. The effects of participation by college students of both sexes in endurance-building physical education classes such as jogging and calisthenics classes were monitored over one semester by Engs and Mulhall (1981), who found that 15 weeks of vigorous exercise had no effect on smoking and drinking patterns of the participants.

Those studies that measure the orientation toward sports in psychological terms collectively report considerably more varied results than those using a behavioral measure. In a broad survey of students in five colleges, Blum et al. (1970) found that those for whom sports are either of very little or no importance report more experience with all classes of drugs including alcohol, while those for whom athletics were extremely important were the least experienced in drug use.

Similar findings have been reported for the relationship between marijuana use and attitudes toward athletics. Tec's (1972) survey revealed that those high-school students who aspired to become the "best athlete" had the lowest rate of marijuana use. Different results were reported when students were surveyed at two colleges. Male heavy drinkers described themselves as more athletic than abstainers, but female heavy drinkers described themselves as less athletic and more poised than female abstainers.

There is little definite evidence regarding the nurturant effects of sports competition upon positive character traits in later life. Based upon a review of the literature of all systematic psychological studies of sports and ideal character traits, Edwards (1973) reported that of a total 12 traits evaluated by the various studies of current or former school athletes, none was substantiated; results regarding 11 traits were inconclusive, and one (physical fitness) was found not to result in later life on the part of former university athletes.

Indeed the evidence is not clear regarding the relationship of sports participation to conforming or ideal behavior. Differences in findings among studies may in part result from measurement procedures, in that results differ systematically according to whether the orientation to sports is measured by actual participation or measured psychologically in terms of interests or self-perception. The former group of studies generally found a negative relationship between athletic participation and drug use, while the psychological studies collectively report mixed findings.

The research presented here investigates this issue in terms of use or avoidance of mood-altering drugs. Nonmedical use of mood-altering substances is generally considered physically unhealthy and socially as deviant behavior. If participation in sports serves as an inducement to enhancement of physical health and to conforming social behavior, and conversely as a deterrent to deviant behavior, the following hypotheses are expected to be true: (1) the greater the number of sports participated in, the lower the rate of illegal substance use, (i.e., of marijuana, amphetamines, barbiturates, LSD and cocaine), (2) the greater the number of sports participated in, the lower the rate of alcohol use, (3) the greater the number of sports participated in, the lower the rate of cigarette use. These hypotheses are expected to be valid especially for participants in intramural sports, and in out-of-school sports, and are expected to be true for both sexes. Roger Bannister (1973), however, holds that out-of-school sports and non-organised sports participated in entirely voluntarily hold the most meaning and the most benefit for the participant. As reported earlier, Biener's four-year longitudinal survey in Switzerland (1975) demonstrated the effectiveness of voluntary participation in sports clubs in deterring youth from initiating smoking and drinking. A test of this proposition follows. (4) Participation in out-of-school sports is associated with a greater diminishment of illegal substance use, alcohol use, and cigarette use than is participation in interscholastic sports or intramural sports. If it is found that those involved in more sports use illegal substances as frequently as those involved in fewer sports, it is nevertheless possible that the quantity of a substance consumed per occasion would be smaller, resulting in fewer problems following use. From this line of reasoning follows: (5) the greater the number of sports participated in, the fewer the number of problems resulting from substance use.

Research Procedures

Sample

The data presented in this report are based upon a sample of 4,941 high-school seniors from 30 high-schools in six states in the northeast region of the U.S. A self-reporting questionnaire was administered to the entire senior classes present on the day of the survey during the spring of 1977. The 30 schools differed in type of school (71% of respondents in public schools,

29% in Catholic schools), size of senior class (14,793), and type of place (rural, suburban, and central city). The respondents' median age was 17 years. The total response rate was 76 percent, based on the proportion of usable questionnaires to the total senior enrollment. The 24 percent loss represents absentees (20%), those handing in blank questionnaires (2%), and those giving erratic and unusable responses (2%).

The questionnaire consisted of 227 items, which measured many phases of adolescent drug, social, athletic, and school activities. Participation in sports was measured in terms of the number of interscholastic sports, the number of intramural sports, and the number of out-of-school sports participated in over the past year. A summary of these three measures was computed to represent total sport participation for each respondent. The use of marijuana, amphetamines, barbiturates, LSD and cocaine was measured on a seven-point frequency scale: (1) daily or nearly every day, (2) a few times a week, (3) about once a week, (4) about once a month, (5) a few times a year, (6) once a year or less, (7) never. Alcohol use was measured on the frequency scale listed above as well as by the average quantity consumed per occasion for beer, wine, and hard liquor. The quantity and frequency measures were multiplied for each alcoholic beverage, and the products were summed to produce a total alcohol consumption score. Cigarette use was measured on a six-point scale: (0) has never smoked and does not smoke now, (1) used to smoke but has quit, (2) only one or two cigarettes each week or on rare occasions, (3) a few cigarettes each day, (4) about one pack a day, (5) about two or more packs a day.

Since the data consisted of self-reports collected by anonymous questionnaires, it was not possible to test for reliability by direct questioning of respondents, nor to test for validity by direct observation of behavior. The frequencies, however, are very similar to those obtained for high-school seniors in other general surveys (e.g. Kandel et al., 1976; *Student drug use surveys,* 1976).

Problems resulting from substance use were measured in terms of the sum of the number of times each of 14 different outcomes occurred. The items were derived from Straus and Bacon (1953) and included problems such as loss of friends, stopped by police, steady use over an entire weekend, and being called before school authorities. Problems resulting from alcohol and marijuana were measured separately for each substance, while problems resulting from barbiturate and amphetamine use were measured jointly, as were those resulting from use of LSD and cocaine. Verimax factor analysis among the 14 types of problems indicated that one general factor accounted for the majority of the variance in the problems for each substance, and that no other factors were significant. Thus, the sum total of problems from each substance per individual case constituted the problem score for the individual user.

Results

The proportions of students who participated in the variously sponsored sports during their senior year are presented in Table 1. For males, approximately 40 percent participated in one or more interscholastic sport, 48 percent participated in at least one intramural sport, and nearly three-quarters of all boys participated in some form of out-of-school sport. For girls in their senior year, the corresponding figures are approximately 22 percent, 28 percent and 45 percent. That the participation rates for girls in these different levels of competition are approximately 60 percent of that of the corresponding male rate can be interpreted as reflecting the overall greater emphasis upon sports on the part of boys. Nevertheless, the pattern of rates of participation is the same for both sexes; the greatest number engage in out-of-school sports, followed by intramural sports, and the fewest play interscholastic sports, reflecting the greater competitiveness of the latter. The greater competitiveness of interscholastic sports is also manifested in the fact that fewer participants engage in two or more such sports during the year than engage in two or more intramural or out-of-school sports.

A combined sports participation rate for each respondent was computed by summing the number of interscholastic, intramural and out-of-school sports engaged in during the year. The overall greater emphasis upon sport participation for males in American culture is shown by the fact that the mean number of total sports participated in by males is twice that of females, 3.2 to 1.6 sports. Similarly, the results presented in Table 1 show that the proportion participat-

Table 1
Participation Rates Percent of High-school Seniors in Interscholastic, Intramural, Out-of-school Sports and Combined Total Sports

No. of sports	Males (N = 2609)				Females (N = 2237)			
	Inter-scholastic sports	Intra-mural sports	Out-of-school sports	Combined total sports	Inter-scholastic sports	Intra-mural sports	Out-of-school sports	Combined total sports
None	59.2	52.0	26.3	19.9	77.8	72.5	54.5	43.8
1	19.8	15.5	29.0	13.6	13.3	11.4	28.7	19.1
2	13.5	13.3	22.1	11.9	5.9	8.1	9.9	12.0
3	5.7	7.8	13.5	12.6	2.1	3.7	4.6	9.1
4+	1.9	11.4	9.0	40.0	0.9	4.3	2.5	16.1

ing in no sport at all is more than twice as great among females than among males, 43.8 percent to 19.9 percent. Also, the proportion participating in four or more sports is likewise much greater for males than for females, 40 percent to 16 percent.

The proportions of respondents who have ever used the various mood-altering substances measured in this survey are displayed on Table 2 for the entire sample and for each sex. Alcohol clearly is the most used substance, with more than 90 percent users, followed by 50 percent who have tried marijuana. Approximately one-sixth have taken barbiturates and amphetamines outside the direction of a physician, and only six percent have used LSD and cocaine. Cigarettes have been used by slightly more than half the sample. Although the usage rates for males is generally higher than that of females, the difference between the sexes in rates of ever using is not great.

Tests of Hypotheses

The correlation coefficients for each class of sponsored sports and use of specific substances are presented separately for each sex on Table 3. Hypothesis 1 holds that participation in sports is associated with a lower rate of use of illegal substances. The correlation coefficients for marijuana, amphetamines, barbiturates, LSD and cocaine with the various forms of sport participation show that although the majority of the coefficients are in the expected negative direction, their very small magnitude indicates only a negligible relationship between the degree of sport participation and illegal substance use. Because of the large sample size, any correlation coefficient of 0.036 or larger is statistically significant. Correlations of this magnitude, however, are related to very little variance. The highest correlation for the illegal substances is that of amphetamines and combined sports among males, $r = -0.076$ which represents a decline of 0.6 percent in use associated with combined sport participation. Among females, the correlation coefficients for these variables are consistently smaller. Clearly, hypothesis 1 is not upheld. There is no substantive relationship between participation in any form of sports and use of illegal drugs.

Hypothesis 2 holds that the greater the number of sports participated in, the lower the rate of alcohol use.

Table 2
Percentages of High-school Seniors Ever Using Various Substances

Substance	Males	Females	Total
Alcohol	94.8	93.3	94.1
Marijuana	55.0	44.5	50.2
Amphetamine	18.0	15.2	16.7
Barbiturate	15.8	15.5	15.7
LSD	7.8	4.8	6.4
Cocaine	7.7	4.9	6.4
Cigarettes	51.0	60.9	55.6

Table 3
Correlation Coefficients, Various Sports Participation and Substance Use

Substance	Inter-scholastic sports	Intra-mural sports	Out-of-school sports	Combined total sports
Males				
Alcohol	–0.013	–0.036*	–0.030	–0.043*
Marijuana	–0.043*	–0.005	–0.058**	–0.055**
Amphetamine	–0.053**	–0.050**	–0.063***	–0.076***
Barbiturate	–0.042*	–0.020	–0.045*	–0.047**
LSD and cocaine	–0.014	0.016	0.014	0.010
Cigarettes	–0.171***	–0.069***	–0.105***	–0.148***
Females				
Alcohol	–0.009	–0.023	–0.035	–0.037*
Marijuana	–0.029	0.004	0.006	0.000
Amphetamine	–0.007	0.019	0.014	0.013
Barbiturate	–0.002	–0.006	0.010	0.007
LSD and cocaine	–0.012	–0.008	–0.018	–0.016
Cigarettes	–0.089***	–0.043*	–0.104***	–0.106***

*P < 0.05; **P < 0.01; ***P < 0.001.

The data on Table 3 show only very small correlations between alcohol use and any type of sports, indicating that these relationships are best described by the null hypothesis.

Hypothesis 3 holds that cigarette usage declines with increased sport participation. The correlations on Table 3 do give some degree of support to this hypothesis. The strongest relationship is found in the case of interscholastic sport participation among males, $r = -0.171$, and combined sports among males is related to cigarette use, $r = -0.148$. The correlations for females for these variables are slightly smaller, $r = -0.089$ and $r = -0.106$. Hypothesis 3 is upheld, but it must be cautioned that the degree of diminishment of the variance of cigarette use associated with sport participation is in the range of one percent up to three percent.

An analysis of the cross-tabulations (not shown) reveals that the negative relationship of sports and cigarette use lies principally in that sports recruit disproportionately from those who have never smoked, and least from those smoking one pack a day or more. There is no significant difference in the proportions who have quit smoking for either sex between those participating and those not participating in either interscholastic, intramural or out-of-school sports. These findings closely parallel those of Biener (1975), who found that participation in sports clubs among Swiss youth increased the proportion who remained abstinent from tobacco from ages 16 to 20, but cessation of tobacco use occurred on the part of very few of those who were already smokers at age 16. Sports programs, therefore, appear successful in reinforcing abstinence among those already abstinent, but in their present form do not induce cessation among those who have already begun smoking.

Hypothesis 4 holds that participation in out-of-school sports is associated with a greater diminishment of illegal substance use, alcohol use, and cigarette use than is participation in varsity sports or intramural sports. This is based on the expectation that sports engaged in on a purely voluntary and less structured basis involve a greater commitment on the part of the participant. A comparison of the correlation coefficients for out-of-school sports with those for interscholastic sports and intramural sports reveals that for males there is a greater degree of decline for marijuana, amphetamine, and barbiturate use associated with out-of-school sports, but these differences are of insignificant magnitude because of the small correlations in all instances. The only significant difference in magnitude for sport sponsorship occurs in the case of cigarette use, but this difference goes against the hypothesis. The correlation coefficient among males for cigarette use and varsity sports (r= -0.171) exceeds that for out-of-school sports (r = -0.105). Among girls, all correlation coefficients except those for cigarette use are extremely low. In the case of cigarettes, the correlation coefficient for out-of-school sports (r = -0.104) does not sufficiency exceed that for interscholastic sports (r = -0.089) to achieve a significant difference. Clearly, hypothesis 4 regarding possible superior benefits of out-of-school sports is not upheld.

The conditions for testing hypothesis 5 have been met in that there are no substantial variations in alcohol and in illegal drug use associated with any form of sport participation. However, it is possible that athletes may consume smaller quantities of drugs per occasion of use and thereby experience fewer problems. Therefore, hypothesis 5 holds that the greater the number of sports participated in, the fewer the number of problems resulting from drug use.

The correlation coefficients for sports and drug problems presented on Table 4 give very little support to this hypothesis in that all coefficients are small, especially so for females. The largest coefficient, that of amphetamine and barbiturate problems and combined sports among males, r = 0.167, goes against the hypothesis, indicating that the number of problems experienced from these substances increases slightly with participation in a greater number of sports. The second largest coefficient, combined sports and LSD and cocaine problems among males, r = -0.124, is in the expected direction. Considering all 32 coefficients for both sexes, however, a total of 13 achieve statistical significance, and seven of these are in the direction of the hypothesis, while six go against the hypothesis. Given the fact that the statistically significant coeffi-

Table 4
Correlation Coefficients, Various Sports Participation and Drug Problems

Problems resulting from	Inter-scholastic sports	Intra-mural sports	Out-of-school sports	Combined total sports
Males				
Alcohol	0.018	0.052**	0.030	0.051**
Marijuana	–0.043*	0.052**	0.058**	0.005
Amphetamine and barbiturates	0.056**	0.014	0.014	0.167***
LSD and cocaine	–0.058**	–0.034	–0.050**	–0.124***
Females				
Alcohol	0.001	0.001	0.004	0.055**
Marijuana	0.000	0.006	0.000	0.043*
Amphetamine and barbiturates	0.000	0.000	0.000	–0.050**
LSD and cocaine	0.000	0.001	0.000	–0.026

*P < 0.05; **P < 0.01; ***P < 0.001.

cients are nearly equally distributed in favor of and against the hypothesis, and that the magnitude of all significant coefficients is very small, clearly the hypothesis is not upheld by the results.

Discussion and Conclusions

The degree of participation in sports of any type appears to have very little relationship to use of mood-altering drugs on the part of high-school seniors of both sexes. The only exception to this finding occurs in the case of cigarette use, which declines to a small degree with greater participation in interscholastic sports and also with the total number of sports. Neither the use of alcohol or of any of the illegal drugs or the problems resulting from their use are diminished substantially by the degree of participation in any class of sports. Clearly, except for diminished use of cigarettes, athletics is not related to either greater adherence to community norms for teenagers or to a greater concern for health as measured by use of mood-altering drugs.

These findings appear not to concur with an important group of studies. In the literature review, it was noted that, although studies with a psychological focus had mixed results, most studies that measured the orientation toward sports in terms of actual participation reported lower rates of deviancy. The present report becomes the sole exception. This difference in findings may be due to a difference in measurement, to a normative change over time, or to the region of the country surveyed. Of prior studies that measured athletic participation, most did so only for interscholastic sports, and these were measured in dichotomous terms of athlete vs. non-athlete. The current study took account of all classes of sports, measured the number of sports participated in by each respondent, and correlated these with the degree of substance use. Another possibility is that perhaps the norms of students had changed by the time this study was conducted, and consequently drug use was accorded greater acceptance among students. Being defined as less deviant, drug use may have become less subject to control by athletics and other conventional activities. The lack of relationship of athletics and drug use may also be influenced by the region of the country surveyed, the Northeast, which has higher rates of drug use than the South or the Midwest (NTIS, 1978), which greater usage rate again may be related to a greater degree of acceptance.

Regardless of the nature of the findings, they need not diminish the function of athletics in representing the ideal of good behavior and serving as a form of civil religion that transcends economic class, race, sex, and regional differences, and thereby serving to unify members of the society. Novak (1976) observes that because organized athletics is accorded the symbolic function of representing goodness, faith, fair play and fun, it supports the human spirit and thus is healthy and essential for the culture. Athletics as a social institution can continue to carry this public symbolic function irrespective of the private behavior of the participants.

The overall findings may best be interpreted in terms of a major theme of Edwards' analysis of sports in society (1973). Edwards observes that sports reflect the general American profile at a given time, particularly the relationship between the social and economic realities and the nation's value priorities, attitudes and perspectives. Since the many classes of mood-altering drugs have experienced widespread increase in use and acceptance among adolescents and young adults over the past 20 years, should we expect athletes to be different?

References

Bannister, R. (1973). The meaning of athletic performance. In J. T. Talamini, & C. H. Page (Eds.), *Sport and society: An anthology* (pp. 326–335). Boston, MA: Little, Brown & Co.

Biener, K. J. (1975). Sportungfalle in Jugendalter. *Sozial-und Praeventiuniedzin, 20*(1), 9–10.

Blum, R. H., et al. (1970). *Students and drugs.* San Francisco: Jossey-Bass.

Cozens, F. W., & Stumpf, F. S. (1953). *Sports in American life.* Chicago, IL: University of Chicago Press.

Educational Policies Commission, National Educational Association. (1954). *School athletics: Problems and policies.* New York: Greenwood Press.

Edwards, H. (1973). *Sociology of sport.* Homewood, IL: The Dorsey Press.

Engs, R. C., & Mulhall, P. F. (1981). Again—let's look before we leap: The effects of physical activity on smoking and drinking patterns. *Journal of Alcohol and Drug Education, 26,* 65.

Friedenberg, E. (1973). The adolescent and high school athletics. In J. T. Talamini, & C. H. Page (Eds.), *Sport and society: An anthology.* Boston, MA: Little, Brown.

Jessor, R., & Jessor, S. L. (1977). *Problem behavior and psychosocial development: A longitudinal study of youth.* New York: Academic Press.

Kandel, D. B., Treiman, D., Faust, R. & Single, E. (1976, December). Adolescent involvement in legal and illegal drug use: A multiple classification analysis. *Social Forces, 55,* 438.

Leavitt, N. M., & Price, H. D. (1958). *Intramural and recreational sport for high school and college* (2nd ed.). New York: Roland Press.

McCann H. G. et al. (1977). Drug use: A model for a deviant sub-culture. *Journal of Alcohol and Drug Education, 23,* 29.

National Technical Information Services (NTIS). (1975). *A national study of adolescent drinking behavior, attitudes and correlates.* Order Number PB-246-002/AS, Springfield, VA: Research Triangle Institute.

Novak, M. (1976). *The joy of sports.* New York: Basic Books.

Straus, R., & Bacon, S. D. (1953). *Drinking in college.* Westport, CT: Greenwood.

Student drug use surveys. San Mateo County, CA, (1976).

Talamini, J. T., & Page, C. H. (Eds.). (1973). School athletics: Public policy versus practice. *Sport and society: An anthology.* Boston: Little, Brown.

Tec, N. (1972). Some aspects of high school status and differential involvement with marijuana: A study of suburban teenagers. *Adolescence, 7,* 1–28.

Discussion Questions

1. What basic assumption do most Americans make regarding the physical and moral effects of participation in sports?
2. The mean number of total sports participated in by high-school boys is twice that of female students: 3.2 sports to 1.6 sports. Why do males have a higher rate of participation in sports? Relate your answer to traditional American sex roles.
3. How do the positive conforming effects of sports relate to the fact that sports participation diminishes drug use, other than cigarettes, to a very small degree?
4. How can you explain Rooney's finding that especially in interscholastic sports cigarette use is significantly diminished?

Creating Fetal Rights and Protecting Pregnant Women's Constitutional Rights

An Analysis of Drug-related Cases and Issues

Emilio Viano

Emilio C. Viano is a professor in the Department of Justice, Law and Society at the American University in Washington D.C., and Editor-in-Chief of *Victimology: An International Journal.* He has been active in the field of victimology and victim/witness services since the early 1970s. Presently, he is conducting comparative research on biomedical and bioethical issues. He has organized and chaired several national and international meetings, has directed many training and information programs, and has served as a national and international expert on various projects. Professor Viano has published several articles, books, and monographs on various justice-related issues and is the recipient of various international honors and awards.

Drugs, Pregnancy, and Fetal Rights

For centuries, the justice system has been groping with difficult legal issues related to children. However, the last 15 years have seen the courts drawn into a growing number and variety of hard questions related to parents and children, and to women and fetuses. Presently, law, politics, and scientific advances in medicine are creating considerable pressures for a larger legal involvement in women's pregnancies. This is taking place during a period of deep disagreement and doubt about basic questions affecting birth, motherhood, and the family. Compounding this situation is the drug epidemic sweeping the country and inevitably involving women who are pregnant or who are expected to care for small children as the sole parent.

The U.S. Supreme Court has generated even more tension with the July 3, 1989, ruling *Webster v. Reproductive Health Services* [57 U.S.L.W. 5023 (U.S. July 3, 1989) No. 88–605] , which handed states greater freedom to supervise and control abortion. The ruling has the potential not only to lead to new laws governing when, where, and how women can have an abortion, but also to make possible *considerable regulation of the pregnancies* of the women who do not have abortions.

Encouraged by the *Webster* opinion, a number of prosecutors, judges, social services personnel, doctors, and legal experts have begun to aggressively expand the concept of "fetal rights," the basic concept that has stoked the anti-abortion movement, to support the courts' right to oversee women's decisions during pregnancy and hold them accountable in case the fetus is harmed.

The activities of these "interventionists" have led to the arrest and/or prosecution of an increasing number of women for pregnancy-related behavior under various "fetal abuse" theories. Most of the cases allege that the women took illegal drugs during pregnancy.

These attempts to protect the fetus affirmatively during pregnancy with the introduction of so-called "fetal abuse" laws are justified, according to some, by the large and ever increasing number of "drug babies." The National Association for Perinatal Addiction Research and Education recently conducted a survey of 36 hospitals in the United States, located in both urban and suburban areas and serving patients from all socio-economic groups. It found that the average reported incidence of drug use by pregnant women is 11 percent. The study estimated the number of infants born with drugs in their body at 375,000 per year ("Widespread abuse," 1988) . It is important to realize that a new type of illegal behavior is being created here: *illegal drug use plus pregnancy.* There are those who want to go even further and pass laws that would penalize a woman for "fetal abuse," broadly defined to include even legal actions such as drinking and smoking that are known to jeopardize the fetus's healthy growth.

Fetal Rights Used against Drug-using Pregnant Women

In the United States since 1988 some 48 women have been arrested on criminal charges because of their behavior during pregnancy. Previously, there were only three documented cases of this type (ACLU, 1990). In 1989, at least 10 women faced criminal prosecution in California, Florida, Illinois, Massachusetts, and South Carolina because of their use of cocaine, heroin or alcohol during pregnancy. One has been found guilty.

In Rockford, Illinois, Melanie Green, a 24-year-old alleged cocaine user, was charged with manslaughter and delivery of a controlled substance to a minor when her daughter died two days after birth. The prosecutor sought an involuntary manslaughter indictment against Green because of what he defined as the drug-related death of her daughter. He alleged that Green's use of cocaine during pregnancy constituted a reckless act that demonstrated negligence and carelessness for the life of her child. However, a Winnabago County grand jury refused to indict her because it did not find a connection between the child's death and possible cocaine use. The jurors also rejected the charge of delivering an illegal substance to a minor.

An attempt to build a criminal charge of child endangerment against a woman was undertaken by a prosecutor in San Diego, California, in 1986. Pamela Rae Stewart had used drugs during her pregnancy. Her child died shortly after being born. Just like Green, Stewart had received little prenatal care. She was using marijuana and amphetamines, and she ignored her physician's advice to abstain from sexual intercourse and to seek medical care in case of vaginal bleeding. However, Judge E. MacAmos Jr. decided that the statute did not extend to fetuses and that Stewart's failure to comply with medical advice was not illegal under the statute the prosecution had cited [*People v. Stewart,* No. M508197 (San Diego Mun. Ct. Feb. 23, 1987)] . At the same time, the judge urged the state legislature to adopt legislation specifically aimed at making similar prosecutions of pregnant women possible in the future.

The California case of *Reyes v. Superior Court* [75 Cal. App. 3d 214, 141 Cal. Rptr. 912 (1977)] is an example of an actual criminal prosecution of a woman who gave birth to a drug dependent child. Margaret Reyes was a heroin addict who continued to use the drug during her pregnancy. A public health nurse warned her that if she did not seek prenatal care, the health of her child would be jeopardized. She did not seek care and continued to use the narcotic during the last months of her pregnancy. Reyes eventually gave birth to twin boys, both addicted to heroin and suffering from withdrawal. She was charged with two counts of felony child endangerment. The Court of Appeals ordered the case dismissed because it reasoned that the crime of child endangering "was not intended to apply to conduct endangering an unborn child" (Id. at 219, 141 Cal. Rptr. at 914).

On July 13, 1988, a 23-year-old cocaine addict, Jennifer C. Johnson, was found guilty by a Sanford, Florida, judge of delivering a controlled substance to a minor, on the grounds that she had delivered drugs to her two children through their umbilical cords before the cords were severed after delivery. Johnson had admitted smoking cocaine the evening before giving birth and also after she had already gone into labor. In this case a charge which is generally reserved for drug dealers was declared applicable because the judge held that "a child who is born but whose umbilical cord has not been severed is a person (under Florida law)" (*State v. Johnson,* 89-890CFA, Cir. Ct. Seminole County). Similar cases in Florida include that of Toni Hudson, arraigned near Orlando in January, 1989, on charges of providing drugs to a minor: her baby was born with cocaine in its body. Hudson was alleged to have smoked cocaine an hour before delivery. In Broward county, similar charges were filed against a woman who gave birth to her second "cocaine baby."

In Washington D.C. in the summer of 1988, Superior Court Judge Peter Wolf sentenced Brenda Vaughn, a first offender convicted of second-degree theft, to jail, not so much because of her crime, for which the prosecutor had recommended a sentence of probation, but because she had tested positive for cocaine in a presentencing drug screening and was also pregnant. The judge stated that he wanted to protect the fetus in Vaughn's womb from her destructive habit. Vaughn spent almost four months in jail (*U.S. v. Vaughn,* Sup. Ct. D.C., Crim. No. F-2172-88B) .

Those who support women's reproductive rights find these legal actions to be a wrong, and even an unconstitutional, invasion of one of the most personal aspects of a woman's life, precisely like restrictive abortion laws. They see the state taking away from women highly personal decisions and empowering instead the courts and state legislatures to make these decisions for women. Thus, women who are pregnant end up being treated as less than full legal persons simply because of their pregnancy. Reproductive rights supporters maintain that expectant women are entitled to the same control of their body that persons have in other situations. Intrusions should be carefully justified and highly restricted.

The "pro-life" advocates instead stress the fact that there are two human beings involved in the case of a pregnancy—the woman and the unborn child—and that therefore the rights and interests of both of them should be taken into account. They also emphasize that self-determination when it comes to one's body can be legitimately limited if it has a harmful impact on someone else.

The recent backing away from *Roe* by the Supreme Court's *Webster* decision strengthens the interventionists' position. The central passage of the court's opinion calls for the recognition of an overwhelming state interest in potential life during pregnancy, not only after the fetus is viable, as in *Roe.*

The role of medical technology should not be underestimated. Dramatic progress in fetal medicine permits earlier and more accurate diagnosis of problems in the development of the fetus, and even therapeutic intervention to correct some fetal defects by means of surgery in the uterus. These advances can also supply a better factual base for intervening and regulating pregnancies.

More regulation naturally leads to a larger role for the judiciary. As an example, during the last decade, the courts have been approached some 20 times by doctors and hospitals seeking the power to overrule pregnant women's wishes and deliver a baby by cesarean section. The reasons used to support these requests are generally complications that appear during labor or even earlier. The majority of the judges have agreed with the medical personnel, stating that the fetus's stake in life has precedence over the right of the mother to have control over her body.

It is clear that technology is advancing rapidly and outracing the capacity of ethics and the law to keep up. Moreover, pregnancy law is being made in the midst of a drug epidemic, and there is no clear indication of where it will lead.

The Creation of Fetal Rights: Recent Trends

The U.S. legal system historically has considered the fetus as part of the woman carrying it and has provided it no rights as a being independent and separate from her. However, recently courts and state legislatures have increasingly awarded fetuses rights that historically have belonged only to persons. The novel element here is that the *fetus is seen as a being, independent from the woman who is bearing it,* with interests that may differ from or even be contrary to hers. As a consequence, some states have limited the self-determination of women during pregnancy to promote opposite fetal interests.

It is particularly since the *Roe* decision that legislation has increasingly protected the fetus. For example, a majority of states' wrongful death statutes presently hold fetuses that have died in the uterus to be "persons" (Keeton, 1984: at 370 and n. 32 listing the states).

A similar trend has appeared in criminal law. Common law traditionally holds that destroying a fetus in the uterus is not a homicide. It is necessary for the victim to be "born alive." However, the Supreme Judicial Court of Massachusetts recently broke with this long-standing precedent, holding that a fetus is a person according to the state's vehicular homicide statute, and consequently a potential victim of homicide [*Commonwealth v. Cass,* 467 NE 2d, 1328 (1984)]. Additionally, several states have enacted legislation that imposes criminal penalties for the destruction of a fetus that are the same as those used for the murder of a person.

Certainly, creating fetal rights not dependent on subsequent live birth could stem from a legitimate demand to protect the rights of the expectant mother and father. The recognition of fetuses in wrongful death actions makes it possible to compensate parents for their loss, to deter and punish tortious behavior, and also to protect pregnant women from physical attack and from having their pregnancies aborted against their will and violently by a third party, as has happened in some cases of domestic violence. In this sense, protecting the fetus is equivalent to protecting the pregnant woman's interests. However, there is a clear potential that fetal rights may be expanded or interpreted in ways that conflict with women's interests. This happens basically when the fetus and not the mother is considered the locus of the right, independent of the pregnant woman. In other words, the law has begun to bestow rights upon the fetus as a fetus, and not only when it is necessary to protect the interests of the newborn and those of the parents. Once we accept that the fetus is a being with legal rights independent of the pregnant woman, then it is entirely possible and likely that fetal rights will be created or discovered that are adverse to the interests of the pregnant woman, and that possibly they will be used to oppose her rights. This potential has already been realized, particularly when the pregnant woman is an addict or a habitual drug user (*EPR*, 1988) .

Drug Use and the Removal of Newborns under Child Abuse Statutes

While presently there is no national study to determine how frequent such immediate removals are, child protective services in Nassau County, New York, and Los Angeles County, California, immediately seek to take away children with positive drug tests.

The view that *drug use by the mother is child neglect* is supported by the California case *Solomon L. v. Brenda L.* [190 Cal. App. 3d 1106, 236 Cal. Rptr. 2 (1987)]. When it terminated parental rights, the court stated that "neglect was shown by her use of drugs during pregnancy, and that child's withdrawal from drugs after birth and neglect in the early days of the child's life." (Id. at 1111, 236 Cal. Rptr. at 3–4) . The abuse that is prosecuted is to the newborn.

Depending on well-accepted common law principles, the courts have steadily held that criminal laws forbidding certain actions against "human beings" preclude prosecutions for acts committed against fetuses [See, for example, *Keeler v. Superior Court of Amador County,* 2 Cal. 3d 619, 470 P. 2d 617, 87 Cal. Rptr. 481 (1970)] . Accordingly, the California appellate court in *Reyes v. Superior Court of San Bernardino County* [75 Cal. App. 3d 214, 141 Cal. Rptr. 912 (1977)] dismissed all the charges brought against Margaret Reyes, the addicted mother. Similarly, the California Department of Justice in 1987 issued a directive stating that it would no longer accept Child Abuse Investigative Reports that cite "acts or negligence by a pregnant woman or other person(s) which adversely affect the well-being of a fetus" (Cal. Dept. of Justice, Bulletin A-87-8-BCS, May 15, 1987, see also Bolton, 1987) .

To correct this situation, California Senator Ed Royce (Anaheim) introduced Senate Bill 1070 [S.B. 1070, 1987 Reg. Sess. (Cal. April 10, 1987)] imposing criminal liability where it is proven that physical or mental damage has been caused to a fetus. Thus, the bill explicitly incorporates the fetus in child endangerment laws [Cal. Penal Code #273 (a) (West Supp. 1987)]. The amended bill passed on September 30, 1989, making a newborn who is drug addicted subject to child abuse reporting laws and to the jurisdiction of the juvenile court.

In Florida, as well, the Florida Department of Health and Rehabilitative Services (HRS) did not permit its social workers to investigate cases of "drug or cocaine babies," because state law did not acknowledge these children as abused or neglected. Efforts to correct this situation began with the filing of House Bill 155 and of its companion Bill 323 in the Senate. The original version of Bill 155 broadened the meaning of "harm" constituting "child abuse and neglect" so that protective services could be extended to cases of "injury sustained by a newborn infant as a result of being born dependent" on drugs such as cocaine, marijuana, LSD, morphine, and heroin. After major changes, the House version of the Bill was passed unanimously by both the House and the senate, was signed into law by the Governor, and became effective October 1, 1987 (Spitzer, 1987).

State intervention to remove a child because of the infant's drug addiction have often been successful. Michigan courts, in *In re Baby X* [97 Mich. App. 111,

113, 293 NW2d 736, 738 (1980)], determined that there was enough evidence of neglect to take temporary custody of a newborn that was showing signs of withdrawal within 24 hours of being born. The mother appealed, contending that prenatal conduct could not constitute neglect or abuse under Michigan's Probate Code and that consequently the court lacked jurisdiction. The court of appeals agreed that the statute did not extend to the unborn but at the same time overruled this objection stating: "Since Baby K was born before the instant petition was filed . . . this aspect of jurisdiction is not properly at issue" (Id. at 114–15, 293 NW 2d at 738]. Then, it decided that "a newborn suffering narcotics withdrawal symptoms as a consequence of prenatal maternal drug addiction may properly be considered a neglected child" (Id. at 116, 293 NW 2d at 739).

In New York State, *In re Male R* [102 Misc. 2d 1, 2, 422 NYS 2d 819, 820 (NY Fam. Ct. 1979)] was the case of a drug dependent infant whose mother never actually had physical custody of him. Regardless, the court ruled that the child was neglected, that the mother's addiction to prescription drugs made her unable to look after the infant, and that therefore the child was in imminent danger of neglect (Id. at 6, 422 NYS 2d at 823) .

With *In re Smith* [128 Misc. 2d 1976, 979, 492 NYS 2d 331, 334 (NY Fam. Ct. 1985)], the court went a step further, first of all by holding that the mother's refusal to seek treatment for her alcoholism or to provide appropriate medical care for her child was "sufficient to establish an 'imminent danger' of impairment of physical condition, including the possibility of fetal alcohol syndrome, to the unborn child," and that therefore the child was "neglected." Secondly and even more importantly, the court held that an unborn child is a "person" under New York's abuse and neglect statute (128 Misc. 2d at 980, 492 NYS 2d at 335) . A court in Ohio reached the same conclusion *In re Ruiz* [27 Ohio Misc. 2d 31, 33, 500 NE 2d 936, 936 (1986)].

The far-reaching implications of drug use during pregnancy can be seen in a New York case, *Maureen Dunn on behalf of Baby Girl Dunn v. Catholic Home Bureau for Dependent Children* [133 Misc. 2d 399; 506 NYS 805 (1986)] . Dunn, the unmarried natural mother, was seeking to revoke her consent to the adoption of her child. While the court had some reservations about the manner in which the adoption had been carried out, it decided that baby Dunn should remain with her adoptive parents "both 29 years old, [who] enjoy a stable marriage and are financially secure." One of the reasons for denying the petition of the natural mother was that "at least through the first trimester of her pregnancy, she continued *smoking, drinking and using cocaine*" (Id. at 805; emphasis added).

The court opinion indicates that the court concluded that the natural mother's legal and illegal drug habits had negatively impacted the development of the fetus. The court went even further and predicted that the child "may develop health defects" caused by the way in which the pregnancy had unfolded.

Many states have child abuse and neglect statutes that can be construed to provide protection for infants negatively affected by maternal prenatal drug abuse.

The Debate Over Fetal Rights

The establishment of fetal rights that can be used to the disadvantage of pregnant women is a very recent development, and still a limited one. However, the current fierce disagreement over abortion and related issues will certainly lead to more activities in this new area.

The Reasoning of the Interventionists

Interventionists feel that existing laws in most states do not adequately protect the unborn against acts that constitute abuse and neglect. In their opinion, one of the major reasons for this situation is a continuing misunderstanding of the *Roe v. Wade* decision [410 US 113 (1973)] . They admit that *Roe* supports the position that the human unborn are not "persons" who enjoy the protection of the federal Constitution and particularly of the 14th Amendment. However, they also reason that the *Roe* decision permits the states, and of course the federal government, to freely pass laws on behalf of the human unborn, because the Supreme Court clearly acknowledges that a state may have an "important and legitimate interest in potential life" (Id. at 163).

Naturally this legislative power is not absolute but is limited by having to take into account other legitimate and competing interests. Particularly at stake are privacy interests in the area of individual decision making about the family, such as a woman's interest in deciding whether or not to bear a child; personal decision making about bodily integrity; and the autonomy of the family unit (Parness, 1986) .

Consequently, the interventionists reason, state laws can define the unborn as persons and confer their protection upon potential human life provided that such laws are *rational, comprehensible,* and either *compatible* with interests protected by the Constitution or based on *overriding justifications* if there is a conflict. While it is easiest to safeguard potential human life by including the newborn in the definition of "person," a recommended alternative is to base those laws on the rationale of supporting the state interest in ensuring live and healthy births.

Thus, interventionists propose that the states extend protection to the unborn, for example, by abolishing the "born alive" common law requirement; enacting laws punishing acts that cause abuse or neglect of the unborn; permitting compensation for injuries that may result from those acts; encouraging higher concern for and consciousness of measures by which abuse of the unborn can be diminished or eradicated; and providing financial subsidies to people who take actions that support, rather than devalue, the potentiality of human life. Most existing state laws are seen as quite inadequate in this respect. When it comes to punishment in particular, it is felt that most states neglect to criminalize, and consequently to deter, acts of abuse and neglect that damage the unborn.

These shortcomings, the interventionists say, are not limited to criminal law. Tort laws of many states, for example, do not allow recovery by those born alive but injured because of actions that occurred prior to the time when they were viable fetuses. Child protective laws generally do not demand that parents provide the unborn what is necessary for sustaining its potential life. At the same time the jurisdiction of social service agencies over abuse and neglect by parents-to-be is normally non-existent, with the result that these agencies cannot intervene on behalf of the fetus.

In conclusion, the interventionists call for state legislatures to take the primary role in protecting the unborn in the criminal, civil, and child protection spheres, and for the courts to adhere to these protective laws while upholding the restraints imposed by the Constitution on actions by the government. Ideally, they would like to see potential life protected through the enactment of "a distinct statutory scheme covering crimes against the unborn" (Parness, 1986, p. 172), like the recently enacted Minnesota laws (H.F. No. 1844) .

Moreover, those laws mandate that, in Minnesota, any pregnant woman reported to be "chemically dependent" must be given drug treatment and prenatal care. State agencies are further mandated to seek involuntary civil commitment of a "chemically dependent" pregnant woman who refuses or fails to undergo the recommended treatment. Treatment is then compulsory, and women have a right to appointed counsel to contest the civil commitment.

The Reasoning of the Advocates of Reproductive Freedom

When it comes to legislative proposals or court opinions restricting the reproductive rights of women because of their use of illegal drugs, advocates of reproductive freedom emphasize the *public health consequences* more than the legal ones. These policies, they say, would not actually advance the welfare of women and babies because they would deter pregnant women from seeking prenatal medical care. Furthermore, such policies brush aside the real problems, such as lack of prenatal care for certain segments of the population and also the scarcity of drug treatment programs for those seeking help. Punitive policies constitute a short-term solution that has political appeal but does not truly address the underlying problems. It also allows society to overlook genuine solutions such as education, treatment, and prenatal care.

This approach would also instigate criminal charges against women solely because they may not be taking good care of themselves and of their unborn babies while pregnant. Moreover, it seems arbitrary to assume that signs of drug use necessarily mean that there is a risk of impending injury to the baby, without making a case-by-case assessment of the dangers.

Also, since state intervention would be justified by a concern for the well-being of the fetus and by the view that women can be guilty of a crime for harming or engaging in behavior potentially harmful to the developing child, it could reach quite far and proscribe behaviors that are presently legal, such as the consumption of alcohol, nicotine, caffeine, and non-prescription drugs. It could forbid ordinary activities normally deemed to be healthy or at least lawful, such as exercising, having sexual intercourse, and working. Women who have health or weight problems that require the use of drugs that could be harmful to the fetus, or who are too destitute to eat properly or obtain prenatal care, could be considered fetal abusers. Those who resist could be imprisoned or institutionalized to ensure compliance with the approved regimen.

Pregnant women would conceivably live in constant fear that any mishap or mistake in judgment on their part could be considered unacceptable or deviant and provoke a criminal investigation and eventual prosecution by the state or a civil suit by the father-to-be or a relative. Basically, advocates of reproductive freedom state that introducing criminal sanctions, initially because of illegal drug use during pregnancy, inevitably opens the door to *transforming pregnancy itself into a crime* for the simple reason that *no woman can provide the perfect womb.*

To those who would argue that at least using illegal drugs is obviously harmful and therefore can be singled out, these advocates point out that no substance can be considered in isolation. How harmful a certain drug may be depends on several variables, such as how much of the substance was taken, how it was taken, whether the woman was healthy or not, and whether or not prenatal care was available to her.

The enforcement of fetal rights would ultimately call for a system of surveillance, intrusion and coercion that would affect and oppress all women of childbearing age and require impermissible invasions of the basic constitutional rights of liberty and privacy recognized by the Supreme Court in *Roe* and other cases. The poor and the racial minorities would bear a disproportionate burden of the implementation of these policies, since they are those most easily subjected to scrutiny and state intrusions. Moreover, the major or only option open to a woman accused of prenatal abuse, in order to avoid prosecution and imprisonment, particularly if she is poor, may be an abortion, an outcome that deeply contradicts the stated purpose of those accusing her of a crime.

It is also felt that the policies advocated by the interventionists represent a deeply inhuman and anti-woman perspective since they consider women simply and solely as though they were vessels, agents under the control of others for the purpose of breeding and delivering "perfect" babies.

Fetal rights laws, it is argued, would also unfairly single out women of childbearing age as such, and stigmatize and penalize them for no other reason than their ability to bear children. This would perpetuate a pernicious system of sex inequality, since men would escape these restrictions, although the use of legal and illegal drugs can also affect their ability to procreate or to father a healthy baby. Women's ability to conceive and bear children would be used once more to deny them equality. By controlling women as if their lives were characterized exclusively by their capacity to reproduce, the state would preserve a system of sex discrimination based on biological differences between the sexes. This in effect would strip women of their constitutional right of equal protection under the law.

Finally, fetal rights based on the view that the fetus is a being completely separate from the mother, with interests that may be contrary to hers, effectively creates an adversarial relationship between the mother-to-be and her baby-to-be, a situation that can be traumatic and unnatural.

Because of the serious threat that the legal recognition of the fetus poses for women, advocates of reproductive rights demand that "laws governing reproductive biology be scrutinized to ensure that (1) the law has no significant impact in perpetuating either the oppression of women or culturally imposed sex-role constraints on individual freedom or (2) if the law has this impact, it is justified as the best means of serving a *compelling* state purpose" (Law, 1984, pp. 1008–9). In other words, the state must bear the burden of making sure that legislation extending rights to the fetus does not disadvantage women or in any way encroach on the self-determination of pregnant women (Johnsen, 1986). (Table 1 and Table 2 summarize the main positions of the interventionists and reproductive rights groups.)

Table 1
Summary of the Positions of the Interventionists

During pregnancy, two human beings are involved: the woman and the unborn child. The rights and interests of *both* of them must be taken into account.

Self-determination should be limited when it has a harmful impact on someone else.

The large and ever increasing number of drug babies requires the intervention of the state to protect them.

A majority of states' wrongful death statutes hold fetuses that died in the uterus to be "persons."

A fetus is a person according to the vehicular homicide statute and thus a potential victim of homicide (Supreme Court of Massachusetts).

Several states impose the same criminal penalties for the destruction of a fetus as for the murder of a person.

Fetal rights protect the rights of the expectant mother and father, by making compensation possible when the baby is born injured because of harmful actions against the mother-to-be, by deterring harmful behavior, and by protecting pregnant women from violence and forced abortion.

Protecting the fetus means protecting the pregnant woman's interests, particularly in wrongful death and domestic violence cases.

Existing laws in most states do not adequately protect the unborn against abuse and neglect. *Roe* permits the states and federal government to pass laws on behalf of the unborn because a state may have an "important and legitimate interest in potential life" [*Roe v. Wade,* 410 US 113 (1973) at 163].

Severe battering of a pregnant woman can also lead to postnatal injury to the child and warrant state intervention against the perpetrator. Similarly, maternal abuse during pregnancy of legal or illegal substances can have serious postnatal effects on children and should trigger protective intervention.

Social service agencies should be given jurisdiction over abuse and neglect by parents-to-be so that they can intervene and protect the fetus.

Drug use by the expectant mother is child abuse or neglect and justifies termination of parental rights. State intervention to remove a child because of drug addiction at birth has often been successful in the courts.

State laws that are rational, comprehensible, and either compatible with the Constitution or based on overriding justifications can and should *define the unborn as persons* and protect potential human life by abolishing the "born alive" common law requirement, criminalizing abuse and neglect that damage the unborn, permitting compensation for injuries to the unborn, subsidizing financially those who support the potentiality of human life, and reforming tort laws accordingly.

The ideal is to enact a comprehensive statutory scheme covering crimes against the unborn and providing drug treatment and prenatal care to "chemically dependent" mothers, as Minnesota has done.

If the biology of pregnancy has been used to give women—to the exclusion of any claims of biological fathers—a special right to decide whether or not to undergo abortion, surely that same biology imposes special obligations on them as well.

Protecting the unborn and holding those harming a fetus accountable is a clear obligation of society that should be legislated.

Table 2
Summary of the Positions of Advocates of Reproductive Rights

Roe supports the position that the human unborn are not "persons" who enjoy the protection of the federal Constitution.

Negative public health consequences may occur if state intervention deters pregnant women from seeking prenatal medical care.

Lack of prenatal medical care and of drug treatment programs for certain segments of the population (poor, minorities) poses a real problem.

Punitive policies are a short-term solution with political appeal but they do not address the underlying problem, and they overlook genuine solutions such as education, treatment, and prenatal care.

It is unfair to instigate criminal charges against women solely because they may not be taking good care of themselves and of their unborn while pregnant.

It is arbitrary to assume that drug use necessarily means there is risk of impending injury to the baby without a case-by-case assessment.

State intervention could forbid behaviors presently legal, such as consumption of alcohol, nicotine, caffeine, and non-prescription drugs, as well as ordinary, lawful, and even healthy behaviors such as exercising, sex, and working.

Women addressing health and weight problems by using drugs, and women who are too poor to eat properly or obtain prenatal care could be considered child abusers, imprisoned or institutionalized to ensure compliance.

Introducing criminal sanctions because of illegal drug use during pregnancy transforms pregnancy itself into a crime because *no woman can provide the perfect womb.*

No substance can be considered in isolation. How harmful a drug may be depends on several variables.

Enforcing fetal rights would entail surveillance, intrusion, and coercion affecting all women of childbearing age, and require impermissible invasions of basic constitutional rights. Poor and minorities would bear a disproportionate burden.

Abortion would be the only option for women accused of prenatal abuse, to avoid prosecution and imprisonment.

The interventionists' position reflects an anti-woman perspective controlling women to breed and produce "perfect" babies.

Fetal rights laws will unfairly single out, control, and penalize women of childbearing age, simply because they can bear children.

Legislation based exclusively on women's capacity to reproduce is sexist, based as it is only on biological differences between the sexes, and it strips women of equal protection under the law.

Fetal rights create an adversarial relationship between the mother-to-be and her baby-to-be.

Laws governing reproductive biology must not perpetuate the oppression of women or culturally imposed sex-role constraints, unless there is a *compelling* state purpose.

Self-determination and control over one's life are paramount values that must be carefully protected.

Conclusion

Both camps, those we have called the interventionists and the advocates of reproductive rights, reflect genuine concerns and disagreements on critical issues facing our society in the midst of a drug epidemic. The reality of the "drug babies," expressed by the alarming and exponential growth of their numbers, cannot be denied. The human, financial, educational, rehabilitative and, in many cases, criminal justice costs generated by them have not yet been calculated but will be staggering.

An important value of our moral and legal civilization is that of *responsibility*. We have rights but they are hollow and precarious if they are not balanced by our acceptance of personal responsibility. It appears reasonable to ask women who intend to carry a pregnancy to term to commit themselves, within reason, to a healthy lifestyle, provided of course that society commits itself as well to making available appropriate support systems such as prenatal health care and treatment and rehabilitation programs for the addict seeking help. Just as we are finally holding people responsible for the consequences of their drunk or intoxicated driving, so we may find it reasonable to hold parents-to-be responsible at least for the most egregious instances of their negligence and its outcome.

On the other hand, there is no question that criminalizing behaviors we know are unhealthy for the developing fetus raises serious constitutional and practical problems. Realistically, one can doubt that society is willing to pay the price in invasion of privacy and autonomy that the effective enforcement of lifestyle requirements would demand. Even if society were willing, the destruction of legal concepts and practices that are central to a free and democratic type of society would be irreparable. Moreover, the justice system would be overwhelmed by the number of cases, if the estimates of the magnitude of the problem prove to be correct. The system simply cannot handle some 400,000 prosecutions each year on this issue alone.

Clearly, there are many more legal issues emerging as a consequence of the large number of women who abuse drugs during pregnancy. This chapter is not intended to answer all of the questions raised. Rather, its purpose is to outline the conflicting interests and rights involved, stimulate discussion, and present some ideas as to how these interests could be balanced.

While state courts have recognized that unborn children have rights in some areas, we can anticipate that efforts to grant unborn children more protection from possibly harmful actions undertaken by their mothers during pregnancy will be strictly scrutinized. It can be expected that the only restrictions on maternal conduct that will survive a constitutional challenge are those very narrowly tailored and requiring a minimum of intrusion into the private lives of the mothers-to-be. However, one cannot predict which side the Supreme Court would ultimately support.

Furthermore, we must carefully examine whether bringing the force of the law to bear on this issue will truly serve its intended objective, or merely deter pregnant women from seeking prenatal care. The likelihood that there may not be sufficient drug and alcohol treatment programs should also give society pause before imposing all the burden of responsibility on the pregnant woman. On the other hand, the requirements to report child abuse and neglect should be enhanced and extended to infants born dependent on drugs.

Our society must also increase the level, quality, and availability of prenatal care services and of outreach efforts that educate women and men about the consequences of drug use and abuse during pregnancy.

Ultimately, the basic flaw in the interventionists' argument is that *it simply does not make sense to assume that two distinct persons can inhabit the same body at the same time and control it.* To use such an assumption to develop laws and decide court cases will not and cannot work. As the Committee on Ethics of the American College of Obstetrics and Gynecology in 1987 has aptly stated, for example, "Clinicians should be aware of the destructive effects of court orders on the pregnant woman's autonomy and on the physician-patient relationship . . . The use of judicial authority to implement treatment regimens in order to protect the fetus violates the pregnant woman's autonomy. Furthermore, inappropriate reliance on judicial authority may lead to undesirable societal consequences, such as the criminalization of non-compliance with medical recommendations" (ACOG, 1987) .

To ask the law to support and enforce the interventionists' position runs contrary to well-established legal and philosophical tenets and deeply demeans the dignity and autonomy of any person.

However, the other side of the story—that babies *born* to crack addicts do face permanent damage from growing up in uncaring, drug-riddled environments—raises critical questions that our child welfare system must address. There is no question that biological parents are the first and best resource for raising children successfully. In those cases where poverty, unemployment, and other such pressures cause families to break down, family preservation services can often succeed at keeping biological families together.

However, it is an appalling modern reality that parents who abuse drugs—especially crack—are often both incompetent at and uninterested in raising their children. In those sad cases where drugs have made a travesty of the very notion of family, it is imperative that judges and social workers insist on the immediate removal of children from their parents' custody. Children must not be allowed to stay in hard-core drug environments that can damage them for life, physically, emotionally, and mentally.

No one would dispute that it is difficult to decide whether to try to preserve a family or remove a child from his or her parents. In those cases where such calls have to be made, however, it is the responsibility of those involved to put the children first. Depending on the situation, that might call for family preservation, temporary foster care or a group home, or it might call for the termination of parental rights and adoption by a caring family. In any case, we must *think of the children first,* not just for their sake, but for the sake of our society and its future.

References

ACLU (American Civil Liberties Union). (1990). *Overview of ACLU national survey of criminal prosecutions brought against pregnant women.* Unpublished memorandum.

ACOG—American College of Obstetricians & Gynecologists. (1987). *Patient choice: Maternal-fetal conflict.* Committee Opinion No. 55.

Bainham, A. (1987). Protecting the unborn: New rights in gestation? *Modern Law Review, 50*(3), 361–368

EPR—Editorial Research Reports. (1988, July). *Do pregnant women lose legal rights?* Washington, DC: Congressional Quarterly.

Johnsen, D. B. (1986). The creation of fetal rights: Conflicts with women's constitutional rights to liberty, privacy, and equal protection. *Yale Law Journal, 95,* 599–625

Keeton, W. P., Dobbs, D., Keeton, R., & Owen, D. (1984). *Prosser and Keaton on the law of torts* (5th ed.). St. Paul MN: West.

Law, S. (1986). Rethinking sex and the constitution. *132 University of Pennsylvaia Law Review, 4*(6), 955–1040.

Parness, J. A. (1986). The abuse and neglect of the human unborn: Protecting potential life. *Family Law Quarterly, 20*(2), 197–212.

Spitzer, B. C. (1987). A response to cocaine babies—amending Florida's child abuse and neglect laws to encompass infants born drug dependent. *Florida State Univiversity Law Review, 15*(4), 865–884.

Widespread abuse of drugs by pregnant women is found. (1988, October 30). *New York Times,* p. 1.

Discussion Questions

1. Summarize in narrative (essay) form and through charts and/or diagrams the positions of the interventionists and of the advocates on this issue. Which position has the most validity for you? Why? What recommendations could be made that differ from both positions outlined in the chapter to help solve this problem?
2. How would you go about researching this issue to determine if arresting and/or prosecuting drug-using women for child abuse is effective? If arresting and/or prosecuting them were effective, would that justify such measures in your opinion? Has the use of the law to repress certain behaviors solved major social problems in the past?
3. Discuss the position that the intervention of the criminal law against pregnant drug users is just another example of the repression of women and the violation of their civil rights. Have minority groups in the past been threatened with the loss of newly acquired rights? Develop guidelines for arresting, prosecuting, and sentencing pregnant drug users. Would your proposed laws also extend to their husbands, boyfriends, or drug suppliers?
4. How has the U.S. legal system historically considered the fetus: as a part of the woman carrying it,

or as a being independent and separate from her? Is there any change nowadays in that historic position on the part of courts and state legislatures? How might dramatic advances in fetal medicine affect moral opinions and legal norms?

5. Assuming that both the so-called interventionists and their opponents, the advocates, are addressing important and crucial points in the relationship mother-fetus, how would you balance the interests of both the mother and the fetus, so that neither one of them is harmed either by the law or by the behavior of the adult? Is it possible to balance these interests? How could it be done best?

6. Our society is based on a strong foundation of *individual rights.* There are those who feel that we have gone too far in stressing the rights of the individual, and that it is time that we emphasize our *responsibilities* towards the community and those who rightly depend on us, as children do on parents. What would you change to take into account our responsibility to the community? Would this entail major changes in lifestyle, career, and mental outlook? Is it fair to ask women to limit their behavior while pregnant simply because they happen to be those carrying a developing child?

Unintended Consequences

The Prosecution of Maternal Substance Abuse

Maureen A. Norton Hawk

Maureen Norton Hawk is a doctoral candidate in sociology at Northeastern University. She holds a Masters degree in Social Work and a Masters of Science degree in Counseling, and has done extensive work with addicted populations. Her area of interest and research continues to be substance abuse, especially in the area of addiction and pregnancy.

In 1988 in the United States 375,000 babies were born addicted to drugs. In Massachusetts in 1989 the number of drug-addicted newborns was 600, and at Boston City Hospital 30 percent of the 2,000 babies delivered had traces of cocaine in their system (Kong, 1989). Because of the prevalence of poly-drug use, it is difficult to determine the effects of one particular drug on the unborn child. Studies do indicate, however, a relationship between the use of various illicit drugs and spontaneous abortions, lower birth weight and smaller head circumference, irritability, hyperreflexia and tremulousness, negative responses to multiple stimuli (Howard et al., 1989), and a potential for the malformation of developing systems (Zuckerman, 1991). It is important to note that while a relationship between illicit drug use and physiological problems in newborns does exist, causality in some cases has not been established because other variables, such as the lack of prenatal care, and poor maternal nutrition, are difficult to rule out.

These physiological/psychological effects on newborns who have been exposed to drugs prenatally can result in dramatic social and medical costs. The medical cost to provide care for a full-term infant suffering symptoms of drug exposure, who requires 10 days hospitalization, is estimated to be $6,000 (Novick, 1989), with the cost rising as high as $135,000 for a drug-exposed premature infant needing intensive care for several months (Halfon, 1989). The cost grows considerably as we consider the problem of boarder babies—those children abandoned at the hospital at birth. For a group of 9,000 identified crack-exposed infants, the Office of the Inspector General estimated that the total cost of hospital and foster care for this group till the age of five could amount to $500 million (Getting Straight, 1990).

Prenatal exposure to illicit drugs is not the only concern. Five to 10 percent of pregnant women continue to drink heavily (Balisy, 1987), resulting in Fetal Alcohol Syndrome (FAS) which affects nearly 5,000 babies each year (Getting Straight). This disorder is marked by dysfunction of the central nervous system, and prenatal and postnatal growth deficiency and facial malformations (Day, 1992; Abel, 1984); it is the third leading cause of birth defects associated with mental retardation (Getting Straight). It was estimated that in 1980 it cost the United States $2.7 billion for medical, educational and custodial services for children born with Fetal Alcohol Syndrome and Fetal Alcohol Effect (Balisy, 1987). In an attempt to grapple with the "discovery" of maternal substance abuse, whether this use involves illicit substances or alcohol, a number of punitive court decisions have been handed down in recent years.

However, the trend toward punitive intervention strategies currently being utilized by the courts to deal with the problems associated with maternal substance abuse may not have the intended effect, and in fact this policy may increase the severity of the problem. To show this we will first present an overview of some of the recent court decisions and, secondly, we will examine the possible results of the punitive intervention strategies aimed toward reducing drug use during pregnancy and improving infant health. Sieber's work on the unanticipated consequences of social intervention will provide a framework for this analysis (Sieber, 1981).

Court Cases

Recently, attempts have been made to legislate against and prosecute drug-using expectant mothers on the charge of child abuse/neglect, or of delivering a controlled substance to a minor. Several case examples are used for the purpose of illustration.

In Massachusetts, in September, 1989, Josephine Pellegrini was charged with providing an illegal drug to a child in the womb. Ms. Pellegrini was charged with delivering cocaine to a minor after the substance was found in her newborn shortly after birth. The indictment was based on a 1983 law originally designed not to deal with expectant mothers but to combat drug pushers, and this law carries a minimum three-year sentence (Coakley & Hart, 1989).

Brenda Vaughan, a Washington, D.C., resident, who was originally arrested for writing bad checks, tested positive for cocaine and was sent to jail until the date her baby was due, to protect her unborn child from drug abuse. The judge stated: "I'm going to keep her locked up until the baby is born because she's tested positive for cocaine . . . She's apparently an addictive personality, and I'll be darned if I'm going to have a baby born that way" (Cassen Moss, 1988, p. 20).

In Florida, in July, 1989, a woman who gave birth to two children with traces of cocaine in their systems was convicted on charges of delivering a drug to a minor, and could have received up to 30 years in jail. The judge stated "that a child who is born but whose umbilical cord has not been severed is a person within the intent and meaning of Florida law" (Drugs Found in Babies, 1989, p. A10).

> All over the country, pregnant women who use illegal drugs and/or alcohol are targeted by the criminal justice system. They are preventively detained by judges who mete out jail sentences for minor crimes that would ordinarily result in probation or a fine; charged with child abuse or neglect (although by law the fetus is not a child) and threatened with manslaughter charges should they miscarry . . . . (Pollitt, 1990, p. 410)

The results of these punitive intervention strategies will be discussed within the framework of Sieber's book *Fatal Remedies.*

Fatal Remedies

In his book *Fatal Remedies,* Sieber develops a general framework for discussing and interpreting the negative effects of various social policy strategies. Sieber is not interested in social policies that fail to improve a situation, nor is his aim to evaluate the side effects of social policies, rather he is interested in regressive interventions—interventions that make the original aim of the social policy less attainable or cause a worsening in the condition that the policy was supposed to alleviate (Sieber, 1981).

For example, the poor quality of education in some of the schools in Boston historically has been of great concern. It was theorized that the reason for the substandard education in a number of these schools was the segregated nature of the school system. Thus, to alleviate the problem, the goal was set to desegregate Boston city schools. The social policy that was instituted was to bus children from one school district to another, to ensure integrated classrooms. The result of this social intervention was the movement of whites to the suburbs, or the placement of their children into private schools as a means of preventing them from being bused to other school districts. This "white flight" created an even more segregated school system, making the goal of integration less attainable and making the social problems caused by segregation even worse.

We can apply this same framework of regressive interventions to maternal substance abuse. Most Americans would agree that excessive use of drugs, licit or illicit, by pregnant women may harm the child and thus may be defined as a social problem. The goal we as a society would most like to attain in dealing with this social problem is to decrease the use of drugs and alcohol by pregnant women, thus ensuring infant health. Currently the primary means of addressing the problem of maternal substance abuse focuses on punishment and incarceration, as evidenced by the fact that the ratio of federal money is weighted toward law enforcement over treatment, 70 percent versus 30 percent (Kong & Ellement, 1989). It is the argument of this article that this punitive approach to dealing with maternal substance abuse may make the goal of decreasing maternal drug use less likely, that it will not ensure healthy babies, and that it may actually increase the severity of the problem of maternal substance abuse.

How does this happen? What are the dynamics of this process of regressive interventions? How can a social policy actually make the goal of the intervention less attainable, or make the original social problem worse? To deal with these questions, Sieber develops the notion of a "conversion mechanism." A conversion mechanism is a feature or characteristic of the intervention or social policy that interacts with the environment and results in a regressive intervention. Sieber suggests at least six types of conversion mechanisms: functional imbalance, exploitation, goal displacement, provocation, derogatory classification, and placation. We will now examine each of these conversion mechanisms and will discuss how they relate to maternal substance abuse.

Conversion Mechanisms

Functional Imbalance

Sieber suggests that one characteristic of social policies that can have regressive effects is an overemphasis on a specific goal, which in turn causes planners to ignore other aspects of the social problem. For example, in our nation's war against drugs one of the goals has been to stem the flow of drugs into this country by eliminating drugs at their source. This goal was the rationale that the Nixon administration used to support the eradication of marijuana fields in Mexico. While the United States was successful in diminishing the supply of marijuana across our southern borders, not only did other countries replace Mexico as our primary supplier, but, additionally, domestic production increased. Thus the intervention undertaken, to eliminate drugs at their source, while successful in one area, may have actually made the overall problem worse by failing to address the "demand" side of the drug problem (Goode, 1989).

The emphasis in addressing the problem of maternal substance abuse has been on punishment and incarceration. In discussing maternal substance abuse, Dr. Ben Sachs notes that ". . . we are more willing to build prison cells and set up prisons than to set up treatment programs" (Kong, 1989). By concentrating almost exclusively on retribution, needs and issues that are created by this position are overlooked. There exists little consideration for the fact that there are few treatment facilities that deal with pregnant drug abusers and fewer jails and prisons than can effectively deal with an expectant mother. Ellen Barry, director of Legal Services for Prisoners with Children stated that "it is very short-sighted on the part of the judiciary to consider that placing a woman in a county jail or state prison is beneficial to the pregnancy."

In one case brought by Prisoners with Children, the plaintiff delivered her baby on the floor of the Kern County Jail in Bakersfield, California (Cassens Moss, 1988). In the case of Brenda Vaughan, while at D.C. jail she received no drug treatment, was allowed to detox with no medical supervision, and received only spotty prenatal care (Smith, 1990). Thus the fetus may be in as much danger, if not more, from the intervention as it is from the behavior of the expectant mother.

Exploitation

Another aspect of social policies that may bring about regressive effects can be interventions that become exploited by those they are meant to help. In either case the intervention may be used for personal or ideological benefits. For example, pregnant women who are prosecuted and incarcerated for their drug use may have little desire to stop using drugs, and drugs are probably as, if not more, available in jails than elsewhere. Thus, women who do not want to stop using drugs are being placed in a position where their drug use can be continued if not accelerated. As noted by Candice Cason, Executive Director of Women Inc., "It seems crazy to me to lock them up. Drugs are more readily available in jail" (Kong, 1989). Not only may the women have as great or even greater accessibility to drugs, but, because of contact with a diverse inmate subculture, they may also have the opportunity to experiment with different drugs and may make drug connections in jail that can carry on after release. Thus, the potential for greater abuse of drugs by women who are reluctant to stop using is inherent in the design of this punitive approach, making resolution of the problem less likely.

Goal Displacement

In addition to regressive effects resulting from either functional imbalance or exploitation, another possible cause of regressive interventions can occur when the goal of efficiency overshadows the goal of effectiveness. In other words, the benefits of providing an efficient and inexpensive means of dealing with a problem become more important than whether or not the policy is effective. As Sieber (1981) suggests, "Less efficient but more effective means are replaced by more efficient but less effective means" (p. 116). For example, in dealing with the marijuana problem, spraying the plants with paraquat, a toxic herbicide, may have seemed like an efficient strategy to deter use of the drug. However, this strategy, because it did not change patterns of use, may have been less than effective in improving the health of marijuana users, decreasing social and medical costs of drug use, or decreasing the demand for the drug.

Likewise, the practice of dealing with maternal substance abusers through indictments and prosecution may appear at first glance to be the most efficient and cost-saving strategy to decrease use, if one assumes that fear of legal consequences can deter one from use. "What people like about doing it this way (incarceration) is it doesn't cost any money. You don't have to raise taxes. You just have to bring down a couple of indictments" (Kennedy, 1989, p. 1).

But is the incarceration of maternal substance abusers effective in reducing their drug use? Or does our punitive social policy simply give the picture that something is being done about the problem, without really addressing the underlying issues that are the basis of continued maternal substance abuse? The women who are prosecuted are overwhelmingly low-income single women, primarily women of color who are dependent on public facilities for their care. "Incarceration does not address the possible roots of the problem: poverty, unemployment and lack of educational and vocational opportunities" (Smith, 1990). Additionally, pregnant women are seldom welcomed in treatment programs. Pregnant and addicted women were refused service by 54 percent of 78 treatment programs surveyed in New York City. Sixty-seven percent of the programs denied treatment to pregnant addicts on Medicaid, and 87 percent denied treatment to pregnant women on Medicaid and addicted specifically to crack (Chavkin, 1989). Rather than allocate monies for social programs and treatment rather than demand legislation forcing treatment facilities to accept these women, we employ the method that appears the most efficient: prosecution and incarceration. "The focus on maternal behavior allows the government to appear to be concerned about babies without having to spend any money, change any priorities or challenge any vested interests" (Pollitt, 1990, p. 410).

Provocation

The fourth possible characteristic of interventions that can result in regressive effects is the stirring up of emotions that lead to behavior that causes a reversal of intended outcomes. For example, if the practice of indictments and prosecution of maternal substance abusers continues, pregnant mothers who use drugs may refrain from any form of prenatal care, thus increasing the risks to the child (Pollitt, 1990).

Sieber also suggests that when any threat or display of force is viewed as illegitimate, this action tends to engender counter force in the form of collective defiance and deviance on an increased scale (Sieber, 1981). For example, in the recent Charles Stuart case, where it was initially thought that a young black male was the perpetrator of the murder, the black community of Mission Hill and Roxbury were angered by what was perceived as a racially biased sweep of the area. Rather than making the area safer, the police involvement may well have increased anger and potential violence, directed especially at the white community.

The same negative response has been experienced as a result of prosecution of pregnant women, and many groups have come forth in protest. Paltrow of the American Civil Liberties Union argues that "it was not acceptable for the government to come in and take over pregnant women's lives" (Kennedy, 1989). The indictment of a Brockton woman for motor vehicle homicide, after an accident where the woman was driving under the influence of alcohol and where her unborn child was killed, raised a controversy among advocates of women's rights. Eight groups filed a friend of the court brief (Langer, 1989). Though the goal of these groups may in fact be to protect women's rights, the focus on constitutional and legal issues detracts from some resolution of the original problem—to reduce maternal substance use. People may become so involved in protecting women's rights that the social/medical problems confronting pregnant substance abusers and their babies become a secondary consideration. That is, one protects rights but still offers no solution.

Additionally, subcultures may engage in certain illicit behavior primarily to symbolize their rejection of dominant group motives. Drug use among minorities may symbolize a rejection of the dominant middle-class values of health and abstinence, which are ignored. If this is the case, focusing on addicted babies, who in Massachusetts are more often minority than white (Kong, 1989), may simply be a way of perpetuating the symbolic function of drug-using behavior.

Derogatory Classification

Another characteristic of interventions that can have regressive effects is derogatory classification. "A system of derogatory classification may induce a change in the expectations of others as well as a change in self perception" (Sieber, 1981, p. 141). This process can be examined by using Wilkins' notion of deviance amplification.

Wilkins argues that once a behavior is defined and accepted as deviant, the tendency of the society's non-deviant members is to isolate the individuals who fit the deviant definition. With the separation from the larger population, those defined as meeting the criteria for inclusion in the deviant group not only cease to have information regarding normal behavior and acceptable norms, but in fact develop a value system that supports and enhances the deviant behavior (Wilkins, 1988).

This may be the case with maternal substance abusers. By focusing on the pregnant substance abuser we have created a new deviant classification. She is not simply a drug user but a maternal drug user, one so deviant that she would gratify her own desires at the expense of her child. She is isolated from the larger society for her deviant behavior and may find support only with other substance abusers. This newly formed group of deviant individuals, since they have less and less contact with mainstream society, will establish group norms that explain, rationalize, and justify their substance abuse. Once the behavior of using drugs while pregnant is justified, continued substance abuse is more likely, and the problem of maternal substance abuse worsens.

Placation

The final conversion mechanism that, according to Sieber's theory, has a regressive effect on social interventions is "interventions that are chiefly a means of placating certain parties whose support is considered necessary or whose attacks require neutralization" (Sieber, 1981, p. 165). An example of this process of placation is the legislative support of the organization Mothers Against Drunk Driving. MADD is a group composed initially of significant others who had lost a family member to a drunk driver and who, as a group, demanded that action be taken, not against the liquor companies, but rather against those individuals who choose to drink and drive. Under pressure from MADD, President Reagan appointed a Presidential Commission on drunk driving that recommended changes in legislation also aimed at the individual (Reinarman, 1988). Thus this legislative strategy of focusing on the individual as the source of the problem, i.e. individual pathology, was consistent with the policies supported by MADD, and this consistency effectively neutralized some of the potential legislative power of MADD. Further, this legislative action gave the appearance to the general public that steps were being taken to resolve drunk driving, thus quieting their fears. However, the legislation avoided addressing a potentially more significant aspect of drunk driving, the role of liquor companies.

This same process of placating certain groups, and at the same time scarcely addressing and possibly exacerbating the problem of maternal substance abuse, may be best examined on a macro level and can be understood within the framework of our current policy toward drug abuse.

Since the 1960s our government has been waging a war on drugs (Czajkoski, 1990) with questionable and variable results. However, even if we are not winning the war, a war on drugs, like any war, may serve a number of useful control purposes. For example, during a "war" the general population is often willing to accept an abridgment of civil liberties and a subordination of the individual. Such abridgment would never be accepted by the general public in more stable times. For example, Czajkoski argues that the war mentality after Pearl Harbor clouded any concern for due process and elementary fairness, as evidenced by our internment of Japanese Americans (Czajkoski, 1990). Today in the name of the war on drugs and zero tolerance the general population appears willing to accept random drug screens, which seem to many a clear violation of self-incrimination and privacy rights.

In such a "war" mentality, the maternal substance abuser is targeted as an enemy and is punished. Through this punishment the illusion that the battle is being won is perpetuated. As a result, the public is placated by war victories.

Furthermore, by punishing these expectant mothers, usually members of poor and disenfranchised groups, we are focusing on a group whose political power is minimal. The likelihood of protest of the current punitive policy or consideration of violations of civil rights is minimized. In terms of placation the punishment of maternal substance abusers: (1) shows that something is being done about the drug problem (even if nothing is being accomplished), (2) satisfies the public, and (3) avoids addressing central problems in the social system, such as poverty, unemployment, and racism, that may in fact exacerbate the drug problem.

Conclusion

In this article I have examined, using Sieber's *Fatal Remedies,* the notion that a punitive intervention to deal with maternal substance abusers may not only be ineffective, but may actually exacerbate the problem we hope to solve. Evidence indicates that time and time again, whether we are dealing with desegregation of schools, fighting the war on drugs, or confronting the issue of poverty, certain features of our social policies bring about a worsening of the problem. In the case of maternal substance abusers, we have examined the possibility that punitive measures do not take into consideration other factors such as (1) the lack of proper facilities for incarcerated pregnant addicts, (2) the fact that, while incarceration may seem the most efficient method of intervention, its effectiveness is questionable, (3) the fact that the intervention can be exploited, (4) the emotional response of the target group, a response that may lessen the likelihood that the maternal substance abuser will obtain prenatal care, (5) the instituting of a social policy, not because it is effective, but as a means of placating powerful segments of the population, and (6) the consequences for the maternal substance abuser and the social problem when we classify individuals in a derogatory manner.

References

Abel, E. (1984). *FAS and FAE.* New York: Plenum Press.

Balisy, S. S. (1987). Maternal substance abuse: The need to provide legal protection for the fetus. *Southern California Law Review. 60,* 1209–1238.

Cassens Moss, D. (1988). Pregnant? Go directly to jail. *American Bar Association Journal, 59,* 20.

Chavkin, W. (1989, April 27). Testimony born hooked: Confronting the impact of perinatal substance abuse. *Hearing Select Committee on Children, Youth, and Families.* U. S. House of Representatives.

Coakley, T., & Hart, J. (1989, September 27). Mother indicted on cocaine charge. *Boston Globe,* p. 31.

Czajkoski, E. H. (1990). Drugs and the warlike administration of justice. *Journal of Drug Issues, 20*(1).

Day, N. L. (1992). The effect of prenatal exposure to alcohol. *Alcohol, Health, and Research Works, 16*(3), 238–244.

Drugs found in babies, and mother is guilty. (1989, July 14). *New York Times.,* p. A10.

Getting straight: Overcoming treatment barriers for addicted women and their children (fact sheet). (1990, April 23). *Hearing Select Committee on Children, Youth, and Families.* U. S. House of Representatives.

Goode, E. (1989). *Drugs in American society.* New York: Alfred A. Knopf Inc.

Halfon, N. (1989, April 27). Testimony born hooked: Confronting the impact of perinatal substance abuse *The Select Committee on Children, Youth, Families.* U. S. House of Representatives.

Howard, J., & Beckwith, L. (1989). The development of young children of substance-abusing parents: Insights from seven years of intervention and research *Zero to three, 1*(5), 8–12.

Keating, D. (1990, January 13). Woman faces charges of abuse of newborn. *The Miami Herald,* p. B1.

Kennedy, J. (1989, August 23). Cloudy future after infant-cocaine case. *Boston Globe,* p. 1.

Kong, D. (1989, October 11, 25). Mass reports 600 infants born addicted each year. *Boston Globe.*

Kong, D., Ellemont, J. (1989, December 12). Bennett take infant if mother is on drugs. *Boston Globe,* pp. 1,13.

Langer, P. (1989, December 5). Charges dropped in death of fetus. *Boston Globe,* pp. 29, 39.

Novick, E. (1989). *Crack addiction in pregnant women: An analysis of the problem, model programs and proposed legislation in California.* Unpublished master's thesis, University of California at Berkeley.

Pollitt, K. (1990, March 26). Fetal rights—a new assault on feminism. *The Nation,* pp. 409–418.

Reinarman, C. (1988). The social construction of an alcohol problem *Theory and Society, 17,* 91–120.

Sieber, S. (1981). *Fatal remedies.* New York: Plenum Press.

Smith, B. V. (1990, May 17). Testimony law and policy affecting addicted women and their children. *Hearing Select Committee on Children, Youth, and Families.* U. S. House of Representatives.

Wilkins, L. (1965). The deviance amplifying system. In R. Farrell, & V. Swigert (Eds.), *Social Deviance* (pp. 182–184) Belmont, CA: Wadsworth.

Woman charged after giving birth to addict. (1989, October 7). *The Indianapolis Star,* p. 1.

Zuckerman, B. (1991). Drug-exposed infants: Understanding the medical risks. *Future of Children, 1*(1), 26–35.

Discussion Questions

1. Would you support a punitive approach to controlling what women do when they are pregnant? What policies do you think would better address the problem of maternal substance abuse?
2. What factors—social, biological, or psychological—do you think cause women to use drugs and alcohol when they are pregnant? Where did you obtain the information on which you are basing your beliefs? Could your source of information be problematic?
3. Are there other factors that have an impact on infant health? Does our society scrutinize these factors and prosecute the offender?
4. Can you use Sieber's framework to examine other social policies? What other social policies have had a regressive effect?

The Politics of Needle Exchange in New York City

Cherni Gillman

Dr. Cherni Lynne Gillman served as a contributing editor at the *International Journal on Drug Policy.* She has taught on the university level and held research positions at New York State Psychiatric Institute, Columbia University School of Public Health, and Narcotic and Drug Research, Inc. Dr. Gillman's particular area of interest is beginning social movements. Her presentations and published work have addressed lessons from the war on drugs, the sexual transmission of AIDS, and how ethnographic methods can be utilized to identify policy options.

It took New York City three years to approve a needle exchange experiment. In earlier work I discussed the ideological conflicts that caused this delay (Gillman, 1989). Later, I documented what happened during the one year the needle exchange was allowed to operate (Gillman, 1990). Now, since Mayor Dinkins closed the needle exchange in February 1990, I am returning to the topic of the relationship between the ideological war on drugs and health policy in New York City.

But I want to begin further back. My reading of history is that our country's political system is driven by the values of religious fundamentalism. The first settlers to arrive in the Native Americans', the Indians', homeland, came as individuals fleeing religious persecution. These Puritans regarded their fellow human beings as morally frail creatures constantly tempted by the devil and sin. Redemption could be procured only by strict adherence to the God-fearing ways they advocated.

Literature and history show us that transgressors were dealt with harshly by the Puritans. So-called sinners could be banished from the community, as with the "adulteress" in the novel *The Scarlet Letter*, or even, as in the Salem witch trials, publicly executed. It is my opinion that this rigid doctrine polarized the community into "us" versus "them," dividing those who appeared to conform to prevailing values against those who did not.

Why have I started with a not-so-original interpretation of cultural history? Because two epidemics characterize our time—drugs and AIDS—(Eaton, 1990), and, historically, bifurcating the community into "us" against "them" explains how policy regarding drug use and the transmission of AIDS is formulated.

Our political heritage of rigid fundamentalism affects how science is used to inform public policy. Indeed, fundamentalism affected whether science—the theory of evolution—would be allowed to be taught in schools in the United States. I will offer some disquieting observations about how science is used to inform, in this case, health policy (Eaton, 1990).

It is conservatively estimated that 50 percent of New York City's 200,000 injection drug users (IDUs) are infected with the virus that causes AIDS. But the response to the AIDS epidemic has not been based on epidemiological strategies (Eaton, 1990). Instead, the response is based on politics. Politics has turned the issue into a choice between combating AIDS or addiction.

This essay is an expanded version of a plenary address given during the First International Conference on the Reduction of Drug-Related Harm, held in Liverpool, England, April 9–12, 1990.

In the United States, dominant public opinion remains entrenched between those who regard addiction as a crime and those who view it as a disease. Proponents of a moral/legal perspective are the dominant group. They believe that drug use indicates moral weakness (Nancy Reagan's famous "Just Say No"), and that laws should punish addicts as criminals. Advocates of the disease model see addicts as individuals with a biochemical problem that requires physiological treatment. Nonetheless, adherents of both models disapprove of addiction and agree that it must be stopped—even though fewer than 40,000 drug treatment slots exist for the City's 200,000 IDUs.

I argue that the impasse on preventing AIDS among injection drug users, their sex partners, and children is ideological. The division in the power structure that impedes its response to AIDS among IDUs reflects irreconcilable attitudes that are held by the American public. Typically, the American public regards drug users as criminals. Yet 40 percent of Americans surveyed favor giving needles to injection drug users if the purpose is to slow the spread of AIDS (Kagay, 1988).

Given the different priorities of the medical and criminal ideologies, I contend that the power structure (of elected officials, the law enforcement community, and the medical establishment) is aligned in such a way that an external individual or agent is necessary for initiating change warranted by the AIDS epidemic. When a political system is unable to respond to a health crisis, public policy can be influenced by an individual or organization that represents a competing ideology (Gillman, 1989).

In New York, Health Department officials were prodded by ADAPT, an advocacy group for the rights of injection users, to establish a government program to address the plight of users because of AIDS.

Treating AIDS and drug use as public health problems instead of legal or medical issues was not easily achieved. (Nor was it retained.) The city's narcotics prosecutor delayed the start of the needle exchange for six months with legal objections. "The Health Commissioner can designate whoever he wants to have needles, but you cannot take a legal instrument and use it for an illegal purpose," the prosecutor asserted. Making a pun, he noted with satisfaction, "I think that's stopped them in their tracks." The Commissioner was then forced to concede, "Without the cooperation of law enforcement officials so that addicts are not arrested the moment they walk out the program's door, the plan cannot work" (Gillman, 1989, p. 30).

Before it had operated even a month, the City Council voted to end the needle exchange program. The vote was 30 to zero. However, the vote was nonbinding and therefore only symbolic. Former Mayor Koch chose to invoke the moral authority of science by having a representative retort, "We're glad it's nonbinding because we need to follow the advice of the medical community and try this plan." (Council Calls for End to Free Needles Plan, 1988).

What happened at the needle exchange during the one year the City tried this plan? Very briefly: Three hundred and eighteen drug injectors enrolled. Half of them tested positive for HIV. Nearly 80 percent accepted referral to drug treatment programs.

What did we learn from this experiment? To begin, we learned that, *yes*, it is possible to operate a needle exchange—even located under the worst circumstances. Outside the needle exchange is probably the largest concentration of narcotics detectives in the Western world. And there's Criminal Court, Civil Court, Family Court, and the Supreme Court. Not to forget the Tombs, a prison where all drug users who are arrested are taken in handcuffs. In short, the city placed the needle exchange in the HEART of the drug war.

Getting clients to come to the needle exchange was a daunting task. But the program surpassed its quota of 200 participants. Three hundred and eighteen injection drug users came. Charles ("Chuck") Eaton, the project's director, explained, "You learn to become a lawyer in this business. We decided that 200 meant 200 active participants." (Gillman, 1990, p. 19). (Clients left active status when they entered drug treatment or were out of contact with the program for more than 10 working days.)

The needle exchange got participants to come by chauffeuring them in the Commissioner's car and literally walking them through the building. Otherwise, Eaton said, the project would not have had participants. If they were ferried by car, one out of two clients (versus one out of 12) would appear. It cost the project four and a half cents per needle. "Our gasoline bill for driving clients to the project was higher than our needle budget," said Eaton (Gillman, 1990, p. 19).

Eaton, who still directs the "Bridge to Treatment" that the exchange has become, says, "I don't like military metaphors. What I learned is that fighting in this war does not mean marching in a parade with the sun gleaming off your rifle barrel. Instead, it's sneaking around the barn and finding your way through the woods" (Eaton, 1990).

What else was learned from the needle exchange experiment? We found out that drug injectors would enroll even though they were limited to receiving *one* sterile needle per visit. "If time is money," Eaton observed, "these were the most expensive needles in the world."

Usually, the program had two contacts with clients: one for needle exchange, and the other to get clients placed in the drug modality they chose. Demonstrating that the program could function as a supportive "bridge" to treatment became a primary objective. Since placement into drug treatment often took place in a single visit, the project was in direct contact with clients for an average of one to three days. Out of a sample of 250 clients, 78 percent accepted referral to a drug treatment program.

It is quite likely that injection drug users attended the program because the staff could be helpful and deliver services. The new Bridge to Treatment program is still able to retain clients because it provides them with primary health care.

Who came to the needle exchange? Again, out of a sample of 250 clients, two-thirds were male; one-third were homeless. At intake, 11 percent had infectious syphilis. Their mean age was 33 (New York City Department of Health, 1989). ("Our clients are curious and adventurous people," commented Eaton. "Who else would go through all this hassle for one free needle?") Lastly, the needle exchange demonstrated that most users are willing to enter treatment, and that teaching needle hygiene is a difficult task which requires a context.

Now let's examine the objectives of the needle exchange experiment. When we look at the Department of Health's official report, we find something unexpected: There are none. There were never measurable, observable criteria for evaluating the needle exchange program. Agreement never existed among the community, the political structure, and the people running the program, on *anything.*

The needle exchange program was established as a scientific experiment, but for experiments to qualify as science, experts must share standards for measuring methodology and outcomes. That's why we have peer review. What occurred at the needle exchange was that an experiment was implemented. Over 300 addicts enrolled, and *no one else* paid attention. Success or failure of the program could not be determined because politicians never bothered to consider what it would have to accomplish to prove its value.

Well, how did we get here? Here's a different history from the one I opened with. In the 1830s, morphine was isolated. In the 1840s, the hypodermic syringe was invented. In the 1860s, for the first time, the new discovery of injectable morphine was applied in a major war, during the United States Civil War. In the 1870s, a play featured a cowboy who was a morphine addict. The moral of this short list of events is that injection drug use is as American as apple pie (Eaton, 1990).

Jumping to the present, there are two popular ways that people ideologically view the AIDS epidemic. (Let me warn you that I'll ask you to think over how you would apply these explanatory schemes to drug use.)

The dominant group regards AIDS as punishment for sin, the sin of homosexuality or the sin of drug use. These people do not believe that treatment or therapy is needed, because the problem solves itself. Sinners live short lives. Those holding a medical view see AIDS as caused by a retrovirus that is not transmitted by casual contact and is hard to contract. Supportive therapies can have an impact, but they cannot eradicate the virus. Prevention is through education.

I would like to ask you to consider: Where are the parallels to drug use? How do you think people who believe that AIDS is caused by selfish, sinful behavior regard drug use?

At least in the United States, the dominant view is that drug use is pleasure-seeking behavior engaged in by people of weak character. Marijuana, heroin, crack—historically, each has been seen as easy to get addicted to, both seductive and insidious.

What is the treatment for this type of behavior? *Religion.* Or at least reform. People have to get their values and strength of character from somewhere; failing that, incarceration is deserved.

Now let's analyze the structure of the rhetoric used by the U.S. Secretary of Health when he commented on the viability of needle exchange programs. Here is Sullivan being quoted from an inner office memo:

> Getting into drugs is easy for young people. Take no action that will even remotely suggest that use of illegal drugs is acceptable. Solving the problem of HIV infection in these communities involves more than fighting a virus. We must take every reasonable step, but we cannot in this battle lose sight that our war is against drug use in America. There is a danger that the controversy surrounding needle exchange will overshadow the greater issue of drug abuse in society. We cannot have a solution become part of the problem. (Eaton, 1990)

This position contrasts sharply with that of the Chief of Police in San Francisco, who says, "I don't arrest people who give out needles. I've got real crime to worry about. These people are part of the solution, not the problem."

Getting back to Sullivan, it is important to recognize that he is the top health official in the United States, stating his perspective on the nature of drug use and our policy for addressing the AIDS epidemic. To quote Sullivan again, "The greater issue is ZERO tolerance of drug use in society" (Eaton, 1993).

So, here we have the party line. Where does science fit in this? Sterile needles are the most expedient agent that can stop the AIDS virus from being transmitted by injection, but our government prohibits people from taking advantage of the best information and technology we have for slowing the AIDS epidemic.

I began by saying that I would offer some disquieting observations about science and policy.

Mayor Dinkins declared, when he closed the pilot program, that "Providing needles to addicts *is to surrender* [emphasis mine] to drug abuse," and that the test project had not changed his mind. "I don't want to give people [injection] paraphernalia," he announced (Purdum, 1990, p. A21).

Thus, there are no criteria, no data, no findings that can influence New York City's policymakers. Although the rhetoric was given out that we needed scientific data to demonstrate the effectiveness of needle exchange, so as to inform public policy, we have every evidence that public policy does not respond to scientific data (Eaton, 1990). Instead, another perspective dominates and defines the situation.

The aftermath of New York City's needle exchange experiment is that we cannot presume that science will inform public policy. "The outcome for our program will be politically determined," Eaton had predicted. "We interact with politicians, not scientists" (Eaton, 1990). One year later, after ending the needle exchange, its real status was obvious. The exchange was a feasibility study that was crippled at the start. It was never a public health measure. What this exposes is that we are not even at the first step of seriously addressing the transmission of HIV. We have no strategy, no program, no policy. What are we doing to stop the behavior that transmits the virus? Nothing remarkable is being done.

Until AIDS has an impact outside the injecting drug community, until prompt treatment is not available to those we think of as middle-class—heart bypass, gall bladder, prostate patients, for example—until the health care delivery system experiences crisis, I believe that large-scale prevention efforts won't be legislated. When no one can get a hospital bed in New York City, then we can expect effective prevention tactics.

Instead of being addressed by government action, the fate of an issue like AIDS among injection users may hinge on "non-decisions," that is, the demands for change may be suffocated before they ever gain access to the relevant decision-making arenas. It has been theorized that until a group influences public opinion to support a social movement aimed at changing a condition—no matter how intolerable that condition appears—the condition will not be recognized as a social "problem" (Maus, 1975).

The demographics of illness on the HIV spectrum may offer another explanation for government's lack of response to AIDS among IDUs. In New York City during 1989, 57 percent of the known AIDS cases had died. That left 6,000 people with full-blown AIDS. Although hospital beds were at 95 percent capacity, it appears that, so far, HIV-infected individuals have remained asymptomatic long enough to allow hospitals to accommodate the number of full-blown AIDS cases. This is because other AIDS patients who have died have freed up hospital beds (Josephs, 1989). But how long can we count on the dead continuing to empty hospital beds to make room for the dying?

Luckily, New York is not the world, and other strategies have been adopted. In March 1990, 10 people were arrested in New York for trying to give out sterile needles (Lambert, 1990). This action may have more consequences than anything that preceded this event. The issue will be processed through the courts. If fighting AIDS with sterile injection equipment becomes recognized as a medical and not a criminal act, if fighting AIDS is decriminalized, city officials and health departments will be allowed broad, expanded powers for fighting medical epidemics. In Boston, John Parker was exonerated of a criminal charge for distributing needles. Needle exchanges are slated to begin in Hawaii, Connecticut, and Baltimore. Already, needle exchanges are operating in Tacoma, Portland, Boulder and Seattle. These cities in the West were settled by homesteaders and cattle ranchers, *not* by Puritans.

The mission of public health is to protect the health of all citizens, not to reform their lifestyles. One impact of the AIDS epidemic may be that public health officials will have to continue considering nonstandard, politically volatile strategies (such as needle exchanges) to slow the contagion of AIDS.

To conclude, one of the main forces that is determining health policy is the war on drugs. But there is a rumor that the former Drug Czar, Bennett, wanted to declare defeat in the war, and then resign. And one colleague tossed off the prediction that George Bush grew bored with the war on drugs and wanted to declare that he'd won it (Klein, 1990)!

In our prohibitionist climate, our task is to educate our leadership, yet at the same time realize that the movement for constructive change will not come from leadership. If government officials formulate their policy recommendations on their perception of public sentiment, the rational aspects of a policy stance different from their own may fail to be persuasive. We must also recognize that there can be rigid ideological stances that refuse to brook new evidence or information.

We need to engender a different reaction to AIDS and drug use, aside from short-sighted punishment or neglect. New York City's mayor implied that he was protecting schoolchildren by refusing to situate a needle exchange near a school. But many of the students have parents who are injection drug users. So instead of being harmed by needle exchange, these schoolchildren could have benefited from proximity to needle exchange services (Eaton, 1990).

Because the criteria on which to debate its merit were never specified or agreed on, the data from the needle exchange experiment had no impact on the decision to end it. Community empowerment is about agreeing, directing, strategizing. We need some level of agreement before politicians will take leadership. We must break through social isolation to come to this sense of agreement, a direction, a strategy. Without this process, no policy—whether it is based on science or not—will be accepted or approved.

Acknowledgments

The author thanks Charles Eaton for his contribution to the analysis presented in this paper.

References

Council calls for end to free needles plan. (1988, December 7). *The New York Times*, p. 2.

Eaton, C. (1990, March 29). *Drugs and society.* [Seminar lecture]. Columbia University, New York.

Gillman, C. (1989, September/October). Genesis of New York City's experimental needle exchange program. *The International Journal on Drug Policy*, 28–32.

Gillman, C. (1990, March/April). After one year: New York City's needle exchange pilot programme. *The International Journal on Drug Policy, 1*, 19–21.

Josephs, H. (1989, October). Personal communication.

Kagay, M. R. (1988, October 14). Poll finds antipathy towards some AIDS victims. *The New York Times*, p. 6.

Klein, D. (1990, April 6). Personal communication.

Lambert, B. (1990, March 7). Ten seized in demonstration to give away new needles. *The New York Times*, p. B3.

Maus, A. (1975). *Social problems as social movements.* Philadelphia, PA: J. B. Lippincott Company.

The pilot needle exchange study in New York City: A bridge to treatment. (1989, December). Report to the New York City Department of Health.

Purdum, T. (1990, February 14). Dinkins decides to cancel needle-exchange program. *The New York Times*, p. A21.

Discussion Questions

1. Why does so much controversy surround the City Department of Health's needle exchange program?
2. What objective criterion was used for evaluating the needle exchange experiment?
3. How do you think the needle exchange program can be evaluated?
4. What public health interventions would you suggest for curtailing the increasing rate of HIV infections among drug injectors and their families?

Summary and Postscript

Peter J. Venturelli

Peter J. Venturelli (University of Chicago Ph.D., 1981; M.A., 1978) is currently Chair and Associate Professor of Sociology at Valparaiso University. His areas of specialization are: substance abuse, ethnicity, urban community and social psychology. Publications include: *Drugs and Society* (1988 second edition coauthored with Weldon Witters and the 1992 edition coauthored with Weldon Witters and Glen Hanson, Boston & London, Jones & Bartlett Publishers, Inc.); *Drugs in America: Social, Cultural and Political Perspectives,* editor, 1994, Jones & Bartlett Publishers, Inc. He has also written articles in *Human Organization* and *Family and Community* (edited by Richard Juliani), and presented dozens of research papers on ethnicity and substance abuse at regional, national and international professional association conferences. Currently Venturelli is writing a book-length manuscript entitled *Social Construction of Ethnicity: Negotiating Generational Ethnic Identity.*

For this volume, 29 research articles were written by contributors, and six introductory chapters and this conclusion were written by the editor. The goal for this publication has been to raise the level of discussion and incite meaningful dialogue concerning drug use and abuse. Emphasis has been placed on discussing this problem from social, cultural, and political perspectives.

While, collectively, the larger more pragmatic goal of the readings is to increase the readers' knowledge of societal aspects of substance abuse, readers can extrapolate the following findings from this anthology:

1. Society pays very dearly for alcohol abuse in terms of premature deaths, reduced productivity, accidental deaths, suicides, and homicides. Alcohol's continuing status as the most widely used and abused psychoactive drug does little to encourage any optimistic predictions for its role in future generations.
2. When we shift our perception of alcohol addiction from viewing it as moral degeneracy to viewing it as a disease or as a career, methods of prevention, treatment and rehabilitation come into focus.
3. Patterns of excessive alcohol consumption and the excessive use of other drugs are now linked to: situational and social factors, cultural dissimilarities and practices, normative expectations, religious differences, and certain occupational fields where the non-medical use of drugs is common.
4. Marital problems, stressful occupations and peer pressure are other examples of situational and social factors.
5. Effective methods for reducing adolescent alcohol-related injuries include: (1) increasing the minimum drinking age to 21, (2) restrictions on physical and economic availability of alcoholic beverages, (3) more educational and mass media advertising and public announcement programs against drug use, and (4) development of more government funded treatment programs for adolescent alcohol abusers.
6. Differential association theory, emphasizing deviant behavior as *learned from* social associations with deviant friends, appears to be among the more insightful theories for explaining drug and alcohol use among adolescents.
7. The desire for novel experiences and the need for excitement are directly related to adolescent drug use.
8. The process of ethnic assimilation affects the amount of alcohol consumption in different ethnic groups. The more traditional and restrictive

ethnic groups adapt to the permissive U.S. alcohol-drinking culture, the more these ethnic groups will develop liberalized attitudes about drinking.

9. Members of disenfranchised minority groups, minority members who have experienced prejudice, discrimination and racism, have a greater likelihood of becoming substance abusers.
10. The social influence approach appears to be the most successful drug prevention approach. This approach involves teaching refusal or resistance techniques coupled with bolstering self-esteem and improving interpersonal skills.
11. The media continue to be an underutilized resource for diminishing substance abuse in American society. The media's potential for persuasion against drug use and abuse has not been fully realized.
12. One leading cause of death and disability among teenagers and young adults is alcohol-impaired driving. Among the most successful methods for deterring drunk driving are teaching personal responsibility and employing peer intervention techniques.
13. The degree of public commitment to drug prevention has an independent influence on strategies for curbing drug use. Strategic planning clarifies and upholds major goals and strategies for drug abuse prevention programs.
14. Predominant in the United States for over 75 years, the punitive model postulates that drug use is widespread because American society is too lenient with drug users and suppliers. As a result, our current justice system applies punishment instead of treatment and rehabilitation for drug violations.
15. Several articles show that major drug busts increase the demand by diminishing the supply. When drug supplies are diminished, price increases, and in turn new dealers are enticed to enter the selling market.
16. *Opponents of* legalization argue that the elimination of criminal prosecution for drug use would be elitist, racist, and immoral, because legalization would have its most devastating effects on the economically deprived. According to this view, we would be condemning hundreds of thousands of poor children to lifelong drug addiction.
17. *Proponents of* legalization emphasize that we need to give decriminalization a chance, since punishment for drug use has not worked in the past 75 years. There has been greater success in diminishing the effects of legalized drugs than in diminishing the use of prohibited types of drugs.
18. From a social control perspective, the criminal justice system has become overwhelmed and preoccupied with drug offenses. This single concern of the criminal justice system has adversely affected such branches of the criminal justice system as state prosecutors, the courts, and the prison system.
19. Regarding substance abuse in the medical profession and in sports, several research articles found that, generally, the belief is that health care professionals have double and triple the rates of drug dependence of our general population. Current estimates are that between 50 percent and 90 percent of athletes in basketball, baseball, and football use drugs.
20. Supervised recreational and sport activity does not necessarily reduce drug use and abuse. More predictive factors are: the proportion of time spent in such activities, in comparison to the total amount of available leisure time; whether the recreational activity requires active or passive participation; and whether peer group norms either support or conflict with drug use.
21. The general conclusion of many medical research studies on the topic of maternal substance abusers is that the use of marijuana and cocaine during pregnancy has an independent effect on, and is strongly associated with, impaired fetal growth.
22. An unexpected 22 percent of U.S. adult AIDS cases result from intravenous (I.V.) drug users who share needles; "another 52 percent of heterosexual AIDS cases, and 59 percent of nationwide pediatric cases are related to I.V. drug use" (Hagan, DesJarlais, Purchase, et al., 1991). In New York alone, it is conservatively estimated that 50 percent of New York City's 200,000 injecting drug users are infected with the AIDS virus. The most important goals sought in needle exchange programs are to reduce sharing, halt the spread of AIDS that results from needle sharing, and establish successful educational intervention techniques

that will alter the behavior of severely drug-addicted individuals.

The 22 noteworthy findings above clearly show how drug use is linked with many other aspects affecting our lives. In part, this linkage can be explained by the fact that drug use does not occur in a vacuum. Drug abusers are embroiled within a constellation of social, cultural, political, historical and legal conflicts as well. Their interpersonal involvements and attachments to family members, peers, neighborhood and community residents, including interpersonal relationships with schoolmates or fellow workers, often comprise this larger network of interaction. Using drugs is hardly ever an isolated act. In part, this explains why drug use is effected by and affects so many aspects of our lives. In an effort to develop the initial discussion in the preface, this final section concludes with some observations on the broader socio-cultural dimensions of drug use.

Much of the information on substance abuse traces the potential reason(s) for drug consumption to such obvious causes as peer influence, rebellion, status frustration, inadequate socialization, child abuse, dysfunctional and divorced families, juvenile delinquency, and the like. Often these explanations fail to account for other larger, interacting "root" causes and situations for drug use.

From a substantive and holistic perspective, drug users are enveloped within larger social problems. In effect, the scourge of drug use in our society is a symptom of the shortcomings and failures occurring on multiple levels. Such personality characteristics as low self-esteem, low self-confidence, insatiable need for social approval, high anxiety, and inadequate assertiveness often lead to drug abuse (Abadinsky, 1989). Thus, when substance abuse is viewed from a substantive and holistic perspective, we find that it is not for example peer group influence *per se* causing substance abuse. Instead, it is a shortcoming located in the personality structure coupled with social or economic deprivation that compels like-minded individuals to band together and influence one another to abuse drugs. In this example, drug abuse and peer influence are not only symptomatic of personality shortcomings but of other situational, social and economic factors as well.

Personality, family, and community are not autonomous entities without interconnections. Healthy as well as addictive personality structures are surrounded by and located within other social structures, such as the family system, neighborhood, and the community. While sometimes personality appears to be the major reason for drug abuse, often the abuse of drugs stems from additional aggravating root causes that go unrecognized. Included as root causes are the effects of poverty, racism, sexism, and even ageism. Further, when these larger causes are not taken into account, the spread of drug use is assured.

Spread of drug abuse can occur on at least three levels: First, people who are poor, for example, reside and associate with others affected by the same economic circumstances. Thus, if one individual is addicted to drugs, other residents in these neighborhoods are influenced as well. Second, commonly affected residents in poverty-stricken communities sharing multiple psychological, social, and economic problems use drugs as a manifestation of their plight in a social and economic system that bars them from membership in middle-class society. Finally, selling drugs is a lucrative business. Allegedly, young drug dealers can earn as much as $20,000 a week at age l6 (Williams, 1989).

Drug abuse is a symptom, and not the cause of aberrant behavior and ruined lives. Neighborhoods and communities infested with drug use are often the same areas populated by poverty-stricken minorities who experience a severe lack of standard educational facilities, employment opportunities, and decent housing. On the topic of crime, Professor Reinarman of the University of California at Santa Cruz states that "Crime is a function of the social class of the users, not the pharmacology of the drug. People who have a stake in conventional life don't throw it all away" (Raymond, 1991, p. A10).

Massive efforts to control drug use based on the punitive model, which relies on the criminal justice system for enforcement, have been very disappointing. Attacking drug use with "strong-arm" tactics does not work. This form of attack on drug use and abuse will accomplish little unless we attempt to help dysfunctional families, curb the spread of poverty, implement urban policies that address structural unemployment within the inner cities (Wilson, 1988), and legislate against blatant and disguised forms of racism. Taking singular approaches to eliminating drug use is akin to removing a layer of cancerous tissue and hoping that the remaining layers will dissipate on their own. After so many years of failed measures to lessen drug use and abuse, it is now time that we view the problem more substantively and create strategies that attack concomitant root causes.

Unfortunately, tackling the widespread use and abuse of drugs involves solving the larger problems that in the past were either ignored or unrecognized as root causes. Tackling poverty for example through skill training, creation of inner city jobs, family support programs and other humane programs will not only lessen drug use and abuse, but will also lower juvenile delinquency, adult crime, and urban violence rates.

As a sociologist, humanist, and the editor of this anthology, I wholeheartedly embrace Amatai Etzioni's communitarian approach. Etzioni has inspired a social reform movement that led to the publication of "The Responsive Communitarian Platform" (1991/1992, pp. 4–20). The preamble to the journal, *The Responsive Community,* calls upon us to reclaim a moral sense of community spirit and action for restoring all that has gone astray in our society. In applying the responsive communitarian platform to drug abuse in our society, I hold steadfastly to the view that as responsible citizens we must collectively *lead* government in restoring the moral strength and stamina of such major socializing institutions as our families, schools, and communities. The framework for restructuring our society should be modeled on the responsive communitarian preamble, which advocates responsible social reform. This platform is resistant to political corruption and the blind application of our currently ineffective punitive model for solving drug abuse in our society. A communitarian approach advocates moral responsibility and seeks to attack drug abuse through education and rehabilitation.

I join with the 29 contributors to this volume and with most other social scientists in hoping that in the remaining years of this century, we will begin to approach the drug problem in a more substantive and holistic manner and that as a society we will permanently halt naive and failed "band-aid" solutions of the past. Lessening drug abuse requires responsible collective agreement on comprehensive and multifaceted educational and practical programs, strategies, and procedures.

To effectively tackle and begin solving the current drug epidemic, we first need to view the drug problem as *our* problem. Second, as a society of responsible citizens we need to develop strategies that directly attack the complexity of this problem on many levels, and finally, there is a need to approach the task with serious moral, social, political, and economic commitment. Nothing short of this type of commitment will ever alleviate the drug scourge afflicting our nation's citizens.

References

Abadinsky, H. (1989). *Drug abuse: An introduction.* Chicago, IL: Nelson-Hall.

Hagan, H., Des Jarlais, D. C., Purchase, D., Reid, T., & Friedman, S. R. (1991). The Tacoma syringe exchange. *Journal of Addictive Disease, 10,* 81–88.

Raymond, C. (1991, December 22). Researchers say debate over drug war and legalization is tied to Americans' cultural and religious values. *Chronicle of Higher Education,* pp. A6, A10.

Responsive Communitarian Platform (The). (1991/92). *The Responsive Community 2,* 4–20.

Tovares, R. (1989). How to solve the drug problem. *National Catholic Reader.* Kansas City, MO.

Williams, T. (1989). *The cocaine kids.* New York: Addison-Wesley.

Wilson, W. J. (1988). *The truly disadvantaged.* Chicago, IL: University of Chicago Press.

Index